Lecture Notes in Computer Science 4307

Commenced Publication in 1973
Founding and Former Series Editors:
Gerhard Goos, Juris Hartmanis, and Jan van Leeuwen

Peng Ning   Sihan Qing   Ninghui Li (Eds.)

Information and Communications Security

8th International Conference, ICICS 2006
Raleigh, NC, USA, December 4-7, 2006
Proceedings

 Springer

Volume Editors

Peng Ning
North Carolina State University
Raleigh, NC 27695-8206, USA
E-mail: pning@ncsu.edu

Sihan Qing
Chinese Academy of Sciences
Beijing 100080, P.R. China
E-mail: qsihan@ercist.iscas.ac.cn

Ninghui Li
Purdue University
West Lafayette, Indiana 47907-2066, USA
E-mail: ninghui@cs.purdue.edu

Library of Congress Control Number: 2006936899

CR Subject Classification (1998): E.3, G.2.1, D.4.6, K.6.5, F.2.1, C.2, J.1

LNCS Sublibrary: SL 4 – Security and Cryptology

ISSN   0302-9743
ISBN-10   3-540-49496-0 Springer Berlin Heidelberg New York
ISBN-13   978-3-540-49496-6 Springer Berlin Heidelberg New York

Springer is a part of Springer Science+Business Media

springer.com

© Springer-Verlag Berlin Heidelberg 2006
Printed in Germany

Typesetting: Camera-ready by author, data conversion by Scientific Publishing Services, Chennai, India
Printed on acid-free paper   SPIN: 11935308   06/3142   5 4 3 2 1 0

Preface

It is our great pleasure to welcome you to the Eighth International Conference on Information and Communications Security (ICICS 2006), held in Raleigh, North Carolina, USA, December 4–7, 2006. The ICICS conference series is an established forum that brings together researchers and scholars involved in multiple disciplines of Information and Communications Security in order to foster exchange of ideas. The past seven ICICS conferences were held in Beijing, China (ICICS 1997); Sydney, Australia (ICICS 1999); Xi'an China (ICICS 2001); Singapore (ICICS 2002); Hohhot City, China (ICICS 2003); Malaga, Spain (ICICS 2004); and Beijing, China (ICICS 2005). The conference proceedings of the past seven events have been published by Springer in the *Lecture Notes in Computer Science series*, in LNCS 1334, LNCS 1726, LNCS 2229, LNCS 2513, LNCS 2836, LNCS 3269, and LNCS 3783, respectively.

This year we received a total of 119 submissions on various aspects of ad-hoc and sensor network security. The Program Committee selected 22 regular papers and 17 short papers that cover a variety of topics, including security protocols, applied cryptography and cryptanalysis, access control in distributed systems, privacy, malicious code, network and systems security, and security implementations.

Putting together ICICS 2006 was a team effort. First of all, we would like to thank the authors of every paper, whether accepted or not, for submitting their papers to ICICS 2006. We would like to express our gratitude to the Program Committee members and the external reviewers, who worked very hard in reviewing the papers and providing suggestions for their improvements. We would also like to thank the Organizing Committee members, who did a wonderful job in organizing the conference. We would like to thank our sponsor, North Carolina State University (NCSU)/Duke University Center for Advanced Computing and Communications (CACC), for supporting the conference. Finally, we would like to express our gratitude to the US Army Research Office and the US National Science Foundation for the generous financial support of this conference. Their grants provided travel supports for graduate students to attend the conference.

We hope that you will find these proceedings interesting and thought-provoking.

September 2006

Peng Ning and Sihan Qing
Program Chairs, ICICS 2006

External Reviewers

Abdulhran Alarifi
Abdulraham Alarifi
Elli Androulaki
Joonsang Baek
Kun Bai
Abhilasha
   Bhargav-Spantzel
Marina Blanton
Mike Burmester
Matt Burnside
Su Chang
Shu Chen
Shuo Chen
Jong Youl Choi
Gabriela Cretu
Deepak Kumar Dalai
Kanti Das
Christophe Doche
Markus Duermuth
Yann Duponchel
Sarah Edwards
Min Feng
Keith Frikken
Tim van der Horst
Jeff Horton

Jeffrey Horton
Hungyuan Hsu
Zhengli Huang
Sotiris Ioannidis
Pandurang Kamat
Kameswari Kotapati
Fengjun Li
Lunquan Li
Zhuowei Li
Anyi Liu
Michael Locasto
Liang Lu
Andreas Moser
Karsten Nohl
Joseph Pamula
Chi-Chun Pan
Nathanael Paul
James Riordan
Sankardas Roy
Farzad Salim
Emre Sezer
Siamak Fayyaz
   Shahandashti
Nicholas Sheppard
Stelios Sidiroglou

Hui Song
Alok Tongaonkar
Mercan Topkara
Umut Topkara
Dominique Unruh
Hai Wang
Haodong Wang
Huaxiong Wang
Pan Wang
Ronghua Wang
Shuhong Wang
Xinran Wang
Yawen Wei
Liang Xie
Mengjun Xie
Ping Xie
Yongqiang Xiong
Wenyuan Xu
Yi Yang
Chao Yao
Zhen Yu
Chuan Yue
Linfeng Zhang
Qinghua Zhang
Yukai Zou

Organization

ICICS 2006 was organized by the North Carolina State University (NCSU)/Duke University Center for Advanced Computing and Communication (CACC), with support from the US Army Research Office (ARO) and the US National Science Foundation (NSF).

Organizing Committee

General Chair
Douglas S. Reeves   North Carolina State University, USA

Program Chairs
Peng Ning   North Carolina State University, USA
Sihan Qing   Chinese Academy of Sciences, China

Publication Chair
Ninghui Li   Purdue University, USA

Panel and Keynote Chair
David Evans   University of Virginia, USA

Publicity Chair
Haining Wang   College of William and Mary, USA

Local Arrangement Chair
Errin Fulp   Wake Forrest University, USA

Posters and Demos Chair
Yong Guan   Iowa State University, USA

Financial Chair
Donggang Liu   University of Texas at Arlington, USA

Program Committee

Mikhail Atallah   Purdue University, USA
Vijay Atluri   Rutgers University, USA

Table of Contents

Security Protocols

Applied Crytography

Access Control and Systems Security

Privacy and Malicious Code

Network Security

Systems Security

Cryptanalysis

Applied Cryptography and Network Security

Security Implementations

Strong and Robust RFID Authentication Enabling Perfect Ownership Transfer

Chae Hoon Lim and Taekyoung Kwon*

Dept. of Computer Engineering, Sejong University, Seoul 143-747, Korea
{tkwon, chlim}@sejong.ac.kr

Abstract. RFID technology arouses great interests from both its advocates and opponents because of the promising but privacy-threatening nature of low-cost RFID tags. A main privacy concern in RFID systems results from clandestine scanning through which an adversary could conduct silent tracking and inventorying of persons carrying tagged objects. Thus, the most important security requirement in designing RFID protocols is to ensure untraceability of RFID tags by unauthorized parties (even with knowledge of a tag secret due to no physical security of low-cost RFID tags). Previous work in this direction mainly focuses on backward untraceability, requiring that compromise of a tag secret should not help identify the tag from past communication transcripts. However, in this paper, we argue that forward untraceability, i.e., untraceability of future events even with knowledge of a current tag secret, should be considered as an equally or even more important security property in RFID protocol designs. Furthermore, RFID tags may often change hands during their lifetime and thus the problem of tag ownership transfer should be dealt with as another key issue in RFID privacy problems; once ownership of a tag is transferred to another party, the old owner should not be able to read the tag any more. It is rather obvious that complete transfer of tag ownership is possible only if some degree of forward untraceability is provided. We propose a strong and robust RFID authentication protocol satisfying both forward and backward untraceability and enabling complete transfer of tag ownership.

1 Introduction

Radio Frequency Identification (RFID) is an automated identification technology in which a small transponder, attached to a real world object, receives and responds to radio-frequency queries from a transceiver. The transponder is usually called an RFID *tag* while the transceiver is an RFID *reader*. The RFID tag incorporates silicon chips with radio antennas for electronic operations and wireless data transmissions. It tends to have extremely limited capabilities in every aspect of computation, communication, and storage for economic viability. Passive tags are not equipped with an internal power source, contrary to

---

* Research by the 2nd author was supported by grant No. R01-2005-000-11261-0 from Korea Science and Engineering Foundation in Ministry of Science & Technology.

semi-passive or active tags with built-in batteries. They store authentic data and respond for identification and authentication, with neither physical nor visual contact. The RFID reader communicates with tags and cooperates with a backend database which contains information on the tagged objects.

In fact, this technology is not fundamentally new; rather it has been around since the late 1960s and is being used in the public domain [11]. Recently, RFID has aroused a great interest from various communities due to the promising nature of small low-cost RFID tags in future smart applications. Rapid RFID progress has already been made in retail sectors, such as Wal-Mart and Procter & Gamble, as well as in government sectors, such as U.S. DoD and Postal Service [14]. The U.S. government also has mandated adoption by Oct 26, 2006 of *e-passports* (biometrically-enabled RFID tags) by the 27 countries in the Visa-Waiver Program [16]. It is widely believed that RFID tags will more rapidly spread over and its cost will go down fast in the near future.

RFID systems however raise a lot of privacy concerns, mainly due to the possibility of clandestine tracking and inventorying of tags [27,30,24,5,15,16,14]. For example, adversarial parties equipped with commodity RFID readers may trace a person carrying a tagged item by recognizing the same tag in different places at different times. This traceability problem is considered as the biggest security challenge to general acceptability and wide-scale deployment of RFID technology. Actually the boycott movement from those fearing privacy infringement made companies like Benetton and Gillette drop or reconsider their RFID-tagging plans [7,29]. Fortunately, a number of studies have also been done for handling such security and privacy issues in RFID systems [17,24,10,13,19,4,8,23]. The approaches taken in these studies vary, from schemes based on weak but realistic models to strong cryptographic techniques, and each approach may have its own merit and demerit.

In this paper, we are more interested in a stronger security model, assuming that tag secrets may be read by an adversary, since most low-cost RFID tags have no protection capability of the tag memory. Since reading the tag memory content endows the adversary with full capability of the tag from the moment, it is very important to see how the past and the future transactions of the tag are related with the current internal state of the tag at the time of memory break-in. This observation brings us the security notions of backward (resp. forward) untraceability, meaning that knowledge of a tag's current internal state must not help identify the tag's past (resp. future) interactions.[1] Most previous studies focus on backward untraceability and, as far as we know, no attention has been paid explicitly to forward untraceability yet. In this paper, we would like to call our attention to the importance of forward untraceability and related issues.

We argue that *forward untraceability* is even more important than backward untraceability in RFID systems. Suppose that compromise of tag secrets results in complete loss of control over the tags. Then, it may be catastrophic if tag secrets are compromised in some point of tag deployment or during their cir-

---

[1] Note that we used the terms 'forward' and 'backward' opposite to usual definitions. See Section 2 for our justification.

culation within supply chains; then it would be much easier to trace the tags and reproduce cloned tags. Another important related issue is the problem of *ownership transfer*. Since tags may change hands frequently during their lifetime, it is certainly necessary to provide some means of ownership transfer of a tag from one party to another. Ownership of a tag means the ability to read the tag and thus ownership transfer should guarantee that once ownership of a tag is transferred, the tag should be able to be read only by the new owner but never by the old owner. Such a complete transfer of tag ownership would be impossible unless some degree of forward untraceability is provided, since the old owner would have already owned all the information necessary to control the tag. Note that we are talking about perfect ownership transfer between users, contrary to Molnar et al.'s temporary ownership transfer or time-limited access delegation [23] (See Section 4 for more details).

Our Contribution. As discussed above, there is of no doubt on the importance of forward untraceability, in addition to traditional backward untraceability, in designing RFID authentication protocols. Backward untraceability is easy to achieve by updating tag secrets based on a one-way key chain and has been widely studied in the literature. However, it is never easy to achieve forward untraceability using cryptographic techniques in low-cost RFID tags, due to the very limited resources available in such tags. The mobility of tagged items is our primary finding as a means of achieving forward untraceability with little increase of complexity. That is, even if an adversary learns the tag secret of a particular person's belonging, he will not be able to physically track the target item all the way from the moment of tag break-in. Thus, assuming that it is not possible for the adversary to eavesdrop all the interactions of the target tag afterwards, we will be able to completely refresh the tag secret in synchronization with the backend database by injecting into the tag secret the shared randomness involved in every successful authentication. In this paper, we first bring the notion of forward untraceability explicitly and rigorously in the design of RFID authentication protocols and propose such a protocol achieving both requirements of forward and backward untraceability. Furthermore, we show that our protocol enables perfect transfer of tag ownership between users. This feature will be essential in trading tagged objects in the real world. We also show that this feature can be used to delegate access to tags to potentially untrustworthy readers for distributed processing of a central database and may help thwart tag cloning by refreshing the tag secret whenever necessary.

2   RFID Systems and Security

2.1   The Communication Model

An RFID system consists of three main entities such as RFID tags, RFID readers, and a backend database server, along with communication channels between them. Figure 1 depicts the high-level view of the communication and security model for conducting RFID authentication in general. The channels between the

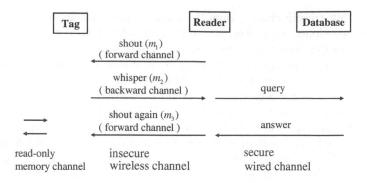

Fig. 1. The top-level communication and security model for RFID systems

tag and the reader are wireless radio channels which can be read or engaged by an adversary, while those between the reader and the database might be wired channels which are usually assumed secure. The channel from a reader to a tag is called the forward channel and its opposite is the backward channel. Due to the difference of signal strengths flowing in different directions, the adversary may have in general more chances to read the forward channel. Since we can't imagine physically secure tag chips in most low-cost RFID tags, it is reasonable to assume that the tag memory could be read by an adversary. In this respect, we may view read access to the tag memory as another hypothetical channel, called the memory channel [2], wiretapable by the adversary.

It is still a challenging task to design and analyze RFID authentication protocols since the capabilities of passive tags are extremely limited. The problem becomes rather paradoxical in the context of tag authentication without public key cryptography. Actually a legitimate reader cannot authenticate itself to a tag until it knows which key to use, requiring the tag's identity ahead, while the tag does not want to reveal its identity to an unauthenticated reader for privacy reasons. In Figure 1, the reader may shout without knowing the tag's identity in the first flow, and the tag should not reveal its identity to an illegitimate reader while whispering in the second flow. The third flow may be necessary for authenticating the reader and possibly updating the tag's internal state.

2.2 Forward Versus Backward Untraceability

In the above communication model, an adversary is able to collect a set of readings on both the forward and backward communication channels and also to tamper with a target tag's memory channel to learn its internal state at a certain moment. Thus we need to define untraceability of a tag in either direction of time travels from the moment of tag memory break-in. This brings us the notions of backward and forward untraceability. Unfortunately, the terms 'forward' and 'backward' have been used in security definitions somewhat ambiguously and are still controversial [28,1]. The cryptographic community has long time used the term 'forward security' loosely to mean the protection capability of past traffic even with disclose of a current secret in many public key designs, in order to mitigate the damage from the long-term secret key exposure (e.g., key exchange protocols, public key encryption and digital signatures). However, the opposite concept, 'backward security', is rarely used explicitly (though some key-evolving signatures introduce an external trusted authority to achieve such a security property; e.g., see [22]). This might be one reason for the lack of efforts in establishing agreed-upon concrete definitions for both security notions. Note however that these definitions are exactly opposite to the verbatim meaning of the words and also to our intuition. They are awkward in particular when used in conjunction with untraceability. We will thus use the terms 'forward' and 'backward' untraceability literally as defined below (more general and formal definitions on various untraceability notions are provided in Appendix A).

Backward and forward untraceability are concerning the indistinguishability of past and future interactions of a tag with knowledge of the current internal state of the tag at the time of memory break-in. Backward untraceability states that even if given all the internal states of a target tag at time t, the adversary should not be able to identify the target tag's interactions that occurred at time $t' < t$. That is, it requires that knowledge of a tag's current internal state should not help identify the tag's past interactions. Backward untraceability has been considered as the most important security requirement in strong RFID authentication, since otherwise the past transcripts of a tag (e.g., from readers' logs) may allow tracking of the tag owner's past behaviors.

On the other hand, to our best knowledge, the opposite concept, forward untraceability, has not yet brought explicitly in the research community of RFID security. Forward untraceability can be similarly defined as requiring that knowledge of a tag's internal state at time t should not help identify the tag's interactions that occurred at time $t' > t$. In fact, not much attention has been paid to this security notion, since it is obvious that there exists no way (without the help of some external trusted authority) to maintain the future security once the current secret is exposed. The only thing we can do is to detect key compromise a.s.a.p. and to replace the exposed key with a fresh one to protect future transactions. However, this may not be easy in RFID systems; it is almost impossible to detect compromise of a tag secret and the tag secret may not be manageable by the tag owner.

Obviously, perfect forward untraceability makes no sense, since the adversary ia able to trace the target tag at least during the authentication immediately following a compromise of the tag secret. Thus the minimum restriction that may be imposed to achieve forward untraceability would be such that there should exist some non-empty gap between the time of memory break-in and the attack time in which the adversary could not hear the interactions (see Appendix for more details). Forward untraceability is thus harder to achieve than backward untraceability in general, in particular under the very constrained environment such as RFID tags. Nevertheless, we note that forward untraceability is never less important than backward untraceability in RFID systems. There may exist some situations in which forward untraceability is even more important.

Both security requirements will be equally important in fighting against the universal surveillance threat by some powerful organizations (such as intelligence agencies) capable of collecting a huge amount of interaction logs (legally or illegally) almost without limitation in time and coverage. On the other hand, in the case of target tracing, we may not need such a power. It suffices to somehow steal the tag secret attached to a particular target's always-carry-on item and collect interaction logs from the target's frequently visiting places to trace the future behaviors of the particular target. Such a target tracing is trivial without forward untraceability. An even catastrophic scenario without forward untraceability would be such a case that tag secrets are leaked at some point of tag deployment or during the stay in supply chains. Then, all such tags could be traced afterwards. We thus raise a strong motivation to the need of forward untraceability in RFID protocol designs (even if not perfect), in addition to the well-recognized backward untraceability. This property is also closely related to the problem of ownership transfer of tags as we will see in Section 4.

2.3   Previous Work

There have been proposed a number of RFID security protocols in the literature [30,25,17,24,12,13,6,8,21,19,23]. They can be classified into two broad classes; a class of protocols trying to enhance privacy and security in RFID systems without using standard cryptographic primitives, e.g., [17,24,13,19], and a class of protocols relying on symmetric-key primitives such as block ciphers and hash functions, e.g., [30,25,24,12,6,8,21,23]. The former proposals aim at finding some security enhancements best achievable and easy to implement under the current hardware and functionality of RFID tags (e.g., EPC UHF Gen2 tags) but they still have a number of practical issues to be addressed for actual implementations and not so easy to implement in the current standard tags either. On the other hand, the latter protocols assume enhanced tags with built-in hardware circuits for a symmetric primitive and pursue stronger security under still resource-constrained environments. There also exist some work on optimized design and implementation of block ciphers for low-cost RFID tags, e.g., [10,20].

We do not survey previous work in detail, but refer the reader to, e.g., [5,2,15,14]. We briefly examine the Ohkubo-Suzuki-Kinoshita (OSK, for short) protocol [25,6] however, as it is most relevant to and the starting point of our proposed protocol. The basic idea of the scheme is to use a one-way key chain to evolve a tag secret in response to every query request. Then, only the backend database can identify the tag since it is the only other party with knowledge of the initial tag secret for the one-way key chain. More specifically, a tag T_i is initialized with a random secret s_i and, whenever queried, emits $r_i = h(0, s_i)$ and evolves the tag secret s_i as $s_i \leftarrow h(1, s_i)$, where h is a one-way function. If the backend server keeps a key chain of length m for each tag T_i, i.e., $\{r_i^k\}_{k=0}^{m-1}$, where $r_i^j = h(0, s_i^j)$, $s_i^j = h(1, s_i^{j-1})$ and $s_i^0 = s_i$, then a tag can be identified just by searching the database for each query response r_i. Once the tag T_i is identified, the backend server updates the precomputed key chain so that it now contains m key chain values starting from the verified tag secret s_i. Thus the parameter m specifies the maximum number of authentication failures allowable between two valid sessions. Actually, this protocol should be modified into a challenge-response type to get resistance against replay attacks and there may exist more efficient time-memory tradeoffs to enhance the efficiency of the backend server (see [6,4]). It is easy to see that this protocol is backward untraceable due to the tag secret evolution through a one-way key chain.

3   The Proposed Authentication Protocol

3.1   Design Rationale

Our proposed protocol starts with the simple OSK protocol and augments it with mutual authentication and further protection capability in view of forward untraceability, thus making the resulting protocol immune against both the forward and the backward tracking attacks. First note that the OSK protocol achieves backward untraceability by updating a tag secret deterministically in response to every authentication request. The backend database then maintains a key chain of length m evolved from the tag secret of the last successful authentication, so that desynchronization up to m times can be resolved within this key chain.

The basic idea to enhance the protocol with forward untraceability is to refresh the tag secret simultaneously within both the tag and the central database, whenever the authentication is completed successfully, using the authentic random numbers exchanged during the protocol execution. Note that we use the term *update* to mean deterministic evolution of tag secrets while *refresh* to mean probabilistic evolution. That is, in every authentication session, the tag secret is evolved using a one-way key chain in two different ways; If the authentication succeeds, then both the tag and the database refresh the tag secret probabilistically using the exchanged random numbers, while, if the protocol fails anyway, the tag updates its secret deterministically as in the OSK protocol. Then, the resulting protocol would be made forward untraceable from the moment that an adversary is missing even one successful authentication session after compromising the tag secret.

One problem still remains in the above approach. If the adversary executes the protocol with a tag immediately after compromising the tag secret (she can do it successfully since she knows the tag secret), then the tag secret will be permanently desynchromized in the tag and the backend database, and the tag can be read only by the adversary.[2] This is because the tag refreshes its secret probabilistically using the randomness only shared with the adversary. To repair this problem, we introduce another one-way key chain maintained by the database and verified by the tag. The tag then refreshes its secret only if a received key chain value is verified. Note that this key chain is used in reverse

---

[2] This very property can be used to transfer tag ownership from the database to a consumer, as we can see later.

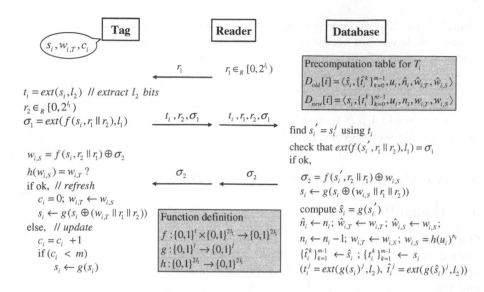

Fig. 2. The proposed protocol

order, contrary to the key chain for tag secret update, so we call it as a *backward key chain* while the latter as a *forward key chain*. We thus use the forward key chain for tag secret evolution and the backward key chain for server validation which triggers a refresh of the tag secret.

Finally, we note that there may still exist some subtle desynchronization problem in the case that the protocol message in the third flow is lost during transmission due to either unreliable medium or denial-of-service attacks by an adversary. The loss of the last protocol message in transit again results in permanent desynchronization of the tag secret, since then the tag will update the tag secret while the server will refresh it. We solve this problem by making the database keep two key chains of length m of relevant secrets, one based on the old secret and the other based the new secret, and examine both key chains in the next authentication. The problem can then be resolved, since the tag secret will belong to one of the two key chains, depending on whether or not the last protocol message arrives correctly.

3.2   Protocol Description

Parameters. The following parameters are used in the proposed protocol.

– m : The maximum number of allowable authentication failures between two valid sessions. If the protocol fails more than this threshold after the last successful interaction with the server (via an honest reader), then the tag stops evolving its secret and keeps using the last updated secret until the next successful authentication.

- n : The length of the backward key chain used for server authentication. This value can be set around the maximum number of successful authentications (not counting failed sessions) expected during the tag lifetime.
- ℓ : The bit-length of a tag secret.
- ℓ_1 : The bit-length of random challenges and responses.
- ℓ_2 : The bit-length of the tag secret transmitted in clear to help the backend server to identify the tag secret in its database. This value may depend on the tag population managed by the server (e.g., $\ell_2 \simeq \log_2 2mN$, where N is the maximum expected number of tags). The tag secret of length $\ell = \ell_2 + \ell'$ thus has the effective key length of ℓ' bits.

Pseudorandom Functions. Our protocol makes use of three pseudorandom functions f, g and h, all of which may be constructed from a single lightweight block cipher as can be seen later. We denote by $g(x)^n$ n-times applications of the function g on x :

- $f : \{0,1\}^\ell \times \{0,1\}^{2\ell_1} \to \{0,1\}^{2\ell_1}$: A pseudorandom function to generate authenticators.
- $g : \{0,1\}^\ell \to \{0,1\}^\ell$: A pseudorandom function to build the forward key chain used to evolve tag secrets.
- $h : \{0,1\}^{2\ell_1} \to \{0,1\}^{2\ell_1}$: A pseudorandom function to build the backward key chain used to authenticate the server.

Tag & Database Initialization. Each tag T_i is initialized by the backend database server as follows:

- The server chooses a random secret s_i (say, of 128 bits) for the tag T_i, evaluates $(m-1)$ evolutions of s_i, $s_i^0 = s_i$ and $s_i^j = g(s_i^{j-1})$ for $1 \le j \le m-1$, and extracts the key identifiers t_i^j for s_i^j as $t_i^j = ext(s_i^j, \ell_2)$ for $0 \le j \le m-1$, where $ext(x, \ell)$ denotes a simple extract function returning ℓ bits out of x (e.g., $x \bmod 2^\ell$).
- The server also chooses a random $u_i \in [0, 2^{2\ell_1})$ for each tag T_i and computes a key chain of length n, $\{w_i^j\}_{j=0}^{n-1}$, such that $w_i^n = u_i$ and $w_i^j = h(w_i^{j+1})$ for $0 \le j < n$. This key chain is used in reverse order to authenticate the server and to trigger a refresh of a tag secret.
- The tag then stores the pair of (tag secret, server validator) $\langle s_i, w_{i,T} \rangle$ and initializes the failure counter c_i as $c_i = 0$, where $w_{i,T} = w_i^0$.
- The server makes two entries for T_i, $D_{old}[i]$ (initially empty) and $D_{new}[i]$, in its database and stores the T_i's identification data $\langle s_i, \{t_i^j\}_{j=0}^{m-1}, u_i, n_i, w_{i,T}, w_{i,S} \rangle$ in the entry $D_{new}[i]$, where $w_{i,S} = w_i^1$ and $n_i = n$. Here, the variable n_i maintains the depth of the current $w_{i,S}$ in the key chain (i.e., $w_{i,S} = h(u_i)^{n_i}$). Note that $w_{i,T} = h(w_{i,S})$.

Authentication Procedures

1. The reader picks $r_1 \in_R [0, 2^{\ell_1})$ and sends it to the tag.
2. The tag chooses $r_2 \in_R [0, 2^{\ell_1})$, computes $t_i = ext(s_i, \ell_2)$ and $\sigma_1 = ext(f(s_i, r_1 \| r_2), \ell_1)$ and sends $\langle t_i, r_2, \sigma_1 \rangle$ to the reader.

3. The reader then queries $\langle t_i, r_1, r_2, \sigma_1 \rangle$ to the database server.

4. The server searches its database to find an entry containing the received key identifier t_i. If no match is found, the server responds with $\sigma_2 = \perp$ (denoting 'failure') and stops. Suppose that a match of $t_i = t_i^j$ for some j is found in one of T_i's entries, $D_{old}[i]$ or $D_{new}[i]$, containing $\langle s_i, \{t_i^k\}_{k=0}^{m-1}, u_i, n_i, w_{i,T}, w_{i,S} \rangle$. Then, the server computes the tag secret corresponding to t_i^j by $s_i' = g(s_i)^j$ and checks that $ext(f(s_i', r_1 \parallel r_2), \ell_1) = \sigma_1$. If the check fails, the server stops with output $\sigma_2 = \perp$. If the check succeeds, the server sends the response σ_2 to the reader, where $\sigma_2 = f(s_i', (r_2 \parallel r_1)) \oplus w_{i,S}$. The server then updates the two entries, $D_{old}[i]$ and $D_{new}[i]$, of the identified tag T_i as follows:

   1) The server moves the set of data found in the identified entry to $D_{old}[i]$ after updating the key identifiers t_i^j's according to the verified tag secret s_i'; $\hat{t}_i^k = t_i^{j+k+1}$ for $0 \le k \le m - j - 1$, $\hat{s}_i = g(s_i')$ and $\hat{t}_i^k = ext(g(\hat{s}_i)^{k-m+j}, \ell_2)$ for $m - j \le k \le m - 1$. Thus, we have $D_{old}[i] = \langle \hat{s}_i, \{\hat{t}_i^k\}_{k=0}^{m-1}, u_i, n_i, w_{i,T}, w_{i,S} \rangle$.

   2) The server then generates new data for $D_{new}[i]$ as follows: $s_i \leftarrow g(s_i \oplus (w_{i,S} \parallel r_1 \parallel r_2))$, $t_i^j = ext(g(s_i)^j, \ell_2)$ for $0 \le j \le m - 1$, $n_i \leftarrow n_i - 1$, $w_{i,T} \leftarrow w_{i,S}$ and $w_{i,S} = h(u_i)^{n_i}$ and stores the set of data $\langle s_i, \{t_i^k\}_{k=0}^{m-1}, u_i, n_i, w_{i,T}, w_{i,S} \rangle$ in the entry $D_{new}[i]$.

5. If $\sigma_2 = \perp$, the reader stops. Otherwise, it forwards the received σ_2 to the tag.

6. The tag computes $w_{i,S}' = \sigma_2 \oplus f(s_i, r_2 \parallel r_1)$ and checks that $h(w_{i,S}') = w_{i,T}$. If the check succeeds, then the tag sets $c_i = 0$ and updates its secret and validator pair $\langle s_i, w_{i,T} \rangle$ as $w_{i,T} \leftarrow w_{i,S}'$ and $s_i \leftarrow g(s_i \oplus (w_{i,T} \parallel r_1 \parallel r_2))$. If the check fails, the tag increases the failure counter $c_i \leftarrow c_i + 1$ and, if $c_i < m$, updates its secret by $s_i \leftarrow g(s_i)$, and, if $c_i \ge m$, does nothing, keeping its current state unchanged.

Construction of Functions f, g and h. We may use a block cipher as a building block for construction of the functions f, g and h. Note that block ciphers usually allow more compact hardware implementations than hash functions and that we only need to implement the encryption function for our purpose. In particular, it was shown that a lightweight block cipher deigned for resource-constrained environments could be implemented using just a few thousand (NAND-equivalent) gates [20] (see also [10]).

Suppose that we have chosen parameters of $l = 128, l_1 = l_2 = 32$ and that we have a 64-bit block cipher with 128-bit key length, denoted by $E : \{0,1\}^{128} \times \{0,1\}^{64} \rightarrow \{0,1\}^{64}$. The function f can then be simply the encryption function E, so $f(k, x) = E_k(x)$. The one-way function g may be constructed by $g(k) = f(k, c_0) \parallel f(k, c_1)$ for some 64-bit constants c_0 and c_1. Similarly, we may construct the half-sized key chain function h by $h(k) = f(k \parallel k, c_2)$ for another 64-bit constant c_2. If the encryption function is secure, then inversion of functions g and h would require an exhaustive search for the keys involved. Also note that even if 32 bits of k are disclosed, there remain large enough secret bits so that an exhaustive search is still infeasible.

3.3   Security and Privacy

It is easy to see that the proposed protocol works correctly if both the tag and the backend server behave honestly. We show in this section that our protocol is secure, and backward and forward untraceable under some reasonable assumption. For the security analysis, we assume that the functions f, g and h are one-way and behave like random functions.

Attacks on tag authentication. We first consider possible attacks by the adversary impersonating a tag. The aim of the adversary in these attacks in the context of authentication is to make the backend database accept a fake tag as valid. First note that the tag secret constantly evolves in every query request from readers and thus past tag responses may be assumed uniformly distributed irrespective of the queries requested (thus of no use for future attacks). Thus a fake tag $\tilde{T}_i$ without knowledge of a valid secret s_i has no better strategy than to reply with random $\tilde{t}_i \in [0, 2^{\ell_2})$ and $\tilde{\sigma}_1 \in [0, 2^{\ell_1})$. Let N be the total number of tags managed by the backend server. Then the probability of this reply being accepted by the server is at most $2mN/2^{\ell_1+\ell_2}$ for each query response, since for a random tag identifier $\tilde{t}_i$ there exist at most $2mN/2^{\ell_2}$ matching tag identifiers in the database and for each matching tag identifier the probability of a random $\tilde{\sigma}_1$ being verified is $1/2^{\ell_1}$. Thus, our protocol achieves tag authentication with a cheating probability of at most $2mN/2^{\ell_1+\ell_2}$.

Attacks on reader authentication. We next consider possible attacks by the adversary impersonating a legitimate reader. The aim of the adversary in these attacks in the context of authentication is to make an honest tag accept the adversary as a legitimate reader. Possible results of a successful attack may include tracking a tag or illegal modification of tag's internal states. A fake reader without knowledge of valid secrets $(s_i, w_{i,S})$ associated with an honest tag T_i again has no better strategy than to send a random $\tilde{\sigma}_2$ in the final protocol flow. The probability of such a response being accepted by the tag is negligible (around $1/2^{2\ell_1}$ on average).

We now consider an adversary tampering with a tag T_i at some point. Suppose that the adversary somehow obtains T_i's secrets $(s_i, w_{i,T})$ at time t. Obviously, this information becomes useless if T_i has completed even one valid session (with a legitimate reader) at time $t' > t$ which the adversary could not eavesdrop, since then the tag secret s_i would have been refreshed with a random number of length $2\ell_1$ unknown to the adversary. We thus only consider the case of the adversary attacking T_i immediately after compromising the tag secrets. Even in this case, the adversary cannot successfully cheat T_i without knowledge of the corresponding server validator $w_{i,S}$. The only way to get a live value of $w_{i,S}$ would be to intercept a valid σ_2 (sent by a legitimate reader) and then to invalidate it immediately so that it cannot be accepted by T_i. Then the adversary can recover a live value of $w_{i,S}$ from σ_2 which can be used later to trigger a refresh of the tag secret by T_i. This is the only potential threat identified but inevitable in our protocol. However, the feasibility of such an attack requiring instant intercept-then-invalidate operation over the air is highly questionable for proximate wireless transmissions in typical RFID tag environments.

Other attacks. Our protocol has strong resistance against Denial-of-Service (DoS) attacks on the last protocol message. Any alteration of this message may cause desynchronization of tag secrets in the tag and the backend server, but such a desynchronization problem can be resolved by dual copies of tag state information maintained in the server. Authentication failures more than the threshold m just cause the tag secret to remain static, which may break untraceability, but the tag secret is restored to a fresh after a secure reading of the tag.

Tag cloning is also ineffective in our protocol. Cloned tags are made useless as soon as tag secrets of the original tags are refreshed by a legitimate reading.

Forward and backward untraceability. From the above discussions, it is obvious that our protocol is backward untraceable and also forward untraceable under a reasonable assumption. Tag secrets at time t does not help identify tag interactions executed at time $t' < t$, as far as the one-wayness of the function g remains intractable, thus resulting in backwrad untraceability.

Forward untraceability is also provided to some extent under the natural assumption that the adversary compromising a tag cannot eavesdrop all the future interactions of the tag. The tag secret is refreshed upon every successful interaction with the server and thus a compromised tag becomes untraceable from the moment that the adversary misses even a single valid session of the tag. That is, forward untraceability of a tag, even if broken at any point during its lifetime, can be restored just by a single secure reading of the tag. However, we should be careful for the potential threat to this nice property as explained above (i.e., a possibility of intercept-then-invalidate of wireless signals over the air), since its realization would result in complete loss of control over the tag.

3.4   Efficiency Considerations

Suppose that the function f is implemented as the encryption function of a 64-bit block cipher supporting 128-bit keys and the functions g and h are derived from f as explained at the end of Section 3.2. Also suppose that we choose the parameters $\ell = 128$ and $\ell_1 = \ell_2 = 32$. Each tag T_i then needs to store 196 bits of rewritable data (a 128-bit s_i and a 64-bit $w_{i,T}$) and exchange 192 bits of data per session (send 96 bits and receive 96 bits). A tag requires 5 blocks of encryption for each session.

Consider an RFID system with $N = 2^{20}$ tags. The length m of precomputed key chains stored in the backend server controls untraceability between two refreshes and determines the storage requirement of the server; it need not be chosen too large, since the tag owner can refresh the tag secrets whenever necessary (e.g., $m = 64$). The server requires at least $(m + 3)$ invocations of the function g for each successful query from the reader to update the precomputation table entries. The length n for the backward key chain determines the number of valid authentications during the whole tag lifetime and thus may be chosen quite large for long-lived tags, say $n = 2^{20}$. The server requires n_i invocations of the function h to update the current server validator $w_{i,S}$ in each successful authentication. This workload however can be reduced to a fixed c invocations if the server precomputes (say, at every midnight) and stores the c-th upward value in addition, assuming that at most c legitimate readings of the tag in a day are sufficient (e.g., $c = 100$). The server then requires storage of just around 620 Mbytes for tag identification data (i.e., $D_{old}[i]$'s and $D_{new}[i]$'s) and less than 250 evaluations of the encryption function for each successful query on average. Note that the storage requirement of the server never exceeds tens of gigabytes (still easily available even in potable devices such as PDAs) even if we take a larger value of m and store full values in both forward and backward key chains for computational efficiency and robustness against DoS attacks.

4 Ownership Transfer, Delegation and Anti-cloning

4.1 Ownership Transfer

Ownership of RFID tags may be changed frequently during their lifetime. For example, tags are initially created and attached to objects by manufacturers and tagged objects are then handed over to retailers, and finally consumers buy tagged objects in shopping malls. The owner of a tagged object may also transfer its ownership to another party (e.g., by buying an object and giving it to his friend as a birthday present, or by selling or swapping used objects via a garage sale or in a swap meet). Ownership transfer of a tag means transfer of authorization to read the tag. Thus, such an ownership transfer must guarantee that once ownership is transferred to another party, the old owner should not be able to read the tag any more.

The problem of ownership transfer seems not extensively studied in the RFID security community yet, but we argue that this problem is in fact in the core of the RFID privacy problem. Suppose that Alice bought an tagged item from a shopping mall. The ideal consequence of this transaction would be such that Alice should take over the complete control of the tag via her portable RFID reader[3] and then even the backend server of the shopping mall should not be able to trace the sold tag any longer. Once receiving all the necessary information to control the tag, the new owner's reader can now take the place of the server. Obviously, this problem is closely related to forward untraceability, since the backend server still maintains all the secret information on the tag, which should be made useless (at least in tracing the tag) after the sales transaction. This requirement is more obvious in the case of ownership transfer between users.

It is rather simple to transfer tag ownership in our protocol. Suppose that Alice wants to take over a tag T_i from the database server since she bought

---

[3] Commodity mobile RFID readers will be available soon in various mobile devices, such as mobile handsets and PDAs. In particular, mobile phones with built-in RFID readers will constitute the majority of mobile readers. Mobile phones could also be the best place to host RFID proxy for various personal belongings (e.g., see [26,18]).

the tagged item. Alice then uses her mobile reader to securely communicate with the server via the checkout reader and receives all the relevant information from the server via the secured channel. The information received will certainly include the T_i's table entries, $D_{old}[i]$ and $D_{new}[i]$, and the tag ID. Alice can then take over the ownership of the tag simply by reading the tag via her mobile reader. This will make the tag refresh its secret based on the randomness shared only with Alice's mobile reader and thus no one else can read the tag from the moment. Note that no eavesdropper, except the backend server, can refresh the tag secret, since the backward key chain needed for this operation is only known to Alice's reader (and the backend server; thus tag reading may be done outside the communication range of the checkout reader for safety).

We note that no previous work explicitly deals with this kind of perfect ownership transfer between users. Molnar et al.'s pseudonym protocol [23] is the only one we found that deals with the problem of ownership transfer explicitly. However, their method for ownership transfer is not complete in the sense that the backend server still maintains all the control power of the tag. Only partial information is delivered to a reader, so that the reader can read the tag by some predetermined number of times without on-line connectivity to the server. Thus, strictly speaking, their scheme corresponds to time-limited access delegation rather than ownership transfer. Contrary to this, ownership transfer in our protocol is perfect. Ownership transfer can be carried out every time tagged objects change hands during their lifetime.

4.2   Access Delegation and Anti-cloning

In most RFID authentication scenarios, an RFID reader tends to act as a dumb relay, just passing protocol messages back and forth between a tag and a central database server. This may overburden the server in both computing and communication complexities. Availability may also be a big issue; on-line access to the database server should be always available in a reliable way but readers may have intermittent connectivity for various reasons. It is however not easy to distribute the functionality of the database into a large number of readers scattered over the RFID infrastructure. Readers may not be always trustworthy and consistency of the database is hard to manage in such a large scale distribution.

Time-limited access delegation may be useful in such a case. We may delegate access to a set of tags to a particular reader, so that the reader can read the tags in a limited time span without on-line connectivity to the server. After the specified time span, however, the reader's access to the tags should expire and thus the reader should not be able to read the tags any more without interaction with the server. Molnar et al. proposed such a time-limited access delegation in their pseudonym protocol [23].

In our protocol, we propose a different approach to time-limited access delegation. Due to the probabilistic nature of tag secret evolution, it is not possible in our protocol to delegate access authorization that automatically expires after a specified time limit. However, our protocol has such a nice feature that only the server can refresh tag secrets using the backward key chain for server validators.

We may thus deliver only two forward key chains for the tag secret and the tag ID to the reader but not the backward key chain for server validation. Then, the reader may identify the tag from the first two protocol flows but cannot respond with a valid answer in the third flow. We note that our protocol works correctly even if the third protocol message is suppressed (the reader may send an arbitrary dummy answer as σ_2 for the tag to proceed without waiting until the timeout). This makes the tag secret evolved deterministically and eventually remain static after m readings. Thus the server never loses its control over the tag. Though untraceability may be broken by more than m readings, this may not be a problem, since untraceability is in fact not much necessary before tagged objects are handed over to consumers.

A remaining issue in the above scenario is how to cancel access authorization given to the reader. The solution is fairly simple. We can just read the tag as before using a reader on-line connected to the server to refresh the tag secret, so that the access delegated reader cannot read the tag any more. This method of distributed processing can be effectively used to manage a large volume of tags as well. For example, suppose the case of warehouse inventory of tagged objects. The database server makes a copy of its database only containing two forward key chains for the tag secret and the tag ID for each tag and delivers it to a local database or a set of readers used for inventorying the warehouse (even hand-held readers (say, PDAs) may have storage of several or tens of gigabytes, so they can easily hold a copy of the database). The distributed local databases can be made useless at any time by scanning the tags using a reader on-line connected to the central server as before.

The authorized refreshability of tag secrets in our protocol may also be used to thwart tag cloning. Suppose that a warehouse employee in the above example steals a set of tag secrets from the local database and reproduces cloned tags. These cloned tags however can be made easily obsolete by refreshing tag secrets in both the original tags and the central database, say, before tagged objects leave the warehouse. This time, we may need two readings in order to wipe out old tag secrets in the central database as well. Note that tag refresh cannot be done by the malicious employee, instead, to make the original tags obsolete, since he is not given any value of the backward key chain.

5   Conclusion

We have introduced the concept of forward untraceability and its importance in designing RFID security protocols. It has also been shown that forward untraceability is the key ingredient for perfect ownership transfer of RFID tags. Based on these observations and requirements, we presented a strong and robust RFID security protocol providing both forward and backward untraceability. As far as we know, our protocol achieves the strongest possible security in RFID authentication. The proposed protocol also has several nice features such as complete ownership transfer between users and distributed processing capability of the central database maintaining tag identification information. Though our protocol may not be easy to implement in low-end RFID tags under the current standard and technology, we expect that it could be used right away in high-end tags for stronger security and probably low-end tags as well in the near future as hardware technology advances.

References

1. R. Anderson, "Two remarks on public key cryptology," Technical Reports, UCAM-CL-TR-549. Univ. of Cambridge, http://www.cl.cam.ac.uk/TechReports/, 2002.
2. G. Avoine, "Adversarial model for radio frequency identification," *Cryptology ePrint Archive*, Report 2005/049, 2005.
3. G. Avoine, Security and privacy in RFID systems (A complete list of related papers), http://lasecwww.epfl.ch/ gavoine/rfid/, Last Access: May 2006.
4. G. Avoine, E. Dysli, and P. Oechslin, "Reducing time complexity in RFID systems," *Selected Areas in Cryptography - SAC 2005*, LNCS 3897, Springer-Verlag, pp.291-306, 2005.
5. G. Avoine and P. Oechslin, "RFID traceability: A multilayer problem," *Financial Cryptography - FC 2005*, LNCS 3570, Springer-Verlag, pp.125-140, 2005.
6. G. Avoine and P. Oechslin, "A scalable and provably secure hash based RFID protocol," *The 2nd IEEE International Workshop on Pervasive Computing and Communication Security - PerSec 2005*, IEEE Computer Society Press, pp.110-114, 2005.
7. Boycott Benetton Home Page, http://www.boycottbenetton.com/, 2003.
8. T. Dimitriou, "A lightweight RFID protocol to protect against traceability and cloning attacks," In *IEEE SecureComm*, pp.59-66, 2005.
9. EPCglobal Web site, http://www.EPCglobalinc.org, 2005.
10. M. Feldhofer, S. Dominikus, and J. Wolkerstorfer, "Strong authentication for RFID systems using the AES algorithm," *Workshop on Cryptographic Hardware and Embedded Systems - CHES 2004*, LNCS 3156, Springer-Verlag, pp.357-370, 2004.
11. K. Finkenzeller, *RFID Handbook*, John Wiley & Sons, 1999.
12. D. Henrici and P. Müller, "Hash-based enhancement of location privacy for radio-frequency identification devices using varying identifiers," *Workshop on Pervasive Computing and Communications Security - PerSec 2004*, IEEE Computer Society, pp.149-153, 2004.
13. A. Juels, "Minimalist cryptography for low-cost RFID tags," *The Fourth International Conference on Security in Communication Networks - SCN 2004*, LNCS 3352, Springer-Verlag, pp.149-164, 2004.
14. A. Juels, "RFID security and privacy: a research survey," IEEE Journal on Selected Areas in Communications, 2006.
15. A. Juels, S. Garfinkel, and R. Pappu, "RFID privacy: An overview of problems and proposed solutions," *IEEE Security and Privacy*, 3(3):34- 43, 2005.
16. A. Juels, D. Molnar, and D. Wagner, "Security and privacy issues in e-passports," *IEEE SecureComm'05*, IEEE, 2005, Referenced 2005 at http://www.cs.berkeley.edu/ dmolnar/papers/papers.html.
17. A. Juels, R.L. Rivest, and M. Szydlo, "The blocker tag: Selective blocking of RFID tags for consumer privacy," *8th ACM Conference on Computer and Communications Security*, ACM Press, pp.103-111, 2003.
18. A.Juels, P.Syverson and D.Bailey, High-power proxies for enhancing RFID privacy and utility, In *Privacy Enhancing Technology 2005*, LNCS 3856, Spinger-Verlag, 2005, pp.210-226.

19. A.Juels and S.Weis, Authenticating pervasive devices with human protocols, In *Advances in Cryptology-Crypto 2005*, LNCS 3621, Spinger-Verlag, 2005, pp.293-308.
20. C.H.Lim and T.Korkishko, mCrypton-A lightweight block cipher for security of low-cost RFID tags and sensors, In *WISA 2005*, LNCS 3786, Spinger-Verlag, 2006, pp.243-258.
21. S. Lee, Y. Hwang, D. Lee, and J. Lim, "Efficient authentication for low-cost RFID systems," *Computing System Applications*, LNCS 3480, Springer-Verlag, pp.619-627, 2005.
22. T.Malkin, S.Obana and M.Yung, The hierarchy of key evolving Signatures and a characterization of proxy signatures, In *Advances in Cryptology-EUROCRYPT 2004*, LNCS 3027, pp.306-322. Springer-Verlag, 2004.
23. D. Molnar, A. Soppera, and D. Wagner, "A scalable, delegatable pseudonym protocol enabling ownership transfer of RFID tags," *Selected Areas in Cryptography - SAC 2005*, LNCS 3897, Springer-Verlag, pp.276-290, 2005.
24. D. Molnar and D. Wagner, "Privacy and security in library RFID : Issues, practices, and architectures," *ACM Conference on Communications and Computer Security*, ACM Press, pp.210 - 219, 2004.
25. M. Ohkubo, K. Suzuko, and S. Kinoshita, "Cryptographic approach to "privacy-friendly" tags," In *RFID Privacy Workshop*, 2003.
26. M.Rieback, B.Crispo and A.Tanenbaum, RFID guardian: A battery-powered mobile device for RFID privacy management, In *ACISP 2005*, LNCS 3574, Springer-Verlag, pp.184-194, 2005.
27. S. Sarma, S. Weis, and D. Engels, "RFID systems and security and privacy implications," *Workshop on Cryptographic Hardware and Embedded System - CHES 2002*, LNCS 2523, Springer-Verlag, pp.454-469, 2002.
28. R. Shirey, "Internet Security Glossary," IETF RFC 2828, at http://www.ietf.org/rfc/rfc2828.txt, May 2000.
29. Stop RFID, http://www.stoprfid.org.
30. S. Weis, S. Sarma, R. Rivest, and D. Engels, "Security and privacy aspects of low-cost radio frequency identification systems," *International Conf. on Security in Pervasive Computing - SPC 2003*, LNCS 2802, Springer-Verlag, pp.454-469, 2003.

A   The Security Model for Untraceability

Not much work has been done yet on formal security models for RFID security protocols, though a number of proposals based on varying assumptions have been proposed and analyzed in the literature. Juels have proposed a somewhat weak but realistic security model specific to his pseudonym protocol [13]. On the other hand, Avoine introduced a rather strong cryptographic model to define the strong privacy notion of untraceability in RFID protocols [2]. Here, we would like to take a step toward a generic security model that can cover weak to strongest possible security in RFID protocols. Our model closely follows Avoine's model but makes it more general and flexible by incorporating various possible restrictions existing in RFID systems. We primarily focus on the strongest privacy notion of untraceability, in particular, forward and backward untraceability, but it would be rather easy to extend it to include the general notion of authentication as well.

Oracles. An RFID protocol, $\mathcal{P}$, is formally a probabilistic algorithm that determines how instances of the principals, a tag T and a reader R, behave in response to inputs sent from their environment. The inputs may be given by an adversary, $\mathcal{A}$, that may have complete control over the environment. The adversary is a probabilistic algorithm with a distinguished query tape. Queries written on this tape are answered by principals according to $\mathcal{P}$. Each of the principals can run several instances of $\mathcal{P}$. We denote a tag instance at time i by π_T^i and a reader instance at time j by π_R^j. The adversary $\mathcal{A}$ is allowed to have access to the following oracles:

- Query(π_T^i, m_1, m_3): this query models $\mathcal{A}$ actively querying T. It sends a request m_1 to T through the forward channel and subsequently responds with the message m_3 after having received an answer from T.
- Send(π_R^j, m_2): this query models $\mathcal{A}$ actively querying R. It sends the message m_2 to R through the backward channel and receives an answer from R.
- Execute(π_T^i, π_R^j): this query models $\mathcal{A}$ passively eavesdropping on the communication channels between T and R. It executes an instance of $\mathcal{P}$ between T and R and obtains the messages exchanged on both the forward and the backward channels.
- Execute*(π_T^i, π_R^j): this query models $\mathcal{A}$ passively eavesdropping only on the forward channel. It executes an instance of $\mathcal{P}$ between T and R, but only obtains the messages exchanged on the forward channel. This oracle may be used to model the secure backward channel assumption in some protocols.
- Reveal(π_T^i): this query models $\mathcal{A}$ obtaining the content of T's memory channel. This query is only allowed during the time interval of $\mathcal{A}$'s training phase. Other queries can still be used even after the reveal query (possibly under some restriction).

For simplicity, let Q,S,E,E*, and R represent, respectively, the oracles Query, Send, Execute, Execute* and Reveal. Note that the adversary is passive when using the oracles E and E*, while it is active when using the oracles Q and S. In fact, the oracle E may be simulated using the oracles Q and S by the man-in-the-middle attack, but the reverse is not true.

Attack Models. The adversary attacking untraceability may use the above oracles in arbitrary manner according to its strategy, except the reveal oracle. The aim of the adversary is to distinguish a particular tag or a set of tags from others in different instances of the protocol (a more formal definition will be given below). The adversary's ability to achieve this aim can be characterized by the oracles to which the adversary is given access. We can thus classify the attack models according to the set of oracles available to the adversary. For example, the QSE model and the QSER model may be most intersting among others.

In typical RFID system environments, however, it may be too strong to allow unrestricted access to the oracles provided. Typically, tags and readers operate only at short communication range and for a relatively short period of time. Furthermore, RFID tags may be assumed in many cases highly mobile and thus hard to trace physically (otherwise, we do not need to worry about privacy infringement due to the traceability of tagged items). Therefore, it may not be unrealistic in practice to put some restrictions to the adversary's oracle access in terms of access time and frequency. We thus consider two access models, namely the universal or unrestricted access (UA) model and the restricted access (RA) model. Access restriction in the RA model is hard to define generically and thus a specific RA model should include a description on the imposed restrictions. For example, natural restrictions that could be imposed on the adversary may include some limitation in the number of successive queries to target tags and some limitation in the number of successive valid sessions that can be read by the adversary (e.g., as in the minimalist security model [13]).

We can thus talk of untraceability under the combined model of available oracles and access restriction. For example, we can say that a given protocol is untraceable under the UA-QSE model, meaning that the protocol is untraceable against any adversary who can interact with target tags and readers and eavesdrop interactions between target tags and legitimate readers at any time it wishes.

Attack Games. Let $\omega_i(T)$ be the result of the application of an oracle Q,E,E*, or R on a tag T, where $\omega_i(T) \in \{$Query$(\pi_T^i, *)$, Execute$(\pi_T^i, *)$, Execute*$(\pi_T^i, *)$, Reveal$(\pi_T^i)\}$ (note that tags are involved in all oracles, except the Send oracle). A tag *interaction* is defined as a set of oracle execution results on the same tag (identified by physical tracing or through an active query). More precisely, an interaction is defined by $\Omega_I(T) = \{\omega_i(T)|i \in I\} \cup \{$Send$(\pi_*^i, *)|i \in J\}$, where $I, J \subset \mathbb{N}$. The length of an interaction $\Omega_I(T)$ is equal to $|I|$ by definition. We use the notation $I < J$ for $I, J \subset \mathbb{N}$ to denote that numbers in I precede those in J; i.e., $I = [a, b]$, $J = [c, d]$ such that $a \leq b < c \leq d$.

Untraceability can be formally defined by a game being played between a *Challenger* and an adversary $\mathcal{A}$, where the adversary is allowed to interact with given oracles. The game begins with the *Challenger* randomly choosing a target tag T and providing it to the adversary $\mathcal{A}$. After having experimented with the target T using a set of oracles $\mathcal{O}$ provided (possibly including the reveal oracle R) under some access restriction $\mathcal{R}$ and thus obtaining an interaction $\Omega_I(T)$ over its chosen interval I, the adversary $\mathcal{A}$ requests challenge tags from the *Challenger*, which then provides two tags T_0 and T_1, one of which is T (i.e., $T_b = T$ for some hidden bit $b \in \{0, 1\}$). The adversary continues experimenting with the two tags as before, except that the reveal oracle, if provided, is not allowed to query in this stage, and thus obtains two interactions $\Omega_{I_0}(T_0)$ and $\Omega_{I_1}(T_1)$, where the intervals I_0 and I_1 should not overlap with the interval I. Finally, $\mathcal{A}$ outputs her best guess b' based on the experiments. If the probability of $b = b'$ is negligible for every I_0 and I_1 and for every $\mathcal{A}$, then we say that the protocol is *untraceable under the $\mathcal{R}$-$\mathcal{O}$ model.*

More formally: Let $\mathcal{O}$ be the set of oracles available to the adversary, where $\mathcal{O} \in \{$E*, E, QS, QSE*, QSE, QSER$\}$, and let $\mathcal{R}$ be the (description of) access restriction imposed on the oracles, where $\mathcal{R}$ may be empty. Let $\mathcal{O}'$ be the same as $\mathcal{O}$ except that $\mathcal{O}' = $ QSE in the case of $\mathcal{O} = $ QSER. Let $\mathcal{O}_{\mathcal{R}}$ be the set of oracles

$\mathcal{O}$ under the access restriction $\mathcal{R}$. That is, when a query is received, $\mathcal{O}_{\mathcal{R}}$ first checks the given access restriction $\mathcal{R}$ and returns an answer only if it satisfies the restriction. We use $Oracle$ to simulate the set of oracles to which the adversary has access. More precisely, $Oracle$ takes as inputs a tag T and a time interval I, makes calls to the oracles of $\mathcal{O}_{\mathcal{R}}$ or $\mathcal{O}_{\mathcal{R}}{}'$ and sends back an interaction $\Omega_I(T)$. Let ℓ_{ref} and ℓ_{ch} be security parameters controling the length of interactions that the adversary can execute during the training and the cracking phases of the experiment. We first define a general experiment for untraceability, the strongest privacy notion, and then define forward and backward untraceability based on this experiment.

1. The $Challenger$ randomly picks a target tag T (among all possible random tags) and gives it to the adversary $\mathcal{A}$, together with the permission of oracle accesses to $\mathcal{O}_{\mathcal{R}}$.
2. $\mathcal{A}$ chooses I and calls $Oracle(T, I, \mathcal{O}_{\mathcal{R}}\})$ where $|I| \leq \ell_{ref}$, and gets $\Omega_I(T)$.
3. $\mathcal{A}$ requests the $Challenger$ to provide challenge tags and receives T_0 and T_1 such that $T_b = T$ for a hidden bit $b \in \{0, 1\}$.
4. $\mathcal{A}$ chooses I_0 and I_1 such that $|I_0|, |I_1| \leq \ell_{ch}$ and $(I_0 \cup I_1) \cap I = \emptyset$, calls $Oracle(T_0, I_0, \mathcal{O}_{\mathcal{R}}{}')$ and $Oracle(T_1, I_1, \mathcal{O}_{\mathcal{R}}{}')$, and gets $\Omega_{I_0}(T_0)$ and $\Omega_{I_1}(T_1)$.
5. $\mathcal{A}$ finally outputs her best guess b'.

Note that the reveal oracle R, if provided, can only be queried during the training phase (step 2) but never in the cracking phase (step 4). The advantage of $\mathcal{A}$ for a given protocol $\mathcal{P}$ under the $\mathcal{R}$-$\mathcal{O}$ model is defined by $\mathsf{Adv}_{\mathcal{P}}^{\mathcal{UNT}}(\mathcal{A}^{\mathcal{O}_{\mathcal{R}}}) = \Pr(b' = b) - \frac{1}{2}$, where the probability is taken over the coin tosses of $\mathcal{A}$ and $Challenger$ and over the choice of random intervals and random tags. In general, we say that $\mathcal{P}$ is $\mathcal{O}$-untraceable under the restriction $\mathcal{R}$ if this advantage is negligible w.r.t the security parameters ℓ_{ref} and ℓ_{ch}. We simply say that $\mathcal{P}$ is untraceable if $\mathcal{R} = \emptyset$ (the UA model) and $\mathcal{O} = \mathsf{QSE}$, since this is the best achievable untraceability notion without the reveal oracle.

When the reveal query is allowed (i.e., if $\mathcal{O} = \mathsf{QSER}$), we make a further distinction according to the additional restriction on the choice of experiment time intervals. If I, I_0 and I_1 are chosen such that $I > I_0$ and $I > I_1$, then the protocol is said to be backward untraceable under the restriction $\mathcal{R}$ (simply backward untraceable if $\mathcal{R} = \emptyset$). If the restriction is such that $I < I_0$ and $I < I_1$, then we say that the protocol is forward untraceable under the restriction $\mathcal{R}$. Note that forward untraceability under the UA model makes no sense, since once obtaining the tag secret by the reveal query, the adversary takes all the power of the tag itself and thus can trace the target tag at least during the authentication immediately following the attack. Thus, the minimum restriction for forward untraceability is such that there should exists some non-empty gap not accessible by the adversary between the time of a reveal query and the attack time. That is, there should exist some non-empty intervals J_0 and J_1 such that $I < J_0 < I_0$ and $I < J_1 < I_1$. Forward untraceability under this restriction would be the best one we can achieve in any RFID authentication protocol.

A Robust and Secure RFID-Based Pedigree System (Short Paper)

Chiu C. Tan and Qun Li

Department of Computer Science
College of William and Mary

Abstract. There has been considerable interest recently on developing a system to track items like pharmaceutical drugs or food products. Such a system can help prevent counterfeits, aid product recall, and improve general logistics. In this paper, we present such system based on radio frequency identity (RFID) technology. Our solution provides the means of storing the entire movement of the item from original manufacturer to final consumer on the RFID tag itself, and also makes it more difficult to introduce large numbers of counterfeits. The solution also allows the end user to easily verify the authenticity of the item.

1 Introduction

A tracking system, or electronic pedigree system, is an architecture for creating digital documentation for movement of goods. With this documentation, the entire route from beginning to end can be recreated. For instance, consider the case of some cargo shipped from a supplier to a customer. The electronic pedigree tracks the journey from the supplier's warehouse until it reaches the customer. It includes information like which intermittent stops were made and possibly more detailed information like which trucks were used. This form of documentation is useful for routine inventory control and tracking, as well as rare time-sensitive operations like product recalls. An electronic pedigree that tracks goods on an individual packaging basis can be used to defend against the counterfeits. Instead of relying on random checks at large warehouses, a per item electronic pedigree allows the end user who just purchased a product to verify the authenticity using electronic pedigree, thus improving the detection of counterfeits.

Recent developments in radio frequency identity (RFID) technology have made it possible to implement an electronic pedigree on a per item basis. RFID technology is made up of small powerless tags and their corresponding readers. These tags can be attached to different products like shipping crates or bottles of medication, and can contain information like the unique identity number of the product, origin, transit locations, storage instructions. RFID readers obtain the stored information by querying the tag from a distance without line of sight. One possible method of integrating RFID technology is described in [12] as "track and trace". It uses a central database to keep track of the unique ID number embedded in each tag. When products with attached RFID tags are received,

P. Ning, S. Qing, and N. Li (Eds.): ICICS 2006, LNCS 4307, pp. 21–29, 2006.
© Springer-Verlag Berlin Heidelberg 2006

an RFID reader reads in the ID from each tag. The ID can be verified against the central database containing information like the location of particular ID. An ID that shows up in the wrong location, or does not exist in the database could indicate potential problems. However, the paper also pointed out that this method is not robust enough against inevitable human errors, or instances where access to the database is limited.

Furthermore, the use of RFID tags introduces new security problems. Since an RFID tag can be read from a distance without line of sight, an adversary can steal large numbers of RFID data and then place the real data onto counterfeit RFID tags. This way, both the real and fake RFID tags contain legitimate information. Trials on RFID-enhanced passports reported RFID readers being able to access RFID data from 30 feet away [13]. For an RFID based pedigree system to function, it has to be robust enough to function without constant access to a central database. It also has to defend against counterfeits which can be introduced anywhere inside the supply chain.

In this paper, we present an RFID-based electronic pedigree system that does not depend on constant access to a database to function. Our system adds pedigree data onto the RFID tag itself in a secure manner. Since the RFID tag is always attached to the object, receiving the object means receiving the tag as well. With more information stored on the tag, pedigree information can be accessed more conveniently. Our solution also provides the end user, or consumer, with a means of easily verifying the authenticity of a tag while preserving his privacy.. The rest of the paper is as follows. The next section discusses some related work on RFID. Section 3 formalizes our problem and section 4 present our basic pedigree scheme. Section 5 improves on the basic scheme and section 6 concludes.

2   Related Work

There has been relatively little research that explicitly addresses using RFID for tracking purposes. Gonzalez et. al [3] addresses the problem of managing large quantities of RFID data generated when RFID tags are widely used for tracking. The work focuses on techniques for aggregating and indexing RFID data and query processing. Staake et. al [12] discusses how RFID used in tracking inventory can also be used for anti-counterfeiting purposes.. It described the track and trace method whereby each object is tagged with its own RFID tag embedded with some unique data. A main database is used to keep track of the tag data. As each object moves through the supply chain, information like object location can be matched against the tag unique data and database. This makes introducing counterfeits more difficult. However, this method requires all entities to update the database promptly, making it less robust to inevitable errors.

Texas Instruments (TI) [8] presented the *authenticated RFID* model which combines public key and RFID, and is targeted at pharmaceutical products. Under this model, the unique id of each RFID is first hashed, and then digitally signed with private key. This signature is stored onto the RFID tag itself together with the tag unique id before leaving the drug manufacturer. Later, authorized RFID readers like the pharmacist receiving the RFID tag authenticate the tag by reading in the digital signature and unique id. The pharmacist decrypts the signature with the public key, and compares the value against the hashed result of the unique id. If they match, then the tag is considered genuine. This model also allows additional information like timestamps to be signed and placed onto the RFID tag for additional security. However, as Juels [6] pointed out, this model has a vulnerability. An adversary will be unable to forge the signature, but is perfectly able to copy it. This means that an adversary could simply copy the genuine RFID tag data, and then place them onto the counterfeit drugs. Our solution also uses public key cryptography, but specifically addresses the problem of copying.

The copying of data from real RFID tags is know as skimming the tag, and placing real tag data onto fake RFID tags is known as cloning the tag. Juels [5] discusses the risks of RFID tag cloning, and provided solutions for a reader to authenticate a tag. The basic solution assumes that each RFID tag has a secret that is not reveled when queried. An authenticated reader will know this secret, and challenges the tag with it. The RFID tag is designed to return a 1 bit if the challenge secret matches its own secret, otherwise returns 0. So the RFID reader issues a series of challenges, some using the the tag secret, others not. A real tag will be able to return the correct answer each time. A counterfeit tag which was cloned from the real tag will not know this secret. However, this particular solution may require several interactions between reader and tag before the reader is satisfied that the tag is genuine, make it less efficient.

Another cloning resistant scheme by Dimitriou [2] uses a different approach. His approach uses a secure external server for authentication. The RFID tag returns a reply that can only be decrypted by the external server. The server releases the tag data to the reader only after authenticating him. This means that an adversary will not be able to obtain the RFID tag data without going through the secure server, thus preventing skimming. However, this scheme like track and trace, requires persistent access to a database.

There are other security protocols that can prevent cloning, and we refer interested readers to the excellent website maintained by Avoine [1], and recent survey papers [6,11]. In general, they all rely on only having authenticated RFID readers having access to RFID tag data. However, this concept can create potential privacy problems when applied to the electronic pedigree system. The problem lies in authenticating the RFID readers. Consider the example of a drug company shipping drugs to the clinic. After a patient purchases the medication, he would like to read the RFID tag data to make sure it is genuine. If only authenticated readers can read the RFID tag, then the patient will have to authenticate himself to the drug company, thus violating his privacy. Allowing *any* RFID reader to reader the tag protects the patient's privacy, but also allow malicious agents to clone the RFID tags. To prevent large scale RFID tag data to be stolen without use authorized RFID readers, we borrow a similar idea from [7] that uses both a optical and radio channel. Their paper focuses on banknotes embedded with an RFID tag. The RFID data is changed periodically so that it does not always return the same value, thus serving as a pseudo identifier for the banknote. The serial number is the optical channel that controls the changing of RFID data so that the data cannot be changed by malicious agents remotely.

3 Problem Formulation and Assumptions

We can abstract the problem of moving products from manufacturer to consumer as

$$D_0 \rightarrow (D_1 \cdots D_n) \rightarrow C$$

where D_0 is the original manufacturer, and C is the final consumer. D_0 is assumed to be always trusted, and C is assumed to always verify his purchase. $D_1 \cdots D_n$ are the different intermediaries that the product goes through before reaching the consumer. These intermediaries are entities that come into contact with the product, for example resellers, warehouse operators or delivery trucks. Each individual product has a unique RFID tag, T, with identity, id. Subscripts are used to distinguish one tag from another. Since every product has an RFID tag, referring to a particular tag, T_i, refers to both the RFID tag and the product. We consider an adversary denoted as α that can attack anywhere between $(D_1 \cdots D_n)$. The goal of α is to create large numbers of counterfeit RFID tags that are indistinguishable from real RFID tags.

We assume that different intermediaries like D_i and D_j can verify each other's identity and create a secure channel to exchange information. We also assume that consumers will have easy access to RFID readers and barcode readers. This is a realistic assumption since these readers are beginning to be integrated with cell phones [9],[10]. The RFID tags used in this paper are assumed to have a memory divided into multiple cells. This division of RFID memory into different cells was also adopted in [7] in which the RFID attached to a banknote has two memory cells. Finally the memory cells in the basic pedigree scheme are write once only, while the cells in the improved scheme can be written multiple times. Both types of RFID tags are currently available [4].

4 Basic Pedigree Scheme

In the basic scheme, the tags attached to each product have multiple memory cells, in which each cell can only be written once. We assume that the tag has n memory cells, and there are less than n intermediaries. Furthermore, each product also contains a 2D barcode which stores more data than a conventional 1D barcode. This 2D barcode is place in such a manner that is difficult to read without damaging the packaging. In a packet of medication, for example, the RFID tag can be attached to the outside packaging while the barcode is placed inside the packaging. The only way to read the 2D barcode is to open the packaging.

Consider the case when D_0 is manufacturing a product with a particular tag T_i. D_0 first generates an id_i and stores the pairing of id_i and T_i. It then creates a 2D barcode embedded with id_i and attaches the barcode to the product. Finally, D_0 stores the hashed result of id_i, $h(id_i)$ into the first cell of T_i. Figure 1 illustrates T_i and barcode after preprocessing. When D_0 prepares to hand T_i

Barcode	Memory Cell 1	Memory Cell 2	$\cdots$	Memory Cell n
id_i	$h(id_i)$		$\cdots$	

Fig. 1. T_i after preprocessing

off to D_1, both parties first authenticate each other. Then, D_1 sends a random number n_{D_1} to D_0. D_0 signs the concatenation of this random number and D_1's identity using his private key, $(n_{D_1}||D_1)_{D_0}$, and stores the result into the next empty memory cell of T_i. When D_1 receives T_i, he reads in the last written memory cell in T_i and applies D_0 public key to the result. If D_1 gets back n_{D1}, he is convinced that T_i comes from D_0. This entire transaction can occur in real time just as D_0 hands off T_i to D_1. Figure 2 illustrates T_i when D_1 receives it. Figure 2 illustrates T_i when D_1 receives it. The same authentication process is

Barcode	Memory Cell 1	Memory Cell 2	$\cdots$	Memory Cell n
id_i	$h(id_i)$	$(n_{D_1}, D_1)_{D_0}$	$\cdots$	

Fig. 2. T_i after D_0 passes off to D_1

performed by the remaining intermediaries when they receive T_i. Thus when D_1 hands T_i off to D_2, D_1 will add $(n_{D_2}||D_2)_{D_1}$ to T_i, and so on. D_2 can also verify that D_1 is supposed to possess T_i by checking the earlier memory cells in T_i. D_2 first asks D_1 who it receive T_i from. Then, D_2 can use D_0's public key to open the package $(n_{D_1}||D_1)_{D_0}$ found in the earlier memory cell and check if the D_1 identity is indeed stored the earlier memory cell. More generally, an intermediary D_i can *backtrack* back to D_0 by reading the data off the RFID tag and asking earlier intermediaries and thus recreating the entire movement of a particular product from the data stored in the RFID tag. This approach is feasible when the intermediaries are related and their public keys easily available., for example when T_i is passed from one FedEx truck to another, or when intermediaries are compelled to cooperate by the relevant authorities.

When the consumer receives T_i, he opens the package to reveal the 2D barcode. He then checks if the hashed result of the 2D barcode is equivalent to the data stored in the first memory cell of T_i. If they match, he then checks $h(id_i)$ against a public website managed by D_0. Since D_0 stores the pairing of id_i and T_i during preprocessing, D_0 will be able to identify a valid $h(id_i)$. If either test fails, the consumer rejects the package and contacts the relevant authorities.

4.1   Evaluating the Basic Scheme

A robust pedigree system needs to store and recover information from the RFID tag without using a persistent central server. From the scheme above, we see that storing data onto the RFID tag does not require a central server. Here, we show how to obtain information from the RFID tag data. A secure pedigree system has to prevent large number of counterfeit RFID tags from being accepted by intermediaries.

A key function of a pedigree record is to retrieve information about a particular product like which warehouse it was stored in or which truck transported it. The difference of a pedigree system using RFID is that it allows the creation of a pedigree record on a *per item* basis. Thus, an effective pedigree system will be able to easily retrieve this information. Every intermediary D_i, that comes into contact with T_i stores the identity of the next intermediary D_j it passes T_i to by storing $(n_{D_j} || D_j)_{D_i}$. Thus, when there is a need to identify all the products that came into contact with D_j due to a contamination or product recall, the relevant authorities can release the identities and the public keys of the intermediaries around like D_i, D_j, D_k. Concerned consumers can scan the RFID tag of their own products and apply the different public keys to verify if they have a product that passed through D_j. Intermediaries can also verify their inventories since RFID tags can be read quickly without line of sight. Note that the electronic pedigree based on RFID tags does not supplant existing inventory management, but complements it. Thus we can assume that relevant authorities can identify the potential intermediaries and disseminate their public key information. The entire route taken by a particular product can also be recreated by backtracking back to D_0.

For an adversary α to create a large number of counterfeits to flood the system, α will also need to convince the intermediaries that it is a legitimate recipient of the product. Consider the case where D_j is supposed to pass T_i to D_k. α can scan T_i from D_j, attach it to its counterfeits, and try to pass it off to D_k. Assuming that D_j got T_i from D_i, the contents of T_i scanned by α will be

$$\{h(id_i) || (n_{D_1}, D_1)_{D_0} | \cdots | (n_{D_j}, D_j)_{D_i}\}$$

After α passes of T_i to D_k, T_i will become

$$\{h(id_i) || (n_{D_1}, D_1)_{D_0} | \cdots | (n_{D_j}, D_j)_{D_i} | (n_{D_k}, D_k)_{\alpha}\}$$

When D_k asks α to verify that it is a legitimate recipient of T_i, α will have to provide the identity of the intermediary he received the product from. However, the previous memory cell contains $(n_{D_j}, D_j)_{D_i}$, and not $(n_{\alpha}, \alpha)_{D_i}$ which D_k is expecting. Thus, α will not be able to convince D_k is a legitimate recipient of T_i. Since D_k can continue to ask each previous intermediary up till the original D_0 which is always trusted, multiple adversaries colluding can still be identified.

However, the above scheme does not protect against a legitimate intermediary who is also an α. Consider the case where D_k receives a legitimate tag T_i from D_j. D_k is also malicious, so he reads the data from the T_i, and place the data onto another RFID tag attached to a counterfeit product. Let us term this counterfeit product's RFID tag as $\hat{T}_i$. Now, the backtracking approached used above does not work, since T_i and $\hat{T}_I$ both contain the same data. To detect this form of counterfeit, we rely of the consumer verifying the RFID tag. When the consumer wishes to verify his purchase, he will first read the id_i stored in the 2D barcode and compare the hashed result of the 2D barcode against the first memory cell of T_i which is $h(id_i)$. Since a one-way hash is used, α will not be able to derive id_i from $h(id_i)$. Thus, the counterfeit product will not have a 2D barcode whose hashed value matches the value on the RFID tag. An alternative is for α to create a fake id_i termed $\hat{id}_i$, and create a fake tag $\hat{T}_i$ that has $h(\hat{id}_i)$. However, when the consumer checks the hashed value against the public website maintained by D_0, he will discover $h(\hat{id}_i)$ is invalid. Finally, α can obtain a legitimate 2D barcode by physically opening one product, and then replicate the same T_i and 2D barcode on multiple counterfeits. While this form of attack is able to fool a consumer, the scope of such an attack is rather limited. Since barcode contains a unique identifier, all the counterfeit RFID tags by α will have the same $h(id_i)$ stored in the first memory cell, making it easy for intermediaries to detect.

5   Improved Pedigree Scheme

One drawback of the basic scheme is it is unsuitable when there are too many intermediaries. The number of memory cells needed will be too expensive to attach to individual products. The improved scheme limits the number of memory cells needed by compressing the data. The improved scheme retains the use of the 2D barcode, but uses a re-writable RFID tag. This means that the data on a particular cell on the RFID tag can be overwritten.

The improved scheme requires three memory cells on the RFID tag. The first cell is used to store the hashed result of the barcode. The remaining two cells are used to store signatures from the different intermediaries. The improved scheme retains the same preprocessing step as the basic scheme. For sake of brevity, we denote $h(id_i)$ as r_1 and $(n_{D_1}, D_1)_{D_0}$ as d_1. Both r_1 and d_1 are stored in the first memory cell of T_i. This cell cannot be over written. Figure 3 shows T_i when D_1 receives it. When D_1 hands off T_i over to D_2, it will generate $d_2 = (n_{D_2}, D_2)_{D_1}$

Barcode	Memory Cell 1	Memory Cell 2	Memory Cell 3
id_i	$d_1 = (n_{D_1}, D_1)_{D_0}$		
	$r_1 = h(id_i)$		

Fig. 3. T_i when passed to D_1

and $r_2 = h(r_1 \| d_1)$ and store it into the next empty memory cell. The $\|$ denotes concatenation. D_2 handing off to D_3 will have $d_3 = (n_{D_3}, D_3)_{D_3}$ and $r_3 = h(r_2 \| d_2)$. Figure 4 shows T_i when D_3 receives the it from D_2. When D_3 prepares to pass T_i to D_4, there are no more empty cells left in T_i. D_3 then replaces the contents of memory cell 2 with information regarding $d_4 = (n_{D_4}, D_4)_{D_3}$ and

Barcode	Memory Cell 1	Memory Cell 2	Memory Cell 3
id_i	$d_1 = (n_{D_1}, D_1)_{D_0}$	$d_2 = (n_{D_2}, D_2)_{D_1}$	$d_3 = (n_{D_3}, D_3)_{D_2}$
	$r_1 = h(id_i)$	$r_2 = h(r_1 \| d_1)$	$r_3 = h(r_2 \| d_2)$

Fig. 4. D_3 getting T_i from D_2

$r_4 = h(r_3 \| d_3)$. Figure 5 illustrates T_i when D_4 receives it. D_4 can verify that d_4 is correct by applying D_3's public key and checking the random number n_{D_4}. D_4 uses r_3 and d_3, both found in memory cell 3, to verify that D_3 computed the correct r_4 value. Using r_4, we can derive the structure shown in Figure 6, where the information captured in the basic scheme can be derived.

As in the basic scheme, T_i can be backtracked to D_0 by having the intermediary ask each previous intermediary whom they received T_i from. This information is then checked against the data found in the tag. The consumer can verify the product using the 2D barcode and r_i found in memory cell 1 as in the basic scheme. However, unlike the basic scheme, this solution does not permit the consumer or an intermediary from checking whether T_i had passed through any particular intermediary simply by releasing the identity and public keys. This information can only be found via backtracking.

Barcode	Memory Cell 1	Memory Cell 2	Memory Cell 3
id_i	$d_1 = (n_{D_1}, D_1)_{D_0}$	$d_4 = (n_{D_4}, D_4)_{D_3}$	$d_3 = (n_{D_3}, D_3)_{D_2}$
	$r_1 = h(id_i)$	$r_4 = h(r_3 \| d_3)$	$r_3 = h(r_2 \| d_2)$

Fig. 5. D_4 getting T_i from D_3

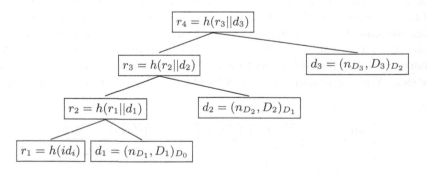

Fig. 6. Building pedigree from r_3

6   Conclusion

In this paper, we examine how RFID tags can be used to establish an electronic pedigree. We present two schemes that allow pedigree information to be stored directly onto the RFID tag itself. The end user can verity the authenticity of his purchase. Finally, both schemes make large scale counterfeits difficult to accomplish.

Acknowledgment. The authors would like to thank all the reviewers for their helpful comments. This project was partially supported by US National Science Foundation award CCF-0514985.

References

1. G. Avoine. http://lasecwww.epfl.ch/~gavoine/rfid/.
2. T. Dimitriou. A lightweight RFID protocol to protect against traceability and cloning attacks. In *Conference on Security and Privacy for Emerging Areas in Communication Networks – SecureComm*, Athens, Greece, September 2005. IEEE.
3. H. Gonzalez, J. Han, X. Li, and D. Klabjan. Warehousing and analyzing massive rfid data sets. In *ICDE '06: Proceedings of the 22nd International Conference on Data Engineering (ICDE'06)*, page 83, Washington, DC, USA, 2006. IEEE Computer Society.
4. T. Hassan and S. Chatterjee. A taxonomy for rfid. *hicss*, 8:184b, 2006.
5. A. Juels. Strengthening EPC tags against cloning. In *WiSe '05: Proceedings of the 4th ACM workshop on Wireless security*, pages 67–76, New York, NY, USA, 2005. ACM Press.
6. A. Juels. RFID security and privacy: A research survey. *IEEE Journal on Selected Areas in Computing*, 24(2):381–394, February 2006.
7. A. Juels and R. Pappu. Squealing euros: Privacy protection in RFID-enabled banknotes. In R. N. Wright, editor, *Financial Cryptography – FC'03*, volume 2742 of *Lecture Notes in Computer Science*, pages 103–121, Le Gosier, Guadeloupe, French West Indies, January 2003. IFCA, Springer-Verlag.
8. Texas Instruments Incorporated. Securing the pharmaceutical supply chain with rfid and public-key infrastructure (PKI) technologies. In *http://www.ti.com/rfid/docs/customer/eped-form.shtml*.
9. MobileMagazine. http://www.mobilemag.com/content/100/104/c2607/.
10. Nextel. *http : //www.nextel.com/en/solutions/special_devices/roadrunner.shtml*.
11. M. Rieback, B. Crispo, and A. Tanenbaum. The evolution of RFID security. *IEEE Pervasive Computing*, 5(1):62–69, January–March 2006.
12. T. Staake, F. Thiesse, and E. Fleisch. Extending the EPC network: the potential of rfid in anti-counterfeiting. In *SAC '05: Proceedings of the 2005 ACM symposium on Applied computing*, pages 1607–1612, New York, NY, USA, 2005. ACM Press.
13. J. Yoshida. Tests reveal e-passport security flaw. *EE Times*, 2004.

A Topological Condition for Solving Fair Exchange in Byzantine Environments

Benoît Garbinato and Ian Rickebusch

Université de Lausanne
CH-1015 Lausanne, Switzerland
{benoit.garbinato, ian.rickebusch}@unil.ch

Abstract. In this paper, we study the solvability of fair exchange in the context of Byzantine failures. In doing so, we first present a generic model with trusted and untrusted processes, and propose a specification of the fair exchange problem that clearly separates safety and liveness, via fine-grained properties. We then show that the solvability of fair exchange depends on a necessary and sufficient topological condition, which we name the *reachable majority* condition. The first part of this result, i.e., the condition is necessary, was shown in a companion paper and is briefly recalled here. The second part, i.e., the condition is sufficient, is the focal point of this paper. The correctness proof of this second part consists in proposing a solution to fair exchange in the aforementioned model.

1 Introduction

Intuitively, a fair exchange is an exchange of items among two or more parties where the only possible outcome is either that all parties obtain their items, or none of them do. In our modern daily lives, the notions of fair exchange and trust are ubiquitous: everyday, without even noticing, we participate in numerous commercial exchanges, which we expect to be fair (and most actually are). Such exchanges range from buying a coffee to spending a significant part of our savings in buying a house. A key enabler to make all these exchanges occur is the notion of *trust*. In the physical world, this trust is supported by the identification and the implicit reputation of tangible exchange partners.

In the digital world, on the contrary, fair exchange is a surprisingly difficult problem. This can be explained by the lack of trust that characterizes the digital realm. In an e-commerce environment, an exchange partner behaving unfairly can vanish without a trace, in contrast with a physical commercial environment where a partner can be approached physically and held accountable for a misbehavior. Yet, fair exchange is a fundamental problem that has constantly been studied over the past decades and that has recently regained interest [1,2,3,4]. This is partly due to the advent of m-business as a natural evolution of e-business, i.e., extending the possibilities of e-business through the use of mobile devices, e.g., cellular phones. When it comes to solving fair exchange in such semi-open environments, i.e., where all parties are not necessarily identified a priori, carefully modeling and analyzing trust relationships between peers is a key issue.

P. Ning, S. Qing, and N. Li (Eds.): ICICS 2006, LNCS 4307, pp. 30–49, 2006.

Contribution and Roadmap. This paper propose a generic model in order to study fair exchange in different network settings and also provides a topological condition, both necessary and sufficient, for solving fair exchange. In Section 2, we introduce a synchronous distributed model where processes are divided into two categories, namely *participants*, which can be Byzantine, and *trustees*, which are known a priori to be correct. In that section, we then formally define the fair exchange problem via fine-grained properties that separately capture the liveness and safety requirements of the problem. In Section 3, based on an impossibility result shown in a companion paper, we present a necessary and sufficient topological condition for solving fair exchange in a model with trustees. Section 4 then presents a solution to fair exchange under the aforementioned condition: this solution and its proof provide the correctness proof for the condition. Finally, Section 5 discusses related work, while Section 6 summarizes our contribution and sketches ongoing and future work.

2   Model and Problem Statement

Intuitively, our model consists in a synchronous distributed system composed of two types of processes: *participants*, which are processes potentially subject to Byzantine failures, and *trustees*, which are known a priori to be correct (and which can thus be trusted). The addition of trusted processes in our model is motivated by the fact that fair exchange is impossible in the absence of trust, i.e., without at least one correct process trusted a priori by all other processes [4]. Adding only a single trusted process would however limit the scope of our model and imply a specific role for that trustee, i.e., that of a Trusted Third Party (TTP). For this reason, we associate a trustee with each process, hence uniformly splitting the notion of trust among participants of the exchange and allowing for fully decentralized approaches.

A Generic Yet Realistic Model. The notion of trustees allows us to produce a generic model applicable to various trust and network topologies [2,5]. In particular, this model does not dictate the role of trustees in the fair exchange protocol, i.e., how trustees are connected or the amount of computation they bear. As a consequence, most existing solutions, either centralized or decentralized, can be described in our model. For example, Figure 1(a) shows a classical centralized trust setting, typically via a TTP as in [5], and the equivalent setting in our model. Figure 1(b) then illustrates a distributed trust setting, as with Guardian Angels [2]. By splitting the trust among all participants, via their respective trustees, we can show that the existence of a decentralized solution to fair exchange depends on a rather simple topological condition.

In practice, a trustee is typically implemented via a tamperproof piece of hardware embedded in each host, e.g., a specialized chip or a smart card. This hardware-based approach is gaining momentum in the industry, as illustrated by efforts from IBM, with both its PCI 4758 and PCI-X 4764 cryptographic coprocessors [6], and from Intel, with its Trusted Platform Module [7]. Such solutions are expected to

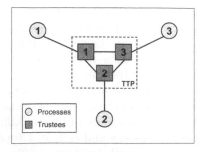
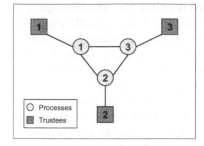

(a) Classical TTP in our model.   (b) Distributed TTP.

Fig. 1. Examples of trust topologies

eventually become mainstream, as the urge to go beyond software-based security increases, in particular in the realm of digital rights management, and as fully decentralized peer-to-peer architectures are being deployed.

2.1 System Model

More formally, we consider a distributed system consisting of a set Π of n *processes*, $\Pi = \{p_1, p_2, \ldots, p_n\}$. Processes of Π are called *participants*. We complete our model with a set Π' of n trusted processes, $\Pi' = \{p'_1, p'_2, \ldots, p'_n\}$, i.e., a *trusted process* is known to be correct a priori by all other processes. Processes of Π' are called *trustees*. Furthermore, each p'_i is matched in a one-to-one relationship with the corresponding participant p_i and is directly connected to it. The set Π^+ is then the set of all $2n$ processes, i.e., $\Pi^+ = \Pi \cup \Pi'$. Participants are processes actually taking part in the exchange by offering and demanding items, and they may exhibit Byzantine behaviors. Trustees on the contrary are *trusted processes* that have no direct interest in the exchange. Their role is to decide when it is appropriate to provide their associated participant with its expected item. We also assume the existence of a *Public Key Infrastructure* (PKI), i.e., each process (participants and trustees) owns a private key and made the corresponding public key accessible to all other processes. Among other things, this assumption provides message unforgeability.

Topology and Synchrony. Processes are interconnected by a communication network and communicate by message passing. The system is *synchronous*: it exhibits *synchronous computation* and *synchronous communication*, i.e, there exists upper bounds on processing and communication delays. To help our reasoning, we also assume the existence of some global real time clock, whose tick range, noted T, is the set of natural numbers.[1]

Regarding the network topology, we assume that processes of Π^+ form a connected graph and that there exists a direct link between any participant and

---

[1] This global clock is virtual in the sense that processes do not have access to it.

its trustee. Links are reliable bidirectional communication channels, i.e, if both the sender and the receiver are correct, any message inserted in the channel is *eventually* delivered by the receiver. The *synchronous* system assumption further tells us that the delivery will occur within some known time bound Δ_{PL}. Formally, such channels are said to be *perfect links* (PL), which provide *send* and *deliver* primitives (respectively PL.send() and PL.deliver() functions) and ensure the well-known *termination* and *no creation* properties.

Executions and Failure Patterns. We define the *execution* of algorithm A as a sequence of steps executed by processes of Π^+. In each step, a process has the opportunity to atomically perform all three following actions: (1) send a message, (2) receive a message and (3) update its local state.[2] Based on this definition, a *Byzantine process* is one that deviates from A in any sort of way, so a Byzantine process is Byzantine against a specific algorithm A. It is a known result that Byzantine failures can only be defined with respect to some algorithm [8]. A *Byzantine failure pattern* f is then defined as a function of T to 2^Π where $f(t)$ denotes a set of Byzantine processes that have deviated from A through time t. In a way, a failure pattern f can be seen as a projection of all process failures during some execution of A. Once a process starts misbehaving, it cannot return to being considered correct, i.e., $f(t) \subseteq f(t+1)$. We also define F as the set of all possible failure patterns of A, so $f \in F$. Let $\mathsf{Byz}(f) = \bigcup_{t \in T} f(t)$ denote the set of Byzantine processes in f. We then define the set F_b of all failure patterns where no more than b processes are Byzantine. More formally, F_b is the largest subset of F such that, for any failure pattern $f \in F_b$, $|\mathsf{Byz}(f)| \leq b$, with $0 \leq b \leq n$:

$$F_b = \{f \in F \ : \ |\mathsf{Byz}(f)| \leq b\} \ with \ 0 \leq b \leq n \ .$$

Note that b is bounded by n, the number of processes in Π. From this definition, b is the maximum number of Byzantine processes in any failure pattern of F_b and $F_n = F$. Note that all the above definitions regarding executions and failures are similar to the models of [8,9], but that failures refer exclusively to participants, i.e., processes of Π, since trustees are correct.

2.2   The Fair Exchange Problem

The fair exchange problem consists in a group of processes trying to exchange digital items in a fair manner. The difficulty of the problem resides in achieving fairness. Intuitively, fairness means that, if one process obtains the desired digital item, then all processes involved in the exchange should also obtain their desired digital item. The assumption is made that each process knows both the set Π of processes participating in the fair exchange and the terms of the exchange. The terms of the exchange are defined by a set D of expected item descriptions, $D = \{d_1, d_2, \ldots, d_n\}$, and a set Ω of pairs of processes (p_i, p_j). A description d_i is the description of the item expected by process p_i. Furthermore d_i is unique, so

---

[2] At each step, the process can of course choose to skip any of these actions, e.g., if it has nothing to send.

if $i \neq j$, then $d_i \neq d_j$. A pair (p_i, p_j) defines the receiver p_j of the item offered by p_i. Elements of Ω are defined such that p_j is the image of p_i through a bijective map (or permutation) of Π, with $i \neq j$. Finally, let M denote the set of digital items m_i actually offered by process p_i during an execution of fair exchange, $M = \{m_1, m_2, \ldots, m_n\}$. Note that, accordingly, for each description in D there does not necessarily exist a corresponding item in M, since M includes items that might have been offered by Byzantine processes. Finally, let $\mathsf{desc}(m)$ be the function returning the description of item m.

Fair Exchange as Service. Fair exchange can be seen as a service allowing processes to exchange digital items in a fair manner. Each process offers an item in exchange for a counterpart of which it has the description. The exchange is completed when every process releases the desired counterpart or all processes release the abort item φ, meaning that the exchange has aborted. To achieve this, the service offers the two following primitives.

> **offer**(m_i, p_j) – Enables the process p_i to initiate its participation in the exchange with processes of Π by offering item m_i to p_j, in exchange for the item matching description d_i, with d_i and Π known a priori.[3]
>
> **release**(x) – Informs the process that the exchange completed and works as a callback. Process p_i receives item x, which is either an item matching d_i or the abort item φ.

Note that, at the end of an exchange, we say that p_i *releases* an item, meaning that the service calls back the *release* operation of p_i. This convention is similar to the one used for typical *deliver* primitives, e.g., with reliable broadcast primitives [10].

Fair Exchange Properties. We now specify the formal properties of the fair exchange problem. While several other specifications exist in the literature [2,3,11], our specification differs in that it separates safety and liveness via *fine-grained properties*. Such elemental properties then allow us to better reason about the correctness of our solution.

Validity. If a correct process p_i releases an item x, then either $x \in M$ and x matches d_i, or x is the abort item φ.

Uniqueness. No correct process releases more than once.

Non-triviality. If all processes are correct, no process releases the abort item φ.

Termination. Every correct process *eventually* releases an item.

Integrity. No process p_j releases an item m_i, with process p_i correct, if m_i matches description d_k of some correct process p_k, with $p_k \neq p_j$.

Fairness. If any process p_i releases an item m_j matching description d_i, with p_i or p_j correct, then every correct process p_k releases an item matching description d_k.

---

[3] When defining the FE problem, trustees are not required since they have no direct interest in the exchange.

Among these six properties, the last two, *integrity* and *fairness*, are specific to the problem of fair exchange and define precisely the possible outcomes of fair exchange algorithms. Other specifications of fair exchange usually rely on a single property to capture the notion of fairness [2,5,11]. However we argue that if those specifications are suitable for cases where $n = 2$, they are impossible to satisfy in models allowing more than one Byzantine process. In [2], for example, the *fairness* property requires that if any correct process does not obtain its item, then no process obtains any items from any other process. This is clearly unsustainable in the presence of two or more Byzantine processes because one cannot prevent two Byzantine processes from conspiring in order for one of them to obtain the item of the second one. A simple but flawed fix would be to modify this definition as follows: if any correct process does not obtain its item, then no process obtains any items from any *correct* process. If it first seems correct, this definition of *fairness* now allows a correct process to obtain the item of a Byzantine process, even if other correct processes do not obtain anything.

Coming back to our specification, *integrity* ensures that no process obtains an item offered by a correct process and matching the description of some other correct process. Notice that this does not prevent a Byzantine process from illicitly obtaining the item destined to or offered by some other Byzantine process, since such a behavior cannot be prevented and does not prejudice any correct process. Then, *fairness* guarantees that if any process obtains its desired item offered by some other process, with at least one of them being correct, then every correct process also obtains its desired item. In other words this property prevents a Byzantine process from taking advantage of a correct process but does not protect other Byzantine processes from their own incorrect behaviors. More trivially, it also ensures that no correct process takes advantage of any process.

3   The *Reachable Majority* Condition

In a companion paper [4], we showed that a *necessary* condition to solve fair exchange in the model with trustees is to have every correct participant reliably connected to a majority of trustees. To formally define this condition, named the *reachable majority* (RM) condition, we must first define the notion of *reliable path* as follows. Let p_i and p_j be two correct processes of Π^+. We say that p_i and p_j are connected by a *reliable path*, if there exists at least one path between p_i and p_j such that no process along that path is Byzantine. The RM condition is then formally defined as follows.

Definition 1 (Reachable majority condition). *Topological condition under which, for any correct process* $p \in \Pi$ *and any failure pattern* $f \in F_b$, *p is connected by a reliable path to a strict majority of trustees, i.e.,* $\lfloor \frac{n}{2} + 1 \rfloor$, *even in the presence of up to b Byzantine processes.*

Note that trustees described in Definition 1 are called *major* trustees, whereas others are called *minor* trustees. The strict majority of Definition 1 ensures that the set of major trustees is identical for all correct processes, since if two processes have a single major trustee in common, then they have all their major trustees in common. The main focus of this paper is to show that not only is this condition necessary, it is also sufficient (Theorems 1 and 2 hereafter). This condition then allows us to better reason on the solvability of fair exchange and to compare different topologies. Indeed, given a topology and a number of Byzantine processes, one can infer whether a solution exists in that context. Or maybe more interestingly, it is possible to determine the maximum number of Byzantine processes that a specific network topology may sustain and yet still allow true fair exchange (by opposition to probabilistic fairness). Note that if the RM condition is met, it implies that all correct processes and a majority of trustees are interconnected by reliable paths. However, it is important to note that it does not imply, nor require, a majority of correct processes. Figure 2 gives examples of topologies allowing true fair exchange, including their respective upper bounds on the number of Byzantine processes. As illustrated in Figure 2(a), a TTP is able to sustain any number of Byzantine processes, whereas Figure 2(b) and (c) show topologies sustaining respectively a minority of Byzantine processes and up to the parity between correct and Byzantine processes.

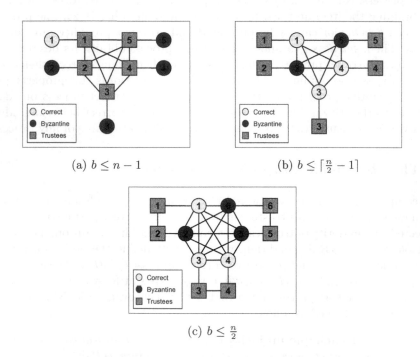

(a) $b \leq n - 1$ (b) $b \leq \lceil \frac{n}{2} - 1 \rceil$

(c) $b \leq \frac{n}{2}$

Fig. 2. Topologies allowing true fair exchange

3.1 Impossibility and Solvability Theorems

As already mentioned, in [4] we showed that the RM condition is a *necessary* condition in order to deterministically solve fair exchange in the model with trustees. Hereafter, Theorem 1 gives an informal reading of this result. Furthermore, in this paper, we argue through Theorem 2 that the RM condition is also *sufficient* in order to solve fair exchange.

Theorem 1 (Impossibility). *In the context of a synchronous model with trustees and Byzantine failures, there is no deterministic solution to the fair exchange problem, if the reachable majority condition is not satisfied.*

The formal proof of Theorem 1 falls outside the scope of this paper and can be found in [4]. However, to give an intuition of its correctness, first observe that, in order to ensure fairness, trustees must make a *consistent* decision whether to allow their respective processes to obtain their items or not. Then, since a process and its trustee are directly connected, if some correct process p is not reliably connected to a majority of trustees, neither is its trustee p'. So, either p' is not allowed to make a decision and p ends up violating the termination property of fair exchange; or p' is indeed allowed to make a decision in the absence of a majority, in which case there is no means to prevent fairness from being violated, e.g., if another group of reliably connected trustees make a contradictory decision.

Theorem 2 (Solvability). *In the context of a synchronous model with trustees and Byzantine failures, there exists a deterministic solution to the fair exchange problem under the reachable majority condition.*

Proof. In Section 4, we present Algorithms 1 and 2, which combine to produce a generic solution to fair exchange, for any topology and any number of Byzantine processes respecting the RM condition. We then prove the correctness of Theorem 2 by proving that our solution preserves the *validity*, *uniqueness*, *non-triviality*, *termination*, *integrity* and *fairness* properties of fair exchange.

4   Fair Exchange Under the RM Condition

In this section, we propose a solution to fair exchange that relies on the use of trustees. As described in Section 2.1 (system model), participants communicate by message passing and the network is a connected graph with respective participants and trustees connected directly. Our solution is composed of Algorithm 1 and Algorithm 2 and, other than *perfect links* presented in the model, they rely on two communication modules described hereafter, i.e., a *best-effort multicast* module and a *Byzantine agreement* module. Note that we merely aim at proving that a generic solution does exist under the RM condition and are thus not concerned with performance.

Best-Effort Multicast (BM). In order to solve fair exchange, Algorithms 1 and 2 rely on a *best-effort multicast* module that provides processes (participants and trustees) with the means to send messages to any group of processes with best effort. As described in our model, directly connected processes communicate via reliable channels. However, two processes that do not benefit from a direct link are not necessarily reliably connected, since paths between them might go through a Byzantine process, making communications potentially unreliable. The BM module provides a means to reliably send messages to processes accessible through at least one reliable path.[4] The module provides two primitives, *send* and *deliver*, described hereafter.

BM.send($p_i, S,$ 'TYPE', m) – Enables a process p_i to multicast a message m to a defined set S of processes. The message type prevents confusion among different messages.

BM.deliver($p_i, p_j,$ 'TYPE', m) – Works as a callback and enables a process p_j of S to receive a message m from process p_i.

Hereafter, we present the *validity* and *agreement* properties of best-effort multicast, which are the two main properties ensured by the BM module. A *no creation* property is also part of the specification of the best-effort multicast abstraction but is not detailed here. Note that one can ensure that the *validity* property of BM is achieved within some maximum time bound Δ_{BM}, e.g., by having $\Delta_{BM} = n \times \Delta_{PL}$ in the worst case.

Validity. Let p_i and p_j be any two correct processes connected by a reliable path, if p_i BM.sends a message m to a set S, with $p_j \in S$, then p_j eventually delivers m.

Agreement. Let p_i and p_j be any two correct processes of some set S that are connected by a reliable path, if p_i BM.delivers a message m BM.sent to S, then p_j BM.delivers m.

Byzantine Agreement (BA). In Algorithm 2, we use a Byzantine Agreement module that provides trustees with a means to reach agreement among major trustees, in spite of Byzantine failures that may occur along the various paths. This version of Byzantine agreement is largely based on [13]. However it differs in the sense that no Byzantine processes participate in the agreement (only trustees) but communications along unreliable paths may be blocked by Byzantine processes. Now, by considering minor trustees responsible for Byzantine failures happening along the unreliable paths leading to them, one can then apply Byzantine agreement to our model, i.e., by considering major trustees as correct processes, minor trustees as Byzantine processes and unreliable paths as reliable. The BA module provides three primitives, BA.start(), BA.send() and BA.deliver(), described hereafter in details.

BA.start(p_j') – Enables a trustee p_i' to start an execution of BA in order to receive a message from a trustee p_j'. For each execution of the protocol, every trustee calls the *start* primitive at the same time (see explanation below) and trustee p_j' calls the *send* primitive.

BA.send(p_i', m) – Enables a trustee p_i' to reliably broadcast a message m to all trustees.

---

[4] This can be achieved using flooding as presented in Appendix A or some more sophisticated algorithm [12].

BA.deliver(p'_i, M) – Works as a callback and enables a trustee p'_j to receive a set M of messages as the result of a reliable broadcast by trustee p'_i. Possible outcomes of the broadcast are twofold: (1) M is a singleton, meaning that transmissions from the sender were not blocked, so that message can be used; (2) M is the empty set, meaning that the sender did not call the *send* primitive in a timely fashion or that messages from the sender were blocked.

Intuitively, the goal consists in preventing Byzantine processes along unreliable paths from causing major trustees to receive different sets M. When relying on unforgeable signed messages, a solution is known to exists for any number of Byzantine processes [13], i.e., in our case minor trustees. Hereafter, we recall the two interactive consistency (IC) properties ensured by the BA module.

IC1 – Agreement. If a major trustee BA.delivers a set of messages M, then every major trustee BA.delivers M.

IC2 – Validity. If a major trustee BA.sends a message m, then every major trustee *eventually* BA.delivers the set $\{m\}$.

An implicit assumption in [13] is that all trustees roughly start at the same time to allow the absence of messages to be detected. Since all trustees roughly start Algorithm 2 at the same time, the *start* primitive of BA enables us to explicitly ensure this assumption by having all trustees calling the primitive at the same time (line 13 of Algorithm 2), i.e., at time $t_0 + \Delta_{BM}$. This ensures *termination* of BA, even if a trustee does not send any vote or messages are blocked by some Byzantine processes.

4.1   Fair Exchange Algorithm

Algorithms 1 and 2 provide a generic solution to the fair exchange problem for any topology and any number of Byzantine processes meeting the RM condition. For sake of simplicity, we assume that all correct processes – including all trustees – have local clocks that are synchronized within some fixed maximum error, as discussed in [14], so they are able to start the algorithms at the same time. We also assume that *upon* actions are executed atomically with respect to one another. Participants execute Algorithm 1, which initiates the fair exchange protocol, and trustees execute Algorithm 2. In Algorithm 1, each participant sends an encrypted version of its offered item to the trustee of the corresponding participant, according to Ω (the terms of the exchange). It then waits to receive and release the content of the first message sent by its trustee. The termination of Algorithm 1 is ensured by the timeout contained in Algorithm 2. In Algorithm 2, each trustee waits to receive the item expected by its associated participant. Algorithm 2 is then structured in two phases described hereafter: (1) the voting phase, and (2) the clue exchange phase.

Voting Phase. In this phase, trustee p'_i sends its vote to every trustee to inform them that it holds the expected item, and waits to receive the vote of every trustee. In Algorithm 2, once trustee p'_i receives the encrypted item (line 7), it

---

Algorithm 1. Fair Exchange executed by participant p_i, with $(p_i, p_j) \in \Omega$

1: **Uses:** Perfect Link (PL), Best-effort Multicast (BM)
2: Initialisation:
3:    released ← 'false'

4: **function offer**(item, p_j)
5:    BM.send(p_i, {p_j'}, 'ITEM', encrypt(p_j', item))   {*sends its encrypted item to p_j'*}

6: **upon** PL.deliver(p_i', p_i, item) **do**   {*callback from PL*}
7:    **if** ¬released **then**   {*avoids releasing*}
8:       released ← 'true'   {*more than once*}
9:       **release**(item)   {*releases the item received*}

---

deciphers it using its private key, checks if it matches its description and starts the voting process. The trustee signs and broadcasts its PROCEED vote (line 12) using BA, indicating that it holds the expected item. It also starts BA for each trustee to ensure termination of all executions of BA. Then, upon reception of a vote, the validProceedVote() function checks if the delivered set is a singleton containing the PROCEED vote of the sender (line 17). If the vote is valid, it is added to the set of votes. Once all votes are gathered, a trustee knows that every trustee voted PROCEED and that they thus hold the expected item. With that information, trustee p_i' enters the final phase by signing and then sending the n votes – called the i-th clue – to every trustee (line 21).

Clue Exchange Phase. In this phase, trustee p_i' sends its clue to all trustees to inform them that it received all n votes, and waits to receive the clues from a majority of trustees (line 27). Upon reception of a clue, the validClue() function checks if the clue contains a signed set of all n PROCEED votes (line 25). With $\lfloor \frac{n}{2} + 1 \rfloor$ clues, it sends the deciphered item to its corresponding participant (line 28). The majority is necessary to ensure that at least one major trustee was able to produce its i-th clue in order for any process to release its item. At this stage, no Byzantine process is able to prevent trustees of correct processes to send the expected item to their respective process.

4.2   Correctness Proof

In the following, we prove that Algorithms 1 and 2 solve fair exchange under the *reachable majority* condition. Our correctness proof shows that Algorithms 1 and 2 preserve the *validity*, *uniqueness*, *non-triviality*, *termination*, *integrity* and *fairness* properties of fair exchange. Based on Lemma 1, the respective theorems hereafter validate each of these properties. Note that, hereafter, the term *process* is only used to designate participants, i.e., processes of Π, unless specifically mentioned otherwise.

Algorithm 2. Fair Exchange protocol executed by trustee p'_i

1: **Uses:** Perfect Link (PL), Best-effort Multicast (BM), Byzantine Agreement (BA)
2: Initialisation:
3:     $t_0 \leftarrow$ time()   *{sets t_0 to starting time}*
4:     $d_i \leftarrow ...$ *{sets description to known value}*
5:     item $\leftarrow \perp$ *{sets variable to null}*
6:     votes, clues $\leftarrow \emptyset$ *{sets variables to empty set}*

7: **upon** BM.deliver(p_j, p'_i, 'ITEM', sealedItem) **do**   *{callback from BM}*
8:     **if** (item $= \perp$) **then**   *{checks for duplicate send}*
9:        item $\leftarrow$ decipher(sealedItem)   *{deciphers and stores received item}*
10:        **if** desc(item) $= d_i$ **then**   *{check if item matches description}*
11:           vote $\leftarrow$ sign('PROCEED')   *{produces PROCEED vote}*
12:           BA.send(p'_i, vote)   *{sends vote}*

13: **upon** $time() > t_0 + \Delta_{BM}$ **do**   *{item exchange phase is over}*
14:     **for all** $p'_j \in \Pi'$ **do**   *{for all trustees}*
15:        BA.start(p'_j)   *{starts BA}*

16: **upon** BA.deliver(p'_j, vote) **do**   *{callback from BA}*
17:     **if** validProceedVote(vote) **then**   *{checks vote}*
18:        votes $\leftarrow$ votes $\cup$ vote   *{adds p'_j's vote to set}*
19:        **if** ($|$votes$| = n$) **then**   *{if all votes are PROCEED}*
20:           clue $\leftarrow$ sign(votes)   *{produces clue}*
21:           BM.send(p'_i, Π', 'CLUE', clue)   *{sends clue}*
22:     **else**
23:        PL.send(p'_i, p_i, φ)   *{sends φ to p_i}*

24: **upon** BM.deliver(p'_j, p'_i, 'CLUE', clue) **do**   *{callback from BM}*
25:     **if** validClue(clue) **then**   *{checks if message is valid}*
26:        clues $\leftarrow$ clues $\cup$ {clue}   *{adds p_j's clue to set}*
27:        **if** ($|$clues$| > n/2$) **then**   *{checks for majority of clues}*
28:           PL.send(p'_i, p_i, item)   *{sends item to p_i}*

Lemma 1. *If some trustee does not receive the expected encrypted item, then no trustee sends an item at line 28 of Algorithm 2.*

Proof. If some trustee does not receive the expected item, it does not send the PROCEED vote. Hence no trustee receives all n PROCEED votes, so no trustee sends its i-th clue. If no trustee sends its i-th clue, then no trustee receives any clue. Without a majority of clues, no trustee sends the item to its corresponding participant at line 28 of Algorithm 2.

Theorem 1 (Validity). *If a correct process p_i releases an item x, then either $x \in M$ and x matches d_i, or x is the abort item φ.*

Proof. In Algorithm 1, a process p_i only releases an item at line 9. Process p_i releases upon reception of an item from its trustee p'_i, so the possible items are those sent by p'_i in Algorithm 2. In Algorithm 2, trustee p'_i explicitly sends the abort item φ at line 23 so p_i would release φ. The only other case of item transmission is at line 28: p'_i sends the item that is stored in variable item. From Lemma 1, if a trustee sends an item at line 28, it has previously received the expected item and stored it in variable item. Since, from line 8, no two different items can be stored in variable item, p'_i sends the expected item at line 28. So p_i would release the expected item.

Theorem 2 (Uniqueness). *No correct process releases more than once.*

Proof. The boolean variable released in Algorithm 1 and the atomic execution of upon statements prevent any correct process from releasing more than once.

Theorem 3 (Non-triviality). *If all processes are correct, no process releases the abort item φ.*

Proof. Since every process is correct, every process sends the correct encrypted item at line 5 of Algorithm 1 as agreed in the terms of the exchange. From the *validity* property of BM, every trustee p'_i receives an item matching description d_i before time $t_1 = t_0 + \Delta_{BM}$, so every trustee produces and sends its PROCEED vote at line 12 of Algorithm 2 in a timely fashion. From the IC2 property of BA, no process receives an invalid PROCEED vote. So finally, no trustee sends the abort item φ (line 23) of Algorithm 2 and thus no process releases φ.

Theorem 4 (Termination). *Every correct process eventually releases an item.*

Proof. The assumption that participants and trustees start Algorithms 1 and 2 at the same time and the timeout at line 13 of Algorithm 2 ensures that every trustee starts all n executions of BA at the same time. This implies that, from the existence of a time bound for the termination of BA and the IC1 property, there is a time after which: either every trustee of correct processes receives at least one invalid PROCEED vote and sends the abort item φ, prompting the corresponding correct process to release φ; or every major trustee receives all n valid PROCEED votes. In the latter case, every major trustee produces and sends its i-th clue at line 21 of Algorithm 2. From the *validity* property of BM and the *reachable majority* condition, every trustee of correct processes receives a majority of clues and then sends the item at line 28 of Algorithm 2. Finally, from the *termination* property of PL, every correct process releases the item.

Theorem 5 (Integrity). *No process p_j releases an item m_i, with process p_i correct, if m_i matches description d_k of some correct process p_k, with $p_k \neq p_j$.*

Proof. Firstly, since any process p_k and its trustee p'_k are directly connected, no process p_j intercepts the transmission of any deciphered item m_i by p'_k at line 28 of Algorithm 2. Secondly, only in a single step of Algorithm 1, i.e., at line 5, does a correct process p_i transmit its item m_i through the network. Since p_i is correct, p_i encrypts m_i using the public key of p'_k in order to send it through the network. So no process other than p_i and p_k holds a deciphered version of

m_i and, since both are correct, they do not send a deciphered version of m_i to p_j. From assumption on the PKI unforgeability, p_j is not capable of obtaining a deciphered version of m_i and thus does not release m_i.

Theorem 6 (Fairness). *If any process p_i releases an item m_j matching description d_i, with p_i or p_j correct, then every correct process p_k releases an item matching description d_k.*

Proof. The proof is by contradiction.

Assume that some correct process p_k does not release an item matching description d_k and that some other process p_i releases an item m_j matching description d_i, with p_i or p_j correct. If p_i releases m_j (line 9 of Algorithm 1), either p_i is correct and only releases an item received from its trustee p'_i; or p_j is correct and encrypted m_j before sending it to p'_i (line 5 of Algorithm 1) and thus p_i is only capable of releasing m_j by receiving it from its trustee p'_i. So in either cases, if p_i releases m_j, m_j is received from trustee p'_i, which sends m_j at line 28 of Algorithm 2. Trustee p'_i thus receives a majority of clues in some previous steps. From the *reachable majority* condition, at least one of these clues is produced by some major trustee p'_x. Trustee p'_x thus receives all n PROCEED votes. So, from the IC1 property of BA, every major trustee also receives all n PROCEED votes, including all trustees of correct processes. This implies that no trustee of correct processes sends the abort item φ (line 23 of Algorithm 2), including p'_k, so p_k does not release φ. From the validity and termination properties of FE, if p_k does not release φ, then p_k releases an item matching description d_k. A contradiction.

4.3   Discussion

As presented in Section 4, our generic solution relies both on best-effort multicast (BM) and Byzantine agreement (BA) modules. The BM module is used in Algorithms 1 and 2, i.e., by participants and trustees, whereas the BA module is only used in Algorithm 2, i.e., by trustees.

Since both modules share very similar *validity* and *agreement* properties, a reasonable question is: could we have done with only one module? The answer is: yes, a modified version of BM would be sufficient. To understand why, let us first point out a key guarantee offered by BA: trustees always *eventually* deliver a set of messages, even if the sender did not call the send primitive or all its messages where blocked by Byzantine processes (in which case the set is empty). The eventual delivery of BA is achieved through the use of the *start* primitive, allowing trustees to detect the absence of messages.[5]

The BM module, on the contrary, offers no such guarantee. However, by adding a *start* primitive to BM and by slightly changing its semantics, we could rely on the BM module to reach deterministic agreement among major trustees.

---

[5] Major trustees are thus able to agree on the votes of all trustees, including minor trustees, even if some (or all) messages sent by minor trustees are blocked.

However, since the BM module already accomplishes two different tasks, i.e., point-to-point and multicast communication, overloading it with a third semantics would make our solution more difficult to understand.

5   Related Work

Research on fair exchange has produced an impressive body of work over the past decades, as testified by several surveys [15,16]. At least three different communities of researchers are showing major interest in this problem, namely people active in *e*-business solutions, in cryptographic algorithms and in distributed systems. This diversity results in a variety of problem statements and underlying assumptions, as well as an even larger number of approaches to solve fair exchange.

Modeling Fair Exchange. The fair exchange problem comes basically in two flavors, namely a *weak* variant and a *true* variant [16]. Weak fair exchange does not require the exchange to be fair but rather that honest peers are able to gather evidence of potential misbehaviors. This variant thus assumes that misbehaving peers can be brought to justice, which is not the case in our approach. The problem we address in this paper is true fair exchange, which on the contrary requires a strong enforcement of fairness.

Within the realm of true fair exchange, various specifications have been proposed, with slightly different sets of properties [15]. Among these properties, fairness is the most difficult to capture and hence where most specifications tend to differ, as in [2,5,11]. Despite what is sometimes claimed, several such specifications are really meaningful for exchanges involving only two processes, i.e., they are impossible to satisfy in models allowing more than one Byzantine process. Note also that many researches explicitly aimed at the fair exchange variant involving only two peers [5,17,18,19,20], in particular when it comes to specific applications of fair exchange, e.g., exchanges of digital signatures, of emails and their receipts, etc. Our specification of the fair exchange problem, on the contrary, considers the general case where more than two peers might be involved, as already discussed in Section 2.2.

Besides proposing a specification, some authors also discuss the difficulty of fair exchange and propose impossibility results in various models. In [11], fair exchange is measured against consensus, and an impossibility result on fair exchange in asynchronous models is shown by comparison with the FLP impossibility [21]. In [22], fair exchange is shown to be impossible to solve *deterministically* in an asynchronous system with no Trusted Third Party (TTP). In another feasibility study [23], complex exchanges are broken into sub-exchanges – each relying on a different TTP – and represented as a graph. Reduction rules are then applied to the graph in order to demonstrate the feasibility of the exchange. This method also makes it possible to illustrate how closely exchange feasibility relies on trust. Along that line, we have shown that fair exchange is insolvable in a synchronous model in the absence of some identified process that every other process can trust *a priori* [4].

Before moving to the discussion on existing fair exchange solutions, let us clarify an often misunderstood specificity of fair exchange. Indeed, this misunderstanding leads some people to believe that the above impossibility results are in fact contradicting an important result by Chaum et al. in [24]. Intuitively, this result states that any multiparty protocol can be achieved in an unconditionally secure manner, provided that the system is synchronous and that at least $\frac{2}{3}$ of the peers are honest. The key difference here is in what one is really trying to achieve. Indeed, the problem considered by Chaum et al. consists in having a set of peers compute a multiparty function while preserving *privacy* regarding each peer's input and output [25]. However, fairness is out of their scope, i.e., they do not achieve it, nor discuss it, hence the confusion, since the absence of discussion may unintentionally lure the reader into thinking otherwise.

Solving Fair Exchange. Most solutions to fair exchange rely on some kind of Trusted Third Party (TTP). A TTP is a process directly accessible to all processes. Fairness is thus trivially ensured by having processes send their items to the TTP, which forwards the items, if the terms of the exchange are fulfilled [26]. A TTP brings synchronism and control over terms of the exchange in order to ensure fairness but constitutes a bottleneck and a single point of failure. For this reason, various so-called *optimistic* algorithm have been proposed that only involve the TTP when something goes wrong, i.e., when an attempt to cheat is detected [5,19,26,27,28]. However *optimistic* approaches are based on the strong assumption that the environment is mostly honest. To weaken the role of the TTP, in [18] for instance, Franklin and Reiter propose a solution using a *semi-trusted* third party that can misbehave on its own but does not conspire with either of the two participant peers. Similarly, the authors of [29] propose a solution based on a cluster of untrusted servers acting as third parties. In the latter paper, however, the authors recognize that they are merely solving a variant of the weak fair exchange.

By relying on fully decentralized tamperproof modules, other approaches depart from the traditional TTP-based approach [1,2,3], assuming fully connected processes but embedded tamperproof modules dependant of their process for communicating. A very interesting feature of the approach proposed in [2] lies in its ability to gracefully degrade its quality of service from true fairness to probabilistic fairness.

6   Concluding Remarks

In this paper, we extended a previous result [4] by proposing a necessary and sufficient topological condition – the *reachable majority* condition – on the solvability of fair exchange in a synchronous model with Byzantine failures and trustees. We gave a solution to fair exchange under the *reachable majority* condition, along with its correctness proof. This result thus validates the correctness of our *reachable majority* condition. Currently, we are further studying the relationship between various topologies and the *reachable majority* condition. We are also further investigating the relationship between our results and those found in the domain of *secure multiparty computation* and *fair computation* [30]. In [24] for instance, Chaum et al. show that any multiparty protocol can be achieved in an unconditionally secure manner, provided that the system is synchronous and that at least $\frac{2}{3}$ of the peers are honest.

Acknowledgements

This research is partly funded by the Swiss National Science Foundation, in the context of Project number 200021-104488.

References

1. Avoine, G., Gärtner, F., Guerraoui, R., Kursawe, K., Vaudenay, S., Vukolic, M.: Reducing fair exchange to atomic commit. Technical report, Swiss Federal Institute of Technology (EPFL) (2004)
2. Avoine, G., Gärtner, F., Guerraoui, R., Vukolic, M.: Gracefully degrading fair exchange with security modules (extended abstract). In: In Proceedings of the 5th European Dependable Computing Conference - EDCC 2005. (2005)
3. Avoine, G., Vaudenay, S.: Fair exchange with guardian angels. Technical report, Swiss Federal Institute of Technology (EPFL) (2003)
4. Garbinato, B., Rickebusch, I.: Impossibility results on fair exchange. In: Proceedings of the 6th International Workshop on Innovative Internet Community Systems (I2CS'06). Volume LNCS., Springer (2006)
5. Asokan, N., Shoup, V., Waidner, M.: Optimistic fair exchange of digital signatures. IEEE Journal on Selected Area in Communications **18** (2000) 593–610
6. Dyer, J., Lindemann, M., Perez, R., Sailer, R., van Doorn, L., Smith, S., Weingart, S.: Building the IBM 4758 secure coprocessor. Computer **34**(10) (2001) 57–66
7. Bajikar, S.: Trusted Platform Module (TPM) based Security on Notebook PCs – White Paper. Intel Corporation – Mobile Platforms Group. (2002)
8. Doudou, A., Garbinato, B., Guerraoui, R.: Tolerating Arbitrary Failures with State Machine Replication. In: Dependable Computing Systems: Paradigms, Performance Issues, and Applications. Wiley (2005) 27–56
9. Chandra, T.D., Toueg, S.: Unreliable failure detectors for reliable distributed systems. Journal of the ACM **43**(2) (1996) 225–267
10. Hadzilacos, V., Toueg, S.: Fault-tolerant broadcasts and related problems. (1993) 97–145
11. Pagnia, H., Gärtner, F.: On the impossibility of fair exchange without a trusted third party. Technical report, Swiss Federal Institute of Technology (EPFL) (1999)
12. Drabkin, V., Friedman, R., Segal, M.: Efficient byzantine broadcast in wireless ad-hoc networks. In: DSN '05: Proceedings of the 2005 International Conference on Dependable Systems and Networks (DSN'05), Washington, DC, USA, IEEE Computer Society (2005) 160–169
13. Lamport, L., Shostak, R., Pease, M.: The byzantine generals problem. ACM Transactions on Programming Languages and Systems **4**(3) (1982) 382–401
14. Pease, M., Shostak, R., Lamport, L.: Reaching agreement in the presence of faults. Journal of the ACM **27**(2) (1980) 228–234

15. Markowitch, O., Gollmann, D., Kremer, S.: On fairness in exchange protocols. In: Proceedings of the 5th International Conference Information Security and Cryptology (ICISC 2002). Volume 2587 of Lecture Notes in Computer Science., Springer (2002) 451–464
16. Ray, I., Ray, I.: Fair exchange in e-commerce. SIGecom Exchanges **3**(2) (2002)
17. Ateniese, G.: Efficient verifiable encryption (and fair exchange) of digital signatures. In: CCS '99: Proceedings of the 6th ACM conference on Computer and communications security, New York, NY, USA, ACM Press (1999) 138–146
18. Franklin, M., Reiter, M.: Fair exchange with a semi-trusted third party (extended abstract). In: CCS '97: Proceedings of the 4th ACM conference on Computer and communications security, New York, NY, USA, ACM Press (1997) 1–5
19. Micali, S.: Simple and fast optimistic protocols for fair electronic exchange. In: PODC '03: Proceedings of the twenty-second annual symposium on Principles of distributed computing, New York, NY, USA, ACM Press (2003) 12–19
20. Ray, I., Ray, I., Natarajan, N.: An anonymous and failure resilient fair-exchange e-commerce protocol. Decision Support Systems **39**(3) (2005) 267–292
21. Fischer, M., Lynch, N., Paterson, M.: Impossibility of Distributed Consensus with One Faulty Process. J. ACM **32** (1985) 374–382
22. Even, S., Yacobi, Y.: Relations among public key signature systems. Technical report, Technion - Israel Institute of Technology (1980)
23. Ketchpel, S., García-Molina, H.: Making trust explicit in distributed commerce transactions. In: Proceedings of the International Conference on Distributed Computing Systems. (1995)
24. Chaum, D., Crépeau, C., Damgard, I.: Multiparty unconditionally secure protocols. In: STOC '88: Proceedings of the 20th ACM symposium on Theory of computing, New York, NY, USA, ACM Press (1988) 11–19
25. Goldreich, O.: The Foundations of Cryptography. Volume 2. Cambridge University Press (2004)
26. Bürk, H., Pfitzmann, A.: Value exchange systems enabling security and unobservability. Computers & Security **9**(9) (1990) 715–721
27. Bao, F., Deng, R.H., Mao, W.: Efficient and practical fair exchange protocols with off-line TTP. In: RSP: 19th IEEE Computer Society Symposium on Research in Security and Privacy. (1998)
28. Baum-Waidner, B., Waidner, M.: Round-optimal and abuse free optimistic multi-party contract signing. In: Automata, Languages and Programming. Number 1853 in Lecture Notes in Computer Science (LNCS), Springer (2000) 524–535
29. Srivatsa, M., Xiong, L., Liu, L.: Exchangeguard: A distributed protocol for electronic fair-exchange. In: 19th International Parallel and Distributed Processing Symposium (IPDPS 2005), IEEE Computer Society (2005)
30. Goldwasser, S., Levin, L.: Fair computation of general functions in presence of immoral majority. In: CRYPTO '90: Proceedings of the 10th International Cryptology Conference on Advances in Cryptology, London, UK, Springer-Verlag (1991) 77–93

A   Best-Effort Multicast

Algorithm 3 provides a solution to the *best-effort multicast* abstraction presented in Section 4 and thus shows that the BM module is implementable in the context of our model. We assume that every process knows its direct neighbors and we define V_{p_i} as the set of neighbors of process p_i. Intuitively Algorithm 3 satisfies the properties of best-effort multicast by having correct processes flooding the network with the message. Flooding is achieved by forwarding any received message the first time it is received. Upon reception of that message, if the process is included in the set S of recipients, it also delivers the message. Note that having a Byzantine process deliver a message it was not suppose to does not jeopardize the validity of BM, nor cause any sort of problems.

Algorithm 3. Best-effort multicast protocol executed by process p_i

---

```
1: Uses:
2:    Perfect Link (PL)

3: Initialisation:
4:    forwarded ← ∅                                      {set of forwarded messages}

5: function send(pᵢ, S, m)
6:    for all pⱼ ∈ Vₚᵢ do                                          {for all neighbors}
7:       PL.send(pᵢ, pⱼ, ⟨pᵢ, S, signᵢ(m)⟩)           {sign and send the message}
8:    if pᵢ ∈ S then                                {check if message destined to self}
9:       deliver(m)                                          {deliver the message}

10: upon PL.deliver(pⱼ, pᵢ, ⟨pₖ, S, signₖ(m)⟩) do
11:    if m ∉ forwarded then                                {check if not forwarded}
12:       forwarded ← forwarded ∪ {m}            {add the message to forwarded set}
13:       for all pₓ ∈ Vₚᵢ − {pⱼ} do                  {for all neighbors except pⱼ}
14:          PL.send(pᵢ, pₓ, ⟨pₖ, S, signₖ(m)⟩)             {forward the message}
15:       if pᵢ ∈ S then                             {check if message destined to self}
16:          deliver(m)                                       {deliver the message}
```

Correctness Proof. In the following, our correctness proof aims at showing that Algorithm 3 preserves the Agreement and Termination properties of best-effort multicast and that such a module is thus implementable in our model. Note that in Lemma 1 the term 'receive a message' does not imply that the message is delivered but it relates to messages that are either obtained from the send() function (line 5 of Algorithm 3) or from the PL.deliver() callback (line 10 of Algorithm 3).

Lemma 1. *Let p_i and p_j be any two correct processes that are connected through a reliable path, if p_i receives a message m, then p_j receives m.*

Proof. The proof is by induction.

Basis step. Assume that some correct process p_i receives a message m (line 5 or 10) and that p_i and p_j are directly connected. So either p_i is the originator of m and sends m to processes of V_{p_i}; or p_i receives m from some process p_x and sends m to processes of $V_{p_i} - \{p_x\}$. In both cases, from the termination property of perfect links, all processes of V_{p_i} eventually receive m. From our initial assumption, since $p_j \in V_{p_i}$, p_j receives m.

Inductive step. Assume that any two correct processes p_i and p_j are connected through a reliable path. From definition of reliable paths, there exists a process p_k such that p_k is on that reliable path and $p_j \in V_{p_k}$. Moreover, p_k is correct and connected to p_i through a reliable path. So now assume that p_i and p_k receive a message m. Again either p_k is the originator of m and sends m to processes of V_{p_k}; or p_k receives m from some process p_y and sends m to processes of $V_{p_k} - \{p_y\}$. In both cases, from the termination property of perfect links, all processes of V_{p_k} eventually receive m. From our initial assumption, since $p_j \in V_{p_k}$, p_j receives m.

Theorem 1 (Agreement). *Let p_i and p_j be any two correct processes of S that are connected through a reliable path, if p_i delivers a message m, then p_j delivers m.*

Proof. Assume that any two correct processes p_i and p_j of S are connected through a reliable path and that p_i delivers a message m. So p_i receives m in a previous step of Algorithm 3 (line 5 or 10). From Lemma 1, p_j also receives m. Since p_j is a correct process of S, either m is in the forwarded set of p_j and p_j has delivered m, or m is not in the forwarded set of p_j and p_j delivers m at line 16.

Theorem 2 (Termination). *Let p_i and p_j be any two correct processes connected through a reliable path, with $p_j \in S$, if p_i sends a message m, then p_j eventually delivers m.*

Proof. Assume that any two correct processes p_i and p_j of S that are connected through a reliable path and that p_i sends a message m. So p_i receives m, as the originator of m. From Lemma 1, p_j also receives m. Since p_j is a correct process of S, either m is in the forwarded set of p_j and p_j has delivered m, or m is not in the forwarded set of p_j and p_j delivers m at line 16.

A Security Analysis of the
Precise Time Protocol (Short Paper)

Jeanette Tsang and Konstantin Beznosov

Laboratory for Education and Research in Secure Systems Engineering
University of British Columbia
Vancouver, Canada
tsangj@interchange.ubc.ca, beznosov@ece.ubc.ca
https://lersse.ece.ubc.ca

Abstract. This paper reports on a security analysis of the IEEE 1588 standard, a.k.a. Precise Time Protocol (PTP). We show that attackers can use the protocol to (a) incorrectly resynchronize clocks, (b) rearrange or disrupt the hierarchy of PTP clocks, (c) bring the protocol participants into an inconsistent state, or (d) deprive victim slave clocks from synchronization in ways undetectable by generic network intrusion detection systems. We also propose countermeasures for the identified attacks.

Keywords: IEEE 1588, Precise Time Protocol, Network Time Protocol, security analysis, time synchronization.

1   Introduction

The ability to precisely synchronize clocks among distributed components is critical for electrical power systems, industrial automation, telecommunication systems, military applications, and other fields where timing is crucial to their correctness and performance. The components of these distributed systems often contain real-time clocks that control their performance and coordination.

The IEEE 1588 standard [1] specifies a precision clock synchronization protocol for networked measurement and control systems that may utilize non-IP networks. It is equivalent to the IEC 61588 standard [6]. Both standards are known as "Precise Time Protocol" (PTP). In this paper, we use the terms "PTP" and "IEEE 1588" interchangeably. Networked heterogeneous systems can employ this protocol to synchronize clocks with accuracy in the sub-microsecond range. Real-world examples of PTP applications can be found in [9,10].

Although existing protocols such as the Network Time Protocol (NTP) [7] and the Global Positioning System (GPS) are used to synchronize clocks within networks, PTP is the only one that offers accuracy at the sub-microsecond level for small self-administered networks [4,5]. NTP also requires the underlying network to be IP-based, whereas PTP does not have this restriction.

Even though PTP is being positioned by the industry to serve as a key time synchronization technology for automation and control [10], its resilience to security attacks has not yet been publicly studied. For PTP to serve its intended

P. Ning, S. Qing, and N. Li (Eds.): ICICS 2006, LNCS 4307, pp. 50–59, 2006.

role, the automation and control community needs to be aware of the protocol's security properties.

In this paper, we report on the results of our security analysis of the 2002 revision of the IEEE 1588 specification [1]. The analysis focused on PTP's message transmission period, i.e., when networked devices exchange synchronization messages. The results of this analysis can assist the developers and users of PTP-based technologies in identifying the security requirements and developing the necessary security mechanisms for the protocol.

We made several assumptions for the purpose of analysis. In order to focus on PTP-related attacks and to exclude attacks specific to other protocols from our analysis, we assumed that the network being analyzed is a "closed network," i.e., none of the network nodes is connected to other external networks, such as the Internet. For those environments where the above assumption does not hold, additional types of attacks (e.g., distributed denial of service), including those specific to general-purpose network protocols, such as IP, UDP, and TCP, have to be taken into account. As a consequence of the first assumption, our second assumption was that only adversaries who have direct access to the PTP network can initiate attacks. Our third assumption was that the attacker(s) can mount passive (message eavesdropping) as well as active (message modification, removal, and injection) attacks. On the other hand, we could not make the assumption that IPSec [8] and its supporting services (e.g., key management) are available in the automation and control system that uses PTP because the PTP specification does not mandate IPSec.

Due to the lack of built-in protection, PTP messages can be easily tampered with by anyone who has access to the network. More importantly, the results of our analysis also suggest that attackers can easily use this weakness to incorrectly resynchronize clocks or to illegally rearrange (or even disrupt) the hierarchy of PTP clocks. Additionally, the protocol lacks a mechanism for detecting and compensating "out of range" data that can result in an inconsistent state of PTP participants. Furthermore, we discovered several PTP-specific attacks that, we believe, are very hard to detect by a network intrusion detection system, unless it maintains the state of the victim PTP clock hierarchy, which could be expensive.

The rest of the paper is organized as follows. Background on the PTP is provided in Section 2. Section 3 describes the attacks that we identified PTP to be vulnerable to. We draw conclusions and outline future work in Section 4.

2   Background on the Precise Time Protocol

This brief overview of the standard is based on the 2002 revision of the IEEE 1588 specification [1]. A more detailed description can be found in [12]. The main two elements of any PTP network are the *clock* and *port*. The *clock* is a network node that can provide measurements of time. An example of a clock is a network switch connected to two or more subnets. Its connections with the subnets are referred to as *ports*. The switch is referred to as a *boundary clock*, which has more than one port. *Ordinary clocks* have only a single port.

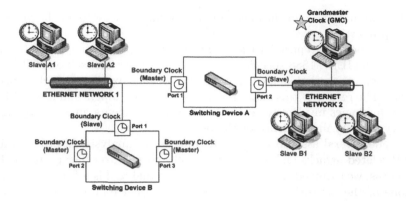

Fig. 1. A hypothetical PTP network (adapted from [3])

Each clock port serves as either a master or slave clock. The *master clock* is used as a reference for calibrating all of the *slave clocks*. Above all, the *grand master clock* (GMC) is the root clock that all the master clocks of the subnets are synchronized to. The master clock and the GMC are elected via the best master clock (BMC) algorithm, which is executed by every port individually and autonomously. The algorithm ensures that there is only one master clock active at any given moment on any subnet. The BMC algorithm is explained in detail in [12], and its vulnerabilities are analyzed in Section 3.1 of this paper.

Figure 1 shows a hypothetical PTP network with two subnets connected via one switch. Switching Device A is a boundary clock with two ports. Port 2 acts as a slave, and port 1 acts as the master clock. The standard allows messages to be transmitted either directly in Ethernet frames or as UDP payload. PTP defines both management and time synchronization messages. For the purposes of this paper, we are concerned only with the latter. There are four types of synchronization messages used in the PTP protocol: Sync, Follow_Up, Delay_Req, and Delay_Response. They are used for the regular synchronization procedure, and are propagated only within one PTP subnet. The contents of these messages are listed in Appendix B of [12]. Time synchronization is performed over three phases: master clock selection, time offset correction, and communication delay measurement. The first two phases are executed every synchronization interval, which by default is 2 seconds [5]. Delay measurement is initiated by each slave individually on irregular bases, between 4 and 60 seconds by default [5]. The message flow during time synchronization is illustrated by the example shown in Figure 2.

The Sync message is multicasted by the master clock to all of the slaves on the subnet. The main purpose of the message is to deliver the estimated time that it has left the master clock. Upon receipt of this message, the slave clocks record the reception time, which is used to calculate the offset between the slave and master clocks. The optional Follow_Up message is sent immediately following the Sync message by the master , and contains the precise sending time of the Sync message. After receiving the Follow_Up message, the slave clock calculates

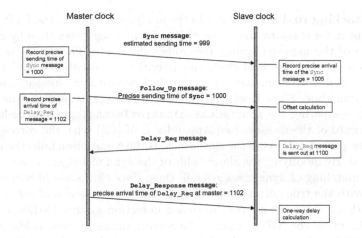

Fig. 2. An example of message flow during time synchronization

the offset. Communication delay between each slave and the master clock is computed with the aid of delay request and response messages.

Referring again to the example in Figure 2, the one-way delay was calculated from the **Delay_Req** and **Delay_Response** messages as $[(1005 - 1000) + (1102 - 1100)]/2 = (5 + 2)/2 = 3.5$ time units, whereas the offset was $1005 - 1000 - delay = 5 - 3.5 = 1.5$ time units. The slave's clock was then recalibrated using the offset value.

3   Threat Analysis

Like Bishop's security analysis [2] of the NTPv2, we studied the goals, attack methods, effects of attacks, and possible countermeasures for the following five types of threats: modification, masquerading, delay, replay, and denial of service. Specifically, we analyzed how these attacks could jeopardize synchronization objectives of PTP participants. The following subsections discuss results of our analysis for each of the five threat types. A more detailed analysis of the threats can be found in the long version of this paper [12].

3.1   Modification

The goal of a modification attack could be to: (a) cause denial of service, (b) cause slave clocks(s) to incorrectly resynchronize, or (c) alter the hierarchy of the master and slave clocks. The attack can be launched by manipulating the content of messages. Furthermore, the modification of the messages sent by a master clock would produce the greatest effect, since a master clock can send messages used for both time synchronization and management.

(a) **Attacking to deny service:** In the analyzed version of the PTP, there is no mechanism for checking the authenticity of a message other than by checking the source of the message against the node's data sets. The data sets contain information such as the local clock and parent clock attributes, and information about the "current master", i.e., the clock whose Sync messages are used for correcting time. Slave clocks verify that a message came from the correct master by comparing the sourceCommunicationTechnology, sourceUuid and sourcePortId of the message (see Appendix B of [12]) with the corresponding fields in the parent data set of the slave clock. If the comparison fails, the message is discarded. By modifying the above fields of the Sync messages, an attacker can make the matching of Sync messages fail; thus, slave clocks would refuse to synchronize with the true current master. This can cause a denial of service (DoS) attack without a generic network intrusion detection system (NIDS) detecting the attack, unless the NIDS "knows" the correct values of these fields. Furthermore, modifying the sequence ID of the message can also lead to a PTP-specific DoS attack variant, which we discuss in detail in Section 3.5.

(b) **Attacking to cause incorrect resynchronization:** Tampering with the timestamp clock and variance fields of Sync messages can cause an incorrect resynchronization of the slave clock(s) or a miscalculation of the network latency. The originTimestamp field serves as the record of time at which the Sync message leaves the master clock.

(c) **Attacking to alter the hierarchy of the master and slave clocks:** Wrong information about the grandmaster clock within Sync messages can lead to setting the port to a different mode, e.g., slave or passive. Each slave clock executes the BMC algorithm for electing the best master clock for the next round of synchronization. Since the BMC algorithm uses information about the grandmaster clock, by altering the grandmaster clock information in a Sync message, an attacker can easily make this message "better" than other Sync messages received by most clocks in the given PTP subnet. As a result, this crafted Sync message could become the best message for all local clocks from the attacker's subnet. Then, by winning all the comparisons used in the BMC algorithm (Figure 3 of [12]), the attacker can make the victim clock(s) switch into passive mode or slave mode. As a result, the attacker could disrupt or even destroy the synchronization hierarchy of clocks on the victim PTP network.

To illustrate the above attack, consider the PTP network depicted in Figure 1. If, say, the attacker controls Slave A_2, it can start sending Sync messages that are "better" than those sent by the true GMC. As a result, Slave A_1 as well as switching devices A and B will elect Slave A_2 as their new master clock. Switching device A will also change its port 1 into slave mode and port 2 into master mode. As a result, the true GMC will switch into slave mode, and the original hierarchy of PTP clocks shown in Figure 3(a), will transform into the hierarchy shown in Figure 3(b), with Slave A_2 being a rogue GMC.

Suggested countermeasures: We recommend employing cryptographic integrity protection on all PTP messages as a basic countermeasure. However, it is not obvious how the issue of key management can be addressed in PTP

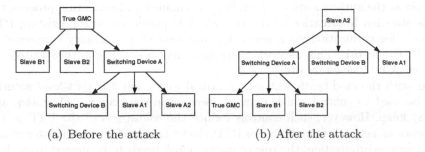

(a) Before the attack   (b) After the attack

Fig. 3. PTP clock hierarchy before and after a hypothetical attack on the PTP network shown in Figure 1

networks, as the protocol does not have any provisions for registering slave or master clocks, or binding their identities to keys. Efficiency is another issue to be considered when cryptographic integrity protection is employed. Further investigation is needed to decide which cryptographic integrity protection scheme is most suitable for PTP. An alternative countermeasure is to employ port-level security [11] to enforce such simple rules as "only the network interfaces of the true GMC, port 1 of the switching device A, as well as ports 2 and 3 of the switching device B can send Sync messages." These access controls based on port-level security might be more effective performance-wise than those based on cryptography. In addition, key management can be avoided. However, the use of port-level security might fall short of enforcing all rules necessary to counter attacks on PTP clock hierarchies. For instance, if switching device A is compromised, then its port 1 can send bogus Sync messages even with the above rule enforced. Port-level security also increases the overhead of configuring network switches, and, as a result, increases the risk of "friendly denial of service" due to configuration errors.

3.2   Masquerading

The goal of a masquerading attack in a PTP network is to masquerade as the master clock and use the false identity to launch other attacks. To launch the attack, an adversary can first obtain information about the "true" master clock, and then eavesdrop on Sync, Delay_Req, and Delay_Resp messages that are sent to the slave clocks from the master. Once necessary data are obtained, the attacker can spoof Sync, Delay_Req, and Delay_Resp messages to masquerade as a master clock. Masquerading as a master clock could permit the attacker to send out incorrect timing and management messages to other slave clocks, causing different kinds of damage to the system. For example, the attacker could send out incorrect timing information to slave clocks, leading to errors in the synchronization process.

Suggested countermeasures: We recommend using a centralized or chained authentication process. For centralized authentication, the grandmaster clock can act as the authentication server. For the chained authentication process, the authentication information of the new clock is passed on to the existing PTP network for verification via a network component that is already connected to the PTP network. This network component has previously authenticated the new clock by its own means.

As with the modification attack described in Section 3.1, port-level security can be used to control which network device can send Sync, Delay_Req, and Delay_Resp. However, such controls reduce the robustness of the PTP in the presence of network failures. Since PTP clocks locally elect best master clocks for time synchronization, the role of master clock needs to be passed from clock to clock as the network topology changes due to device additions and failures.

3.3   Delay

The goal of a delay attack in a PTP network is to delay the arrival of messages at the recipient nodes, thus causing an increase in the values used in the offset and one-way delay calculations. The attack can be carried out through the use of hardware or software to interrupt the transmission of a message between nodes and later re-inject it into the communication channel. By intentionally delaying the reception time of the Sync message by a certain slave clock, the attacker may dramatically increase the offset of the slave clock with respect to the master clock, setting the slave clock off synchronization with the rest of the system.

Delaying the reception of the Follow_Up message at the slave clock can cause a timeout of the synchronization event. If this condition continues, it may lead to the slave clock being denied synchronization with the master. The slave will either pick the wrong clock on the subnet to synchronize with, or operate based on its local clock, eventually drifting from the true master clock.

A delay caused in the transmission of the Delay_Req message has a similar effect as a delay in the Sync message. Yet, a delay attack in the Delay_Req message can cause a more significant disruption of the synchronization process, because the calculation of the one-way delay is not done as frequently as the offset correction synchronization process. An incorrect value of one-way delay can cause errors in all upcoming offset calculations.

Finally, if the Delay_Response message is not received back at the slave clock after a fixed delay-request interval, the whole calibration process of the one-way delay would be voided. An adversary can even launch this attack, and then add in more delay fluctuations, such as new network components, to the system. Since the one-way delay is not being recalculated due to the timeout of the delay request interval, the additional delay from the new components is not being accounted for in the calculation of the offset.

Suggested countermeasures: PTP can be modified to have a backup plan to compensate for the missing or delayed messages. For example, by taking the averages of the Delay_Req and Delay_Response messages in combination with previous values, the effects of timed out or postponed messages can be reduced.

Also, there should be an algorithm in PTP to determine any abnormal values of the timestamps in the messages. If any abnormality is found for an extended period of time (e.g., the last four one-way delays are significantly higher than the first four), validation of the data against other neighboring nodes might be helpful.

3.4 Replay

The goal of a replay attack is to either create congestion in the network stacks of the clocks, or to desynchronize clocks. The attack can be executed by recording legitimate message(s) being transmitted on the communication path and, at a later time, slightly modifying and then re-injecting the recorded message(s) into the network. The replayed messages would be interpreted as genuine messages. Any occurrence of events caused by the messages would be processed in a First-In-First-Out order. For example, when the Sync message is being replayed to the slave clock, the slave clock would record the precise reception time of it. However, we were uncertain how the precise reception time is stored. If there is one storage location for it, then the later replayed message would overwrite the precise reception time of the first Sync message. If there are multiple storage places, then the precise recorded times can be queued up and would not lead to a problem. Furthermore, replaying messages can saturate the processing queue at the clocks and congest their network stacks, which may result in dropping authentic synchronization messages from the true master clocks.

Suggested countermeasures: We suggest using an integrity protected network path, e.g., a VPN connection, to prevent messages from being spoofed or injected into the network. An alternative would be to use a capable message authentication mechanism to ensure the authenticity of the PTP messages.

3.5 Denial of Service (DoS)

In addition to generic DoS attacks through flooding communication channels and overflowing communication stacks, an adversary can also deny PTP clock(s) time synchronization service in a protocol-specific way. The significance of this attack is that generic NIDS's are unlikely to detect it.

An adversary could trick the attacked slave clock into rejecting Sync and Follow_Up messages from the true master clock. Since the attack is the same for both types of messages, we explain it using the Sync message case.

For performing DoS using Sync messages, the adversary first spoofs the victim slave clock with a Sync message using the true master clock address, albeit with a sequenceID value greater than the one in the previous Sync message. Upon processing this message, the victim clock updates its parent data set accordingly. Denial of service occurs when the true master sends its next Sync message to the victim. Since the parent_last_sync_sequence in the slave clock has already been incremented upon receiving the spoofed Sync message, the Sync message from the true master clock has sequenceID value less than or at most equal to the parent_last_sync_sequence. Therefore, this Sync message is rejected by the victim slave without the master being notified. No synchronization can take place until the true master's Sync message has a sequenceID greater than the parent_last_sync_sequence in the slave clock. The greater the sequenceID in the adversary's Sync messages, the longer the synchronization service is denied. If the adversary keeps on sending Sync messages to increase the victim's value of parent_last_sync_sequence before the true master can catch up with it, the victim can be permanently deprived of synchronization with the true master. The adversary starts controlling the time of the slave clock without the victim or its master clock realizing this.

A small-scale DoS attack may cause time synchronization to be less accurate across the system. If only slave clocks are affected, they may then be set to run on a local clock, drifting away from each other due to the differences in each clock's skew. The bigger the scale of the attack, the greater the number of PTP clocks that would have to run on local clocks. Furthermore, the tree-like hierarchical organization of PTP networks allows attacker(s) to increase the scale of the attack dramatically by denying synchronization to just a few boundary clocks that are close to the GMC.

Suggested countermeasures: Employ message authenticity and integrity protection or use port-level security to limit the set of the devices authorized to send synchronization messages. The limitations and drawbacks of both types of countermeasures were discussed in the previous sections.

4   Conclusions and Future Work

Since it is able to provide synchronization accuracy in the sub-microsecond range, the PTP has been deployed in a wide range of application domains, from factory automation to avionics, to power grids, and to military systems. However, the protocol lacks security mechanisms necessary to ensure the integrity of transmitted messages and to validate the authenticity of the sender. We analyzed the effects of five different types of attacks on a PTP network in this paper: modification, masquerading, delay, replay, and denial of service. It can be seen that PTP alone is weak against these attacks, and that additional security mechanisms are necessary to protect a PTP network. Damage caused by failure in time synchronization can be dramatic.

We did not implement the discovered attacks or countermeasures due to the lack of publicly available PTP implementations. When the situation changes, developing a proof of concept for our attacks and countermeasures could be very helpful for evaluating their feasibility and for testing corresponding countermeasures. Because of the critical nature of the PTP application domains [9,10], we prefer to make the community of security professionals aware of our results now.

We limited our analysis to synchronization messages. The damage caused by corrupting management messages or using them to launch attacks (e.g., to change information on data sets of PTP clocks) can be much greater than that resulting from corrupted time synchronization messages, because they can control all of the data sets as well as the status of a PTP clock. Analysis of management messages is a promising avenue for future research. Another interesting direction is to validate the feasibility of cryptographic countermeasures applied to PTP.

Acknowledgments. The authors would like to thank the following people who provided comments on earlier versions of the paper: Galina Antonova, Matt Bishop, and John Eidson. Craig Wilson helped us to improve the readability of the paper.

References

1. A Precision Clock Synchronization Protocol for Networked Measurement and Control Systems, IEEE Standard 1588-2002, November 2002.
2. M. Bishop, "A Security Analysis of the NTP Protocol Version 2," Proceedings of the Sixth Annual Computer Security Applications Conference, 3-7 December 1990, pp. 20-29, Tucson, AZ, USA.
3. P. Doyle, "Introduction to Real-Time Ethernet II," The Extension—A Technical Supplement to Control Network, vol.5, issue. 4, July-August 2004. Available: www.ccontrols.com/pdf/Extv5n4.pdf
4. J. Eidson, M.C. Fischer, and J. White, "IEEE-1588 Standard for a precision clock synchronization protocol for networked measurement and control systems," Proceedings of the 34th Annual Precise Time and Time Interval Systems and Applications Meeting, December 3-5, 2002, Reston, Virginia.
5. D. Mohl, "IEEE 1588-Precise Time Synchronization as the Basis for Real Time Application in Automation," Available: www.industrialnetworking.com/support/general_faqs_info/Precise_Time_Sync.pdf
6. IEC, "Precision clock synchronization protocol for networked measurement and control systems" IEC 61588, First Edition, 2004, pp. 158.
7. "NTP: Network Time Protocol," Available: www.ntp.org
8. N. Dunbar, "IPsec Networking Standards—An Overview, " Information Security Technical Report, Volume 5, Issue 1, 1 March 2001, pp.35-48.
9. K. R. Harris, S. Balasubramanian, and A. Moldovansky, "The Application of IEEE 1588 to a Distributed Motion Control System," presented at the ODVA CIP Networks Conference, Nov. 16-18, 2004.
10. G. Gaderere, T. Sauter, G. Bumiller, "Clock Synchronization in Powerline Networks," Proceedings of International Symposium on Power Line Communications and Its Application, 2005, pp. 71-75.
11. J. B. Hansen and S. Young, The Hacker's Handbook, CRC Press, 2004, pp.512.
12. J. Tsang and K. Beznosov, "A Security Analysis of the Precise Time Protocol," LERSSE technical report, Electrical and Computer Engineering, University of British Columbia, Vancouver, Canada, LERSSE-TR-2006-02, October., 2005, pp.20, http://lersse-dl.ece.ubc.ca.

An Identity-Based Proxy Signature Scheme from Pairings

Kyung-Ah Shim*

Department of Mathematics, Ewha Womans University,
Seoul, Korea
kashim@ewha.ac.kr

Abstract. A proxy signature enables an original signer to delegate her signing capability to a proxy signer and then the proxy signer can sign a message on behalf of the original signer. In this paper we propose an ID-based proxy signature scheme from bilinear pairings. We provide exact security proof of the proposed ID-based proxy signature scheme in the random oracle model under the Computational Diffie-Hellman assumption without using Forking Lemma.

1 Introduction

In 1984, Shamir [11] introduced the concept of ID-based cryptography. In traditional public key cryptosystems, Alice's public key is a random string. When Bob wishes to send a message to Alice, he must first obtain her authenticated public key in public directories. The central idea in ID-based cryptosystems is to eliminate the public key distribution problem by making Alice's public key derivable from some known aspect of her identity, such as her email address. Such cryptosystems alleviate the certificate overhead and solve the problems of Public Key Infrastructure (PKI) technology: certificate management, including storage and distribution, and the computational cost of certificate verification. Over the years a number of researchers tried to propose secure and efficient ID-based encryption schemes, but with little success. This state of affairs changed in 2001 when an ID-based encryption scheme based on Weil pairing was proposed by Boneh and Franklin [4]. The pairings of algebraic curves have initiated some completely new fields in cryptography, making it possible to realize cryptographic primitives that were previously unknown or impractical. In particular, the pairing-based cryptosystems provide solutions for construction of special-purposed signature schemes; short signature, aggregate signature, multisignature, verifiably encrypted signature, etc. [6,5,1,3,13,15].

The concept of proxy signature was first introduced by Mambo, Usuda, and Okamoto in 1996 [8]. The proxy signature schemes allow a proxy signer to sign messages on behalf of an original signer within a given context (the context and limitations on proxy signing capabilities are captured by a certain warrant

---
* This work was supported by the Korea Research Foundation Grant funded by the Korean Government(MOEHRD).(KRF-2005-217-C00002).

P. Ning, S. Qing, and N. Li (Eds.): ICICS 2006, LNCS 4307, pp. 60–71, 2006.
© Springer-Verlag Berlin Heidelberg 2006

issued by the delegator which is associated with the delegation act). Proxy signatures have found numerous practical applications, particularly in distributed computing where delegation of rights is quite common; distributed systems, Grid computing, mobile agent applications, distributed shared object systems, global distribution networks, and mobile communications. Since Mambo *et al.*'s scheme, many proxy signature schemes have been proposed [14,7,9,13,14,15]. Almost all of these works only provide informal security analysis, i.e., there are no provensecure proxy signature schemes. The first work to formally define the model of proxy signatures, is the work of Boldyreva, Palacio, and Warinschi [2]. However, the security of almost all of (ID-based) signature and proxy signature schemes including Boldyreva *et al.*'s triple Shnorr proxy signature scheme is proved by using Forking Lemma [10], i.e., they do not provide tight security reductions. Recently, Xu *et al.* [12] proposed an ID-based proxy signature scheme from pairings. They extended Boldyreva *et al.*'s security model for proxy signature schemes to the ID-based setting and proved its security in that model without using Forking Lemma. In this paper we define a new security model for ID-based proxy signature schemes and propose a more efficient ID-based proxy signature scheme from pairings with a tight security reduction to the intractability of the Computational Diffie-Hellman problem without using Forking Lemma.

The rest of this paper is organized as follows. In the following Section, we describe basic tools and new security notions for ID-based proxy signature schemes. In Section 3, we propose an ID-based proxy signature scheme from pairings. We then provide exact security proof of the proposed ID-based proxy signature scheme in the random oracle model under the Computational Diffie-Hellman assumption. A concluding remark is given in Section 4.

2   Preliminaries

2.1   Definition and Assumption

Let $\mathbb{G}_1$ and $\mathbb{G}_2$ be two cyclic groups of a large prime order q. We write $\mathbb{G}_1$ additively and $\mathbb{G}_2$ multiplicatively. We assume that the discrete logarithm problems in both $\mathbb{G}_1$ and $\mathbb{G}_2$ are hard.

Admissible Pairing: We call e an *admissible pairing* if $e : \mathbb{G}_1 \times \mathbb{G}_1 \to \mathbb{G}_2$ is a map with the following properties:

1. Bilinearity: $e(aP, bQ) = e(P, Q)^{ab}$ for all $P, Q \in \mathbb{G}_1$ and for all $a, b \in \mathbb{Z}$.
2. Non-degeneracy: There exists $P \in \mathbb{G}_1$ such that $e(P, P) \neq 1$.
3. Computability: There is an efficient algorithm to compute $e(P, Q)$ for any $P, Q \in \mathbb{G}_1$.

The Weil and Tate pairings associated with supersingular elliptic curves or abelian varieties can be modified to create such admissible pairings, as in [4].

We consider the following problem and assumption in $(\mathbb{G}_1, +)$.

Definition 2.1. [Computational Diffie-Hellman (CDH) Problem]. Given (P, xP, yP), to compute xyP, where $x, y \in_R \mathbb{Z}_q^*$, and P is a generator of $\mathbb{G}_1$.

Definition 2.2. [Computational Diffie-Hellman (CDH) Assumption].
Let $\mathcal{G}$ be a CDH parameter generator. We say that an algorithm $\mathcal{A}$ has advantage $\epsilon(k)$ in solving the CDH problem for $\mathcal{G}$ if for a sufficiently large k,

$$Adv_{\mathcal{G},\mathcal{A}}(t) = Pr\left[\begin{array}{c} \mathcal{A}(q, \mathbb{G}_1, \ P, \ xP, yP) = xyP \\ |(q, \mathbb{G}_1) \leftarrow \mathcal{G}(1^k), \ P \leftarrow \mathbb{G}_1, \ x, y \leftarrow \mathbb{Z}_q^* \end{array} \right] \geq \epsilon(k)$$

We say that $\mathcal{G}$ satisfies the CDH assumption if for any randomized polynomial-time in t algorithm $\mathcal{A}$ we have that $Adv_{\mathcal{G},\mathcal{A}}(t)$ is a negligible function. When $\mathcal{G}$ satisfies the CDH assumption we say that CDH is hard in $\mathbb{G}_1$ generated by $\mathcal{G}$.

2.2 Security Notions

We define the security notion for ID-based proxy signature schemes by simplifying Boldyeva et al's and Xu et al's ones [1,12]. An ID-based proxy signature scheme consists of three kinds of participants, an original signer, a proxy signer and a verifier, and the following five algorithms: Setup, Extract, Proxy Key Extract, Sign, and Verify. We remove the Proxy Designation Protocol and Standard Signature Signing Algorithm from Boldyeva et al's and Xu et al's ones by adding the Proxy Key Extract algorithm whose roles are designation of a proxy signer and to extract a proxy signing key for the designated proxy signer.

COMPONENT OF ID-BASED PROXY SIGNATURE SCHEMES. An ID-based proxy signature scheme IBPS=(Setup, Extract, Proxy Key Extract, Sign, Verify) is specified by five polynomial time algorithms with the following functionality;

1. The randomized parameter generation algorithm Setup takes input 1^k, where $k \in \mathbb{Z}$ is the security parameter and outputs some publicly known system parameters Params. These may contain a security parameter, the description of a cyclic group and a generator, and the description of a hash function.
2. The randomized private key extraction algorithm Extract takes input system parameters Params and an identity ID and outputs a pair (Q_{ID}, S_{ID}) consisting of a public key and the corresponding private key, respectively.
3. The randomized proxy signing key extraction algorithm Proxy Key Extract takes input system parameters Params and a pair of identities $\{ID_i, ID_j\}$ with a warrant w (it implies that an original signer ID_i designates ID_j as a proxy signer) and outputs a proxy signing key σ_P for ID_j. The order of $\{ID_i, ID_j\}$ is important, i.e, $\{ID_i, ID_j\}$ and $\{ID_j, ID_i\}$ are different inputs in the Proxy Key Extract algorithm.
4. The randomized proxy signing algorithm Sign takes input a proxy signing key corresponding to an identity ID_j, a message $m \in \{0,1\}^*$ and outputs a proxy signature $\sigma \leftarrow$ Sign(σ_P, m).
5. The randomized verification algorithm Verify takes input a set of identities $\{ID_i, ID_j\}$ with a warrant w, a message $m \in \{0,1\}^*$ and a proxy signature σ of m for $\{ID_i, ID_j\}$, and outputs True if the signature is correct, or $\perp$ otherwise, i.e., $\{$True, $\perp\} \leftarrow$ Verify$(w, m, ID_i, ID_j, \sigma)$.

The most general security notion of a standard signature scheme is existential unforgeability under an adaptively chosen-message attack. We extend this notion to an ID-based proxy signature scheme, namely, existential unforgeability under an adaptively chosen-message and an adaptively chosen-ID attack, where an adversary can adaptively choose identities as well as messages. Informally, existential forgery here means that the adversary attempts to forge an ID-based proxy signature on identities and messages of his choice, i.e., adversary's goal is the existential forgery of a proxy signature. We give the adversary the power to choose identities on which it wishes to forge a proxy signature and the power to request private keys and proxy signing keys on all these identities. The adversary is also given access to a Sign oracle on any desired identity. All designation phases defined in Boldyeva *et al*'s and Xu *et al*'s ones are unified into the Proxy Key Extract. We formalize the ID-based proxy signature model as follows.

UNFORGEABILITY OF ID-BASED PROXY SIGNATURE SCHEMES. Adversary's advantage $Adv_{IBPS,A}$ is defined as its probability of success in the following game between a challenger C and an adversary A;

1. C runs Setup algorithms and its resulting system parameters are given to A.
2. A issues the following queries;
   - Hash Query: C computes the hash value of the requested input and sends the value to A.
   - Extract Query: Given an identity ID, C computes its private key S_{ID} corresponding to Q_{ID} derived from ID.
   - Proxy Key Extract Query: Proceeding adaptively, for a given pair of identities $\{ID_i, ID_j\}$ with a warrant w, i.e., it implies that an original signer ID_i designates ID_j as a proxy signer, C computes ID_j's proxy signing key.
   - Sign Query: Given a message m for $\{ID_i, ID_j\}$ with a warrant w, C returns a proxy signature σ.
3. A outputs σ on a message m for $\{ID_i, ID_j\}$ with a warrant w such that
   i) m is not equal to the inputs of any query to Sign under ID_j,
   ii) $\{ID_i, ID_j\}$ with a warrant w is not requested to Proxy Key Extract query, i.e., ID_j was not designated by ID_i as a proxy signer.
   A wins the game if σ is a valid proxy signature.

Definition 2.3. A forger $A(t, q_E, q_{PE}, q_S, q_H, \varepsilon)$-breaks an ID-based proxy signature scheme $IBPS$ if A runs in time at most t, A makes at most q_E Extract queries, q_{PE} Proxy Key Extract queries, q_S Sign queries and at most q_H queries to the hash function, and $Adv_{IBPS,A}$ is at least ε. An ID-based proxy signature scheme is $Adv_{IBPS,A}(t, q_E, q_{PE}, q_S, q_H, \varepsilon)$-existentially unforgeable under an adaptively chosen-message and an adaptively chosen-ID attack if no forger $Adv_{IBPS,A}(t, q_E, q_{PE}, q_S, q_H, \varepsilon)$-breaks it.

SECURITY REQUIREMENTS OF ID-BASED PROXY SIGNATURE SCHEMES. Like the general proxy signature, an ID-based proxy signature scheme should satisfy the following requirements [7,8];

1. **Distinguishability:** Proxy signatures are distinguishable from normal signatures by everyone.

2. **Verifiability:** From the proxy signature, the verifier can be convinced of the original signers agreement on the signed message.

3. **Strong Non-Forgeability:** A designated proxy signer can create a valid proxy signature for the original signer. But the original signer and other third parties who are not designated as a proxy signer cannot create a valid proxy signature.

4. **Strong Identifiability:** Anyone can determine the identity of the corresponding proxy signer from the proxy signature.

5. **Strong Non-Deniability:** Once a proxy signer creates a valid proxy signature of an original signer, he/she cannot repudiate the signature creation.

6. **Prevention of Misuse:** The proxy signer cannot use the proxy key for other purposes than generating a valid proxy signature. That is, it cannot sign messages that have not been authorized by the original signer.

3   New ID-Based Proxy Signature Scheme from Pairings

3.1   Proposed ID-Based Proxy Signature Scheme: $\mathcal{NIBPS}$

We propose a new ID-based proxy signature scheme $\mathcal{NIBPS}$ from pairings. Let A and B be an original signer and a proxy signer with identities ID_A and ID_B, respectively. The scheme consists of five algorithms; Setup, Extract, Proxy Key Extract, Sign, and Verify. We let k be the security parameter given to the Setup algorithm. The proposed ID-based proxy signature scheme $\mathcal{NIBPS}$ runs as follows;

Setup. Given a security parameter $k \in \mathbb{Z}$, the algorithm works as follows;

1. Run the parameter generator $\mathcal{G}$ on input k to generate a prime q, two groups $\mathbb{G}_1$, $\mathbb{G}_2$ of order q, two different generators P and Q in $\mathbb{G}_1$ and an admissible pairing $e : \mathbb{G}_1 \times \mathbb{G}_1 \to \mathbb{G}_2$.
2. Pick a random $s \in \mathbb{Z}_q^*$ and set $P_{Pub} = sP$.
3. Choose cryptographic hash functions $H_1 : \{0,1\}^* \to \mathbb{G}_1$ and $H_i : \{0,1\}^* \to \mathbb{Z}_q$, $i = 2, 3$. The security analysis will view H_1, H_2 and H_3 as random oracles. The system parameters is Params$=< q, \mathbb{G}_1, \mathbb{G}_2, e, P, Q, P_{Pub}, H_1, H_2, H_3 >$.

Extract. For a given string $ID \in \{0,1\}^*$, the algorithm does;

1. Compute $Q_{ID} = H_1(ID) \in \mathbb{G}_1$.
2. Set the private key S_{ID} to be $s \cdot Q_{ID}$, where s is a master secret.

Proxy Key Extract

1. The original signer, A prepares a warrant w which is explicit description of the delegation relation.

2. A chooses $r_A \in_R \mathbb{Z}_q^*$ and computes

$$U = r_A P \in \mathbb{G}_1, \ h_A = H_2(w, U_A) \in \mathbb{Z}_q, \ V_A = h_A S_A + r_A Q \ \in \mathbb{G}_1.$$

Then A sends (w, U_A, V_A) to the proxy signer B.

3. The proxy signer verifies whether

$$e(V_A, \ P) = e(h_A Q_A, \ P_{Pub}) \cdot e(U_A, Q)$$

holds or not. If it holds, B computes $h_B = H_3(w, U_A)$ and

$$\sigma_P = V_A + h_B S_B \in \mathbb{G}_2$$

and keeps it as a proxy signing key.

Sign. Given its proxy signing key V_P, and a message $M \in \{0,1\}^*$, B does;

1. Choose a random $r \in \mathbb{Z}_q^*$ and compute $U = rP \in \mathbb{G}_1, h = H_3(w, M, U) \in \mathbb{Z}_q$.
2. Compute $V = h \cdot \sigma_P + rQ \in \mathbb{G}_1$.
3. Output the proxy signature (w, M, U_A, U, V).

Verify. Given a proxy signature (w, M, U_A, U, V) for the original signer A and the proxy signer B, a verifier does;

1. Compute $Q_A = H_1(ID_A)$, $Q_B = H_1(ID_B)$ and $h_A = H_2(w, U_A)$, $h_B = H_3(w, U_A)$, $h = H_3(w, M, U) \in \mathbb{Z}_q$.
2. Verify whether

$$e(V, \ P) = e(h[h_A Q_A + h_B Q_B], \ P_{Pub}) \cdot e(hU_A + U, \ Q)$$

holds or not. If it holds, accept the signature.

Correctness. By bilinearity of the pairing e, the consistency of the signature scheme is easy to verify;

$$e(V, \ P) = e(h \cdot \sigma_P + rQ, \ P) = e(h[h_A S_A + r_A Q + h_B S_B] + rQ, \ P)$$

$$= e(h[h_A Q_A + h_B Q_B], \ P_{Pub}) \cdot e(hU_A + U, \ Q).$$

3.2   Security Proof

Now, we prove the security of the proposed ID-based proxy signature scheme $\mathcal{NIBPS}$. Let an adversary $\mathcal{A}$ be a probabilistic polynomial time algorithm whose input is Params$=< q, \mathbb{G}_1, \mathbb{G}_2, e, P, Q, H_1, H_2, H_3 >$, where $q \geq 2^k$. $\mathcal{A}$ can make q_S queries to the Sign, q_{H_1} queries to the H_1-hash, q_{H_2} queries to the H_2-hash, q_{H_3} queries to the H_3-hash, q_E queries to the Extract and q_{PE} queries to the Proxy Key Extract.

Theorem 3.1. *If the CDH problem is (t', ε')-hard, the proposed proxy signature scheme $\mathcal{NIBPS}$ is $(t, q_{H_1}, q_{H_2}, q_{H_2}, q_E, q_{PE}, q_S, \varepsilon)$-secure against existential forgery under an adaptively chosen-message and an adaptively chosen-ID attack, for any t and ε satisfying*

$$\varepsilon \geq e \cdot (q_E + 1) \cdot \varepsilon',$$

$$t \leq t' - c_{\mathbb{G}_1}(q_{H_1} + q_E + 4q_{PE} + 6q_S + 5),$$

where e is the base of natural logarithms, and $c_{\mathbb{G}_1}$ is the time of computing a scalar multiplication $\mathbb{G}_1$ and an inversion in $\mathbb{Z}_q^*$.

Proof. Suppose that $\mathcal{A}$ is a forger who breaks the proposed ID-based proxy signature scheme $\mathcal{NIBPS}$. A CDH instance (P, xP, yP) is given for $x, y \in_R \mathbb{Z}_q^*$. By using the forgery algorithm $\mathcal{A}$, we will construct an algorithm $\mathcal{B}$ which outputs the CDH solution xyP in $\mathbb{G}_1$. Algorithm $\mathcal{B}$ performs the following simulation by interacting with forger $\mathcal{A}$.

Setup. Algorithm $\mathcal{B}$ choose a random $t \in \mathbb{Z}_q^*$, computes tP and sets $P_{Pub} = xP$ and $Q = tP$. $\mathcal{B}$ starts by giving $\mathcal{A}$ the system parameters including $\langle Q, P_{pub} \rangle$.

At any time, algorithm $\mathcal{A}$ can query the random oracles H_1, H_2 and H_3 and **Extract, Proxy Key Extract** and **Sign** queries. To answer these queries, $\mathcal{B}$ does the following;

H_1**-queries.** To respond to H_1-queries, algorithm $\mathcal{B}$ maintains a list of tuples $\overline{(ID, W, b, c)}$ as explained below. We refer to this list as the H_1-list. The list is initially empty. When $\mathcal{A}$ queries the oracle H_1 at a point $ID \in \{0, 1\}^*$, algorithm $\mathcal{B}$ responds as follows;

1. If the query ID already appears on the H_1-list in a tuple (ID, W, b, c) then algorithm $\mathcal{B}$ responds with $H_1(ID) = W \in \mathbb{G}_1$.
2. Otherwise, $\mathcal{B}$ picks a random coin $c \in \{0, 1\}$ with $Pr[c = 0] = \frac{1}{q_E + 1}$.
   - If $c = 0$ then $\mathcal{B}$ computes $W = b(yP)$ for a random $b \in \mathbb{Z}_q^*$.
   - If $c = 1$ then $\mathcal{B}$ computes $W = bP$ for a random $b \in \mathbb{Z}_q^*$.
   $\mathcal{B}$ adds the tuple (ID, W, b, c) to the H_1-list and responds to $\mathcal{A}$ with $H_1(ID) = W$.

H_2**-queries.** To respond to H_2-queries, algorithm $\mathcal{B}$ maintains a list of tuples $\overline{(m, U, h)}$ as explained below. We refer to this list as the H_2-list. The list is initially empty. When $\mathcal{A}$ queries the oracle H_2 at a point $m \in \{0, 1\}^*$, algorithm $\mathcal{B}$ responds as follows;

1. If the query m already appears on the H_2-list in a tuple (m, U, h) then algorithm $\mathcal{B}$ responds with $H_2(m, U) = h \in \mathbb{Z}_q$.
2. Otherwise, $\mathcal{B}$ picks a random $h \in \mathbb{Z}_q$ and adds the tuple (m, U, h) to the H_2-list and responds to $\mathcal{A}$ with $H_2(m, U) = h$.

H_3**-queries.** To respond to H_3-queries, algorithm $\mathcal{B}$ maintains a list of tuples $\overline{(m, U, h')}$ as explained below. We refer to this list as the H_3-list. The list is initially empty. When $\mathcal{A}$ queries the oracle H_3 at a point $m \in \{0,1\}^*$, algorithm $\mathcal{B}$ responds as follows;

1. If the query m already appears on the H_3-list in a tuple (m, U, h') then algorithm $\mathcal{B}$ responds with $H_3(m, U) = h' \in \mathbb{Z}_q$.
2. Otherwise, $\mathcal{B}$ picks a random $h' \in \mathbb{Z}_q$ and adds the tuple (m, U, h') to the H_3-list and responds to $\mathcal{A}$ with $H_3(m, U) = h'$.

Extract Queries. When $\mathcal{A}$ queries the private key corresponding to ID, $\mathcal{B}$ first finds the corresponding tuple (ID, W, b, c) from the H_1-list;

- If $c = 0$ then $\mathcal{B}$ fails and halts.
- Otherwise, it means that $H_1(ID) = bP$ was previously determined. Then algorithm $\mathcal{B}$ computes $S_{ID} = bP_{pub} = b(xP)$ and responds to $\mathcal{A}$ with S_{ID} as a private key of ID.

Proxy Key Extract Queries. When $\mathcal{A}$ queries a proxy signing key with inputs $\{ID_i, ID_j, w\}$ (it means that an original signer ID_i designates ID_j as a proxy signer), $\mathcal{B}$ first finds (ID_i, W_i, b_i, c_i) and (ID_j, W_j, b_j, c_j) from the H_1-list;

- If $c_i = 0$ or $c_j = 0$ then $\mathcal{B}$ fails and halts.
- Otherwise, it means that $H_1(ID_i) = b_i P$ and $H_1(ID_j) = b_j P$ were previously determined. Then algorithm $\mathcal{B}$ chooses $r_i \in_R \mathbb{Z}_q^*$, computes $U_i = r_i P$ and chooses $h_i, h'_i \in_R \mathbb{Z}_q$. If the tuples containing h_i and h'_i already appear in H_2-list and H_3-list, respectively then $\mathcal{B}$ chooses another r_i and tries again. Then $\mathcal{B}$ computes

$$\sigma_P = h_i(b_i P_{Pub}) + r_i Q + h'_i(b_j P_{Pub})$$

and stores (w, U_i, h_i) and (w, U_i, h'_i) in H_2-list and H_3-list, respectively. Finally, $\mathcal{B}$ responds to $\mathcal{A}$ with (U_i, σ_P) as ID_j's proxy signing key.

Sign Queries. When $\mathcal{A}$ makes a Sign-query on M with $\{ID_i, ID_j, w\}$, $\mathcal{B}$ first finds the corresponding tuples (ID_i, W_i, b_i, c_i) and (ID_j, W_j, b_j, c_j) from the H_1-list;

- If $c_i = 0$ or $c_j = 0$ then $\mathcal{B}$ fails and halts.
- Otherwise, it means that $H_1(ID_i) = b_i P$ and $H_1(ID_j) = b_j P$ were previously determined. Then algorithm $\mathcal{B}$ chooses $r_i, r_j \in_R \mathbb{Z}_q^*$ and computes $U_i = r_i P$, $U_j = r_j P$.
  - If the queries w already appear on the H_2-list and H_3-list in a tuple (w, U_i, h_i), (w, U_i, h'_i) and (w, m, U_j, h'_j), respectively, then $\mathcal{B}$ uses such h_i, h'_i and h'_j.
  - Otherwise, $\mathcal{B}$ chooses random $h_i, h'_i, h'_j \in_R \mathbb{Z}_q$ and stores (w, U_i, h_i), (w, U_i, h'_i), and (w, m, U_j, h'_j) in the H_2-list and H_3-list, respectively. Then, $\mathcal{B}$ computes

$$V = h'_j[h_i(b_i P_{Pub}) + r_i Q + h'_i(b_j P_{Pub})] + r_j Q$$

and responds to $\mathcal{A}$ with $\sigma = (U_i, U_j, V)$.

All responses to Sign queries are valid; indeed, the output (w, m, U_i, U_j, V) of Sign query is a valid proxy signature on m for $\{ID_i, ID_j, w\}$, to see this,

$$e(V,\ P) = e(h'_j[h_i(b_i P_{Pub}) + r_i Q + h'_i(b_j P_{Pub})] + r_j Q,\ P)$$

$$= e(h'_j V_P,\ P_{Pub}) \cdot e(h'_j U_i + U_j,\ Q).$$

If $\mathcal{B}$ does not abort as a result of $\mathcal{A}$'s Sign queries, Extract queries and Proxy Key Extract queries then $\mathcal{A}$'s view is identical to its view in the real attack.

Output. Eventually $\mathcal{A}$ outputs a forgery σ on a message M for $\{ID_i, ID_j, w\}$. Again by assumption, $\mathcal{A}$ has previously issued hash-queries for $\{ID_i, ID_j\}$. If the coins flipped by $\mathcal{B}$ for the query to ID_k, where k is one of i and j, did not show 0 then $\mathcal{B}$ fails (in fact, $c_i = 0$ and $c_j = 0$ do not appear simultaneously because $Pr[c = 0] = \frac{1}{q_E+1}$). Otherwise, $(c_i = 0, c_j = 1)$ or $(c_i = 1, c_j = 0)$.

- If $(c_i = 0, c_j = 1)$ then $H_1(ID_i) = b_i(yP)$ and $H_1(ID_j) = b_j P$ and $\mathcal{B}$ outputs

$$(h'_j \cdot h_i \cdot b_i)^{-1}[V - h'_j t U_i - h'_j h'_i(b_j P_{Pub}) - t U_j]$$

$$= (h'_j \cdot h_i \cdot b_i)^{-1}[h'_j h_i S_{ID_i}] = (h'_j \cdot h_i \cdot b_i)^{-1} h'_j h_i x(b_i yP) = xyP.$$

- If $(c_i = 1, c_j = 0)$ then $H_1(ID_i) = b_i P$ and $H_1(ID_j) = b_j(yP)$ and $\mathcal{B}$ outputs

$$(h'_j \cdot h'_i \cdot b_j)^{-1}[V - h'_j h_i(b_i P_{Pub}) - h'_j t U_i - t U_j]$$

$$= (h'_j \cdot h'_i \cdot b_j)^{-1}[h'_j h'_i S_{ID_j}] = (h'_j \cdot h'_i \cdot b_j)^{-1} h'_j h'_i x(b_j yP) = xyP.$$

This completes the description of algorithm $\mathcal{B}$. It remains to show that $\mathcal{B}$ solves the given instance of the CDH problem with probability at least ε'. To do so, we analyze five events needed for $\mathcal{B}$ to succeed;

- E_1: $\mathcal{B}$ does not abort as a result of any of $\mathcal{A}$'s Extract queries.
- E_2: $\mathcal{B}$ does not abort as a result of any of $\mathcal{A}$'s Proxy Key Extract queries.
- E_3: $\mathcal{B}$ does not abort as a result of any of $\mathcal{A}$'s Sign queries.
- E_4: $\mathcal{A}$ generates a valid signature forgery $(w, M, ID_i, ID_j, U_i, U_j, V)$.
- E_5: Event E_4 occurs and $c_k = 0$, where k is one of i and j such that $c_k = 0$ for the tuple containing ID_k on the H_1-list.

$\mathcal{B}$ succeeds if all of these events happen. The probability $Pr[E_1 \wedge E_1 \wedge E_3 \wedge E_4 \wedge E_5]$ is decomposed as

$$Pr[E_1 \wedge E_1 \wedge E_3 \wedge E_4 \wedge E_5] = Pr[E_1] \cdot Pr[E_2|E_1] \cdot Pr[E_3|E_1 \wedge E_2]$$

$$\cdot Pr[E_4|E_1 \wedge E_2 \wedge E_3] \cdot Pr[E_5|E_1 \wedge E_2 \wedge E_3 \wedge E_4] \quad \cdots\cdots \quad (1).$$

The following claims give a lower bound for each of these terms.

Claim 1. The probability that algorithm $\mathcal{B}$ does not abort as a result of $\mathcal{A}$'s Extract queries is at least $(1 - \frac{1}{q_E+1})^{q_E}$. Hence, $Pr[E_1] \geq (1 - \frac{1}{q_E+1})^{q_E}$.

Claim 2. The probability that algorithm $\mathcal{B}$ does not abort as a result of $\mathcal{A}$'s Proxy Key Extract queries is 1 since it is simulated so that $\mathcal{B}$ does not abort as a result of any of $\mathcal{A}$'s Proxy Key Extract queries under the aborted result of any of $\mathcal{A}$'s Extract queries. Hence, $Pr[E_2|E_1] = 1$.

Claim 3. The probability that algorithm $\mathcal{B}$ does not abort as a result of $\mathcal{A}$'s Sign queries is 1.

Proof. It is simulated so that $\mathcal{B}$ does not abort as a result of any of $\mathcal{A}$'s Sign queries under the aborted result of any of $\mathcal{A}$'s Extract and Proxy Key Extract queries. Hence, $Pr[E_2|E_1 \wedge E_2] = 1$.

Claim 4. If $\mathcal{B}$ does not abort as a result of $\mathcal{A}$'s Sign queries, Extract queries and Proxy Key Extract queries then $\mathcal{A}$'s view is identical to its view in the attack. Hence, $Pr[E_4|E_1 \wedge E_2 \wedge E_3] \geq \varepsilon$.

Claim 5. The probability that algorithm $\mathcal{B}$ does not abort after $\mathcal{A}$ outputs a valid and nontrivial forgery is at least $(1 - \frac{1}{q_E+1}) \cdot \frac{1}{q_E+1}$. Hence, $Pr[E_5|E_1 \wedge E_2 \wedge E_3 \wedge E_4] \geq (1 - \frac{1}{q_E+1}) \cdot \frac{1}{q_E+1}$.

Proof. Algorithm $\mathcal{B}$ succeeds only if $\mathcal{A}$ generates a forgery such that $c_k = 0$, where k is one of i and j for $\{ID_i, ID_j\}$. Hence, $Pr[E_5|E_1 \wedge E_2 \wedge E_3 \wedge E_4] \geq (1 - \frac{1}{q_E+1}) \cdot \frac{1}{q_E+1}$.

Algorithm $\mathcal{A}$ produces the correct forgery with probability at least

$$(1 - \frac{1}{q_E + 1})^{q_E} \cdot \varepsilon \cdot \frac{1}{q_E + 1}(1 - \frac{1}{q_E + 1})$$

$$\geq (1 - \frac{1}{q_E + 1})^{q_E+1} \cdot \varepsilon \cdot \frac{1}{q_E + 1} \geq \frac{1}{e} \cdot \frac{\varepsilon}{(q_E + 1)} \geq \varepsilon'$$

as required.

Algorithm $\mathcal{B}$'s running time is the same as $\mathcal{A}$'s running time plus the time is takes to respond to $(q_{H_1} + q_{H_2} + q_{H_2} + q_S)$ hash queries, q_E Extract queries, q_{PE} Proxy Key Extract queries and q_S Sign queries, and the time to transform $\mathcal{A}$'s final forgery into the CDH solution. The H_1, Extract, Proxy Key Extract and Sign queries requires 1, 1, 4, and 6 scalar multiplications. The output phase requires 4 scalar multiplications and an inversion. We assume that a scalar multiplication in $\mathbb{G}_1$ and an inversion in $\mathbb{Z}_q^*$ take time $c_{\mathbb{G}_1}$. Hence, the total running time is at most $t + c_{\mathbb{G}_1}(q_{H_1} + q_E + 4q_{PE} + 6q_S + 5) \leq t'$ as required. $\square$

3.3 Further Security Analysis

Now, we show that our ID-based proxy signature scheme satisfies all the requirements described in the section 2.

1. **Distinguishability:** This is obvious, because there is a warrant w in a valid proxy signature, at the same time, this warrant w and the public keys of the

original signer and the proxy signer must occur in the verification equations of proxy signatures.

2. **Verifiability:** It derived from correctness of the proposed ID-based proxy signature scheme. In general, the warrant contains the identity information and the limitation of the delegated signing capacity and so satisfies the verifiability.
3. **Strong Non-Forgeability:** It derived from correctness of the Theorem 3.1.
4. **Strong Identifiability:** It contains the warrant w in a valid proxy signature, so anyone can determine the identity of the corresponding proxy signer from the warrant w.
5. **Strong Non-Deniability:** As the identifiability, the valid proxy signature contains the warrant w, which must be verified in the verification phase, it cannot be modified by the proxy signer. Thus once a proxy signer creates a valid proxy signature of an original signer, he cannot repudiate the signature creation.
6. **Prevention of Misuse:** In our proxy signature scheme, using the warrant w, we had determined the limit of the delegated signing capacity in the warrant w, so the proxy signer cannot sign some messages that have not been authorized by the original signer.

4   Conclusion

We have proposed a new ID-based proxy signature scheme from bilinear pairings with a tight security reduction without using the Forking Lemma [10]. The proposed scheme requires a scalar multiplication (two scalar multiplications can be precomputed) in signing and 3 scalar multiplications and 3 pairing computation in verification.

References

1. A. Boldyreva, Efficient threshold signature, multisignature and blind signature schemes based on the Gap-Diffie-Hellman-group signature scheme, PKC'03, LNCS 2567, Springer-Verlag (2003), pp. 31-46. 8.
2. A. Boldyreva, A. Palacio and B. Warinschi, Secure Proxy Signature Scheme for Delegation of Signing Rights, IACR ePrint Archive, available at http://eprint.iacr.org/2003/096/, 2003.
3. D. Boneh, X. Boyen, and H. Shacham, Short group signatures, Advances in Cryptology: Crypto'04, LNCS 3152, Springer-Verlag (2004), pp. 41-55.
4. D. Boneh and M. Franklin, Identity-based encryption from the Weil pairing, Advances in Cryptology: Crypto'01, LNCS 2139, Springer-Verlag (2001), pp. 213-229.
5. D. Boneh, C. Gentry, B. Lynn, and H. Shacham, Aggregate and verifiably encrypted signatures from bilinear maps, Advances in Cryptology: Eurocrypt'03, LNCS 2656, Springer-Verlag (2003), pp. 416-432.
6. D. Boneh, B. Lynn, H. Shacham, Short signatures from the Weil pairing, Advances in Cryptology: Asiacrypt'01, LNCS 2248, Springer-Verlag (2002), pp. 514-532.

7. B. Lee, H. Kim and K. Kim, Secure mobile agent using strong non-designated proxy signature, ACISP'01, LNCS 2119, Springer Verlag (2001), pp. 474-486.
8. M. Mambo, K. Usuda, and E. Okamoto, Proxy signature: Delegation of the power to sign messages, In IEICE Trans. Fundamentals, E79-A(9), pp. 1338-1353, 1996.
9. T. Okamoto, M. Tada and E. Okamoto, Extended proxy signatures for smart cards, ISW'99, LNCS 1729, Springer-Verlag (1999), pp. 247-258.
10. D. Pointcheval, and J. Stern, Security proofs for signature schemes, Advances in Cryptology: Eurocrypt'96, LNCS 1070, Springer-Verlag (1996), pp. 387-398.
11. A. Shamir, Identity-based cryptosystems and signature schemes, Advances in cryptology: Crypto'84, LNCS 196, Springer-Verlag (1884), pp. 47-53.
12. Jing Xu, Zhenfeng Zhang, Dengguo Feng, ID-Based Proxy Signature Using Bilinear Pairings, ISPA Workshops, LNCS 3559, Springer-Verlag (2005) pp. 359-367
13. F. Zhang and K. Kim, Efficient ID-based blind signature and proxy signature from pairings, ACISP'03, LNCS 2727, Springer-Verlag (2003), pp. 312-323.
14. F. Zhang, R. S. Naini and C. Y. Lin, New proxy signature, proxy blind signature and proxy ring signature schemes from bilinear pairings, Cryptology ePrint Archive, Report 2003/117.
15. F. Zhang, R. Safavi-Naini, and W. Susilo, An efficient signature scheme from bilinear pairings and its application, PKC'04, LNCS 2947, Springer-Verlag (2004), pp. 277-290.

Finding Compact Reliable Broadcast in Unknown Fixed-Identity Networks (Short Paper)

Huafei Zhu and Jianying Zhou

Institute for Infocomm Research, A-star, Singapore
{huafei, jyzhou}@i2r.a-star.edu.sg

Abstract. At PODC'05, Subramanian, Katz, Roth, Shenker and Stoica (SKRSS) introduced and formulated a new theoretical problem called reliable broadcast problems in unknown fixed-identity networks [3] and further proposed a feasible result to this problem. Since the size of signatures of a message traversing a path grows linearly with the number of hops in their implementations, this leaves an interesting research problem (an open problem advertised by Subramanian et al in [3]) − how to reduce the communication complexity of their reliable broadcast protocol?

In this paper, we provide a novel implementation of reliable broadcast problems in unknown fixed-identity networks with lower communication complexity. The idea behind of our improvement is that we first transfer the notion of path-vector signatures to that of sequential aggregate path-vector signatures and show that the notion of sequential aggregate path-vector is a special case of the notion of sequential aggregate signatures. As a result, the currently known results regarding sequential aggregate signatures can be used to solve the open problem. We then describe the work of [3] in light of sequential aggregate signatures working over independent RSA, and show that if the size of an node $v_{i,j}$'s public key $|g(v_{i,j})|$ is $t_{i,j}$ and the number of hops in a path p_i is d_i in the unknown fixed-identity graph G (with k adversaries), the reduced communication complexity is approximate to $\sum_{j=1}^{d_i-1} t_{i,j}$ while the computation (time) complexity of our protocol is the same as that presented in [3].

Keywords: aggregate path-vector signatures, path-vector signatures, reliable broadcast problem.

1 Introduction

At PODC'05, Subramanian, Katz, Roth, Shenker and Stoica (SKRSS) introduced and formulated a new theoretical problem called reliable broadcast problems in unknown fixed-identity networks [3] and then proposed a feasible result such that given a bound k on the number of adversaries, there exists a distributed algorithm that achieves reliable broadcast in an unknown fixed-identity network if and only if G is $(2k + 1)$ vertex connected. The key idea behind their construction is that − if a node u propagates a path-vector message (m, s, p) to

P. Ning, S. Qing, and N. Li (Eds.): ICICS 2006, LNCS 4307, pp. 72–81, 2006.
© Springer-Verlag Berlin Heidelberg 2006

v, then v's identity is already appended to the path p by u signifying that u has propagated the message to v. As a result, the signatures' size of the message over the path grows linearly with the number of hops and thus increases communication overheads. This leaves an interesting research problem (an open problem advertised by Subramanian et al in [3]) − how to reduce the communication complexity of the proposed reliable broadcast protocol?

1.1 More on SKRSS' Assumptions

To remove the public key infrastructure (PKI) assumption, Subramanian, Katz, Roth, Shenker and Stoica further made the followings two assumptions on mobile nodes:

- **Assumption 1:** the identity of a node is fixed which cannot be forged;
- **Assumption 2:** a node knows the identities of its neighbors in the underlying graph.

We stress that the second assumption can be absorbed by a broadcasting protocol itself and thus can be implemented without any difficulty. For example, an initiator node broadcasts a message "hello, every neighbor node sends me a reply message please". Each node within one hop that receives this request for the first time appends its identifier to the received message and then sends it back to the initiator.

We also stress that an implementation of the first assumption however is a difficult task in the non-PKI setting since if the identity of a node cannot be forged, then some kinds of digital signatures or commitment schemes should be involved just like the certificates in the PKI setting. A simple way here is that we allow a device manufactory (serving as a trusted third party) to sign individual device id. The concatenation of a device id and its signature in turn is viewed as a fixed device id which can be publicly verified. Since a verifier cannot check the validation of the manufactory's public key on time in the non-PKI setting (yet this verification can be made off-line or with the help of proxies of the device, i.e., via delegation technique), we refer to this kind of signatures as obliviously committed signatures. Intuitively, an obliviously committed signature is a digital signature that is used for signing an id of a device by a third party (need not to be trusted), and the validity of the signer's public key is questionable from the point view of a verifier at the current time, and thus it is oblivious (1-out-of 2, validity (1) or invalidity (0)), however the verifier will obtain a correct answer (0 or 1) with the help of others. Since there is no satisfactory solution to this problem, we thus leave an interesting problem to the research community − how to implement secure yet efficient (with low computation and communication complexities) obliviously committed signatures in the non-PKI environment?

1.2 This Work

The goal of this paper is to provide a solution to Subramanian et al's open problem. We employ sequential aggregate signatures to accomplish this task. The contribution of this paper is twofold.

- In the first fold, we transfer the notion of path-vector signatures to that of sequential aggregate path-vector signatures and show that the notion of sequential aggregate path-vector is a special case of the notion of sequential aggregate signatures. As a result, the currently known results regarding sequential aggregate signatures can be used to solve the open problem.
- In the second fold, we describe the work of [3] in light of the best result regarding sequential aggregate signatures that are working over independent RSA moduli presented in [4] and show that assuming that $v_{i,j}$'s public key size is $|g(v_{i,j})| = t_{i,j}$ and the number of hops in a path p_i is d_i in the unknown fixed-identity graph G (with k adversaries), the reduced communication complexity is approximate to $\sum_{j=1}^{d_i-1} t_{i,j}$ while the computation (time) complexity of our protocol is the same as that presented in [3]. We thus, provide a solution to the open problem presented in [3].

2   From Path-Vector Signatures to Sequential Aggregate Signatures

2.1   Path-Vector Signatures

The basic tool used to solve the reliable broadcast problem in unknown fixed-identity networks is the notion of path-vector signatures introduced in [3]. Informally, a path-vector signature consists of the following three algorithms [2]:

- Public-key initialization: By m, we denote a message sent by v_1 to v_n over a path $(v_1, \cdots, v_n)$. Every node v_i generates its public key $g(v_i)$, and communicates it to its neighbor v_{i-1}.
- Message initialization: The source node v_1 sends the message $m_1 = [(m, s, p), sig_1]$ to its neighbor v_2 where $s = (v_1, g(v_1))$, $p_1 = [(v_1, g(v_1)), (v_2, g(v_2))]$, and $sig_1 = sig((m, s, p_1), g(v_1))$;
- Incremental update: Node v_i receives message $m_{i-1} = [(m, s, p_{i-1}), sig_{i-1}]$ from its predecessor v_{i-1}. It then sends message $m_i = [(m, s, p_i), sig_i]$ to its successor v_{i+1} where $p_i = [(p_{i-1}, (v_{i+1}, g(v_{i+1})]$ and $sig_i = (sig_{i-1}, sig((m, s, p_i), (v_i, g(v_i)))$.

We stress that the notion of a path-vector signatures presented in [3] is order specified. Furthermore, it allows multi-signer to sign same message m. As a result, the notion of a path-vector signatures is equivalent to that of order-specified multi-signature schemes and thus notion of sequential aggregate path-vector is a special case of the notion of sequential aggregate signatures.

To reduce communication complexity of the reliable broadcasting problem, we need to compress the size of the underlying path-vector signature. Motivated by this consideration, a new notion which we called sequential aggregate path-vector signatures can be introduced and formalized (where the same message m is signed by all nodes along the path p) in a natural way. We however derive this new notion from the standard notion of sequential aggregate signatures so that currently known results regarding sequential aggregate signatures can be used for our purpose, rather than formalize the stand-alone notion of sequential aggregate path-vector signatures.

2.2 Syntax of Sequential Aggregate Signatures in the Public-Key Infrastructure (PKI) Environment

Syntax. A sequential aggregate signature scheme (KG, AggSign, AggVf) consists of the following algorithms [2]:

- Key generation algorithm (KG): On input l and k_i, KG outputs system parameters param (including an initial value $\mathcal{IV}$, without loss of generality, we assume that $\mathcal{IV}$ is a zero strings with length l-bit), on input param and user index $i \in \mathcal{I}$ and k_i, it outputs a public key and secret key pair (PK_i, SK_i) of a trapdoor one-way permutation f_i for a user i.
- Aggregate signing algorithm (AggSign): Given a message m_i to sign, and a sequential aggregate σ_{i-1} on messages $\{m_1, \cdots, m_{i-1}\}$ under respective public keys $PK_1, \cdots, PK_{i-1}$, where m_1 is the inmost message. All of m_1, $\cdots, m_{i-1}$ and $PK_1, \cdots, PK_{i-1}$ must be provided as inputs. AggSign first verifies that σ_{i-1} is a valid aggregate for messages $\{m_1, \cdots, m_{i-1}\}$ using the verification algorithm defined below (if $i=1$, the aggregate σ_0 is taken to be zero strings 0^l). If not, it outputs $\perp$, otherwise, it then adds a signature on m_i under SK_i to the aggregate and outputs a sequential aggregate σ_i on all i messages $m_1, \cdots, m_i$.
- Aggregate verifying algorithm (AggVf): Given a sequential aggregate signature σ_i on the messages $\{m_1, \cdots, m_i\}$ under the respective public keys $\{PK_1, \cdots, PK_i\}$. If any key appears twice, if any element PK_i does not describe a permutation or if the size of the messages is different from the size of the respective public keys reject. Otherwise, for $j = i, \cdots, 1$, set $\sigma_{j-1} = f_j(PK_1, \cdots, PK_j, \sigma_j)$. The verification of σ_{i-1} is processed recursively. The base case for recursion is $i = 0$, in which case simply check that σ_0. Accepts if σ_0 equals the zero strings.

A sequential aggregate signature is called a sequential aggregate path-vector signature if all nodes over a path $p=(PK_1, \cdots, PK_n)$ sign any same message (i.e., $m_1 = \cdots = m_n$).

The Definition of Security. The following security definition of sequential aggregative signature schemes is due to [2]. The aggregate forger $\mathcal{A}$ is provided with a initial value $\mathcal{IV}$, a set of public keys $PK_1, \cdots, PK_{i-1}$ and PK, generated at random. The adversary also is provided with $SK_1, \cdots, SK_{i-1}$; PK is called target public key. $\mathcal{A}$ requests sequential aggregate signatures with PK on messages of his choice. For each query, he supplies a sequential aggregate signature σ_{i-1} on some messages $m_1, \cdots, m_{i-1}$ under the distinct public keys $PK_1, \cdots,$ PK_{i-1}, and an additional message m_i to be signed by the signing oracle under public key PK. Finally, $\mathcal{A}$ outputs a valid signature σ_i of a message m_i which is associated with the aggregate σ_{i-1}. The forger wins if $\mathcal{A}$ did not request $(m_i,$

σ_{i-1}) in the previous signing oracle queries. By $\mathsf{AdvAggSign}_\mathcal{A}$, we denote the probability of success of an adversary.

We say a sequential aggregate signature scheme is secure against adaptive chosen-message attack if for every polynomial time Turing machine $\mathcal{A}$, the probability $\mathsf{AdvAggSign}_\mathcal{A}$ that it wins the game is at most a negligible amount, where the probability is taken over coin tosses of KG and $\mathsf{AggSign}$ and $\mathcal{A}$. The security of sequential aggregate path-vector signatures can be defined in a similar way as that of sequential aggregate signatures with the restriction $m_i = m$ for the jth oracle query over a path $p = (PK_1, \cdots, PK_n)$.

Sequential Aggregate Signatures from RSA. In [2], Lysyanskaya, Micali, Reyzin, Shacham proposed two approaches to instantiate their generic construction from RSA trapdoor one-way permutations:

- the first approach is to require the user's moduli to be arranged in increasing order: $N_1 < N_2 < \cdots < N_t$. At the verification, it is important to check that the i-th signature σ_i is actually less than N_i to ensure the signatures are unique if H is fixed. As long as $\log(N_1) - \log(N_t)$ is constant, the range of H is a subset of Z_{N_1} whose size is the constant fraction of N_1, the scheme will be secure;
- the second approach does not require the moduli to be arranged in increasing order, however they are required to be of the same length. The signature will expanded by n bits $b_1, \cdots, b_n$, where n is the total number of users. Namely, during signing, if $\sigma_i \geq N_{i+1}$, let $b_i = 1$; else, let $b_i = 0$. During the verification, if $b_i = 1$, add N_{i+1} to σ_i before proceeding with the verification of σ_i. Always, check that σ_i is in the correct range $0 \leq \sigma_i \leq N_i$ to ensure the uniqueness of signatures.

For applications of aggregate path-vector signature schemes in reliable communication where a graph G is unknown, the choice of a claimed public key of a node v_i is completely independent on the choice of a claimed public key of another node v_j in the Internet. Thus, for any RSA-based aggregate path-vector signature that works over an unknown fixed-identity graph, a reasonable assumption should be that the sizes of all moduli are bounded by a fixed size (this requirement does not violate the unknown of underlying graph G). We stress that there is efficient implementation of sequential aggregate signatures presented in [4], which is sketched below:

Sequential aggregate signatures working over independent RSA moduli

Let $H: \{0,1\}^* \to \{0,1\}^l$ be a cryptographic hash function and $\mathcal{IV}$ be the initial vector that should be pre-described by an aggregate path-vector signature scheme. The initial value could be a random l-bit string or an empty string. Without loss of generality, we assume that the initial value $\mathcal{IV}$ is 0^l. Our aggregate path-vector signature is described as follows:

- Key generation: Each user i generates an RSA public key (N_i, e_i) and secret key (N_i, d_i), ensuring that $|N_i| = k_i$ and that $e_i > N_i$ is a prime. Let G_i:

$\{0,1\}^{t_i} \rightarrow \{0,1\}^{k_i}$, be cryptographic hash function specified by each user i, $t_i = l - k_i$.

- AggPVSig: User i is given an aggregate path-vector signature g_{i-1} and $(b_1, \cdots, b_{i-1})$, a sequence of messages $m_1, \cdots, m_{i-1}$, and the corresponding keys $(N_1, e_1), \cdots, (N_{i-1}, e_{i-1})$. User i first verifies σ_{i-1}, using the verification procedure below, where $\sigma_0 = 0^l$. If this succeeds, user i computes $H_i = H(m_1, \cdots, m_i, (N_1, e_1), \cdots, (N_i, e_i))$ and computes $x_i = H_i \oplus g_{i-1}$. Then it separates $x_i = y_i || z_i$, where $y_i \in \{0,1\}^{k_i}$ and $z_i \in \{0,1\}^{t_i}$, $t_i = l - k_i$. Finally, it computes $g_i = f_i^{-1}(y_i \oplus G_i(z_i))||z_i$. By $\sigma_i \leftarrow (g_i, b_i)$, we denote the aggregate path-vector signature(if $y_i \oplus G_i(z_i) > N_i$, then $b_i = 1$, if $y_i \oplus G_i(z_i) < N_i$, then $b_i = 0$; again we do not define the case $y_i \oplus G_i(z_i) = N_i$ since the probability the event happens is negligible), where $f_i^{-1}(y) = y^{d_i}$ mod N_i, the inverse of the RSA function $f_i(y) = y^{e_i}$ mod N_i defined over the domain $Z_{N_i}^*$.
- AggPVf: The aggregate path-vector verification algorithm is given as input an aggregate path-vector signature g_i, $(b_1, \cdots, b_i)$, the messages $m_1, \cdots, m_i$, the correspondent public keys $(N_1, e_1), \cdots, (N_i, e_i)$ and proceeds as follows. Check that no keys appears twice, that $e_i > N_i$ is a prime. Then it computes:
  - $H_i = H(m_1, \cdots, m_i, (N_1, e_1), \cdots, (N_i, e_i))$;
  - Separating $g_i = v_i || w_i$;
  - Recovering x_i form the trapdoor one-way permutation by computing $z_i \leftarrow w_i$, $y_i = B_i(f_i(v_i) + b_i N_i) \oplus G_i(z_i)$, and $x_i = y_i || z_i$, where $B_i(x)$ is the binary representation of $x \in \mathcal{Z}$ (with k_i bits).
  - Recovering g_{i-1} by computing $x_i \oplus H_i$. The verification of (g_{i-1}, b_{i-1}) is processed recursively. The base case for recursion is $i = 0$, in which case simply check that $\sigma_0 = 0^l$.

Lemma 1. *([4]): Let $\cup_{i \in I} f_i$ be a certificated homomorphic trapdoor permutation family, the sequential aggregate signature scheme described above is secure in the random oracle model.*

2.3 Optimal Result

Let f be an RSA trapdoor one-way permutation defined over Z_N^*, where $N = PQ$, P and Q are two large prime numbers and $|N| = k$. Let $H: \{0,1\}^* \rightarrow \{0,1\}^l$ be a cryptographic hash function. Let $f(x) = x^e$ mod N and $f^{-1}(x) = x^d$ mod N, where $ed \equiv 1$ mod $\phi(N)$, e is a public key, and d is the correspondent secret key. Throughout this section, we assume that $l \geq k + 1$.

On input a message $m \in \{0,1\}^*$, we obtain a string $H(m) \in \{0,1\}^l$ which in turn can be rewritten as the form $qN + r$ $(= H(m))$, where $0 \leq r < N$. Let $g_1(m) = f^{-1}(r)$ and $g_2(m) = \mathcal{P}(q)$, where $\mathcal{P}$ is a padding algorithm ($\mathcal{UP}$ is the correspondent un-padding algorithm) which is further defined below.

- Padding algorithm $\mathcal{P}$: on input a random string $q \in \{0,1\}^\tau$, $\mathcal{P}$ outputs a $(l-k)$-bit codeword $0^{l-k-\tau}||q$ of q which is denoted by $\mathcal{P}(q)$;
- Un-padding algorithm $\mathcal{UP}$: on input $(l-k)$-bit string $\mathcal{P}(q)$, $\mathcal{UP}(\mathcal{P}(q))$ outputs a τ-bit string q, i.e., $\mathcal{UP}(\mathcal{P}(q)) = q \in \{0,1\}^\tau$.

By $(N, e, H, k, l, (\mathcal{P}, \mathcal{UP}))$, we denote the public key of a signature scheme. The secret key is (d, N). Our signature scheme working in an extended domain is defined as follows:

- **Signing algorithm:** on input a message m, the signer computes $H(m)$, and then writes $H(m)$ as the form $qN + r$ ($0 \leq r < N$, $|N| = k$); Finally it computes $g_1(m) \leftarrow f^{-1}(r)$ and $g_2(m) \leftarrow \mathcal{P}(q)$, where $\mathcal{P}(q)$ is a padding of q; The signature σ of message m is $(g_1(m), g_2(m))$;
- **Verification algorithm:** given a putative signature $\sigma(m)$, a verifier computes $r \leftarrow f(g_1(m))$, and $q \leftarrow \mathcal{UP}(g_2(m))$; Finally, the verifier checks $H(m) \overset{?}{=} qN + r$.

Using the same technique presented in [4], we show that assuming that the RSA function is a trapdoor one-way permutation defined over Z_N^*, our signature scheme defined above is provably secure against existential forgery under an adaptive chosen-message attack in the random oracle model. This ordinary signature can be further transferred to a sequential aggregate signature without bit-expansion. For simplicity, in the following discussion, we provide our solution to the open in light of the base signature case and leave an exercise to readers in the optimal case.

3   Reliable Broadcast in Unknown Fixed-Identity Networks

Given an undirected graph G, two vertices u and v are called connected if there exists a path from u to v; Otherwise they are called disconnected. The graph G is called connected graph if every pair of vertices in the graph is connected. A vertex cut for two vertices u and v is a set of vertices whose removal from the graph disconnects u and v. A vertex cut for the whole graph is a set of vertices whose removal renders the graph disconnected. The vertex connectivity $k(G)$ for a graph G is the size of minimum vertex cut. A graph is called k vertex connected if its vertex connectivity is k or greater.

3.1   Removal of Certificated Public Keys

We stress that a collection of claimed public keys within a path-vector signature must be certificated. Thus, either a trusted third party (a certificate authority) or a public key infrastructure is required. To remove the concept of certificated identity graph G_x from path-vector signatures, a new notion called keyed-identity graph G_x is first introduced and formalized in [3]. To do so, the fixed-identity assumption is critical. The fixed-identity assumption states the following thing: each node in an undirected graph G has a unique identity it cannot fake and it knows the identities of its neighbors in G. If this assumption is not met and an adversary uses different identities to different neighbors, then for any given integer $m > 0$, there exists an m-vertex connected network G on n nodes where each node is initially aware of the identities if only its neighbors such that, a single adversary using multiple identities is sufficient to disrupt reliable broadcast in G.

With the help of fixed-identity assumption, an algorithm determining genuine keyed-identity can be proposed [3]. Suppose the underlying graph G is $2k + 1$ vertex connected with k adversaries, then, between every pair of good nodes, there exists at least $k + 1$ vertex disjoint paths that traverse only good nodes (the fact that adversaries can at most prove k disjoint paths to a fake node is critical for the solvability of this problem.).

3.2   Sequential Aggregate Based Broadcast Protocols

Now we can embed sequential aggregate signatures into the SKRSS asynchronous broadcast algorithm presented in [3]. That is, given a path-vector message (m, s, p) and its signature, we define the keyed identity path $P_I(m, s, p)$ associated with (m, s, p) to consist of vertices $(v_i, g(v_i))$, where v_i is the identity of a node in p and $g(v_i)$ is the public key of v_i in the signature. We borrow the notation G_x from [3] to denote the keyed-identity graph computed by a node x with a set of neighbors $N(x)$. Every good node x performs the following set of operations.

Sequential aggregate based broadcast protocol in identity-fixed networks.

- Asynchronous node wake up: A node can either begin broadcast by itself or begin transmissions upon receipt of the first message from a neighbor.
- Initiation: G_x consists of one vertex $(x, g(x))$.
- For every $u \in N(x)$, x transmits $(m(x), x, [x, u])$ to u along with its sequential aggregate signature sas.
- Propagation: For every path-vector message (m, s, p) with sequential aggregate signature sas that x receives from $u \in N(x)$, x performs:
    - Immediate-neighbor key check: Check if public-key of u in S matches the same public-key used in previous messages. If not, reject (m, s, p); if $v \in N(x) \setminus \{u\}$ appears in p, then the public-key of v should also match the one directly advertised by v.
    - Verify S using the verification algorithm of the aggregate path-vector signature.
    - Learn one vertex at a time: Accept the message only if $P_I(m, s, p)$ contains at most one new keyed identity (at the end of the path) not present in G_x. If so, update G_x with $P_I(m, s, p)$.
    - Message suppression: If $P_I(m, s, p)$ adds no new vertices or edges to G_x, ignore the message.
    - To every $u \in N(x)$, x transmits (m, s, p') where $p' = p \cup \{u\}$ after updating the signature.
- Flow computation: If the number of identity-disjoint paths to $(v, g(v))$ in G_x is at least $k + 1$, then x deems v to be a genuine identity and $g(v)$ to be its public key. By identity disjoint paths, we mean that no two paths should contain two different vertices $(v, g(v))$ and $(v, g'(v))$ which share the same identity v. The immediate-neighbor key check is necessary to ensure that if

an adversary $v \in N(x)$, then v uses only a single keyed-identity $(v, g(v))$ in all its messages propagated to x. Any other message that x receives (from other neighbors) which contains the identity v is accepted only if it contains the same public key $g(v)$.

Theorem 1. *Given a bound k on the number of adversaries, the algorithm described above achieves reliable broadcast in an unknown fixed-identity network $U(n, G, N)$ if and only if G is $2k + 1$ vertex connected.*

Proof. The necessary condition can be argued as follows: the structure of graph G is unknown but each node knows the identities of its neighbors in our model while the entire graph G is known to all nodes in Dolev's model [1]. Clearly, Dolev's model is a special case of our model. It follows that the assumption that G is $(2k+1)$-vertex connected is a necessary condition for reliable communication in our model.

The sufficient condition can be argued as follows: Let G' be a subgraph of G consisting of all edges between honest nodes. since the underlying graph G is $(2k + 1)$-vertex connected with k adversaries, it follows that G' is at least $(k+1)$-vertex connected. If every good node u can learn all the edges in G', then it can definitely compute $(k+1)$ identity disjoint paths to every other good node and hence, can successfully determine every other good node v. Consequently, to show the proposed routing algorithm achieving reliability, it is sufficient to show that every good node will eventually learn all edges in G'. Now we consider the presence of $k > 0$ adversaries and two good nodes u and v are separated by τ hops. By the broadcasting algorithm described above, we know that at the ith hop, an individual node exchanges the new sequential aggregate signature it learnt from the $(i-1)^{th}$ with its neighbors. Recursively, every good node learns all edges in G' eventually since G' is at least $(k+1)$-vertex connected subgraph.

4   Computation and Communication Complexity

Assuming that $v_{i,j}$'s public key size is $|g(v_{i,j})| = t_{i,j}$ and the number of hops in a path $p_i = \{v_{i,1}, \cdots, v_{i,d_i}\}$ is d_i. The message flow of the original SKRSS protocol is that:

- message flow generated by $v_{i,1}$: $m_{i,1} = \; <m_i, (v_{i,1}, g(v_{i,1})), (v_{i,2}, g(v_{i,2}))>$, and $< sig_{i,1}(m_{i,1}) >$;
- message flow generated by $v_{i,2}$: $m_{i,2} = \; < m_i, (v_{i,1}, g(v_{i,1})), (v_{i,2}, g(v_{i,2})),$ $(v_{i,3}, g(v_{i,3})) >$ and $< sig_{i,1}(m_{i,1})$ and $sig_{i,2}(m_{i,2}) >$;
- $\cdots$;
- message flow generated by v_{i,d_i-1}: $m_{i,d_i-1} = \; < m_i, (v_{i,1}, g(v_{i,1})), \cdots, (v_{i,d_i-1},$ $g(v_{i,d_i-1})) >$, and $< sig_{i,1}(m_{i,1}), \cdots, sig_{i,d_i-1}(m_{i,d_i-1}) >$.

The message flow along the path p_i of our reliable broadcast protocol are that:

- message flow generated by $v_{i,1}$: $v_{i,1}$: $m_{i,1} = <m_i, (v_{i,1}, g(v_{i,1})), (v_{i,2}, g(v_{i,2})) >$, $< sig_{i,1}(m_{i,1}) >$;

- message flow generated by $v_{i,2}$: $m_{i,2} = \; < m_i, \; (v_{i,1}, g(v_{i,1})), \; (v_{i,2}, \; g(v_{i,2})),$
  $(v_{i,3}, \; g(v_{i,3})) >$ and $< b_{i,1}, \; sig_{i,2}(m_{i,2}) >$, where $b_{i,1} \in \{0,1\}$;
- $\cdots$
- message flow generated by v_{i,d_i-1}: $m_{i,d_i-1} = \; < m_i, \; (v_{i,1}, g(v_{i,1})), \cdots, (v_{i,d_i-1},$
  $g(v_{i,d_i-1})) >$, and $< b_{i,1}, \; \cdots, \; b_{i,d_i-2}, \; sig_{i,d_i-1}(m_{d_i-1}) >$, where $b_{i,i} \in \{0,1\}$,
  $1 \le i \le d_i - 2$;

By $comp_i$, we denote the communication complexity of original scheme along
the path p_i; and by $\widetilde{comp}_i$, we denote the communication complexity of our
scheme along the same path p_i. Thus, we have the following estimation (typically,
$d_i - 1 \ll min\{t_{i,1}, \cdots, t_{i,d_i-1}\}$): $comp_i - \widetilde{comp}_i = t_{i,1} + \cdots + t_{i,d_i-1} - (d_i - 1)$
(the term $(d_i - 1)$ is eliminated in case that our optimal sequential aggregate
signature scheme is applied).

5   Conclusion

In this paper, we have transferred the notion of path-vector signatures to that of
sequential aggregate signatures and have also shown that the notion of sequential
aggregate path-vector is a special case of the notion of sequential aggregate
signatures. We have described the work of [3] in light of sequential aggregate
signatures to realize the same functionality of path-vector signatures. We have
presented alternative solution to reliable broadcast problem with nearly optimal
communication complexity and thus provided an efficient solution to the open
problem addressed in the introduction section.

References

1. D.Dolev: The Byzantine Generals Strike Again. J. Algorithms 3(1): 14-30 (1982)
2. A.Lysyanskaya, S.Micali, L.Reyzin, H.Shacham: Sequential Aggregate Signatures
   from trapdoor one-way permutations. EUROCRYPT 2004: 74-90.
3. L.Subramanian, R.Katz, V.Roth, S.Shenker, I.Stoica: Reliable broadcast in unknown fixed-identity networks. PODC2005: 342- 351.
4. H.Zhu, F.Bao, R.H.Deng: Sequential Aggregate Signatures Working over Independent Homomorphic Trapdoor One-Way Permutation Domains. ICICS 2005: 207-219

Formal Analysis and Systematic Construction of Two-Factor Authentication Scheme (Short Paper)

Guomin Yang[1], Duncan S. Wong[1,*], Huaxiong Wang[2], and Xiaotie Deng[1]

[1] Department of Computer Science
City University of Hong Kong
Hong Kong, China
{csyanggm, duncan, deng}@cs.cityu.edu.hk
[2] Department of Computing
Macquarie University
Australia
hwang@ics.mq.edu.au

Abstract. One of the most commonly used two-factor authentication mechanisms is based on smart card and user's password. Throughout the years, there have been many schemes proposed, but most of them have already been found flawed due to the lack of formal security analysis. On the cryptanalysis of this type of schemes, in this paper, we further review two recently proposed schemes and show that their security claims are invalid. To address the current issue, we propose a new and simplified property set and a formal adversarial model for analyzing the security of this type of schemes. We believe that the property set and the adversarial model themselves are of independent interest.

We then propose a new scheme and a generic construction framework. In particular, we show that a secure password based key exchange protocol can be transformed efficiently to a smartcard and password based two-factor authentication scheme provided that there exist pseudorandom functions and collision-resistant hash functions.

1 Introduction

Password authentication with smart card is one of the most convenient and effective *two-factor authentication* mechanisms. This technology has been widely deployed for various kinds of authentication applications which include remote host login, online banking, access control of restricted vaults, activation of security devices, and many more. Although some smart-card-based password authentication systems have already been in use, many of them are having issues on both security and performance aspects.

A smart-card-based password authentication scheme involves a server S and a client A with identity ID_A. At the very beginning, S issues a smart card to

---

* The author was supported by a grant from CityU (Project No. 7001959).

P. Ning, S. Qing, and N. Li (Eds.): ICICS 2006, LNCS 4307, pp. 82–91, 2006.

A with the smart card being personalized with respect to ID_A and some initial password. This phase is called the *registration phase* and is carried out only once for each client in some secure way. After obtaining the smart card, A can access S in the *login-and-authentication phase*. This phase can be carried out as many times as needed. However, in this phase, there could have various kinds of passive and active adversaries in the communication channel between A and S. They can eavesdrop messages and even modify, remove or insert messages into the channel. The security goal of the scheme in this phase is to ensure mutual authentication between A and S in the presence of these adversaries. In particular, it is required to both *have* A's smart card and *know* A's password in order to carry out the smart-card-based password authentication scheme successfully with server S, that is, maintaining *two-factor security* that the scheme should provide. There are also some other desirable properties people would like the scheme to possess. We will discuss these properties shortly.

Besides registration phase and login-and-authentication phase, A may want to *change password* from time to time. Conventionally, this activity usually has S involved and requires S to maintain a database for storing the passwords or some derived values of the passwords of its clients. In this paper, we promote the idea of letting A change the password at will without interacting with or notifying S (while ensuring two-factor security), and also eliminating any password database at the server side.

Current systems also suffer from other potential security vulnerabilities. One prominent issue is security against *offline guessing attack* (also known as offline dictionary attack). The purpose of offline guessing attack is to compromise a client's password through exhaustive search of all possible password values. In the context of a password-based cryptosystem, we consider that passwords are short in the sense that they are human memorizable. In other words, we assume that the password space is so small that an adversary is able to enumerate all possible values in the space within some reasonable amount of time.

A stronger notion of security against offline guessing attack is to require that compromising a client's smart card does not help the adversary launch offline guessing attack against the client's password. In practice, the adversary may steal the smart card and extract all the information stored in it through reverse engineering. This notion is reminiscent of password-based key exchange protocols [6]. The difference is that for password-based key exchange protocols, the focus is on preventing adversaries from getting any useful information about the password mainly from the transcripts of protocol runs, while for smart-card-based password authentication schemes, in addition to thwarting related attacks against password-based key exchange protocols, we also need to protect the password from being known even after the client's smart card is compromised.

Since Lamport [9] introduced a remote user authentication scheme in 1981, there have been many smart-card-based password authentication schemes proposed (some recent ones are [2,14,15,10]). These schemes are aimed for different security goals and properties, and noticeably, there is no common set of desirable security properties that has been widely adopted for the construction of this type of schemes. Although the construction and security analysis of this type of schemes have a long history, recently proposed schemes are still having various security weaknesses being overlooked, and we can find many of these schemes broken shortly after they were first proposed [4,5,12,11,15].

1.1   Our Results

In this paper, we contribute on three areas:

1. We propose a new and simplified set of desirable security properties for a smart-card-based password authentication scheme. We also propose an adversarial model for formal analysis of the security of this type of schemes.
2. We show that two recently proposed schemes are insecure with respect to their claimed security properties which have also been captured in our desirable property set.
3. We propose a generic construction framework and show that a secure smart-card-based password authentication scheme can be constructed by *transforming* a proven secure password based key exchange protocol (under some appropriate security model which will be specified) provided that there exist pseudorandom unctions and collision-resistant hash functions. The transformation is very efficient. It essentially adds in only two additional hash evaluations and one pseudorandom function evaluation.

Paper Organization: In Sec. 2, we propose a set of desirable properties and an adversarial model for smart-card-based password authentication schemes. In Sec. 3, we review a scheme proposed by Liao et al. in [10] and show that the scheme is insecure. In Sec. 4, we propose a new scheme and show its security. In Sec. 5, we propose a generic construction framework that can be used to convert a proven secure password-based mutual authentication protocol to a smart-card-based password authentication scheme.

2   Security Properties

As introduced in Sec. 1, there are two phases and one activity in a smart-card-based password authentication system. The two phases are *registration phase* and *login-and-authentication phase*, and the activity is called *password-changing activity*.

In the registration phase, an authenticated and secure environment is assumed to present, and all parties are assumed to be honest and perform exactly according to the scheme specification. In the real world, this stage may require the client who is requesting for registration to show up in person at the server's office and then have a smart card initialized and personalized using a secure and isolated machine. The smart card is finally issued to the client at the end of the stage. After this phase is completed, the client is said to be *registered*. In the login-and-authentication phase, the communication channel between server

S and a registered client A is no longer considered to be secure. Both passive and active adversaries are present and their objective is to compromise the scheme's primary security goal, that is, mutual authentication between S and A. During the password-changing activity, a registered client A change the password and updates the smart card accordingly. A may need to interact with S for changing the password. However, this is undesirable due to the scalability issue and the concern of user friendliness. It will be better if A can change the password freely without the help or notification of S. In the following, we describe what we want a secure smart-card-based password authentication system to achieve (i.e. security goals / desirable properties) and what the capabilities of the adversary are (adversarial model).

2.1   Desirable Properties and Adversarial Model

Below are the five desirable properties that a smart-card-based password authentication system should achieve.

1. (*Client Authentication*) The server is sure that the communicating party is indeed the registered client that claims to be at the end of the protocol.
2. (*Server Authentication*) The client is sure that the communicating party is indeed the server S at the end of the protocol.
3. (*Server Knows No Password*) S should not get any information of the password of a registered client or anything derived from the password.
4. (*Freedom of Password Change*) A client's password can freely be changed by the client without any interaction with server S. S can be totally unaware of the change of the client's password.
5. (*Short Password*) The password space is small enough so that the underlying adversary can enumerate all the possible values of the space in a reasonable amount of time. We consider a human-memorizable password to be a value in this password space.

Adversarial Model. Consider an adversary $\mathcal{A}$ who has the full control of the communication channel between the server S and any of the *registered* clients. $\mathcal{A}$ can obtain all the messages transmitted between the server S and a registered client; $\mathcal{A}$ can also modify or block those transmitted messages; and $\mathcal{A}$ can even make up fake messages and send to any entity in the system while claiming that the messages are from another entity in the system (i.e. impersonation). To simulate insider attack [1], we also allow $\mathcal{A}$ to know the passwords and all information stored in the smart cards of all the clients except those of a client who is under attack from $\mathcal{A}$. In addition, we also allow $\mathcal{A}$ to *either* compromise the password *or* the smart card of the client under attack, but not both. However, $\mathcal{A}$ is not allowed to compromise S.

Discussions.   In the list of desirable properties above, the first two constitute the primary security requirement of a secure smart-card-based password authentication scheme, that is, mutual authentication between the server S and a registered client A. The third property helps solve the scalability problem at the server side. In addition, since there is no information about clients' passwords stored at the server side, the property also alleviate damage entailed to the clients if the server is compromised. The fourth property will help improve the user friendliness of the system as there is no additional communication overhead when a client changes her password. One should note that property 3 does not imply property 4. It is always possible to construct a scheme such that the server does not have any information of a client's password while the client cannot change the password either once after registration. The fifth property means that we always consider that if an adversary launches an attack which needs to search through the password space (for example, an offline guessing attack), the adversary can always evaluate all the possible values in the space within the running time of the adversary. To prevent an adversary from launching offline guessing attack, we therefore need to make sure that the scheme is not going to leak any information useful about the client's password to the adversary, even though the password is considered to be weak and low-entropy.

Note that the adversary can always launch the *online* guessing attack. In this attack, the adversary impersonates one of the communicating parties and sends messages based on a trial password chosen by the adversary. If the trial password is guessed incorrectly, the other party will reject the connection. If so, the adversary will try another password and repeat the steps until a trial password leads to an acceptance of connection. Online guessing attack is easy to defend against in practice. Conventionally, a system can set up a policy mandating that if the password of a client is entered incorrectly for three times in a row, then the client will be blocked and refused to connect any further. This policy works well in practice and can effectively defend against online guessing attack if the attack only allows the adversary to try one password in each impersonation attack. However, we should also note that a secure scheme should not allow the adversary to test two passwords or more in each of this impersonation attack.

In our full paper [13], we also present a comparison between our model and a set of requirements for smart-card-based password authentication schemes recently proposed by Liao et al. [10].

3   Offline Guessing Attack Against a Smart-Card-Based Password Authentication Scheme

In this section, we show that the scheme proposed by Liao et al. [10] is insecure against offline guessing attack. In our full paper [13], we show that another scheme recently proposed by Yoon and Yoo [15] is insecure either.

Here are the notations that we will use for describing Liao et al.'s scheme. Let p be a 1024-bit prime. Let g be a generator of $\mathbb{Z}_p^*$. The server S chooses a secret key x. In [10], the authors did not specify the length of x, however, in order to prevent brute-force search, we assume x to be a random string of at least 160 bits long. Let h be a hash function (e.g. SHA-256) and $a\|b$ denote the concatenation of a and b.

Registration phase: Server S issues a smart card to a client A as follows.

1. A arbitrarily chooses a *unique* identity ID_A and password PW_A. PW_A is a short password that is appropriate for memorization. A then calculates $h(PW_A)$ and sends $(ID_A, h(PW_A))$ to S.
2. S calculates $B = g^{h(x\|ID_A)+h(PW_A)} \bmod p$ and issues A a smart card which has (ID_A, B, p, g) in it.

Login-and-authentication phase: A attaches the smart card to an input device and keys in ID_A and PW_A. Afterwards, S and A (the smart card) carry out the following steps.

1. A sends a login request to S.
2. On receiving the login request, S calculates $B'' = g^{h(x\|ID_A)R} \bmod p$ where $R \in \mathbb{Z}_p^*$ is a random number, and sends $h(B'')$ and R to A.
3. Upon receiving the message from S, A calculates $B' = (Bg^{-h(PW_A)})^R \bmod p$ and checks if $h(B'') = h(B')$. If they are not equal, S is rejected. Otherwise, A calculates $C = h(T\|B')$ where T is a timestamp, and sends (ID_A, C, T) to S.
4. Let T' be the time when S receives (ID_A, C, T). S validates A using the following steps.
   (a) S checks if ID_A is in the correct format[1]. If it is incorrect, S rejects.
   (b) Otherwise, S compares T with T'. If $T' - T \geq \Delta T$, S rejects, where ΔT is the legal time interval for transmission delay.
   (c) S then computes $C' = h(T\|B'')$ and checks if $C = C'$. If they are not equal, S rejects. Otherwise, S accepts.

3.1   Offline Guessing Attack

Malicious user offline guessing attack. In [10], the scheme above is claimed to be secure against offline guessing attack even if the client's smart card is compromised. In the following, we show that this is not true. Suppose client A's smart card is compromised by an adversary $\mathcal{A}$. $\mathcal{A}$ can carry out the offline guessing attack as follows.

1. $\mathcal{A}$ impersonates A and sends a login request to S.
2. S calculates $B'' = g^{h(x\|ID_A)R} \bmod p$ and sends back $(h(B''), R)$.
3. $\mathcal{A}$ then carries out offline guessing attack by checking if

$$h(B'') = h((Bg^{-h(PW_A^*)})^R \bmod p)$$

for each trial password PW_A^* (i.e. $\mathcal{A}$'s guess of PW_A).

---

[1] In [10], the format of identity ID_A was not given. We hereby assume that there is some pre-defined format for all the identities used in their system.

Note that after $\mathcal{A}$ receives the message from S in step (2), $\mathcal{A}$ does not need to provide any response to S and therefore S does not know whether the communicating party is launching an attack or simply the message sent by S is lost during transmission. This makes the guessing attack described above difficult to detect. Also notice that if $\mathcal{A}$ possesses a past communication transcript Trans between A and S, $\mathcal{A}$ can perform the offline guessing attack directly without interacting with S.

4   A New Scheme

In this section, we propose a new smart-card-based password authentication scheme which is proven secure and also satisfies all the properties we described in Sec. 2. This new scheme can also be extended to a generic construction framework which allows us to convert most of the proven secure password-based key exchange protocols [6] to smart-card-based versions. The significance of this framework is that we can now design provably secure smart-card-based password authentication scheme in a systematic way and make use of those proven secure password-based key exchange protocols as the main building blocks. The schemes constructed in this framework will also have session keys established that are generally useful for target applications. More details of the generic construction framework will be given in Sec. 5. In this section, we focus on describing how the new scheme is constructed.

In [3], Halevi and Krawczyk defined a security model for password-based authentication and also proposed a protocol of this type. The definition of security in this model essentially says that the "best" possible strategy for the adversary to compromise user authentication is online guessing attack, which can be thwarted in practice by limiting the number of consecutive authentication failures that each user is allowed. Based on the Halevi-Krawczyk one-way password-based authentication protocol, we build a proven secure password-based authenticated key exchange (PWAKE) protocol, and then "upgrade" the PWAKE protocol to our final smart-card-based password authentication scheme. Here we merely present the PWAKE protocol and the final smart-card-based password authentication scheme, for all the details, readers can refer to our full paper [13].

A PWAKE Protocol. Let G be a subgroup of prime order q of a multiplicative group $\mathbb{Z}_p^*$. Let g be a generator of G. Let $(\mathrm{PK}_S, \mathrm{SK}_S)$ denote a public/private key pair of the server S. User A has a password PW_A which is shared with S.

$$A \rightarrow S : A, sid, g^{\hat{x}}$$
$$A \leftarrow S : S, sid, g^{\hat{y}}, \mathrm{SIG}_{\mathrm{SK}_S}(S, A, sid, g^{\hat{x}}, g^{\hat{y}})$$
$$A \rightarrow S : A, sid, c = \mathrm{ENC}_{\mathrm{PK}_S}(PW_A, A, S, sid, g^{\hat{x}}, g^{\hat{y}})$$

The session key is calculated as $\sigma = g^{xy}$.

4.1   A Smart-Card-Based Password Authentication Scheme

Notations: let p, G, g, q be the group parameters defined as above. Besides a public/private key pair (PK_S, SK_S), the server S also maintains a long-term secret x which is a random string of length k. Let $H : \{0,1\}^* \rightarrow \{0,1\}^k$ denote a collision resistant hash function and $PRF_K : \{0,1\}^k \rightarrow \{0,1\}^k$ a pseudorandom function keyed by K.

Registration phase: Server S issues a client A as follows.

1. A arbitrarily chooses a unique identity ID_A and sends it to S.
2. S calculates $B = PRF_x(H(ID_A)) \oplus H(PW_0)$ where PW_0 is the initial password (e.g. a default such as a string of all '0').
3. S issues A a smart card which contains PK_S, ID_A, B, p, g, q. In practice, we can have all these parameters except B be "burned" in the read-only memory of the smart card when the smart card is manufactured.
4. On receiving the smart card, A changes the password immediately by performing the password-changing activity (described below).

Login-and-authentication phase: A attaches the smart card to an input device, and then keys in ID_A and PW_A. The smart card checks if the identity is equal to the value stored in it. If not, the smart card will refuse carrying out any further operation. Otherwise, the smart card retrieves the value $LPW = B \oplus H(PW_A)$. A (actually performed by the client's smart card) and S then use LPW as the password to perform the PWAKE protocol.

Password-changing activity: If A wants to change the password, A carries out the following steps.

1. Select a new password PW'_A.
2. Compute $Z = B \oplus H(PW_A) \oplus H(PW'_A)$, where PW_A is the old password.
3. Replace B with Z in the smart card.

Remarks: The "password" used in the login-and-authentication phase is LPW, instead of the real password PW_A. Note that S can compute the value of LPW once after receiving ID_A. Hence it does not violate property 3 (Server Knows No Password) in Sec. 2. From the password-changing activity above, it is obvious that the scheme also satisfies property 4 (Freedom of Password Change).

In the two-factor security, we do not consider the case that both the password and the smart card are compromised, but we need to consider the other three cases: (1) neither the password nor the smart card is compromised; (2) the password is leaked while the smart card remains secure; (3) the smart card is compromised but the password remains secure. It is obvious that security under case (1) can be ensured if security under either case (2) or case (3) is guaranteed. And our goal is to achieve security under both case (2) and case (3). In other words, compromising one factor should not affect the other.

Case (2) Security. If the smart card is not compromised (even when the password is leaked), our proposed scheme deduces the success probability of the adversary to a negligible level by assuming that pseudo-random functions exist.

Theorem 1. *If the smart card is not compromised, and $PRF_K(\cdot)$ is a pseudorandom function, then the adversary has only a negligible success probability in the Halevi-Krawczyk model.*

The proof is given in our full paper [13].

Case (3) Security. If the smart card is compromised while the password remains secure, there is no security "upgrade" when compared with a password-based protocol. It is easy to see that if $PRF_K(\cdot)$ is replaced by a random function, then the protocol provides the same security as the password protocol. And by using the same approach as in the proof of Theorem. 1, we can show that our scheme provides almost the same security level (with at most a negligible gap) when compared with the password-based protocol.

5   A Generic Construction Framework

Up to this point, readers may have already realized that a smart-card-based password authentication scheme can readily be built from a proven secure password-based mutual authentication protocol by applying the *upgrading technique* of Sec. 4.1. The resulting scheme will then be secure under a model similar to the security model for the original password-based protocol, but extended according to the discussions in Sec. 4.1.

For example, we may choose an efficient password-based mutual authentication (and key exchange) protocol, such as [8,7], then we "upgrade" it to an efficient smart-card-based password authentication scheme using the technique described in Sec. 4.1. Interestingly, both of the protocols in [8,7] are proven secure without random oracle. Our upgrading technique does not rely on random oracle either. The "upgraded" smart-card-based scheme will then be secure with security statements similar to that of Theorem 1 (but now in the corresponding model of the original password-based authentication protocol) and also with respect to Case (2) as well as Case (3) Security. We refer readers to [6] for other examples of password-based mutual authentication (and key exchange) protocols.

Efficiency. The "upgrading" technique proposed in Sec. 4.1 is very efficient. During the login-and-authentication phase, the smart card only needs to carry out one pseudorandom function evaluation and two hashes in addition to the operations incurred by the underlying password-based protocol. The generic construction framework allows us to choose a password-based protocol which is efficient enough when implemented on smart cards.

A Practical Issue. In the description above, we consider the server S to maintain one single long-term secret x for communication with all the clients. As a result, the secrecy of x is utmost important because the security of the entire system essentially relies on the security of x. In practice, we can alleviate the damage caused to a system by using multiple values of x to partition the system, and in each partition, a randomly generated x is used by a disjoint set of clients. Each partition is to be handled by a distinct and independent server. Compromising one server will therefore only affect the security of the corresponding partition of clients rather than the entire system. Note that this partitioning method does not affect the fulfillment of any of the desirable properties for a secure smart-card based password authentication scheme proposed in Sec. 2. Another mechanism which can be used in conjunction with the mechanism above is to set each long-term secret x with a validity period. Usually, smart cards are used such that they are valid only for a period of time. Hence for a different period of time, a fresh long-term secret x can be used.

References

1. C. Boyd and A. Mathuria. *Protocols for Authentication and Key Establishment.* Springer-Verlag, 2003.
2. H. Y. Chien, J. K. Jan, and Y. M. Tseng. An efficient and practical solution to remote authentication: Smart card. *Computers and Security,* 21(4):372–375, 2002.
3. S. Halevi and H. Krawczyk. Public-key cryptography and password protocols. *ACM Trans. Inf. Syst. Secur.,* 2(3):230–268, 1999.
4. M.-S. Hwang. Cryptanalysis of remote login authentication scheme. *Computer Communications,* 22(8):742–744, 1999.
5. M.-S. Hwang, C.-C. Lee, and Y.-L. Tang. An improvement of SPLICE/AS in WIDE against guessing attack. *Internat. J. Inform.,* 12(2):297–302, 2001.
6. IEEE. *P1363.2 / D23: Standard Specifications for Password-based Public Key Cryptographic Techniques,* March 2006. Available at http://grouper.ieee.org/groups/1363/passwdPK/draft.html.
7. S. Jiang and G. Gong. Password based key exchange with mutual authentication. In *11th International Workshop on Selected Areas in Cryptography (SAC 2004),* pages 267–279. Springer-Verlag, 2005. LNCS 3357.
8. J. Katz, R. Ostrovsky, and M. Yung. Efficient and secure authenticated key exchange using weak passwords. *Journal of the ACM, to appear,* 2006.
9. L. Lamport. Password authentication with insecure communication. *Communications of the ACM,* 24(11):770–771, November 1981.
10. I-En Liao, Cheng-Chi Lee, and Min-Shiang Hwang. A password authentication scheme over insecure networks. *J. Comput. Syst. Sci.,* 72(4):727–740, 2006.
11. M. Scott. Cryptanalysis of an id-based password authentication scheme using smart cards and fingerprints. *SIGOPS Oper. Syst. Rev.,* 38(2):73–75, 2004.
12. B. Wang, J. H. Li, and Z. P. Tong. Cryptanalysis of an enhanced timestamp-based password authentication scheme. *Comput. Secur.,* 22(7):643–645, 2003.
13. G. Yang, D. S. Wong, H. Wang, and X. Deng. Formal analysis and systematic construction of two-factor authentication scheme. Cryptology ePrint Archive, Report 2006/270, 2006.
14. E. J. Yoon, E. K. Ryu, and K. Y. Yoo. Efficient remote user authentication scheme based on generalized elgamal signature scheme. *IEEE Transactions on Consumer Electronics,* 50(2):568–570, May 2004.
15. E.-J. Yoon and K.-Y. Yoo. New authentication scheme based on a one-way hash function and Diffie-Hellman key exchange. In *4th International Conference of Cryptology and Network Security (CANS 2005),* pages 147–160. Springer-Verlag, 2005. LNCS 3810.

Hierarchical Key Assignment for Black-Box Tracing with Efficient Ciphertext Size

Tatsuyuki Matsushita[1] and Hideki Imai[2,3]

[1] Corporate Research & Development Center, Toshiba Corporation
1, Komukai Toshiba-cho, Saiwai-ku, Kawasaki 212-8582, Japan
tatsuyuki.matsushita@toshiba.co.jp
[2] Faculty of Science and Engineering, Chuo University
1-13-27 Kasuga, Bunkyo-ku, Tokyo 112-8551, Japan
h-imai@elect.chuo-u.ac.jp
[3] Research Center for Information Security, National Institute of Advanced
Industrial Science and Technology
1-18-13 Sotokanda, Chiyoda-ku, Tokyo 101-0021, Japan

Abstract. We propose a hierarchical key-assignment method to reduce the ciphertext size in a black-box tracing scheme presented at ASIA-CRYPT 2004. Applying the proposed method to this scheme, the ciphertext size is reduced from $O(\sqrt{n})$ to $O(k+\log(n/k))$ without a substantial increase in the decryption-key size, where k, n denote the maximum number of colluders in a coalition and the total number of receivers respectively. The resulting scheme also supports black-box tracing and enjoys the following properties: Even if a pirate decoder does not respond any further queries when it detects itself being examined, the pirate decoder can be traced back to a person who participated in its construction. A tracer's key, which is necessary for black-box tracing, is public.

Keywords: Hierarchical key assignment, black-box tracing, reduced ciphertext size.

1 Introduction

The piracy becomes a serious threat in an increasing number of applications where a sender broadcasts data to many receivers and the data should be available only to authorized receivers. As an example of the applications, consider a content-distribution system illustrated in Fig. 1. A broadcaster encrypts (i) a digital content with a session key and (ii) the session key itself with a broadcaster's key. We call the ciphertext as a header. The broadcaster broadcasts the encrypted content and the header to authorized receivers (users). The users decrypt the header (and consequently the encrypted content) by using their decryption boxes (decoders) which contain their decryption keys (personal keys). In this system, malicious users (traitors) may build a pirate decoder by illegally using their personal keys and sell it at the black market. The redistribution of the personal key is serious since this piracy enables the non-users who possess the pirate decoder to have illegal access to the content.

P. Ning, S. Qing, and N. Li (Eds.): ICICS 2006, LNCS 4307, pp. 92–111, 2006.

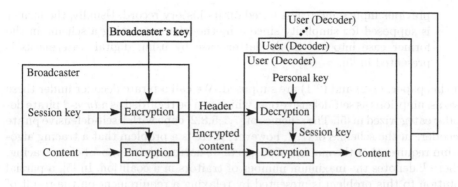

Fig. 1. Content-distribution system

To combat against this piracy, traitor tracing [4] has been studied extensively. Its goal is to develop a scheme in which, from the confiscated pirate decoder, a tracer can identify at least one of its producers by executing a tracing algorithm with a tracer's key. (We give a formal definition in 2.2.) The efficiency is evaluated on the following criteria: the header size, the personal-key size, the broadcaster's-key size, the computational cost for decryption, etc. One of the most important criteria is the header size. To construct a traitor-tracing scheme with $O(n)$ header size is straightforward, where n denotes the total number of users. Such a scheme is inefficient since the transmission overhead becomes linearly larger as the number of users increases. Therefore, to achieve the sublinear header size is a minimum requirement. If the bandwidth of a broadcast channel is limited, the header size must not greatly be affected by n. This is required in the case of satellite broadcasting and other wireless transmissions. In this paper, we seek a scheme with more efficient header size than $O(\sqrt{n})$.

We mention related work from the viewpoints of assumptions on a pirate decoder and the public availability of a broadcaster's key and a tracer's key. It is desirable that a traitor-tracing scheme support black-box tracing, in which the tracer can identify the traitor(s) without breaking open the pirate decoder and thus it is assured that the traitor(s) is traced no matter how the pirate decoder is implemented. There are two kinds of assumptions on a pirate decoder in black-box tracing.

(1-1) The pirate decoder always output a plaintext or (1-2) if it detects itself being examined, it may give the tracer intentionally incorrect outputs or no output for further inputs by activating a self-defensive mechanism[1].

(2-1) A test during black-box tracing is done independently of the other tests by resetting the pirate decoder or (2-2) the pirate decoder memorizes the

---

[1] Note that (i) for simplicity we assume that the reaction is triggered deterministically, i.e., it is activated once the pirate decoder detects tracing and (ii) a tracing algorithm in the deterministic case can be extended to the general probabilistic case under an assumption that plural pirate decoders constructed by the same traitors are available in tracing.

previous inputs and reacts based on its history record. Usually, the former is supposed for simplicity since a method for converting a scheme in the former case into one in the latter case by using digital watermarks is presented in [5].

In this paper, (1-2) and (2-1) are supposed. We call a pirate decoder under these two assumptions as self-defensive one, which can be regarded as a *type-2* pirate decoder categorized in [5]. The schemes of [7,1,5,8,2] cope with a self-defensive pirate decoder. In the schemes of [7,1], however, there is a problem that a tracing algorithm requires that the number of suspects be narrowed down to k before tracing, where k denotes the maximum number of traitors in a coalition. In [5], a partial solution to this problem is presented by relaxing a requirement on the result of tracing, i.e., the tracing algorithm outputs a list of suspects and it is assured that at least one of the traitors is included in the list. This scheme achieves the $O(\sqrt{n})$ header size. Unfortunately, this relaxation causes another problem that there exists a trade-off between the header size and the suspect-list size, i.e., the detection probability. The schemes of [8,2] solve both of the above problems and generates a header of size $O(\sqrt{n})$. (We mention the difference between the two schemes in 1.1.) Our interest is in reducing the header size in this kind of scheme.

The public availability of a broadcaster's key and a tracer's key enhances the scalability of a system. It is desirable that the broadcaster's key be public since plural broadcasters can use the same system without sharing any secret information. For example, in the schemes of [7,1] the broadcaster's key is public. Note that even in a scheme (e.g., [4]) where the broadcaster's key is designed to be secret, it can be publicized by replacing a symmetric-key cryptosystem used to build a header with a public-key cryptosystem. Among the schemes in which the broadcaster's key is public, the schemes of [6,2] require that the tracer's key be secret, while it is also public in other schemes (e.g., [8,3])[2]. It is desirable that the tracer's key be public since plural entities can be delegated to do tracing without sharing any secret information and the existence of a larger number of tracers is a stronger deterrent to the piracy. In this paper, we consider a scheme in which both of them are public.

1.1 Our Contributions

The construction of the scheme of [8] is algebraic, while that of [2] is not. Since the algebraic construction is suited to reduce the header size, we extend the scheme of [8] to the one which generates a header of size less than $O(\sqrt{n})$. In order to achieve this, we propose a hierarchical key-assignment method which can be applied to the scheme of [8]. The header size cannot be reduced by straightforwardly extending the scheme of [8]. We explain this in Sect. 3.

The resulting scheme achieves that the header size is reduced from $O(\sqrt{n})$ to $O(k + \log(n/k))$ while allowing the personal-key size to increase from $O(1)$ to $O(\log(n/k))$. Since the resulting scheme is based on the scheme of [8], it also has

---

[2] In the multi-user case in the scheme of [3], a private procedure by a trusted party is required in order to decide a traitor, as pointed out in [3].

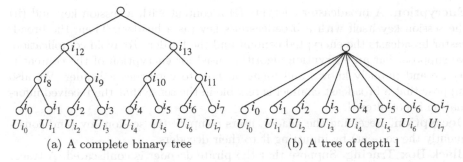

(a) A complete binary tree   (b) A tree of depth 1

Fig. 2. Structure of T ($L = 8$)

the following inherent properties: (i) The scheme supports black-box tracing even
if the pirate decoder is self-defensive, (ii) in contrast to the scheme of [2], both the
broadcaster's key and the tracer's key are public, (iii) the maximum coalition size
is limited to k, while that of [2] is fully collusion resistant, and (iv) the computational cost for decryption is linear in k, while it is constant in that of [2].

The rest of the paper is organized as follows. In Sect. 2, definitions are given.
We clarify what to be resolved in Sect. 3. The proposed key-assignment method
and the resulting scheme are shown in Sect. 4. The resulting scheme is analyzed
in terms of security and efficiency in Sect. 5 and Sect. 6 respectively. In Sect. 7,
conclusions are presented.

2 Definitions

2.1 Tree Structure

We define notations on a tree structure used in this paper.

Definition 1 (Notations on a Tree Structure). *We define* $T, \mathcal{N}_T$ *as a tree
with L leaves and a set of all of the nodes including the leaves but not the root
in T respectively. We simply suppose that* $\mathcal{N}_T = \{0, \ldots, |\mathcal{N}_T| - 1\}$. *For a node,
v ($v \in \mathcal{N}_T$), $\mathcal{U}_v$ is defined as a set of the users who correspond to the leaves of the
subtree rooted at v. For a given T, we define a collection, Y_T, of subsets of users as
$Y_T = \{\mathcal{U}_0, \ldots, \mathcal{U}_{|\mathcal{N}_T|-1}\}$. We define $\mathcal{U}$ as a set of all of the users. The depth of a
node means the number of branches on the path from the root to the node.*

Figure 2 illustrates a structure of T in the case where $L = 8$. For example, in
Fig. 2(a), $\mathcal{N}_T = \{0, \ldots, 2L - 3 \,(= 13)\}$, $\mathcal{U}_{i_0}$ is a set of the users who correspond
to the leftmost leaf, and $\mathcal{U}_{i_8} = \mathcal{U}_{i_0} \cup \mathcal{U}_{i_1}$. In Fig. 2(b), $\mathcal{N}_T = \{0, \ldots, L - 1 \,(= 7)\}$.

2.2 Black-Box Tracing

Black-box tracing consists of four processes.

Key Generation. A trusted party generates and secretly gives every user a
personal key. The personal key is stored in the decoder.

Encryption. A broadcaster encrypts (i) a content with a session key and (ii) the session key itself with a broadcaster's key (as a header). Then, the broadcaster broadcasts the encrypted content and the header. To avoid complication, we suppose that an encryption algorithm used for encryption of the content is secure and publicly known and focus on how to construct a header. We also suppose that a broadcast channel is reliable in the sense that the received information is not altered.

Decryption. Receiving the header, users compute the session key (and consequently the content) by inputting it to their decoders.

Black-Box Tracing. Suppose that the pirate decoder is confiscated. A tracer builds a header for tracing with a tracer's key, gives the header to the pirate decoder, and observe whether it decrypts correctly or not. The tracer decides a traitor based on its outputs.

This model is described formally as follows.

Definition 2 (BBTS). *A black-box tracing scheme (BBTS) is a 4-tuple of polynomial-time algorithms, $(\mathsf{Gen}, \mathsf{Enc}, \mathsf{Dec}, \mathsf{BBT})$, s.t.*

Gen, *the key-generation algorithm, is a probabilistic algorithm which takes as input a security parameter, ℓ, the total number of users, n, and the maximum number of colluders in a coalition, k. It returns a broadcaster's key, BK, n personal (secret) keys, $d_{u_1}, \ldots, d_{u_n}$, a tracer's key, TK, and a collection, Y, of subsets of users.*

Enc, *the encryption algorithm, is a probabilistic algorithm which takes as input BK, Y, and a session key (a message), s. It returns a header (a ciphertext), H.*

Dec, *the decryption algorithm, is a deterministic algorithm which takes as input d_{u_i} and H. It returns s or an incorrect one, We require that $\mathsf{Dec}(d_{u_i}, \mathsf{Enc}(BK, Y, s)) = s$ for all of the session keys (unless the user, u_i, is revoked).*

BBT, *the black-box tracing algorithm, is a probabilistic algorithm which takes as input TK, Y, and a pirate decoder, PD, as a black box. It returns one of the traitors' IDs, u_j.*

In this paper, we consider a BBTS in which (i) Y is represented by a tree structure and (ii) both BK and TK are public.

2.3   Security

We describe security definitions of a BBTS. A BBTS is said to be secure if it satisfies indistinguishability and black-box traceability defined as follows.

Definition 3 (Indistinguishability). *Let $\Pi = (\mathsf{Gen}, \mathsf{Enc}, \mathsf{Dec}, \mathsf{BBT})$ be a BBTS. Given a header, Π is said to be indistinguishable if no non-users (eavesdroppers) can distinguish a session key corresponding to the header from a random session key with non-negligible advantage.*

Definition 4 (Black-Box Traceability). *Let $\Pi = (\mathsf{Gen}, \mathsf{Enc}, \mathsf{Dec}, \mathsf{BBT})$ be a BBTS and PD be a pirate decoder. When PD is constructed by a coalition of at most k traitors, Π is said to be black-box traceable if at least one of them is identified, only by observing inputs and outputs of PD, with probability $1 - \varepsilon$ where ε is negligible.*

3 Basic Scheme

First, we review the scheme of [8]. Secondly, we explain why its simple extension is not a satisfactory solution and clarify what to be resolved.

3.1 The Scheme of [8]

$\mathsf{Gen}(1^\ell, n, k)$: Generate two primes, p, q, s.t. $|q| = \ell$, $q|p - 1$, and $q \geq n + 2k - 1$. Let G_q be a subgroup of $\mathbb{Z}_p^*$ of order q. Generate a generator, g, of G_q. In the paper, $\in_R$ denotes a random selection of an element of the set on its right side, and the calculations are done over $\mathbb{Z}_p^*$ unless otherwise specified.

Let $\mathcal{U}$ be a set of all of the users. Split $\mathcal{U}$ into L disjoint subgroups each of which has at most $2k$ elements, define an L-ary tree, T, of depth 1 and generate a collection, Y_T, of subsets of users. T is depiced in Fig. 2(b), and each split subgroup corresponds to a different leaf.

Choose $a_0, \ldots, a_{2k-1}, b_0, \ldots, b_{L-1} \in_R \mathbb{Z}_q$ and compute a public key, e (= $BK = TK$), as follows.

$$e = (p, q, g, \{y_{0,i} = g^{a_i}\}_{i=0,\ldots,2k-1}, \{y_{1,i} = g^{b_i}\}_{i=0,\ldots,L-1}).$$

Suppose that $u \in \mathcal{U}_v$. The subscriber u's personal key is $(u, v, f_v(u))$ where

$$f_v(x) = \sum_{i=0}^{2k-1} a_{v,i} x^i \bmod q, \tag{1}$$

$$a_{v,i} = \begin{cases} a_i & (i \neq v \bmod 2k), \\ b_v & (i = v \bmod 2k). \end{cases}$$

$\mathsf{Enc}(e, Y_T, s)$: Suppose that $s \in_R G_q$. Select $R_0, R_1 \in_R \mathbb{Z}_q$. For each leaf, v_j ($1 \leq j \leq L$), in T, set bit_{v_j} to 0 or 1 at random. Then, calculate H_{v_j} as follows.

$$H_{v_j} = (\bar{h}_{v_j}(= g^{r_{v_j}}), h_{v_j,0}, \ldots, h_{v_j,2k-1}),$$

$$h_{v_j,i} = \begin{cases} y_{0,i}^{r_{v_j}} & (i \neq v_j \bmod 2k), \\ s y_{1,v_j}^{r_{v_j}} & (i - v_j \bmod 2k), \end{cases}$$

$$r_{v_j} = \begin{cases} R_0 & (bit_{v_j} = 0), \\ R_1 & (bit_{v_j} = 1). \end{cases}$$

A header, H, is a collection of H_{v_j}'s computed in the above procedure.

$\mathsf{Dec}(d_u, H)$: Suppose that $u \in \mathcal{U}_{v_j}$. The user, u, correctly computes the session key, s, by using $(u, v_j, f_{v_j}(u)) \in d_u$ and $H_{v_j} \in H$ as follows.

$$\left(\frac{\prod_{i=0}^{2k-1} h_{v_j,i}^{u^i}}{\bar{h}_{v_j}^{f_{v_j}(u)}} \right)^{1/u^{v_j} \bmod 2k} = s \left(\frac{g^{r_{v_j} \sum_{i=0}^{2k-1} a_{v_j,i} u^i}}{g^{r_{v_j} f_{v_j}(u)}} \right)^{1/u^{v_j} \bmod 2k}$$

$$= s.$$

BBT(e, Y_T, PD): First, we give an outline of the algorithm and secondly a concrete description. The tracer examines whether a user is a traitor one by one. In the jth test, where $1 \le j \le n$, the tracer chooses a user, u_j, and builds the header in which all of the users in $\mathcal{X} = \{u_1, \ldots, u_j\}$ are revoked and the others are not, where $u_1, \ldots, u_{j-1}$ has been selected in the $(j-1)$th test. Throughout this paper, $\mathcal{X}$ means a set of revoked users in a header for tracing. The tracer inputs this header to the pirate decoder and observes whether it decrypts correctly or not. If its output is (i) correct for the input where $\mathcal{X} = \{u_1, \ldots, u_{j-1}\}$ and (ii) incorrect for the input where $\mathcal{X} = \{u_1, \ldots, u_j\}$, then the tracer decides that the user, u_j, is a traitor.

The algorithm is concretely described as follows. Let i_t be the $(t+1)$th leaf from the left in T as illustrated in Fig. 2. For simplicity, we suppose that $|\mathcal{U}_{i_t}| = 2k$ for all t's ($0 \le t \le L-1$) and $n = 2kL$. Label all of the elements in $\mathcal{U}_{i_t}$'s as follows.

$$\mathcal{U}_{i_t} = \{u_{2kt+1}, \ldots, u_{2k(t+1)}\} \ (0 \le t \le L-1). \tag{2}$$

For $1 \le j \le n$, repeat the following procedure.

- Set $ctr_j = 0$ and then repeat the following test m times[3].
  1. Set $\mathcal{X} = \{u_1, \ldots, u_j\}$ and choose a session key, $s \in_R G_q$. Then build the header, H. (We omit the construction of H.)
  2. Give H to the pirate decoder and observe its output.
  3. If it decrypts correctly, then increment ctr_j by one. (If a self-defensive reaction is triggered, then decide that the user, u_j, is a traitor.)

Finally, find an integer, $j \in \{1, \ldots, n\}$, s.t. $ctr_{j-1} - ctr_j$ is the maximum and then decide that u_j is a traitor, where $ctr_0 = m$.

3.2   Simple Extension

As illustrated in Fig. 2(b), the depth of a tree in the scheme of [8] is 1. Therefore, it can be expected that the header size will be reduced by constructing a multi-level version of the scheme of [8], i.e., introducing a complete binary tree and applying the complete subtree method presented in [10] to the scheme of [8][4]. We try constructing a simple extension of the scheme of [8].

Gen'$(1^\ell, n, k)$: Define a complete binary tree, T, as illustrated in Fig. 2(a) and generate a collection, Y_T, of subsets of users. Define a key-generation polynomial, $F_v(x)$. (We discuss how to build $F_v(x)$ below.) The personal key of a user, u, is represented as $d_u = \{(u, v, F_v(u)) | v \in \mathcal{N}_T, u \in \mathcal{U}_v\}$. For example, in Fig. 2(a), if $u \in \mathcal{U}_{i_0}$, then $d_u = \{(u, i_0, F_{i_0}(u)), (u, i_8, F_{i_8}(u)), (u, i_{12}, F_{i_{12}}(u))\}$.

---

[3] It is shown in [5] that at least one traitor is identified with overwhelming probability if $m = O(n^2 \log^2 n)$.

[4] One would wonder if the subset difference method, which is the other covering method presented in [10], can be applied to the scheme of [8] with efficient personal-key size. Our current answer would be negative since it seems hard to support the personal-key derivation, by which the size of the personal key is reduced.

There are two simple methods for constructing $F_v(x)$. One is that $F_v(x)$ is generated from a single system. For instance, in Fig. 2(a), if $u \in \mathcal{U}_{i_0}$, then $d_u = \{(u, i_0, f_{i_0}(u)), (u, i_8, f_{i_8}(u)), (u, i_{12}, f_{i_{12}}(u))\}$, where $f_v(x)$ is defined in (1). Unfortunately, this is insecure against the following collusion attack: Suppose that colluders, $x_1, \ldots, x_k$, belong to the same subgroup, $\mathcal{U}_{i_0}$. They can reveal a value of each coefficient of the key-generation polynomial by solving the following system of equations.

$$\begin{cases} f_{i_j}(x_1) = \sum_{t=0}^{2k-1} a_{i_j,t} x_1^t \\ f_{i_j}(x_2) = \sum_{t=0}^{2k-1} a_{i_j,t} x_2^t \\ \quad \vdots \\ f_{i_j}(x_k) = \sum_{t=0}^{2k-1} a_{i_j,t} x_k^t \end{cases} \quad (j = 0, 8, 12). \tag{3}$$

Since the number of equations and that of variables are $3k, 2k + 3$ respectively, they can compute another user's personal key if $k \geq 3$.

The other is to use plural systems, i.e., $F_v(x)$ is generated from the δth system where v is a node at depth δ. For example, in Fig. 2(a), $d_u = \{(u, i_0, f_{i_0}^{(3)}(u)), (u, i_8, f_{i_8}^{(2)}(u)), (u, i_{12}, f_{i_{12}}^{(1)}(u))\}$, where $f_v^{(\delta)}(x)$ denotes a key-generation polynomial assigned to a node, v, at depth δ. Since the number of variables in (3) is $6k$ (with overwhelming probability), the above collusion attack is impossible. Hereafter, we consider the simple extension by using the latter key-generation method. Let $e^{(\delta)}$ be a public key which corresponds to $f_v^{(\delta)}(x)$.

$\mathsf{Enc}'((e^{(1)}, \ldots, e^{(\log_2 L)}), Y_T, s)$: Execute an algorithm, Sel, described as follows. Sel takes as input Y_T and returns ID's of $\log_2 L + 1$ nodes in T.

$\mathsf{Sel}(Y_T)$: Select $\log_2 L + 1$ nodes including one or more leaves, $v_1, \ldots, v_{\log_2 L+1}$, which satisfy the condition that $\bigcup_{i=1}^{\log_2 L+1} \mathcal{U}_{v_i} = \mathcal{U}^5$. In Fig. 2(a), 4 ($= \log_2 8 + 1$) nodes, e.g., i_0, i_1, i_9, i_{13} ($\bigcup_{j \in \{0,1,9,13\}} \mathcal{U}_{i_j} = \mathcal{U}$), are selected.

Execute Enc in 3.1 with the following two relations: (i) H_{v_j} is calculated for each selected nodes, v_j ($1 \leq j \leq \log_2 L + 1$), and (ii) $e^{(\delta)}$ is used as a public key when computing H_{v_j} where v_j is a node at depth δ.

The header size in the simple extension is $O(k \log L)$ since each H_{v_j} is calculated from a corresponding $e^{(\delta)}$. This is inefficient as shown in Fig. 3.

To summarize, (i) if the key-generation polynomial is generated from a single system, the resultant scheme is vulnerable to the collusion attack, and (ii) the collusion attack is avoided by running $\log_2 L$ systems in parallel, but the header size in the resultant scheme is inefficient. It is non-trivial to avoid the collusion attack and reduce the header size at the same time.

---

[5] If the number of H_{v_j}'s in H for broadcasting is always less (or greater) than that for tracing, this difference enables the pirate decoder to distinguish one from the other. This is why we fix the number of selected nodes. We set the number of selected nodes to $\log_2 L + 1$ because a leaf has to be chosen in building a header for tracing, as described in BBT″ in Sect. 4.

4   The Hierarchical Key-Assignment Method

We present the hierarchical key-assignment method and apply it to the scheme of [8]. Let $(\mathsf{Gen}'', \mathsf{Enc}'', \mathsf{Dec}'', \mathsf{BBT}'')$ be the resulting scheme. The proposed method is shown in Gen''. The other algorithms than Gen'' are so constructed as to adapt the scheme of [8] to the hierarchical key assignment.

$\mathsf{Gen}''(1^\ell, n, k)$: Generate two primes, p, q $(q \geq n + 2k)$, and a generator, g, and split $\mathcal{U}$ into L disjoint subsets in the same way as in Gen in 3.1.

Define a complete binary tree, T, as depicted in Fig. 2(a) and generate a collection, Y_T, of subsets of users.

Choose $a_i, b_i \in_R \mathbb{Z}_q$ for $0 \leq i \leq 2k - 1$, and $c_i, \lambda_i \in_R \mathbb{Z}_q$ for $0 \leq i \leq 2L - 3$. Compute a public key, e $(= BK = TK)$, as follows.

$$e = (p, q, g, \{y_{0,i} = g^{a_i}\}_{i=0,\ldots,2k-1}, \{y_{1,i} = g^{c_i}\}_{i=0,\ldots,2L-3}, \{y_{2,i} = g^{\lambda_i}\}_{i=0,\ldots,2L-3}).$$

Next, define key-generation polynomials, $A_v(x), B(x)$, as follows.

$$A_v(x) = \sum_{i=0}^{2k-1} (a_{v,i} - \lambda_v b_i)x^i \bmod q,$$

$$B(x) = \sum_{i=0}^{2k-1} b_i x^i \bmod q,$$

$$a_{v,i} = \begin{cases} a_i & (i \neq v \bmod 2k), \\ c_v & (i = v \bmod 2k), \end{cases}$$

Note that it always holds that

$$A_v(x) + \lambda_v B(x) = \sum_{i=0}^{2k-1} a_{v,i} x^i \bmod q. \tag{4}$$

This relation enables the decryption algorithm to work. A personal key, d_u, of a user, u, is represented as $d_u = \{(u, v, A_v(u), B(u)) | v \in \mathcal{N}_T, \ u \in \mathcal{U}_v\}$. In Fig. 2(a), for instance, if $u \in \mathcal{U}_{i_0}$, then

$$d_u = \{(u, i_0, A_{i_0}(u), B(u)), (u, i_8, A_{i_8}(u), B(u)), (u, i_{12}, A_{i_{12}}(u), B(u))\}.$$

Remark 1. We explain the rationale behind introducing $A_v(x), B(x)$. Consider the same collusion attack as described in 3.2. Suppose that colluders, $x_1, \ldots, x_k$, belong to the same subgroup, $\mathcal{U}_{v_1}$, where v_1 is a leaf. They also belong to $\mathcal{U}_{v_2}, \ldots, \mathcal{U}_{v_{\log_2 L}}$ where $v_2, \ldots, v_{\log_2 L}$ are the nodes on the path from the leaf to the root. They try to determine the coefficients of $A_{v_j}(x), B(x)$ by solving the following system of equations.

$$\begin{cases} A_{v_j}(x_1) + \lambda_{v_j} B(x_1) = \sum_{i=0}^{2k-1} a_{v_j,i} x_1^i \\ A_{v_j}(x_2) + \lambda_{v_j} B(x_2) = \sum_{i=0}^{2k-1} a_{v_j,i} x_2^i \\ \qquad\qquad\qquad \vdots \\ A_{v_j}(x_k) + \lambda_{v_j} B(x_k) = \sum_{i=0}^{2k-1} a_{v_j,i} x_k^i \end{cases} \qquad (1 \leq j \leq \log_2 L). \tag{5}$$

In (5), however, the coefficients remain indeterminate even though the number of equations exceeds that of variables. Therefore, this collusion attack is impossible.

$Enc''(e, Y_T, s)$: Execute Sel in 3.2 and then do Enc in 3.1 with the following two relations: (i) H_{v_j} is calculated for each selected nodes, v_j ($1 \leq j \leq \log_2 L + 1$), and (ii) $H_{v_j} = (\bar{h}_{v_j}, \hat{h}_{v_j} (= y_{2,v_j}^{r_{v_j}}), h_{v_j,0}, \ldots, h_{v_j,2k-1})$.

Note that in this paper we do not consider changes in group membership in the normal broadcast, although arbitrary revocation can be supported by integrating the mechanism of flexible revocation presented in [9] into the resulting scheme. If we focus on black-box tracing, it is not necessarily required to support arbitrary revocation since BBT in 3.1, which is also used in BBT'', only requires that suspects be examined (i.e., revoked) in such a way that each user is added to a set of revoked users one by one.

$Dec''(d_u, H)$: Suppose that $u \in \mathcal{U}_{v_j}$. The user, u, correctly computes the session key, s, by using $(u, v_j, A_{v_j}(u), B(u)) \in d_u$ and $H_{v_j} \in H$ as follows.

$$\left(\frac{\prod_{i=0}^{2k-1} h_{v_j,i}^{u^i}}{\bar{h}_{v_j}^{A_{v_j}(u)} \hat{h}_{v_j}^{B(u)}} \right)^{1/u^{v_j} \bmod 2k} = s \left\{ \frac{g^{r_{v_j} \sum_{i=0}^{2k-1} a_{v_j,i} u^i}}{g^{r_{v_j}(A_{v_j}(u) + \lambda_{v_j} B(u))}} \right\}^{1/u^{v_j} \bmod 2k}$$

$$= s \quad (\because (4)).$$

$BBT''(e, Y_T, PD)$: Execute BBT in 3.1, where H is built by executing Enc''' defined as follows.

$Enc'''(e, Y_T, s)$: Execute Enc'' with the following two relations: (i) The following two conditions are added in selecting nodes: (a) $\mathcal{X} \cap \mathcal{U}_{v_j} = \emptyset$, $0 < |\mathcal{U}_{v_j} \backslash (\mathcal{X} \cup \mathcal{V}_{v_j})| < 2k$, or $\mathcal{X} \cap \mathcal{U}_{v_j} = \mathcal{U}_{v_j}$ and (b) at most one node, v_j, s.t. $0 < |\mathcal{U}_{v_j} \backslash (\mathcal{X} \cup \mathcal{V}_{v_j})| < 2k$ is chosen, where $\mathcal{V}_{v_j}$ is defined as $\mathcal{V}_{v_j} = \bigcup_{1 \leq t \leq \log_2 L + 1, t \neq j} \mathcal{U}_{v_t}$. For example, in Fig. 2(a), if $\mathcal{X} = \{u_1, \ldots, u_{7k}\}$, four nodes, i_2, i_3, i_8, i_{13} ($\bigcup_{j \in \{2,3,8,13\}} \mathcal{U}_{i_j} = \mathcal{U}$, $\mathcal{X} \cap \mathcal{U}_{i_2} = \mathcal{U}_{i_2}$, $|\mathcal{U}_{i_3} \backslash (\mathcal{X} \cup \bigcup_{j \in \{2,8,13\}} \mathcal{U}_{i_j})| = |\{u_{7k+1}, \ldots, u_{8k}\}| = k$, $\mathcal{X} \cap \mathcal{U}_{i_8} = \mathcal{U}_{i_8}$, $\mathcal{X} \cap \mathcal{U}_{i_{13}} = \emptyset$), can be selected and (ii) the process of calculating $h_{v_j,i}$ branches as follows[6].

– If $\mathcal{X} \cap \mathcal{U}_{v_j} = \emptyset$, then

$$h_{v_j,i} \left(\overset{\triangle}{=} h'_{v_j,i} \right) = \begin{cases} y_{0,i}^{r_{v_j}} & (i \neq v_j \bmod 2k), \\ s y_{1,v_j}^{r_{v_j}} & (i = v_j \bmod 2k), \end{cases}$$

where if there exists a node, v_i, among the selected ones s.t. $0 < |\mathcal{U}_{v_i} \backslash (\mathcal{X} \cup \mathcal{V}_{v_i})| < 2k$, then set $bit_{v_j} = 0$. Otherwise (there is no such v_i), set bit_{v_j} to 0 or 1 at random.

– If $0 < |\mathcal{U}_{v_j} \backslash (\mathcal{X} \cup \mathcal{V}_{v_j})| < 2k$, first, suppose that $\mathcal{U}_{v_j} \backslash (\mathcal{X} \cup \mathcal{V}_{v_j}) = \{\alpha_1, \ldots, \alpha_m\}$ and choose $2k - m - 1$ distinct elements, $\alpha_{m+1}, \ldots, \alpha_{2k-1} \in_R \mathbb{Z}_q \backslash (\mathcal{U} \cup$

---

[6] The branched processes are also similar to those in the scheme of [8].

$\{0\}$), when $2k - m - 1 > 0$. Secondly, find elements, $L_0, \ldots, L_{2k-1} \in \mathbb{Z}_q$, s.t. $\sum_{i=0}^{2k-1} L_i \alpha_t^i = 0 \bmod q$ for $1 \leq t \leq 2k - 1$. Finally, set $bit_{v_j} = 1$ and compute $h_{v_j,i}$ as follows.

$$h_{v_j,i} \left(\stackrel{\triangle}{=} h''_{v_j,i} \right) = \begin{cases} g^{L_i} y_{0,i}^{r_{v_j}} & (i \neq v_j \bmod 2k), \\ sg^{L_i} y_{1,i}^{r_{v_j}} & (i = v_j \bmod 2k). \end{cases} \tag{6}$$

We explain how a user, $u \in \mathcal{U}_{v_j} \cap \mathcal{X}$, is revoked. The user, u, tries to compute the session key as follows.

$$\left\{ \prod_{i=0}^{2k-1} h_{v_j,i}^{u^i} \Big/ \left(\bar{h}_{v_j}^{A_{v_j}(u)} \hat{h}_{v_j}^{B(u)} \right) \right\}^{1/u^{v_j} \bmod 2k}$$

$$= s \left\{ g^{\sum_{i=0}^{2k-1} L_i u^i} g^{r_{v_j} \sum_{i=0}^{2k-1} a_{v_j,i} u^i} \Big/ g^{r_{v_j} \left(A_{v_j}(u) + \lambda_{v_j} B(u) \right)} \right\}^{1/u^{v_j} \bmod 2k}.$$

Since it does not hold that $\sum_{i=0}^{2k-1} L_i u^i = 0 \bmod q$, the session key cannot be obtained.

- If $\mathcal{X} \cap \mathcal{U}_{v_j} = \mathcal{U}_{v_j}$, then set bit_{v_j} to 0 or 1 randomly. Set $h_{v_j,i} = h'_{v_j,i}$ with the exception that (i) if $bit_{v_j} = 1$ and there exists a node, v_i, among the selected ones s.t. $0 < |\mathcal{U}_{v_i} \setminus (\mathcal{X} \cup \mathcal{V}_{v_i})| < 2k$, then set $h_{v_j,i} = h''_{v_j,i}$ and (ii) if $bit_{v_j} = 1$ and there is no such v_i, then the following procedure can optionally be performed for one v_j only: Choose $\alpha_1, \ldots, \alpha_{2k-1} \in_{\mathrm{R}} \mathbb{Z}_q \setminus (\mathcal{U} \cup \{0\})$ and compute $h''_{v_j,i}$ as in (6). If this optional procedure is done, we regard that there exists a node, v_i, s.t. $0 < |\mathcal{U}_{v_i} \setminus (\mathcal{X} \cup \mathcal{V}_{v_i})| < 2k$. In any case, select $z_{v_j} \in_{\mathrm{R}} \mathbb{Z}_q$ and replace $h_{v_j,v_j \bmod 2k}$ with $g^{z_{v_j}}$.
  Note that all of the users in $\mathcal{U}_{v_j}$ are revoked by replacing the element, $h_{v_j,v_j \bmod 2k}$, which is used only by them, with the random element, $g^{z_{v_j}}$.

5   Security

The security of the resulting scheme shown in Sect. 4 is based on the difficulty of the decision Diffie-Hellman (DDH for short) problem. Proofs are given in the appendix. The proofs of Lemma 3 and Theorem 2 are omitted due to space limitation. Lemma 3 can be proved in a similar way to Lemmas 1 and 2. The proof of Theorem 2 is the same as in [8, Theorem 2].

Theorem 1 (Indistinguishability). *The resulting scheme is indistinguishable as defined in Definition 3 under the assumption that the DDH problem is intractable in G_q.*

The next lemmas are used to prove black-box traceability of the resulting scheme. Let valid and invalid inputs denote headers for broadcasting and those for tracing respectively.

Table 1. Efficiency comparison ($\mathcal{H}$, $\mathcal{S}$, $\mathcal{P}$, $\mathcal{B}$: sets of possible headers, session keys, personal keys, and broadcaster's keys respectively, n: the total number of users, k: the maximum coalition size, L: the total number of leaves in a tree ($L = n/2k$))

	Header size $(\log|\mathcal{H}|/\log|\mathcal{S}|)$	Personal-key size $(\log|\mathcal{P}|/\log|\mathcal{S}|)$	Broadcaster's-key size $(\log|\mathcal{B}|/\log|\mathcal{S}|)$
[8]	$4k + L + 2$	1	$2k + L$
Simple extension of [8]	$(2k+1)(\log_2 L + 1)$	$\log_2 L$	$2(k\log_2 L + L - 1)$
Resulting scheme	$4k + \log_2 L + 5$	$\log_2 L + 1$	$2(k + 2L - 2)$
[2]	$6\sqrt{n}$	1	$3\sqrt{n}$

	Is a tracer's key public?	Collusion resistance (max. coalition size)	Computational cost for decryption
[8]	Yes	Limited to k	$O(k)$
Simple extension of [8]	Yes	Limited to k	$O(k)$
Resulting scheme	Yes	Limited to k	$O(k)$
[2]	No	Unlimited	$O(1)$

Lemma 1 (Indistinguishability of an Input). *Distinguishing a valid input from an invalid one by any coalition of k non-revoked users is as difficult as the DDH problem in G_q.*

Lemma 2 (Indistinguishability in an Invalid Input). *Given an invalid input, distinguishing a session key corresponding to the input from a random element in G_q by any coalition of k users revoked in the input is as difficult as the DDH problem in G_q.*

Lemma 3 (Indistinguishability of a Suspect). *Recall that $\mathcal{X}$ denotes a set of revoked users in an invalid input, H. Suppose that all of the users are labeled as represented in (2). Given a user, u_j, distinguishing an invalid input in which $\mathcal{X} = \{u_1, \ldots, u_{j-1}\}$ from an invalid one in which $\mathcal{X} = \{u_1, \ldots, u_j\}$ by any coalition, $\mathcal{C}$, of k users is as difficult as the DDH problem in G_q, when $u_j \notin \mathcal{C}$.*

From Lemmas 1, 2, and 3, it follows that the next theorem holds.

Theorem 2 (Black-Box Traceability). *The resulting scheme is black-box traceable as defined in Definition 4 under the assumption that the DDH problem is intractable in G_q.*

6   Efficiency

In Table 1, the scheme of [8], its simple extension, the resulting scheme shown in Sect. 4, and the scheme of [2] are compared. The construction of the first three schemes is algebraic, while that of the last one is pairing-based.

Figure 3 numerically shows the header size in each scheme when $n = 10^6$, where we suppose that $L = n/2k$ in the first three schemes. The header size in the resulting scheme can be considered linear only in k. Contrary to this, the depth of

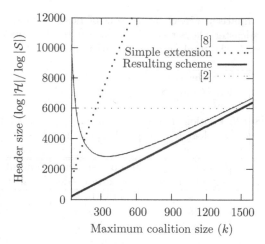

Fig. 3. Header size when the total number of users is 10^6

a tree greatly affects the header size in the simple extension. Compared with the scheme of [8], the resulting scheme is always more efficient if $k < n/11$. Compared with the scheme of [2], the resulting scheme is more efficient if, roughly speaking, k is less than $1.5\sqrt{n}$ or so. Such a value of k can be chosen in real applications.

In the schemes of [8,2], the personal-key size is constant, while in the simple extension and the resulting scheme it is linear in the depth of a underlying tree. However, in the case that e.g., $n = 10^6$, $k = 10^3$, it holds that $\log_2 L < 9$ and thus this is not a heavy storage burden in practice.

In all of the schemes in Table 1, the broadcaster's key is public. The broadcaster's-key size in the scheme of [8] and the resulting scheme is $O(\sqrt{n})$ $(k = O(\sqrt{n}))$ but becomes less efficient than that of [2] as k comes close to n. In Table 1, p, q, g are not included as a broadcaster's key in the first three schemes. Similarly, some public information is not counted as a broadcaster's key in the scheme of [2].

In the resulting scheme, the tracer's key is also public, while it must be kept secret in the scheme of [2]. The secret tracer's key is an obstacle to delegate plural entities to perform tracing since the security is degraded when the tracer's key is compromised.

In the resulting scheme, the number of traitors in a coalition must be limited to k and the number of modular exponentiations required for decryption is linear in k, while in the scheme of [2] there is no upper bound on the coalition size and a constant number of pairing computations are required for decryption. The resulting scheme can be an option to applications where reducing the transmission overhead is a top priority.

7   Conclusions

We have proposed a hierarchical key-assignment method which can be used to reduce the header size in the scheme of [8]. The resulting scheme achieves (i) the header size is reduced from $O(\sqrt{n})$ to $O(k + \log(n/k))$ without a substantial increase in the personal-key size, (ii) the scheme supports black-box tracing even if the pirate decoder is self-defensive, (iii) both the broadcaster's key and the tracer's key are public. The computational cost for decryption is linear in k and remains to be improved.

References

1. D. Boneh and M. Franklin. An efficient public key traitor tracing scheme. In *Proc. CRYPTO'99*, LNCS 1666, pages 338–353. Springer-Verlag, 1999.
2. D. Boneh, A. Sahai, and B. Waters. Fully collusion resistant traitor tracing with short ciphertexts and private keys. In *Proc. EUROCRYPT 2006*, LNCS 4004, pages 573–592. Springer-Verlag, 2006.
3. H. Chabanne, D. Phan, and D. Pointcheval. Public traceability in traitor tracing schemes. In *Proc. EUROCRYPT 2005*, LNCS 3494, pages 542–558. Springer-Verlag, 2005.
4. B. Chor, A. Fiat, and M. Naor. Tracing traitors. In *Proc. CRYPTO'94*, LNCS 839, pages 257–270. Springer-Verlag, 1994.
5. A. Kiayias and M. Yung. On crafty pirates and foxy tracers. In *Security and Privacy in Digital Rights Management: Revised Papers from the ACM CCS-8 Workshop DRM 2001*, LNCS 2320, pages 22–39. Springer-Verlag, 2002.
6. A. Kiayias and M. Yung. Traitor tracing with constant transmission rate. In *Proc. EUROCRYPT 2002*, LNCS 2332, pages 450–465. Springer-Verlag, 2002.
7. K. Kurosawa and Y. Desmedt. Optimum traitor tracing and asymmetric schemes. In *Proc. EUROCRYPT'98*, LNCS 1403, pages 145–157. Springer-Verlag, 1998.
8. T. Matsushita and H. Imai. A public-key black-box traitor tracing scheme with sublinear ciphertext size against self-defensive pirates. In *Proc. ASIACRYPT 2004*, LNCS 3329, pages 260–275. Springer-Verlag, 2004.
9. T. Matsushita and H. Imai. A flexible-revocation scheme for efficient public-key black-box traitor tracing. *IEICE Trans. Fundamentals*, E88-A(4):1055–1062, 2005.
10. D. Naor, M. Naor, and J. Lotspiech. Revocation and tracing schemes for stateless receivers. In *Proc. CRYPTO 2001*, LNCS 2139, pages 41–62. Springer-Verlag, 2001.

A   Security Proofs

A.1   Definitions

We define the DDH problem and the MDDH problem, which is a modified version of the DDH problem. Subsequently, we prove that the MDDH problem is computationally equivalent to the DDH problem and use it to proof Lemmas 1, 2, and 3.

Definition 5 (DDH). *The DDH problem is the following: Given a generator, $g \in G$, where G is a cyclic group of prime order, q, and a 4-tuple, $(g_1, g_2, g_3, g_4) = (g_1, g_2, g_1^a, g_2^b)$, where $g_1, g_2 \in_R G$, $a, c \in_R \mathbb{Z}_q$, and $b = a$ or c, decide whether $b = a$ or not. A probabilistic polynomial-time (PPT for short) algorithm, Alg, solves the DDH problem if it satisfies, for some fixed $\alpha > 0$ and sufficiently large n,*

$$|\Pr[\mathsf{Alg}(q, g, g_1, g_2, g_1^a, g_2^a) = \text{``}b = a\text{''}]$$
$$-\Pr[\mathsf{Alg}(q, g, g_1, g_2, g_1^a, g_2^c) = \text{``}b = a\text{''}]| > 1/n^\alpha.$$

We call a 4-tuple coming from the distribution, $\langle g_1, g_2, g_1^a, g_2^a \rangle$, as a Diffie-Hellman tuple.

Definition 6 (MDDH). *The MDDH problem is the following: Given a generator, $g \in G$, where G is a cyclic group of prime order, q, and a 6-tuple, $(g_1, g_2, g_3, g_4, g_5, g_6) = (g_1, g_2, g_1^a, g_2^b, g_1^c, g_2^c)$, where $g_1, g_2 \in_R G$, $a, c, d \in_R \mathbb{Z}_q$, and $b = a$ or d, decide whether $b = a$ or not. A PPT algorithm, Alg, solves the MDDH problem if it satisfies, for some fixed $\alpha > 0$ and sufficiently large n,*

$$|\Pr[\mathsf{Alg}(q, g, g_1, g_2, g_1^a, g_2^a, g_1^c, g_2^c) = \text{``}b = a\text{''}]$$
$$-\Pr[\mathsf{Alg}(q, g, g_1, g_2, g_1^a, g_2^d, g_1^c, g_2^c) = \text{``}b = a\text{''}]| > 1/n^\alpha.$$

We also call a 6-tuple coming from the distribution, $\langle g_1, g_2, g_1^a, g_2^a, g_1^c, g_2^c \rangle$, as a Diffie-Hellman tuple. In Definitions 5 and 6, we assume that G is a multiplicative group. If G is an additive one, these definitions can be rewritten additively. In the proposed schemes, one can take an additive group of points of an elliptic curve over a finite field instead of G_q.

Let DDH, MDDH be PPT algorithms which solve the DDH problem and the MDDH problem in G_q respectively. For two PPT algorithms, A, B, we mean by A $\Rightarrow$ B that the existence of A implies that of B and by A $\Leftrightarrow$ B that A $\Rightarrow$ B and B $\Rightarrow$ A.

Lemma 4. *The DDH problem in G_q is as difficult as the MDDH problem in G_q.*

Proof. We prove that DDH $\Leftrightarrow$ MDDH. First it is clear that DDH $\Rightarrow$ MDDH. Secondly, we show that MDDH $\Rightarrow$ DDH by constructing DDH using MDDH as a subroutine. The construction of DDH is as follows.

Algorithm 1
Input: A challenge 4-tuple, (g_1, g_2, g_3, g_4).
Output: "Diffie-Hellman tuple" or "Random tuple."

1. Select $r \in_R \mathbb{Z}_q$ and build a 6-tuple $(g_1, g_2, g_3, g_4, g_1^r, g_2^r)$. Observe that if the challenge 4-tuple is a Diffie-Hellman tuple, the 6-tuple is also a Diffie-Hellman tuple. Otherwise, it is not.
2. Give the 6-tuple to MDDH. If MDDH decides that the 6-tuple is a Diffie-Hellman tuple, then output "Diffie-Hellman tuple." Otherwise, output "Random tuple." Since MDDH behaves differently for Diffie-Hellman tuples and random ones in G_q, DDH can solve the given challenge. □

A.2   Proof of Theorem 1

Let Dis be a PPT algorithm the non-users use to distinguish between the session key corresponding to the header and a random element in G_q. We prove that Dis $\Leftrightarrow$ DDH. First, it is clear that DDH $\Rightarrow$ Dis. Secondly, we show that Dis $\Rightarrow$ DDH by constructing DDH using Dis as a subroutine. The construction of DDH is as follows.

Algorithm 2
Input: A challenge 4-tuple, (g_1, g_2, g_3, g_4).
Output: "Diffie-Hellman tuple" or "Random tuple."

1. Define T and generate Y_T.
2. Select $\beta \in_R \mathbb{Z}_q$, $a_i \in_R \mathbb{Z}_q$ for $0 \leq i \leq 2k - 1$, and $\alpha_v, \lambda_v \in_R \mathbb{Z}_q$ for $0 \leq v \leq 2L - 3$. Then, compute e as follows.

$$e = (p, q, g_1, \{g_1^{a_i}\}_{i=0,\dots,2k-1}, \{g_1^{\alpha_i} g_2^{\beta}\}_{i=0,\dots,2L-3}, \{g_1^{\lambda_i}\}_{i=0,\dots,2L-3}).$$

3. Select $s \in_R G_q$ and execute Enc'' in Sect. 4 with the relation that H_{v_j} is computed as follows.

$$H_{v_j} = \left(g_1^r g_3, (g_1^r g_3)^{\lambda_{v_j}}, h_{v_j,0}, \dots, h_{v_j,2k-1} \right),$$

$$h_{v_j,i} = \begin{cases} (g_1^r g_3)^{a_i} & (i \neq v_j \bmod 2k), \\ s \, (g_1^r g_3)^{\alpha_i} (g_2^r g_4)^{\beta} & (i = v_j \bmod 2k), \end{cases}$$

where $r = R_0$ if $bit_{v_j} = 0$. Otherwise $(bit_{v_j} = 1)$, r is set to 0.
Observe that if the challenge 4-tuple is a Diffie-Hellman tuple, the session key corresponding to the header is s. Otherwise, it is a random element in G_q.

4. Give e, H, s to Dis. If Dis decides that s is the session key corresponding to H, then output "Diffie-Hellman tuple." Otherwise, output "Random tuple." Since Dis behaves differently for session keys and random elements in G_q, DDH can solve the given challenge. $\square$

A.3   Proof of Lemma 1

Let $\mathcal{C}$ be a set of k non-revoked colluders and $\mathsf{Dis}_\mathcal{C}$ be a PPT algorithm the colluders use to distinguish a valid input from an invalid one. We prove that $\mathsf{Dis}_\mathcal{C} \Leftrightarrow$ DDH for any $\mathcal{C}$ with $\mathcal{X} \cap \mathcal{C} = \emptyset$, $|\mathcal{C}| = k$. First, it is clear that DDH $\Rightarrow \mathsf{Dis}_\mathcal{C}$ for any $\mathcal{C}$ with $\mathcal{X} \cap \mathcal{C} = \emptyset$, $|\mathcal{C}| = k$. Secondly, since it is proved in Lemma 4 that DDH $\Leftrightarrow$ MDDH, we use MDDH instead and show that $\mathsf{Dis}_\mathcal{C} \Rightarrow$ MDDH for any $\mathcal{C}$ with $\mathcal{X} \cap \mathcal{C} = \emptyset$, $|\mathcal{C}| = k$ by constructing MDDH using $\mathsf{Dis}_\mathcal{C}$ as a subroutine. The construction of MDDH is as follows.

Algorithm 3
Input: A challenge 6-tuple, $(g_1, g_2, g_3, g_4, g_5, g_6)$.
Output: "Diffie-Hellman tuple" or "Random tuple."

1. Choose $\mathcal{U}$, define T, and generate Y_T in the same way as in Gen'' in Sect. 4. Then, choose $\mathcal{C}$.
2. We plan to generate a public key, e, only from the colluders' personal keys. Suppose that $\mathcal{C} = \{x_1, \dots, x_k\}$. Choose $k - 1$ distinct elements, $x_{k+1}, \dots, x_{2k-1} \in_R \mathbb{Z}_q \backslash \mathcal{C}$, $\theta, \mu \in_R \mathbb{Z}_q$, $z_{A,t} \in_R \mathbb{Z}_q$ for $1 \leq t \leq k$, and $\varphi_t, \psi_t \in_R \mathbb{Z}_q$

for $k + 1 \leq t \leq 2k - 1$. Then, there exists a unique polynomial, $A_R(x) = \sum_{i=0}^{2k-1} \alpha_i x^i \bmod q$, s.t.

$$
\begin{aligned}
(A_R(x_1), \ldots, A_R(x_{2k-1}))^{\mathrm{T}} &= (z_{A,1}, \ldots, z_{A,2k-1})^{\mathrm{T}} \\
&= (\alpha_0, \ldots, \alpha_0)^{\mathrm{T}} + W(\alpha_1, \ldots, \alpha_{2k-1})^{\mathrm{T}} \bmod q, \\
g_1^{z_{A,0}} &= g_1^{\theta} g_2^{\mu}, \\
g_1^{z_{A,t}} &= g_1^{\varphi_t} g_2^{\psi_t} \qquad (k + 1 \leq t \leq 2k - 1),
\end{aligned}
$$

where

$$
W = \begin{pmatrix} x_1 & \cdots & x_1^{2k-1} \\ \vdots & \ddots & \vdots \\ x_{2k-1} & \cdots & x_{2k-1}^{2k-1} \end{pmatrix} \bmod q.
$$

Since W is a Vandermonde matrix, we obtain

$$
(\alpha_1, \ldots, \alpha_{2k-1})^{\mathrm{T}} = W^{-1}(z_{A,1} - z_{A,0}, \ldots, z_{A,2k-1} - z_{A,0})^{\mathrm{T}} \bmod q.
$$

Let $(w_{t,1}, \ldots, w_{t,2k-1})$ be the tth row of W^{-1}. For $1 \leq t \leq 2k - 1$, α_t is represented as follows.

$$
\begin{aligned}
\alpha_t &= w_{t,1}(z_{A,1} - z_{A,0}) + \cdots + w_{t,2k-1}(z_{A,2k-1} - z_{A,0}) \\
&= w_{t,1} z_{A,1} + \cdots + w_{t,2k-1} z_{A,2k-1} - z_{A,0}(w_{t,1} + \cdots + w_{t,2k-1}) \bmod q.
\end{aligned}
$$

Therefore, $g_1^{\alpha_t}$ is calculated as follows.

$$
\begin{aligned}
g_1^{\alpha_t} &= g_1^{w_{t,1} z_{A,1} + \cdots + w_{t,2k-1} z_{A,2k-1}} \Big/ (g_1^{z_{A,0}})^{w_{t,1} + \cdots + w_{t,2k-1}}, \\
&= \prod_{\ell=1}^{k} \left(g_1^{w_{t,\ell} z_{A,\ell}} \right) \prod_{\ell=k+1}^{2k-1} \left(g_1^{\varphi_\ell} g_2^{\psi_\ell} \right)^{w_{t,\ell}} \Big/ \left(g_1^{\theta} g_2^{\mu} \right)^{w_{t,1} + \cdots + w_{t,2k-1}}.
\end{aligned}
$$

Recall that $\mathcal{N}_T = \{0, \ldots, 2L - 3\}$. Define $\mathcal{N} = \{v | v \in \mathcal{N}_T, \ x_i \in \mathcal{C}, \ x_i \in \mathcal{U}_v\}$ and suppose that $x_i \in \mathcal{U}_v$ ($x_i \in \mathcal{C}$, $v \in \mathcal{N}$). Choose $\eta, \sigma, \omega \in_{\mathrm{R}} \mathbb{Z}_q$, $\eta_v \in_{\mathrm{R}} \mathbb{Z}_q$ for each $v \in \mathcal{N}$, and $\sigma_t, \omega_t \in_{\mathrm{R}} \mathbb{Z}_q$ for $0 \leq t \leq 2L - 3$, $t \notin \mathcal{N}$. Then, there exist a unique element, $\zeta \in \mathbb{Z}_q$, for each $v \in \mathcal{N}$ s.t.

$$
\begin{aligned}
\eta &= \lambda - \zeta \bmod q, \\
\eta_v &= \lambda_v - \zeta \bmod q, \\
g_1^{\lambda} &= g_1^{\sigma} g_5^{\omega}, \\
g_1^{\lambda_t} &= \begin{cases} g_1^{\lambda + \eta_t - \eta} & (t \in \mathcal{N}), \\ g_1^{\sigma_t} g_5^{\omega_t} & (0 \leq t \leq 2L - 3, \ t \notin \mathcal{N}), \end{cases}
\end{aligned}
$$

Select $\delta_v \in_{\mathrm{R}} \mathbb{Z}_q$ for each $v \in \mathcal{N}$. Then, there exists a unique element, $\gamma_v \in \mathbb{Z}_q$, for each $v \in \mathcal{N}$ s.t.

$$
\delta_v = \gamma_v - \alpha_{v \bmod 2k} \bmod q.
$$

Choose $z_{B,i} \in_R \mathbb{Z}_q$ for $1 \leq i \leq k$. We plan to compute each colluder's personal key, d_{x_i}, as follows.

$$d_{x_i} = \{(x_i, v, A_v(x_i), B(x_i)) | v \in \mathcal{N}, \ x_i \in \mathcal{U}_v\},$$
$$B(x_i) = z_{B,i} \bmod q \quad (1 \leq i \leq k),$$
$$A_v(x_i) = A_R(x_i) + \delta_v x_i^{v \bmod 2k} - \eta_v B(x_i)$$
$$= \alpha_0 + \alpha_1 x_i + \cdots + \gamma_v x_i^{v \bmod 2k} + \cdots + \alpha_{2k-1} x_i^{2k-1} - \lambda_v z_{B,i}$$
$$+ \zeta z_{B,i} \bmod q.$$

Note that it is allowed to give the values of η_v, δ_v to the colluders since they can compute them from their personal keys. Select $\theta_t, \mu_t \in_R \mathbb{Z}_q$ for $0 \leq t \leq 2L - 3$, $t \notin \mathcal{N}$. To satisfy the relation in (4) for each $x_i \in \mathcal{C}$, a_t and c_t are represented as follows.

$$g_1^{a_t} = g_1^{\alpha_t + \beta_t} \quad (0 \leq t \leq 2k - 1),$$
$$g_1^{c_t} = \begin{cases} g_1^{\delta_t + \alpha_t \bmod 2k + \beta_t \bmod 2k} & (t \in \mathcal{N}), \\ g_1^{\theta_t} g_2^{\mu_t} & (0 \leq t \leq 2L - 3, \ t \notin \mathcal{N}), \end{cases}$$

where we can set $g_1^{\beta_0}, \ldots, g_1^{\beta_{2k-1}}$ to any of the solutions of the following system of equations.

$$g_1^{\sum_{t=0}^{2k-1} \beta_t x_i^t} = g_1^{\zeta z_{B,i}},$$
$$= \left(g_1^\sigma g_5^\omega / g_1^\eta \right)^{z_{B,i}} \quad (1 \leq i \leq k).$$

Finally, set $e = (p, q, g_1, \{g_1^{a_i}\}_{i=0,\ldots,2k-1}, \{g_1^{c_i}\}_{i=0,\ldots,2L-3}, \{g_1^{\lambda_i}\}_{i=0,\ldots,2L-3})$.
3. Choose $s \in_R G_q$ and $r \in_R \mathbb{Z}_q$. Set bit_{v_j} to 0 or 1 at random, and compute H_{v_j} as follows.

$$H_{v_j} = \begin{cases} (g_1^r, g_1^{\lambda_{v_j} r}, g_1^{a_0 r}, \ldots, sg_1^{c_{v_j} r}, \ldots, g_1^{a_{2k-1} r}) & (bit_{v_j} = 0), \\ (g_3, g_3^{\lambda_{v_j}}, g_3^{a_0}, \ldots, sg_3^{c_{v_j}}, \ldots, g_3^{a_{2k-1}}) & (bit_{v_j} = 1), \end{cases}$$
$$g_3^{\lambda_{v_j}} = \begin{cases} g_3^\sigma g_6^\omega g_3^{\eta_{v_j} - \eta} & (v_j \in \mathcal{N}), \\ g_3^{\sigma_{v_j}} g_6^{\omega_{v_j}} & (0 \leq v_j \leq 2L - 3, \ v_j \notin \mathcal{N}), \end{cases}$$
$$g_3^{a_i} = g_3^{\alpha_i + \beta_i},$$
$$g_3^{\alpha_i} = \prod_{\ell=1}^{k} \left(g_3^{w_{i,\ell} z_{A,\ell}} \right) \prod_{\ell=k+1}^{2k-1} \left(g_3^{\varphi_\ell} g_4^{\psi_\ell} \right)^{w_{i,\ell}} / \left(g_3^\theta g_4^\mu \right)^{w_{i,1} + \cdots + w_{i,2k-1}},$$
$$g_3^{c_{v_j}} = \begin{cases} g_3^{\delta_{v_j} + \alpha_{v_j} \bmod 2k + \beta_{v_j} \bmod 2k} & (v_j \in \mathcal{N}), \\ g_3^{\theta_{v_j}} g_4^{\mu_{v_j}} & (0 \leq v_j \leq 2L - 3, \ v_j \notin \mathcal{N}), \end{cases}$$

where we can set $g_3^{\beta_0}, \ldots, g_3^{\beta_{2k-1}}$ to any of the solutions of the following system of equations.

$$g_3^{\sum_{t=0}^{2k-1} \beta_t x_i^t} = \left(g_3^\sigma g_6^\omega / g_3^\eta \right)^{z_{B,i}} \quad (1 \leq i \leq k).$$

Observe that if the challenge 6-tuple is a Diffie-Hellman tuple, H is a valid input. Otherwise, it is an invalid one in which the k colluders in $\mathcal{C}$ are not revoked, i.e., $\mathcal{X} \cap \mathcal{C} = \emptyset$.

4. Give $d_{x_1}, \ldots, d_{x_k}, e, H$ to $\mathsf{Dis}_{\mathcal{C}}$. If $\mathsf{Dis}_{\mathcal{C}}$ decides that H is a valid input, then output "Diffie-Hellman tuple." Otherwise output "Random tuple." Since $\mathsf{Dis}_{\mathcal{C}}$ behaves differently for valid inputs and invalid ones, MDDH can solve the given challenge. Since $\mathcal{C}$ with $\mathcal{X} \cap \mathcal{C} = \emptyset$, $|\mathcal{C}| = k$ can be chosen arbitrarily, it holds that $\mathsf{Dis}_{\mathcal{C}} \Rightarrow$ MDDH for any $\mathcal{C}$ with $\mathcal{X} \cap \mathcal{C} = \emptyset$, $|\mathcal{C}| = k$. $\qquad \square$

A.4   Proof of Lemma 2

Let $\mathcal{C}$ be a set of k colluders revoked in the invalid input and $\mathsf{Dis}'_{\mathcal{C}}$ be a PPT algorithm the colluders use to distinguish a session key corresponding to the input from a random element in G_q. We prove that $\mathsf{Dis}'_{\mathcal{C}} \Leftrightarrow$ DDH for any $\mathcal{C}$ with $\mathcal{C} \subseteq \mathcal{X}$, $|\mathcal{C}| = k$. First, it is clear that DDH $\Rightarrow \mathsf{Dis}'_{\mathcal{C}}$ for any $\mathcal{C}$ with $\mathcal{C} \subseteq \mathcal{X}$, $|\mathcal{C}| = k$. Secondly, since it is proved in Lemma 4 that DDH $\Leftrightarrow$ MDDH, we use MDDH instead and show that $\mathsf{Dis}'_{\mathcal{C}} \Rightarrow$ MDDH for any $\mathcal{C}$ with $\mathcal{C} \subseteq \mathcal{X}$, $|\mathcal{C}| = k$ by constructing MDDH using $\mathsf{Dis}'_{\mathcal{C}}$ as a subroutine. The construction of MDDH is as follows.

Algorithm 4
Input: A challenge 6-tuple, $(g_1, g_2, g_3, g_4, g_5, g_6)$.
Output: "Diffie-Hellman tuple" or "Random tuple."

1. Choose $\mathcal{U}$, define T, and generate Y_T in the same way as in Gen'' in Sect. 4. Suppose that all of the users are labeled as represented in (2). Select $m \in_R \{1, \ldots, n\}$ and define a set of revoked users, $\mathcal{X} = \{u_1, \ldots, u_m\}$. Then, choose $\mathcal{C}$ s.t. $\mathcal{C} \subseteq \mathcal{X}$.
2. Suppose that $\mathcal{C} = \{x_1, \ldots, x_k\}$. Compute $d_{x_1}, \ldots, d_{x_k}$, and e by executing the same procedure as in Algorithm 3.
3. Choose $s \in_R G_q$ and $r, x, y \in_R \mathbb{Z}_q$. Execute Enc''' in Sect. 4, where $\mathcal{X} = \{u_1, \ldots, u_m\}$, with the following relation:

$$\bar{h}_{v_j} = \begin{cases} g_3^r & (bit_{v_j} = 0), \\ g_1^x g_3^y & (bit_{v_j} = 1), \end{cases}$$

$$\hat{h}_{v_j} = \begin{cases} g_3^{\lambda_{v_j} r} & (bit_{v_j} = 0), \\ (g_1^x g_3^y)^{\lambda_{v_j}} & (bit_{v_j} = 1), \end{cases}$$

$$h'_{v_j, i} = \begin{cases} g_3^{a_i r} & (i \neq v_j \bmod 2k, \, bit_{v_j} = 0), \\ s g_3^{c_{v_j} r} & (i = v_j \bmod 2k, \, bit_{v_j} = 0), \\ (g_1^x g_3^y)^{a_i} & (i \neq v_j \bmod 2k, \, bit_{v_j} = 1), \\ s (g_1^x g_3^y)^{c_{v_j}} & (i = v_j \bmod 2k, \, bit_{v_j} = 1), \end{cases}$$

$$h''_{v_j, i} = \begin{cases} g_1^{L_i} (g_1^x g_3^y)^{a_i} & (i \neq v_j \bmod 2k), \\ s g_1^{L_i} (g_1^x g_3^y)^{c_{v_j}} & (i = v_j \bmod 2k). \end{cases}$$

In this procedure, $g_3^{\lambda_{v_j}}, g_3^{a_t}$, and $g_3^{c_{v_j}}$ are computed in the same manner as in Algorithm 3. Observe that if the challenge 6-tuple is a Diffie-Hellman tuple, s is the session key corresponding to H. Otherwise, it is not.

4. Give $d_{x_1}, \ldots, d_{x_k}, e, H, s$ to $\mathsf{Dis}'_{\mathcal{C}}$. If $\mathsf{Dis}'_{\mathcal{C}}$ decides that s is the session key corresponding to H, then output "Diffie-Hellman tuple." Otherwise output "Random tuple." Since $\mathsf{Dis}'_{\mathcal{C}}$ behaves differently for session keys and random elements in G_q, MDDH can solve the given challenge. Since $\mathcal{C}$ with $\mathcal{C} \subseteq \mathcal{X}$, $|\mathcal{C}| = k$ can be chosen arbitrarily, it holds that $\mathsf{Dis}'_{\mathcal{C}} \Rightarrow$ MDDH for any $\mathcal{C}$ with $\mathcal{C} \subseteq \mathcal{X}$, $|\mathcal{C}| = k$. □

Trace-Driven Cache Attacks on AES
(Short Paper)

Onur Acıiçmez[1] and Çetin Kaya Koç[1,2]

[1] Oregon State University, School of EECS
Corvallis, OR 97331, USA
[2] Information Security Research Center, Istanbul Commerce University
Eminönü, Istanbul 34112, Turkey
aciicmez@eecs.oregonstate.edu, koc@cryptocode.net

Abstract. Cache based side-channel attacks have recently been attracted significant attention due to the new developments in the field. In this paper, we present an efficient trace-driven cache attack on a widely used implementation of the AES cryptosystem. We also evaluate the cost of the proposed attack in detail under the assumption of a noiseless environment. We develop an accurate mathematical model that we use in the cost analysis of our attack. We use two different metrics, specifically, the expected number of necessary traces and the cost of the analysis phase, for the cost evaluation purposes. Each of these metrics represents the cost of a different phase of the attack.

Keywords: Side-channel Analysis, cache attacks, trace-driven attacks, AES.

1 Introduction

There are various cache based side-channel attacks in the literature, which are discussed in detail in the next section. Trace-driven attacks are one of the three types of cache based attacks that had been distinguished so far. We present a trace-driven cache based attack on AES in this paper. There are already two trace-driven attacks on AES in the literature [5,12]. However, our attack requires significantly less number of measurements (e.g. only 5 measurements in some cases) and is much more efficient than the previous attacks. We show that trace-driven attacks have indeed much more power than what was stated in the previous studies.

Furthermore, we present a robust computational model for trace-driven attacks that allows one to evaluate the cost of such attacks on a given implementation and platform. Although, we only apply our model to a single attack on AES in this paper, it can also be used for other symmetric ciphers like DES. The main contribution of our model to the field is that it can be used to quantitatively analyze the cost of trace-driven attacks on different implementations of a cipher. Therefore, we can analyze the effectiveness of various mitigations that can be used against such attacks. Thus, a designer can use our model to determine which mitigations she needs to implement against trace-driven attacks to achieve a predetermined security level.

P. Ning, S. Qing, and N. Li (Eds.): ICICS 2006, LNCS 4307, pp. 112–121, 2006.

2   Background and Previous Work

The feasibility of the cache based side-channel attacks, abbreviated to "cache attacks" from here on, was first mentioned by Kocher and then Kelsey et al. in [10,11]. D. Page described and simulated a theoretical cache attack on DES [16]. Actual cache based timing attacks were implemented by Tsunoo et al. [18,19]. The original attack on MISTY1 proposed in [19] has recently been improved in [20].

Although, cache side-channel threat had been known for a couple of years, the first efficient and realistic attacks were not developed until 2005. Bernstein showed the vulnerability of AES software implementations on various platforms [4]. There was a common belief that Bernstein's attack is a realistic remote attack and it can recover an entire AES key. However, Neve et al. showed in [13] that this is only a fallacy. They described the circumstances in which the attack might work and also the limitations of the Bernstein attack. A realistic general remote cache attack was developed by Acıiçmez et al [3].

Osvik et al. described various local cache attack variants in [15]. They made use of a local array and exploited the collisions between the table lookups and the access operations to this array. Neve et al. improved these attacks by taking the last AES round into consideration [14]. The same idea of exploiting collisions between two different processes was also used by Colin Percival in [17] to develop an attack on RSA.

Similar to external collisions between different processes, the internal collisions inside a cipher can also be taken advantage of. Internal cache collisions were first used in [18] and [19]. The attacks presented in [3,12,6] are also based on internal collisions.

There are three different types of cache attacks, namely time-driven, trace-driven, and access-driven. Time-driven and trace-driven attacks were first described by Page in [16]. Access-driven attacks are relatively new and first seen in [15]. The difference between these attack types are the capabilities of the adversary.

The adversary is assumed to be able to capture the profile of the cache activity during an encryption in trace-driven attacks. This profile includes the outcomes of every memory access the cipher issues in terms of cache hits and misses. Therefore, the adversary has the ability to observe if a particular access to a lookup table yields a hit and can infer information about the lookup indices, which are key dependent. This ability gives an adversary the opportunity to make inferences about the secret key.

Time-driven attacks, on the other hand, are less restrictive because they do not rely on the ability of capturing the outcomes of individual memory accesses. Adversary is assumed to be able to observe the aggregate profile, i.e., total numbers of cache hits and misses or at least a value that can be used to approximate these numbers. For example, the total execution time of the cipher can be measured and used to make inferences about the number of cache misses in a time-driven cache attack.

In access-driven attacks, the adversary can determine the cache sets that the cipher process modifies. Therefore, she can understand which elements of the lookup tables or S-boxes are accessed by the cipher. Then, the wrong key assumptions that would cause an access to unaccessed parts of the tables can be eliminated.

2.1 Overview of Trace-Driven Cache Attacks

Trace-driven attacks on AES were first presented in [12,5]. Bertoni et al. implemented a cache based power attack that exploits external collisions between different processes [5]. Their attack requires 256 power traces to reveal the secret AES key. Lauradoux's power attack exploits the internal collisions inside the cipher but only considers the first round AES accesses and can reduce the exhaustive search space of a 128-bit AES key to 80 bits.

We described much more efficient trace-driven attacks on AES in [2]. Our two-round attack is a known-plaintext attack and exploits the collisions among the first two rounds of AES. A more efficient version, which we call the last round attack, considers last round accesses and is a known-ciphertext attack. Due to the space limitation, we only present our last round attack in this paper.

In trace-driven cache attacks, the adversary obtains the traces of cache hits and misses for a sample of encryptions and recovers the secret key of a cryptosystem using this data. We define a trace as a sequence of cache hits and misses. For example,

$$MHHM, HMHM, MMHM, HHMH, MMMM, HHHH$$

are examples of a trace of length 4. Here H and M represents a cache hit and miss respectively. The first one in the first example is a miss, second one is a hit, and so on. If an adversary captures such traces, she can determine whether a particular access during an encryption is a hit or a miss.

The trace of an encryption can be captured by the use of power consumption measurements as done in [5,12]. In this paper, we do not get into the details of how to capture cache traces. We analyze trace-driven attacks on AES under the assumption that the adversary can capture the traces of AES encryption. This assumption corresponds to clean measurements in a noiseless environment. In reality, an adversary may have noise in the measurements in some circumstances, in which case the cost of the attack may increase depending on the amplitude of the noise. However, an analysis under the above assumption gives us a more clear understanding of the attack cost. Assumption of a noiseless environment also enables us to make more reliable comparison of different attacks.

In a side-channel attack, there are essentially two different phases:

– Online Phase: consists of the collection of side-channel information of the target cipher. This phase is also known as the sampling phase of the attack. The adversary encrypts or decrypts different input values and measures the side-channel information, e.g., power consumption or execution time of the device.

- Offline Phase: is also known as the analysis phase. In this phase, the adversary processes the data collected in the online phase and makes predictions and verifications regarding the secret value of the cipher.

An adversary usually performs the former phase completely before the latter one. However, in some cases, especially in adaptive chosen-text attacks (e.g. [7,1]), these two phases may overlap and may be performed simultaneously.

We use two different metrics to evaluate the cost of our last round attack presented in this paper. The first metric is *the expected number of traces* that we need to capture to narrow the search space of the AES key down to a certain degree. The second metric is *the average number of operations* we need to perform to analyze the captured traces and eliminate the wrong key assumptions. These metrics basically represent the cost of the online and offline phases of our attack. As the reader can clearly see in this paper, there is a trade-off between the costs of these two phases.

3   Trace-Driven Cache Attacks on the AES

In this paper, we present a trace-driven attack on the most widely used implementation of AES, and estimate its cost. We assume that the cache does not contain any AES data prior to each encryption, because the captured traces cannot be accurate otherwise. Therefore, the adversary is assumed to clean the cache (e.g., by loading some garbage data as done in [5,19,18,15,17]) before the encryption process starts.

Another assumption we make is that the data in AES lookup tables cannot be evicted from the cache during the encryption once they are loaded into the cache. This assumption means that each lookup table can only be stored in a different non-overlapping location of the cache and there is no context-switch during an encryption or any other process that runs simultaneously with the cipher and evicts the AES data. These assumptions hold if the cache is large enough, which is the case for most of the current processors. An adversary can also discard a trace if a context-switch occurs during the measurement.

We also assume that each measurement is composed of the cache trace of a single message block encryption. In this paper, we only consider AES with 128-bit key and block sizes. Our attack can easily be adapted to longer key and block sizes; however we omit these cases for the sake of simplicity.

The implementation we analyze is described in [9] and it is suitable for 32-bit architectures. It employs 4 different lookup tables in the first 9 rounds and a different one in the last round. In this implementation, all of the component functions, except AddRoundKey, are combined into four different tables and the rounds turn to be composed of table lookups and bitwise exclusive-or operations.

The S-box lookups in the final round are implemented as table lookups to another 1KB-large table , called T4, with 256 many 32-bit elements. Four repetations of the same 8-bit long Sbox element are concatenated to each other to form the corresponding 32-bit long element of T4. There are 16 accesses to T4 in that round. The indices of these accesses are S_w^{10}, where S_w^t is the byte w of the intermediate state value that becomes the input of round t and $w \in \{0, .., 15\}$. Let C be the ciphertext, i.e. the output of the last round, and represented as an array of 16 bytes, $C = (c_0, c_1, ..., c_{15})$. Individual bytes of C are computed as:

$$c_i = Sbox[I_i] \oplus RK_i^{10} ,$$

where RK_i^{10} is the ith byte of the last round key, $Sbox[I_i]$ is the S-box output for the input index I_i, and $I_i = S_w^{10}$ for known $w, i \in \{0, 1, ..., 15\}$.

I_i is equal to S_w^{10} for known values of i and w, but the actual mapping between these variables is not relevant for our purposes. In this paper, we present our attack under the assumption that the AES memory accesses in the last round are issued by the processor in a given order, i.e., first T4$[I_0]$, second T4$[I_1]$, etc. However, the actual order is implementation specific and may differ from our assumption. Our attack can easily be adapted to any given order without any performance loss. We also need to mention that the S-box in AES implements a permutation, and therefore its inverse, i.e. $Sbox^{-1}$, exists.

The outcomes of the last round accesses to T4 leak information about the values of the last round key bytes, i.e., RK_i^{10} where $i \in \{0, .., 15\}$. For example, if the second access to T4 results in a cache hit, we can conclude that the indices I_0 and I_1 are equal. If it is a cache miss, then the inequality of these values becomes true. We can use this fact to find the correct round key bytes RK_0^{10} and RK_1^{10} as the following.

We can write the value of I_i in terms of RK_i^{10} and c_i:

$$I_i = Sbox^{-1}[c_i \oplus RK_i^{10}] ,$$

If I_0 and I_1 are equal, so are $Sbox^{-1}[c_0 \oplus RK_0^{10}]$ and $Sbox^{-1}[c_1 \oplus RK_1^{10}]$, which also mandates the equality of $c_0 \oplus RK_0^{10}$ and $c_1 \oplus RK_1^{10}$. This equality can also be written as

$$c_0 \oplus RK_0^{10} = c_1 \oplus RK_1^{10} \Rightarrow c_0 \oplus c_1 = RK_0^{10} \oplus RK_1^{10}$$

Since the value of C is known to the attacker, $RK_0^{10} \oplus RK_1^{10}$ can directly be computed from the values of c_0 and c_1 if the second access to T4 results in a cache hit. In case of a cache miss, we can replace the $=$ sign in the above equations with $\neq$ and we can use the inequalities to eliminate the values that cannot be the correct value of $RK_0^{10} \oplus RK_1^{10}$.

In a real environment, even if the index of the second access to a certain lookup table is different than the index of the first access, a cache hit may still occur. Any cache miss results in the transfer of an entire cache line, not only one element, from the main memory. Therefore, whenever an access retrieves an element, which lies in the same cache line of the previously accessed data, a cache hit occurs.

Let δ be the number of bytes in a cache line and assume that each element of the table is k bytes long. Under this situation, there are δ/k elements in each line, which means any access to a specific element will map to the same line with $(\delta/k - 1)$ different other accesses. If two different accesses to the same array read the same cache line, the most significant parts of their indices, i.e., all of the bits except the last $\ell = \log_2(\delta/k)$ bits, must be identical.

Therefore, we observe a cache hit in the second access to T4 whenever

$$\langle I_0 \rangle = \langle I_1 \rangle \,,$$

and so

$$\langle Sbox^{-1}[c_0 \oplus RK_0^{10}] \rangle = \langle Sbox^{-1}[c_1 \oplus RK_1^{10}] \rangle \,,$$

where $\langle A \rangle$ stands for the most significant part of A. However due to the non-linearity of the AES S-box, only the correct RK_0^{10} and RK_1^{10} values obey the above equation for every ciphertext sample. Therefore, we can find the correct RK_0^{10} and RK_1^{10} values instead of their difference. This increases the search space of this initial guessing problem from 8 bits to 16 bits. However, once we find these round key bytes, we only need to search through 8 bits to find each of the remaining round key bytes.

The value of RK_2^{10} can also be determined by analyzing the first three accesses to T4 after the correct values of RK_0^{10} and RK_1^{10} are found. Similarly, if we extend our focus to the first four accesses, we can find RK_3^{10}. Then we can find RK_4^{10} and so on. After revealing the entire round key, it becomes trivial to compute the actual secret key, because the key expansion of the AES cipher is a reversible function.

We want to explain some details of our attack that are not mentioned above. We call all possible values that can be the correct value of a round key byte as the hypotheses of that particular round key byte or shortly round key byte hypotheses. Incorrect values are called wrong hypotheses. Initially all of the 256 possible values are considered as the round key byte hypotheses for a particular round key byte. During the course of the attack, we distinguish some of these values as wrong hypotheses; thus decrease the number of hypotheses and increase that of wrong hypotheses.

In our attack, we consider each access to T4 separately, starting from the second one. The first access is always a miss because of the cache cleaning and the assumptions explained above. We start a search on all possible hypotheses of (RK_0, RK_1) pair by assigning $RK_0 = x$, $RK_1 = y$ and checking whether (x, y) obeys the captured traces, $x, y \in \{0, ..., 255\}$. We then eliminate the wrong hypotheses those do not obey the traces. Then we extend our focus to the third access and perform a similar search on $((RK_0, RK_1), RK_2)$. Again we eliminate the wrong hypotheses of RK_2 for each remaining (RK_0, RK_1) pairs and end up only with (RK_0, RK_1, RK_2) values those obey the traces. We continue this method by considering fourth access and so on. After we determine all of the round key hypotheses actually obeying the traces, we perform an exhaustive search on the final remaining set. The above method is the same as AC-3 algorithm, which is an optimal propogation algorithm for binary constraints just like our case.

4   Analysis of the Attacks

In this section we estimate the number of traces need to be capture to recover the secret key. In other words, we determine the cost of the attack presented above. We first present a computational model that allows us to determine the cost of trace-driven attacks and then we use this model to perform the cost analysis of the proposed attack.

4.1   Our Model

Let m be $2^{(8-\ell)}$, i.e. the number of blocks in a table. A block of elements of a lookup table that are stored together in a single cache line is defined as a block of this table. The cost of a trace-driven attack is a function of m. The two most common values of m are 16 and 32 today and thus we evaluate the cost of the attacks for these two values of m.

In order to calculate the expected number of traces, first we need to find an equation that gives us the expected number of table blocks that are loaded into the cache after the first k accesses. We denote this expected number as $\#_k$.

The probability of being a single table block not loaded into the cache after k accesses to this table is $(\frac{m-1}{m})^k$. The expected number of blocks that are not loaded becomes $m * (\frac{m-1}{m})^k$. Therefore,

$$\#_k = m - m * (\frac{m-1}{m})^k .$$

Let $R^k_{expected}$ be the expected fraction of the wrong key hypotheses that obeys a captured trace in k^{th} step of the attack. In other words, a wrong key hypothesis that generated the same trace with the correct key in the first k accesses of an encryption has a chance of generating the captured outcome for the next access with a probability of $R^k_{expected}$. Therefore, if the adversary captures the outcomes of the first $(k + 1)$ accesses $(1 \le k \le 15)$ to T4 during a single encryption, she can eliminate $(1 - R^k_{expected})$ fraction of the wrong key hypotheses in the kth step of the attack, where

$$R^k_{expected} = \frac{\#_k}{m} * \frac{\#_k}{m} + (1 - \frac{\#_k}{m}) * (1 - \frac{\#_k}{m}) , 1 \le k \le 15 .$$

Notice that $R^k_{expected}$ is not the kth power of a constant $R_{expected}$ here, but it is defined as a variable that is specified by the parameter k. The left (right) side of the above summation is the product of the probability of a cache hit (miss, resp.) and the expected ratio of the wrong hypotheses that remain after eliminating the ones that do not cause a hit (miss, resp.).

Figure.1 shows the approximations of $R^k_{expected}$ and $\#_k$ for different values of k and m. We want to mention again that these values are experimentally verified. The differences between the calculated and empirical values of $R^k_{expected}$ are less than 0.2% in average. We can use these values to find the expected number of remaining wrong key hypotheses after t measurements or the expected number of measurements to reduce the key space down to a specific number or in any such calculations.

k	m=32		m=16	
	$R^k_{expected}$	$\#_k$	$R^k_{expected}$	$\#_k$
1	0.939453	1.000000	0.882813	1.000000
2	0.884523	1.968750	0.787140	1.937500
3	0.834806	2.907227	0.709919	2.816406
4	0.789923	3.816376	0.648487	3.640381
5	0.749522	4.697114	0.600528	4.412857
6	0.713273	5.550329	0.564035	5.137053
7	0.680868	6.376881	0.537265	5.815988
8	0.652021	7.177604	0.518709	6.452488
9	0.626464	7.953304	0.507063	7.049208
10	0.603946	8.704763	0.501197	7.608632
11	0.584236	9.432739	0.500138	8.133093
12	0.567116	10.137966	0.503050	8.624775
13	0.552384	10.821155	0.509209	9.085726
14	0.539850	11.482994	0.517999	9.517868
15	0.529340	12.124150	0.528890	9.923002

Fig. 1. The calculated values of $\#_k$ and $R_{expected}$ for different values of m

4.2   Trade-Off Between Online and Offline Cost

There is an obvious trade-off between online and offline cost of the attack. If an adversary can capture a higher number of traces, it becomes easier to find the key. Eliminating more wrong hypotheses in early steps reduces the cost of the later steps. The change in the offline cost of the attack with the number of captured traces can be seen in Figure.2.

As shown in the figure, the last round attack requires only 5 measurements to reduce the computational effort of breaking the entire 128-bit key below the recommended minimum security levels (c.f. [8]). NSA and NIST recommends a minimum key length of 80 bits for symmetric ciphers so that the computational effort of an exhaustive search should not be lower than 2^{80}.

5   Experimental Details

We performed experiments to test the validity of the values we have presented above. The results show a very close correlation between our model and empirical results and confirm the validness of our model and calculations.

Bertoni et al. showed that the cache traces could be captured by measuring power consumption [5]. In our experimental setup, we did not measure the power consumption, instead we assumed the correctness of their argument. We simply modified the AES source code of OpenSSL. The purpose of our modifications was not to alter the execution of the cipher, but to store the values of the access indices. These index values were then used to generate the cache traces. This process allows us to capture the traces and obtain the empirical results.

We generated one million randomly chosen cipherkeys and encrypted 100 random plaintext under each of these keys. In other words, we performed the

m=16		m=32	
Number of traces	Cost $\approx$	Number of traces	Cost $\approx$
1	$2^{117.68}$	1	$2^{120.93}$
5	$2^{74.51}$	5	$2^{90.76}$
10	$2^{35.12}$	10	$2^{56.16}$
20	$2^{24.22}$	20	$2^{33.97}$
30	$2^{21.36}$	30	$2^{27.77}$
40	$2^{20.08}$	40	$2^{24.88}$
50	$2^{19.46}$	50	$2^{23.25}$
75	$2^{19.13}$	75	$2^{21.22}$
100	$2^{19.12}$	100	$2^{20.39}$

Fig. 2. The cost analysis results of the last round attack

attack steps with 100 random plaintext. After each encryption, we determined the ratio of the number of remaining wrong key hypotheses to the number of wrong key hypotheses that were present before the encryption. We call this ratio the reduction ratio, which is denoted as $R^k_{expected}$. We calculated the average of these measured values. Our results show very close correlation between the measured and calculated values. The average difference between the empirical and calculated values of $R^k_{expected}$, i.e, the error rate, is less than 0.2%. The calculated $R^k_{expected}$ values are given in Subsection 4.1.

6 Conclusion

We have presented a trace-driven cache attack on the most widely used software implementation of AES cryptosystem. We have also developed a mathematical model, accuracy of which is experimentally verified, to evaluate the cost of the proposed attack. We have analyzed the cost using two different metrics, each of which represents the cost of a different phase of the attack.

Our analysis shows that such trace-driven attacks are very efficient and require very low number of encryptions to reveal the secret key of the cipher. To be more specific, an adversary can reduce the strength of 128-bit AES cipher below the recommended minimum security level by capturing the traces of only 5 encryptions. Having more traces reduces the total cost of the attack significantly. Our results also show this trade-off between the online and offline cost of the attack in detail.

References

1. O. Acıiçmez, W. Schindler, and Ç. K. Koç. Improving Brumley and Boneh Timing Attack on Unprotected SSL Implementations. Proceedings of the 12th ACM Conference on Computer and Communications Security, pages 139-146, Alexandria, Virginia, November 7-11, 2005.
2. O. Acıiçmez and Ç. K. Koç. Trace-Driven Cache Attacks on AES. Cryptology ePrint Archive, Report 2006/138, 2006.

3. O. Acıiçmez, W. Schindler, and Ç. K. Koç. Cache Based Remote Timing Attack on the AES, Topics in Cryptology - CT-RSA 2007, The Cryptographers' Track at the RSA Conference 2007, to appear.
4. D. J. Bernstein. Cache-timing attacks on AES. April, 2005. Available at: http://cr.yp.to/antiforgery/cachetiming-20050414.pdf
5. G. Bertoni, V. Zaccaria, L. Breveglieri, M. Monchiero, and G. Palermo. AES Power Attack Based on Induced Cache Miss and Countermeasure. International Symposium on Information Technology: Coding and Computing - ITCC 2005, Volume 1, 4-6 April 2005, Las Vegas, Nevada, USA.
6. J. Bonneau and I. Mironov. Cache-Collision Timing Attacks against AES. Cryptographic Hardware and Embedded Systems - CHES 2006, to appear.
7. D. Brumley and D. Boneh. Remote Timing Attacks are Practical. Proceedings of the 12th Usenix Security Symposium, pages 1-14, 2003.
8. Cryptographic Key Length Recommendation. Available at: http://www.keylength.com
9. J. Daemen and V. Rijmen. "The Design of Rijndael". Springer-Verlag, 2002.
10. J. Kelsey, B. Schneier, D. Wagner, and C. Hall. Side Channel Cryptanalysis of Product Ciphers. Journal of Computer Security, vol.8, pages 141-158, 2000.
11. P. C. Kocher. Timing Attacks on Implementations of Diffie–Hellman, RSA, DSS, and Other Systems. Advances in Cryptology - CRYPTO '96, N. Koblitz, editors, pages 104-113, Springer-Verlag, LNCS Nr. 1109, 1996.
12. C. Lauradoux. Collision attacks on processors with cache and countermeasures. Western European Workshop on Research in Cryptology - WEWoRC 2005, C. Wolf, S. Lucks, and P.-W. Yau, editors, pages 76-85, 2005.
13. M. Neve, J.-P. Seifert, and Z. Wang. A refined look at Bernstein's AES side-channel analysis. Proceedings of ACM Symposium on Information, Computer and Communications Security - ASIACCS'06, Taipei, Taiwan, March 21-24, 2006.
14. M. Neve and J.-P. Seifert. Advances on Access-driven Cache Attacks on AES. Selected Areas of Cryptography - SAC'06, to appear.
15. D. A. Osvik, A. Shamir, and E. Tromer. Cache Attacks and Countermeasures: The Case of AES. Topics in Cryptology - CT-RSA 2006, The Cryptographers' Track at the RSA Conference 2006, D. Pointcheval, editor, pages 1-20, Springer-Verlag, LNCS Nr. 3860, 2006.
16. D. Page. Theoretical Use of Cache Memory as a Cryptanalytic Side-Channel. Technical Report CSTR-02-003, Department of Computer Science, University of Bristol, June 2002.
17. C. Percival. Cache missing for fun and profit. BSDCan 2005, Ottawa, 2005. Available at: http://www.daemonology.net/hyperthreading-considered-harmful/
18. Y. Tsunoo, T. Saito, T. Suzaki, M. Shigeri, and H. Miyauchi. Cryptanalysis of DES Implemented on Computers with Cache. Cryptographic Hardware and Embedded Systems - CHES 2003, C. D. Walter, Ç. K. Koç, and C. Paar, editors, pages 62-76, Springer-Verlag, LNCS Nr. 2779, 2003.
19. Y. Tsunoo, E. Tsujihara, K. Minematsu, and H. Miyauchi. Cryptanalysis of Block Ciphers Implemented on Computers with Cache. ISITA 2002, 2002.
20. Y. Tsunoo, E. Tsujihara, M. Shigeri, H. Kubo, and K. Minematsu. Improving cache attacks by considering cipher structure. International Journal of Information Security, February 2006.

A Construction for General and Efficient Oblivious Commitment Based Envelope Protocols

Jiangtao Li[1,*] and Ninghui Li[2]

[1] Intel Corporation, 2111 NE 25th Avenue, Hillsboro, OR 97124
jiangtao.li@intel.com
[2] Department of Computer Science, Purdue University, West Lafayette, IN 47907
ninghui@cs.purdue.edu

Abstract. The notion of Oblivious Commitment Based Envelope (OCBE) was recently proposed; it enables attribute-based access control without revealing any information about the attributes. Previous OCBE protocols are designed by taking zero-knowledge proof protocols that prove a committed value satisfies some property and changing the protocols so that instead of one party proving to the other party, the two parties compute two keys that agree if and only if the committed value indeed satisfy the property. In this paper, we introduce a more general approach for designing OCBE protocols that uses zero-knowledge proof protocols in a black-box fashion. We present a construction such that given a zero-knowledge proof protocol that proves a committed value satisfies a predicate, we have an OCBE protocol for that predicate with constant additional cost. Compared with previous OCBE protocols, our construction is more general, more efficient, and has wide applicability.

1 Introduction

In attribute-based access control systems, access decisions are based on attributes of the requester, which are established by digitally signed certificates through which certificate issuers assert their judgements about the attributes of entities. Each certificate associates a public key with the key holder's identity and/or attributes such as employer, group membership, credit card information, date of birth, citizenship, and so on. Because these certificates are digitally signed, they can serve to introduce strangers to one another without online contact with the attribute authorities. In many scenarios, the attribute information in a certificate is sensitive and needs to be protected. The requester may want to disclose only the information that is absolutely necessary to obtain the resource from the server.

Recently, Li and Li [20] proposed a cryptographic primitive called Oblivious Commitment Based Envelope (OCBE) that enables oblivious access control; that is, it enables attribute-based access control without revealing any information about the attributes. Informally, in an OCBE scheme, the receiver has a private attribute value a which has been committed to the sender; the sender has a public predicate b (i.e., her access control policy) and a private message M. The sender and the receiver engage in an interactive protocol such that in the end, the receiver gets the message M if and only

---

* Most of this work was done while the author was at Purdue University.

P. Ning, S. Qing, and N. Li (Eds.): ICICS 2006, LNCS 4307, pp. 122–138, 2006.

if her attribute value satisfies the predicate, i.e., $b(a) = $ true. Furthermore, the sender learns nothing about the receiver's attribute value. Formal definition of OCBE will be reviewed in Section 2.

Li and Li [20] developed OCBE protocols for the Pedersen commitment scheme [25] and predicates such as $=, \neq, <, >, \leq, \geq$ as well as logical combinations of them. Their approach for designing the OCBE protocols is to take zero-knowledge proof protocols that prove a committed value satisfies some property and change the protocols so that instead of one party proving to the other party, the two parties compute two keys that agree if and only if the committed value indeed satisfy the property.

In this paper, we introduce a more general approach for designing OCBE protocols. Rather than taking zero-knowledge proof protocols and finding ways to change them, we use these protocols in a black box fashion. The basic idea is as follows. The receiver first sends a commitment of another attribute value to the sender, and then uses zero-knowledge proof protocols to prove that the committed value in the new commitment satisfies the policy. Finally, the receiver and the sender run a protocol such that the receiver can retrieve the message if and only if the values in the two commitments are the same, and the sender does not learn whether the two committed values are the same.

We apply this approach to the commitment scheme introduced by Fujisaki and Okamoto [17] and later extended by Damgård and Fujisaki [14]. We prove that our protocol is secure under the Strong RSA assumption and the Computational Diffie-Hellman assumption modulo an RSA modulus in the Random Oracle Model.

Compared with previous work [20], our approach has the following advantages:

- Our OCBE construction achieves a general result; i.e., if there exists a zero-knowledge proof of knowledge protocol that can prove a committed value satisfies a predicate, then we can build an OCBE protocol for that predicate with constant additional cost. As a result, one does not need develop new OCBE protocols for each new families of predicates from the scratch and prove their security. Instead, one can directly take advantage of the existence of efficient zero-knowledge proof protocols for properties of committed values.
- Our OCBE protocol is more efficient than the previous OCBE protocols [20]. The OCBE protocols in [20] for the comparison predicates other than the equality predicates have linear computation and communication costs; i.e., both the sender and the receiver need to perform $O(\ell)$ modular exponentiations where ℓ is the maximum length of the receiver's attribute. In comparison, our OCBE protocol has constant computation cost for comparison predicates.
- Unlike the OCBE protocols in [20] where the input range for the receiver is limited to $\mathbb{Z}_q$, where q is a prime; the set of the receiver's committed input in our OCBE protocol can be $\mathbb{Z}$, the set of all integers. This feature is particularly important for linear relation predicates, i.e., to test whether a committed value satisfies a linear relation over $\mathbb{Z}$.
- Our OCBE protocols are compatible with the anonymous credentials [24,8,11]. The OCBE scheme in [20] is designed primarily for Oblivious Attribute Certificates (OACerts) [20] and is not compatible with the anonymous credential systems. The reason is that, in [20], the commitment is computed by the trusted third party rather

than the receiver. We modify the definition of OCBE to let the receiver commit, so that the new definition is compatible with the anonymous credentials.

The rest of this paper is organized as follows. We first give our notations and review the definition of OCBE in Section 2. We next review in Section 3 cryptographic assumptions and tools that we use. In Section 4, we present our OCBE protocol and prove that it is secure. In Section 5, we describe how the OCBE protocol can be applied in attribute-based access control systems and automated trust negotiation systems, in particular, we show how our OCBE protocol can be used together with the anonymous credentials. We discuss the related work in Section 6 and conclude our paper in Section 7.

2   Review the Definition of OCBE

2.1   Notation

In the rest of this paper, we use the following notations. We say that $\mu(k)$ is a negligible function, if for every polynomial $p(k)$ and for all sufficiently large k, $\mu(k) < 1/p(k)$. We say $\nu(k)$ is overwhelming if $1 - \nu(k)$ is negligible.

If S is a probability space, then the probability assignment $x \leftarrow S$ means that an element x is chosen at random according to S. If S is a finite set, then $x \leftarrow S$ denotes that x is chosen uniformly from S. Let A be an algorithm, we use $y \leftarrow A(x)$ to denote that y is obtained by running A on input x. In case A is deterministic, then y is unique; if A is probabilistic, then y is a random variable. Let A and B be interactive Turing machines, we use $(a \leftarrow A(\cdot) \leftrightarrow B(\cdot) \rightarrow b)$ to denote that a and b are two random variables corresponding to the outputs of A and B as a result of their joint computation.

Let p be a predicate and $A_1, A_2, \ldots, A_n$ be n algorithms, We use $\Pr\left[\{x_i \leftarrow A_i(y_i)\}_{1 \leq i \leq n} : p(x_1, \cdots, x_n)\right]$ to denote the probability that $p(x_1, \cdots, x_n)$ will be true after running sequentially algorithms $A_1, \ldots, A_n$ on inputs $y_1, \ldots, y_n$.

2.2   Definition of OCBE

We now briefly review the definition of OCBE [20]. We slightly modify the definition to make the OCBE scheme compatible with the anonymous credential schemes. The difference between our new definition and the OCBE definition in [20] is that, in our new definition, we let the sender to commit rather than the trusted third party. Please refer to Section 5 for the detailed explanation. Note that, our OCBE protocol presented in Section 4 works both this new definition and the original definition in [20].

Definition 1 (OCBE). An OCBE scheme is parameterized by a commitment scheme commit. An OCBE scheme involves a sender, a receiver, and a trusted third party, and has the following four phases:

Setup. The trusted third party takes a security parameter k and outputs public parameters P for commit, a set S of possible values, and a set B of predicates (i.e., boolean functions). Each predicate $b \in B$ maps each element in S to either true or false. The domain of commit contains S as a subset. The trusted third party sends $\langle P, S, B \rangle$ to the sender and the receiver.

Initialization. The receiver chooses a value $a \in S$, computes the commitment $c = \text{commit}(a, r)$ where r is a random number, and sends c to the sender. The sender chooses a message $M \in \{0, 1\}^*$ and a predicate $b \in B$ and then reveals b to the receiver.

The sender has b, c, and M. The receiver has a, b, c, and r.

Interaction. The sender and the receiver run an interactive protocol, during which an envelope containing an encryption of M is delivered to the receiver.

Open. After the interaction phase, if $b(a)$ is true, the receiver outputs the message M. Otherwise, the receiver does nothing.

Note that, in the initialization phase, it is crucial for the sender to reveal the predicate b after the receiver has committed a. Otherwise, the receiver could choose a value a' that satisfies the predicate and commit a' rather than a, so that she can always open the envelope and obtain M in the end.

An OCBE scheme must satisfy the following three properties [20]. It must be sound, oblivious, and semantically secure against the receiver.

Sound. An OCBE scheme is *sound* if in the case that $b(a)$ is true and both the sender and the receiver are honest, the receiver can output the message M with overwhelming probability.

Oblivious. An OCBE scheme is *oblivious* if the sender learns nothing about a. More precisely, no adversary sender $\mathcal{A}$ has a non-negligible advantage against the challenger $\mathcal{C}$ in the following game: $\mathcal{C}$ first runs the setup program and sends $\langle P, S, B \rangle$ to $\mathcal{A}$. Then $\mathcal{A}$ chooses a random message $M \in \{0, 1\}^*$, two values $a_0, a_1 \in S$, and a predicate $b \in B$, and sends a_0, a_1, b to $\mathcal{C}$. Next $\mathcal{C}$ chooses randomly $a \in \{a_0, a_1\}$, computes the commitment c for a, and interacts with $\mathcal{A}$ by emulating the receiver. In the end, $\mathcal{A}$ outputs $a' \in \{a_0, a_1\}$. The adversary wins the game if $a = a'$. An OCBE scheme is oblivious if

$$\left| \Pr \left[a' \leftarrow \mathcal{A}(1^k) \leftrightarrow \mathcal{C}(1^k) \rightarrow a : a' = a \right] - 1/2 \right| = \mu(k)$$

where the symbols $\leftarrow, \leftrightarrow, \rightarrow$ are defined in Section 2.1, and $\mu(k)$ is negligible function in k. In other words, the adversary cannot do substantially better than random guessing whether the receiver's committed value is a_0 or a_1.

Secure against the receiver. An OCBE scheme is *secure against the receiver* if the receiver learns nothing about M when $b(a)$ is false. More precisely, no adversary sender $\mathcal{A}$ has a non-negligible advantage against the challenger $\mathcal{C}$ in the following game: $\mathcal{C}$ first runs the setup program and sends $\langle P, S, B \rangle$ to $\mathcal{A}$. Then $\mathcal{A}$ chooses a value $a \in S$ and a value r^1, computes the commitment $c = \text{commit}(a, r)$, and sends a, r, c to $\mathcal{C}$. $\mathcal{A}$ also chooses two equal length messages $M_0, M_1 \in \{0, 1\}^*$ and sends M_0, M_1 to $\mathcal{C}$. Next, $\mathcal{C}$ chooses a predicate $b \in B$ such that $b(a)$ equals to false, chooses randomly a message $M \in \{M_0, M_1\}$, and interacts with $\mathcal{A}$ by emulating the sender. In the end, $\mathcal{A}$ outputs

---

[1] In [20], r is chosen by the challenger rather than the adversary. This is because in the original definition of OCBE [20], the trusted third party chooses r; whereas in our new definition, the receiver chooses r and computes the commitment.

$M' \in \{M_0, M_1\}$. The adversary wins the game if $M = M'$. An OCBE scheme is secure against the receiver if

$$| \Pr\left[M' \leftarrow \mathcal{A}(1^k) \leftrightarrow \mathcal{C}(1^k) \rightarrow M : M' = M \right] - 1/2 | = \mu(k)$$

where $\mu(k)$ is negligible function in k. In other words, even if we give the adversary the power to pick two equal-length messages M_0 and M_1 of her choice, she still cannot distinguish an envelope containing M_0 from one containing M_1.

3   Cryptographic Assumptions and Tools

In this section, we first review some standard assumptions in cryptography that we use, then review two cryptographic tools that shall be used in our OCBE protocol, one is the integer commitment scheme, the other is zero-knowledge proofs of knowledge.

3.1   Security Assumptions

In the rest of this paper, we shall use the following cryptographic assumptions and models, namely, the computational Diffie-Hellman assumption, the strong RSA assumption, and the random oracle model. The strong RSA assumption was introduced by Barić and Pfitzmann [3] and has been used in proving the security of many cryptographic schemes (e.g., [17,10], to list a few).

Computational Diffie-Hellman (CDH) Assumption. Given a finite cyclic group G, a group generator g, and group elements g^a, g^b; there exists no polynomial-time algorithm that can compute g^{ab} with non-negligible probability.

Strong RSA Assumption. Given an RSA modulus n and a random value x in $\mathbb{Z}_n^*$, there exists no polynomial-time algorithm that can compute $e > 1$ and $y \in \mathbb{Z}_n^*$ with non-negligible probability such that $y^e = x \bmod n$.

Random Oracle Model. The random oracle model is an idealized security model introduced by Bellare and Rogaway [5]. Roughly speaking, a random oracle is a function $H : X \rightarrow Y$ chosen uniformly at random from the set of all functions $\{h : X \rightarrow Y\}$. Random oracles are used to model cryptographic hash functions such as SHA-1.

3.2   Integer Commitment Scheme

Our OCBE protocol use the following integer commitment scheme introduced by Fujisaki and Okamoto [17] and later extended by Damgård and Fujisaki [14]. The reasons we choose this integer commitment scheme instead of the Pedersen commitment scheme [25] used in [20] are that: first, the input domain of this commitment scheme is the set of all integers rather than a set of values in a group; and second, this commitment scheme supports efficient proof that a committed value lies in a given interval [6]. This second feature shall be used to construct efficient OCBE protocol for greater-than-or-equal-to predicates.

Definition 2 (Integer Commitment Scheme)

Setup. This step takes a security parameter k and outputs a special RSA modulus $n = pq$, such that $p = 2p'+1$ and $q = 2q'+1$ where p, q, p', q' are primes. It also outputs $h \leftarrow QR_n$ and $g \leftarrow \langle h \rangle$, where QR_n is the set of quadratic residues modulo n and $\langle h \rangle$ is the group generated by h. The public parameters of this commitment scheme are (n, g, h).

Commit. The domain of the committed values is $\mathbb{Z}$. To commit an integer $a \in \mathbb{Z}$, the prover chooses $r \leftarrow \mathbb{Z}$ and computes the commitment $c = \text{commit}(a, r) = g^a h^r \bmod n$.

Open. To open a commitment c, the prover reveals a and r; then the verifier verifies whether $c = g^a h^r \bmod n$.

The integer commitment scheme is *statistically hiding*: under the factoring assumption, $\text{commit}(a, r)$ statistically reveals no information to the verifier. More formally, there exists a simulator which outputs simulated commitments to a which are statistically indistinguishable from true commitments to a. This commitment scheme is *computationally binding*: the prover cannot commit herself two distinct values a_0 and a_1 by the same commitment unless she can factorize n. In other words, under the factoring assumption, it is computationally infeasible for the prover to compute a_0, a_1, r_0, r_1 where $a_0 \neq a_1$ such that $\text{commit}(a_0, r_0) = \text{commit}(a_1, r_1)$.

3.3 Zero-Knowledge Proofs of Knowledge

We now list a few known proof of knowledge protocols based on the Fujisaki and Okamoto commitment scheme. In the rest of this paper, all the computations are modulo n unless explicitly specified.

- Proof of knowledge on how to open a commitment [14]. That is, given the parameters (n, g, h) of the integer commitment scheme and a commitment c, the prover proves the knowledge of a and r such that $c = g^a h^r$. We denote the protocol as

$$PK\{(a, r) : c = g^a h^r\}$$

- Proof that a committed value is equal to a given integer [14]. That is, given the parameters (n, g, h) of the integer commitment scheme, a commitment c, and an integer a_0; the prover proves the knowledge of a and r such that $c = g^a h^r$ and $a = a_0$. We denote the protocol as

$$PK\{(a, r) : c = g^a h^r \wedge a = a_0\}$$

- Proof that a committed value lies in a given integer interval [6]. That is, given the parameters (n, g, h) of the integer commitment scheme, a commitment c, and integers a_0 and a_1; the prover proves the knowledge of a and r such that $c = g^a h^r$ and $a_0 \leq a \leq a_1$. We denote the protocol as

$$PK\{(a, r) : c = g^a h^r \wedge a_0 \leq a \leq a_1\}$$

- Proof that a committed value is the product of two other committed values [14]. That is, given the parameters (n, g, h) of the integer commitment scheme and three commitments c, c_0, c_1, the prover proves the knowledge of a_0, a_1, r, r_0, r_1 such that $c = g^{a_0 a_1} h^r$, $c_0 = g^{a_0} h^{r_0}$, and $c_1 = g^{a_1} h^{r_1}$. We denote the protocol as

$$PK\{(a_0, a_1, r, r_0, r_1) : c = g^{a_0 a_1} h^r \wedge c_0 = g^{a_0} h^{r_0} \wedge c_1 = g^{a_1} h^{r_1}\}$$

- Proof that a committed value has a linear relation with n committed values [14]. That is, given the parameters (n, g, h) of the integer commitment scheme, $n + 1$ commitments $c, c_1, \ldots, c_n$, and integers $z_0, z_1, \ldots, z_n$; the prover proves the committed values $a, a_1, \ldots, a_n$ satisfy the equation $a = z_0 + a_1 z_1 + \cdots + a_n z_n$. We denote the protocol as

$$PK\{\begin{matrix} (a, r, a_1, r_1, \ldots, a_n, r_n) : \{c_i = g^{a_i} h^{r_i}\}_{1 \leq i \leq n} \wedge c = g^a h^r \wedge \\ a = z_0 + a_1 z_1 + \cdots + a_n z_n \end{matrix}\}$$

All the above described protocols have constant computational and communication costs. These protocols are secure under the strong RSA assumption.

4   Our OCBE Protocol

In this section, we first present a construction that turns any zero-knowledge proof protocol that proves a committed value satisfies some predicate into an OCBE protocol for that predicate. Then we prove that our protocol is secure and compare our protocol with the several OCBE protocols described in [20].

4.1   Construction of OCBE Protocol

In [20], Li and Li developed several OCBE protocols for comparison predicates, i.e., one OCBE protocol for each type of predicates. In this paper, we present a more general and more efficient result:

Our result. Let S be a set of integers and B be a set of predicates, such that each predicate $b \in B : S \rightarrow \{\text{true, false}\}$. Let commit be an integer commitment scheme described in Section 3.2. Suppose for every predicate $b \in B$, there exists an efficient zero-knowledge proof of knowledge protocol that can prove a committed value $a \in S$ satisfies the predicate b, i.e., $PK\{(a, r) : c = \text{commit}(a, r) \wedge b(a) = \text{true}\}$. Then with constant additional cost, we can develop an efficient OCBE protocol for predicates set B.

Before we present the OCBE protocol, we briefly describe the intuition how the protocol works. Let (n, g, h) be the public parameters of the integer commitment scheme, a be the receiver's private input, c be the corresponding commitment. Consider the following scheme: If $b(a)$ is true, The receiver first proves to the sender that the value committed in c satisfies the predicate b; then the sender sends the message M to the receiver. Such scheme is secure against the receiver, but not oblivious; i.e., the sender learns some information about a.

In our proposed scheme, if $b(a)$ is true, then the receiver chooses $a' = a$; otherwise, she chooses a' such that $b(a') = $ true. Then the receiver commits a' to the sender; i.e., she chooses r, computes $c' = g^{a'} h^{r'}$, and gives c' to the sender. The receiver also proves that the value committed in c' satisfies the predicate b. Observe that the sender learns nothing about a — all she learns so far is that the value committed under c' satisfies b. Also note that, if $b(a)$ is true, then $a = a'$ and $c/c' = g^a h^r / g^{a'} h^{r'} = h^{r-r'}$; otherwise, $c/c' = g^{a-a'} h^{r-r'}$. In other words, if $b(a)$ is true, the receiver has the knowledge of $\log_h(c/c')$. The sender can use this fact to build a Diffie-Hellman style key-agreement, so that only $b(a)$ is true can the receiver obtain the encryption key.

Protocol 1 (OCBE). Let E be a semantically secure symmetric encryption scheme with keyspace $\{0,1\}^s$. Let $H : \mathbb{Z}_n \to \{0,1\}^s$ be a cryptographic hash function that extracts a key for E from an element in the group $\mathbb{Z}_n$. The OCBE protocol involves a sender, a receiver, and a trust third party.

Setup. The trusted third party takes a security parameter k and runs the setup algorithm of the integer commitment scheme in Section 3.2 to create $P = (n, g, h)$. The third party also outputs an integer set $S \subseteq \mathbb{Z}$, and a set B of predicates. For each $b \in B$, $b : S \to \{\text{true}, \text{false}\}$. The trusted third party sends $\langle P, S, B \rangle$ to the sender and the receiver.

Suppose for each $a \in S$ and $b \in B$, if $b(a) = $ true, there is an efficient zero-knowledge proof of knowledge protocol $\text{PK}\{(a, r) : c = g^a h^r \wedge b(a) = \text{true}\}$.

Initialization. The receiver chooses a value $a \in S$ and a value $r \in \mathbb{Z}$, computes the commitment $c = g^a h^r$, and sends c to the sender. The sender chooses a message $M \in \{0,1\}^*$ and a predicate $b \in B$ and then reveals b to the receiver. The sender has b, c, and M. The receiver has a, b, c, and r.

Interaction. The sender and the receiver run the following steps:

1. If $\forall a \in S, b(a) = $ false; then the sender and the receiver terminate the protocol immediately.

2. If $b(a) = $ true, the receiver set $a' = a$, otherwise the receiver randomly chooses a' such that $b(a') = $ true. The receiver chooses $r' \leftarrow \mathbb{Z}$ and computes the commitments $c' = g^{a'} h^{r'}$. The receiver sends c' to the sender.

3. The sender and the receiver runs the zero-knowledge proof of knowledge protocol

$$\text{PK}\{(a', r') : c' = g^{a'} h^{r'} \wedge b(a') = \text{true}\}$$

   to prove that the value committed in c' satisfies the predicate b.

4. The sender picks $y \leftarrow \mathbb{Z}_n$, computes $\sigma = (c/c')^y$, and then sends to the receiver the pair $\langle \eta = h^y, C = E_{H(\sigma)}[M] \rangle$.

Open. The receiver receives $\langle \eta, C \rangle$ from the interaction phase. If $b(a) = $ true, in other words $a = a'$, the receiver computes $\sigma' = \eta^{r-r'}$, decrypts C using $H(\sigma')$, and obtains M.

Observe that the computational cost of the above OCBE protocol is close to the cost of the zero-knowledge proof sub-protocol. More specifically, suppose in the zero-knowledge proof sub-protocol, the sender and the receiver need to perform ℓ_s and ℓ_v modular exponentiations, respectively; then in the OCBE protocol, the sender and the receiver need to perform at most $\ell_s + 2$ and $\ell_v + 1$ modular exponentiations, respectively.

4.2 Security Proofs

Our OCBE protocol invokes the zero-knowledge proof protocol $PK\{(a,r) : c = g^a h^r \wedge b(a) = \text{true}\}$ as a sub-protocol. We here need to examine the security properties of this zero-knowledge proof protocol, before we prove the security of the OCBE protocol. The security definition of a zero-knowledge proof of knowledge protocol derives from Bellare and Goldreich [4].

Given a commitment c and a predicate b as input. Let R be a polynomially computable relation defined as, given a and r, $R(a,r,c,b) = 1$ if and only if $c = g^a h^r$ and $b(a) = \text{true}$. A zero-knowledge proof of knowledge of witness (a,r) such that $R(a,r,c,b) = 1$ is a probabilistic polynomial-time protocol between a prover P and a verifier V with the following properties:

1. Completeness: For all possible a and r such that $R(a,r,c,b) = 1$

$$\Pr\left[P(a,r,c,b) \leftrightarrow V(c,b) \to x : x = \text{accept}\right] = 1 - \mu(k),$$

   where $\mu(k)$ is a negligible function.

2. Zero-knowledge: Intuitively, the verifier should not learn any information about a and r other than the fact that $R(a,r,c,b) = 1$. Formally speaking, there exists a probabilistic, expected polynomial-time simulator S such that, for every probabilistic polynomial-time verifier V_k, for all $(a,r,c,b) \in R$, the distribution $P(a,r,c,b) \leftrightarrow V_k(c,b)$ and $S(c,b) \rightarrowtail V_k(c,b)$ are computationally indistinguishable, where $S \rightarrowtail V$ means S has black-box access to algorithm V.

3. Soundness: Intuitively, if the prover does not know (a,r) such that $R(a,r,c,b) = 1$, the probability that the prover can convince the honest verifier is negligible. More formally, for all (c,b), for all probabilistic polynomial-time prover P_k, if there is a function $\epsilon(k)$ such that

$$\Pr\left[P_k(c,b) \leftrightarrow V(c,b) \to x : x = \text{accept}\right] = \epsilon(k);$$

   then there exists a polynomial-time extractor E and a negligible function $\mu(k)$ such that

$$\Pr\left[P_k(c,b) \leftarrowtail E(c,b) \to (a,r) : R(a,r,c,b) = 1\right] = \epsilon(k) - \mu(k).$$

   In other words, if the prover can convince the verifier with probability $\epsilon(k)$, then the extractor can compute (a,r) with probability close to $\epsilon(k)$.

Theorem 1. *The OCBE protocol in Section 4.1 is sound.*

Proof. To show the OCBE protocol is sound, we consider two cases. In the first case, suppose for any $a \in S \Rightarrow b(a) = \text{false}$, then both the sender and the receiver know that the receiver should not receive M, as the receiver's input will never satisfy the predicate b. Therefore, the sender and the receiver simply quit the protocol on step 1 of the interaction phase. In the second case, there exists some $a \in S$ such that $b(a) = \text{true}$. In this case, steps 2-4 of the interaction phase will be executed. By the completeness property of the zero-knowledge proof protocol, the zero-knowledge proof protocol almost always succeeds. If the value a committed by the receiver satisfies the predicate b, then $a' = a$. It follows that

$$\sigma = (c/c')^y = (g^{a-a'} h^{r-r'})^y = (h^{r-r'})^y = (h^y)^{r-r'} = \eta^{r-r'} = \sigma'.$$

The sender and the receiver share the same symmetric key that is used to encrypt the message M. Therefore, if $b(a) = \text{true}$, the receiver can obtain the message M.

Theorem 2. *The OCBE protocol in Section 4.1 is oblivious.*

Proof. An OCBE scheme is oblivious if the sender learns nothing about the value the receiver committed. Let us first see which messages the sender receives during the initialization and interaction phases. In the initialization phase, the sender receives c, the commitment of a, from the receiver. In the interaction phase, the sender receives from the receiver c', the commitment of a'. The sender also involves in the zero-knowledge proof protocol $\text{PK}\{(a', r') : c' = g^{a'} h^{r'} \wedge b(a') = \text{true}\}$ as the verifier.

More formally, an OCBE scheme is oblivious if we can show that the view of the sender can be simulated. We build a simulator S as follows: Given a set S of integers and a predicate b, S chooses a random number $a_0 \leftarrow S$ and computes the commitment $c_0 = \text{commit}(a_0)$. Then S chooses another value $a_0' \leftarrow S$ such that $b(a_0') = \text{true}$ and computes the commitment $c_0' = \text{commit}(a_0')$. Finally, S calls the simulator for the zero-knowledge proof protocol. As the commitment scheme is statistically hiding, the joint distribution of (c, c') is statistically indistinguishable from the joint distribution of (c_0, c_0'). By the zero-knowledge property of the zero-knowledge proof protocol, it is easy that the transcripts generated by the sender when interacting with the receiver is computationally indistinguishable with the transcripts generated by the simulator S. Therefore, the OCBE protocol is oblivious.

Theorem 3. *The OCBE protocol in Section 4.1 is secure against the receiver.*

Proof. The preceding OCBE protocol uses a semantically secure symmetric encryption algorithm. Suppose H is modeled as a random oracle, the OCBE protocol is secure against the receiver when no receiver, whose committed value does not satisfy the predicate b, can compute with non-negligible probability the secret that the sender uses to derive the encryption key.

More precisely, the OCBE protocol is secure against the receiver if no polynomial-time adversary wins the following game against the challenger with non-negligible probability: The challenger runs the setup phase and sends $\langle P, S, B \rangle$ to the adversary, where $P = (n, g, h)$ is the public parameter of the integer commitment scheme. The adversary picks integers $a \in S$ and $r \in \mathbb{Z}$, computes the commitment $c = g^a h^r$, and sends a, r, and c to the challenger. The challenger responds by picking a predicate $b \in B$ such that $b(a) = \text{false}$. The adversary chooses a value a' such that $b(a') = \text{true}$, chooses $r \in \mathbb{Z}$, and computes $c' = g^{a'} h^{r'}$. The adversary sends c' to the challenger and also runs $\text{PK}\{(a', r') : c' = g^{a'} h^{r'} \wedge b(a') = \text{true}\}$ to prove that the value committed in c' satisfies the predicate b. The challenger then picks $y \leftarrow \mathbb{Z}_n$ and sends to the adversary h^y. The adversary then outputs σ, and the adversary wins the game if $\sigma = (c/c')^y$.

By the soundness property of the zero-knowledge proof protocol, the challenger can extract a' and r' from the zero-knowledge proof using the standard rewinding technique. That is, we can replace the zero-knowledge proof protocol in the above game with that the adversary sends a', r', and c' to the challenger. Note that, as $b(a) = $ false and $b(a') = $ true, it follows that $a \neq a'$. Also note that, since the challenger runs the setup program of the integer commitment scheme, she knows how to factorize n.

Given an attacker $\mathcal{A}$ that wins the above game with probability ϵ, we construct another attacker $\mathcal{B}$ that can solve the computational Diffie-Hellman problem in $\langle h \rangle$, the group generated by h, with the same probability. $\mathcal{B}$ does the following:

1. $\mathcal{B}$, when given p, q, h, h^x, h^y where $n = pq$ is a special RSA modulus used in the commitment scheme and h is an element in QR_n, gives $P = (n, h^x, h)$, $S = \mathbb{Z}$, and B to $\mathcal{A}$. We use g to denote h^x.
2. $\mathcal{B}$ receives a, r, and c from $\mathcal{A}$, and verifies that $c = g^a h^r$. $\mathcal{B}$ chooses a predicate $b \in B$ such that $b(a) = $ false and sends b to $\mathcal{A}$.
3. $\mathcal{B}$ receives a', r', and c' from $\mathcal{A}$. $\mathcal{B}$ verifies that $c' = g^{a'} h^{r'}$ and $b(a') = $ true. Then $\mathcal{B}$ sends h^y to $\mathcal{A}$.
4. $\mathcal{B}$ receives σ from $\mathcal{A}$, computes $\tau = \sigma h^{(r'-r)y}$ and outputs $\tau^{(a-a')^{-1} \bmod \phi(n)}$. If $\mathcal{A}$ wins the game, we get

$$\sigma = (c/c')^y = (g^{a-a'} h^{r-r'})^y = (g^y)^{a-a'} h^{(r-r')y}$$

$$\tau = \sigma h^{(r'-r)y} = (g^y)^{a-a'} = (h^{xy})^{a-a'}$$

$\mathcal{B}$ outputs $\tau^{(a-a')^{-1} \bmod \phi(n)} = h^{xy}$.

$\mathcal{B}$ succeeds in solving the computational Diffie-Hellman problem if and only if $\mathcal{A}$ wins the above game, i.e., successfully compute $(c/c')^y$. Therefore, under the CDH assumption, the OCBE protocol is secure against the receiver.

4.3   Comparison with Previous OCBE Protocols

To compare the OCBE protocol with the OCBE protocols proposed by Li and Li [20], we first list all families of predicates that our OCBE protocol supports. All the zero-knowledge proof protocols listed below are summarized in Section 3.3; and they have constant computation and communication costs.

– *Equality Predicates*: Let B be the family of equality predicates. Each predicate b in B takes a_0 as a parameter, and $b(a)$ is equal to true if and only if $a = a_0$. As there exists an efficient zero-knowledge proof protocol

$$PK\{(a, r) : c = g^a h^r \land a = a_0\},$$

we can build an efficient OCBE protocol for this family of predicates. In this OCBE protocol, the receiver can open the sender's message if and only if her committed number a is equal to a_0.

- *Greater-Than-Or-Equal-To Predicates*: Let B be the family of Greater-Than-Or-Equal-To predicates. Each predicate b in B takes a_0 as a parameter, and $b(a)$ is equal to true if and only if $a \geq a_0$. As there exists an efficient zero-knowledge proof protocol

$$PK\{(a, r) : c = g^a h^r \,\wedge\, a \geq a_0\},$$

we can build an efficient OCBE protocol for this family of predicates. In this OCBE protocol, the receiver can open the sender's message if and only if her committed number a is greater than or equal to a_0.
- *Other Comparison Predicates*: Besides $=$ and $\geq$, the other comparison operations include $<, >, \leq, \neq$. Since there exists efficient zero-knowledge protocols for these comparison operations, the corresponding OCBE protocols can be built.
- *Range Predicates*: Let B be the family of range predicates. Each predicate b in B takes a_0 and a_1 as parameters, and $b(a)$ is equal to true if and only if $a_0 \leq a \leq a_1$. As there exists an efficient zero-knowledge proof protocol

$$PK\{(a, r) : c = g^a h^r \,\wedge\, a_0 \leq a \leq a_1\},$$

we can build an efficient OCBE protocol for this family of predicates. In this OCBE protocol, the receiver can open the sender's message if and only if her committed number a is in the range of (a_0, a_1).
- *Square Predicate*: Given an input a, this predicate outputs true if and only if a is a square, i.e., $a = x^2$ for some integer x. Note that

$$PK\{(a, r, x) : c = g^a h^r \,\wedge\, a = x^2\}$$

can be constructed using the zero-knowledge proof that a committed value is the product of two other committed values as

$$PK\{(a, r, x, r_x) : c = g^a h^r \,\wedge\, c_x = g^x h^{r_x} \,\wedge\, a = x \cdot x\}$$

Therefore, we can build an efficient OCBE protocol for the square predicate. In this OCBE protocol, the receiver can open the sender's message if and only if her committed number a is a square number.
- *Modular Equality Predicates*: Let B be the family of range predicates. Each predicate b in B takes z_0 and z_1 as parameters, and $b(a)$ is equal to true if and only if $a \equiv z_0 \pmod{z_1}$. For example, if $z_0 = 0$ and $z_1 = 2$, this predicate tests whether a is an even number. Note that

$$PK\{(a, r) : c = g^a h^r \,\wedge\, a \equiv z_0 \pmod{z_1}\}$$

can be constructed using the zero-knowledge proof that a committed value has a linear relation with another committed value as

$$PK\{(a, r, x, r_x) : c = g^a h^r \,\wedge\, c_x = g^x h^{r_x} \,\wedge\, a = z_0 + x z_1\}$$

Therefore, we can build an efficient OCBE protocol for this family of predicates. In this OCBE protocol, the receiver can open the sender's message if and only if her committed number a is equal to z_0 modulo z_1.

In Table 1, we give a detailed comparison between our OCBE protocols and the OCBE protocols developed by Li and Li [20]. For equality predicates, the OCBE protocol in [20] is slightly better than ours, although they have the same complexity. For other comparison predicates and range predicates, the OCBE protocols in [20] are more expensive than ours, i.e., their protocols have linear cost whereas ours require only constant computation. Also note that the OCBE protocols for the square predicate and the modular equality predicates are first developed in this paper.

Table 1. Comparison between the OCBE protocols in [20] with our OCBE protocol in terms of computation and communication costs. In the table, ℓ is the length of the committed value, $*$ denotes that such predicates are not supported in the OCBE protocols.

	OCBE Protocols in [20]	Our OCBE Protocols
Equality Predicates	$O(1)$	$O(1)$
Other Comparison Predicates	$O(\ell)$	$O(1)$
Range Predicates	$O(\ell)$	$O(1)$
Square Predicate	$*$	$O(1)$
Modular Equality Predicates	$*$	$O(1)$

5   Applications of Our OCBE Protocol

In this section, we discuss the applications of OCBE to attribute-based access control, right after we present how the OCBE protocol is used in access control systems.

5.1   How to Use the OCBE Protocol

Recall that in the initialization phase of an OCBE scheme, the receiver sends the commitment of her attribute to the sender. To use OCBE in attribute-based access control, the sender needs to make sure that the commitment from the receiver is indeed the commitment of the receiver's attribute. In other words, the receiver needs to show that the attribute committed to the sender is certified by a certificate authority. This can be done using either OACerts [20] or anonymous credentials [24,8,11].

OACerts. OACerts is a certificate scheme developed by Li and Li [20]. In the OACerts scheme, instead of storing attribute values directly in the certificate, a certificate authority stores the commitments of these values in the certificate. These commitments arc computed by the certificate authority. When the receiver interacts with the sender, she first reveals her OACerts; then she runs the OCBE protocol with the sender based on the commitments in the certificates.

Anonymous Credentials. An anonymous credential system [24,8,11] is a credential system in which the transactions carried out by the same user cannot be linked. In the anonymous credential system proposed by Camenisch and Lysyanskaya [8], the attributes of a user are signed by a certificate authority using a specially designed signature scheme. To show an attribute, the user commits the attribute and proves that the attribute in the commitment is the same as the attribute in the anonymous credential. When the receiver interacts with the sender, she first commits her attribute, then proves that the committed attribute is the same as in the anonymous credentials. In the end, the receiver runs the OCBE protocol with the sender based on that commitment. Note that the attribute is committed by the receiver, instead of by the certificate authority. That is the reason that, in the new definition of OCBE, the receiver chooses r and computes the commitment.

5.2 Applications to Attribute-Based Access Control

We list two applications of OCBE to attribute-based access control. The ideas of these applications come from [20]; we only sketch here.

Oblivious Access Control. Suppose Alice is a client and Bob is a server. Alice wants to access some resources from Bob whose policy is based on Alice's attribute. Alice can first show her OACerts or anonymous credentials, then based on commitment of her attribute, she runs an OCBE protocol with Bob. In the OCBE protocol, Bob sends Alice an encrypted envelope such that Alice could open the envelope only if her attribute satisfies Bob's policy. That is, Bob can perform access control based on Alice's attribute values while being oblivious about Alice's attribute information.

Breaking Policy Cycles. OCBE can be used to break policy cycles (see [23] for definition) in automated trust negotiation [29,28,30]. Consider the following scenario: Alice's policy is based on Bob's attribute and Bob's policy is based on Alice's attribute. As a result, none of them wants to reveal their attributes. Alice and Bob can run an OCBE protocol to break such cycles. See [22] for detailed discussions on how OCBE can be integrated into automated trust negotiation.

6   Related Work

An OCBE scheme can be seen as a special oblivious transfer. The oblivious transfer protocol was first introduced by Rabin [26]. In an oblivious transfer between Alice and Bob, Alice wants to send a message to Bob in such a way that with half probability Bob will receive the message, and with half probability Bob will receive nothing. Furthermore, Alice does not know which of the two events really happened.

Crescenzo, Ostrovsky, and Rajagopalan [13] introduced a variant of oblivious transfer called conditional oblivious transfer; in which Alice has a private input x_a and Bob has a private input x_b, they and shares with each other a public predicate b that evaluates over x_a and x_b. In the conditional oblivious transfer of a message M from Alice to Bob, Bob receives M only when the predicate holds, i.e., $b(x_a, x_b) = $ true; furthermore, Alice learns nothing about x_b or $b(x_a, x_b)$. OCBE is different from conditional oblivious transfer in that, in OCBE, Bob's private input is committed to Alice. Besides, the conditional oblivious transfer protocol for great-than-or-equal-to predicates [13] has the computation cost linear to the size of x_a and x_b, whereas our OCBE protocol for great-than-or-equal-to predicates has constant time performance.

Crépeau [12] introduced the notion of committed oblivious transfer. In committed oblivious transfer, Alice commits two bits: a_0 and a_1, and Bob commits a bit b. All three commitments are shared by Alice and Bob. In the end, Bob learns a_b without learning anything else, and Alice learns nothing. Garay, MacKenzie, and Yang [18] gave an efficient construction of committed oblivious transfer under the universal composability framework. OCBE differs from committed oblivious transfer in that Bob's input is an arbitrary integer rather than a single bit.

Our work is also somewhat related to several cryptographic schemes that have been recently proposed for attribute-based access control. For example, oblivious signature based envelopes [23], hidden credentials [7,19], secret handshakes [2,9], pairing-based cryptography [27], anonymous identification [15], certified input private policy evaluation [21], hidden policies with hidden credentials [16], and policy-based cryptography [1] were proposed to address the privacy issues in access control, in particular, these schemes can be used to protect the requester's identities or attributes.

7 Conclusion

The OCBE scheme has been proved to be a useful primitive for privacy protection in attribute-based access control. In this paper, we improved the OCBE protocols in [20] and gave an efficient and general construction of OCBE. Our construction replies on the existence of efficient zero-knowledge proof of knowledge protocols that prove a committed value satisfying certain predicate. Our construction is secure under the CDH assumption and the strong RSA assumption in the random oracle model.

Acknowledgement

This work is supported by NSF IIS-0430274, NSF CCR-0325951, and sponsors of CERIAS. We thank the anonymous reviewers for their helpful comments.

References

1. Walid Bagga and Refik Molva. Policy-based cryptography and applications. In *Proceedings of the 9th International Conference on Financial Cryptography and Data Security*, February 2005.
2. Dirk Balfanz, Glenn Durfee, Narendar Shankar, Diana Smetters, Jessica Staddon, and Hao-Chi Wong. Secret handshakes from pairing-based key agreements. In *Proceedings of the IEEE Symposium and Security and Privacy*, pages 180–196, May 2003.
3. Niko Barić and Birgit Pfitzmann. Collision-free accumulators and fail-stop signature schemes without trees. In *Advances in Cryptology: EUROCRYPT '97*, volume 1233 of *LNCS*, pages 480–494. Springer, 1997.
4. Mihir Bellare and Oded Goldreich. On defining proofs of knowledge. In *Advances in Cryptology: CRYPTO '92*, volume 740 of *LNCS*, pages 390–420. Springer, 1992.
5. Mihir Bellare and Phillip Rogaway. Random oracles are practical: A paradigm for designing efficient protocols. In *Proceedings of the 1st ACM Conference on Computer and Communications Security*, pages 62–73. ACM Press, 1993.
6. Fabrice Boudot. Efficient proofs that a committed number lies in an interval. In *Advances in Cryptology: EUROCRYPT '00*, volume 1807 of *LNCS*, pages 431–444, May 2000.
7. Robert Bradshaw, Jason Holt, and Kent Seamons. Concealing complex policies with hidden credentials. In *Proceedings of 11th ACM Conference on Computer and Communications Security*, pages 146–157, October 2004.

8. Jan Camenisch and Anna Lysyanskaya. An efficient system for non-transferable anonymous credentials with optional anonymity revocation. In *Advances in Cryptology: EUROCRYPT '01*, volume 2045 of *LNCS*, pages 93–118. Springer, 2001.

9. Claude Castelluccia, Stanislaw Jarecki, and Gene Tsudik. Secret handshakes from CA-oblivious encryption. In *Advances in Cryptology: ASIACRYPT '04*, pages 293–307, December 2004.

10. Ronald Cramer and Victor Shoup. Signature schemes based on the strong RSA assumption. In *Proceedings of the 6th ACM Conference on Computer and Communications Security*, pages 46–51. ACM Press, November 1999.

11. Jason Crampton and George Loizou. Administrative scope and role hierarchy operations. In *Proceedings of 7th ACM Symposium on Access Control Models and Technologies*, pages 145–154, June 2002.

12. Claude Crépeau. Verifiable disclosure of secrets and applications (abstract). In *Advances in Cryptology: EUROCRYPT '89*, volume 434 of *LNCS*, pages 150–154. Springer, 1990.

13. Giovanni Di Crescenzo, Rafail Ostrovsky, and S. Rajagopalan. Conditional oblivious transfer and timed-release encryption. In *Advances in Cryptology: EUROCRYPT '99*, volume 1592 of *LNCS*, pages 74–89, March 1999.

14. Ivan Damgård and Eiichiro Fujisaki. An integer commitment scheme based on groups with hidden order. In *Advances in Cryptology: ASIACRYPT '02*, volume 2501 of *LNCS*, pages 125–142. Springer, December 2002.

15. Yevgeniy Dodis, Aggelos Kiayias, Antonio Nicolosi, and Victor Shoup. Anonymous identification in ad hoc groups. In *Advances in Cryptology: EUROCRYPT 2004*, pages 609–626, May 2004.

16. Keith B. Frikken, Mikhail J. Atallah, and Jiangtao Li. Hidden access control policies with hidden credentials. In *Proceedings of the 3rd ACM Workshop on Privacy in the Electronic Society*, October 2004.

17. Eiichiro Fujisaki and Tatsuaki Okamoto. Statistical zero knowledge protocols to prove modular polynomial relations. In *Advances in Cryptology: CRYPTO '97*, volume 1294 of *LNCS*, pages 16–30. Springer, 1997.

18. Juan Garay, Philip MacKenzie, and Ke Yang. Efficient and universally composable committed oblivious transfer and applications. In *Theory of Cryptography, TCC 2004*, volume 2951 of *LNCS*, pages 297–316. Springer, 2004.

19. Jason E. Holt, Robert W. Bradshaw, Kent E. Seamons, and Hilarie Orman. Hidden credentials. In *Proceedings of the 2nd ACM Workshop on Privacy in the Electronic Society*, pages 1–8, October 2003.

20. Jiangtao Li and Ninghui Li. OACerts: Oblivious attribute certificates. In *Proceedings of the 3rd Conference on Applied Cryptography and Network Security*, volume 3531 of *LNCS*, pages 301–317. Springer, June 2005.

21. Jiangtao Li and Ninghui Li. Policy-hiding access control in open environment. In *Proceedings of the 24nd ACM Symposium on Principles of Distributed Computing*, pages 29–38. ACM Press, July 2005.

22. Jiangtao Li, Ninghui Li, and William H. Winsborough. Automated trust negotiation using cryptographic credentials. In *Proceedings of the 12th ACM Conference on Computer and Communications Security*, pages 46–57. ACM Press, November 2005.

23. Ninghui Li, Wenliang Du, and Dan Boneh. Oblivious signature-based envelope. In *Proceedings of the 22nd ACM Symposium on Principles of Distributed Computing*, pages 182–189. ACM Press, July 2003.

24. Anna Lysyanskaya, Ronald L. Rivest, Amit Sahai, and Stefan Wolf. Pseudonym systems. In *Proceedings of the 6th Workshop on Selected Areas in Cryptography*, volume 1758 of *LNCS*, pages 184–199. Springer, 1999.

25. Torben P. Pedersen. Non-interactive and information-theoretic secure verifiable secret sharing. In *Advances in Cryptology: CRYPTO '91*, volume 576 of *LNCS*, pages 129–140. Springer, 1991.
26. Michael O. Rabin. How to exchange secrets by oblivious transfer. Technical Report Memo TR-81, Aiken Computation Laboratory, Harvard University, 1981.
27. Nigel Smart. Access control using pairing based cryptography. In *Proceedings of the Cryptographers' Track at the RSA Conference 2003*, pages 111–121. Springer-Verlag LNCS 2612, April 2003.
28. William H. Winsborough and Ninghui Li. Safety in automated trust negotiation. In *Proceedings of the IEEE Symposium on Security and Privacy*, pages 147–160, May 2004.
29. William H. Winsborough, Kent E. Seamons, and Vicki E. Jones. Automated trust negotiation. In *DARPA Information Survivability Conference and Exposition*, volume I, pages 88–102. IEEE Press, January 2000.
30. Ting Yu, Marianne Winslett, and Kent E. Seamons. Supporting structured credentials and sensitive policies through interoperable strategies for automated trust negotiation. *ACM Transactions on Information and System Security*, 6(1):1–42, February 2003.

Defining and Measuring Policy Coverage in Testing Access Control Policies

Evan Martin, Tao Xie, and Ting Yu

Department of Computer Science
North Carolina State University
Raleigh, NC 27695
eemartin@ncsu.edu,
{xie,yu}@csc.ncsu.edu
http://ase.csc.ncsu.edu

Abstract. To facilitate managing access control in a system, security officers increasingly write access control policies in specification languages such as XACML, and use a dedicated software component called a Policy Decision Point (PDP). To increase confidence on written policies, certain types of policy testing (often in an ad hoc way) are usually conducted, which probe the PDP with some typical requests and check PDP's responses against expected ones. This paper develops a first step toward systematic policy testing by defining and measuring policy coverage when testing policies. We have developed a coverage-measurement tool to measure policy coverage given a set of XACML policies and a set of requests. We have developed a tool for request generation, which randomly generates requests for a given set of policies, and a tool for request reduction, which greedily selects a nearly minimal set of requests for achieving the same coverage as the originally generated requests. To evaluate coverage-based request reduction and its effect on fault detection, we have conducted an experiment with mutation testing on a set of real policies. Our experimental results show that the coverage-based test reduction can substantially reduce the size of generated requests and incur only relatively low loss on fault detection. We also conduct a study on the policy coverage achieved by manually generated requests.

1 Introduction

Access control is one of the most fundamental and widely used security mechanisms. It controls which principals (users, processes, etc.) have access to which resources in a system. To better manage access control, systems often explicitly specify access control policies using policy languages such as XACML [1] and Ponder [14]. Whenever a principal requests access to a resource, that request is passed to a software component called a Policy Decision Point (PDP). PDP evaluates the request against access control policies, and grants or denies the request accordingly.

The specification of access control policies is often a challenging problem. It is common that a system's security is compromised due to the misconfiguration of access control policies instead of the failure of cryptographic primitives or protocols. This problem becomes increasingly severe as software systems become more and more complex, and are deployed to manage a large amount of sensitive information and resources that are organized into sophisticated structures.

P. Ning, S. Qing, and N. Li (Eds.): ICICS 2006, LNCS 4307, pp. 139–158, 2006.

Formal verification is an important means to ensuring the correct specification of access control policies. Recently, several tools have been developed to verify XACML access control policies against user-specified properties [16, 22, 42]. However, it is often beyond the capabilities of these tools to verify complex access control policies in large-scale information systems. Furthermore, user-specified properties are often not available [16].

Like in software development, errors in access control policies may also be discovered through testing. In fact, once access control policies are specified, they are often tested with some access requests so that security officers may manually check the PDP's responses against expected ones [6]. However, current policy testing practice tends to be ad hoc. Although there exist various coverage criteria [43] for software programs, there are no criteria or good heuristics to guide systematic generation of high-quality policy test suites. With an ad hoc policy testing, it is questionable that high confidence could be gained on the correctness of access control policies.

This paper presents a first step toward systematic policy testing. We propose the concept of *policy coverage* to measure the quality of policy test suites, which are sets of request-response pairs. Intuitively, the more policy rules (as well as their components such as subjects, resources, and conditions) are involved when evaluating a test suite, the more likely it is to discover errors in access control policies. We have developed a coverage-measurement tool to measure the coverage of XACML policies achieved by a set of access requests. We have also developed a request-generation tool that randomly generates policy test suites for a given set of policies.

Although the randomly generated test suites can achieve high policy coverage, and are effective in detecting a variety of policy specification errors, it may potentially include a huge number of requests, which makes it difficult to efficiently inspect and verify the correctness of responses from the PDP. To mitigate this problem, we further propose a request reduction technique to significantly reduce the size of a test suite while maintaining its policy coverage.

Previous experiments [35] showed that test reduction based on program code coverage can severely compromise the fault-detection capabilities of the original test suite. To evaluate the impact of the proposed request reduction technique on the quality of policy testing, we conduct an experiment on a set of real policies with mutation testing [15], which is a specific form of fault injection that consists of creating faulty versions of a policy by making small syntactic changes. In the experiment, we compare the fault-detection capabilities of the reduced set and original set of requests. Our experimental results show that our coverage-based request reduction technique can substantially reduce the size of generated requests but incur only relatively low loss in fault detection capabilities. We also conduct a study that measures the policy coverage of an XACML conformance test suite as well as a conference reviewing system's policy. Our results show that the measurement of policy coverage can effectively identify uncovered parts of policies. Such results can be used to guide the development of further test cases, significantly improving the quality of policy testing.

The rest of the paper is organized as follows. Section 2 presents background information on XACML, a widely used and standardized meta policy language for expressing domain-specific access control requirements. Section 3 proposes the concept of policy testing and policy coverage based on a general access control model. In Section 4, we instantiate the concept of policy coverage in the context of XACML. We also present the design of a coverage measurement tool. Sections 5 and 6 describe the request-generation tool and our request reduction technique, respectively. Section 7 presents a set of initial mutation operators developed for policies. Section 8 presents the experiment conducted to assess request reduction and its effect on fault detection capabilities. Section 9 illustrates the study of measuring the policy coverage achieved by manually generated requests. Section 10 discusses related work and Section 11 concludes the paper with future directions.

2 XACML

XACML (eXtensible Access Control Markup Language) is a language specification standard designed by OASIS. It can be used to express domain-specific access control policy languages as well as access request languages. Besides offering a large set of built-in functions, data types, and combining logic, XACML also provides standard extension interfaces for defining application-specific features. Since it was proposed, XACML has received much attention from both the academia and the industry. Many domain-specific access control languages have been developed using XACML [32, 30]. Open source XACML implementations are also available for different platforms (e.g., Sun's XACML implementation [2] and XACML.NET [3]). Therefore, XACML provides an ideal platform for the development of policy testing techniques that can be easily applied to multiple domains and applications.

The basic concepts of access control in XACML include *policies*, *rules*, *targets*, and *conditions*. A single access control policy is represented by a policy element, which includes a target element and one or more rule elements. A target element contains a set of constraints on the subject (e.g., the subject's role is equal to faculty), resources (e.g., the resource name is grade), and actions (e.g., the action name is assign)[1]. A target specifies to what kinds of requests a policy can be applied. If a request cannot satisfy the constraints in the target, then the whole policy element can be skipped without further examining its rules.

We next describe how a policy is applied to a request in details. A policy element contains a sequence of rule elements. Each rule also has its own target, which is used to determine whether the rule is applicable to a request. If a rule is applicable, a *condition* (a boolean function) associated with the rule is evaluated. If the condition is evaluated to be true, the rule's *effect* (Permit or Deny) is returned as a *decision*; otherwise, NotApplicable is returned as a decision. If an error occurs when a request is applied against policies or their rules, Indeterminate is returned as a decision.

More than one rule in a policy may be applicable to a given request. To resolve conflicting decisions from different rules, a *rule combining algorithm* can be specified to combine multiple rule decisions into a single decision. For example, a deny overrides algorithm determines to return Deny if any rule evaluation returns Deny or no rule is applicable. A first applicable algorithm determines to return what the evaluation of

---

[1] Conditions of "AnySubject", "AnyResource", and "AnyAction" can be satisfied by any subject, resource, or action, respectively.

```
1<Policy PolicyId="demo" RuleCombinationAlgId="first-applicable">
2 <Target>
3    <Subjects> <AnySubjects/> </Subjects>
4    <Resources>
5     <Resource>
6      <ResourceMatch MatchId="equal">
7       <AttributeValue>demo:5</AttributeValue>
8       <ResourceAttributeDesignator AttributeId="objectid"/>
9      </ResourceMatch>
10     </Resource>
11    </Resources>
12    <Actions> <AnyAction/></Actions>
13 </Target>
14 <Rule RuleId="1" Effect="Deny">
15  <Target> <Subjects><AnySubject/></Subjects>
16    <Resources> <AnyResource/> </Resources>
17    <Actions>
18     <Action>
19      <ActionMatch MatchId="equal">
20       <AttributeValue>Dissemination</AttributeValue>
21       <ActionAttributeDesignator AttributeId="actionid"/>
22      </ActionMatch>
23     </Action>
24    </Actions>
25  </Target>
26  <Condition FunctionId="not">
27   <Apply FunctionId="at-least-one-member-of">
28    <SubjectAttributeDesignator AttributeId="loginid"/>
29    <Apply FunctionId="string-bag">
30     <AttributeValue>testuser1</AttributeValue>
31     <AttributeValue>testuser2</AttributeValue>
32     <AttributeValue>fedoraAdmin</AttributeValue>
33    </Apply>
34   </Apply>
35  </Condition>
36 </Rule>
37 <Rule RuleId="2" Effect="Permit"/>
38</policy>
```

Fig. 1. An example XACML policy

the first applicable rule returns. In general, an XACML policy specification may also include multiple policies, which are included with a container element called *PolicySet*. When a request can also be applied to multiple policies, a *policy combining algorithm* can also be specified in a similar way.

Figure 1 shows an example XACML policy, which is revised and simplified from a sample Fedora[2] policy (to be used in our experiment described in Section 8). This policy has one policy element which in turn contains two rules. The rule composition function is "first-applicable", whose meaning has been explained earlier. Lines 2-13 define the target of the policy, which indicates that this policy applies only to those access requests of an object "demo:5". The target of Rule 1 (Lines 15-25) further narrows the scope of applicable requests to those asking to perform a "Dissemination" action on object "demo:5". Its condition (Lines 26-35) indicates that if the subject's "loginId" is "testuser1", "testuser2", or "fedoraAdmin", then the request should be denied. Otherwise, according to Rule 2 (Line 37) and the rule composition function of the policy (Line 1), a request applicable to the policy should be permitted.

---

[2] http://www.fedora.info

3   Access Control Policies and Policy Coverage

Besides XACML, a generic policy language, many access control policy languages have been proposed for different application domains. Policies in these languages are usually composed of a set of rules, which specify under what conditions a subject is allowed or denied access to certain objects in a system. To discuss policy coverage criteria in general, we model access requests and policies in this paper as follows.

Let S, O and A denote respectively the set of all the subjects, objects and actions in an access control system. Each subject, object, or action is associated with a set of attributes that may be used for access control decisions. For example, a subject's attributes may include a user's role, rank, and security clearance. An object's attributes may include a file's type, a document's security class, and a printer's location.

An access request q is a tuple (s, o, a), where $s \in S$, $o \in O$ and $a \in A$. A request (s, o, a) means that subject s requests to take action a on object o.

An access control policy P is a sequence of rules, each of which is of the form $(Cond_s, Cond_o, Cond_a, decision, Cond_g)$. $Cond_s$, $Cond_o$ and $Cond_a$ are constraints over the attributes of a subject, object, and action, respectively. $Cond_g$ is a general constraint that may potentially be over all the attributes of subjects, objects, actions, and other properties of a system (e.g., the current time and the load of a system). A *decision* is either *deny* or *permit*. Given a request (s, o, a), if $Cond_s(s)$, $Cond_o(o)$, $Cond_a(a)$, and $Cond_g$ are all evaluated to be *true*, then the request is either permitted or denied, according to *decision* in the rule.

One may wonder that since $Cond_g$ can be a general constraint over the attributes of subjects, objects, and actions as well as other properties of a system, why do we still need $Cond_s$, $Cond_o$, and $Cond_a$ in a rule? The reason is that, although conceptually those conditions can be merged with the general condition $Cond_g$, by separating them, it makes it easy to quickly locate relevant rules to a request. For example, given a request (s, o, a), if one of $Cond_s$, $Cond_o$ and $Cond_a$ is evaluated to be false, then we do not need to further evaluate $Cond_g$ that sometimes may be much more complex than the former three. Such a form of access control rules is commonly supported in access control policy languages. If a request satisfies $Cond_s$, $Cond_o$ and $Cond_a$ of a rule, then we say the rule is *applicable* to the request.

A policy may have multiple rules that are applicable to a request. These rules may in fact offer conflicting decisions. The final decision regarding the request depends on application-specific conflict resolution functions. Commonly used conflict resolution functions include denial overriding permission (where a request is denied if it is denied by at least one rule), permission overriding denial (where a request is permitted if it is permitted by at least one rule) and first applicable (where the final decision is the same as that of the first applicable rule in a sequence of rules whose condition $Cond_g$ is evaluated true). We use PDP (Policy Decision Point) to denote the component of a system where final decisions are made according to the decision of each rule and a specific confliction resolution function. Conceptually, given a policy P and a request q, a PDP returns the access control decision of q.

Since we are interested in capturing potential errors in policy specifications, we assume that PDP is correctly implemented in the rest of the paper. In practice, generic PDP implementations are often available, which have been scrutinized by the public.

We next start our discussion on policy testing based on the preceding model. The basic idea of policy testing is simple. Like software testing, given a policy, we would like to generate a set of requests, and check whether the access control decisions on these requests are expected. Any unexpected decision indicates potential errors in the specification of the policy.

If no requests are evaluated against a rule during testing, then potential errors in that rule cannot be discovered. Thus, it is important to generate requests so that a large portion of rules are involved in the evaluation of at least one of the requests. In other words, we are interested in requests that cause a rule's conditions to be evaluated to be true. Recall that if a request satisfies $Cond_s$, $Cond_o$, and $Cond_a$ of a rule, then we say the rule is *applicable* to the request.

Definition 1. *Given a request q and a rule m in a policy P, we say q covers m if m is applicable to q. Given a set of requests Q, the rule coverage of P by Q is the ratio between the number of rules covered by at least one request in Q and the total number of rules in P.*

Intuitively, the higher the rule coverage of a set of requests, the better chance specification errors may be discovered. Like software testing, it is often infeasible to have exhausted policy testing when the space of possible requests is large. Therefore, policy specification errors may still exist even after testing with requests that cover all the rules.

To improve the quality of policy testing, it helps to further examine potential errors in the specification of conditions in each rule, which can also be tested by requests.

Definition 2. *Given a request q and a rule $m(Cond_s, Cond_o, Cond_a, decision, Cond_g)$, we say $Cond_g$ is positively (negatively) covered by q if m is covered by q and $Cond_g$ is evaluated to be true (false). Given a set of requests Q, the condition coverage of P by Q is the ratio between the numbers of general conditions positively or negatively covered by at least one request in Q and two times of the total number of rules in P.*

The intuition behinds the above definition is as follows. An error in the condition of a rule may have two types of impacts on a request. Suppose $Cond'_g$ is the condition when an error is introduced to the original condition $Cond_g$. Given a request q, $Cond'_g(q)$ may be evaluated to be true while $Cond_g(q)$ is false, or vice versa. That is why we concern with both positive and negative coverage of a condition in the preceding definition.

Our definition of condition coverage corresponds to clause coverage or condition coverage [33] in program testing. Note that there exist more complicated coverage criteria for logical expressions. For example, in program testing, predicate coverage (also called decision coverage or branch coverage) [33] requires to cover both true and false of compound conditions in a logical expression. In policy testing, predicate coverage requires that the whole compound condition for a rule needs to be evaluated to be true and false, respectively. In program testing, combinatorial coverage (also called multiple condition coverage) [33] requires to cover each possible combination of outcomes of each condition in a logical expression. In policy testing, combinatorial coverage requires to cover each possible combination of outcomes of each condition for a rule. In our existing approach, we use basic, simple criteria for conditions in rules; in future work, we plan to investigate these more complicated alternatives in terms of their effects on fault-detection capability.

4   Policy Coverage in XACML

In XACML languages, we can see there are three major entities: policies, rules for each policy, and a condition for each rule. We define policy coverage as follows:

- *Policy hit percentage.* A policy is hit by a request if the policy is applicable to the request; in other words, all the conditions in the policy's target are satisfied by the request. Policy hit percentage is the number of hit policies divided by the number of total policies.
- *Rule hit percentage.* A rule for a policy is hit by a request if the rule is also applicable to the request; in other words, the policy is applicable to the request and all the conditions in the rule's target are satisfied by the request. Rule hit percentage is the number of hit rules divided by the number of total rules.
- *Condition hit percentage.* The evaluation of the condition for a rule has two outcomes: true and false, which are called as the true condition and false condition, respectively. A true condition for a rule is hit by a request if the rule is applicable to the request and the condition is evaluated to be true. A false condition for a rule is hit by a request if the rule is applicable to the request and the condition is evaluated to be false. Condition hit percentage is the number of hit true conditions and hit false conditions divided by twice of the number of total conditions.

Note that a policy has at least one rule but a rule can have no condition, indicating an implicit condition `true`, which is always satisfied when the rule is applicable. Therefore, when there are no conditions defined within the policies under consideration, the condition hit percentage is always the same as the rule hit percentage. Normally a policy tester shall be able to generate requests to achieve 100% for all three types of policy coverage. In other words, all the to-be-covered entities defined in the policy coverage are feasible to be covered in principle; otherwise, those infeasible parts of policy specifications could be removed like dead code in programs.

To automate the measurement of policy coverage, we have developed a measurement tool by instrumenting Sun's open source XACML implementation [2]. Sun's implementation facilitates the construction of a PDP. We instrument several methods throughout their implementation that collect policy, rule, and condition information when a policy is loaded into the PDP. Then coverage information is collected and stored in a singleton as requests are evaluated by a PDP against the policy under test.

After the PDP returns the decision, we output the coverage information into a text file, whose name is determined by the names of given policies; if a text file with the same name exists, the coverage information in the text file is updated by incorporating the new coverage information. Therefore, when PDP receives several requests separately against the same set of policies, the aggregated coverage information achieved by these requests is collected. Besides the basic coverage information, we also output the details of covered entities and their covering requests as well as the details of uncovered entities. The extra information can help developers or external tools in generating or selecting requests for achieving higher policy coverage.

5   Request Generation

Because manually generating requests for testing policies is tedious, we have developed a technique for randomly generating requests given only the policy under test. The random request generator analyzes the policy under test and generates requests on demand by randomly selecting requests from the set of all combinations of attribute id-value pairs found in the policy. A particular request is represented as a vector of bits. The length of this vector is equal to the number of different attribute values found in the policy set targets,policy targets, rule targets, and rule conditions of the policy under test. Each attribute value appears in the request if its corresponding bit in the vector is 1; otherwise, the value is not present.

More specifically, all possible combinations can be represented by integers from 0 to 2^n where n is the number of attribute values found in the policy. Each request is generated by setting each bit in the vector to 0 or 1 with probability 0.5. The number of randomly generated requests can be configured by the user and the configured number can be considerably smaller than the total number of combinations. To help achieve adequate coverage with a small set of random requests, we modified the random test generation algorithm to ensure that each bit was set to 1 and 0 at least once. In particular, we explicitly set the ith bit to 1 for the first n generated requests where $i = 1, 2, ...n$. Similarly, for the next n requests, we explicitly set the $(i - n)^{th}$ bit to 0 where $i = n + 1, n + 2, ...2n$. This improved algorithm guarantees that each attribute value is present and absent at least once as long as the number of randomly generated requests is greater than $2n$.

6   Request Reduction

The request reduction problem can be stated similar to the test minimization problem for program testing [20]:

Given: request set QS, a set of requirements r_1, r_2, ..., r_n that must be satisfied to provide the desired test coverage of the policies, and subsets of QS, Q_1, Q_2,..., Q_n, one associated with each of the r_is such that any one of the request q_j belonging to Q_i can be used to test r_i.
Problem: Find a representative set of requests from QS that satisfies all of r_is.

In the problem statement, the r_is can represent policy coverage requirements, such as covering a certain policy, a certain rule, and a certain condition. In a representative set of requests that satisfies all of the r_is, at least one request satisfies each r_i. We call a representative set is *minimal* if removing any request from the set causes the set not to be a representative set. Given a request set QS, there can be several minimal representative sets $QS' \subseteq QS$. Among the minimal representative request sets, we could find a request set that has the smallest possible number of requests. Finding such request tests reduces to optimization problems called "minimum set cover" and "minimum exact cover", respectively; these problems are known to be NP complete, and in practice approximation algorithms are used [27].

In our implementation of coverage-based request reduction, we use a greedy algorithm for selecting requests as they are generated by the random request factory if and only if the generated request increases any of the coverage metrics described in Section 4. More specifically, we iteratively generate a random request and add it to the large set. We then evaluate that request against the policy in order to both compute the response and measure the coverage. If the coverage increases due to the evaluation of the request, then that request is added to the reduced request set.

We note that this greedy algorithm may not produce a minimal representative set. In practice, it does, however, often produce a representative set whose size is near the size of a minimal representative set. We call our reduced set as a *nearly minimal* representative set.

7 Measuring Fault-Detection Capability

In order to investigate the effect of request reduction on fault-detection capabilities, we can inject faults into the original policy thereby creating faulty policies. Since fault detection is the central focus of any testing process, it provides an external measure of the effectiveness of that process. We aim to demonstrate that reduced request sets based on coverage can detect a large percentage of the faults detected by the original request set. We use mutation testing [15] as a mechanism to compare request sets in terms of fault detection.

Mutation testing [15] has historically been applied to general-purpose programming languages. The program under test is iteratively mutated to produce numerous mutants, each containing one fault. A test input is independently executed on the original program and each mutant program. If the output of a test executed on a mutant differs from the output of the same test executed on the original program, then the fault is detected and the mutant is said to be killed. The fundamental premise of mutation testing as stated by Geist et al. [17] is that, in practice, if the software contains a fault, there will usually be a set of mutants that can only be killed by a test that also detects that fault. In other words, the ability to detect small, minor faults such as mutants implies the ability to detect complex faults. Because fault detection is the central focus of any testing process, mutation testing provides an external measure of the effectiveness of that process. The higher the percentage of killed mutants, the more effective the test set is at fault detection.

In policy mutation testing, the program under test, test inputs, and test outputs correspond to the policy, requests, and responses, respectively. We first define a set of mutation operators shown in Table 1. Given a policy and a set of mutation operators, a mutator generates a number of mutant policies. Given a request set, we evaluate each request in the request set on both the original policy and a mutant policy. The request evaluation produces two responses for the request based on the original policy and the mutant policy, respectively. If these two responses are different, then we determine that the mutant policy is killed by the request; otherwise, the mutant policy is not killed.

Table 1. Index of mutation operators

ID	Description
PSTT	Policy Set Target True. The policy set is applied to all requests.
PSTF	Policy Set Target False. The policy set is not applied to any requests.
PTT	Policy Target True. The policy is applied to all requests.
PTF	Policy Target False. The policy is not applied to any requests.
RTT	Rule Target True. The rule is applied to all requests.
RTF	Rule Target False. The rule is not applied to any requests.
RCT	Rule Condition True. The condition always evaluates to true.
RCF	Rule Condition False. The condition always evaluated to false.
CPC	Change Policy Combining Algorithm. Each policy combining algorithm is tried in turn.
CRC	Change Rule Combining Algorithm. Each rule combining algorithm is tried in turn.
CRE	Change Rule Effect. The rule effect is inverted (e.g. permit for deny).

Unfortunately, there are various expenses and barriers associated with mutation testing. The first and foremost is the generation and execution of a large number of mutants. For general-purpose programming languages, the number of mutants is proportional to the product of the number of data references and the number of data objects in the program [34]. For XACML policies, the number of mutants is proportional to the number of policy elements, namely policy sets, policies, targets, rules, conditions, and their associated attributes.

8   Experiment on Request Reduction and Its Effect on Fault Detection

The objective of the experiment is to examine whether the reduced request set is as effective at fault detection as the original request set. Similar to the goals of Hennessy et al. [21] for grammar-based software, we wish to investigate the following hypotheses:

Hypothesis 1. *We can achieve a significant reduction in request-set size for large randomly generated request sets while maintaining equivalent policy, rule, and condition coverage.*

Hypothesis 2. *Reducing a request set based on coverage will not proportionately decrease its fault detection capability.*

8.1   Metrics

In order to investigate our hypotheses, we need to measure the reduction in request-set size, the coverage metrics, and the reduction in fault detection capability. The following metrics are measured for each policy under test, each request set, and each mutation operator.

- *Policy hit percentage.* The policy hit percentage or policy coverage is the number of applicable policies when evaluating the request set divided by the total number of policies.

- *Rule hit percentage.* The rule hit percentage or rule coverage is the number of applicable rules when evaluating the request set divided by the total number of rules.
- *Condition hit percentage.* The condition hit percentage is the number of hit true and hit false conditions when evaluating the request set divided by two times of the total number of conditions.
- *Test count.* The test count is the size of the request set or the number of generated tests. For testing access control policies, a test is synonymous with request.
- *Reduced-test count.* Given a policy and the generated set of requests, the reduced test count is the size of the reduced request set based on policy coverage.
- *Mutant-killing ratio.* Given a request set, the policy under test, and the set of generated mutants, the mutant-killing ratio is the number of mutants killed by the request set divided by the total number of mutants.

Intuitively a set of requests that achieve higher policy coverage are more likely to reveal faults. This notion is easy to understand because a fault in a policy element that is never covered by a request would never contribute to a response and thus a fault in that element cannot possibly be revealed. There is a direct correlation between the test count and the test evaluation time. Furthermore, a low test count is highly desirable because the request-response pairs may need to be inspected manually to verify that the policy specification exhibits the intended policy behavior. An ideal request set should have a low test count, high structural coverage, and high fault-detection capability.

8.2   Results

We used 10 XACML policies collected from three different sources as subjects in our experiment. Table 2 summarizes the basic statistics of each policy. The first column shows the subject names. Columns 2-5 show the numbers of policy sets, policies, rules, and conditions, respectively. Five of the policies, namely simple-policy, codeA, codeB, codeC, and codeD are examples used by Fisler et al. [16,18]. The remaining policies are examples of real XACML policies used by Fedora[3]. Fedora is an open source software that gives organizations a flexible service-oriented architecture for managing and delivering digital content. Fedora uses XACML to provide fine-grained access control to the digital content that it manages. The Fedora repository of default and example XACML policies provides a useful resource of realistic subjects.

We preprocessed each policy to ensure unique policy element identifiers in order to correctly measure structural coverage. Once each policy has been preprocessed, we randomly generate requests for each policy as outlined in Section 5 (we configure that 50 requests are randomly generated for each policy). As these requests are generated and evaluated, we greedily select a smaller set of requests with equivalent coverage as outlined in Section 6. If we define the size of the entire request set as r and the size of the reduced request set as r' then we can define the reduction in request-set size, $SizeReduction$, as follows:

$$SizeReduction = 1 - \frac{r'}{r}$$

---

[3] http://www.fedora.info

Table 2. Policies used in the experiment

Subject	# PolSet	# Pol	# Rule	# Cond
codeA	5	2	2	0
codeB	7	3	3	0
codeC	8	4	4	0
codeD	11	5	5	0
default-2	1	13	13	12
demo-11	0	1	3	4
demo-26	0	1	2	2
demo-5	0	1	3	4
mod-fedora	1	13	13	12
simple-policy	1	2	2	0

Table 3. Structural coverage, number of requests, and size reduction for each policy

Subject	Policy Hit	Rule Hit	Cond Hit	#Req	#Reduced Req	Size Reduction
codeA	100.00%	100.00%	-	50	2	0.96
codeB	100.00%	100.00%	-	50	3	0.94
codeC	100.00%	100.00%	-	50	6	0.88
codeD	100.00%	100.00%	-	50	6	0.88
default-2	100.00%	92.31%	75.00%	50	6	0.88
demo-11	100.00%	100.00%	75.00%	50	2	0.96
demo-26	100.00%	100.00%	50.00%	50	1	0.98
demo-5	100.00%	100.00%	75.00%	50	3	0.94
mod-fedora	100.00%	84.62%	58.33%	50	7	0.86
simple-policy	100.00%	100.00%	-	50	4	0.92

Columns 2-7 of Table 3 show the three structural coverage metrics, size of the generated request set, the size of the reduced request set, and the computed size reduction for each policy, respectively. A dash indicates that there are no policy elements of that type and thus coverage cannot be computed. The random request set achieves 100% policy coverage for all subjects because it is the most coarse measure of structural coverage. Rule coverage and condition coverage are a finer measure of structural coverage and thus more difficult to achieve with randomly generated requests. The results show that we can achieve an average 92% size reduction for the ten policies. The results suggest that we can indeed greatly reduce the request set size of relatively large randomly generated request sets while maintaining equivalent policy, rule, and condition coverage.

The second objective of the experiment is to investigate if the reduced request set can still effectively detect faults in policies compared to the full set. We perform the experiment illustrated in Figure 2. The basic approach is to exploit mutation testing as a mechanism to compare the fault-detection capability of various request sets. As discussed in Section 7, we create several mutant policies using the mutation operators listed in Table 1 for each of the experimental subjects. Each request set is executed against each mutant policy and their corresponding responses are recorded. If the

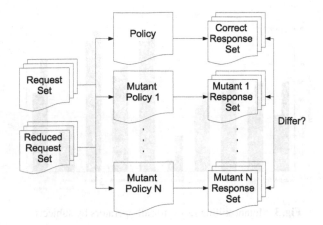

Fig. 2. Overview of fault detection experiment

response for any request evaluated against the original policy differs from the response for the request evaluated against the mutant policy, then the mutant is said to be killed. We define the $CapabilityReduction$ as a metric that quantifies the relative fault detection capability of the reduced set compared to its original set. If we define the total number of mutants detected by the original set as m and the total number of mutants detected by the reduced set as m', then we compute the reduction in fault detection as:

$$CapabilityReduction = 1 - \frac{m'}{m}$$

Figure 3 illustrates the average mutant-killing ratios for each request set grouped by subjects. We observe that the mutant-killing ratios across all subjects for the random and reduced random request sets are quite similar. Unfortunately the mutant-killing ratio is still low when considering the high structural coverage. The observation indicates that a stronger criteria is needed. Specifically the average mutant-killing ratios for the Random, and Reduced Random request sets are 51.8% and 42.1%, respectively. Table 4 lists the mutant-kill ratios in tabular format along with the computed capability reduction. In summary, we observe a 92% reduction in size of the requests while only a 23% reduction in fault detection capability.

In summary, the results indicate that structural coverage is indeed correlated to fault-detection capability. But structural coverage is still not strong enough to achieve an acceptable level of fault detection. Note that the structural coverage investigated in this experiment is essentially equivalent to statement coverage in general-purpose programming languages. In future work, we plan to investigate stronger criteria that correspond to path coverage. We expect these stronger criteria to be much more effective at achieving higher killing ratios.

8.3   Threats to Validity

The threats to external validity primarily include the degree to which the subject policies, mutation operators, coverage metrics, and test sets are representative of true

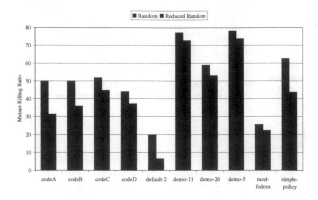

Fig. 3. Mutant-killing ratios for all operators by subjects

Table 4. Mutant-killing ratios and capability reduction for each request set and each policy

Subject	Random	Reduced Random	Capability Reduction
codeA	50.00%	31.25%	37.50%
codeB	50.00%	35.87%	28.26%
codeC	51.79%	44.64%	13.79%
codeD	43.92%	37.16%	15.38%
default-2	19.75%	6.37%	67.74%
demo-11	77.27%	72.73%	5.88%
demo-26	58.82%	52.94%	10.00%
demo-5	78.26%	73.91%	5.56%
mod-fedora	25.48%	22.29%	12.50%
simple-policy	62.50%	43.75%	30.00%

practice. These threats could be reduced by further experimentation on a wider type and larger number of policies and an larger number of mutation operators. In particular, lower level mutation operators are needed to operate on the subject, resource, and action attributes found in various policy elements. Currently the proposed mutation operators operate only on higher level policy elements. The threats to internal validity are instrumentation effects that can bias our results such as faults in Sun's XACML implementation as well as faults in our own policy mutator, policy coverage measurement tool, and request generator.

9 Empirical Study of Manually Generated Requests' Policy Coverage

We have applied the coverage-measurement tool on the whole set of the XACML committee specification conformance test suite [6] and a conference paper review system's policy and its requests developed by Zhang et al. [41].

Table 5. Policy coverage of the XACML conformance test suite

type	100% all	50% cond	non-0% rule/cond	0% rule/cond	total
policies	24	172	24	14	234
Permit	31	144	6		181
Deny			6		6
NotApp	13	28	6	10	57
Indet	1	2	6	4	13

The XACML conformance test suite includes 337 distinct policies[4], 374 requests, their expected responses from the application of the policies. Among these 337 distinct policies, we show the results of 234 policies in this section because for the requests of the remaining 103 policies, Sun's XACML implementation [2] responded different decisions than the ones specified in their expected responses. Applying the requests on these 103 policies failed to conform with expected responses because Sun's XACML implementation does not support some optional features of XACML specifications.

The conference paper review system's policy specified by Zhang et al. [41] has 11 requests and 15 rules, which have 10 conditions. These 10 conditions involve the execution of SQL statements that access an external database. Because it is not trivial to adapt Sun's XACML implementation to support these conditions, we simply remove these 10 conditions as well as some attributes that are not parsed by Sun's XACML implementation, in order to allow us to focus on the measurement of rule hit percentage.

We fed 374 requests in the XACML conformance test suite to the coverage-measurement tool. Table 5 shows the reported statistics of policy coverage. Note that all policies in the conformance test suite are hit by the requests, achieving 100% policy hit percentage. Column 1 shows the type of data and Columns 2-5 show the data for different types of coverage. Row 2 shows the number of policies. Rows 3-6 show the number of requests whose returned decisions are `Permit`, `Deny`, `NotApplicable`, and `Indeterminate`, respectively. When a data entry has a zero value, we do not show the zero value but leave the entry empty.

Column 2 shows the data for policies whose policy, rule, and condition hit percentages reach 100%. These policies have achieved the optimal policy coverage. Column 3 shows the data for policies whose policy and rule hit percentages reach 100% but condition hit percentage reaches 50%. Column 4 shows the data for policies whose rule or condition hit percentage is less than 100% but not equal to 0% (but we do not include the cases shown in Column 3 here). The coverage of these policies needs to be improved. Column 5 shows the data for policies whose rule or condition hit percentage is equal to 0%. These policies are especially in need for improvement. The last column shows the sum of all the data in Columns 2-5.

From the results shown in Table 5, we observed that a majority of policies fell into the category of Column 3, where policy and rule hit percentages reach 100% but

---

[4] In the XACML conformance test suite, there are 374 policies, each of which receives a single request. We have reduced those policies with the same policy content into a single policy, which can then receive multiple requests.

condition hit percentage reaches 50%. Many polices in the XACML conformance test suite contain single rules each of which has a condition. Often each of these policies receives only one request, which basically cover the policy's rule and the rule's true condition.

We took a close look at the details of 14 policies in Column 5. Two of them had 100% for rule hit coverage but 0% for condition hit percentage. Their coverage results were against our expectation because if their conditions were applicable, we expected that either a true or false condition would be hit. We inspected their requests and found that a subject's age was specified twice and their conditions access the subject's age. When evaluating the conditions, PDP encountered an error and returned a decision of Indeterminate; therefore, neither true or false condition was hit.

Note that the XACML conformance test suite was not specifically constructed to achieve high coverage of policies but the measurement results still give us some insights of the common coverage distribution, reflecting policy portions that are commonly hit by manually created requests.

After we fed to the coverage-measurement tool 11 requests for the conference paper review system's policy [41], 73% rule hit percentage was achieved: 4 out of 15 rules were not hit. These four uncovered rules included the case of permitting a PC chair to read papers and no request matched this case. Interestingly one of these uncovered four rules was the last rule, which has the effect of Deny and this rule's target can be matched by any request. This rule is often used for the permit-overrides rule combination algorithm [1]. Given the measurement results of the coverage-measurement tool, we could construct new requests without much difficulty to cover these uncovered rules in the policy of the conference paper review system as well as those uncovered rules or conditions in many policies of the XACML conformance test suite.

10   Related Work

Much work has been done in the modeling and verification of access control policies. A variety of policy languages and models have been proposed. Some of them are generic [1,25,26,14,37] while others are designed for specific applications [11,36,38,7] or data models [8,29,9,19].

One important aspect of policy verification is to formally check general properties of access control policies, such as inconsistency and incompleteness [31,29,25,10]. In the former case, an access request can be both accepted and denied according to the policy, while in the latter case the request is neither accepted nor denied. Although efficient algorithms have been proposed to perform such verification for specific systems [26, 24], this problem can be intractable or even undecidable when dealing with policies that involve complex constraints.

Besides the verification of general properties, several tools have been developed to verify properties for XACML policies [1]. Hughes and Bultan translated XACML policies to the Alloy language [23] and checked their properties using the Alloy Analyzer. Fisler et al. [16] developed a tool called Margrave that uses multi-terminal binary decision diagrams [13] to verify user-specified properties and perform change-impact analysis. Zhang et al [42] developed a model-checking algorithm and tool support to evaluate access control policies written in *RW* languages, which can be converted to XACML [41]. These existing approaches assume that policies are specified using a simplified version of XACML. It is challenging to generalize these verification approaches to support full-feature XACML policies with complex conditions. In addition, most of these approaches require users to specify a set of properties to be verified; however, policy properties often do not exist in practice. The systematic policy testing approach proposed in this paper works on full-feature XACML policies without requiring properties, complementing the existing policy verification approaches.

A test adequacy or coverage criterion provides a stopping rule for testing and a measurement of a test suite's quality [43]. A test coverage criterion can be used to guide test selection. A coverage criterion typically specifies testing requirements based on whether all the identified features in a program or specification have been fully exercised. Identified features in a program can be statements, branches, paths, or definition-use paths. Identified features in a specification can be choices for categories [4, 5] or conditions [12] in specifications.

The importance of test coverage criterion in fault detection can be shown through a fault propagation model such as the PIE (Propagation, Infection, and Execution) model [40]. For example, in order to expose a bug in a statement in a program, a test needs to at least cover the buggy statement. Note that the coverage of a buggy statement is not a sufficient condition to expose the buggy behavior in program outputs; additionally the execution of the buggy statement needs to produce a wrong data state and the wrong data state needs to have an effect on program outputs.

Within our knowledge, our approach is the first that proposes policy coverage and develops an automatic measurement tool and a request reduction tool for it. But there exist several approaches for defining and measuring coverage of rules for grammar-based software or SQL statements for database applications. For example, Hennessy and Power [21] defined rule coverage for context-free grammar and used rule coverage to reduce a test suite for grammar-based software such as C++ compilers. Suarez-Cabal and Tuya [39] defined coverage of SQL queries and developed a tool to automate the measurement. Kapfhammer and Soffa [28] defined a family of test adequacy criteria for database-driven applications based on dataflow information that is associated with entities in a database. Different from these existing coverage measurement approaches for grammars, SQL queries, or database entities, our new approach defines and measures coverage information for policies.

11 Conclusion

In this paper, we have developed a first step toward systematic policy testing by defining and measuring policy coverage. We have proposed the concept of policy testing and policy coverage based on a general access control model. We further defined three levels of specific policy coverage for XACML policies: policy hit percentage, rule hit percentage, and condition hit percentage. To support systematic policy testing based on policy coverage automatically, we have developed a coverage-measurement tool, a request-generation tool, and a request-reduction tool. By using mutation testing, we have conducted an experiment that assesses the coverage-based request reduction and its effect on fault-detection capabilities. The experimental results showed that the coverage-based request reduction substantially reduce the size of the request set but incur only relatively low loss of fault-detection capabilities. We also conducted a study on the policy coverage achieved by manually generated requests for policies in a conformance test suite for XACML specifications [6] and a conference reviewing system [41]. Our results showed that our measurement results can pinpoint uncovered areas of policies and guide the development of new requests to achieve higher policy coverage.

In future work, we plan to develop a comprehensive suite of techniques and tools for systematic policy testing. In particular, we plan to extend our policy coverage to consider cases that reflect the interactions of different rules or different policies, which are not focused by our existing policy coverage. We also plan to conduct experiments on a larger scope of policies.

References

1. OASIS eXtensible Access Control Markup Language (XACML). http://www.oasis-open.org/committees/xacml/, 2005.
2. Sun's XACML implementation. http://sunxacml.sourceforge.net/, 2005.
3. XACML.NET. http://mvpos.sourceforge.net/, 2005.
4. N. Amla and P. Ammann. Using Z specifications in category partition testing. In *Proc. 7th Annual Conference on Computer Assurance*, pages 3–10, June 1992.
5. P. Ammann and J. Offutt. Using formal methods to derive test frames in category-partition testing. In *Proc. 9th Annual Conference on Computer Assurance*, pages 69–80, June 1994.
6. A. Anderson. XACML 1.1 committee specification conformance tests. http://www.oasis-open.org/committees/xacml/ConformanceTests/, 2002.
7. R. J. Anderson. A security policy model for clinical information systems. In *Proc. IEEE Symposium on Security and Privacy*, pages 30–43, 1996.
8. E. Bertino, F. Buccafurri, E. Ferrari, and P. Rullo. A logical framework for reasoning on data access control policies. In *Proc. 12th IEEE Computer Security Foundations Workshop*, pages 175–189, 1999.
9. E. Bertino, S. Castano, and E. Ferrari. On specifying security policies for web documents with an XML-based language. In *Proc. 6th ACM Symposium on Access Control Models and Technologies*, pages 57–65, Chantilly, VA, May 2001.
10. P. Bonatti, S. Vimercati, and P. Samarati. A modular approach to composing access control policies. In *Proc. ACM Conference on Computer and Communication Security*, pages 164–173, Athens, Greece, November 2000.
11. C. Bussler and S. Jablonski. Policy resolution for workflow management systems. In *Proc. Hawaii International Conference on System Science*, pages 831–840, Maui, Hawaii, January 1995.
12. J. Chang and D. J. Richardson. Structural specification-based testing: automated support and experimental evaluation. In *Proc. 7th ESEC/FSE*, pages 285–302, 1999.
13. E. Clarke, M. Fujita, P. McGeer, J. Yang, and X. Zhao. Multi-terminal binary decision diagrams: An efficient data structure for matrix representation. In *Proc. International Workshop on Logic Synthesis*, pages 1–15, 1993.
14. N. Damianou, N. Dulay, E. Lupu, and M. Sloman. The Ponder policy specification language. In *Proc. International Workshop on Policies for Distributed Systems and Networks*, pages 18–38, 2001.
15. R. A. DeMillo, R. J. Lipton, and F. G. Sayward. Hints on test data selection: Help for the practicing programmer. *IEEE Computer*, 11(4):34–41, April 1978.

16. K. Fisler, S. Krishnamurthi, L. A. Meyerovich, and M. C. Tschantz. Verification and change-impact analysis of access-control policies. In *Proc. 27th International Conference on Software Engineering*, pages 196–205, 2005.
17. R. Geist, A. J. Offutt, and F. Harris. Estimation and enhancement of real-time software reliability through mutation analysis. *IEEE Transactions on Computers*, 41(5):55–558, 1992.
18. M. M. Greenberg, C. Marks, L. A. Meyerovich, and M. C. Tschantz. The soundness and completeness of Margrave with respect to a subset of XACML. Technical Report CS-05-05, Department of Computer Science, Brown University, 2005.
19. P. Griffiths and B. Wade. An authorization mechanism for a relational database systems. *ACM Transactions on Database Systems*, 1(3), 1976.
20. M. J. Harrold, R. Gupta, and M. L. Soffa. A methodology for controlling the size of a test suite. *ACM Trans. Softw. Eng. Methodol.*, 2(3):270–285, 1993.
21. M. Hennessy and J. F. Power. An analysis of rule coverage as a criterion in generating minimal test suites for grammar-based software. In *Proc. 20th IEEE/ACM International Conference on Automated Software Engineering*, pages 104–113, November 2005.
22. G. Hughes and T. Bultan. Automated verification of access control policies. Technical Report 2004-22, Department of Computer Science, University of California, Santa Barbara, 2004.
23. D. Jackson, I. Shlyakhter, and M. Sridharan. A micromodularity mechanism. In *Proc. 8th ESEC/FSE*, pages 62–73, 2001.
24. T. Jaeger, X. Zhang, and F. Cacheda. Policy management using access control spaces. *ACM Transactions on Information and System Security*, 6(3), 2003.
25. S. Jajodia, P. Samarati, and V. S. Subrahmanian. A logical language for expressing authorizations. In *Proc. 1997 IEEE Symposium on Security and Privacy*, pages 31–42, 1997.
26. S. Jajodia, P. Samarati, V. S. Subrahmanian, and E. Bertino. A unified framework for enforcing multiple access control policies. In *Proc. ACM SIGMOD International Conference on Management of Data*, pages 474–485, 1997.
27. D. S. Johnson. Approximation algorithms for combinatorial problems. *J. Comput. System Sci.*, 9:256–278, 1974.
28. G. M. Kapfhammer and M. L. Soffa. A family of test adequacy criteria for database-driven applications. In *Proceedings of the 9th ESEC/FSE*, pages 98–107, 2003.
29. M. Kudo and S. Hada. XML document security based on provisional authorization. In *Proc. ACM Conference on Computer and Communication Security*, pages 87–96, Athens, Greece, November 2000.
30. M. Lorch, D. Kafura, and S. Shah. An XACML-based policy management and authorization service for globus resources. In *Proc. International Workshop on Grid Computing*, pages 208–212, Phoenix, AZ, Nov 2003.
31. E. C. Lupu and M. Sloman. Conflict in policy-based distributed systems management. *IEEE Transaction on Software Engineering*, 25(6):852–869, 1999.
32. T. Moses, A. Anderson, S. Proctor, and S. Godik. XACML Profile for Web-Services (WSPL). OASIS Working Draft, Sept. 2003.
33. G. J. Myers. *Art of Software Testing*. John Wiley & Sons, Inc., 1979.
34. J. Offutt and R. H. Untch. Mutation 2000: Uniting the orthogonal. In *Mutation 2000: Mutation Testing in the Twentieth and the Twenty First Centuries*, pages 45–55, October 2000.
35. G. Rothermel, M. J. Harrold, J. Ostrin, and C. Hong. An empirical study of the effects of minimization on the fault detection capabilities of test suites. In *Proc. International Conference on Software Maintenance*, pages 34–43, 1998.
36. T. Ryutov and C. Neuman. Representation and evaluation of security policies for distributed system services. In *Proc. DARPA Information Survivability Conference and Exposition*, pages 172–183, January 2000.

37. R. Sandhu, V. Bhamidipati, and Q. Munawer. The ARBAC97 model for role-based aminis-tration of roles. *ACM Transactions on Information and Systems Security*, 2(1):105–135, Feb. 1999.
38. E. Sirer and K. Wang. An access control language for web services. In *Proc. 7th ACM Symposium on Access Control Models and Technologies*, pages 23–30, Monterey, CA, June 2002.
39. M. J. Suarez-Cabal and J. Tuya. Using an SQL coverage measurement for testing database applications. In *Proc. ACM SIGSOFT International Symposium on Foundations of Software Engineering*, pages 253–262, 2004.
40. J. M. Voas. PIE: A dynamic failure-based technique. *IEEE Transactions on Software Engineering*, 18(8):717–727, 1992.
41. N. Zhang, M. Ryan, and D. P. Guelev. Synthesising verified access control systems in XACML. In *Proc. 2004 ACM workshop on Formal Methods in Security Engineering*, pages 56–65, 2004.
42. N. Zhang, M. Ryan, and D. P. Guelev. Evaluating access control policies through model checking. In *Proc. 8th International Conference on Information Security*, pages 446–460, September 2005.
43. H. Zhu, P. A. V. Hall, and J. H. R. May. Software unit test coverage and adequacy. *ACM Comput. Surv.*, 29(4):366–427, 1997.

Distributed Credential Chain Discovery in Trust Management with Parameterized Roles and Constraints (Short Paper)

Ziqing Mao[1], Ninghui Li[1], and William H. Winsborough[2]

[1] CERIAS and Department of Computer Science, Purdue University
{zmao, ninghui}@cs.purdue.edu
[2] Department of Computer Science, University of Texas at San Antonio
wwinsborough@acm.org

Abstract. Trust management (TM) is an approach to access control in decentralized distributed systems with access control decisions based on statements made by multiple principals. Li et al. developed the RT family of Role-Based Trust-management languages, which combine the strengths of Role-Based Access Control and TM systems. We present a distributed credential chain discovery algorithm for RT_1^C, a language in the RT family that has parameterized roles and constraints. Our algorithm is a combination of the logic-programming style top-down query evaluation with tabling and a goal-directed version of the deductive database style bottom-up evaluation. Our algorithm uses hints provided through the storage types to determine whether to use a top-down or bottom-up strategy for a particular part of the proof; this enables the algorithm to touch only those credentials that are related to the query, which are likely to be a small fraction of all the credentials in the system.

1 Introduction

In [1], Blaze, Feigenbaum, and Lacy coined the term "trust management" to group together some principles dealing with access control in decentralized distributed systems. In the TM approach, access control decisions are based on the attributes (rather than the identity) of the requester, such as citizenship, credit status, date of birth, employment, group membership, security clearance, etc. These attributes need to be certified: they are documented by digitally-signed credentials issued by appropriate authorities, which may have their own attributes documented in other credentials. When one requests a resource from a server, the access is granted if the requester's attributes in its credentials satisfy the server's policy. TM systems allow the authority to certify attributes to be delegated. Like attributes themselves, such delegation relationships are documented in credentials. For example, a university can issue a credential to delegate to its registrar the authority to certify who are students of the university. The process of making an access control decision involves finding a chain of credentials that together prove that the requester satisfies the server's policy. Thus, a central problem in trust management is to determine whether such a chain exists and, if so, to find it. We call this the *credential chain discovery problem*.

P. Ning, S. Qing, and N. Li (Eds.): ICICS 2006, LNCS 4307, pp. 159–173, 2006.

In a series of papers [12,11,10], Li et al. developed the RT family of Role-Based Trust-management languages, which combine the strengths of Role-Based Access Control (RBAC) [16] and TM systems. Two central concepts in RT are *principals* and *roles*. Each principal represents a uniquely identified entity in the system. A role is designated by a principal and a *role term*. For example, HospB.physician is the physician role defined by principal HospB and can be read as HospB's physician role. In RT_0, the most basic language in the RT family, each role term is a string. Li et al. [12] introduced an approach for doing distributed credential chain discovery in RT_0. In credential chain discovery, one needs to determine whether a requester has the attributes that satisfy the policy. One approach is to use *backward search*, which starts with the policies that govern the requested resource and tries to enumerate all principals that are entitled to access the resource. One difficulty of this approach is that because of recursive dependency in policies, the search may never terminate. Clarke et al. [4] proposed an algorithm that addresses the problem by doing a full-scale *forward search*, which tries to compute all facts entailed by all the credentials and policies in the system. These approaches have two drawbacks: First, using either forward or backward search alone, one may evaluate a large number of credentials unrelated to the query. Second, when credentials are stored in a distributed manner, one may not know the existence of some relevant credentials. The approach in [12] addresses these problems by using a goal-directed chain discovery algorithm that combines goal-directed back search and goal-directed forward search.

In [11,10], a number of other components of RT were introduced. In particular, RT_1 adds parameterized roles to RT_0. Parameterized roles can represent attributes that have fields. For example, if HospB has a policy that allows the primary care physician (pcp) of a patient to access the patient's medical record, then HospB needs to define the pcp role. Without parameterized roles, HospB needs to define a pcp role for each patient and to grant access to each of these roles individually. In RT_1, one can parameterize the role HospB.pcp by patient id, and then use only one statement to express the policy. RT_1^C enhances RT_1 with constraints. This enables one to succinctly express permissions regarding structured resources and potentially unbounded domains. For example, using one statement, one can grant the permission to connect to any port over 1024 at any host in the domain abc.dom. Clearly these are essential capabilities in a real-world policy language.

While introducing parameterized roles and constraints greatly increases the expressive power of the RT family, credential chain discovery was also made significantly more challenging. In this paper, we present a distributed credential chain discovery algorithm for RT_1^C. Our algorithm is a novel combination of goal-directed backward search with tabling and goal-directed forward search, using a storage typing system and a mechanism for communicating results between the two search directions and managing search in the two directions. We describe this algorithm in detail; in our specification of the algorithm, we state logical invariants that ensure correctness.

The rest of this paper is organized as follows. Related work is discussed in Section 2. We give a detailed example scenario in Section 3. In Section 4, we describe the syntax and semantics of the RT_1^C language. Distributed credential chain discovery algorithms are given in Section 5. We conclude in Section 6.

2 Related Work

Clarke et al. [4] gave an algorithm for credential chain discovery in SPKI/SDSI 2.0 [5]. Their algorithm views discovery as a term-rewriting problem. Each certificate is viewed as a rewriting rule. Determining whether there is a credential chain that proves a role expression e has a member D is equivalent to whether there is a way to rewrite e into D. In order to avoid potential nontermination caused by recursive definitions, the algorithm in [4] computes a closure the member-sets of all roles in C. This may be suitable when large numbers of queries are made about a slowly changing credential pool of modest size. However, when the credential pool is large, or when the frequency of changes to the credential pool (particularly deletions, such as credential expirations or revocations) approaches the frequency of queries against the pool, the efficiency of the bottom-up approach deteriorates rapidly. The algorithm in [4] also requires that evaluation begin by collecting all credentials in the system at a single location, where the evaluation will be carried out. This is a common problem with many evaluation techniques. In an open system, it will typically be the case that a large number of credentials have nothing to do with the current query. Evaluation methods should not require these irrelevant credentials to be collected. However, because there are no restrictions on the delegation of authority that credentials can specify, there is no simple means of determining which credentials are relevant without examining the chains and partial chains in which they participate. This is the principle our approach uses to avoid collecting irrelevant credentials.

Jha and Reps [7] pointed out that SDSI string rewriting systems correspond exactly to the class of string rewriting systems modeled using push-down systems [2], and therefore, one could use techniques for model checking pushdown systems to do credential chain discovery. This approach, however, does not extend to parameters and constraints.

Query Certificate Managers (QCM) [6] and Secure Dynamically Distributed Datalog (SD3) [8] also consider distributed storage of credentials. The approach in QCM and SD3 assumes that issuers initially store all credentials and every query is answered by doing a form of backward search.

Li et al. [12] gave a distributed credential chain discovery algorithm for RT_0. Extending the algorithm in [12] to deal with parameterized roles and constraints turns out to be quite challenging. One can compare RT_0 to a propositional language, and RT_1^C to a first-order language.

As RT languages have a logic programming semantics, chain discovery in RT_1^C is closely related to deduction in logic programming and deductive databases. Backward search is top-down evaluation, which is used in Prolog engines; and forward search is similar to bottom-up evaluation, which is used in deductive databases. Issues such as tabling and goal-directed evaluation have been extensively studied. For example, top-down evaluation with tabling is studied in [3], and goal-directed bottom-up evaluation is studied in [13]. The uniqueness of our problem lies in the fact that it dictates a combination of top-down evaluation and bottom-up evaluation, because of the distributed storage of credentials. The search algorithm needs to be able to manage searches in both directions and to pass solutions from the search in one direction to the search in the other direction. Also, as RT_1^C has constraints; the search algorithm needs to incorporate ideas from the evaluation algorithms for constraint datalog (e.g., [17]). On the other hand, our problem is simpler than the general problem in that our algorithm only needs to handle four types of logical rules corresponding to the four types of statements in RT.

3   An Example

In this section, we describe an example scenario we will use throughout this paper to illustrate credentials and policy statements in RT and the distributed credential chain discovery process. This example is given in Figure 1 and explained below.

DC is a data center that maintains medical data about patients. The data maintained by it includes patient's personal information (such as name and birthdate), contact info, as well as other medical data such as test results and images. These data are labeled with category information, and the category information is organized in a hierarchy. Some sample categories are shown in the Figure 1(a). There are 3 categories at the top level: person, contact, and medical; each contains subcategories. For example, one's blood test result will be labeled with the category 'medical.testresult.blood' and one's email address will be labeled with the category 'contact.online.email'.

In the discussions below, we distinguish between policy statements and credentials. Policy statements are issued by DC and used by DC locally, thus they do not need to digitally signed. On the other hand, credentials are digitally signed, and DC needs to verify the signatures before accepting them. Other than the above difference, policy statements and credentials can be handled in exactly the same way in the chain discovery process. Note that credentials support the full generality of policy statements, and typically must be collected from distributed storage during chain discovery.

Policies. DC's policy about accessing the data includes the following two rules:

– The primary care physician (PCP) of a patient has access to all information about a patient.
– The PCP of a patient is allowed to delegate access to medical info to another physician in an affiliated clinic or hospital.

These two rules are encoded using policy statements (p1) and (p2) in Figure 1(c). The statement (p1) [DC.access(pname=$?x$, data=$?y$)⟵DC.pcp(pname=$?x$)] states that any principal that is the PCP of a patient X can access any data about the patient X. In the statement $?x$ and $?y$ are two variables. DC.access(pname=$?x$, data=$?y$) is a parameterized role. Note that the same variable $?x$ appears both in the head (the part to the left of ⟵) and the body (the part to the right of ⟵).

The statement (p2) [DC.access(pname=$?x$, data=$?y$) ⟵ DC.delAcc(pname=$?x$, data=$?y$) ∩ DC.physician ; $?y \preceq$ ⟨medical⟩] states that if a principal is being delegated access to certain medical data, and is a physician, then the principal is allowed to access the data. The symbol ∩ denotes set intersection, if one views each role as the set of principals who are members of the role; it can also be equivalently viewed as a logical AND. Note that (p2) includes a constraint $?y \preceq$ ⟨medical⟩, which means that $?y$ must be a subcategory of medical. This syntax for constraints will be explained in Section 4. One cannot use (p2) to gain access to data other than those under the medical category; for example, even if a physician is being delegated access to the contact information by the PCP, the physician still cannot use this rule to gain access to the information.

(a) The Category Hierarchy for the Patient Data

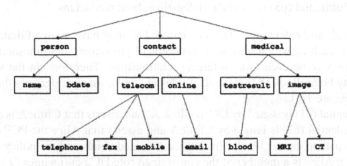

(b) Principals

DC	a data center that maintains medical data
ClinicA	a clinic that is affiliated with DC
HospB	a hospital that is affiliated with DC
Alice	a physician at ClinicA and the PCP of the patient 'Paul'
Bob	a physician at HospB, and is referred by Alice to access image data of 'Paul'

(c) Policy Statements and Credentials

label	statement	stored by
(p1)	DC.access(pname=?x, data=?y) ⟵ DC.pcp(pname=?x). where pname stands for "patient name"	DC
(p2)	DC.access(pname=?x, data=?y) ⟵ DC.delAcc(pname=?x, data=?y) ∩ DC.physician ; ?y ⪯ ⟨medical⟩.	DC
(p3)	DC.delAcc(pname=?x, data=?y) ⟵ DC.pcp(pname=?x).refAcc(pname=?x, data=?y).	DC
(p4)	DC.pcp(pname=?x) ⟵ DC.affil.pcp(pname=?x).	DC
(p5)	DC.physician ⟵ DC.affil.physician.	DC
(c1)	DC.affil ⟵ ClinicA.	ClinicA
(c2)	DC.affil ⟵ HospB.	HospB
(c3)	ClinicA.pcp(pname=?x) ⟵ Alice ; ?x = 'Paul'.	ClinicA
(c4)	HospB.physician ⟵ Bob.	Bob
(c5)	Alice.refAcc(pname=?x, data=?y) ⟵ Bob ; ?x = 'Paul' ∧ ?y ⪯ ⟨medical.image⟩.	Bob

(d) The Inference Process:

label	conclusion	using
(r1)	DC.pcp(pname=?x) ; ?x = 'Paul' ⟵ Alice	(p4), (c1), (c3)
(r2)	DC.physician ⟵ Bob.	(p5), (c2), (c4)
(r3)	DC.delAcc(pname=?x, data=?y) ; ?x = 'Paul' ∧ ?y ⪯ ⟨medical.image⟩ ⟵ Bob.	(p3), (r1), (c5)
(r4)	DC.access(pname=?x, data=?y) ; ?x = 'Paul' ∧ ?y ⪯ ⟨medical.image⟩ ⟵ Bob.	(p2), (r3), (r2)

Fig. 1. A Running Example. This example is explained in detail Section 3.

Policies (p1) and (p2) refer to the three roles: DC.delAcc(· · ·), DC.pcp(· · ·), and DC.physician. They are defined in (p3), (p4), and (p5), respectively. The policy (p3) states that one can be delegated access to a patient's data by the PCP of the patient; (p4) states that DC delegates the authority to certify the PCP relationship to members of the role DC.affil; and (p5) is a similar delegation about physicians.

Credentials and Inferences. The data center DC may have many affiliated clinics and hospitals, each of which may have hundreds of physicians and thousands of patients, and there may be even more referring relationships. Therefore, in the whole system there may be millions of credentials. In this example, we consider only the five credentials in Figure 1(c).

Credential (c1) is issued by DC to ClinicA, and asserts that ClinicA is affiliated with DC. Credential (c3) is issued by ClinicA and asserts that Alice the PCP of the patient who has patient name[1] 'Paul'. From these two credentials and the policy (p4), one can infer (r1): Alice is a member of the constrained role DC.pcp(pname=$?x$); $?x =$ 'Paul'. (In Figure 1(c), this is denoted by the syntax DC.pcp(pname=$?x$); $?x =$ 'Paul' $\leftarrow$ Alice.) Similarly, from credentials (c2) and (c4), together with the policy (p5), one can infer (r2): Bob is a member of the role DC.physician.

Credential (c5) is issued by Alice when Alice wants Bob to look at the medical image date of patient 'Paul', maybe for a second opinion. From (p3), (r1), and (c5), one can infer (r3): Bob is a member of the role DC.delAcc(pname=$?x$, data=$?y$); $?x =$ 'Paul' $\wedge$ $?y \preceq \langle$medical.image$\rangle$.

Finally, using (p2), (r3), and (r2), one can infer that Bob is able to get access to the medical image data of the patient 'Paul'. For example, if Bob requests to access the MRI image, then the access should be allowed.

Credential Storage and Discovery. The first question that we need to address to enable the above access is: Suppose that DC maintains all credentials that are issued by everyone, when Bob requests access to the MRI image of patient 'Paul', how can one make the authorization decision efficiently? We point out that there may be tens of thousands of patients in the system, most of which are unrelated to the above access query; therefore, even if an algorithm runs in time linear in the total number of credentials, it is still not efficient enough. We need an algorithm that touches only the small fraction of credentials that are related to the query.

Furthermore, it is unreasonable to have DC maintain all credentials. For example, credentials (c3), (c4), and (c5) do not even mention DC. It is illogical to have DC store these credentials. The second question that we need to address is then how to find these credentials that are needed. For example, credential (c4) is issued by HospB and certify that Bob is a physician with HospB. Intuitively, it should be stored either by HospB or Bob. When we say a principal *stores* a credential, it means that we can find the credential once we know the principal. Some system, such as a directory, may actually house the credential on the principal's behalf. We require that one can find the directory's address once knowing the principal. One approach to do this is to require the representation of a principal to include both the public key and the directory server address. See [15] for more discussions on this.

In [12], a storage type system and a notion of well-typed credentials were presented to address these problems. They guarantee that credential chains can be discovered

---

[1] In practice, patient records are more likely to be identified with unique patient ids, rather than names. We use patient names here to make the presentation smoother.

even when credentials are stored in a distributed manner. The types also guide search in the right direction, avoiding huge fan-outs. See [12] for description of the storage type system.

4   An Overview of RT_1^C

Constraints. RT_1^C uses constraints to support finite expression of authorizations over infinite or unbounded domains, such as integer ranges or directory hierarchies. Each role parameter has a data type, which is associated with a constraint domain. For example, in the role DC.access(pname=?x, data=?y), ?x has the data type corresponding to patient names and we can use equality constraints of the form ?$x =$ 'Paul', and ?y has the data type corresponding to patient data categories, and we can use constraints of the form ?$y \preceq \langle$medical$\rangle$.

Intuitively, a constraint domain is a domain of objects, such as numbers, points in the plane, or files in a file hierarchy, together with a language for speaking about these objects. The language is typically defined by a set of first-order constants, function symbols, and relation symbols. See [10] for a formal definition of constraint domains. For the purpose of this paper, it suffices to say that each constraint domain has a set of primitive constraints, and these primitive constraints can be conjuncted to form more complicated constraints. We now give several classes of constraint domains that have been defined in RT_1^C.

Tree domains.   Each constant of a tree domain takes the form $\langle a_1.a_2.\cdots .a_k \rangle$. Imagine a tree in which every edge is labeled with a string value. The constant $\langle a_1.\cdots .a_k \rangle$ represents the node for which $a_1.\cdots .a_k$ are the strings on the path from root to this node. A primitive constraint is of the form $x = y$ or $x\theta\langle a_1.\cdots .a_k \rangle$, in which x and y are variables and $\theta \in \{=, <, \leq, \prec, \preceq\}$.

The primitive constraint $x < \langle a_1.\cdots .a_k \rangle$ means that x is a child of the node $\langle a_1.\cdots .a_k \rangle$, and $x \leq \langle a_1.\cdots .a_k \rangle$ means that either $x = \langle a_1.\cdots .a_k \rangle$ or $x < \langle a_1.\cdots .a_k \rangle$. Similarly, the primitive constraint $x \prec \langle a_1.\cdots .a_k \rangle$ means that x is a descendant of $\langle a_1.\cdots .a_k \rangle$ (*i.e.*, the latter is a prefix of x), and $x \preceq \langle a_1.\cdots .a_k \rangle$ means that either $x = \langle a_1.\cdots .a_k \rangle$ or $x \prec \langle a_1.\cdots .a_k \rangle$.

Tree domains are used in the running example for the hierarchically organized data categories.

Discrete domains with sets.   Such a domain has a set of constants and one predicate $=$. A primitive constraint has the form $x = y$, or $x \in \{c_1, \ldots, c_\ell\}$, in which x and y are variables, and $c_1, \ldots, c_\ell$ are constants.

In our running example, the patient name is a discrete domain with sets. In our examples, we use the constraint ?$x =$ 'Paul', which is a shorthand for ?$x \in \{$'Paul'$\}$.

A constraint is a conjunction of primitive constraints, possibly from multiple constraint domains. Given a constraint $\phi(\boldsymbol{x})$, where $\boldsymbol{x}$ is a tuple of variables including all variables that occur free in ϕ, and a tuple $\boldsymbol{t}$ of constants, we say that $\phi(\boldsymbol{t})$ is satisfied if each primitive constraint in $\phi(\boldsymbol{x})$ evaluates to true when the variables in it are replaced with the corresponding constants in $\boldsymbol{t}$. For example, given the constraint $\phi(\langle x_1, x_2 \rangle) = x_1 \leq \langle a_1.a_2 \rangle \wedge x_2 \in (1, 10)$, and the tuple $\boldsymbol{t} = \langle\langle a_1.a_2.a_3 \rangle, 2\rangle$, we have $\phi(\boldsymbol{t})$ is satisfied, because $\langle a_1.a_2.a_3 \rangle \leq \langle a_1.a_2 \rangle$ and $2 \in (1, 10)$ both evaluate to true.

Syntax. In RT_1^C, a ground role is a role in which each parameter is constrained to be equal to one constant. A ground role defines a set of principals who are members of this ground role. Given a tuple of type-compatible constants t, we use $members(A.r(t))$ informally in the following to refer to the set of principals that are member of $A.r(t)$.

Credentials define role membership. (Here we use "credentials" to refer to both unsigned policy statements and to digitally signed credentials.) The variables that occur in a credential are local to that credential in the sense that they are implicitly universally quantified at the outermost level of the credential. In the following, x, y, x_1, and x_2 are tuples of variables that are all distinct. We now describe the four kinds of credentials in RT_1^C:

- *Type-1*: $A.r(x) \longleftarrow B; \psi(x)$

  $A.r(x)$ is a role with each parameter being a variable, B is a principal, and $\psi(x)$ is a constraint over the variables in x.

  This means that $B \in members(A.r(t))$, for any n-tuple of constants t such that $\psi(t)$ is satisfied.
- *Type-2*: $A.r(x) \longleftarrow B.r_2(y); \psi(x, y)$

  $A.r(x)$ and $B.r_2(y)$ are both roles, and $\psi(x, y)$ is a constraint (over the variables in x and y).
  This means that

  $$members(A.r(t)) \supseteq members(B.r_2(s)),$$

  for every constant-tuple t and s such that $\psi(t, s)$ is satisfied.
- *Type-3*: $A.r(x) \longleftarrow A.r_1(y).r_2(z); \psi(x, y, z)$

  $A.r(x)$ and $B.r_1(y)$ are both roles, $r_2(z)$ is a role term, and $\psi(x, y, z)$ is a constraint. We call $B.r_1(y).r_2(z)$ a *linked role*.
  This means that

  $$members(A.r(t)) \supseteq members(D.r_2(w))$$

  for all $D \in members(B.r_1(s))$ for every t, s, and w such that $\psi(t, s, w)$ is satisfied.
- *Type-4*: $A.r(x_0) \longleftarrow A_1.r_1(x_1) \cap A_2.r_2(x_2);$
  $$\psi(x_0, x_1, x_2)$$

  $A.r(x_0)$, $A_1.r_1(x_1)$ and $A_2.r_2(x_2)$ are roles, and $\psi(x_0, x_1, x_2)$ is a constraint. We call $A_1.r_1(x_1) \cap A_2.r_2(x_2)$ a *role intersection*.
  This means that

  $$members(A.r(s_0)) \supseteq (members(A_1.r_1(s_1)) \cap members(A_2.r_2(s_2))),$$

  for all constant-tuple s_0, s_1, s_2 such that $\psi(s_0, s_1, s_2)$ is satisfied.

We use σ to denote a credential, $Head(\sigma)$ to denote the role to the left of "$\longleftarrow$" in the credential σ, and $Body(\sigma)$ to denote the list of roles and constraints to the right of "$\longleftarrow$".

Semantics. Given a set $\mathcal{P}$ credentials, its semantics is formally defined by translating each credential into a constraint datalog clause [9,10,14,17]. We call the set of all resulting clauses the semantic program of $\mathcal{P}$.

Definition 1 (Semantic Program). Given a set $\mathcal{P}$ of policy statements, the *semantic program*, $SP(\mathcal{P})$, of $\mathcal{P}$, has one predicate r of arity $n + 2$ for each n-ary role name r. Intuitively, $r(A, D, t)$ means that D is a member of the role $A.r(t)$. $SP(\mathcal{P})$ is the set of all constraint datalog clauses produced from policy statements in $\mathcal{P}$. The Semantic Program $SP(\mathcal{P})$ can be generated from $\mathcal{P}$ as follows.

For each $A.r(\boldsymbol{x}) \longleftarrow D; \phi(\boldsymbol{x})$ in $\mathcal{P}$, add
$$r(A, D, \boldsymbol{x}) :- \phi(\boldsymbol{x}) \tag{m1}$$
For each $A.r(\boldsymbol{x}) \longleftarrow B.r_1(\boldsymbol{y}); \phi(\boldsymbol{x}, \boldsymbol{y})$ in $\mathcal{P}$, add
$$r(A, z_1, \boldsymbol{x}) :- r_1(B, z_2, \boldsymbol{y}), z_1 = z_2, \phi(\boldsymbol{x}, \boldsymbol{y}) \tag{m2}$$
For each $A.r(\boldsymbol{x}) \longleftarrow A.r_1(\boldsymbol{y}).r_2(\boldsymbol{z}); \phi(\boldsymbol{x}, \boldsymbol{y}, \boldsymbol{z})$ in $\mathcal{P}$, add
$$r(A, z_0', \boldsymbol{x}) :- r_1(A, y_1', \boldsymbol{y}), r_2(y_2', z_2', \boldsymbol{z}), y_1' = y_2', z_0' = z_2', \phi(\boldsymbol{x}, \boldsymbol{y}, \boldsymbol{z}) \quad (m3)$$
For each $A.r(\boldsymbol{x}) \longleftarrow B_1.r_1(\boldsymbol{y}) \cap B_2.r_2(\boldsymbol{z}); \phi(\boldsymbol{x}, \boldsymbol{y}, \boldsymbol{z})$ in $\mathcal{P}$, add
$$r(A, z_0', \boldsymbol{z}) :- r_1(B_1, z_1', \boldsymbol{y}), r_2(B_2, z_2', \boldsymbol{z}), z_0' = z_1', z_1' = z_2', \phi(\boldsymbol{x}, \boldsymbol{y}, \boldsymbol{z}) \quad (m4)$$

An algorithm for evaluating a semantic program (which is a constraint Datalog program) is given in [10]. The algorithm requires using existential quantifier elimination to project constraints onto variables of interest. It is shown in [10] that existential quantifier elimination can be done efficiently in the three constraint domains mentioned in Section 4 and that the evaluation of constraint datalog programs such as $SP(\mathcal{P})$ is tractable when using these domains. However, the algorithm in [10] is a bottom-up algorithm that computes all logical implications of a semantic program. The algorithm is not goal-directed; thus, it is inefficient in practice and cannot deal with distributed storage of credentials.

5   Description of the Algorithms

Given a set of RT_1^C credentials, the goal of our algorithms is to answer the next three common kinds of queries:

1. Given a constrained role $A.r(\boldsymbol{x}); \psi(\boldsymbol{x})$, determine the set of principals that are members of the given constrained role and the associated constraints. More precisely, this query asks for a set of principal/constraint pairs Θ such that
   (a) $\langle D, \varphi(\boldsymbol{x}) \rangle \in \Theta$ implies $\varphi(\boldsymbol{x}) \Rightarrow \psi(\boldsymbol{x})$ and,
   (b) for each principal D and each tuple of constants t such that $\psi(t)$ is satisfied, $SP(\mathcal{P}) \models r(A, D, t)$ if and only if there exists $\langle D, \varphi(\boldsymbol{x}) \rangle \in \Theta$ such that $\varphi(t)$ is satisfied.
2. Given a principal D, determine a set of constrained roles that D is a member of. This query asks for a set Λ of constrained roles such that
   (a) $A.r(\boldsymbol{x}); \varphi(\boldsymbol{x}) \in \Lambda$ implies $\varphi(\boldsymbol{x}) \Rightarrow \psi(\boldsymbol{x})$, and
   (b) for each tuple of constants t, $SP(\mathcal{P}) \models r(A, D, t)$ if and only if there exists $A.r(\boldsymbol{x}); \varphi(\boldsymbol{x}) \in \Lambda$ such that $\varphi(t)$ is satisfied.

3. Given a constrained role $A.r(x); \psi(x)$ and a principal D, determine the set of constraints under which D is a member of $A.r(x); \psi(x)$. More precisely, this query asks for a set of constraints Ω such that
   (a) $\varphi(x) \in \Omega$ implies $\varphi(x) \Rightarrow \psi(x)$, and
   (b) for each tuple of constants t such that $\psi(t)$ is satisfied, $SP(\mathcal{P}) \models r(A, D, t)$ if and only if there exists $\varphi(x) \in \Omega$ such that $\varphi(t)$ is satisfied.

To answer queries of the first form, we can apply a backward search algorithm starting from the constrained role $A.r(x); \psi(x)$. For queries of the second form, we can apply a forward search algorithm starting from the principal D. For queries of the third form, we can use either a backward search or a forward search. For queries of the third form, we also have the alternative of using a bidirectional search algorithm, which simultaneously searches backwards from $A.r(x); \psi(x)$ and forwards from D.

When credential storage is distributed, the bidirectional search algorithm can find some chains that cannot be found by either forward or backward search alone.

5.1   The Backward Search Algorithm

The backward search algorithm constructs a proof graph, each node of which is given by (and represents) a constrained role $A.r(x); \psi(x)$. (The nodes in this proof graph are called *role nodes*. This is the only kind of node constructed by the backwards search algorithm; the forward search algorithm also uses "principal nodes," which, as their name suggests, represent principals.)

Role nodes. Each role node stores a set of solutions. A *solution* comprises a principal and a constraint. The algorithm maintains the following invariant. If the node $A.r(x); \psi(x)$ has a solution $\langle D, \varphi(x) \rangle$, then $\varphi(x) \Rightarrow \psi(x)$ and $SP(\mathcal{P}) \models r(A, D, t)$ for each t such that $\varphi(t)$ is satisfied. When the algorithm terminates, it will also be the case that for each t such that $SP(\mathcal{P}) \models r(A, D, t)$, the node $A.r(x); \psi(x)$ has a solution $\langle D, \varphi(x) \rangle$ such that $\varphi(t)$ is satisfied. Thus, queries of type 1 can be answered by taking Θ to be the set of solutions associated with $A.r(x); \psi(x)$. Similarly, queries of type 3 can be answered by taking Ω to be the set of constraints $\varphi(x)$ such that $\langle D, \varphi(x) \rangle$ is a solution associated with $A.r(x); \psi(x)$. When there are certain kinds of edges between nodes, solutions can be propagated through the edges. Whenever a solution is about to be added to a node, we first check whether the solution is implied by a solution that already exists. A solution $\langle D, \varphi_1(x) \rangle$ is implied by a solution $\langle D, \varphi_2(x) \rangle$ if and only if $\varphi_1(x) \Rightarrow \varphi_2(x)$. If so, then we do not add the new solution. Otherwise, the new solution is added, and the solution is propagated through outgoing edges.

The backward search algorithm maintains a queue of nodes that require further consideration, called the *backward processing queue*. The algorithm removes nodes from the queue one by one and processes them, repeating this until the queue is empty. Both the proof graph and the queue initially contain just one node, which corresponds to the query role. The algorithm also maintains a set of *backward expanded nodes*, which is initially empty.

To process a node $\eta_1 = A.r(\boldsymbol{x}); \psi_1(\boldsymbol{x})$, the algorithm does the following:

1. For each backward expanded node in the graph that has the form $\eta_2 = A.r(\boldsymbol{x})$ $\psi_2(\boldsymbol{x})$, it checks whether $\psi_1(\boldsymbol{x}) \Rightarrow \psi_2(\boldsymbol{x})$. If so, we know that all solutions for η_1 are also solutions to η_2, in which case we say that the node η_2 *subsumes* η_1. The algorithm adds a *specialization edge* from η_2 to η_1.

   The effect of this edge is that each solution $\langle D, \varphi_2(\boldsymbol{x}) \rangle$ that is currently associated with or subsequently added to η_2 is propagated to η_1 as follows: let $\varphi_1(\boldsymbol{x}) = \psi_1(\boldsymbol{x}) \wedge \varphi_2(\boldsymbol{x})$; if $\varphi_1(\boldsymbol{x})$ is satisfiable, then add the solution $\langle D, \varphi_1(\boldsymbol{x}) \rangle$ to η_1.

2. If no backward expanded node subsumes $\eta_1 = A.r(\boldsymbol{x}); \psi_1(\boldsymbol{x})$, then the algorithm adds η_1 to the set of backward expanded nodes, and examines all credentials defining $A.r(\boldsymbol{x})$. For each such credential, there are four cases.

   - *Case-1*: The credential takes the form
     $$A.r(\boldsymbol{x}) \longleftarrow B; \psi_2(\boldsymbol{x})$$
     Let $\varphi(\boldsymbol{x}) = \psi_1(\boldsymbol{x}) \wedge \psi_2(\boldsymbol{x})$; if $\varphi(\boldsymbol{x})$ is satisfiable, then add the solution $\langle B, \varphi(\boldsymbol{x}) \rangle$ to the node η_1.

   - *Case-2*: The credential takes the form
     $$A.r(\boldsymbol{x}) \longleftarrow B.r_2(\boldsymbol{y}); \psi_2(\boldsymbol{x}, \boldsymbol{y})$$
     Let $\psi_3(\boldsymbol{y}) = \exists \boldsymbol{x} \, [\, \psi_1(\boldsymbol{x}) \wedge \psi_2(\boldsymbol{x}, \boldsymbol{y}) \,]$. If $\psi_3(\boldsymbol{y})$ is satisfiable (which can be determined by the existential quantifier elimination procedures of the constraint domains used in ψ_3), create a node $\eta_2 = B.r_2(\boldsymbol{y}); \psi_3(\boldsymbol{y})$, add it to the queue, and add an implication edge from η_2 to η_1.

     The effect of this edge is that each solution $[D, \varphi_2(\boldsymbol{y})]$ currently associated with or subsequently added to the node η_2 is propagated to η_1 as follows. Let $\varphi_1(\boldsymbol{x}) = \exists \boldsymbol{y} \, [\, \psi_1(\boldsymbol{x}) \wedge \psi_2(\boldsymbol{x}, \boldsymbol{y}) \wedge \varphi_2(\boldsymbol{y}) \,]$. If $\varphi_1(\boldsymbol{x})$ is satisfiable, then add the solution $\langle D, \varphi_1(\boldsymbol{x}) \rangle$ to the node η_1.

   - *Case-3*: The credential takes the form
     $$A.r(\boldsymbol{x}) \longleftarrow A.r_1(\boldsymbol{y}).r_2(\boldsymbol{z}); \psi_2(\boldsymbol{x}, \boldsymbol{y}, \boldsymbol{z})$$
     Let $\psi_3(\boldsymbol{y}) = \exists \boldsymbol{x} \exists \boldsymbol{z} \, [\, \psi_1(\boldsymbol{x}) \wedge \psi_2(\boldsymbol{x}, \boldsymbol{y}, \boldsymbol{z}) \,]$. If $\psi_3(\boldsymbol{y})$ is satisfiable, then create a node $\eta_2 = A.r_1(\boldsymbol{y}); \psi_3(\boldsymbol{y})$, add it to the queue, and create a backward monitoring edge from η_2 to η_1.

     The effect of the backward monitoring edge is that for each solution $\langle B, \varphi_1(\boldsymbol{y}) \rangle$ currently associated with or subsequently added to the node η_2, the algorithm does the following. Let $\psi_4(\boldsymbol{z}) = \exists \boldsymbol{x} \exists \boldsymbol{y} \, [\, \psi_1(\boldsymbol{x}) \wedge \psi_2(\boldsymbol{x}, \boldsymbol{y}, \boldsymbol{z}) \wedge \varphi_1(\boldsymbol{y}) \,]$. If $\psi_4(\boldsymbol{z})$ is satisfiable, create a node $\eta_3 = B.r_2(\boldsymbol{z}); \psi_4(\boldsymbol{z})$, add it to the queue, and create a linked implication edge from η_3 to η_1 with $\varphi_1(\boldsymbol{y})$ attached to it.

     The linked implication edge from η_3 to η_1 does the following. Whenever a solution $\langle D, \varphi_3(\boldsymbol{z})) \rangle$ is added to the node η_3, it is propagate to η_1 as follows. Let $\varphi_5(\boldsymbol{x}) = \exists \boldsymbol{y} \exists \boldsymbol{z} \, [\, \psi_1(\boldsymbol{x}) \wedge \psi_2(\boldsymbol{x}, \boldsymbol{y}, \boldsymbol{z}) \wedge \varphi_3(\boldsymbol{z}) \wedge \varphi_1(\boldsymbol{y}) \,]$. If $\varphi_5(\boldsymbol{z})$ is satisfiable, then add the solution $\langle D, \varphi_5(\boldsymbol{x}) \rangle$ to the node η_1.

   - *Case-4*: The credential takes the form
     $$A.r(\boldsymbol{x}) \longleftarrow B_1.r_1(\boldsymbol{y}) \cap B_2.r_2(\boldsymbol{z}); \psi_2(\boldsymbol{x}, \boldsymbol{y}, \boldsymbol{z})$$
     Let $\psi_3(\boldsymbol{y}) = \exists \boldsymbol{x} \exists \boldsymbol{z} \, [\, \psi_1(\boldsymbol{x}) \wedge \psi_2(\boldsymbol{x}, \boldsymbol{y}, \boldsymbol{z}) \,]$, $\psi_4(\boldsymbol{z}) = \exists \boldsymbol{x} \exists \boldsymbol{y} \, [\, \psi_1(\boldsymbol{x}) \wedge \psi_2(\boldsymbol{x}, \boldsymbol{y}, \boldsymbol{z}) \,]$. If both $\psi_3(\boldsymbol{y})$ and $\psi_4(\boldsymbol{z})$ are satisfiable, then create two nodes $\eta_2 = B_1.r_1(\boldsymbol{y}); \psi_3(\boldsymbol{y})$ and $\eta_3 = B_2.r_2(\boldsymbol{z}); \psi_4(\boldsymbol{z})$, add them to the queue,

create an intersection edge from η_2 to η_1 with η_3 attached to it, and create an intersection edge from η_3 to η_1 with η_2 attached to it.

The effect of the intersection edge from η_2 to η_1 is that for each solution $\langle D, \varphi_1(\boldsymbol{y}) \rangle$ currently associated with or subsequently added to the node η_2, the algorithm does the following. It examines the solutions of the node η_3. For each solution of η_3 taking the form $\langle D, \varphi_2(\boldsymbol{z}) \rangle$, let $\varphi_5(\boldsymbol{x}) = \exists \boldsymbol{y} \, \exists \boldsymbol{z} \, [\, \psi_1(\boldsymbol{x}) \wedge \psi_2(\boldsymbol{x}, \boldsymbol{y}, \boldsymbol{z}) \wedge \varphi_1(\boldsymbol{y}) \wedge \varphi_2(\boldsymbol{z}) \,]$. If $\varphi_5(\boldsymbol{x})$ is satisfiable, the algorithm adds the solution $\langle D, \varphi_5(\boldsymbol{x}) \rangle$ to the node η_1.

5.2   The Forward Search Algorithm

The forward search algorithm constructs a proof graph that contains the following two kinds of nodes.

Principal nodes.   Each principal node corresponds to a principal; there is only one principal node for each principal.

Each principal node has a set of solutions. Each solution in a principal node is a constrained role. The invariant is that when the principal D has the solution $A.r(\boldsymbol{x})$; $\varphi(\boldsymbol{x})$, then we have $SP(\mathcal{P}) \models r(A, D, t)$ for all t such that $\varphi(\boldsymbol{x})$ is satisfied.

Furthermore, when the algorithm terminates, it is also true that for each t such that $SP(\mathcal{P}) \models r(A, D, t)$, the node D has a solution $\langle A.r(\boldsymbol{x}); \varphi(\boldsymbol{x}) \rangle$ such that $\varphi(t)$ is satisfied. Thus, queries of type 2 can be answered by taking Λ to be the set of solutions associated with D. Similarly, queries of type 3 can be answered by taking Ω to be the set of constraints $\varphi(\boldsymbol{x})$ such that $\langle A.r(\boldsymbol{x}); \varphi(\boldsymbol{x}) \rangle$ is a solution associated with D.

Role nodes.   In the forward search algorithm, a role node is similar to that in the backward search algorithm. Each such node represents a constrained role $A.r(\boldsymbol{x}); \psi(\boldsymbol{x})$ and contains a list of solutions of the form $\langle D, \varphi(\boldsymbol{x}) \rangle$. The invariant here is as follows: if the node $A.r(\boldsymbol{x}); \psi(\boldsymbol{x})$ has a solution $\langle D, \varphi(\boldsymbol{x}) \rangle$, then $\varphi(\boldsymbol{x}) \Rightarrow \psi(\boldsymbol{x})$ and $SP(\mathcal{P}) \models r(A, D, t)$ for each t such that $\varphi(t)$ is satisfied.

Whenever a solution $\langle D, \varphi(\boldsymbol{x}) \rangle$ is added to a role node $A.r(\boldsymbol{x}); \psi(\boldsymbol{x})$; it will find the principal node for D (and create one if one does not already exist), and add $A.r(\boldsymbol{x}); \varphi(\boldsymbol{x})$ as a solution to D. Notice that the invariant on the latter solution follows from the invariant on the former.

The forward search algorithm maintains a forward processing queue and proceeds by removing nodes from the queue and processing them one by one until the queue is empty. Initially, both the proof graph and the queue contain just a principal node. The forward search algorithm also maintains a set of forward expanded nodes, which is initially empty. Nodes are process as follows:

Forward Processing a Principal Node D

1. Consider all *Type-1* credentials with the principal D in their bodies. For each such $A.r(\boldsymbol{x}) \longleftarrow D; \psi(\boldsymbol{x})$, the algorithm creates a role node $\eta_1 = A.r(\boldsymbol{x}); \psi(\boldsymbol{x})$, adds η_1 to the forward processing queue, and adds the solution $\langle D, \psi(\boldsymbol{x}) \rangle$ to η_1.
2. Each time a principal node D receives a new solution, the algorithm examines all credentials of *Type-4*. For each such $A.r(\boldsymbol{x}) \longleftarrow B_1.r_1(\boldsymbol{y}) \cap B_2.r_2(\boldsymbol{z}); \psi_1(\boldsymbol{x}, \boldsymbol{y}, \boldsymbol{z})$,

if the node D has two forward solutions taking the forms $\{B_1.r_1(\boldsymbol{y}); \varphi_1(\boldsymbol{y})\}$ and $\{B_2.r_2(\boldsymbol{z}); \varphi_2(\boldsymbol{z})\}$, respectively, and one of these is the new solution received by D, then the algorithm proceeds as follows. Let $\psi_2(\boldsymbol{x}) = \exists \boldsymbol{y} \, \exists \boldsymbol{z} \, [\psi_1(\boldsymbol{x}, \boldsymbol{y}, \boldsymbol{z}) \wedge \varphi_1(\boldsymbol{y}) \wedge \varphi_2(\boldsymbol{z})]$. If $\psi_2(\boldsymbol{x})$ is satisfiable, the algorithm creates the node $\eta = A.r(\boldsymbol{x}); \psi_2(\boldsymbol{x})$, adds η to the forward processing queue, and adds the solution $\langle D, \psi_2(\boldsymbol{x}) \rangle$ to the node η.

Forward processing a role node $\eta_2 = B.r_2(\boldsymbol{y}); \psi(\boldsymbol{y})$.

In the following the effects of specialization, implication, and linked implication edges are to propagate solutions from one role node to another just as they do in the backward search algorithm.

1. If there exists a forward expanded node $\eta_1 = B.r_2(\boldsymbol{y}); \psi'(\boldsymbol{y})$ such that $\psi(\boldsymbol{y}) \Rightarrow \psi'(\boldsymbol{y})$, then add a specialization edge from η_2 to η_1. The node η_2 is removed from the queue.
2. If the node η_2 is still in the queue, add it to the set of forward expanded nodes, and examine all *Type-2* credentials with $B.r_2$ in the bodies. For each such credential $A.r(\boldsymbol{x}) \longleftarrow B.r_2(\boldsymbol{y}); \psi_2(\boldsymbol{x}, \boldsymbol{y})$, let $\psi_1(\boldsymbol{x}) = \exists \boldsymbol{y} \, [\psi(\boldsymbol{y}) \wedge \psi_2(\boldsymbol{x}, \boldsymbol{y})]$. If $\psi_1(\boldsymbol{x})$ is satisfiable, create a role node $\eta_1 = A.r_1(\boldsymbol{x}); \psi_1(\boldsymbol{x})$, add it to the forward processing queue, and add an implication edge from η_2 to η_1.
3. Create a principal node $\eta_1 = B$. Add a forward monitoring edge from η_2 to η_1. The effect of the forward monitoring edge is such that whenever the node η_1 receives a forward solution $A.r_1(\boldsymbol{x}); \varphi_1(\boldsymbol{x})$, the algorithm examines all credentials of *Type-3* with $A.r_1(\cdot).r_2(\cdot)$ in their bodies. For each such $A.r(\boldsymbol{z}) \longleftarrow A.r_1(\boldsymbol{x}).r_2(\boldsymbol{y}); \psi_1(\boldsymbol{x}, \boldsymbol{y}, \boldsymbol{z})$, the algorithm proceeds as follows. Let $\psi_2(\boldsymbol{z}) = \exists \boldsymbol{x} \, \exists \boldsymbol{y} \, [\varphi_1(\boldsymbol{x}) \wedge \psi(\boldsymbol{y}) \wedge \psi_1(\boldsymbol{x}, \boldsymbol{y}, \boldsymbol{z})]$. If $\psi_2(\boldsymbol{z})$ is satisfiable, then create a node $\eta_3 = A.r(\boldsymbol{z}); \psi_2(\boldsymbol{z})$, add it to the forward processing queue, and add a linked implication edge from η_2 to η_3 with $\varphi_1(\boldsymbol{x})$ attached to it.

5.3 Bidirectional Search Algorithm

The bidirectional search algorithm integrates the backward and forward searches. The backward search algorithm and the forward search algorithm are executed simultaneously, starting with the query role and the query principal, respectively. As these two searches progress, they typically construct some identical or related nodes. When this occurs, the bidirectional search transfers solutions between the backward proof graph and the forward proof graph. We transfer the solutions as follows:

- **Transfer solutions from the backward proof graph to the forward proof graph:** Whenever the role node $\eta_1 = A.r(\boldsymbol{x}); \psi(\boldsymbol{x})$ in the backward proof graph receives a solution, say $\langle D, \varphi(\boldsymbol{x}) \rangle$, the algorithm creates the principal node $\eta_2 = D$ in the forward search graph, and adds the forward solution $A.r(\boldsymbol{x}); \varphi(\boldsymbol{x})$ to the node η_2.
- **Transfer solutions from the forward proof graph to the backward proof graph:** For each pair of role nodes $\eta_1 = A.r(\boldsymbol{x}); \psi_1(\boldsymbol{x})$ in the forward graph and $\eta_2 = A.r(\boldsymbol{x}); \psi_2(\boldsymbol{x})$ in the backward graph, if $\psi_3(\boldsymbol{x}) = \psi_1(\boldsymbol{x}) \wedge \psi_2(\boldsymbol{x})$ is satisfiable, then add a bidirectional monitoring edge from η_1 to η_2.

  The effect of the bidirectional monitoring edge is that whenever the node η_1 receives a solution $\langle D, \varphi_1(\boldsymbol{x}) \rangle$, let $\varphi_2(\boldsymbol{x}) = \varphi_1(\boldsymbol{x}) \wedge \psi_2(\boldsymbol{x})$. If $\varphi_2(\boldsymbol{x})$ is satisfiable, then add the solution $\langle D, \varphi_2(\boldsymbol{x}) \rangle$ to the node η_2.

Besides transferring the solutions between the backward proof graph and forward proof graph, we need to handle the role intersection specially.

- In the backward proof graph, if there is an intersection edge from η_2 to η_1, whenever the node η_2 receives a solution, say $\langle D, \varphi(x) \rangle$, the algorithm adds the principal node $\eta_3 = D$ to the forward processing queue.
- In the forward proof graph, whenever the principal node $\eta_1 = D$ receives a forward solution, say $B_1.r_1(y); \varphi(y)$, the algorithm examines all credentials of *Type-4*. For each credential having either the form $A.r(x) \longleftarrow B_1.r_1(y) \cap B_2.r_2(z); \psi_1(x, y, z)$ or the form $A.r(x) \longleftarrow B_2.r_2(z) \cap B_1.r_1(y); \psi_1(x, y, z)$, the algorithm proceeds as follows. Let $\psi_2(z) = \exists x \, \exists y \, [\, \psi_1(x, y, z) \wedge \varphi(y) \,]$. If $\psi_2(x)$ is satisfiable, the algorithm creates the role node $\eta_2 = B.r_2(z); \psi_2(z)$ in the backward proof graph and adds η_2 to the backward processing queue.

6   Conclusions

RT_1^C is a language in the RT family of Role-based Trust-management languages. It features rich delegation structures, parameterized roles, and constraints. In this paper we present a goal-directed distributed credential chain discovery algorithm for RT_1^C. We describe this algorithm in detail and illustrate this algorithm with an example.

Comparing it with existing work on logic programming and deductive databases, our algorithm is a combination of the logic-programming style top-down query evaluation with tabling [3] (corresponding to our backward search) and the deductive database style bottom-up evaluation (corresponding to our forward search). Our algorithm uses hints provided through the storage types to determine which directions to use for a particular part of the proof; this enables the algorithm to touch only those credentials that are related to the query, which are likely to be a small fraction of all the credentials in the system.

Acknowledgement

Portions of this work were supported by NSF CCR-0325951, NSF CNS-0448204, NSF CCF-0524010, and sponsors of CERIAS. We thank the anonymous reviewers for their helpful comments.

References

1. M. Blaze, J. Feigenbaum, and J. Lacy. Decentralized trust management. In *Proceedings of the 1996 IEEE Symposium on Security and Privacy*, pages 164–173. IEEE Computer Society Press, May 1996.
2. A. Bouajjani, J. Esparza, and O. Maler. Reachability analysis of pushdown automata: Application to model-checking. In *Proceedings of CONCUR'97*, number 1256 in Lecture Notes in Computer Science, pages 135–150. Springer, 1997.
3. W. Chen and D. S. Warren. Tabled evaluation with delaying for general logic programs. *Journal of the ACM*, 43(1):20–74, Jan. 1996.

4. D. Clarke, J.-E. Elien, C. Ellison, M. Fredette, A. Morcos, and R. L. Rivest. Certificate chain discovery in SPKI/SDSI. *Journal of Computer Security*, 9(4):285–322, 2001.
5. C. Ellison, B. Frantz, B. Lampson, R. Rivest, B. Thomas, and T. Ylonen. SPKI certificate theory. IETF RFC 2693, Sept. 1999.
6. C. A. Gunter and T. Jim. Policy-directed certificate retrieval. *Software: Practice & Experience*, 30(15):1609–1640, Sept. 2000.
7. S. Jha and T. Reps. Analysis of SPKI/SDSI certificates using model checking. In *Proceedings of the 15th IEEE Computer Security Foundations Workshop*, pages 129–144. IEEE Computer Society Press, June 2002.
8. T. Jim. SD3: A trust management system with certified evaluation. In *Proceedings of the 2001 IEEE Symposium on Security and Privacy*, pages 106–115. IEEE Computer Society Press, May 2001.
9. P. C. Kanellakis, G. M. Kuper, and P. Z. Revesz. Constraint query languages. *Journal of Computer and System Sciences*, 51(1):26–52, Aug. 1995.
10. N. Li and J. C. Mitchell. Datalog with constraints: A foundation for trust management languages. In *Proceedings of the Fifth International Symposium on Practical Aspects of Declarative Languages (PADL 2003)*, number 2562 in LNCS, pages 58–73. Springer, Jan. 2003.
11. N. Li, J. C. Mitchell, and W. H. Winsborough. Design of a role-based trust management framework. In *Proceedings of the 2002 IEEE Symposium on Security and Privacy*, pages 114–130. IEEE Computer Society Press, May 2002.
12. N. Li, W. H. Winsborough, and J. C. Mitchell. Distributed credential chain discovery in trust management. *Journal of Computer Security*, 11(1):35–86, Feb. 2003.
13. R. Ramakrishnan. Magic templates: a spellbinding approach to logic programs. *Journal of Logic Programming*, 11(3-4):189–216, 1991.
14. P. Z. Revesz. Constraint databases: A survey. In L. Libkin and B. Thalheim, editors, *Semantics in Databases*, number 1358 in LNCS, pages 209–246. Springer, 1998.
15. R. L. Rivest and B. Lampson. SDSI — a simple distributed security infrastructure, Oct. 1996. Available at *http://theory.lcs.mit.edu/~rivest/sdsi11.html*.
16. R. S. Sandhu, E. J. Coyne, H. L. Feinstein, and C. E. Youman. Role-based access control models. *IEEE Computer*, 29(2):38–47, February 1996.
17. D. Toman. Memoing evaluation for constraint extensions of Datalog. *Constraints: An International Journal*, 2:337–359, 1997.

An Operating System Design for the Security Architecture for Microprocessors

Jörg Platte, Raúl Durán Díaz, and Edwin Naroska

Institut für Roboterforschung, Abteilung Informationstechnik,
Universität Dortmund, Germany
{joerg.platte, edwin.naroska}@udo.edu, raul.duran@uah.es

Abstract. *SAM* is a processor extension used to protect execution of dedicated programs by preventing data disclosure and program manipulations in a multitasking environment. This paper presents an operating system design based on the Linux kernel for *SAM*. The design splits the kernel into a very small protected part and an unprotected part used by drivers and high level functions. Using this kernel protected and unprotected programs can be executed in parallel without diminishing the protection. The protection mechanism does not slow down the execution of unprotected programs, since it is only active during the execution of protected programs.

Keywords: Secure Operating Systems, Certified Execution, Encrypted Programs, Secure Processors.

1 Introduction

Protecting software is becoming more important for the future and, therefore, efficient protection schemes are required. Ideally, these schemes should provide a strong protection while keeping to a minimum the number of required modifications at the software layer (both operating system and user applications), and in the hardware layer as well. Some processor extensions, such as AEGIS [1] and *SAM* [2,3], have been so far proposed, providing a secure execution environment for programs. A program running inside a secure execution environment is safe against both software attacks (originating, for example, from a system administrator or even from a malicious kernel) and hardware attacks (for example, hardware supported sniffing on memory bus to bypass operating system protections).

A number of different applications can benefit from these extensions. One of them is the implementation of efficient copy protection schemes, both for static data and for instructions. Another important field is the case of remote execution of programs such as in GRID computing, since then programs can be executed on many different computers spread all over the world, and the submitter of these programs may not trust all the remote systems. Using a security extension, the GRID can be used even for sensitive simulation data or secret algorithms.

This paper presents an organized description of the modifications needed at the operating system level in order to leverage the security capabilities provided

P. Ning, S. Qing, and N. Li (Eds.): ICICS 2006, LNCS 4307, pp. 174–189, 2006.

by the *SAM* architecture. To test the performance of the complete system, a simulation environment has been developed, and several simulations have been conducted.

The paper is organized as follows: Section 2 provides a brief overview about the *SAM* security architecture. Other security architectures are presented in section 3. Section 4 presents a detailed description of the operating system modifications (based on a SPARC-Linux kernel). In sections 5 and 6, the simulation environment and the computed results are presented. Last, some conclusions in section 7 close the paper.

2 *SAM* Overview

SAM provides a secure execution environment for programs based on a standard processor design and a standard operating system. *SAM* aims at preventing tampering attempts as well as data and program disclosure.

The next paragraphs provide a brief description of *SAM's* main attributes. A more detailed architectural description can be found in [2] and the design of the caches in [3].

The current *SAM* processor design is based on a SPARC V8 compatible CPU [4] and was intended to be an optional extension. Hence, no secured bootstrapping or persistent trusted operating system core is required to run *SAM* protected programs. Both protected and normal unprotected programs can be executed in a multitasking environment and small parts of the operating system are protected only while executing protected programs. Therefore, there is no overhead when only unprotected programs are executed since then a *SAM* enhanced processor behaves like a standard processor. As soon as a protected program is started, *SAM* begins to verify the program related data and the protected part of the operating system.

Each verification error or security access violation results in an immediate program termination and the deletion of all data, including program related keys. The processor then issues a special *SAM* TRAP to inform the kernel about the fault and the reasons.

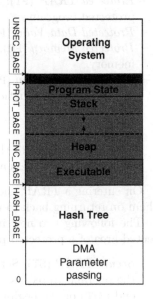

Fig. 1. Memory Layout

The processor core consists of an enhanced ALU supporting additional security instructions, an L1 data and instruction cache as well as an L2 cache. All data inside this core is trusted whereas all data outside is assumed to be untrusted. As described in [3], the L2 cache is endowed with a checked context dictionary to improve the access to shared protected memory. These dictionary entries consists of dynamically assigned context numbers a cache line can be checked for. Each cache lines TAG memory has a corresponding bit for each entry in the dictionary to reduce the number of re-verifications for shared protected memory.

SAM uses a per process fixed virtual memory layout (see figure 1) with two partially overlapping virtual address ranges. In the protected region all data is protected and verified by hash values; in the encrypted region, all data is additionally encrypted. All user instructions located in protected memory regions (protected instructions) are granted access permissions, so that they are supplied with the decrypted values when they access an address located inside an encrypted region. Any other unprotected instruction can not access the cleartext data.

The status of a SPARC processor is maintained using a set of flags, grouped together in a status register, such as the the supervisor flag (S), set when the processor is in supervisor mode. *SAM* introduces a number of additional flags, necessary to support the secure execution environment and to represent its current protection status. These flags, which are only used when a program is executing in protected mode, are the following:

- *Protected Process* (PP): Set for a protected process.
- *Protected TRAP* (PT): Set when executing instructions after a TRAP of a protected program.
- *Protected Data Valid* (PV): Set if all data has been successfully verified.
- *Protected Memory* (PM): Set if the current instruction is located in protected memory.
- *Protected Instruction* (PI): Set depending on the value of other flags, following this boolean equation:

$$PI = PM \wedge (\neg S \vee PT).$$

This flag is passed to the cache to mark protected instructions and used to control register access as described below.

On entering a TRAP, the processor sets the S flag and the PT flag, and resets them on returning back to user mode with a RETT[1].

The following two new instructions are intended to be executed in the protected area of a protected program[2]:

- *Secure TRAP* (ST): Set or clears the PT flag based on the register value of the operand to request or drop additional privileges. It is used to mark the end (STE) or the beginning (STS) of a secure TRAP and can be executed in supervisor mode only.
- *Register Protection* (RPROT): Used to enable or disable register protection for any register in the current register set by using a mask as an operand.

The *SAM* architecture described in [2] has been analyzed with regard to the operating system needs. This analysis showed that the architecture could be

---

[1] Return from TRAP.
[2] Outside the protected area they behave like a NOP.

simplified in many ways without affecting security. The following simplifications have been assumed in the simulation environment: To begin with, the number of additional instructions has been reduced from nine to two. Then, the register protection has been simplified so that the current implementation uses only one additional bit for each physical register. This bit is set to the current value of PI on register write operations. For a register read operation to be successful, both its associated bit and the PI flag must be equal. Otherwise, the processor reports a security access violation.

The SPARC architecture stores the beginning of the TRAP table in the TRAP table base register (TBR). *SAM* XORes this address with the secret program key k [2] to bound the program to the location of the protected TRAP table.

A *SAM* executable is stored in an ELF file like any other executable. But this executable is generated by a "security linker". It reads a statically linked file as input, encrypts it and stores the corresponding sparse hash tree ([5,6]) within the executable. The hash tree covers not only the program code and data, but additionally a small lower part of the operating system. This part contains the trap table and is responsible for basic trap handling like storing or loading registers on or from the stack and saving the program state. The processor ensures that these functions are located in protected memory. As a result, a program is bound to a specific processor and operating system version.

3   Related Work

Intel released their preliminary architecture specification of the LaGrande technology in the year 2006 [7,8]. This technology is connected with Intel's virtualization attempts to provide a hardware protected operating system running in parallel to an unprotected one. LaGrande consists of a processor extension which works in conjunction with a modified chipset, input and output devices to provide a secure execution environment, for example for the Next Generation Secure Computing Base from Microsoft [9], with protected input and output paths. The whole boot process including the BIOS and the bootloaders are protected as well. This results in a very complex system with a huge protected codebase which complicates code auditing. Memory contents are not encrypted, but the chipset is used to control memory access.

Closely related to this architecture is the Trusted Platform Module (TPM) [10] developed by the Trusted Computing Group [11]. The module itself is not able to encrypt memory contents. This has to be done in software by the main processor. The module can only be used to store small amounts of information like encryption keys. Additionally, a TPM provides cryptographic functions, which can be used to protect the boot process and for identification purposes.

Another more related approach is the AEGIS architecture [1], a successor of the XOM architecture [12]. As *SAM*, AEGIS provides transparent data and instruction encryption, decryption and verification of memory contents.

In AEGIS, a program consists of unencrypted, encrypted and protected parts and the architecture provides secure transitions between these parts. Variables and functions can be assigned to these regions at compile time by the programmer. Hence, the programmer needs a profound knowledge about possible attacks to not leak secure data.

In order to prevent software based attacks, AEGIS requires a special bootstrapping mechanism to load a security kernel that has access to the page table and other sensitive information. Memory contents are protected by hash trees based on their physical address. This requires free pages at subsequent physical addresses and precludes paging of these data without reencrypting them.

Each time a new program is started, AEGIS first computes a hash over all secured program related data. This hash is then used in conjunction with processor and operating system hashes to decrypt the program. The initial hashing of a program is a time consuming and complex task, which has been implemented by executing internal microcode instead of a direct hardware implementation.

In addition to the hash values, AEGIS suggests the usage of 32 bit counters to encrypt data, which implies approx. 6 % additional memory consumption. This potentially gives rise to more misses during memory operations. Depending on the number of memory access, this counter can overflow resulting in a time-consuming reencryption, using a new key, of all program related data. Longer counters can prevent this for most programs, but they consume more memory.

Compared to the introduced security architectures SAM does not require a fully protected boot process or modifications to other parts of a computer system than the processor. SAM does require a partly protected operating system, but this part is very small and the protection overhead is minimal, especially when considering that there is no overhead for unprotected programs. -

4   Operating System Design

This section first gives an overview about the basic tasks of the Linux operating system. The subsections point out possible threats and a description of the adjustments to the SPARC-Linux kernel to thwart these. These modifications are kept to a minimum.

4.1   Tasks of Operating Systems

Loosely speaking, an operating system is required whenever resources of any kind must be shared by several concurrently-running processes. In a time-sharing scheme, the operating system scheduler assigns time slots to each runnable process, during which the process is able to execute its own instructions. In several instances (at the end of a time slot, whenever a hardware interrupt is raised or each time the program wants to invoke a system call), the program is interrupted and enters supervisor mode.

On SPARC computers the interrupts are called TRAP's [4]. During a TRAP, the CPU stores the program counters (PC and NPC) in registers and then the operating system[3] typically saves the interrupted program specific data —for

---

[3] The following explanations are based on the Linux kernel.

instance, the contents of a register sets— on the program stack and the current CPU status in kernel structures. Then, the stack pointer is redirected from the user space stack to the kernel stack so that the kernel can safely execute its own code without affecting, or being affected by, the user program. Note that the context remains the same, even when executing instructions in kernel memory area. This allows the kernel to access arbitrary data from user space, which is normally required for parameter passing between user space and kernel space.

After the kernel has finished its tasks, the scheduler selects the next process to be executed. If the selected one is different from the previously executed process, the kernel performs a context switch to change the memory mapping.

4.2   Threats

The *SAM* architecture provides a hardware based protection against external attacks, such as memory modifications and bus sniffing [3]. Another class of attacks are software based attacks originated by the operating system. As described in the subsection 4.1 the operating system is involved in many tasks and can harm the program, for example, in the following ways:

- *Program counter manipulations*: The kernel stores the program counters (PC and NPC) on each TRAP to be able to return to the interrupted instruction. A malicious kernel can modify these values to alter the program flow.
- *Register manipulations*: A modification of register values can alter the program flow as well as resulting in wrong computations.
- *Register value disclosure*: Since the operating system has all access permissions, it could disclose the contents of the register, which should really be kept secret. This is all the more important for a Load/Store architecture, such as SPARC, since then many operands are contained in registers.
- *Register mapping manipulations*: The SPARC architecture uses several physical registers mapped to a (normally much lower) number of logical registers. If a malicious kernel is able to change these mapping, even without directly changing the register values, the result is the same as for the register manipulations case.
- *Forging of memory contents*: There are several places where the kernel is able to forge memory contents. For example:
  - when passing return values to the user program after a system call,
  - when accessing external devices,
  - when setting up the environment variables and command line parameters,
  - by manipulating the page mapping.
- *Manipulating system call return values*: Most system calls return values either in registers or in memory. These values can be tampered with by the operating system to manipulate the program.
- *Tracking the accessed memory area*: The operating system can record all accessed pages using a manipulated page table by forcing a page fault TRAP for each executed instruction.

Unlike a hardware-only approach, which would result in a more complex design and less flexibility, *SAM* exploits a combined hard- and software approach, described in the following subsections. Note that the following sections only apply to protected programs.

4.3   Protected Kernel

Along with some changes in the hardware, *SAM* requires that a (small) part of the operating system is protected and checked automatically by hardware. This part resides in protected memory and, therefore, is protected by hash values, to be provided by the protected program. The protected part has a size of roughly a mere 64 kByte and is located directly over the user stack, at the beginning of the kernel virtual address space. Its main purpose is to ensure a secure transition between the protected user mode and the (mostly) unprotected kernel mode. Using this design, the major part of the operating system kernel, including drivers, can remain unprotected. As a side effect, kernel upgrades, such as bug fixes or additional drivers, are possible without affecting the protected part.

Besides these hash values, each protected program has to provide one additional page located in virtual user space directly before the protected kernel. This page mostly consists of zeros and is used as a protected *compartment* for the corresponding program by the kernel. All data written to this page is protected by *SAM*, since it belongs to the protected and encrypted area. For this reason, the kernel must ensure that this page cannot be paged out. The "security linker" creates this page before encrypting the program and initializes it with the entry point of the program. Then, this page is encrypted along with the rest of the program.

Each time a protected executable is to be started the kernel performs the following steps (cf. [2,3] for more details):

1. Identification of the executable by reading the target architecture. If the executable is not protected, it is loaded in the same manner as an unmodified kernel does. The following steps are performed only if the executable is protected.
2. Assigning an unused secure context number to the new program.
3. Reading the encrypted program dependent secret key from the executable and passing it to the RSA unit for decryption.
4. Loading of the protected program like any other unprotected program by creating the page mappings. At this time the required parts of the sparse hash tree are mapped to memory as well as the protected *compartment*. This is done by the ELF loader in the Linux kernel.
5. When the RSA unit has successfully decrypted the key, the cache automatically loads and decrypts the root hash.
6. Switching to the new secure context to execute an initialization routine, used to check and copy command line parameters and environment variables to the protected stack. A second call of this initialization routine is prevented by setting a lock in the protected *compartment*.

7. Now the new program is ready to be scheduled and will be started by dispatching to the instruction located at the program entry point stored at program linking time.

These steps ensure that the kernel can call the protected initialization routine only one time and the program is started at the intended position.

4.4   User-Supervisor Mode Transitions

As described in the last subsections, the operating system is involved in TRAP handling. To prevent TRAP-based attacks, the *SAM* processor hardware verifies the following conditions for all protected programs when invoking a TRAP and terminates the program immediately, if anyone condition is not satisfied:

1. *Protected TRAP table*: The TRAP table must reside inside the protected area of the program.
2. *Protected TRAP instructions*: All instructions executed in the kernel must be protected, until the ST instruction clears the PT flag. Then, the protected part of the kernel can be quit.
3. *Protected S (supervisor) bit*: This bit can be cleared only when the PI bit is set. Hence, the RETT instruction has to be located in the protected part of the operating system.
4. *Base address of TRAP table*: Write access to the TRAP base register is prevented as long as protected programs are running.

These conditions are used to ensure secure transitions between user and kernel space only. A TRAP for a protected program can be divided into the following transitions:

1. User space to kernel space: This transition requires the TRAP table to be located in protected memory. As a result, the executed kernel code is protected and has full access to registers and memory contents.
2. Protected kernel to unprotected kernel instructions: This transition is preluded with the execution of the STE instruction to clear the PT flag. Hence, this instruction is to be called before leaving the protected area.
3. Unprotected kernel to protected kernel: With this transition the protected part can be reentered by executing the STS instruction again, thus setting the PT flag.
4. Kernel space to user space: This transition is performed by executing the RETT instruction.

These transitions can prevent external manipulations only if the state of the program can not be modified between the second and the third transition. To prevent these modifications, all sensitive data is stored in protected and encrypted memory. This data consists, at least, of the program counters (PC and NPC) of the next instructions to execute and the processor state registers. All register values are stored on the stack located in protected and encrypted memory, too. In this way, *SAM* is able to prevent modifications of any of these values while the program is interrupted and unprotected data is executed.

As stated before, when the kernel has finished its tasks, the scheduler selects the next process to execute. If the selected candidate is other than the interrupted process, a context switch is performed. At each context switch all remaining protected registers are deleted and the protection bits cleared. If the newly selected process is protected, the kernel performs the third transition in order to restore the program state and register values.

Another possible attack to alter the execution of protected programs would be a direct execution of code by jumping into the user program or somewhere into a protected kernel area. But this is prevented by the hardware, since protected instructions in supervisor mode without the PT flag set have no privileges to access encrypted memory or protected registers. Dropping privileges by clearing the supervisor flag in the PSR or by executing a RETT instruction with a cleared PT flag is also forbidden. Hence, a protected user program can only be resumed by following the protected kernel path.

4.5   User Mode

SAM requires only small user mode changes. Compared to an unprotected program, most parts of a program can remain unchanged. The only major difference consists in the system call handling. With each system call, some parameters are passed to the kernel in registers and memory mapped structures. Since major parts of the kernel are located in unprotected areas, direct access to protected registers and protected memory areas is impossible. Fortunately, all system calls are covered by libraries, primarily the libc on Unix compatible systems. So, it mostly suffices to adjust the libraries and the kernel to allow parameter passing, leaving the user code unmodified.

Access to register values can be granted by executing the RPROT instruction in the protected part of the kernel. Just before returning from a system call the registers containing the unprotected return values can be re-protected using the RPROT instruction again.

Data passed in memory to the kernel and vice versa needs a special handling because this data has to be located in unprotected memory to be readable and writable by the kernel. To achieve this, the libc can copy all data into protected memory and adjust the pointers to it before executing the system call. This works in most cases, but it performs poorly. A better solution, which requires modifications to existing code, is the use of a special malloc function provided by the libc returning a pointer to an unprotected memory area. Then, the user program can use this memory area to store all data intended to be passed to the kernel.

The new instructions introduced by *SAM* are not used in user space. Hence, no modified compiler or assembler is required to write *SAM* programs.

4.6   Summary

This subsection summarizes how the threats listed in section 4.2 are prevented by *SAM*:

- *Program counter manipulations*: The program counter is stored in the protected *compartment* and cannot be modified by unprotected instructions.
- *Register manipulations*: Registers are stored on the user stack which is protected by hash values.
- *Register value disclosure*: The hardware register protection prevents reading protected registers outside the protected kernel area.
- *Register mapping manipulations*: The register mapping is stored in the protected *compartment* as well.
- *Forging of memory contents*: *SAM* requires that a program verifies all data read from unprotected sources. All data in protected regions is protected by hashes (which prevent page table attacks) or written and verified by the protected part of the kernel (such as the environment variables and command line parameters).
- *Manipulating system call return values*: This kind of attack cannot be prevented by the current design, because data from unprotected sources can always be manipulated. Fortunately, the number of different system calls used by most programs is fairly low and most direct attacks, such as forged pointers or sizes of these system calls, can be detected by the libc.
- *Tracking the accessed memory area*: This attack cannot be prevented as well but, since *SAM* does not protect the address bus, a prevention of this attack at the operating system level is useless. An attacker could always get the address information by sniffing on the address bus.

5 Simulation Environment

This section briefly describes the simulation environment used to compute the results presented in section 6. The performance evaluation of different cache configurations is based on the SPEC benchmark suite. All benchmarks are executed in a virtual machine emulating a SPARC based computer with peripherals like hard disk, framebuffer and keyboard. This virtual machine is based on the free system emulator QEMU [13]. QEMU translates all instructions of the guest system into native assembler instructions of the host system. Hence, all timing and memory access information are lost. Therefore, QEMU has been extended to add special monitoring instructions during the translation step. They are used to log instruction fetches, read and write data and I/O accesses by the CPU and memory access by simulated peripheral devices as well as context switches and interrupts to a trace file.

This trace file is then used as an input file for the *SAM* cache simulator. It simulates an L1 data and instruction cache as well as the L2 cache with all security related extensions described in [3] to compute the number of simulated clock cycles for these operations. Instruction and data access are passed to the corresponding L1 cache and external device access is simulated by occupying the memory bus. One limitation of using a trace file is a missing feedback from the simulator to QEMU.

The cache simulator is fully configurable in terms of cache sizes, bus widths, number of queue entries and their thresholds, clock divisors to simulate different

Table 1. Cache properties

Cache property	Value
L1 placement	direct mapped
L1 line size	32 bytes
L2 placement	LRU, 4-way-set
L2 line size	64 bytes

Bus	Width	Divisor
L1 ↔ L2 cache	128 bit	2
to memory	64 bit	5
L2 cache ↔ Queues	128 bit	2
to AES units	128 bit	2

Table 2. Cache configurations

Name	L1 size	L2 size	AES units	Check Queue entries
256-*	8k	256k	5	5
1024-*	16k	1024k	5	5
2048-*	32k	2048k	5	5

clock rates for buses and components like the caches, memory latencies or hashing algorithms. The L1 cache runs always with maximum clock speed and all other components are clocked with divisors based on this clock rate. Table 1 lists the basic configuration used for all simulations.

For all simulations, all program data is located between the virtual addresses 0x70000000 and 0xefffffff and has been encrypted. The first 64 KByte of the operating system (0xf0000000–0xf000ffff) are protected. The hash tree starts at address 0x1aaaaab0. Beside the modifications described in the previous sections, the Linux kernel has been modified to allocate memory for the heap starting at address 0x80000000.

In this paper, the multitasking behavior of a *SAM* enabled system has been analyzed. Therefore, for each simulation several benchmarks are executed in parallel. Some benchmarks have a huge memory footprint and paging of protected programs is currently not supported by the modified Linux kernel. Hence, each simulation consists of the execution of one instance of a primary benchmark (out of the SPEC suite) and a number of instances of a secondary benchmark. Due to its reasonable memory footprint, *crafty* has been selected as a secondary benchmark.

After skipping the first 2^{32} simulated instructions, which correspond basically to the initialization routines of each benchmark, each of the started benchmarks has been terminated after a given amount of instructions in user mode resulting in a trace file containing a total of approximately 2^{32} instructions.

Using this trace file, a set of different cache configurations has been simulated to obtain the overall number of simulated cache clock cycles needed for all cache operations. This set includes a configuration without security extensions which is further used as a reference for the speedup computation.

6   Simulation Results

Table 2 gives an overview about the configurations used for all simulations. The Figures 2 and 3 show the simulation results for different cache and benchmark configurations. The results for a particular benchmark in each figure have been

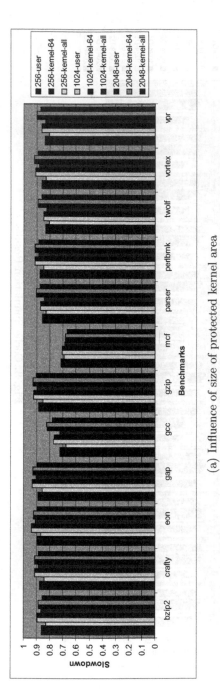

(a) Influence of size of protected kernel area

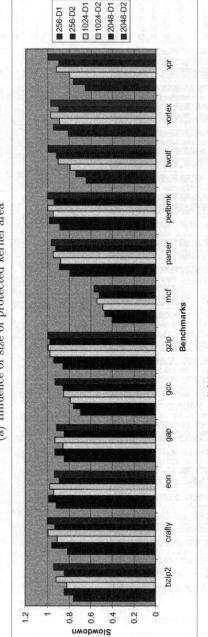

(b) Two protected programs

Fig. 2. Cache Simulation Results

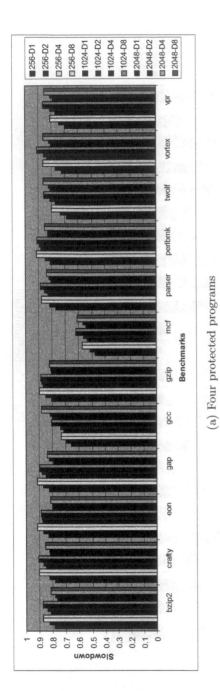

(a) Four protected programs

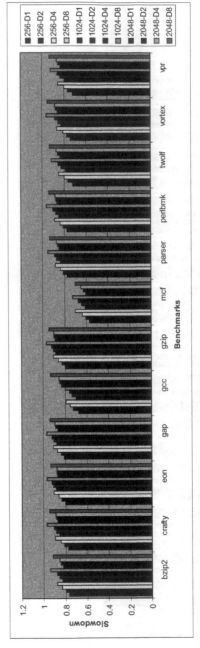

(b) Eight protected programs

Fig. 3. Cache Simulation Results

computed using the same trace file using different cache configurations. The y-axis shows the speedup computed with respect to basically the same cache configuration but without security extensions. Since the speedup is always less than one it is denoted as *slowdown* in all figures.

To measure the influence of the protected part of the kernel, a benchmark configuration with three protected and four unprotected parallel invocations of the secondary benchmark has been started in parallel with the protected primary benchmark.

Figure 2(a) shows the speedups for fully unprotected (*user*), fully protected (*kernel-all*) and partly protected (*kernel-64*) kernel memory running with a cache with four dictionary entries. The partly protected kernel memory covers the protected part of the Linux kernel described in this paper. It can be seen that there is no or only a very small performance degradation for most benchmarks when comparing the *user* and *kernel-64* results. Only a fully protected kernel area displays distinct performance degradation.

The figures 2(b), 3(a), and 3(b) are showing the results for dictionaries with 1, 2, 4, and 8 entries (D1 to D8). Figure 2(b) shows the speedups for two parallel executed protected benchmarks. This figure shows the huge influence of the dictionary, since two entries instead of one can improve the speedup by more than 10 percent points (*crafty*, 256 configuration).

The figures 3(a) and 3(b) are showing the impact of the dictionary for more parallel executed benchmarks. Each benchmark can take an advantage of more dictionary entries up to the number of protected programs. The speedup grows linearly for smaller caches whereas for larger caches the impact is reduced as soon as the number of protected programs exceeds the number of dictionary entries.

In another simulation the overhead of the newly written protected part has been compared with an unmodified Linux kernel. For this comparison each of the simulations listed in figure 3(b) has been started ten times with the unmodified kernel and with the *SAM*-enabled kernel, respectively. Then, the mean values of the number of executed instructions for both kernels have been compared. The comparison proved an almost equal number of clock cycles for both kernels. Hence, the *SAM*-enabled kernel does not result in a performance degradation for unprotected programs.

As a result, *SAM* provides a reasonable performance with a speedup between 0.8 and 1 for most benchmarks.

7   Conclusion

In this paper an operating system kernel design based on Linux for the *SAM* architecture has been introduced. *SAM* consists of a combined hardware and software design providing a secure execution environment for sensitive programs by preventing external modifications or data disclosure. The previous design described in [2] has been optimized and simplified in terms of register protection and the number of additional instructions to reduce the hardware overhead.

For *SAM*, the kernel has to be divided into a small protected and an unprotected part, respectively. Unlike other designs, *SAM's* protected kernel is only protected by the concurrently executed protected programs. When only unprotected programs are executed, the protected part of the kernel is not protected resulting in no additional overhead.

The protected part of the Linux kernel has been redesigned to support the additional instructions of *SAM*. Using these instructions only a defined set of transitions between a protected program, the protected and the unprotected part of the kernel is allowed. During these transitions the execution within the protected part follows only a predefined path. Each time before this path is left, the kernel stores the current state of the program in a security *compartment*. This is a page in protected and encrypted user space used by the kernel. Using this *compartment*, sensitive data like the program counters are protected against attacks while the kernel executes unprotected instructions.

SAM requires that the protected part of the kernel drops its privileges by executing the STE instruction. After executing this instruction in kernel mode, even instructions in protected memory areas lose their ability to access protected registers or encrypted memory. These privileges can only be obtained again by executing the STS instruction in the protected kernel part.

The simulation results show that the cache design of *SAM* with the context dictionary supports the operating design. *SAM* is designed as an extension, used by a limited number of programs. Hence, a limited number of dictionary entries is sufficient to provide a good performance. Even if the number of protected processes is larger than the number of dictionary entries the performance is reasonable.

As a summary, compared to an unprotected kernel, the overhead of the *SAM*-enhanced kernel is negligible and the overall performance of the *SAM* architecture with a speedup between 0.8 and 1 for most configurations is very good.

References

1. Suh, G.E.: AEGIS: A Single-Chip Secure Processor. PhD thesis, Massachusetts Institute of Technology (2005)
2. Platte, J., Naroska, E.: A combined hardware and software architecture for secure computing. In: CF '05: Proceedings of the 2nd conference on Computing frontiers, New York, NY, USA, ACM Press (2005) 280–288
3. Platte, J., Naroska, E., Grundmann, K.: A cache design for a security architecture for microprocessors (SAM). In Grass, W., Sick, B., Waldschmidt, K., eds.: Lecture Notes in Computer Science. Volume 3894 of LNCS. (2006) 435 – 449
4. SPARC International Inc.: The Sparc Architecture Manual Version 8. SPARC International Inc., http://www.sparc.com (1991)
5. Gassend, B., Clarke, D., Suh, G.E., van Dijk, M., Devadas, S.: Caches and Hash Trees for Efficient Memory Integrity Verification. In: Proceedings of the Ninth International Symposium on High Performance Computer Architecture (HPCA-9). (2003)

6. Merkle, R.C.: Protocols for public key cryptosystems. In IEEE, ed.: IEEE Symposium on Security and Privacy, 1109 Spring Street, Suite 300, Silver Spring, MD 20910, USA, IEEE Computer Society Press (1980) 122–134
7. Intel Corporation: LaGrande Technology Preliminary Architecture Specification. `ftp://download.intel.com/technology/security/downloads/PRELIM-LT-SPEC_D52212.pdf` (2006)
8. Intel Corporation: LaGrande Technology Architectural Overview. `ftp://download.intel.com/technology/security/downloads/LT_Arch_Overview.pdf` (2003)
9. Microsoft: Next-generation secure computing base. `http://www.microsoft.com/resources/ngscb/` (2006)
10. Trusted Computing Group: TPM main part 1 design principle, specification version 1.2, revision 94. `https://www.trustedcomputinggroup.org/groups/tpm` (2006)
11. Trusted Computing Group. `https://www.trustedcomputinggroup.org/` (2006)
12. Lie, D., Thekkath, C.A., Mitchell, M., Lincoln, P., Boneh, D., Mitchell, J.C., Horowitz, M.: Architectural support for copy and tamper resistant software (2000)
13. Bellard, F.: QEMU, a fast and portable dynamic translator. In: Proceedings of USENIX 2005 Annual Technical Conference. (2005) 41–46

Point-Based Trust: Define How Much Privacy Is Worth*

Danfeng Yao[1], Keith B. Frikken[2], Mikhail J. Atallah[3], and Roberto Tamassia[1]

[1] Department of Computer Science, Brown University
Providence, RI 02912 USA
{dyao, rt}@cs.brown.edu
[2] Department of Computer Science and Systems Analysis
Miami University
Oxford, OH 45056 USA
frikkekb@muohio.edu
[3] Department of Computer Science, Purdue University
West Lafayette, IN 47907 USA
mja@cs.purdue.edu

Abstract. This paper studies the notion of point-based policies for trust management, and gives protocols for realizing them in a disclosure-minimizing fashion. Specifically, Bob values each credential with a certain number of points, and requires a minimum total threshold of points before granting Alice access to a resource. In turn, Alice values each of her credentials with a privacy score that indicates her reluctance to reveal that credential. Bob's valuation of credentials and his threshold are private. Alice's privacy-valuation of her credentials is also private. Alice wants to find a subset of her credentials that achieves Bob's required threshold for access, yet is of as small a value to her as possible. We give protocols for computing such a subset of Alice's credentials without revealing any of the two parties' above-mentioned private information.

Keywords: Trust management, private multi-party computation, knapsack problem.

1   Introduction

A typical scenario for accessing a resource using digital credentials is for the client, Alice, to send her request to Bob, who responds with the policy that governs access to that resource. If Alice's credentials satisfy Bob's policy, she sends the appropriate credentials to Bob. After Bob receives the credentials and verifies them, he grants Alice access to the resource. Observe that, in this scenario, Alice learns Bob's policy and Bob learns Alice's credentials. However, this mechanism is unacceptable if the credentials or the access control policies are considered to be sensitive information.

The motivation for hiding credentials is individual privacy, e.g., if the credentials are about one's physical impairment or disability, financial distress, political or religious

* Portions of this work were supported by Grants IIS-0325345, IIS-0219560, IIS-0312357, and IIS-0242421 from the National Science Foundation, Contract N00014-02-1-0364 from the Office of Naval Research, by sponsors of the Center for Education and Research in Information Assurance and Security, and by Purdue Discovery Park's e-enterprise Center.

P. Ning, S. Qing, and N. Li (Eds.): ICICS 2006, LNCS 4307, pp. 190–209, 2006.

affiliation, etc. The motivation for hiding the policy is not only security from an evil adversary, but simply the desire to prevent legitimate users from *gaming* the system — e.g., changing their behavior based on their knowledge of the policy (which usually renders an economically-motivated policy less effective). This is particularly important for policies that are not incentive-compatible in economic terms (they suffer from perverse incentives in that they reward the wrong kinds of behavior, such as free-loading). In yet other examples, the policy is simply a commercial secret — e.g., Bob has pioneered a novel way of doing business, and knowledge of the policy would compromise Bob's strategy and invite unwelcome imitators.

It is also important to point out that a process that treats Alice's credentials as confidential is ultimately not only to Alice's advantage but also to Bob's: Bob can worry less about rogue insiders in his organization illicitly leaking (or selling) Alice's private information, and may even lower his liability insurance rates as a result of this. Privacy-preservation is a win-win proposition, one that is appealing even if Alice and Bob are honest and trustworthy entities. This paper gives a trust management model that quantitatively addresses degrees of sensitivity. Moreover, the degree of sensitivity of a given credential is private to each user, and can vary from one user to another.

1.1 Motivations

In a probing attack, Alice can engage in a protocol with Bob multiple times using different credential sets each time (all of which are subsets of her credentials) to gain information about Bob's policy. In the case where Alice is requesting access to a service, Bob will know whether she got access and can therefore also probe (by using different policies and observing their effect) to gain information about Alice's credentials.

One way of mitigating probing attacks is the one followed in the trust negotiation literature [5,37,38,44,45], in which the disclosure of a credential is governed by an access control policy that specifies the prerequisite conditions that must be satisfied in order for that credential to be disclosed. Typically, the prerequisite conditions are a subset of the set of all credentials, and the policies are modeled using propositional formulas. A trust negotiation protocol is normally initiated by a client requesting a service or a resource from a server, and the negotiation consists of a sequence of credential exchanges: Trust is established if the initially requested service or resource is granted and all policies for disclosed credentials are satisfied [38,43].

Although mitigating probing attacks, the requirements of the trust negotiation literature have some practical limitations. (1) Probing is still possible when policies are not treated as sensitive resources, and the client (or server) can game the system in many ways. For example, if the client knows the access control policies for the server's credentials then she will know the path of least resistance to unlock certain credentials. (2) Premature information leaking is difficult to prevent in existing trust negotiation protocols including the recent framework using cryptographic credentials [32]. The premature information leaking refers to the situation when a negotiation is not successful, however sensitive credentials are already disclosed. (3) The service model in trust negotiation is usually limited, that is, the requested service is fixed and independent of the amount of information released by the client at the end of the negotiation session. However, a client may end up disclosing more information than what is required for the initially requested service. The reward or service provided by the server should be dynamically adjustable with the amount of information released from the client.

As will become clear soon, the approach presented in this paper mitigates the above-mentioned problems. The computation for determining whether a user satisfies a policy is privacy-preserving, where *neither* party needs to disclose sensitive information. Of the multiple ways of satisfying the policy, Alice will tend to use the one that utilizes the credentials whose privacy she values least.

1.2   Overview

Quantitatively addressing trust establishment problem has existed in several papers on trust and reputation models [4,17,42,46]. These models have applications in open systems such as mobile ad hoc networks, Peer-to-Peer networks [17], and e-trade systems.

We consider a new point-based trust management policy (rather than a Boolean expression) that is private and should therefore not be revealed to Alice: Bob associates a number of points with every possible credential, and requires the sum of the points of those credentials that Alice uses to reach a minimum threshold before he grants her access to the resource. The resource owner, Bob, defines an admissible threshold, and that threshold is itself private and should not be revealed to Alice. Alice needs to satisfy the threshold requirement to gain access by using a subset of her credentials that gives her the required number of points, but there can be many such subsets: Alice is interested in using the subset that has minimum privacy-value to her, according to her privacy-valuation function; that valuation function is itself private and should not be revealed to Bob. We give a protocol which determines which subset of Alice's credentials *optimally* satisfies Bob's threshold, i.e., it has minimum privacy value to Alice among all subsets that satisfy Bob's threshold. Bob's point-valuation of credentials, his thresholds, and Alice's privacy-valuation of her credentials are private and not revealed.

1.3   Applications

In the point-based model, credentials are mapped with point values defined by the resource owner, therefore the client's reward or service can be dynamically adjusted according to the amount of private information revealed. The flexibility makes the point-based model attractive to the trust management in web-services and e-commerce applications in general, as users have the incentives to carry on the computation for trust establishment, which facilitates business transactions.

Another important type of applications for point-based model is privacy-aware presence systems [27,39,42], where presence data such as the location of a user is collected through devices such as GPS on a cellphone. The management of presence data is crucial, because it concerns not only user privacy, but also safety: presence data can be used to track and profile individuals. In the meantime, there may be emergency situations or extenuating circumstances when certain parties (like emergency workers) should have access to this kind of information, and friends and relatives of a user might be allowed to query his or her location information at any time. Therefore, a desirable feature of a location query system is that it provides different levels of precision based on the requester's trustworthiness or the context of the query. This requires a flexible authorization model for accessing the private location data, which can be offered by the point-based authorization model.

1.4   Our Contributions

1. We propose a point-based trust management model and we formalize the credential selection problem of the model into a knapsack problem. Our point-based trust management model enables users to quantitatively distinguish the sensitivities of different credentials. It also allows a provider to quantitatively assign values to credentials held by clients. The point-based model has several features: (i) Policy specification is simple and easily allows dynamic adjustment of services provided based on released credentials; (ii) A user can proactively decide whether the potential privacy loss is worth the service without disclosing any sensitive information; (iii) To satisfy a policy, a user can select to disclose the *optimal* credential set that minimizes the privacy loss, based on his or her personal measure.

2. We give secure and private dynamic programming protocols for solving the knapsack problem. Our solution, consisting of a basic protocol and an improved protocol, allows the server and user to jointly compute the optimal sum of privacy scores for the released credentials, without revealing their private parameters. The complexity of our basic protocol is $O(nT')$, where n is the total number of credentials and T' is the (private) *marginal threshold*, which corresponds to the sum of the points of the credentials that are *not* disclosed. The protocol uses homomorphic encryptions, and is semantically secure against semi-honest adversaries.

   Our improved protocol, the *fingerprint protocol*, is secure in an adversarial model that is stronger than a semi-honest one (a.k.a honest-but-curious). The improved protocol prevents a participant from tampering with the values used in the dynamic programming computation. That is, while we cannot prevent a participant from lying about her input, we can force *consistency in lying* by preventing capricious use of different inputs during the crucial solution-traceback phase. The complexity of our fingerprint protocol is $O(n^2 T')$.

3. One contribution of this paper that goes beyond the specific problem considered is a general *indexing expansion* method for recovering an optimal solution from any value-computing dynamic programming computation, while detecting cheating by the participants. Using this method, a participant is not required to trust the other party during the back-tracing phase. This is possible because the participant is able to efficiently identify whether the other party has tampered with the computation. For traceback in general dynamic programming problems, our algorithm not only allows a participant to independently and easily recover the optimal traceback solution, once the computed optimal value is given, but also enables the participants to verify the integrity of the optimal value.

Organization of the Paper. Our point-based trust management model is presented in Section 2. The basic protocol for privacy-preserving credential selection is given in Section 3. Fingerprint protocol is given in Section 4. We analyze the security in Section 5. We present an extension to the fingerprint protocol in Section 6. Related work is given in Section 7.

2   Model

In this section, we describe a point-based trust management model, and define the credential selection problem in this model.

2.1   Point-Based Trust Management

In the point-based trust management model, the authorization policies of a resource owner defines an *access threshold* for each of its resources. The threshold is the minimum amount of points required for a requester to access that resource. For example, accessing a medical database requires fifty points. The resource owner also defines a *point value* for each type of credentials, which denotes the number of points or credits a requester obtains if a type of credential is disclosed. For example, a valid ACM membership is worth ten points. This means that a client can disclose his or her ACM membership credential in exchange for ten points. We call this a trust management model as opposed to an access control model, because the resource owner does not know the identities or role assignments of requesters *a priori*.

A requester has a set of credentials, and some of which may be considered sensitive and cannot be disclosed to everyone. However, in order to access a certain resource, the requester has to disclose a number of credentials such that the access threshold is met by the disclosed credentials. Different clients have different perspective on the sensitivity of their credentials, even though the credentials are of the same type. For example, a teenager may consider age information insensitive, whereas a middle-aged person may not be very willing to tell his or her age.

Therefore, in point-based trust management model, each client defines a *privacy score* for each of their credentials. The privacy score represents the inverse of the willingness to disclose a credential. For example, Alice may give privacy score 10 to her college ID, and 50 to her credit card. The client is granted access to a certain resource if the access threshold is met and all of the disclosed credentials are valid. Otherwise, the access is denied. From the requester's point of view, the central question is how to fulfill the access threshold while disclosing the *least* amount of sensitive information. In the next section, we define this as a credential selection problem. The credential selection problem is challenging, because the requester considers his or her privacy scores sensitive, and the server considers its point values and access threshold sensitive.

Where do point values come from? One approach to obtain point values is from reputation systems [4,36,46]. Essentially the point value of a credential represents the trustworthiness of the organization that issues the credential. If a resource owner thinks organization A is more reputable than organization B, the resource owner specifies a higher point value for a credential issued by A than the one issued by B. This idea has been explored in a recent paper that quantitatively studies the connections between computational trust/reputation models with point values in point-based trust management. The paper also discusses the application of such models in privacy-preserving location systems. The work in trust models and reputation systems [4,36,46] serve as a starting point for demonstrating the applicability of point-based trust management.

2.2   Credential Selection Problem

Definition 1. *The credential selection problem is to determine an optimal combination of requester's credentials to disclose to the resource owner, such that the minimal amount of sensitive information is disclosed and the access threshold of the requested resource is satisfied by the disclosed credentials.*

We formalize the credential selection problem as an optimization problem. Our model assumes that the resource owner (or server) and the requester (or client) agree on a set of credential types as the universe of credentials $(C_1, \ldots, C_n)$. We define a binary vector $(x_1, \ldots, x_n)$ as the unknown variable to be computed, where x_i is 1 if credential C_i is selected, and 0 if otherwise. Integer $a_i \geq 0$ is the *privacy score* of credential C_i. It is assigned by the requester *a priori*. If the requester does not have a certain credential C_i, the privacy score a_i for that credential can be set to a large integer. Thus, the (knapsack) algorithm avoids choosing that credential type, as the cost is high. The server defines T that is the *access threshold* of the requested resource. Integer $p_i \geq 0$ is the *point value* for releasing credential type C_i. The requester considers all of a_i values sensitive, and the server considers the access threshold T and all of p_i values sensitive.

The credential selection problem is for the requester to compute a binary vector $(x_1, \ldots, x_n)$ such that the sum of points $\sum_{i=1}^{n} x_i p_i$ satisfies T, and the sum of privacy scores $\sum_{i=1}^{n} x_i a_i$ is minimized. This is captured in the following minimization problem. Compute a binary vector $(x_1, \ldots, x_n)$ such that the following holds:

$$\min \quad \sum_{i=1}^{n} x_i a_i$$

$$\text{subject to } \sum_{i=1}^{n} x_i p_i \geq T$$

The above minimization problem can be rewritten into a knapsack problem with a new variable $y_i = 1 - x_i \in \{0, 1\}$. For i-th credential, $y_i = 1$ represents not disclosing the credential, and $y_i = 0$ represents disclosing the credential.

We define the marginal threshold T', which coarsely correlates to the sum of the points of the credentials that are not disclosed.

Definition 2. *The marginal threshold T' of the credential selection problem is defined as $\sum_{i=1}^{n} p_i - T$, where p_i is the point value for credential type C_i, T is the access threshold for a requested resource, and n is the total number of credential types.*

Let us first review the dynamic programming solution for the 0/1 knapsack problem [15]. Then, we describe our protocol for carrying out private dynamic programming computation of the knapsack problem. The 0/1 knapsack problem is defined as follows. Given items of different integer values and weights, find the most valuable set of items that fit in a knapsack of fixed integer capacity. The dynamic programming solution is pseudo-polynomial: the running time is in $O(nT')$.

In the dynamic programming of knapsack problem, a table is made to track the optimal selection of items so far. A column indicates the range of values, which corresponds to the target weight of the knapsack. A row corresponds to each item. The last table entry has the maximum capacity of the knapsack. The first column and the first row are initialized to zeros, i.e. $M_{0,j}$ and $M_{i,0}$ are zeros, for all $i \in [1, n]$ and $j \in [0, T']$. The table is filled from top to bottom and from left to right. Using the notations defined earlier, the recurrence relation is formally defined as follows. Denote $M_{i,j}$ as the value at i-th row and j-th column, and $i \in [0, n], j \in [0, T']$.

$$M_{i,j} = \begin{array}{ll} M_{i-1,j} & \text{if } j < p_i \\ \max\{M_{i-1,j}, M_{i-1,j-p_i} + a_i\} & \text{if } j \geq p_i \end{array}$$

Each entry of the table stores the total value of a knapsack, which is determined as either the value of a knapsack without the current item (expressed as the value directly to the top of the current entry), or the value of the knapsack with the current item added into it. At the end of the computation, the entry at the lower right corner of the table contains the optimal value of the knapsack. The selections of items can be obtained by bookkeeping the information of where the value of an entry comes from.

For our credential selection problem, the above recurrence relation can be interpreted as follows. If the point value of credential type C_i exceeds j, which is a value in the range of $[0, T']$, then the i-th credential is not selected and the privacy score $M_{i,j}$ is kept the same as $M_{i-1,j}$. Otherwise, the algorithm compares the score $M_{i-1,j}$ for not selecting the i-th credential with the score $M_{i-1,j-p_i} + a_i$ for selecting the i-th credential. The larger value is chosen to be the privacy score $M_{i,j}$.

The standard dynamic programming computation requires values a_i and p_i for all $i \in [1, n]$. However, in our model, the requester considers a_i sensitive, and the server considers p_i sensitive. We present a protocol that allows the completion of the dynamic programming computation without revealing any sensitive information. In addition to protecting sensitive a_i and p_i values, the entries in the dynamic programming table are also protected from both parties.

Once the client has selected the set of credentials to disclose, she reveals them to the server. The server then verifies the validity of the credentials by checking the credential issuers' signatures.

Privacy score of a credential set. In the current model, the privacy score of multiple credentials is the sum of each individual privacy score. The summation is simple to model, and represents the additive characteristic of privacy, i.e., the more personal information revealed, the more privacy lost. Another advantage of the summation of privacy scores is the efficiency; the specification of privacy scores has a size linear in the number of credentials. However, the client may want to explicitly specify an arbitrary privacy score of a certain group of sensitive credentials. The group privacy score may be higher or lower than the sum of individual privacy scores. The latter case can happen when one credential might subsume or include some information that is included in the other credential(s). However, the dynamic programming solution is not clear for the dynamic programming problem with arbitrary constraints. It remains an interesting open question how to formulate the dynamic programming to support arbitrary privacy score specifications.

3   Basic Protocol

We present the basic protocol, which is a secure two-party dynamic-programming protocol for computing the optimal solution of the credential selection problem. The basic protocol has two sub-protocols: recursion and traceback, which represent the two phases of dynamic programming. The protocol maintains the secrecy of sensitive parameters of both parties. Furthermore, neither the server nor the client learns any intermediate result. The main technical challenge is that the server does not want to reveal point values $\{p_i\}$ and the client does not want to reveal privacy scores $\{a_i\}$. As shown by the recurrence relation in Section 2, it seems difficult to compute entry $M_{i,j}$ without knowing p_i and a_i. We overcome the challenge by designing a protocol that hides the conditional testing from the client. The basic protocol is efficient and is secure in the semi-honest adversarial model.

3.1   Building Blocks

In our protocol, we store values in a modularly additively split manner with a large base called L. The additively split manner means that the server and the client each has a share of a value, and the value equals to the sum of their shares modular L. If x^S and x^C represent the share of the server and the client, respectively, then the value equals to $x^S + x^C \bmod L$. We use $L - i$ to represent $-i$ (and use i to represent i). This implies that the range of the values is between $\frac{-L}{2}$ and $\frac{L}{2}$, and L must be chosen so that it is larger enough to prevent accidental wrap-around. Secure two-party private protocols were given in [20] that allow comparison of above described values, in which the comparison result is additively split between the server and the client. It is easy to modify these protocols to compute the maximum of the values in additively split format, which we refer to as the *private two-party maximum protocol*. We use the private two-party comparison and maximum protocols in our paper as a black box.

Our protocols use homomorphic encryption extensively. Recall that a cryptographic scheme with encryption function E is said to be homomorphic, if the following holds: $E(x) * E(y) = E(x + y)$. Another property of such a scheme is that $E(x)^y = E(xy)$. The arithmetic performed under the encryption is modular, and the modulus is part of the public parameters for this system. Homomorphic schemes are described in [16,34]. We utilize homomorphic encryption schemes that are semantically secure. Informally, a homomorphic scheme is *semantically secure* if the following condition holds. Given the public parameters of a homomorphic scheme E, and the encryption of one of the two messages m, m' where m is from a specific message and m' is chosen uniformly random from the message space, then $|(Pr(P(E(m))) = 1) - Pr(P(E(m'))) = 1)|$ is negligible for any probabilistic polynomial time algorithm P.

3.2   Overview of Basic Protocol

The basic protocol consists of two sub-protocols: the basic recursion sub-protocol and the basic traceback sub-protocol.

– Basic recursion sub-protocol: the client and server compute a $(n+1) \times (T'+1)$ matrix M in an additive split form. Let $M_{i,j}$ denote the value stored at the i-th row and

j-th column. Let E_C be the public encryption function of the client's semantically-secure homomorphic encryption scheme. The server learns $E_C(M_{i,j})$ values for all $i \in [1, n]$ and $j \in [1, T']$. From the security of E_C, a computationally-bounded server gains no information from the $E_C(M_{i,j})$ values. The server computes (with the client's help) the value $E_C(M_{i,j})$, when given $E_C(M_{i',j'})$ for all values (i', j') that are dominated by (i, j), for all $i \in [1, n]$ and $j \in [1, T']$. $M_{0,j}$ and $M_{i,0}$ are zeros, for all $i \in [0, n]$ and $j \in [0, T']$.

- Basic traceback sub-protocol: once the dynamic programming table has been filled out, the client discovers (with the server's help) the set of credentials that have been selected to disclose. The optimal selection is revealed to both parties.

Note that the basic recursion sub-protocol should unify the operations in the two cases ($j < p_i$ and $j \geq p_i$) of the recurrence relation. Otherwise, the client can learn p_i from the computation. We solve this by designing a generic and private maximum function and by additively splitting intermediate results between the two parties.

3.3 Basic Recursion Sub-protocol

The basic recursion sub-protocol is described in Figure 1.

When $j > T'$ (recall that $T' = \sum_{i=1}^{n} p_i - T$), the server terminates the protocol. The last entry $M_{n,T'}$ of the dynamic programming matrix has been computed. The

---

Setup: The client has published the public parameters of a semantically secure homomorphic scheme E_C. We will use the base of this scheme as the modulus for the additively split values.

Input: The server has $E_C(M_{i',j'})$ for all values (i', j') that are dominated by (i, j), where $i \in [1, n]$ and $j \in [0, T']$. The sever also has point values $p_1, \ldots, p_n$ and the client has privacy scores $a_1, \ldots, a_n$.

Output: The server learns $E_C(M_{i,j})$.

Steps:

1. The server creates a pair of values α_0 and α_1, where $\alpha_0 = E_C(M_{i-1,j})$, and $\alpha_1 = E_C(-\infty)$ if $p_i > j$, and $\alpha_1 = E_C(M_{i-1,j-p_i})$ otherwise. Without loss of generality, we assume that a_i values defined by the client are always bounded by an integer B that is known to the server, i.e. $a_i \leq B$ for all $i \in [1, n]$. The server then uses $-B-1$ as $-\infty$. The server also chooses random values r_0 and r_1, and sends to the client $\alpha_0 E_C(r_0)$ and $\alpha_1 E_C(r_1)$.

2. The client decrypts the values to obtain β_0 and β_1. The server sets its shares to $-r_0$ and $-r_1$ and the client sets its shares to β_0 and $\beta_1 + a_i$. Note that the two candidate values for $M_{i,j}$ are additively split between the client and the server.

3. The client and the server engage in a private maximum protocol to compute the maximum of these two values in an additively split format. Denote the shares by x^S and x^C.

4. The client sends $E_C(x^C)$ to the server, and the server computes $E_C(x^C + x^S)$ and sets this value as his output.

Fig. 1. Basic recursion sub-protocol

client knows the marginal threshold T', as she keeps her share of the matrix. Yet, the client does not learn the individual point value p_i and access threshold T from the computation so far.

Lemma 1. *The complexity of the basic recursion sub-protocol is $O(nT')$, with $O(1)$ homomorphic encryptions or decryptions at each round, where n is the total number of credentials and T' is the marginal threshold.*

The proof of Lemma 1 is in the full version of the paper [41].

The basic recursion sub-protocol runs in $O(nT')$, where marginal threshold T' or the number of credentials n can potentially be large. We point out that an important advantage of our protocol compared to conventional boolean-based policies lies in the privacy-preserving functionality offered. Our protocol not only computes the optimal selection of credentials, but also does it in a privacy-preserving fashion for both the server and client. For conventional policies, the latter aspect cannot be easily achieved without having the server to publish or disclose unfairly its policies.

The protocol presented here is secure in the semi-honest adversary model, which is improved later by our indexing expansion method in Section 4. The detailed security analysis is given in Section 5.

3.4 Basic Traceback Sub-protocol

To support the back-tracking of the optimal solution (i.e., the optimal credential set to be disclosed), the basic recursion sub-protocol needs to be modified accordingly. At step 3 in the basic recursion sub-protocol, not only the maximum but also the *comparison result* of the two candidate values for $M_{i,j}$ are computed for all $i \in [1, n]$ and $j \in [1, T']$. During the computation, neither the server nor the client knows the result of the comparison tests, as the result is split between them. From the recurrence relation in Section 2, it is easy to see that the comparison result directly indicates whether a_i is contained in $M_{i,j}$ and thus whether credential C_i is selected. Denote F as a matrix that contains the result of the comparisons, we modify the previous basic recursion sub-protocol so that the server learns $E_C(F_{i,j})$ for the entire matrix. In the basic traceback sub-protocol, the server and the client work together to retrieve the plaintext comparison results starting from the last entry of the table, following the computation path of the optimal dynamic programming solution.

Figure 2 describes the basic traceback sub-protocol.

Lemma 2. *The complexity of the basic traceback sub-protocol is $O(n)$, with $O(1)$ homomorphic decryptions at each round, where n is the total number of credentials.*

The following theorem states the overall complexity of the basic protocol.

Theorem 1. *The complexity of the basic protocol is $O(nT')$, where n is the total number of credentials and T' is the marginal threshold.*

The proof of Theorem 1 is in the full version of this paper [41].

The basic traceback sub-protocol assumes that the server does not maliciously alter the computation results. In the case of a malicious server, the server may send $E_C(0)$

Input: The server has matrix entries $\{E_C(M_{i,j})\}$ and $\{E_C(F_{i,j})\}$ encrypted with the client's public key, for all $i \in [1,n]$ and $j \in [1,T']$. The client has her private key.
Output: The client learns the optimal value of the dynamic programming computation of knapsack. The server and the client learn the optimal selection of credentials, or nothing.
Steps:

1. The server sends the client $E_C(M_{n,T'})$. The client decrypts the ciphertext to obtain the result $M_{n,T'}$. $M_{n,T'}$ represents the privacy score associated with the unselected credentials. If this value is acceptable to the client according to some pre-defined privacy standard set by the client, then this sub-protocol continues. Otherwise, this sub-protocol terminates.
2. The server reveals the entry $E_C(F_{n,T'})$ to the client.
3. The client decrypts $E_C(F_{n,T'})$ to obtain $F_{n,T'} \in \{0,1\}$. The client sends the plaintext value $F_{n,T'}$ to the server (The server then knows whether C_n is selected or not.) If $F_{n,T'} = 1$, then credential C_n will not be disclosed. $F_{n,T'} = 1$ also means that entry $M_{n,T'}$ is computed from entry $M_{n-1,T'}$. Therefore, the server next reveals $E_C(F_{n-1,T'})$ to the client. If $F_{n,T'} = 0$, then the server next reveals $E_C(F_{n-1,T'-p_n})$, as the entry $M_{n,T'}$ is computed from entry $M_{n-1,T'-p_n}$.
4. The revealed entries represent the computation path of the optimal knapsack dynamic programming solution. The above process is repeated until n reaches zero.

Fig. 2. Basic traceback sub-protocol

instead of the real values to mislead the client to disclose all credentials. Although the attack might be caught by the client (as the client may find a subset of credentials that still satisfies the threshold constraint), we give a stronger traceback algorithm that proactively prevents this type of attacks in the next section.

4 Fingerprint Protocol

In this section, we give an alternative protocol for privacy-preserving knapsack computation. The new approach is inspired by the *subset sum problem*, yet we stress that this solution does not require the client to solve the general subset sum problem. The main idea is to allow the client (*not the server*) to efficiently identify the selected credentials from the optimal privacy score. The new protocol, which we refer to as the *fingerprint protocol*,[1] is an important step towards a protocol that is secure against malicious servers, because it can be extended to prevent the server from tampering the computation during traceback.

In addition to solving our credential selection problem (and thus the knapsack problem), the fingerprint protocol can be generalized to solve the traceback problem in a large variety of integer linear programming problems. It can be used for one party to securely and privately trace the optimal solution from the final computed value, with very

---

[1] The name is because of the similarities between fingerprinting in forensics and the indexing technique that we use to uniquely identify a subset.

little or no participation from the other party. The technique guarantees the correctness of the traceback results, even though the other party cannot be trusted during traceback.

4.1   Fingerprint Protocol Description

The key idea of the fingerprint protocol is to convert the client's privacy scores $\{a_i\}$ into another set of scores $\{A_i\}$, such that the following two conditions hold. (1) The optimal credential selection computed with $\{A_i\}$ should be the same as the optimal credential selection computed with $\{a_i\}$. (2) The privacy score computed with $\{A_i\}$ should reveal which set of credentials are used to obtain that score. Thus, this transformation process requires the following two properties:

Property 1.   **Ordering consistency:** For two sets S and R in $2^{\{1,\dots,n\}}$, if $\sum_{i \in S} A_i < \sum_{i \in R} A_i$, then $\sum_{i \in S} a_i \leq \sum_{i \in R} a_i$.

Property 2.   **Uniqueness:** For any two distinct sets S and R in $2^{\{1,\dots,n\}}$, $\sum_{i \in S} A_i \neq \sum_{i \in R} A_i$.

The ordering consistency property ensures that the set of revealed credentials computed with the transformed scores is optimal even when the original scores are used. The uniqueness property guarantees that traceback is possible, as only one set of credentials can generate a specific score. Although the above properties do not imply that an efficient traceback is possible, our transformation leads to an efficient traceback method. Our *indexing expansion* method transforms a privacy score a_i to A_i as follows.

$$A_i = a_i * 2^n + 2^{i-1}.$$

In binary representation, the indexing expansion shifts the binary form of a_i to the left by n positions, and gives zeros to n least significant bits except the i-th least significant bit, which is given a one. For example, suppose there are four privacy scores 2, 3, 5, 8 or in binary form 010, 011, 101, 1000. Here $n = 4$. After the transformations, the expanded scores have the binary form 010 0001, 011 0010, 101 0100, 1000 1000, respectively. Readers can verify that the example satisfy the two required properties. We now prove that the indexing expansion has the desired properties.

Lemma 3. *The indexing expansion achieves the ordering consistency property.*

Lemma 4. *The indexing expansion achieves the uniqueness property.*

Proofs of the above two lemmas are in the full version of this paper [41].

Hence, the indexing expansion method allows the client to compute the credentials that are used to achieve a specific privacy score. Although the optimal value obtained from the secure dynamic programming with the A_i scores is different from the one with the original a_i scores, the set of credentials corresponding to the optimal privacy values are the same. We now describe the fingerprint protocol, which makes use of the indexing expansion.

The indexing expansion of privacy scores requires n additional bits for each credential, where n is the total number of credentials. In Lemma 5 below, we prove that in order to satisfy the uniqueness property, the number of bits required for the transformed privacy scores is bounded by $\Omega(n)$.

Input: The server has the marginal threshold T' and point values $p_1, \ldots, p_n$. The client has privacy scores $a_1, \ldots, a_n$.

Output: The client (*not the server*) learns the optimal selection of credentials.

Steps:

1. The client applies the indexing expansion to each of her privacy scores $\{a_i\}$ and obtains the transformed scores $\{A_i\}$.
2. The server and the client carry out the basic recursion sub-protocol (in Figure 1) with the transformed privacy scores $\{A_i\}$. Recall that at the end of the basic recursion sub-protocol, the server has computed $E_C(M_{n,T'})$ in entry (n, T') of the dynamic programming matrix.
3. The server sends the ciphertext $E_C(M_{n,T'})$ to the client.
4. The client decrypts $E_C(M_{n,T'})$ to obtain $M_{n,T'}$.
5. The client expresses the optimal value $M_{n,T'}$ in binary form and identifies the non-zero bits in the last n bits. The positions of such bits give the indices of credentials that give the optimal solution[2]. Note that the i-th least significant bit of $M_{n,T'}$ is true if and only if credential i was used to obtain the optimal value.

Fig. 3. Fingerprint protocol

Lemma 5. *For any transformation of index to satisfy the uniqueness property, the number of additional bits introduced for a privacy score is lower-bounded by $\Omega(n)$, where n is the number of credentials.*

Theorem 2. *The complexity of the fingerprint protocol is $O(n^2 T')$, where n is the total number of credentials and T' is the marginal threshold.*

The proofs of Lemma 5 and Theorem 2 are in the full version of this paper [41].

4.2 Detection of Value Substitution by the Server

In the method described above, although difficult, it is not impossible for a malicious server to forge its share of the optimal value and thus mislead a client to disclose more credentials. The probability of the server correctly guessing a credential's privacy score and its bit position in the indexing expansion may not be negligible. For example, the server may have $1/n$ probability of correctly guessing the bit position of a credential, where n is the total number of credentials. Also, it may have $1/\max\{a_i\}$ probability of correctly guessing the privacy score, where $\{a_i\}$ represents the set of untransformed privacy scores. In Section 6, we describe a simple checksum technique for preventing the server from tampering with the traceback computation. This is done by appending randomized information to privacy scores.

5 Security

We define our security model as a semi-honest (a.k.a. honest-but-curious) model. Intuitively, this means that adversaries follow the protocol but try to compute additional information other than what can be deduced from their input and output alone. A protocol is defined as secure if it implements a function f, such that the information learned by engaging in the protocol can be learned in an ideal implementation where the functionality is provided by a trusted oracle. This definition follows the standard definitions given by Goldreich [24] for private multi-party computation.

Let A be any one of the two parties in our protocol, we use $view_A$ to represent all of the information that A sees during the protocol. A protocol is secure against a semi-honest A, if and only if there exists an algorithm that can simulate $view_A$ when given A's inputs and A's output. To be more precise, two probability ensembles $X \stackrel{\text{def}}{=} \{X_n\}_{n \in \mathcal{N}}$ and $Y \stackrel{\text{def}}{=} \{Y_n\}_{n \in \mathcal{N}}$ are computationally indistinguishable (i.e., a polynomial bounded algorithm cannot distinguish the two distributions) if for any PPT algorithm D, any positive polynomial p, and sufficiently large n it holds that: $|(Pr(D(X_n, 1^n) = 1)) - (Pr(D(Y_n, 1^n) = 1))| < \frac{1}{p(n)}$. Let A's input and output be represented by A_I and A_O respectively. A protocol is secure in the semi-honest model against adversary A, if there is an algorithm SIM_A such that $view_A$ and $SIM_A(A_I, A_O)$ are computationally indistinguishable (i.e., SIM_A simulates A's view of the protocol).

To prove the security of the basic protocol (in Figure 1), we state a lemma about the security of the private two-party maximum protocol used in step 3 of the basic protocol.

Lemma 6. *The private two-party maximum protocol is secure in the semi-honest model.*

The above lemma states that there exists a private two-party maximum protocol such that when given the client's inputs a^C and b^C, there is an algorithm that simulates the client's view of the maximum protocol.

Given such a private two-party maximum protocol, we show that the basic recursion sub-protocol in Section 3 is secure.

Theorem 3. *The basic recursion sub-protocol is secure in the semi-honest adversarial model.*

We have shown that each individual round is secure in the above protocol. The composition follows from the composition theorem [9].

We show the basic traceback sub-protocol (in Figure 2) is secure. Note that the basic traceback sub-protocol makes uses of a matrix F that is computed in the recurrence phase. Each entry of matrix F contains the selection decision of a credential. The computation of F is secure, which can be deduced from Theorem 3.

Theorem 4. *The basic traceback sub-protocol is secure in the semi-honest adversarial model.*

Proofs of Theorem 3 and 4 are in the full version of this paper [41].

Given Theorem 3, the fingerprint protocol (in Figure 3) is secure, because once the server gives $E_C(M_{n,T'})$ to the client, the client carries out the traceback computation without any communication from the server.

Theorem 5. *The fingerprint protocol is secure in the semi-honest adversarial model.*

6 Extension

The checksum technique has applications beyond the specific problem considered, and is a general method for recovering an optimal solution from any value-computing dynamic programming computation, while detecting cheating by the participants. We discuss an extension to fingerprint protocol that is secure against an adversary who is stronger than a semi-honest one. We consider an adversarial model as described follows. An adversary may tamper with private computation by modifying intermediate results during the protocol, which is not allowed in a semi-honest model. An adversary is curious as in a semi-honest model, in that she may store all exchanged data and try to deduce information from it. An adversary is assumed to participate and follow the protocol, which is a weaker assumption than a malicious model.

It is important to define the above adversarial model. While we cannot prevent a participant from lying about her input, we can force *consistency in lying* by preventing capricious use of different inputs during the crucial solution-traceback phase. For complex functions such as the one being studied, lying about one's input wrecks the worthiness of the answer for both participants, and the participant who does so would have been better off not engaging in the protocol in the first place (this is not true for simple functions where the lier can still get the answer by *correcting for her lie*).

Note that our extension does not support a full malicious model, which would require expensive Zero Knowledge Proofs [26]. However, we do raise the bar on common things that a malicious server may try in our model. When the server is not semi-honest, a significant problem with our protocols is that the server has $E_C(M_{i,j})$ for all matrix values. Thus, the server can replace any value of the matrix with another value $E_C(v)$ for any value v. In the fingerprint protocol, the server has to guess the weights used for each credential. The client can easily check if the proposed sum is created by a certain set of credentials. However, as described earlier, the server may have a non-negligible probability of successfully replacing these values. We now describe a technique that reduces the probability of a successful replacement by the server to a negligible value in terms of a security parameter.

The idea is that the client performs transformations on his or her privacy scores. The client creates a new set of value $\hat{A}_1, \ldots, \hat{A}_n$ that satisfy the traceback properties outlined in Section 4. For each value, A_i, the client chooses uniformly a ρ-bit value (where ρ is the security parameter), which we call r_i. The client sets $\hat{A}_i = A_i 2^{\lg n + \rho} + r_i$ (where A_i is the already transformed value for traceback). It is straightforward to show that these values satisfy the properties outlined in Section 4. Furthermore, for the server to substitute a value, it would have to guess a ρ bit value, which it can guess successfully with only negligible probability in the security parameter ρ.

Another attack that the server can launch is that it can send any intermediate value of the matrix to the client, and claim that it is the final result. Because an intermediate value is well-formed, it cannot be detected by the above technique. However, the server does not gain from this type of attacks. If the server chooses a value from a higher row (with a smaller row index), then this attack can be achieved by setting the point values of some credentials to zero (i.e., they are useless to the client and are never used). If a different column is chosen, then this attack can be achieved by increasing the access threshold T. If the intermediate value is from a different row and a different column, then the effect of this attack can be achieved by increasing the threshold and setting the point values of some credentials to zero at the same time. The server may attempt to form linear combinations of row entries, but there is a non-negligible chance of being caught by the client because a repeated entry may be found.

7 Related Work

In the access control area, the closest work to ours is the framework for regulating service access and release of private information in web-services by Bonatti and Samarati [5]. They study the information disclosure in open systems such as Internet using a language and policy approach. In comparison, we design cryptographic solutions to control and manage information exchange. In addition, we focus on solving the optimality in selecting the set of credentials to disclose. Bonatti and Samarati considered two data types in the portfolio of a user: data declaration (e.g., identity, address, credit card number) and credential. Although we only consider credentials in the description of our model, the protocols can be generalized to include data declarations as long as the server and the client agree on their specifications. In general, credentials (e.g., driver's license and credit card) contain a set of data declaration information, which is usually requested as a group. For example, the credit card number and the expiration date are usually asked for at the same time. Using credentials to represent private information may be sufficient in some cases.

Our point-based trust management model quantitatively treats memberships or credentials, which is conceptually different from most existing access control models. Our approach aims to address the fact that different individuals or groups of people have different privacy concerns in terms of protecting sensitive information. This goal differs from conventional access control models. The flexibility provided by the point-based model enables users to proactively protect their private information. Furthermore, thresholds specified by resource owners prevent unqualified users from accessing the resource.

Anonymous credential and idemix systems have been developed [8,10,12] to allow anonymous yet authenticated and accountable transactions between users and service providers. Together with zero-knowledge proof protocols, they can be used to prove that an attribute satisfies a policy without disclosing any other information about the attribute. The work in this paper focuses on finding the optimal credentials to disclose, and can be integrated with anonymous credential systems. A zero-knowledge proof protocol can be used when the necessary information to satisfy a policy is discovered. We can apply anonymous credential techniques to implement membership credentials in the point-based trust management model. These credentials are then used to prove user's memberships without revealing individual identity.

In hidden credentials system [7,28], when a signature derived from an identity based encryption scheme [6,14,35] is used to sign a credential, the credential content can be used as a public encryption key such that the signature is the corresponding decryption key. Hidden credentials can be used in such a way that they are never shown to anyone, thus the sensitive credentials are protected. Frikken et al. [21] give a scheme that hides both credentials and policies. Most recently, a protocol [22] was proposed that allows both the client and the server to define *private* access policies of their credentials.

The setup of hidden credential protocols does not allow the computation of the *optimal* selection of credentials. In addition, as explained in the recent work by Frikken, Li, and Atallah [22], the server learns whether the client obtained access or not in some environments even when hidden credential schemes are used. In this case, the server can make inferences about the client's sensitive credentials. For example, if the server's policy is *one must have top secret clearance and be a FBI agent*, then the server can deduce a significant amount of information about the client when the access control decision is made. Our proposed solution allows the client to estimate potential privacy loss without leaking any sensitive information.

We have compared the trust negotiation protocols [37,38,44,45] with our point-based trust management model in the introduction. Li, Li, and Winsborough introduce a framework for trust negotiation, in which the diverse credential schemes and protocols including anonymous credential systems can be combined, integrated, and used as needed [32]. The paper presents a policy language that enables negotiators to specify authorization requirements. The research on trust negotiation that is closest to ours is by Chen, Clarke, Kurose, and Towsley [13]. They developed heuristics to find an approximation of the optimal strategy that minimizes the disclosure of sensitive credentials and policies [13]. Using their methods, when negotiation fails, premature information disclosure is still a problem. Our protocols prevent premature information leakage, because the computation does not disclose sensitive parameters. Because the selection computation is private, the minimization problem is simpler to define in our point-based model than in trust negotiation frameworks. In addition, the solution computed by our basic and fingerprint protocols, if exists, is the exact optimal solution, not an approximation.

Secure Multi-party Computation (SMC) was introduced in a seminal paper by Yao [40], which contained a scheme for secure comparison. Suppose Alice (with input a) and Bob (with input b) desire to determine whether or not $a < b$ without revealing any information other than this result (this is known as *Yao's Millionaire Problem*). More generally, SMC allows Alice and Bob with respective private inputs a and b to compute a function $f(a, b)$ by engaging in a secure protocol for public function f. Furthermore, the protocol is private in that it reveals no additional information. This means that Alice (or Bob) learns nothing other than what can be deduced from a (or b) and $f(a, b)$. Elegant general schemes are given in [3,11,23,25] for computing any function f privately.

Besides the generic work in the area of SMC, there has been extensive work on the privacy-preserving computation of various functions. For example, computational geometry [1,18], privacy-preserving computational biology [2]. The private dynamic programming protocol given by Atallah and Li [2] is the most relevant work to ours. Their protocol compares biological sequences in an additively split format. Each party maintains a matrix, and the summation of two matrices is the real matrix implicitly used to compute the edit distance. Our protocols also carry out computation in an additively split form. What distinguishes us from existing solutions is that we are able to achieve efficiently a stronger security guarantee without using Zero-Knowledge Proofs [26]. Recently, there are also solutions for privacy-preserving automated trouble-shooting

[29], privacy-preserving distributed data mining [30], private set operations [19,31], and equality tests [33]. We do not enumerate other private multi-party computation work as their approaches significantly different from ours.

Acknowledgements

We would like to thank Nikos Triandopoulos, Seth Proctor, and Kimberly Perzel for helpful comments on an earlier version of the point-based trust management model, and Aris Anagnostopoulos for helpful hints.

References

1. M. J. Atallah and W. Du. Secure multi-party computational geometry. In *Proceedings of the 7th International Workshop on Algorithms and Data Structures (WADS '01)*, volume 2125 of *Lecture Notes in Computer Science*, pages 165–179, 2001.
2. M. J. Atallah and J. Li. Secure outsourcing of sequence comparisons. In *4th Workshop on Privacy Enhancing Technologies (PET)*, volume 3424 of *Lecture Notes in Computer Science*, pages 63–78, 2004.
3. M. Ben-Or and A. Wigderson. Completeness theorems for non-cryptographic fault-tolerant distributed computation. In *The Twentieth Annual ACM Symposium on Theory of Computing (STOC)*, pages 1–10. ACM Press, 1988.
4. T. Beth, M. Borcherding, and B. Klein. Valuation of trust in open networks. In *Proceedings of the Third European Symposium on Research in Computer Security (ESORICS '94)*, pages 3–18, November 1994.
5. P. A. Bonatti and P. Samarati. A uniform framework for regulating service access and information release on the web. *Journal of Computer Security*, 10(3):241–272, 2002.
6. D. Boneh and M. Franklin. Identity-Based Encryption from the Weil Pairing. In *Proceedings of Crypto 2001*, volume 2139 of *Lecture Notes in Computer Science*, pages 213–229. Springer, 2001.
7. R. Bradshaw, J. Holt, and K. Seamons. Concealing complex policies with hidden credentials. In *Proceedings of 11th ACM Conference on Computer and Communications Security (CCS)*, Oct. 2004.
8. J. Camenisch and E. Van Herreweghen. Design and implementation of the *idemix* anonymous credential system. In *Proceedings of the 9th ACM Conference on Computer and Communications Security (CCS)*, pages 21–30, 2002.
9. R. Canetti. Security and composition of multiparty cryptographic protocols. *Journal of Cryptology*, 13(1):143–202, 2000.
10. D. Chaum. Security without identification: transaction systems to make big brother obsolete. *Communications of the ACM*, 28(10):1030–1044, October 1985.
11. D. Chaum, C. Crépeau, and I. Damgard. Multiparty unconditionally secure protocols. In *The twentieth annual ACM Symposium on Theory of Computing (STOC)*, pages 11–19. ACM Press, 1988.
12. D. Chaum and J.-H. Evertse. A secure and privacy-protecting protocol for transmitting personal information between organizations. In *Proceedings of Advances in cryptology—CRYPTO '86*, pages 118–167, January 1987.
13. W. Chen, L. Clarke, J. Kurose, and D. Towsley. Optimizing cost-sensitive trust-negotiation protocols. In *Proceedings of the 24th Annual Joint Conference of the IEEE Computer and Communications Societies (INFOCOM)*, volume 2, pages 1431–1442, 2005.

14. C. Cocks. An identity based encryption scheme based on quadratic residues. In *8th IMA International Conference on Cryptography and Coding*, volume 2260, pages 360–363. Springer, Dec. 2001.

15. T. H. Cormen, C. E. Leiserson, R. L.Rivest, and C. Stein. *Introduction to algorithms*. MIT Press, 2001.

16. I. Damgård and M. Jurik. A generalisation, a simplification and some applications of Paillier's probabilistic public-key system. In *4th International Workshop on Practice and Theory in Public Key Cryptosystems (PKC '01)*, LNCS 1992, pages 119–136, 2001.

17. E. Damiani, S. De Capitani di Vimercati, S. Paraboschi, P. Samarati, and F. Violante. A reputation-based approach for choosing reliable resources in peer-to-peer networks. In *ACM Conference on Computer and Communications Security (CCS '02)*, pages 207–216, 2002.

18. W. Du. A study of several specific secure two-party computation problems, 2001. PhD thesis, Purdue University, West Lafayette, Indiana.

19. M. Freedman, K. Nissim, and B. Pinkas. Efficient private matching and set intersection. In *Advances in Cryptology – Eurocrypt '04*, volume 3027 of *LNCS*, pages 1–19. Springer-Verlag, May 2004.

20. K. B. Frikken and M. J. Atallah. Privacy preserving route planning. In *Proceedings of the 2004 ACM workshop on Privacy in the Electronic Society (WPES)*, pages 8–15. ACM Press, 2004.

21. K. B. Frikken, M. J. Atallah, and J. Li. Hidden access control policies with hidden credentials. In *Proceedings of the 3nd ACM Workshop on Privacy in the Electronic Society (WPES)*, Oct. 2004.

22. K. B. Frikken, J. Li, and M. J. Atallah. Trust negotiation with hidden credentials, hidden policies, and policy cycles. In *Proceedings of the 13th Annual Network and Distributed System Security Symposium (NDSS)*, 2006.

23. O. Goldreich. Secure multi-party computation, Oct. 2002. Unpublished Manuscript.

24. O. Goldreich. *The Foundations of Cryptography*, volume 2. Cambridge University Press, 2004.

25. O. Goldreich, S. Micali, and A. Wigderson. How to play any mental game. In *The nineteenth annual ACM conference on theory of computing*, pages 218–229. ACM Press, 1987.

26. S. Goldwasser, S. Micali, and C. Rackoff. The knowledge complexity of interactive proof-systems. In *Proceedings of the Seventeenth Annual ACM Symposium on Theory of Computing (STOC)*, pages 291–304, 1985.

27. M. Gruteser and D. Grunwald. Anonymous usage of location-based services through spatial and temporal cloaking. In *ACM/USENIX International Conference on Mobile Systems, Applications, and Services (MobiSys)*, 2003.

28. J. E. Holt, R. W. Bradshaw, K. E. Seamons, and H. Orman. Hidden credentials. In *Proceedings of the 2nd ACM Workshop on Privacy in the Electronic Society (WPES)*, Oct. 2003.

29. Q. Huang, D. Jao, and H. J. Wang. Applications of secure electronic voting to automated privacy-preserving troubleshooting. In *Proceedings of the 12th ACM Conference on Computer and Communications Security (CCS)*, November 2005.

30. G. Jagannathan and R. N. Wright. Privacy-preserving distributed k-means clustering over arbitrarily partitioned data. In *Proceeding of the Eleventh ACM SIGKDD International Conference on Knowledge Discovery in Data Mining*, pages 593–599, 2005.

31. L. Kissner and D. Song. Private and threshold set-intersection. In *Advances in Cryptology – CRYPTO '05*, August 2005.

32. J. Li, N. Li, and W. H. Winsborough. Automated trust negotiation using cryptographic credentials. In *Proceedings of 12th ACM Conference on Computer and Communications Security (CCS)*, pages 46–57, 2005.

33. H. Lipmaa. Verifiable homomorphic oblivious transfer and private equality test. In *Advances in Cryptology — Asiacrypt '03*, LNCS, pages 416–433, 2003.

34. P. Paillier. Public-key cryptosystems based on composite degree residuosity classes. *Advances in Cryptology – EUROCRYPT 1999*, LNCS 1592:223–238, 1999.
35. A. Shamir. Identity-based cryptosystems and signature schemes. In *Advances in Cryptology – Crypto'84*, volume 196 of *Lecture Notes in Computer Science*, pages 47–53. Springer, 1984.
36. H. Tran, M. Hitchens, V. Varadharajan, and P. Watters. A trust based access control framework for P2P file-sharing systems. In *Proceedings of the Proceedings of the 38th Annual Hawaii International Conference on System Sciences (HICSS'05) - Track 9*, page 302c. IEEE Computer Society, 2005.
37. W. H. Winsborough and N. Li. Safety in automated trust negotiation. In *Proceedings of IEEE Symposium on Security and Privacy*. IEEE Computer Society Press, May 2004.
38. W. H. Winsborough, K. E. Seamons, and V. E. Jones. Automated trust negotiation. In *DARPA Information Survivability Conference and Exposition*, volume I, pages 88–102. IEEE Press, Jan. 2000.
39. N. Yankelovich, W. Walker, P. Roberts, M. Wessler, J. Kaplan, and J. Provino. Meeting central: making distributed meetings more effective. In *Proceedings of the 2004 ACM Conference on Computer Supported Cooperative Work (CSCW '04)*, pages 419–428, New York, NY, USA, 2004. ACM Press.
40. A. C. Yao. How to generate and exchange secrets. In *Proceedings of the 27th IEEE Symposium on Foundations of Computer Science*, pages 162–167. IEEE Computer Society Press, 1986.
41. D. Yao, K. B. Frikken, M. J. Atallah, and R. Tamassia. Flexible, secure and private point-based trust management, November 2005. Technical Report. Brown University.
42. D. Yao, R. Tamassia, and S. Proctor. Privacy-preserving computation of trust with application to fuzzy location queries, March 2006. Brown University Technical Report.
43. T. Yu, X. Ma, and M. Winslett. PRUNES: An efficient and complete strategy for automated trust negotiation over the internet. In *Proceedings of the ACM Conference on Computer and Communications Security (CCS)*, pages 210–219, November 2000.
44. T. Yu and M. Winslett. A unified scheme for resource protection in automated trust negotiation. In *Proceedings of IEEE Symposium on Security and Privacy*, pages 110–122. IEEE Computer Society Press, May 2003.
45. T. Yu, M. Winslett, and K. E. Seamons. Interoperable strategies in automated trust negotiation. In *Proceedings of the 8th ACM Conference on Computer and Communications Security (CCS '01)*, pages 146–155. ACM Press, Nov. 2001.
46. C. Zouridaki, B. L. Mark, M. Hejmo, and R. K. Thomas. A quantitative trust establishment framework for reliable data packet delivery in MANETs. In V. Atluri, P. Ning, and W. Du, editors, *Proceedings of the Third ACM Workshop on Security of Ad Hoc and Sensor Networks (SASN)*, pages 1–10. ACM, 2005.

Efficient Protocols for Privacy Preserving Matching Against Distributed Datasets

Yingpeng Sang[1], Hong Shen[2], Yasuo Tan[1], and Naixue Xiong[1]

[1] School of Information Science, Japan Advanced Institute of Science and Technology
Asahidai, Nomi, Ishikawa, Japan, 923-1211
{yingpeng, ytan, naixue}@jaist.ac.jp
[2] School of Computer Science, The University of Adelaide
SA 5005, Australia
hong.shen@adelaide.edu.au

Abstract. When datasets are distributed on different sources, finding out matched data while preserving the privacy of the datasets is a widely required task. In this paper, we address two matching problems against the private datasets on N ($N \geq 2$) parties. The first one is the Privacy Preserving Set Intersection (PPSI) problem, in which each party wants to learn the intersection of the N private datasets. The second one is the Privacy Preserving Set Matching (PPSM) problem, in which each party wants to learn whether its elements can be matched in any private set of the other parties. For the two problems we propose efficient protocols based on a threshold cryptosystem which is additive homomorphic. In a comparison with the related work in [18], the computation and communication costs of our PPSI protocol decrease by 81% and 17% respectively, and the computation and communication costs of our PPSM protocol decrease by 80% and 50% respectively. In practical utilities both of our protocols save computation time and communication bandwidth.

Keywords: cryptographic protocol, privacy preservation, distributed database, set intersection, set matching.

1 Introduction

For datasets distributed on different sources, data matching among these sets is always required to gain useful information. Supermarkets need find out the same card numbers which have consuming records in all of their databases, and then provide better service for the card owners. This is a *set intersection* problem among distributed datasets. The tenderees consider that duplicate submission of tenders is a damage of their benefits, so they want to reject those tenderers who have submitted duplicate tenders to any two of them. Such tenderers can be found out by one tenderee by firstly set intersections between his tender set and each set of the others, then a set union on all the intersections. This is a *set matching* problem among distributed datasets.

Privacy may be a critical concern of the data owners, so they are reluctant to directly publish their datasets. Specifically, one supermarket doesn't want other

P. Ning, S. Qing, and N. Li (Eds.): ICICS 2006, LNCS 4307, pp. 210–227, 2006.
© Springer-Verlag Berlin Heidelberg 2006

supermarkets to know the card numbers in its database except those in the intersection. One tenderee A even doesn't like another tenderee B to know that it is him that has a matched tender with B. Therefore, there should be some privacy preserving techniques for them to determine the results of set intersection and matching, without the datasets being directly published. In this paper, we address the two related problems: *privacy preserving set intersection*, and *privacy preserving set matching*. Basically, both of them are solved by efficiently constructing and evaluating polynomials whose roots are elements of the set intersection and matching.

Problem Formulation: Suppose there are N ($N \geq 2$) parties, each party P_i ($i = 1, ..., N$) has a set (or multiset) of inputs of size S: $T_i = \{T(i, j) | j = 1, ..., S\}$. We also assume that all T_i for $i = 1, ..., N$ are subsets of a common set $\mathbb{T}$, and $S \ll |\mathbb{T}|$, such that given two arbitrarily selected subsets T_i and $T_{i'}$, The probability that an input $a \in T_i$ equals any input $a' \in T_{i'}$ is negligible (i.e., $\frac{S}{|\mathbb{T}|} \to 0$). In the following we define our two problems:

1) *Privacy Preserving Set Intersection (PPSI):* All parties want to learn the intersection of their private sets, i.e., $TI = T_1 \cap ... \cap T_N$, without gleaning any information other than those computed from a coalition of parties inputs and outputs.

2) *Privacy Preserving Set Matching (PPSM):* Each party P_i wants to learn whether each element of its can be matched in any set of the other parties, i.e., whether each element $T(i, j) \in \bigcup_{i'=1,...,N, i' \neq i}(T_i \cap T_{i'})$, without gleaning any information other than those computed from a coalition of parties inputs and outputs.

Privacy Requirements: Firstly, in both problems, an honest party shouldn't be subject to the dictionary attack, in which an adversary may defraud the honest party of inputs using the common set $\mathbb{T}$. The dictionary attack can be effectively resisted in assumption of $S \ll |\mathbb{T}|$.

What's more, without colluding with the other parties, an adversary-controlled party P_i shouldn't glean the following information:

1) For PPSI, P_i can't know elements on $P_{i'}$ ($i' = 1, ..., N, i' \neq i$) except TI.
2) For PPSM, if $T(i, j) \in \bigcup_{i'=1,...,N, i' \neq i}(T_i \cap T_{i'})$, P_i can't know the specific matching times, i.e., how many parties $T(i, j)$ has matches on, and the matching originations, i.e., which party $T(i, j)$ has a match on.

If P_i is in a coalition of c ($1 \leq c \leq N - 1$) adversary-controlled parties, it may get more information than above. We analyze these information in Section 6 of this paper.

Our Contributions: Our main contributions in this paper include:

1) We propose an efficient PPSI protocol, which has lower computation and communication costs than the PPSI protocols in [18] and [8].
2) To our knowledge there hasn't been a direct solution for PPSM. Though a PPSM solution can be derived from the techniques in [18], we propose a

more efficient protocol in the computation and communication costs than the derived one.

The remainder of the paper is organized as follows: Section 2 discusses some related work. Section 3 lists the necessary preliminaries for our protocols. Section 4 and Section 5 propose the PPSI protocol and PPSM protocol respectively. In Section 6 we analyze the security of the two protocols. In Section 7 we compare our two protocols with the related work considering the computation and communication costs. Section 8 concludes the whole paper.

2   Related Work

PPSI and PPSM are specific problems belonging to the general *Secure Multiparty Computation* (SMC) problem. There have been general solutions for the SMC problem ([12], [24]). In general SMC, the function to be computed is represented by a circuit, and every gate of the circuit is privately evaluated. However, when this general solution is used for a specific problem, the large size of the circuit and high cost of evaluating all gates will result in a much less efficient protocol than the non-private protocol for this problem. Therefore, many efficient private protocols for the specific problems have been proposed based on the specific properties of these problems.

PPSI and PPSM can be traced back to the specific problem of private equality test (PET) in two-party case, where each party has a single element and wants to test whether they are equal without publishing the elements. The problem of PET was considered in [1], [4], [19] and [20]. PET solutions can't be simply used for the multi-party cases of PPSI and PPSM, otherwise too much sensitive information will be leaked, e.g., any two parties will know the intersection of their private sets.

A solution for the multi-party case of PPSI was firstly proposed in [8]. The solution is based on evaluating polynomials representing elements in the sets. In [18], another solution for PPSI was proposed, in which each polynomial representing each set is multiplied by a random polynomial which has the same degree with the former polynomial. In this paper, to get a solution with lower costs than [8] and [18], we multiply each polynomial representing each set by a random polynomial which has a low enough degree without compromising the security of the solution. We also multiply the randomized polynomials by a non-singular matrix to improve the correctness of our solution. We will compare our solution for PPSI with [8] and [18] in details in Section 7.

Though there hasn't been a direct solution for the PPSM problem, it can be considered as computing a function $\bigcup_{i'=1,...,N,i\neq i'}(T_i \cap T_{i'})$ on P_i for $i = 1, ..., N$, and can be solved by the techniques of privacy preserving set intersection and set union in [18]. Thus we can derive a solution from [18], and we name it *"Solution D1"* in this paper. In [18] the way to securely construct Solution D1 wasn't provided. Solution D1 also requires high cost. We will compare our solution for PPSM with Solution D1 in Section 7.

Other related privacy preserving problems, such as set cardinality, set disjointness, threshold set union, etc, can be found in [8], [18], [17] and [14]. They are different problems from PPSI and PPSM, thus need different solutions.

3 Preliminaries

3.1 Adversary Model

Generally speaking there are two types of adversaries in SMC, depending on whether they take active steps to disrupt the execution of the protocol, or merely gather information. The latter adversary is referred to as semi-honest (or passive, honest-but-curious); the former one is referred to as malicious (or active). A semi-honest party is assumed to follow the protocol exactly as what is prescribed by the protocol, except that it keeps a record of all its intermediate computations. A malicious party may arbitrarily deviate from the specified protocol, including refusing to participate in the protocol, substituting their local inputs and aborting the protocol prematurely. For the security in the malicious model, a general compiler is given in [11] to force each party to either effectively behave in a semi-honest manner or be detected as cheating.

In this paper we assume the parties are semi-honest, and they may compose any coalition of c ($1 \leq c \leq N - 1$) parties ($P_{i_1}, ..., P_{i_c}$). A multi-party protocol is said to *privately compute* a function $\mathfrak{f}$, if whatever a coalition of semi-honest parties can obtain after participating in the protocol could be essentially obtained from the inputs and outputs of these very parties. By [10] and [11], a formal definition of *privacy with respect to semi-honest behavior* is given in the following:

Definition 1. *Let* $\mathfrak{f} : (\{0,1\}^*)^m \rightarrow (\{0,1\}^*)^m$ *be an m-ary functionality, where* $\mathfrak{f}_i(x_1, ..., x_m)$ *is the i-th element of* $\mathfrak{f}(x_1, ..., x_m)$. *For* $I = \{i_1, ..., i_c\} \subseteq \{1, ..., m\}$, $\mathfrak{f}_I(x_1, ..., x_m) = \{\mathfrak{f}_{i_1}(x_1, ..., x_m), ..., \mathfrak{f}_{i_c}(x_1, ..., x_m)\}$. *Let Π be an m-party protocol for computing* $\mathfrak{f}$. *The* **view** *of the i-th party (P_i) after participating in an execution of Π on* $\overline{x} = (x_1, ..., x_m)$, *denoted* $VIEW_i^\Pi(\overline{x})$, *is* $(x_i, r, m_1, ..., m_t)$, *where r are the random bits generated by P_i, $m_1, ..., m_t$ is a sequence of message received by P_i. For* $I = \{i_1, ..., i_c\}$, *we let* $VIEW_I^\Pi(\overline{x}) = (I, VIEW_{i_1}^\Pi(\overline{x}), ..., VIEW_{i_c}^\Pi(\overline{x}))$.

We say that Π **Privately Computes** $\mathfrak{f}$ *if there exists a probabilistic polynomial-time (PPT) algorithm, denoted S, such that for every $I \subseteq \{1, ..., m\}$, it holds that*

$$S(I, (x_{i_1}, ..., x_{i_c}), \mathfrak{f}_I(\overline{x}))_{\overline{x} \in (\{0,1\}^*)^m} \equiv^c VIEW_I^\Pi(\overline{x})_{\overline{x} \in (\{0,1\}^*)^m} \tag{1}$$

In the definition above, "$\equiv^c$" denotes *computationally indistinguishable*, which is also called *indistinguishable in polynomial time*. Given two ensembles $X = \{X_w\}_{w \in S'}$ and $Y = \{Y_w\}_{w \in S'}$ (S' is a set of strings), they are indistinguishable in polynomial time if for every PPT algorithm D, every positive polynomial $p(\cdot)$, and all sufficiently long $w \in S'$, $|Pr[D(X_w, w) = 1]| - |Pr[D(Y_w, w) = 1]| < \frac{1}{p(|w|)}$.

3.2   Homomorphic Encryption

Our protocols are based on an additive Homomorphic Encryption (HE) scheme. Let ε be a probabilistic encryption scheme. Let M be the message space and C the ciphertext space such that M is a group under operation $\oplus$ and C is a group under operation $\odot$. ε is a $(\oplus, \odot)$-HE scheme if for any instance $E_R(\cdot)$ of the encryption scheme, given $c_1 = E_{r_1}(m_1)$ and $c_2 = E_{r_2}(m_2)$, there exists an r such that $c_1 \odot c_2 = E_{r_1}(m_1) \odot E_{r_2}(m_2) = E_r(m_1 \oplus m_2)$. ε is *additive* when it's a $(+, \odot)$ scheme, and *multiplicative* when it's a $(*, \odot)$ scheme.

The HE scheme in our protocols is also required to support secure (N, N)-threshold decryption. The corresponding secret key is shared by a group of N parties, and the decryption can't be performed by any single party, unless all parties act together.

Thus, we can use Paillier's cryptosystem ([21]) for its following properties: 1) it's an additive homomorphic encryption scheme. Given two encryptions $E(m_1)$ and $E(m_2)$, $E(m_1 + m_2) = E(m_1) \cdot E(m_2)$; 2) given an encryption $E(m)$ and a scalar a, $E(a \cdot m) = E(m)^a$; 3) (N, N)-threshold decryption can be supported (by [6],[7]). In this paper, $\mathcal{N}$ is the RSA-modulus which is the multiplication of two large prime numbers, and $\mathbb{Z}_{\mathcal{N}}$ is the plaintext space of Paillier's cryptosystem.

3.3   Calculations on Encrypted Polynomials

In our protocols, we need do some calculations on encrypted polynomials. For a polynomial $f(x) = \sum_{i=0}^{m} a_i x^i$, we use $E(f(x))$ to denote the sequence of encrypted coefficients $\{E(a_i) | i = 0, ..., m\}$. Given $E(f(x))$, where $E(\cdot)$ is an additive HE scheme (e.g., Paillier), some computations can be made as follows (which have also been used in [8] and [18]):

1) At a value v, we can evaluate $E(f(x))$: $E(f(v)) = E(a_m v^m + a_{m-1} v^{m-1} + ... + a_0) = E(a_m)^{v^m} E(a_{m-1})^{v^{m-1}} \cdots E(a_0)$.
2) Given $E(f(x))$, we can compute $E(c \cdot f(x)) = \{E(a_m)^c, ..., E(a_0)^c\}$.

Table 1. Major Notations in This Paper

Notation	Definition
N	Total number of parties
P_i	The i-th party
T_i	The set or multiset on P_i
S	Total number of elements on each party
$T(i, j)$	The j-th element on P_i, $j = 1, ..., S$
c	Total number of colluded parties, $1 \le c \le N - 1$
I	The index set of c colluded parties, $\{i_1, ..., i_c\}$
I'	The index set of honest parties, $\{1, ..., N\} \setminus I$
f_i	The polynomial whose roots are elements in T_i. $f_i = \prod_{j=1}^{S}(x - T(i, j))$
$\mathbb{Z}_{\mathcal{N}}$	The plaintext space of Paillier's cryptosystem

3) Given $E(f(x))$ and $E(g(x))$, $g(x) = \sum_{j=0}^{m} b_j x^j$, we can compute $E(f(x) + g(x)) = \{E(a_m)E(b_m), ..., E(a_0)E(b_0)\}$.

4) Given $f(x)$ and $E(g(x))$, we can compute $E(f(x)*g(x))$. Suppose that $g(x) = \sum_{j=0}^{n} b_j x^j$, $f(x) * g(x) = \sum_{k=0}^{m+n} c_k x^k$, then $E(c_k) = E(a_0 b_k + a_1 b_{k-1} + ... + a_k b_0) = E(b_k)^{a_0} \cdots E(b_0)^{a_k}$. a_i or b_j are treated as zero if $i > m$ or $j > n$.

3.4   Notations

The major notations in this paper are listed in Table 1.

4   Protocol for Privacy Preserving Set Intersection

4.1   Main Idea

Our protocol for PPSI is based on evaluating randomized polynomials representing the intersection, which is a similar way with [8] and [18], but achieves lower cost.

Each P_i can compute a polynomial f_i to represent its set T_i: $f_i = (x - T(i,1)) \cdots (x - T(i, S))$. Then it randomizes f_i to be $f_i * \sum_{j=1}^{N} r_{i,j}$ by the help of other parties, in which $r_{i,j}$ is generated by P_j, $r_{i,j} = a_{i,j} x + b_{i,j}$, $a_{i,j}$ and $b_{i,j}$ are uniformly selected from the plaintext space of the threshold HE scheme (for Paillier's scheme, it's $\mathbb{Z}_N$).

The N parties get a polynomial vector $F = (f_1 * \sum_{j=1}^{N} r_{1,j}, ..., f_N * \sum_{j=1}^{N} r_{N,j})$ and compute $G = FR$, in which R is an $N \times N$ nonsingular matrix whose entries R_{uv} $(1 \le u, v \le N)$ are random numbers. The resulting G is another polynomial vector $(g_1, ..., g_N)$ as following:

$$g_1 = f_1 * \sum_{j=1}^{N} r_{1,j} R_{11} + ... + f_N * \sum_{j=1}^{N} r_{N,j} R_{N1}$$

$$...$$

(2)

$$g_N = f_1 * \sum_{j=1}^{N} r_{1,j} R_{1N} + ... + f_N * \sum_{j=1}^{N} r_{N,j} R_{NN}$$

Then, each P_i evaluates $(g_1, ..., g_N)$ at the element $T(i, j)$. If for $k = 1, ..., N$ $g_k(T(i,j)) = 0$, then P_i determines $T(i,j) \in TI$. The correctness of this determination will be proved in Lemma 1.

In the computation of G, to protect the privacy of each f_i, f_i is encrypted by P_i, and the encryption of $f_i * \sum_{j=1}^{N} r_{i,j}$ is also computed. Then each party P_i generates a random matrix R_i so that $R = \prod_{i=1}^{N} R_i$ is nonsingular but no one knows what R is without publishing all R_i. The encryptions of FR_1, $FR_1 R_2$, ..., $FR_1 \cdots R_N$ are computed respectively on P_1, P_2, ..., P_N. Finally, the N parties get the encryption of $G = FR$. After decryption, each P_i knows G, but not $f_{i'}$ for $i' \neq i$.

4.2   The Protocol

Protocol 1: *Protocol for Privacy Preserving Set Intersection*
Inputs: There are N ($N \geq 2$) semi-honest parties. Each party has a private
set of S elements, denoted T_i. Each party holds the public key and it's own
share of the secret key for the threshold Paillier's cryptosystem.
Output: Each party P_i knows $TI = T_1 \cap ... \cap T_N$.
1) **Computing $E(F)$:** For $i = 1, ..., N$,
   1.1) P_i computes $f_i = (x - T(i,1)) \cdots (x - T(i,S))$, encrypts the coefficients
        to get $E(f_i)$, and sends $E(f_i)$ to all the other $N - 1$ parties.
   1.2) on each P_j ($j \neq i$), $r_{i,j}$ is generated as $a_{i,j}x + b_{i,j}$, in which $a_{i,j}$ and $b_{i,j}$
        are uniformly selected from $\mathbb{Z}_N$. P_j computes $E(f_i * r_{i,j})$ by computation
        4) in Section 3.3, and sends it to P_i.
   1.3) P_i also generates $r_{i,i}$ and computes $E(f_i * r_{i,i})$. Then P_i computes $E(f_i * \sum_{j=1}^{N} r_{i,j})$ by computation 3) in Section 3.3, and sends it to P_1.
        In the end, P_1 gets $E(F)$ in which $F = (f_1 * \sum_{j=1}^{N} r_{1,j}, ..., f_N * \sum_{j=1}^{N} r_{N,j})$.
2) **Computing $E(G)$:** For $i = 1, ..., N$,
   2.1) P_i generates a nonsingular $N \times N$ matrix R_i which is uniformly distrib-
        uted over $\mathbb{Z}_N$ (by the method in [22]).
   2.2) P_i computes $E(FR_1 \cdots R_i)$ according to computation 2) and 3) in Section
        3.3, and sends it to P_{i+1} if $i + 1 \leq N$.
        In the end, P_N gets $E(G) = E(F \prod_{i=1}^{N} R_i)$ and sends it to all the
        other parties.
3) **Decryption and Evaluation:**
   3.1) The parties cooperatively decrypt $E(G)$ and gets $G = F(\prod_{i=1}^{N} R_i)$. Let
        $R = \prod_{i=1}^{N} R_i$, and $R_{u,v}$ ($1 \leq u, v \leq N$) is the (u, v)-th entry of R, G is a
        polynomial vector $(g_1, ..., g_N)$ as described in the equation 2) of Section
        4.1.
   3.2) Every P_i evaluates $T(i,j)$ in G for $j = 1, ..., S$ by computation 1) in
        Section 3.3. If $G(T(i,j)) = (g_1(T(i,j)), ..., g_N(T(i,j))) = (0, ..., 0)$, the
        $T(i,j) \in TI$; otherwise, $T(i,j) \notin TI$.

We prove the correctness of Protocol 1 in the following lemma:

Lemma 1. *Protocol 1 is a correct protocol for the PPSI problem.*

Proof: Protocol 1 determines whether $T(i,j) \in TI$ by $G(T(i,j))$. If $T(i,j) \in TI$,
$T(i,j)$ is a root of all f_i for $i = 1, ..., N$, then $F(T(i,j)) = (f_1(T(i,j)) \sum_{j=1}^{N} r_{1,j},$
$..., f_N(T(i,j)) \sum_{j=1}^{N} r_{N,j}) = (0, ..., 0)$, $G(T(i,j)) = F(T(i,j))R = (0, ..., 0)$. That
is, if the evaluation $G(T(i,j)) \neq (0, ..., 0)$, $T(i,j) \notin TI$.
    Then we prove that if $G(T(i,j)) = (0, ..., 0)$, overwhelmingly $T(i,j) \in TI$.
$G = FR_1 \cdots R_N = F(\prod_{i=1}^{N} R_i) = FR$. Because R_i for $i = 1, ..., N$ are generated
to be nonsingular, $R = \prod_{i=1}^{N} R_i$ is also nonsingular. If $G(T(i,j)) = (0, ..., 0)$, a
linear system $F(T(i,j))R = (0, ..., 0)$ can be made, and it has only one solution:
$F(T(i,j)) = (0, ..., 0)$, i.e., $f_l(T(i,j)) * \sum_{j=1}^{N} r_{l,j}(T(i,j)) = 0$ for $l = 1, ..., N$.

The coefficients of $r_{l,j}$ are uniformly selected from $\mathbb{Z}_\mathcal{N}$. Suppose $\sum_{j=1}^{N} r_{l,j} = a_l x + b_l$, a_l and b_l are also uniformly distributed over $\mathbb{Z}_\mathcal{N}$. The probability that any $T(i,j) \in \mathbb{Z}_\mathcal{N}$ is a root of $a_l x + b_l$ is $1/\mathcal{N}$. If $\exists T(i,j)$, $\forall l \in \{1, ..., N\}$, $f_l(T(i,j)) * \sum_{j=1}^{N} r_{l,j}(T(i,j)) = 0$, because $f_l(T(i,j))$ must be 0 when $l = i$, so the probability that $\forall l \ (l \neq i) \ f_l(T(i,j)) = 0$ is $p = (1 - 1/\mathcal{N})^{N-1}$. N is the number of parties and practically $N \ll \mathcal{N}$. When $\mathcal{N}$ is large enough, $p \to 1$, then overwhelmingly $T(i,j)$ is a root of all f_l and $T(i,j) \in TI$.   ■

5   Protocol for Privacy Preserving Set Matching

5.1   Main Idea

The problem of PPSM can be considered as computing a function $\bigcup_{i'=1,...,N, i' \neq i}(T_i \cap T_{i'})$ on P_i for $i = 1, ..., N$. On each P_i the polynomial f_i is computed whose roots are elements in T_i. Then we can use a polynomial $(f_i * \sum_{k=1}^{N} r_{i'k} + f_{i'} * \sum_{k=1}^{N} r'_{i'k})$ to represent elements in $T_i \cap T_{i'}$, in which $r_{i'k} = \sum_{j=0}^{\alpha} a_j x^j$, $r'_{i'k} = \sum_{j=0}^{\alpha} a'_j x^j$. The degrees of $r_{i'k}$ and $r'_{i'k}$ are both α and $\alpha = \lceil \frac{S}{N-1} \rceil$. The coefficients a_j and a'_j for $j = 0, ..., \alpha$ are uniformly selected from the plaintext space of the threshold HE scheme (for Paillier's scheme, it's $\mathbb{Z}_\mathcal{N}$).

We can also use the multiplication of these polynomials to represent the elements in the union of all $T_i \cap T_{i'}$ for $i' = 1, ..., N, i' \neq i$. The resulting polynomial is F_i as following:

$$F_i = \prod_{i'=1,...,N, i' \neq i} (f_i * \sum_{k=1}^{N} r_{i'k} + f_{i'} * \sum_{k=1}^{N} r'_{i'k}) \qquad (3)$$

The coefficients of F_i should be encrypted in the computations. We can use the evaluation of F_i at $T(i,j)$ to determine whether $T(i,j) \in \bigcup_{i'=1,...,N, i' \neq i}(T_i \cap T_{i'})$. The correctness of the determination will be proved in Lemma 2. For PPSM defined in Section 1, $E(F_i)$ can't be decrypted before evaluations, otherwise P_i will know $T(i,j)$ can be matched by b parties if P_i finds there is a factor $(x - T(i,j))^b$ in F_i, and this will breach the Privacy Requirement 2) in Section 1.

5.2   The Protocol

In the following Protocol 2, each party P_i computes its $E(F_i)$ in $N - 1$ rounds. For example, P_1 firstly computes $E(F_{12}) = E(f_1 * \sum_{k=1}^{N} r_{2k} + f_2 * \sum_{k=1}^{N} r'_{2k})$ in Step 2) of Protocol 2, by summing $E(f_1 * \sum_{k=1}^{N} r_{2k})$ and $E(f_2 * \sum_{k=1}^{N} r'_{2k})$. Then P_1 repeats Step 2), computes $E(F_{13}) = E(F_{12}(f_1 * \sum_{k=1}^{N} r_{3k} + f_3 * \sum_{k=1}^{N} r'_{3k}))$, by summing $E(F_{12} f_1 * \sum_{k=1}^{N} r_{3k})$ and $E(F_{12} f_3 * \sum_{k=1}^{N} r'_{3k})$. After $N - 1$ rounds of Step 2), P_1 gets $E(F_1) = E(F_{1N}) = E((f_1 * \sum_{k=1}^{N} r_{2k} + f_2 * \sum_{k=1}^{N} r'_{2k}) \cdots (f_1 * \sum_{k=1}^{N} r_{Nk} + f_N * \sum_{k=1}^{N} r'_{Nk}))$. Finally, P_1 evaluates each $E(F_1(T(1,j)))$, and decrypts it to see whether it's 0.

Protocol 2: *Protocol for Privacy Preserving Set Matching*

Inputs: There are N ($N \geq 2$) semi-honest parties. Each party has a private set of S elements, denoted T_i. Every party holds the public key and it's own share of the secret key for the threshold Paillier's cryptosystem.

Output: Each party P_i knows whether its tuples belong to $\bigcup_{i'=1,\dots,N, i' \neq i}(T_i \cap T_{i'})$.

Steps:

1) Each party P_i computes its $f_i = (x - T(i,1)) \cdots (x - T(i,S))$.
2) P_1 initializes $E(F_{11}) = E(1)$, and repeats the following for $j = 2, \dots, N$.
   2.1) P_1 computes $E(F_{1(j-1)} * f_1)$ and sends it to all the other parties. Each party P_k ($k \neq 1$) randomly chooses r_{jk} as described in Section 5.1, computes $E(F_{1(j-1)} * f_1 * r_{jk})$ by computation 4) in Section 3.3, and sends it back to P_1. P_1 also randomly chooses r_{j1} and computes $E(F_{1(j-1)} * f_1 * \sum_{k=1}^{N} r_{jk})$ by computation 3) in Section 3.3.
   2.2) P_1 sends $E(F_{1(j-1)})$ to P_j, P_j computes $E(F_{1(j-1)} * f_j)$, sends it to all the other parties. Each of these parties P_k including P_j randomly chooses r'_{jk}, computes $E(F_{1(j-1)} * f_j * r'_{jk})$ and sends it to P_1. P_1 computes $E(F_{1(j-1)} * f_j * \sum_{k=1}^{N} r'_{jk})$.
   2.3) P_1 computes $E(F_{1j}) = E(F_{1(j-1)}(f_1 * \sum_{k=1}^{N} r_{jk} + f_j * \sum_{k=1}^{N} r'_{jk}))$ by summing $E(F_{1(j-1)} * f_1 * \sum_{k=1}^{N} r_{jk})$ and $E(F_{1(j-1)} * f_j * \sum_{k=1}^{N} r'_{jk})$. At the end of $j = N$, P_1 gets $E(F_1) = E(F_{1N}) = E(\prod_{j=2}^{N}(f_1 * \sum_{k=1}^{N} r_{jk} + f_j * \sum_{k=1}^{N} r'_{jk}))$.
3) Each P_i other than P_1 repeats Step 2) and gets $E(F_i) = E(\prod_{i'=1\dots N, i' \neq i}(f_i * \sum_{k=1}^{N} r_{i'k} + f_{i'} * \sum_{k=1}^{N} r'_{i'k}))$.
4) Each P_i evaluates $E(F_i)$ at $T(i,j)$ for $j = 1, \dots, S$, using computation 1) in Section 3.3.
5) Each party decrypts $E(F_i(T(i,j)))$ in the collaboration of the other $N-1$ parties for $j = 1, \dots, S$. If the evaluation $F_i(T(i,j)) = 0$, $T(i,j)$ has a duplicate on the other parties; otherwise, $T(i,j)$ hasn't any duplicate on the other parties.

Lemma 2. *Protocol 2 is a correct protocol for the PPSM problem.*

Proof: Protocol 2 determines whether $T(i,j) \in \bigcup_{i'=1,\dots,N, i' \neq i}(T_i \cap T_{i'})$ by the evaluation $F_i(T(i,j))$. If there is a party $P_{i'}$ who has a duplicate of $T(i,j)$, i.e., $T(i,j) \in \bigcup_{i'=1,\dots,N, i' \neq i}(T_i \cap T_{i'})$, then both $f_{i'}(T(i,j))$ and $f_i(T(i,j))$ are 0, and $f_i(T(i,j)) * \sum_{k=1}^{N} r_{i'k} + f_{i'}(T(i,j)) * \sum_{k=1}^{N} r'_{i'k} = 0$, then $F_i(T(i,j)) = 0$. That is, if $F_i(T(i,j)) \neq 0$, $T(i,j) \notin \bigcup_{i'=1,\dots,N, i' \neq i}(T_i \cap T_{i'})$.

If $F_i(T(i,j)) = 0$, $T(i,j)$ is a root of at least one factor $(f_i * \sum_{k=1}^{N} r_{i'k} + f_{i'} * \sum_{k=1}^{N} r'_{i'k})$ in F_i. In this factor, $f_i(T(i,j)) = 0$, $\sum_{k=1}^{N} r'_{i'k}$ is a polynomial of degree $\lceil \frac{S}{N-1} \rceil$ uniformly distributed over $\mathbb{Z}_\mathcal{N}[x]$. Any $T(i,j) \in \mathbb{Z}_\mathcal{N}$ is a root of $\sum_{k=1}^{N} r'_{i'k}$ with probability $1/\mathcal{N}$ (by [13]). When $\mathcal{N}$ is large enough, overwhelmingly $T(i,j)$ is a root of $f_{i'}$, and the corresponding $P_{i'}$ has a duplicate of $T(i,j)$. ∎

6 Security Analysis

6.1 Security Analysis on Protocol 1

The Inferred Information by the Definition of PPSI. Suppose there are c colluded parties P_I, $I = \{i_1, ..., i_c\}$. It's unavoidable for P_I to combine their inputs and outputs to infer information. However, by the definition of PPSI in Section 1, they should know no more information than TI in each $T_{i'}$, $\forall i' \in I'$, $I' = \{1, ..., N\} \setminus I$. That is,

6.1.1) On $P_i \in P_I$, if $T(i, j) \in TI$, they know each $T_{i'}$ has $T(i, j)$.
6.1.2) On $P_i \in P_I$, if $T(i, j) \notin TI$, they don't know whether $T(i, j) \in T_{i'}$ for $\forall i' \in I'$.

The Inferred Information after Participating in Protocol 1. In Protocol 1, each P_i gets $G = (g_1, ..., g_N)$, so P_I may infer the roots of $f_{i'}$ for $\forall i' \in I'$ by analyzing the coefficients in G. By the following lemma, we prove that G resists such kind of analysis.

Lemma 3. *In Protocol 1, any P_i in the coalition of c $(1 \le c \le N - 1)$ semi-honest parties (P_I) can know no more elements than TI in any $T_{i'}$ for $\forall i' \in I'$.*

Proof: Due to the security of the threshold HE cryptosystem, P_I can't know any information on the plaintexts of the encryptions unless they are decrypted. We use P_i to denote any party in P_I. P_i gets only the decryption of $E(G)$. If $G(T(i, j)) = (0, ..., 0)$, by Lemma 1, P_i knows $T(i, j)$ is a root for all f_l ($l = 1, ..., N$) and each $T_{i'}$ has $T(i, j)$. This accords with the case 6.1.1).

1) We firstly prove that, if $G(T(i, j)) \neq (0, ..., 0)$, P_i doesn't know whether $T(i, j) \in T_{i'}$ for $\forall i' \in I'$, that is, whether $T(i, j)$ is a root of any $f_{i'}$.
   From the view of P_i, $G = F(\prod_{i \in I} R_i \cdot \prod_{i' \in I'} R_{i'})$, $\prod_{i \in I} R_i$ is generated by P_I, and $\prod_{i' \in I'} R_{i'}$ is generated by $P_{I'}$. P_i doesn't know $\prod_{i' \in I'} R_{i'}$, thus if $G(T(i, j)) \neq (0, ..., 0)$, P_i can't compute $F(T(i, j))$. Then P_i can't know any $f_{i'}(T(i, j))$ and whether $T(i, j) \in T_{i'}$ for $\forall i' \in I'$. This accords with the case 6.1.2).

2) P_i may also analyze the coefficients of a single g_l ($l = 1, ..., N$). In P_i's view, $g_l = f_{TI}(\mathcal{F}_I + \mathcal{F}_{I'})$, in which f_{TI} is the polynomial whose roots are TI, $\mathcal{F}_I = \sum_{i \in I}(f_i / f_{TI} * \sum_{j=1}^{N} r_{i,j} R_{il})$, and $\mathcal{F}_{I'} = \sum_{i' \in I'}(f_{i'} / f_{TI} * \sum_{j=1}^{N} r_{i',j} R_{i'l})$. We should also prove that P_i can't know $\mathcal{F}_{I'}$, otherwise he will know $\bigcap_{i' \in I'} T_{i'}$ by factoring $\mathcal{F}_{I'}$.
   From the view of P_i, in $\mathcal{F}_I$, $\forall i \in I$, $\sum_{j=1}^{N} r_{i,j} R_{il}$ can be supposed as $b_{i,1} x + b_{i,0}$, in which $b_{i,1}$ and $b_{i,0}$ are random numbers. Given $f_i / f_{TI} = \sum_{k=0}^{S-|TI|} a_{i,k} x^k$, suppose $f_i / f_{TI} * \sum_{j=1}^{N} r_{i,j} R_{il} = \sum_{k=0}^{S-|TI|+1} c_{i,k} x^k$, then $c_{i,k} = a_{i,k} b_{i,0} + a_{i,k-1} b_{i,1}$. Suppose $\mathcal{F}_I = \sum_{k=0}^{S-|TI|+1} e_k x^k$, then $e_k = \sum_{i \in I} c_{i,k}$. Suppose $\mathcal{F}_{I'} = \sum_{k=0}^{S-|TI|+1} e'_k x^k$, then the k-th coefficient of $\mathcal{F}_I + \mathcal{F}_{I'}$: $e''_k = e_k + e'_k = \sum_{i \in I}(a_{i,k} b_{i,0} + a_{i,k-1} b_{i,1}) + e'_k$.

P_i knows all $e_k^{''}$ from g_l/f_{TI}, and all $a_{i,k}$ from f_i/f_{TI}, but doesn't know all $b_{i,1}$, $b_{i,0}$, and e_k'. Thus from $e_k^{''} = \sum_{i \in I}(a_{i,k}b_{i,0} + a_{i,k-1}b_{i,1}) + e_k'$, P_i gets a set of $S - |TI| + 2$ linear equations with $2c + S - |TI| + 2$ unknowns. For $1 \le c \le N-1$, P_i can't compute the solutions for these unknowns. Therefore, P_i can't know e_k' for $k = 0, ..., S - |TI| + 1$, and can't know any root of $\mathcal{F}_{I'}$. In each g_l ($l = 1, ..., N$), P_i can't know $\mathcal{F}_{I'}$, which makes P_i fail to know any $f_{i'}/f_{TI}$ in $\mathcal{F}_{I'}$.

In sum, in Protocol 1, $P_i \in P_I$ can know no more roots than TI in any $T_{i'}$ for $\forall i' \in I'$.   ∎

Theorem 1. *Protocol 1 is a privacy preserving protocol for the PPSI problem.*

The proof of this theorem is postponed to the Appendix.

6.2   Security Analysis on Protocol 2

The Inferred Information by the Definition of PPSM. If there is any coalition of c semi-honest parties P_I ($I = \{i_1, ..., i_c\}$), by the definition of PPSM, it's unavoidable for P_i ($\in P_I$) to infer the following information by combining inputs and outputs of its coalition parties:

6.2.1) if the determination is $T(i, j)$ has a duplicate on the other parties, and P_i knows $T(i, j)$ also has a duplicate on P_I, then it can't know whether there is any duplicate of $T(i, j)$ on the remaining parties $P_{I'}$ ($I' = \{1, ..., N\}\backslash I$).
6.2.2) if the determination is $T(i, j)$ has a duplicate on the other parties, and P_i knows $T(i, j)$ hasn't any duplicate on P_I, then it knows that $T(i, j)$ must have a duplicate on $P_{I'}$; We denote these $T(i, j)$ on $P_{I'}$ as set $\mathcal{T}$. It's easy to see that $0 \le |\mathcal{T}| \le (N - c)S$.
6.2.3) if the determination is $T(i, j)$ hasn't any duplicate on the other parties, then P_i knows that $T(i, j)$ hasn't any duplicate on $P_{I'}$, that is, $P_{I'}$ can't have $T(i, j)$. We denote these $T(i, j)$ as $\mathcal{T}'$.

Therefore, by the definition P_i ($\in P_I$) knows $\mathcal{T}$ and $\mathcal{T}'$ as above. We assume this kind of information is harmless.

The Inferred Information after Participating in Protocol 2. In Step 3) of Protocol 1, P_i ($\in P_I$) can't directly know the coefficients of F_i because they are encrypted. However, P_i knows S pairs of ($T(i, j), F_i(T(i, j))$), and those $f_{i'}$, $r_{i'k}$ and $r_{i'k}'$ generated by its collation parties. Thus, P_i can do an attack by analyzing the coefficients of F_i. In the following lemma, we prove that Protocol 2 is robust against this attack.

Lemma 4. *In Protocol 2, any P_i in the coalition of c ($1 \le c \le N - 1$) semi-honest parties (P_I) can get only the following information:*

1) the same two sets as $\mathcal{T}$ and $\mathcal{T}'$ in the case 6.2.2) and 6.2.3).
2) guessing elements on $P_{I'}$ other than $\mathcal{T}$ and $\mathcal{T}'$, after randomly choosing at least 1 numbers.

Proof: In this proof P_i is any party in P_I. Due to the security of the threshold HE cryptosystem, P_i can't know any information on the plaintexts of the encryptions they receive.

P_i gets S pairs ($T(i,j), F_i(T(i,j))$) by evaluating F_i at $T(i,j)$. Because $f_i(T(i,j)) = 0$, then $F_i(T(i,j))$ becomes $F_i'(T(i,j))$ for which $F_i' = \prod_{i'=1...N, i' \neq i}(f_{i'} * \sum_{k=1}^{N} r_{i'k}')$. If P_i can know all coefficients of F_i', it can know all roots of F_i' by polynomial factoring, but all coefficients are encrypted. For P_i, there are $(N-1)S$ unknown coefficients in $\prod_{i'=1...N, i' \neq i} f_{i'}$ excluding the leading coefficient ($= 1$). Because $\prod_{i'=1...N, i' \neq i}(\sum_{k=1}^{N} r_{i'k}') = \sum_{j=0}^{\beta} R_j x^j$, $\beta = (N-1)\lceil \frac{S}{N-1} \rceil$, in this part there are at least $S+1$ unknown coefficients. Totally there are at least $(N-1)S + S + 1$ unknown coefficients in F_i'. It's easy to see that P_i can't find a unique F_i' that fits S pairs ($T(i,j), F_i'(T(i,j))$).

However, P_i knows f_{i_t} for $i_t \in I$, and $r_{i'k}'$ generated by P_I. Then in P_i's view, $F_i' = f_{\mathcal{I}} f_{\mathcal{I}'} \prod_{i'=1...N, i' \neq i}(\sum_{k \in I} r_{i'k}' + \sum_{k \in I'} r_{i'k}')$, in which $f_{\mathcal{I}} = \prod_{i_t \in I, i_t \neq i} f_{i_t}$, $f_{\mathcal{I}'} = \prod_{i_t' \in I'} f_{i_t'}$, $\sum_{k \in I} r_{i'k}'$ is generated by P_I, $\sum_{k \in I'} r_{i'k}'$ is generated by $P_{I'}$.

1) if $F_i'(T(i,j)) = 0$, and $f_{\mathcal{I}}(T(i,j)) = 0$, then P_i can't know any root of $f_{\mathcal{I}'}$. This accords with the case 6.2.1).
2) if $F_i'(T(i,j)) = 0$, and $f_{\mathcal{I}}(T(i,j)) \neq 0$, then P_i knows $f_{\mathcal{I}'}(T(i,j)) = 0$. All these $T(i,j)$ are the same as $\mathcal{T}$ in the case 6.2.2).
3) if $F_i'(T(i,j)) \neq 0$, P_i knows $f_{\mathcal{I}'}(T(i,j)) \neq 0$, i.e., $T(i,j)$ isn't one root of $f_{\mathcal{I}'}$. All these $T(i,j)$ are the same as $\mathcal{T}'$ in the case 6.2.3).

Suppose in 2), all P_I know C_1 roots of $f_{\mathcal{I}'}$, then $0 \leq C_1 \leq (N-c)S$. Suppose in 3), P_i knows C_2 pairs ($T(i,j), F_i'(T(i,j))$) for F_i', then $0 \leq C_2 \leq S$. Because P_i knows $f_{\mathcal{I}}(T(i,j))$, P_i can know $C_1 + C_2$ evaluations of F_i'': $F_i'' = F_i'/f_{\mathcal{I}} = f_{\mathcal{I}'} \prod_{i'=1...N, i' \neq i}(\sum_{k \in I} r_{i'k}' + \sum_{k \in I'} r_{i'k}')$. For P_i, there are $(N-c)S$ unknown coefficients in $f_{\mathcal{I}'}$ excluding the leading coefficient ($= 1$). In $\prod_{i'=1...N, i' \neq i}(\sum_{k \in I} r_{i'k}' + \sum_{k \in I'} r_{i'k}') = \sum_{j=0}^{\beta} R_j' x^j$, $\beta = (N-1)\lceil \frac{S}{N-1} \rceil$, there are at least $S+1$ unknown coefficients. Therefore P_i still needs to arbitrarily guess $t = (N-c)S + S + 1 - (C_1 + C_2)$ coefficients in F_i''. It's easy to see that $t \geq 1$. That is, P_i should guess at least 1 random number before inferring other roots in $f_{\mathcal{I}'}$ than $\mathcal{T}$ and $\mathcal{T}'$.   ■

Theorem 2. *Protocol 2 is a privacy preserving protocol for the PPSM problem.*

The proof of this theorem is postponed to the Appendix.

7   Comparisons with Related Work

7.1   Comparisons for Protocol 1

Complexity of Protocol 1

1) *Computation Cost:* Each Paillier's encryption and decryption requires a cost of $2lg\mathcal{N}$ modular multiplications (mod $\mathcal{N}^2$). Each exponentiation has the same cost with the encryption. We compare our protocol with other related

work regarding their computation cost on encryptions and multiplications of ciphertexts, and consider modular multiplication (mod $\mathcal{N}^2$) as a basic computation.

Thus, for each party in Protocol 1, the total encryptions are $(S+2)(N-1)^2-2$, and the total multiplications of ciphertexts are $(S+2)(N^2+2N-3)$. Then the total computation cost for each party is $2((S+2)(N-1)^2-2)lg\mathcal{N}+(S+2)(N^2+2N-3)$ modular multiplications.

2) *Communication Cost*: The length of each encryption is $2lg\mathcal{N}$. Then in Protocol 1, the total communication cost among all parties is $2N(N-1)(4S+5)lg\mathcal{N}$ bits.

Speeding up techniques can be employed in Protocol 1. If all parties ensure that there is a coalition of c ($1 \leq c \leq N-1$) semi-honest parties, in Step 1) of Protocol 1 each $E(f_i)$ can be randomized as $E(f_i * \sum_{j=1}^{c+1} r_{i,j})$ by sending $E(f_i)$ to c parties. In Step 2) $E(G)$ can be computed as $E(F \prod_{i=1}^{c+1} R_i)$. What's more, in Step 1) the iterations $i = 1, ..., N$ can be made in parallel. Then the computation cost is $2(c(S+2)(N-1)-2)lg\mathcal{N} + c(S+2)(N+3)$ modular multiplications. The communication cost is $2cN(4S+5)lg\mathcal{N}$ bits.

Kissner's Protocol. In Kissner's protocol for PPSI ([18]), a single polynomial $F = \sum_{l=1}^{N} f_l * \sum_{k=1}^{N} r_{l,k}$ is constructed and evaluated on each $T(i,j)$. f_l is a polynomial representing elements on P_l, $r_{l,k}$ is a polynomial uniformly selected by P_k and has the same degree with f_l. In this protocol, it's easy to see that $T(i,j) \in TI$ is a sufficient condition for the evaluation $F(T(i,j)) = 0$, but $F(T(i,j)) = 0$ is not even a sufficient condition for $\forall l \in \{1, ..., N\}$ $f_l(T(i,j)) * \sum_{k=1}^{N} r_{l,k}(T(i,j)) = 0$. In Lemma 1 we have proved that if $\forall l \in \{1, ..., N\}$ $f_l(T(i,j)) * \sum_{k=1}^{N} r_{l,k}(T(i,j)) = 0$, the probability that $T(i,j) \in TI$ is $(1 - 1/\mathcal{N})^{N-1}$. Therefore, in Kissner's protocol, if $F(T(i,j)) = 0$, the probability that $T(i,j) \in TI$ is less than the probability achieved by our Protocol 1.

The major cost of this protocol is on computing the encrypted F. It's also based on Paillier's cryptosystem. The computation cost for each party and communication cost among all parties are shown in Table 2.

Freedman's Protocol. Freedman's protocol for PPSI ([8]) is quite different from ours and [18]'s. In their protocol, each party P_i ($i = 1, ..., N-1$) sends the encrypted polynomial f_i representing its elements to P_N. P_N evaluates its elements $T(N,j)$ for $j = 1, ..., S$ on all these polynomials, randomizes the evaluations and sends them to all the other parties. These parties decrypt and combine the evaluations to determine whether $T(i,j) \in TI$. In this protocol each party also generates a random matrix, but the matrices are used in a different way from our Protocol 1 for they aren't full rank and not for multiplications. The XOR of each row of the matrices is required to be zero, and they are used to randomize the decryptions on each party.

The major cost of this protocol is on the evaluations of encrypted polynomials at all elements of P_N. The protocol is also based on Paillier's cryptosystem. The average computation cost for each party and communication cost among all parties are shown in Table 2. In [8] only the protocol for the semi-honest model is given.

Comparisons of 3 protocols. From Table 2, the computation costs of Protocol 1, protocols in [18] and [8] are respectively $O(cSNlg\mathcal{N})$, $O(cS^2lg\mathcal{N})$, $O(S(S + N)lg\mathcal{N})$ modular multiplications. Practically the size of a set, S, may be much larger than the number of parties, N. Then it's easy to see that Protocol 1 is more efficient in computation than [18] and [8], and more efficient in communication than [18].

For a quantitative analysis, we conservatively set $S = 20$, $N = 5$, and set $c = 3$, $lg\mathcal{N} = 1024$, then Protocol 1 saves 81% and 63% computation costs, 17% and 20% communication costs in comparison with [18] and [8]. We also notice that if $c = 4$, i.e., all of the N parties are semi-honest, then the communication cost in Protocol 1 will increase by 6% in comparison with [8]. Thus Protocol 1 can utilize the knowledge on honest relationships among some of the N parties to reduce the communication cost.

Table 2. Comparisons of solutions for the PPSI problem

	Computation Cost	Communication Cost
Our Protocol 1	$2(c(S+2)(N-1) - 2)lg\mathcal{N} + c(S+2)(N+3)$	$2cN(4S+5)lg\mathcal{N}$
Protocol in [18]	$2(c(S+1)^2 + 5S + 3)lg\mathcal{N} + c(S^2 + 4S + 2)$	$2cN(5S+2)lg\mathcal{N}$
Protocol in [8]	$((S+1)(S+2) + 3S(N-1) - 1)2lg\mathcal{N} + S(S+1)$	$10S(N-1)^2lg\mathcal{N}$

7.2   Comparisons for Protocol 2

Complexity of Protocol 2. In Protocol 2, on each party the computation on encryptions and multiplications of ciphertexts requires $2N^2S^2lg\mathcal{N} + N^3S$ modular multiplications (mod $\mathcal{N}^2$). The communication cost among all parties is $4N(N-1)^2Slg\mathcal{N}$ bits.

The complexity of Protocol 2 can be reduced if all parties ensure that there may be a coalition of c $(1 \le c < N - 1)$ parties. In Step 2.1), P_1 can send $E(F_{1(j-1)} * f_1)$ to c parties; in Step 2.2), P_j can send $E(F_{1(j-1)} * f_j)$ to c parties; At the end of Step 2), P_1 gets $E(F_1) = E(\prod_{j=2}^{N}(f_1 * \sum_{k=1}^{c+1} r_{jk} + f_j * \sum_{k=1}^{c+1} r'_{jk}))$. The iterations in Step 3) can also be made in parallel with Step 2). Then the computation cost is $2cNS^2lg\mathcal{N} + cN^2S$ modular multiplications, and the communication cost is $4c(N-1)^2Slg\mathcal{N}$ bits.

Solution D1 Derived from [18]. The main idea of the private set intersection protocol in [18] is to plus the randomized polynomials representing the data sets, and their private set union protocol is mainly to multiply the polynomials representing the data sets. Therefore, Solution D1 (as described in Section 2) should firstly compute $(f_i * \sum_{k=1}^{N} r_{i'k} + f_{i'} * \sum_{k=1}^{N} r'_{i'k})$ for $T_i \cap T_{i'}$ for $i' = 1, ..., N$, $i' \ne i$, then compute $F_i = \prod_{i'=1...N, i' \ne i}(f_i * \sum_{k=1}^{N} r_{i'k} + f_{i'} * \sum_{k=1}^{N} r'_{i'k})$

for $\bigcup_{i'=1...N, i' \neq i}(T_i \cap T_{i'})$, and evaluate it. In [18], the way to privately compute the encryption of F_i wasn't provided, and all $r_{i'k}$ and $r'_{i'k}$ are randomly chosen polynomials with degree S. Because $r_{i'k}$ and $r'_{i'k}$ have the same degree with f_i and f'_i, Solution D1 needs a high cost to compute the encrypted polynomial multiplications and evaluations. The computation and communication costs of Solution D1 are shown in Table 3.

Comparisons. From Table 3, it's easy to see that Protocol 2 is more efficient in computation and communication than Solution D1. Suppose $N = 5$, $c = 4$, $S = 20$, $lg\mathcal{N} = 1024$, then Protocol 2 saves 80% computation cost and 50% communication cost.

Table 3. Comparisons of solutions for the PPSM problem

	Computation Cost	Communication Cost
Our Protocol 2	$2cNS^2lg\mathcal{N} + cN^2S$	$4c(N-1)^2Slg\mathcal{N}$
Solution D1	$2cN^2S^2lg\mathcal{N} + 2cN^2S$	$8c(N-1)^2Slg\mathcal{N}$

8   Conclusions and Open Problems

We address two problems in privacy preserving matching against distributed datasets: Privacy Preserving Set Intersection (PPSI) and Privacy Preserving Set Matching (PPSM) among N parties. The two problems are solved by constructing polynomials representing elements in the set intersection and set matching, and evaluating the polynomials to determine whether an element is in the set intersection and set matching, without publishing the datasets on each party. The security of the two protocols are proved assuming there is a coalition of c $(1 \leq c \leq N-1)$ semi-honest parties. In comparison with related work in [18] and [8], our two protocols have less computation and communication costs.

In the future, we will extend the two protocols in the semi-honest model to the malicious model employing some zero-knowledge proofs. We will also utilize the two protocols to protect the privacy in some practical problems, e.g., internet congestion control ([23]).

In the problem formulation of Section 1, we have assumed that the size of each party's set (S) is much less than the size of the common set $\mathbb{T}$ to prevent the dictionary attack. There are many applications fitting for this assumption, e.g., the intersection among the sets of credit card numbers. It's well known that the common set $\mathbb{T}$ for credit card numbers is large enough, so that given a suitable S, the probability that an adversary arbitrarily chooses a number which equals any number of the honest party is $\frac{S}{|\mathbb{T}|} \to 0$. However, there are also some applications where $\frac{S}{|\mathbb{T}|}$ can't be negligible. Then how can the dictionary attack be prevented? In these cases, our two protocols can effectively resist the semi-honest behaviors of the adversary, and be extended to resist the malicious behaviors, but it's also an important problem to prevent the adversary from defrauding the honest party of inputs using the common set $\mathbb{T}$ when $\frac{S}{|\mathbb{T}|}$ isn't negligible.

Acknowledgments. This research is conducted as a program for the "Fostering Talent in Emergent Research Fields" in Special Coordination Funds for Promoting Science and Technology by Ministry of Education, Culture, Sports, Science and Technology, Japan. We also acknowledge the anonymous reviewers for their helpful suggestions on improving the quality of this paper, and all the other people who contribute to this paper.

References

1. F. Boudot, B. Schoenmakers and J. Traor'e, "A Fair and Efficient Solution to the Socialist Millionaires' Problem", in *Discrete Applied Mathematics*, 111(1-2), pp. 23-36, 2001.
2. R. Cramer, I. Damgard, and J. Nielsen, "Multiparty Computation from Threshold Homomorphic Encryption", in *Advances in Cryptology - EUROCRYPT 2001*, LNCS, Springer, vol. 2045, pp. 280-300, 2001.
3. W. Du and M. Attalah, "Protocols for Secure Remote Database Access with Approximate Matching", in *Proc. of the 7th ACM CCS, the 1st Workshop on Security and Privacy in E-commerce*, 2000.
4. R. Fagin, M. Naor, and P. Winkler, "Comparing Information without Leaking It", in *Communications of the ACM*, 39(5): 77-85, 1996.
5. J. Feigenbaum, Y. Ishai, T. Malkin, K. Nissim, M. Strauss, and R. Wright, "Secure Multiparty Computation of Approximations", in *Proc. of the 28th International Colloquium on Automata, Languages and Programming (ICALP 2001)*, pp. 927-938, 2001.
6. P. Fouque, G. Poupard and J. Stern, "Sharing Decryption in the Context of Voting or Lotteries", in *Proc. of the 4th International Conference on Financial Cryptography*, pp. 90 - 104, 2000.
7. P. Fouque and D. Pointcheval, "Threshold Cryptosystems Secure against Chosen-ciphertext Attacks", in *Proc. of Asiacrypt 2001*, pp. 351 - 368, 2001.
8. M. Freedman, K. Nissim and B. Pinkas, "Efficient Private Matching and Set Intersection", in *Proc. of Eurocrypt '04*, LNCS, Springer, vol. 3027, pp. 1 - 19, 2004.
9. B. Goethals, S. Laur, H. Lipmaa, and T. Mielikainen, "On Secure Scalar Product Computation for Privacy-Preserving Data Mining", in *Proc. of ICISC*, 2004.
10. O. Goldreich, "Foundations of Cryptography: Volume 1, Basic Tools", Cambridge University Press, 2001.
11. O. Goldreich, "Foundations of Cryptography: Volume 2, Basic Applications", Cambridge University Press, 2004.
12. O. Goldreich, S. Micali, and A. Wigderson, "How to Play Any Mental Game", in *Proc. of 19th STOC*, pp. 218-229, 1987.
13. T. Hartman and R. Raz, "On the Distribution of the Number of Roots of Polynomials and Explicit Weak Designs", in *Random Structures and Algorithms*, Vol. 23 (3), pp. 235 - 263, 2003.
14. S. Hohenberger and S. A. Weis, "Honest-Verifier Private Disjointness Testing without Random Oracles", in *Workshop on Privacy Enhancing Technologies (PET)*, 2006.
15. P. Indyk and D. Woodruff, "Polylogarithmic Private Approximations and Efficient Matching", in *Proc. of the Third Theory of Cryptography Conference (TCC 2006)*, LNCS, Springer, vol. 3876, pp. 245-264, 2006.

16. M. Jakobsson, A. Juels, "Mix and Match: Secure Function Evaluation via Cipher-texts", in *ASIACRYPT 2000*, pp 162-177, 2000.

17. A. Kiayias and A. Mitrofanova, "Testing disjointness of private datasets", in *Proc. of Financial Cryptography (FC 2005)*, LNCS, Springer, vol. 3570, pp. 109C124, 2005.

18. L. Kissner and D. Song, "Privacy-Preserving Set Operations", in *Advances in Cryptology - CRYPTO 2005*, LNCS, Springer, vol.3621, pp. 241-257, 2005.

19. H. Lipmaa, "Verifiable Homomorphic Oblivious Transfer and private Equality Test", in *Advances in Cryptography ASIACRYPT 2003*, pp. 416-433, 2003.

20. M. Naor and B. Pinkas, "Oblivious Transfer and Polynomial Evaluation", in *Proc. of the 31st Annual ACM Symposium on Theory of Computing*, pp. 245-254, 1999.

21. P. Paillier, "Public-key Cryptosystems based on Composite Degree Residuosity Classes", in *Proc. of Asiacrypt 2000*, pp. 573-584, 2000.

22. D. Randall, "Efficient Generation of Random Nonsingular Matrices", in *Random Structures and Algorithms*, vol. 4(1), pp. 111-118, 1993.

23. N. Xiong, X. Defago, X. Jia, Y. Yang, and Y. He, "Design and Analysis of a Self-tuning Proportional and Integral Controller for Active Queue Management Routers to support TCP Flows", in *Proc. of IEEE INFOCOM*, 2006.

24. A.C. Yao, "Protocols for Secure Computations", in *Proc. of the 23rd Annual IEEE Symposium on Foundations of Computer Science*, pp. 160 - 164, 1982.

Appendix: Proofs of Theorems

Theorem 1. *Protocol 1 is a privacy preserving protocol for the PPSI problem.*

Proof: By the definition of PPSI, we actually should compute a multi-party function f: $f(T_1, ..., T_N) = f(\overline{T}) = \{PPSI(T(i,j))|T(i,j) \in T_i, i = 1, ..., N, j = 1, ..., S\}$, with the i-th element $f_i(\overline{T}) = \{PPSI(T(i,j))|T(i,j) \in T_i, j = 1, ..., S\}$ for the party P_i, where $PPSI(T(i,j)) = 1$ if $T(i,j) \in TI$, and $PPSI(T(i,j)) = 0$ if $T(i,j) \notin TI$.

Given any coalition of c ($c \leq N - 1$) semi-honest parties indexed by $I = \{i_1, ..., i_c\}$, their views after participating in Protocol 1 are denoted by $VIEW_I^{\Pi}(\overline{T}) = (I, VIEW_{i_1}^{\Pi}(\overline{T}), ..., VIEW_{i_c}^{\Pi}(\overline{T}))$. We also let $f_I(\overline{T}) = (f_{i_1}(\overline{T}), ..., f_{i_c}(\overline{T}))$. From the definition in Section 3.1, we have to show that there exists a PPT algorithm S such that $S(I, (T_{i_1}, ..., T_{i_c}), f_I(\overline{T}))$ and $VIEW_I^{\Pi}(\overline{T})$ are computationally indistinguishable.

$VIEW_I^{\Pi}(\overline{T}) = \{V_1, V_2, V_3, V_4\}$: 1) V_1 is $I = \{i_1, ..., i_c\}$. 2)V_2 are $T_{i_1}, ..., T_{i_c}$. 3)V_3 are $E(G)$ and the intermediate encryptions received by P_I. 4)V_4 are $G(T(i_t, j))$ for any $i_t \in I$. With these views, the coalition can do the following two types of analysis:

1) *Cryptanalysis on* (V_1, V_2, V_3): Due to the semantic security of the threshold HE cryptosystem, P_i can't gain extra information from the encryptions in V_3. That is, supposing V_3 has s encryptions, with only negligible probability, P_i can distinguish V_3 and $\mathcal{ER}_1 = (E(r_1), ..., E(r_s))$ by randomly choosing $\mathcal{R}_1 = (r_1, ..., r_s)$ over the plaintext space of the HE scheme. Thus, $(V_1, V_2, V_3) \equiv^c (V_1, V_2, \mathcal{R}_1, \mathcal{ER}_1)$.

2) *Roots analysis on* (V_1, V_2, V_4): From Lemma 3, P_I can't know roots other than TI in any $f_{i'}$ for $\forall i' \in I'$. Thus, $V_4 = (\mathcal{A}, TI)$. $\mathcal{A} = \{a_{i_t, j} | i_t \in \{i_1, ..., i_c\}, j = 1, ..., S\}$ in which $a_{i_t, j} = 1$ if $G(T(i_t, j)) = (0, ..., 0)$, and $a_{i_t, j} = 0$ otherwise.

In sum, $VIEW_I^\Pi(\overline{T}) \equiv^c (V_1, V_2, \mathcal{R}_1, \mathcal{ER}_1, \mathcal{A}, TI)$.

$f_I(\overline{T})$ also equals $(\mathcal{A}, TI)$ by the analysis of the cases 6.1.1) and 6.1.2) in Section 6.1. Let $\mathcal{R}_1' = \{r_i' | i = 1, ..., s\}$ are randomly chosen by P_I, and $\mathcal{ER}_1'$ are the encryptions of the sequence in $\mathcal{R}_1'$, then $S(I, (T_{i_1}, ..., T_{i_c}), f_I(\overline{T})) \equiv^c (I, (T_{i_1}, ..., T_{i_c}), \mathcal{A}, TI, \mathcal{R}_1', \mathcal{ER}_1') \equiv^c (V_1, V_2, \mathcal{A}, TI, \mathcal{R}_1, \mathcal{ER}_1) \equiv^c VIEW_I^\Pi(\overline{T})$. Then Protocol 1 privately computes PPSI against the coalition of any c ($c \leq N - 1$) semi-honest parties. ∎

Theorem 2. *Protocol 2 is a privacy preserving protocol for the PPSM problem.*

Proof: By the definition of PPSM, we actually should compute a multi-party function f: $f(T_1, ..., T_N) = f(\overline{T})$, with the i-th element $f_i(\overline{T}) = \{PPSM(T(i, j)) | T(i, j) \in T_i, j = 1, ..., S\}$ for the party P_i, where $PPSM(T(i, j)) = 1$ if $T(i, j) \in \bigcup_{i'=1,...,N, i' \neq i}(T_i \cap T_{i'})$, and $PPSM(T(i, j)) = 0$ otherwise. Given any coalition of c ($c \leq N-1$) semi-honest parties indexed by $I = \{i_1, ..., i_c\}$, their views after participating in Protocol 2 are $VIEW_I^\Pi(\overline{T})$. We also let $f_I(\overline{T}) = (f_{i_1}(\overline{T}), ..., f_{i_c}(\overline{T}))$. We show that there exists a PPT algorithm S such that $S(I, (T_{i_1}, ..., T_{i_c}), f_I(\overline{T}))$ and $VIEW_I^\Pi(\overline{T})$ are computationally indistinguishable.

$VIEW_I^\Pi(\overline{T}) = \{V_1, V_2, V_3, V_4\}$: 1) V_1 is $I = \{i_1, ..., i_c\}$. 2)V_2 are $T_{i_1}, ..., T_{i_c}$. 3)V_3 are $E(F_i)$ and the intermediate encryptions received by P_I. 4)V_4 are $F_{i_t}(T(i_t, j))$ for any $i_t \in I$. The coalition can do the following analysis:

1) *Cryptanalysis on* (V_1, V_2, V_3): Due to the semantic security of the threshold HE cryptosystem, supposing V_3 has s encryptions, with only negligible probability, P_i can distinguish V_3 and $\mathcal{ER}_1 = (E(r_1), ..., E(r_s))$ by randomly choosing $\mathcal{R}_1 = (r_1, ..., r_s)$. Thus, $(V_1, V_2, V_3) \equiv^c (V_1, V_2, \mathcal{R}_1, \mathcal{ER}_1)$.
2) *Roots analysis on* (V_1, V_2, V_4): From Lemma 4, $V_4 = (\mathcal{A}, \mathcal{T}, \mathcal{T}', \mathcal{R}_2)$. $\mathcal{A} = \{a_{i_t}^j | i_t \in \{i_1, ..., i_c\}, j = 1, ..., S\}$ in which $a_{i_t}^j = 1$ if $F_{i_t}(T(i_t, j)) = 0$, and $a_{i_t}^j = 0$ otherwise. $\mathcal{R}_2 = \{R_i | i = 1, ..., t\}$, in which R_i is a random number guessed by P_i, $t \geq 1$.

In sum, $VIEW_I^\Pi(\overline{T}) \equiv^c (V_1, V_2, \mathcal{R}_1, \mathcal{ER}_1, \mathcal{A}, \mathcal{T}, \mathcal{T}', \mathcal{R}_2)$. $f_I(\overline{T}) = (\mathcal{A}, \mathcal{T}, \mathcal{T}')$ by the analysis of the cases 6.2.1), 6.2.2) and 6.2.3). Let $\mathcal{R}_1' = \{r_i' | i = 1, ..., s\}$, $\mathcal{R}_2' = \{R_i' | i = 1, ..., t\}$ are randomly chosen by P_I, and $\mathcal{ER}_1'$ are the encryptions of the sequence in $\mathcal{R}_1'$. Then $S(I, (T_{i_1}, ..., T_{i_c}), f_I(\overline{T})) = (I, (T_{i_1}, ..., T_{i_c}), \mathcal{A}, \mathcal{T}, \mathcal{T}', \mathcal{R}_1', \mathcal{ER}_1', \mathcal{R}_2') \equiv^c VIEW_I^\Pi(\overline{T})$. Then Protocol 2 privately computes PPSM against the coalition of any c ($c \leq N - 1$) semi-honest parties. ∎

Quantifying Information Leakage in Tree-Based Hash Protocols (Short Paper)

Karsten Nohl and David Evans

University of Virginia, Computer Science Department
{nohl, evans}@cs.virginia.edu

Abstract. Radio Frequency Identification (RFID) systems promise large scale, automated tracking solutions but also pose a threat to customer privacy. The tree-based hash protocol proposed by Molnar and Wagner presents a scalable, privacy-preserving solution. Previous analyses of this protocol concluded that an attacker who can extract secrets from a large number of tags can compromise privacy of other tags. We propose a new metric for information leakage in RFID protocols along with a threat model that more realistically captures the goals and capabilities of potential attackers. Using this metric, we measure the information leakage in the tree-based hash protocol and estimate an attacker's probability of success in tracking targeted individuals, considering scenarios in which multiple information sources can be combined to track an individual. We conclude that an attacker has a reasonable chance of tracking tags when the tree-based hash protocol is used.

1 Introduction

Radio Frequency Identification (RFID) systems provide more precise identification (right down to the item-level) and superior reliability over existing tracking systems, as well as the possibility of strong authentication. Their capabilities, however, also pose a threat to individual privacy. Several schemes have been proposed that preserve consumer privacy by obfuscating the tag identity from rogue readers. Some proposed schemes, such as Weis et al.'s [13] and Ohkubo et al.'s [8], provide strong privacy but cannot scale to large RFID systems because the workload for the backend system scales linearly with the number of tags in the system. Other schemes, such as the tree-based hash protocol first proposed by Molnar and Wagner [5], provide scalability but sacrifice some privacy. We focus on this protocol and describe it in Section 2.

Avoine et al. analyzed the degree to which privacy is scarified in the tree-based protocol and concluded that a serious privacy threat exists [1]. In this paper, we revisit their assumptions and derive a different attacker model that we believe better captures possible capabilities and motives of real-world attackers. In our model, the attacker wants to track a tag through the system and needs to distinguish that tag from all other tags. We find that the threat to privacy is even higher than Avoine et al.'s estimate.

We assume an active attacker who can send arbitrary messages to readers and tags of the system, but cannot invert the hash function. We also assume our

P. Ning, S. Qing, and N. Li (Eds.): ICICS 2006, LNCS 4307, pp. 228–237, 2006.

attacker can extract secrets from a limited number of tags. The attacker tries to learn as many bits of information as possible about each tag's identity with the final goal of distinguishing among passing tags. The amount of information that the adversary needs to successfully launch an attack depends on properties of the system and environment. The attack becomes harder if the system has more tags and also if more of these appear in the limited environment that the attacker probes. Our attacker model is different from previous models in that we consider the case in which the attacker sees only a subset of all tags in the system and tries to distinguish among those. The probability an attack will be successful increases with the amount of information that each tag leaks, and with the number of tags that are likely to stay together as a group. Our model does not make assumptions about how the attacker learns information about the tags other than that the attacker can extract all the key material from a number of captured tags. We focus on information leaked from the protocol layer; information leaked through side channels may further increase the risk of privacy compromise.

Our main contributions are an improved metric for information leakage that allows us to combine different information sources and that better follows the proposed attacker model (Section 3), an analysis of the tree-based protocol based on this metric (Section 4), and an analysis of the relevance of our results o realistic RFID systems 5. We conclude that the privacy risks associated with the tree-based hash protocol are more severe than previously thought.

2 Private Authentication Protocols

Several protocols have been proposed through which a tag can identify itself to a legitimate reader while preserving the customer's privacy against rogue readers.

Public-key cryptography would provide a clear solution to the privacy problem, but is usually too expensive to implement on RFID tags. All the protocols we consider employ symmetric cryptographic hash functions in which keys are shared between the tag and legitimate readers.

Weis et al. proposed a privacy-preserving RFID protocol in which the tag hashes a random value (nonce) with a secret key that is only known to the tag itself and all legitimate readers [13]. This linear hash protocol provides strong privacy (as defined in Section 3) but fails to provide the needed scalability for large RFID systems. The reader stores one key per tag and has to try all possible keys in the database. Every tag authentication requires $O(N)$ hashing operations where N is the number of tags in the system. Since RFID systems must scale to millions of tags, this cost becomes excessive.

To achieve scalability, Molnar and Wagner [5] proposed a protocol that achieves sub-linear workload in the backend system[1]. The main drawback is that secrets are shared among several tags. Hence, an attacker who can extract secrets from a given

---

[1] Other protocols have been devised that sacrifice reliability for better scalability [8][12]. Since we believe that most RFID applications require high availability, we do not consider these protocols viable solutions.

tag also learns some of the secrets stored on other tags. The tags are structured in a tree where each tree leaf is a tag. Secrets are assigned to each tree branch and every leaf stores all secrets on the path from the root to itself. The tree has a depth d. Each node in the tree (except for the leaves) has k children. Each tag holds d secrets, one for each level of the tree. Using the notation from Avoine et al. [1] we denote the ith secret on the j level of the tree as $r_{j,i}$. The secrets on each tag correspond to a unique path through the tree; hence, every tag has at least one secret that is not shared with any other tag.

To authenticate a tag in the tree, the reader initiates the protocol by sending a nonce, N_R. The tag responds with a second nonce, N_T, and one hash for each level of the tree. The tag response is: $N_T, H\left(r_{1,i}||N_T||N_R\right), \cdots, H\left(r_{d,i}||N_T||N_R\right)$, where H is a cryptographic hash function (our analysis assumes the attack cannot compromise H). The nonce provided by the tag provides privacy by making consecutive responses from the same tag unlinkable. The reader-supplied nonce prevents replay attacks. On reception, the backend system generates hashes for all possible secrets corresponding to the first-level branches with the two session-specific nonces. The one hash that matches the transmitted hash on this level points to a node on the next level. This step is repeated until a leaf is reached.

If the tree is balanced, it holds $N = k^d$ tags. On each of the d levels, up to k hashing operations are needed to find the responding secret. Hence, the database performs up to $dk = d\sqrt[d]{N}$ hashing operations. The tag performs d times the number of hash operations than were required with the linear hash protocol, and the transmitted response is approximately d times larger (ignoring the framing and protocol overhead that does not grow with d). The memory needed to store and process the hashes grows with d. Therefore, it is necessary to keep d small to minimize the tag processing and memory requirements. The parameter k does not affect the tag, but determines the computational cost in the backend database. When designing a tree it can be chosen more freely than d. It can also be dynamically adapted to a changing system size.

Different tags can have different probabilities of being broken. Tags that are more likely to be broken should have fewer secrets (i.e., be placed higher in the tree) than tags that are know to be hard to break. The question of the optimal number of secrets was answered by Poovendran and Baras [9] in the context of multicast keys. If tag i has a probability of being broken of p_i then the optimal number of secrets for this tag is $d_i = -log_k(p_i)$. Note that for the special case in which all tags have the same probability of being broken ($\forall i : p_i = \frac{1}{N}$), this resolves to a balanced tree as introduced earlier $d = -log_k(\frac{1}{N}) = log_k(N)$. The rest of this paper assumes equal probabilities of being captured for all tags and a balanced tree.

3   Privacy Definition

Several different notions of RFID privacy have been developed. The first papers that targeted RFID privacy [13][8] focused on the requirement that tags should protect product information from being disclosed. This is a weak notion because it leaves tags traceable. A stronger property, *unlinkability*, means that an adversary should not be able to differentiate between readings that originated from the same tag and readings that originated from different tags.

A system achieves *strong privacy* when an adversary cannot distinguish between two tags with a probability better than random guessing [4]. Since scalable protocols have to sacrifice strong privacy, we need a more flexible measure of privacy. Our notion captures shades of privacy where a tag can be distinguishable from some tags but not from others.

Our notion of privacy is closely related to anonymity, which has been studied in the context of mix-nets [10][3]. Mix-nets try to make sender and recipient of a message anonymous. The anonymity set is defined as the set of all potential senders of a given message. The degree to which anonymity is achieved depends on the size of the anonymity set. Perfect anonymity is achieved if the set includes all members capable of sending messages in the system. The metric used by Serjantov and Danezis is similar to the metric we propose in this paper. Both are based on Shannon's information theory [11]. They use entropy to describe the number of possible elements in a group (in our case, the set of RFID tags in the system). Nohara et al. were the first to use entropy in the analysis of the tree-based RFID protocols [6][2]. They only considered the case of a single compromised tag and concluded that almost no information is leaked if the number of tags in the system is large enough. Our results are consistent with this, but extend to the more likely scenario where multiple tags are compromised.

Buttyán, Holczer and Vajda recently published an analysis of the privacy of tree-based hash protocols also employing an information-theoretic metric similar to ours [2]. Their notion of privacy is different from ours in that they employ the average anonymity set size as their metric. In this metric the impact of decreasing the anonymity set size is independent of the initial set size. We believe that the attacker's actual incentive is better modeled by a logarithmic measure. Decreasing the size from 100 to 50 should have the same impact as from 2 to 1 since both advances help to distinguish tags twice as well.

Measuring Privacy. We define privacy as the degree to which two authentication sessions of the same tag are not linkable. An authentication session is the interaction between a reader (legitimate or rogue) and a tag at the protocol level. Sessions are unlinkable if an attacker cannot discover whether two responses originated from the same tag with a probability better than random guessing. The highest degree of unlinkability exits if any pair of tags is indistinguishable. The metric that we derive in this paper measures the unlinkability as a value between zero (unlinkable) and $log_2(N)$ (all tags linkable). Our metric closely follows our attacker model as described in Section 1.

We measure privacy as the degree to which a member of the group is indistinguishable from other elements of the group. The degree to which elements in the group are distinguishable can be measured in bits. If we have a group of size N and the adversary can, with absolute certainty, divide our group into two

---

[2] Poovendran and Baras use entropy to analyze multicast keys [9].

disjoint subgroups of size $\frac{N}{2}$ each then we have disclosed 1 bit of information. We can extend this to two arbitrarily sized subgroups, S_1 and S_2, where $\frac{N}{s}$ tags are placed into group S_1 and the remaining $\left(1 - \frac{1}{s}\right) N$ tags are placed into S_2. The adversary can place every tag in either S_1 or S_2. We use I to denote average amount of information disclosed (that is, the amount of information that can be learned about all tags divided by the number of tags). The information disclosed is: $I = \frac{1}{s} \cdot log_2\left(s\right) + \frac{s-1}{s} \cdot log_2\left(\frac{s}{s-1}\right)$.

In general, an attacker will be able to split the group of all tags, G, into k disjoint groups, S_i, of arbitrary size. Then, the information disclosed is:

$$I = \sum_{i=1}^{k}\left(\frac{|S_i|}{|G|} \cdot log_2\left(\frac{|G|}{|S_i|}\right)\right). \tag{1}$$

The amount of disclosed information increases when there are more groups and is maximized when the groups are equal in size (This is consistent with Shannon's information theory that states that the entropy of a source grows as the probabilities of possible symbols become more similar [11]). Information theory also gives us that a $log_2(N)$-bit identifier uniquely identifies elements in a group of size N. The values of I range from $I = 0$ (strong privacy) to $I = log_2(N)$ (no privacy). In the latter case we can identify each tag uniquely, which means that we have N groups of size 1.

4   Information Leakage

The tree-based protocol shares secrets among tags, so extracting the secrets from one tag compromises the privacy of other tags. This section analyzes the amount of information that can be gathered by an adversary. The amount of information depends on the tree-structure and the tree positions of broken tags. We first look at the worst case in which the adversary can select the tags to compromise based on their tree position in Section 4.1 and then at the random case in Section 4.2.

4.1   Selected Tags Scenario

In the selected tag scenario, the attacker can select which tags to compromise. This enables the attacker to select tags such that the number of redundant secrets is minimized, thereby maximizing the information leakage. We consider the information leaked when an attacker breaks b tags, and denote the broken tags as $t_1, t_2, \cdots, t_b$. The first broken tag, t_1, always reveals d new secrets to the adversary. The second through k^{th} broken tags (recall that k is the number of children of a node), can each reveal between 1 and d new secrets. The number of new secrets depends on how many branches are shared between the broken tag and previously broken tags. This can be as few as one new secret if the tags are siblings in the tree. Assuming the worst case the tags $t_{(k^i+1)} \cdots t_{k^{i+1}}$ reveal $d - i$ new secrets each — that is, all secrets at level i are known to the attacker and each newly broken tag adds one secret to each level below i.

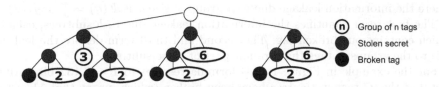

Fig. 1. Distinguishable groups of tags after 4 tags have been broken

For the purpose of our analysis we assume a completely filled k-ary tree with depth d, containing $N = k^d$ tags. The secrets have been extracted from b tags. The adversary always selects tags to break that maximize the number of secrets learned. We define level j of the tree as the deepest level on which all secrets are known: $j = \lfloor log_k(b) \rfloor$ On the next level of the tree, level $j+1$, the adversary knows b secrets. Recall, that we are considering the worst case first in which there exists as little redundancy among the secrets as possible. Each of these secrets is the root to a subtree with height $d - j$ with one known path from the root to one of the leaves. Each of these subtrees split the leaves of the tree into subgroups of size $\frac{N \cdot (k-1)}{k^{j+2}}, \frac{N \cdot (k-1)}{k^{j+3}}, \cdots, \frac{N \cdot (k-1)}{k^d}, \frac{N}{k^d}$. Maximum information is disclosed if the groups of tags are of similar size. Therefore, the remaining tags cluster in groups of only two sizes. These sizes are the ones closest to the average size.

Figure 1 shows an example of the maximal information leakage in a 3-ary tree, in which 4 tags have been broken. For the subgroups in which one of the leaves has been broken, the final level is either the broken tag, or one of two unbroken tags. The remaining unbroken keys at level 2 correspond to tag groups of size 3 and 6. The next broken tag should be selected from one of the groups of size 6.

The unbroken level j keys correspond to tag groups of two sizes, c_1 and c_2, where r_1 and r_2 are the numbers of times these groups appear. The overall number of groups add up to the number of keys at level j $(r_1 + r_2 = k^j)$, because each node on level j has exactly one group (potentially with size 0) below it. Thus, $r_1 = b \bmod k^j$ and $r_2 = k^j - r_1$.

The number of nodes on the next level, k^{j+1}, is equal to the number of groups times their sizes plus the number of broken tags:

$$k^{j+1} = c_1 \cdot r_1 + c_2 \cdot r_2 + b$$

$$c_2 = c_1 + 1 \text{ and } c_1 = \frac{k^{j+1} - b - r_2}{r_1 + r_2}$$

For the example in Figure 1, we get one group of size 3 $(j = 1; r_1 = 1; c_1 = 1 = \frac{3}{k^j})$, two groups of size 6 $(r_2 = 2; c_2 = 2 = \frac{6}{k^j})$; in addition, there are 4 groups of size 2, and 4 groups of size 1 at level $j + 1$.

Using equation 1 we can compute the worst case average information leakage as

$$I(k, d, b) = b \cdot \left(\sum_{i=j+2}^{d} \left(\Psi\left(\frac{k-1}{k^i}\right) \right) + \Psi\left(\frac{1}{k^d}\right) \right) + r_1 \cdot \Psi\left(\frac{c_1}{k^{j+1}}\right) + r_2 \cdot \Psi\left(\frac{c_2}{k^{j+1}}\right)$$

where the information leakage due to a group of size σ is $\Psi(\sigma) = \frac{1}{\sigma} \cdot log_2(\sigma)$.

The first term quantifies the information leakage due to b subtrees, each of which contains one broken tag. The second and third term denote the leakage due to the groups of tags that are not part of these subtrees.

For the example in Figure 1, this formula resolves to $I = 3.132$ bits. After just 4 of the 27 tags in the tree have been broken (which means that 11 of the 39 secrets have been revealed), a significant portion of the maximally achievable information $(= log_2(27)$, approximately 4.75, bits) is disclosed.

The information leakage for a few example cases is shown in Figure 2(a). The figure shows the amount of information leakage over the number of broken tags for several different system sizes. An attacker who compromises 20 tags in a system with 100,000 tags obtains 2.9 bits of information when a tree with depth 3 is used and 4.3 bits when a tree of depth 5 is used. These values are small enough to only allow tracking of individuals in very limited environments.

The worst case scenario will only occur if the attacker can select tags that maximize the number of different secrets compromised. This is entirely possible if the attacker has access to many tags. The attacker could probe every tag for secrets on the tag that match those that were already extracted from other tags, thus identifying a tag to break that has a high number of unknown secrets.

4.2 Random Tags Scenario

The attacker in this scenario breaks tags that are chosen at random. The information disclosure of this scenario cannot be easily captured in a closed-form equation. We choose to simulate this case instead.

We simulated the random case for systems with system sizes in between $N = 10^3$ and $N = 10^7$, and a tree depth $d = 5$, and number of broken tags up to $b = 100$. The results are shown in Figure 2(b). The difference between this simulated random case leakage and the selected tag leakage (Figure 2(a)) is at most 34% (for $N = 10^7$ and $b = 25$) and typically less than 10%. The average difference

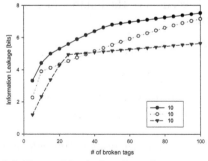

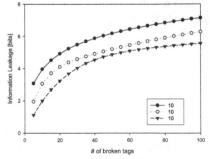

(a) Tree with $d=5$, selected tags scenario

(b) Tree with $d=5$, random tags scenario

Fig. 2. Information leakage in the tree-based hash-protocol

over all simulated cases is 9%. Simulations of trees with different heights lead to similar results [7].

The information leakage in the random tags scenario is always upper-bounded by the selected tags scenario. Our results suggest that the closed-form solution for the selected tags scenario is tight enough, typically within a ten percent, for cases where attackers have no control over which tags they break. Since a smart attacker with access to many tags could obtain nearly the worst case information leakage, the derived closed-form solution can be used to analyze the information leakage in the tree-based protocol in nearly all scenarios.

5 Relevance

An attacker can only track people whose tags can be distinguished from all other people's tags. This definition is different from Avoine et al.'s [1]. They considered an attack to be successful if an attacker can distinguish between two tags. In our model an attacker needs to be able to distinguish a tag from all other tags for a tracking attack to be successful which we believe better captures a realistic attacker. In this section, we estimate the likelihood of a successful attack for different key parameters.

Our threat model and the described tracking attack are not limited to information disclosed at the protocol layer. The most notable additional source of information is the physical layer of a tag. Different tags have different physical characteristics[3].

Few bits of information are encoded in the number of tags that an individual carries. Additional information could be encoded in the timestamp of readings (e.g. if the same tag was always read at around the same time of the day).

Our analysis in limited to the information leaked on the protocol layer. Privacy on this layer can be seen as a required but not sufficient property of RFID privacy.

For simplicity of the analysis we assume that the tags are partitioned into $g = \lfloor 2^I \rfloor$ groups of equal size where I is the amount of information leakage. A second parameter of our attack, η, is the number of tags in the focus of the attacker (e.g. all the tags that have entered the subway system at a given day). Note that this number is typically much smaller than the total number of tags in the system. A tag can be uniquely identified if it is the only tag in one of the g groups. First we look at the case where every individual carries exactly one tag and then we consider the case in which multiple tags stay together as a group.

5.1 Tracking Single Tags

The probability that at least one tag can be uniquely identified (that is, this tag can be distinguished from all other tags) is

---

[3] Based on radio characteristics, several additional bits of information may be extracted from the tag. Our experiment and preliminary results are reported in an extended version of this paper [7].

$$P_1(g, \eta) = \left(\frac{g-1}{g}\right)^{\eta-1}.$$

The probability that at least j tags of the η tags can be identified is

$$P(g, \eta, j) = \prod_{i=1}^{j} \left(\frac{g-i}{g-i+1}\right)^{\eta-i}.$$

Given a system with 100,000 tags of which 20 have been broken, and a tree with depth 5, we get 20 groups ($g = 20$). The probability that in small group of tags ($\eta = 10$), half of the tags can be uniquely identified is 14%. As the number of tags grows, this probability becomes smaller.

5.2   Tracking Collections of Tags

For many RFID applications, it is common for each individual to carry several tags. Even if a given RFID application gives individuals only a single tag, other tags they carry for different RFID applications are equally helpful to the attacker in distinguishing the individual. We assume that these collections comprise randomly selected tags. The number of ways in which l tags can fall into the g groups is given by $\binom{g}{l}$. When combined with the earlier result, the probability that in a group of η individuals who each carry l tags, at least j can be uniquely identified is

$$P(g, \eta, l, j) = \prod_{i=1}^{j} \left(\frac{\binom{g}{l} - i}{\binom{g}{l} - i + 1}\right)^{\eta-i}.$$

Looking at the example from the last section with $N = 10^5$, $d = 5$, $\eta = 10$ but now assuming two tags per individual ($l = 2$), the attacker can uniquely identify 5 individuals ($j = 5$) with a probability of 83%. If each individual carries 5 tags ($l = 5$), this probability exceeds 99%. Looking at an example of larger attack, we assume 50 compromised tags ($b = 50$ and $l = 5$); the probability of identifying half of 1,000 individuals ($\eta = 1000$, $l = 500$) is 88%.

These results illustrate that tracking attacks on large groups of individuals are practical under the assumption that each individual carries a fixed collection of tags.

6   Conclusion

The resource constraints of RFID tags, combined with the strict requirements for large-scale scalability and high availability, mean that strong privacy is not possible. All proposed protocols that provide strong privacy fail to scale to large systems or suffer from a degraded availability. The tree-based protocol provides a trade-off between privacy and scalability, but raises the need to better quantify the amount of privacy compromised.

Privacy must be measured in a way that accounts for a realistic attacker's ability to combine partial information to compromise individuals' privacy without necessarily being able to uniquely distinguish tags. Our proposed metric for information leakage provides useful guidance for estimating the privacy a system provides. An attacker is not likely to distinguish between individuals that each carry only a single tag, but is very likely to be successful in distinguishing individuals that carry several tags. If additional information sources are factored into the attack tracking of very large tag populations becomes entirely possible. Our results indicate that protocol designs previously considered to provide adequate privacy, may in fact be insufficient against more realistic threat models. Designers of RFID applications must be careful to balance the needs for scalability with realistic assessments of the threats of privacy compromise.

References

1. Gildas Avoine, Etienne Dysli, and Philippe Oechslin. Reducing time complexity in RFID systems. In *Selected Areas in Cryptography – SAC*, 2005.
2. Levente Buttyán, Tamás Holczer, and István Vajda. Optimal key-trees for tree-based private authentication. In *Privacy Enhancing Technologies Workshop – PET*, 2006.
3. Claudia Díaz, Stefaan Seys, Joris Claessens, and Bart Preneel. Towards measuring anonymity. In *Privacy Enhancing Technologies Workshop – PET*, 2002.
4. Ari Juels and Stephen Weis. Defining strong privacy for RFID, 2006.
5. David Molnar and David Wagner. Privacy and security in library RFID: Issues, practices, and architectures. In *Conference on Computer and Communications Security – ACM CCS*, 2004.
6. Yasunobu Nohara, Sozo Inoue, Kensuke Baba, and Hiroto Yasuura. Quantitative evaluation of unlinkable id matching schemes. In *Workshop on Privacy in the Electronic Society – WPES*, 2006.
7. Karsten Nohl and David Evans. Quantifying information leakage in tree-based hash protocols. Technical Report CS-2006-20, University of Virginia, Computer Science Department, October 2006.
8. Miyako Ohkubo, Koutarou Suzuki, and Shingo Kinoshita. Cryptographic approach to "privacy-friendly" tags. In *RFID Privacy Workshop*, 2003.
9. Radha Poovendran and John S. Baras. An information-theoretic approach for design and analysis of rooted-tree-based multicast key management schemes. *IEEE Transactions on Information Theory*, 2001.
10. Andrei Serjantov and George Danezis. Towards an information theoretic metric for anonymity. In *Privacy Enhancing Technologies Workshop – PET*, 2002.
11. C. E. Shannon. A mathematical theory of communication. 1948.
12. Gene Tsudik. YA-TRAP: Yet another trivial RFID authentication protocol. In *PerCom*, 2006.
13. Stephen Weis, Sanjay Sarma, Ronald Rivest, and Daniel Engels. Security and privacy aspects of low-cost radio frequency identification systems. In *International Conference on Security in Pervasive Computing – SPC*, 2003.

An Anonymous Authentication Scheme for Identification Card

He Ge

Microsoft Corporation
One Microsoft Way, Redmond, WA 98052
hege@microsoft.com

Abstract. This paper presents the concept of anonymous identification card, a technique enabling a card holder to demonstrates his/her authenticity without disclosing real identity. Anonymous identification card can be used in settings in which people need to demonstrate their eligibility to do certain things, meanwhile they are sensitive to their privacy, not hoping to disclose their identity information to a verifier. We proposed an efficient anonymous authentication scheme for this anonymous identification card, with the support of rogue card revocation. The most advantage of our scheme is its simplicity and efficiency such that all computation can be carried out by a resource-limited identification card. We proved our scheme is secure under the strong RSA assumption and the decisional Diffie-Hellman assumption.

Keywords: Privacy, Anonymous Identification, Identity Management, Group Signature, Cryptographic Protocol.

1 Introduction

Consider the following scenarios: people carry identification cards to prove their authenticity when accessing restricted buildings, using pay parking lots, or driving through tollgates. This identification card is embedded with a cryptographic chip that can carry out computation for authentication. If authentication is associated with a unique identifier (e.g., person's name), transactions by the same user at different places can be tracked and analyzed. To protect a user's privacy, it is desirable to deploy anonymous authentication scheme in such scenarios. That is, a system can verify a user holding a valid card without being able to obtain this person's identity information. A similar scenario happens in Trusted Computing Platforms [18], in which a computer can attest that it holds an original cryptographic chip, Trusted Computing Module (TPM), to a remote server without revealing information for this special chip.

The underlying mechanisms of these applications are cryptographic protocols related to so-called group signature schemes. A group signature is a privacy-preserving signature scheme introduced by Chaum and Heyst [12]. In such a scheme, there are two basic entities: the group manager and certain number of group members. The group manager issues group membership certificate/credential for each group member. Later, based on its own group membership

P. Ning, S. Qing, and N. Li (Eds.): ICICS 2006, LNCS 4307, pp. 238–248, 2006.

certificate, a group member can sign a message on behalf of the group without revealing its identity. That is, a third party can only identify the signature is produced by one group member without being able to find which particular one. Only the group manager can open a signature and reveal its originator. Besides, signatures signed by the same group member cannot be identified as from the same source, i.e, "linked". Recently, the study of group signature schemes has attracted considerable attention, and many solutions have been proposed in the literature (e.g., [10,9,1,7,4,5]).

In our target application, an identification card has extremely limited resource, either computing capability, or memory space. It is desirable that a cryptographic protocol should be lightweight. Trusted Computing Platforms deploy an anonymous authentication technique called "Direct Anonymous Attestation" (DAA), which has been introduced in [6]. The current solution for DAA is a computing intensive construction. To complete all cryptographic calculations in real time, the computation has to be distributed among the TPM and the its host, typically a personal computer. DAA works fine for powerful computing devices, however, it is a too expensive construction for an identification card.

The contribution of this paper includes two parts: (1) we propose a statistical zero-knowledge proof of knowledge protocol, through which a prover can convince a verifier that he knows two integers that are relatively prime without revealing any knowledge for these two integers; (2) based on the result in (1), we devised a lightweight anonymous authentication scheme for anonymous identification card. The new scheme is simple and efficient. As a result, all cryptographic computation can be completed by the card alone. Therefore, the new scheme is more suitable for our target scenarios, i.e., identification card.

The rest of this paper is organized as follows. The next section introduces a security model for our application. Section 3 reviews some definitions, cryptographic assumptions, and building blocks of our proposed scheme. Section 4 presents proposed scheme. Security properties are considered in Section 5. Finally, we summarize and give conclusions in section 6.

2   The Model

In this section, we define a model which captures security requirements for our target application.

Definition 1 (The Model). *A trusted card issuer takes responsibility for issuing anonymous identification card (AID). The issuer and AIDs form a group in which the issuer holds a group master key, while AIDs hold group member keypairs. The system should satisfy the following security requirements.*

1. *(Forgery-resistance) The keypair in the AID can only be produced using the issuer's master key.*
2. *(Anonymous Authentication) The AID can anonymously attest its authenticity to a verifier. It is infeasible to extract AID's identity information, or link transactions by the same AID.*

3. *(Rogue AID Revocation)* *Under certain security policy, the issuer can recover*
   an AID's identity and reveal all malicious behaviors associated with this AID.
   The revoked keypairs should be published on the revocation list to exclude
   rogue AIDs by all verifiers.

Our model could be seen as a simplified group signature model (e.g. [1]). However, we adjust the revocation mechanism in the original model to satisfy our
security requirement. In the classical group signature model, the revocation is
implemented by opening all anonymous signatures in the pool by the group
manager. Just as pointed out by Kiayias *et al.* in [16], this mechanism is either
inefficient (centralized operation by the group manager), or unfair (unnecessarily identifying all innocent group member's signatures). To overcome this short-
coming, they introduced a variant scheme of group signature called traceable
signature, which we refer to as the KTY scheme. However, the new revocation
mechanism in the KTY scheme violates a security requirement called "backward unlinkability" in group signature: disclosing the secret of a group member
should not reveal all this group member's previous behaviors. This conflicting
issue shows in anonymous authentication, suitability of certain feature is more
application oriented, and no sole definition could accommodate all conditions.
In this paper we adopt the revocation mechanism in the KTY scheme since it is
more appropriate for our target application.

3   Definitions and Preliminaries

This section reviews some definitions, widely accepted complexity assumptions,
and building blocks that we will use in this paper.

3.1   Number-Theoretic Assumption

Definition 2 (Special RSA Modulus [8]). *An RSA modulus $n = pq$ is called*
special if $p = 2p' + 1$ and $q = 2q' + 1$ where p' and q' also are prime numbers.
Special RSA modulus is also called safe RSA modulus in some literature [1].

Definition 3 (Quadratic Residue Group QR_n). *Let Z_n^* be the multiplicative*
group modulo n, which contains all positive integers less than n and relatively
prime to n. An element $x \in Z_n^*$ is called a quadratic residue *if there exists an*
$a \in Z_n^*$ such that $a^2 \equiv x \,(\mathrm{mod}\ n)$. The set of all quadratic residues of Z_n^* forms
a cyclic subgroup of Z_n^*, which we denote by QR_n. If n is the product of two
distinct primes, then $|QR_n| = \frac{1}{4}|Z_n^*|$.

We list two properties about QR_n which will be be used in section 5 for the
security proof.

Property 1. *If n is a special RSA modulus, with p, q, p', and q' as in Def-*
inition 2 above, then $|QR_n| = p'q'$ and $(p' - 1)(q' - 1)$ elements of QR_n are
generators of QR_n .

Property 2. *If g is a generator of QR_n, then g^a mod n is a generator of QR_n if and only if $GCD(a, |QR_n|) = 1$.*

The security of our techniques relies on the following security assumptions which are widely accepted in the cryptography literature. (for example, [2,14,9,1]).

Assumption 1 (Strong RSA Assumption). *Let n be an RSA modulus. The Flexible RSA Problem is the problem of taking a random element $u \in Z_n^*$ and finding a pair (v, e) such that $e > 1$ and $v^e \equiv u \pmod{n}$. The Strong RSA Assumption says that no probabilistic polynomial time algorithm can solve the flexible RSA problem with non-negligible probability.*

Assumption 2 (Decisional Diffie-Hellman Assumption over QR_n). *Let n be a special RSA modulus, and let g be a generator of QR_n. For two distributions (g, g^x, g^y, g^{xy}), (g, g^x, g^y, g^z), $x, y, z \in_R Z_n$, there is no probabilistic polynomial-time algorithm that distinguishes them with non-negligible probability.*

3.2   Building Blocks

Our main building blocks are *statistical honest-verifier zero knowledge proofs of knowledge* related to discrete logarithms over QR_n [11,15,9]. They include protocols for things such as knowledge of a discrete logarithm, knowledge of equality of two discrete logarithms, knowledge of a discrete logarithm that lies in an interval, etc. We introduce one of them here. Readers may refer to the original papers for more details.

Protocol 1. *Let n be a special RSA modulus, QR_n be the quadratic residue group modulo n, and g be a generator of QR_n. α, l, l_c are security parameters that are all greater than 1. X is a constant number. A prover Alice knows x, the discrete logarithm of T_1, and $x \in [X - 2^l, X + 2^l]$. Alice demonstrates her knowledge of $x \in [X - 2^{\alpha(l+l_c)}, X + 2^{\alpha(l+l_c)}]$ as follows.*

1. *Alice picks a random $t \in \pm\{0,1\}^{\alpha(l+l_c)}$ and computes $T_2 = g^t \pmod{n}$. Alice sends (T_1, T_2) to a verifier Bob.*
2. *Bob picks a random $c \in \{0,1\}^{l_c}$ and sends it to Alice.*
3. *Alice computes $w = t - c(x - X)$, and $w \in \pm\{0,1\}^{\alpha(l+l_c)+1}$. Alice sends w to Bob.*
4. *Bob checks $w \in \pm\{0,1\}^{\alpha(l+l_c)+1}$ and*

$$g^{w-cX}T_1^c =? \; T_2 \pmod{n}.$$

If the equation holds, Alice proves knowledge of the discrete logarithm of T_1 lies in the range $[X - 2^{\alpha(l+l_c)+1}, X + 2^{\alpha(l+l_c)+1}]$.

Remark 1. It should be emphasized that while Alice knows a secret x in $[X - 2^l, X + 2^l]$, the protocol only guarantees that x lies in the extended range $[X - 2^{\alpha(l+l_c)+1}, X + 2^{\alpha(l+l_c)+1}]$.

Next, we propose a zero-knowledge protocol to show co-primality of two discrete logarithms. That is, a prover demonstrates its knowledge of discrete logarithms of two elements T_1, T_2 in QR_n being relatively prime. The method is based on the following theorem.

Theorem 1. *Let n be an RSA modulus. For a random element $u \in Z_n^*$, if one can find a tuple (T_1, T_2, x, y) such that $T_1^x T_2^y \equiv u \pmod{n}$, then x, y must be relatively prime.*

Proof. By contradiction. If x, y are not co-prime, we assume $GCD(x, y) = e$, $x = k_1 e$, $y = k_2 e$. Then we have $T_1^x T_2^y \equiv (T_1^{k_1} T_2^{k_2})^e \equiv u \pmod{n}$. Thus, we find a pair (v, e) such that $v^e \equiv u \pmod{n}$, where $v \equiv T_1^{k_1} T_2^{k_2} \pmod{n}$, to solve a flexible RSA problem. This contradicts the strong RSA assumption. Therefore x, y must be relatively prime.   □

Protocol 2. (Knowledge of Co-Primality of Two Discrete Logarithms)
(Sketch) Suppose Alice knows a, c are relatively prime. She first uses GCD algorithm to compute b, d, such that $ab + cd = 1$. Then Alice computes

$$T_1 = g^b \pmod{n}, \ T_2 = T_1^a \pmod{n},$$

$$T_3 = g^d \pmod{n}, \ T_4 = T_3^c \pmod{n}.$$

Alice sends (T_1, T_2, T_3, T_4) to Bob, and proves she knows discrete logarithms of T_2, T_4 with base T_1, T_3 respectively. Finally, $T_2 T_4 = g \pmod{n}$, this shows that discrete logarithms of T_2, T_4 are relatively prime.

4   The Authentication Protocol for Anonymous Identification Card

The card issuer, the producer of AIDs, sets various parameters, the lengths of which depend on a *security parameter*, which we denote by σ.

4.1   System Parameter Setting

The system parameters are set by the issuer, these values are:

- n, g, h: n is a special RSA modulus such that $n = pq$, $p = 2p' + 1$, and $q = 2q' + 1$, where p and q are each at least σ bits long (so $p, q > 2^\sigma$), and p' and q' are prime. $g, h \in_R QR_n$ are random generators of the cyclic group QR_n. n, g, h are public values while p, q are kept secret by the issuer.
- α, l_c, l_s: security parameters that are greater than 1.
- X: a constant value. $X > 2^{\alpha(l_c + l_s) + 2}$.

4.2   Key Generation for the AID

The key generation method is straightforward. The card issuer picks a random prime number $s \in_R [X - 2^{l_s}, X + 2^{l_s}]$ and computes

$$E = g^{s^{-1}} \pmod{n},$$

where s^{-1} is the inverse of s modulo $|QR_n| = p'q'$. (E, s) is the keypair of the AID. The issuer feeds (E, s) into the AID, and records (E, s) in its database.

4.3   Anonymous Authentication

The idea of our method to implement anonymous authentication is: the AID generates a random blinding integer b, computes $T_1 = E^b \pmod{n}$, $T_2 = g^b \pmod{n}$. Then the AID sends (T_1, T_2) to a verifier. The AID proves that $T_1^s \equiv T_2 \pmod{n}$ and s lies in the correct interval; $T_2 \equiv g^b \pmod{n}$, and s, b are co-prime.

Protocol 3. (Anonymous Authentication)

1. *The AID picks random* $b \in_R [X - 2^{l_s}, X + 2^{l_s}]$, $t_1, t_2 \in_R \pm\{0,1\}^{\alpha(l_s + l_c)}$. *It uses GCD algorithm to solve* $sa + bd = 1$. *The AID computes (all computations done modulo* n*):*

$$T_1 = E^b, \; T_2 = g^b, \; T_3 = T_1^{t_1},$$
$$T_4 = h^a, \; T_5 = T_4^s, \; T_6 = T_4^{t_1},$$
$$T_7 = h^d, \; T_8 = T_7^b, \; T_9 = T_7^{t_2}, \; T_{10} = g^{t_2}.$$

   $(T_1, T_2, T_3; T_4, T_5, T_6)$ *are used to prove equality of discrete logarithms of* T_2, T_5 *with base* T_1, T_4 *respectively. Also, they are served to prove* s *lies in the correct range.* $(g, T_2, T_{10}; T_7, T_8, T_9)$ *are used to prove equality of discrete logarithms of* T_2, T_8 *with the base* g, T_7, *respectively. The AID sends* $(T_1, T_2, T_3, T_4, T_5, T_6, T_7, T_8, T_9, T_{10})$ *to the verifier.*
2. *The verifier picks number* $c \in \{0,1\}^{l_c}$, *and sends it to the AID.*
3. *The AID computes*

$$w_1 = t_1 - c(s - X), \; w_2 = t_2 - c(b - X),$$

   and sends (w_1, w_2) *to the verifier.*
4. *The verifier checks* $w_1, w_2 \in \pm\{0,1\}^{\alpha(l_s + l_c)+1}$, *and checks (all computations done modulo* n*):*

$$T_1^{w_1 - cX} T_2^c =? \; T_3, \; T_4^{w_1 - cX} T_5^c =? \; T_6,$$

$$g^{w_2 - cX} T_2^c =? \; T_{10}, \; T_7^{w_2 - cX} T_8^c =? \; T_9, \; T_5 T_8 =? \; h.$$

If all these equations hold, this completes the AID's anonymous authentication.

Remark 2. Using the Fiat-Shamir heuristic[13], the authentication scheme can be turned into a non-interactive "signature of knowledge" scheme, which is secure in the random oracle model [3].

4.4   Rogue AID Revocation

If certain behaviors have been identified suspicious, the transaction transcripts should be submitted to the card issuer to reveal the identity. The issuer checks all s in its database

$$T_1^{s_i} =? T_2 \pmod{n}$$

to reveal this AID's identity. Then s_i is published on the revocation list for all the verifiers.

Later, a verifier can check

$$T_1^{s_i} =? T_2 \pmod{n}$$

for all s_i on the revocation list to identify a rouge AID.

4.5   Performance Analysis

Since the computation cost in the protocol is dominated by the modular squaring and multiplication, we can estimate computation cost by counting total modular squarings and multiplications. Let k_1 be the bit length of the binary representation of exponent, and k_2 be the number of 1's in the binary representation, the total computation cost can be treated as k_1 squarings and k_2 multiplications. For example, if $y = g^x \pmod{n}$, and $x \in_R \{0,1\}^{160}$. We assume half of 160 bits of s will be 1. Then the total computation includes 160 squarings and 80 expected multiplications.

In practice, we can choose $\sigma = 512$, then n is 1024 bits long. Suppose we let $\alpha = 9/8$, $l_c, l_s = 160$, and $X = 2^{367}$(46 bytes). Since $s, b \in [X - 2^{l_s}, X + 2^{l_s}]$. We should notice that the actual random part of s, b is the lower 160 bits, and the leading 268 bits are all $0's$ except the first bit. This would save lots of computation as well as memory space. Then computation related to exponents b, s are 368 squarings and 81 expected multiplications. We treat other exponents as 368-bit long. The AID needs at most 3680 (368×10) squarings and 1428 ($81 \times 4 + 184 \times 6$) multiplications. Therefore, total computation cost is 5108 modular multiplication, which can be completed by the AID alone according to the experiment result for the TPM in Trusted Computing Platform [6].

5   Security Properties

We prepare two lemmas that will be used shortly. The first lemma is due to Shamir [17].

Lemma 1. *Let n be an integer. For given values $u, v \in Z_n^*$ and $x, y \in Z_n$ such that $GCD(x, y) = 1$ and $v^x \equiv u^y \pmod{n}$, there is an efficient way to compute the value z such that $z^x \equiv u \pmod{n}$.*

Proof. Since $GCD(x, y) = 1$, we can use the Extended GCD algorithm to find a and b such that $ay + bx = 1$, and let $z = v^a u^b$. Thus

$$z^x \equiv v^{ax} u^{bx} \equiv u^{ay+bx} \equiv u \pmod{n}. \qquad \square$$

We introduce the second lemma for the security of the AID's keypair.

Lemma 2. *If* $X > 2^{\alpha(l_s+l_c)+2}$, $\alpha, l_s, l_c > 1$, *then* $(X - 2^{\alpha(l_s+l_c)+1})^2 > X + 2^{\alpha(l_s+l_c)+1}$.

Proof.

$$(X - 2^{\alpha(l_s+l_c)+1})^2 - (X + 2^{\alpha(l_s+l_c)+1})$$
$$= X^2 - X2^{\alpha(l_s+l_c)+2} + 2^{2\alpha(l_s+l_c)+2} - X - 2^{\alpha(l_s+l_c)+1}$$
$$= X(X - 2^{\alpha(l_s+l_c)+2} - 1) + 2^{2\alpha(l_s+l_c)+2} - 2^{\alpha(l_s+l_c)+1}$$

Since $\alpha, l_s, l_c > 1$, and $X > 2^{\alpha(l_s+l_c)+2}$, the equation is greater than 0.   □

Now, we discuss the security of our scheme. First, we address the issue of keypair forgery. We consider an attack model in which an attacker can obtain a set of legitimate keypairs. A successful attack is one in which a new keypair is generated that is valid and different from current keypairs. The following theorem shows that, assuming the strong RSA Assumption, it is intractable for an attacker to forge such a keypair.

Theorem 2 (Forgery-resistance). *If there exists a probabilistic polynomial time algorithm which takes a list of valid keypairs,* $(s_1, E_1), (s_2, E_2), \ldots, (s_k, E_k)$ *and with non-negligible probability produces a new keypair* (s, E) *such that* $s \in [X - 2^{\alpha(l_s+l_c)+1}, X + 2^{\alpha(l_s+l_c)+1}]$, $E^s = g \,(\mathrm{mod}\, n)$ *and* $s \neq s_i$ *for* $1 \leq i \leq k$, *then we can solve the flexible RSA problem with non-negligible probability.*

Proof. Suppose there exists a probabilistic polynomial-time algorithm $\mathcal{A}$ which computes a new legitimate keypair based on the available keypairs, and succeeds with some non-negligible probability. We can construct an algorithm for solving the flexible RSA problem, given a random input (u, n), as follows:

1. We pick random prime numbers $s_1, s_2, \ldots, s_k$ in the required range $[X - 2^{l_s}, X + 2^{l_s}]$, and compute

$$r = s_1 s_2 \ldots s_k,$$
$$g = u^r = u^{s_1 s_2 \cdots s_k} \,(\mathrm{mod}\, n).$$

   For a random input (u, n), the probability of $u \in QR_n$ is $\frac{1}{4}$. Due to Property 1, u will be a generator of QR_n with probability nearly $\frac{1}{4}$. Since the s_i values are primes strictly less than either p' or q', it must be the case that $GCD(r, |QR_n|) = 1$. Property 2 says that g is a generator of QR_n if and only if u is a generator of QR_n. Then g is a generator of QR_n with non-negligible probability.

2. Next, we create k group keypairs, using the s_i values and E_i values calculated as follows:

$$E_1 = u^{s_2 \cdots s_k} \,(\mathrm{mod}\, n)$$
$$E_2 = u^{s_1 s_3 \cdots s_k} \,(\mathrm{mod}\, n)$$
$$\vdots$$
$$E_k = u^{s_1 s_2 \cdots s_{k-1}} \,(\mathrm{mod}\, n)$$

Note that for all $i = 1, \ldots, k$, $E_i^{s_i} = u^{s_1 s_2 \cdots s_k} = u^r = g \,(\mathrm{mod}\, n)$.

3. We use the assumed forgery algorithm $\mathcal{A}$ for creating a new valid keypair (E, s), where $s \in [X - 2^{\alpha(l_s+l_c)+1}, X + 2^{\alpha(l_s+l_c)+1}]$, and $E^s = g = u^r$ (mod n).
4. If the forgery algorithm succeeds, then s will be different from all the s_i's. By Lemma 2, s cannot be the product of $s_i, s_j, 1 \le i, j \le k$. Therefore, either $\text{GCD}(s, s_1 s_2 \cdots s_k) = 1$, or $GCD(s, s_1 s_2 \cdots s_k) = s_i, 1 \le i \le k$. In the first case, due to Lemma 1, we can find a pair (y, s) such that

$$y^s = u \text{ (mod } n)$$

so the pair (y, s) is a solution to our flexible RSA problem instance. In the second case, assume $s = v \times s_i$, then $v < X - 2^{\alpha(l_s+l_c)+1}$, and $GCD(v, s_1 s_2 \cdots s_k) = 1$ (or $GCD(v, r) = 1$). We then have

$$E^s \equiv E^{vs_i} \equiv (E^{s_i})^v \equiv u^r \text{ (mod } n).$$

Again by Lemma 1, we can find a pair (y, v) such that

$$y^v = u \text{ (mod } n).$$

so the pair (y, v) is a solution to our flexible RSA problem instance.

Through the above steps, assuming the existence of algorithm $\mathcal{A}$, we have solved a random instance flexible RSA problem (u, n) with non-negligible probability. However, this is infeasible under the strong RSA assumption. Therefore, such algorithm $\mathcal{A}$ should not exist under the same assumption. □

Next, we address the security of anonymous authentication scheme which is described as the following theorem.

Theorem 3. *Under the strong RSA assumption, the anonymous authentication protocol is a statistical zero-knowledge honest-verifier proof of a keypair (E, s) such that $E^s \equiv g$ (mod n) and s lies in the correct interval.*

Proof (Sketch). Our protocol directly deploys the standard building blocks to accomplish anonymous authentication.

In the protocol, $(g, T_2, T_{10}; T_7, T_8, T_9)$ are used to prove equality of the discrete logarithms of T_2 with base g, and T_8 with base T_7. This is the statistical honest-verifier zero-knowledge protocol that its security has been proved in the literature under the strong RSA assumption.

$(T_1, T_2, T_3; T_4, T_5, T_6)$ are used to prove equality of discrete logarithms of T_2 with base T_1, and T_5 with base T_4. Also, they are served to prove this discrete logarithm $s \in [X - 2^{\alpha(l_s+l_c)+1}, X + 2^{\alpha(l_s+l_c)+1}]$. This is a generalized version of knowledge protocol of equality of discrete logarithms introduced in [16]. The protocol is also secure under the strong RSA assumption.

Since $T_5 T_8 \equiv h$ (mod n), by Theorem 1, discrete logarithms of T_5, T_8, s and b, respectively, are co-prime.

Putting the above together, the AID demonstrates that it knows s, b such that $T_1^s \equiv g^b$ (mod n), and s, b are relatively prime. Due to Lemma 1, the AID can solve this equation and obtain $E^s \equiv g$ (mod n), which is a valid keypair. □

Finally, we propose the theorem for anonymity property of the scheme. The problem of linking two tuples (T_1, T_2), (T_1', T_2') is equivalent to deciding equality of discrete logarithms of T_2, T_2' with bases T_1, T_1' respectively. This is infeasible under the decisional Diffie-Hellman assumption over QR_n. Therefore, we have the following result.

Theorem 4 (Anonymity). *Under the decisional Diffie-Hellman assumption, the protocol implements anonymous authentication such that it is infeasible link transactions by the same AID.*

6 Conclusion

In this paper, we have presented an efficient protocol to implement authentication for anonymous identification card (AID) with supporting rogue AID revocation. The proposed scheme is simple and efficient enough to be deployed in an identification card to protect user's privacy. The new scheme is proved to be secure under the strong RSA assumption and the decisional Diffie-Hellman assumption.

Theorem 1 is an interesting result in the paper, which is a corollary of the strong RSA assumption. Based on this result, we devised a knowledge proof of co-primality of discrete logarithms. This theorem might be used in other cryptographic construction.

References

1. G. Ateniese, J. Camenisch, M. Joye, and G. Tsudik. A practical and provably secure coalition-resistant group signature scheme. In *Advances in Cryptology — Crypto*, pages 255–270, 2000.
2. N. Baric and B. Pfitzmann. Collision-free accumulators and fail-stop signature schemes without trees. In *Advances in Cryptology — Eurocrypto*, pages 480–494, 1997.
3. M. Bellare and P. Rogaway. Random oracles are practical: A paradigm for designing efficient procotols. In *First ACM Conference On computer and Communication Security*, pages 62–73. ACM Press, 1993.
4. D. Boneh, X. Boyen, and H.Shacham. Short group signatures. In *Advances in Cryptology — Crypto'04, LNCS 3152*, pages 41–55, 2004.
5. D. Boneh and H. Shacham. Group signatures with verifier-local revocation. In *Proc. of the 11th ACM Conference on Computer and Communications Security (CCS 2004)*, pages 168–177, 2004.
6. E. Brickell, J. Camenisch, and L. Chen. Direct anonymous attestation. In *ACM Conference on Computer and Communications Security*, pages 132–145, 2004.
7. J. Camenisch and J. Groth. Group signatures: Better efficiency and new theoretical aspects. In *Security in Communication Networks (SCN 2004), LNCS 3352*, pages 120–133, 2005.
8. J. Camenisch and A. Lysyanskaya. A signature scheme with efficient protocols. In *SCN'02, LNCS 2576*, pages 268–289, 2002.

9. J. Camenisch and M. Michels. A group signature scheme based on an RSA-variants. Technical Report RS-98-27, BRICS, University of Aarhus, Nov. 1998.
10. J. Camenisch and M. Stadler. Efficient group signature schemems for large groups. In *Advances in Cryptology — Crypto'97, LNCS 1294*, pages 410–424, 1997.
11. A. Chan, Y. Frankel, and Y. Tsiounis. Easy come - easy go divisible cash. In *K. Yyberg, editor, Advances in Cryptology – Eurocrypt'98, LNCS 1403*, pages 561 – 574. Sringer-Verlag, 1998.
12. D. Chaum and E. van Heyst. Group signature. In *Advances in Cryptology — Eurocrypt*, pages 390–407, 1992.
13. A. Fiat and A. Shamir. How to prove yourself: practical solutions to identification and signature problems. In *Advances in Cryptology — CRYPTO'86, LNCS 263*, pages 186–194. Springer-Verlag, 1987.
14. E. Fujisaki and T. Okamoto. Statistical zero knowledge protocols to prove modular polynomial relations. In *Advances in Cryptology — Crypto*, pages 16–30, 1997.
15. E. Fujisaki and T. Okamoto. A practical and provably secure scheme for publicly verifable secret sharing and its applications. In *Advances in Cryptology – EUROCRYPTO'98*, pages 32–46, 1998.
16. A. Kiayias, Y. Tsiounis, and M. Yung. Traceable signatures. In *Advances in Cryptology—Eurocypt, LNCS 3027*, pages 571–589. Springer-Verlag, 2004.
17. A. Shamir. On the generation of cryptograpically strong psedorandom sequences. *ACM Transaction on computer systems*, 1, 1983.
18. TCG. http://www.trustedcomputinggroup.org.

A Wireless Covert Channel on Smart Cards
(Short Paper)

Geir Olav Dyrkolbotn and Einar Snekkenes

Norwegian Information Security Lab
Department of Computer Science and Media Technology
Gjovik University College
P.O. Box 191 2802 Gjovik, Norway
geirolav.dyrkolbotn@gmail.com, einar.snekkenes@hig.no

Abstract. Microprocessor devices, such as smart cards, are used more and more to store and protect secret information. This development has its advantages, but microprocessor devices are susceptible to various attacks. Much attention has been devoted to side-channel attacks, exploiting unintentional correlation between internal secret information, such as cryptographic keys, and the various side channels. We present a wireless covert channel attack (WCCA) that intentionally correlates secret information with the electromagnetic side channel. WCCA exploits subversive code hidden on all cards during manufacture, to launch an attack, without physical access, when infected cards are used. Experiments on modern smart cards confirm that an insider with the opportunity to hide subversive code can potentially broadcast the card's internal secrets to a nearby receiver. Security features against side-channel attacks will limit the range but not prevent the attack.

Keywords: Smart Cards, EM Side-Channel, Subversion, Wireless Covert Channel.

1 Introduction

Since the birth of modern side channel attack in the 90's there has been an explosion of proposed attacks exploiting side channels to reveal secret information within a smart card. Current research focuses on exploiting unintended correlations between secret information (cryptographic key) and the side channel, tailoring a specific implementation of a cryptographic algorithm. These attacks often require a "lost or stolen" card and experimental results are often obtained on simple cards of older technology, not on modern smart cards equipped with countermeasures.

By combining the efforts of different fields, electromagnetic side channel attacks , covert channels and subversion, we propose a new attack: wireless covert channel attack (WCCA). We believe that hiding subversive code on cards during manufacture can manipulate the energy leakage from a smart card to create a covert broadcast channel. The channel is activated when cards are used in a normal scenario and will give us access to secret information remotely (i.e. wireless),

P. Ning, S. Qing, and N. Li (Eds.): ICICS 2006, LNCS 4307, pp. 249–259, 2006.

without the need for physical access to the target. The attack is tailored the microprocessor architecture rather than the actual cryptographic algorithm and experiments confirm that the attack will work on modern smart cards equipped with countermeasures against side channel attacks.

This article will explain how to collect and analyze electromagnetic emanation from smart cards to build signatures of individual instruction executed by the microprocessor. These signatures will form a symbol alphabet for a covert communication channel. Subversive code hidden on the smart card will create the covert channel and use it to broadcast secret information to a nearby receiver. Practical result obtained on modern smart cards (identity withheld due to a Non Disclosure Agreement) equipped with counter measures will be shown.

2   Previous Work

The basis for side-channel attacks has been available for a long time. It is possible to use the second law of thermodynamics to show that energy must escape from devices in one way or another(e.g. heat) [1]. The laws of physics explain that it is impossible for any operating device not to leak energy. The goal of side-channel attacks is to look for dependencies between this unavoidable energy leakage and the device's secret parameters.

Exploiting this leakage is not new. Military and government organizations have supposedly used them for a long time, with public interest beginning much later. In 1985 Van Eck [2] published the article on how to eavesdrop video display units via radiation from a considerable distance that attracted much attention. In 1996 Anderson and Kuhn published their work, *"Tamper Resistance - A Cautionary Note"* [3], which showed that trusting tamper resistant devices can be problematic. That same year Kocher [4] published his work on exploiting differences in execution time (Timing Attacks). This work was soon followed up and in 1999 Kocher et al. [5] introduced some powerful attacks through measurement of a device's power consumption. Simple Power Analysis (SPA) and Differential Power Analysis (DPA) received some attention from, among others, the banking industry, and countermeasures were publicly announced. In 2000, Quisquater and Samyde [6,7] applied the analysis technique from SPA and DPA to electromagnetic side-channels, thus introducing electromagnetic analysis (EMA).

In recent years several papers have been published in an ongoing effort to systematically investigate electromagnetic side-channel attacks[8,9,10,11,12]. The experiments have been extended to some distance from the target, implying that physical access to the target may not be necessary. It has been shown that EMA is at least as powerful as power analysis, and that EMA could circumvent power analysis countermeasures [10,13]. At USENIX 2002 [14], Quisquater and Samyde described an automatic method to classify instructions, carried out by a simple CISC processor. The power and electromagnetic signature of instructions were captured and then used to train a neural network. The neural network could automatically recognize, and thus reverse engineer, executed code based on stored electromagnetic and power signatures.

Common for previous attacks is that they exploit unintentional correlations between the side-channel and secret information, often a cryptographic key. Taking a more aggressive approach would be to manipulate the side-channel. It is not difficult to imagine a situation were the code on the smart card is manipulated to give specific results for the neural network of Quisquater and Samyde [14].

Covert communication was first introduced by Lampson in 1973 and was then defined as

> A communication channel is covert if it is neither designed nor intended to transfer information at all

An example can be found in an encrypted packet switched network. An adversary can monitor the packet flow, but can not read the encrypted content of each packet. A covert channel can be created if the following is decided beforehand.

- Packet sent from address A to B - interpret as logic 0
- Packet sent from address A to C - interpret as logic 1

This traffic will appear as regular packet switch traffic (at least to the untrained eye) and hopefully not raise any suspicions, therefore it is covert.

Another example of a covert channel can be the running time of a program. This means that the timing attack of Kocher [4] can be seen as exploiting an unintentional covert channel. Unintentional in the way that the secret information was not intentionally correlated with the timing information. Similarly, other side-channel attacks can also be seen as exploiting unintentional covert channels. Side-channels also fit Lampsons definition from 1973 as stated above.

Kuhn and Andersson [15] talk about attacking a system with malicious code that will use a computer's RF emission to transmit stolen information. The possibility to plant a virus to infiltrate a bank or certificate authority and broadcast key material over an improvised radio channel is mentioned. Practical results are shown with hidden messages in a recovered video signal. This can also be categorized as a covert channel where the electromagnetic side channel has been deliberately manipulated. This approach will be used in WCCA. We introduce the term **wireless covert channel** as *a hidden electromagnetic communication channel, detectable outside the system, as a result of intentional manipulation of valid system parameters.*

Creating a wireless covert channel can be viewed as subversion, described by Myers [16] as

> The subversion of computer systems is the covert and methodical undermining of internal and external controls over a systems lifetime to allow unauthorized and undetected access to system resources and/or information.

In the next chapter the wireless covert channel attack (WCCA) is presented.

3   Wireless Covert Channel Attack

The wireless Covert Channel Attack (WCCA) relies on a highly skilled insider to
undermine the security mechanisms by hiding subversive code in the smart card's
software (SW). This is done during an early stage (design or implementation) of
its life cycle (figure 1) and will affect all cards produced. These infected cards
may be used e.g. in the banking industry as credit cards, loaded with personal
information (cryptographic key, PIN code, account number etc.) when issued to
a customer. The adversary is interested in retrieving the secret, personal information and has an accomplice involved at the use stage of the life cycle. This
will be somebody with access to a smart card terminal, a store owner or maintenance personnel. When a manipulated card is inserted into any terminal, by
the owner, the subversive code exploits characteristic electromagnetic emanation (signatures) from the microprocessor, during execution of instructions, to
broadcasting secret information over a wireless covert channel. The success of
this attack is ensured by the large number of cards infected. If a whole generation of smart cards to the banking industry is infected, there will be enough
cards randomly used in the rigged locations to make the attack worth the effort.

WCCA can be divided into a preparation phase, an implementation phase
and an exploitation phase.

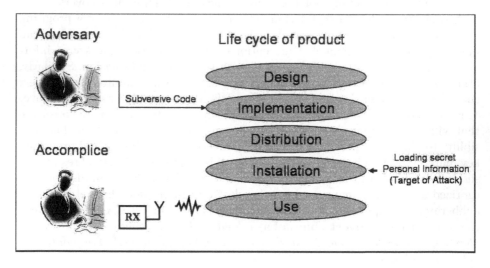

Fig. 1. Scenario: The adversary hides subversive code during an early stage. Later,
secret information is loaded to the card. When the card is used, the subversive code is
activated and broadcasts secret information to the accomplice.

3.1   Preparation Phase

The preparation phase is used to build a library of characteristic electromagnetic
emanation from instructions executed by the microprocessor. WCCA uses the

average power spectrum density (PSD) obtained from a spectrum analyzer to characterize an instruction.

For every instruction of interest, a smart card is prepared with a test code. The card inserted into a customized smart card reader will automatically start executing the test code. A small coil is placed on top of the smart card reader, as close as possible to the microprocessor, without any decapsulation. Using a spectrum analyzer, no synchronization between the executed code and the instrument is needed. The average PSD is stored on a computer for further analysis. The test code is written in assembly language and executes one instruction in a loop. The instruction is repeated several times within the loop to reduce the effect of any unwanted instructions, such as "goto". Each instruction was measured several times, in random order, to enhance the reliability of the data. The signature of an instruction is the mean of all these repetitions.

3.2   Implementation Phase

The implementation phase is used to design and hide the subversive code needed to create the covert channel. A symbol alphabet for the channel, as well as a carrier frequency, is obtained from analysis of the recorded signatures. The smart card executing the subversive code can be considered a bandpass digital system [17], where a carrier is modulated with binary data. In this work we restrict the discussion to a binary system, and leave M-ary bandpass digital systems for future work.

For two possible messages, m_1 and m_2, two possible waveforms $s_1(t)$ or $s_2(t)$ are transmitted in a bit interval, T_b. The waveforms $s_1(t)$ and $s_2(t)$ cannot be chosen freely, but are a result of emitted energy when executing instructions on the smart card. Since the receiver makes the decision based on received energy, it is natural to look for frequencies where the emitted energy can be controlled by execution of different instructions. Given the right receiver it should be possible to take advantage of the energy difference over a large frequency range, but in order to demonstrate the feasibility of the attack a low cost narrow band receiver was chosen. The approach is therefore to look for one carrier frequency, f_c, with a large difference in emitted energy between execution of two instructions. Exploiting the energy emitted in a larger band is subject to work in progress.

Using the recorded signatures, a carrier frequency is easily found. Let diff(i,j) be the spectral difference between signature i and j. Diff(i,j) is simply the magnitude of the difference at each sample of signature i and j. Calculating diff(i,j) for all combinations of instructions, there will be two signatures i=A and j=B that gives the maximum difference at a specific frequency. This frequency is chosen as the carrier frequency, f_c.

The emitted energy at carrier frequency f_c can now be controlled by designing a subversive code that transmits secret information using

– Instruction A - logic 0 - small energy emission at f_c
– Instruction B - logic 1 - large energy emission at f_c

Once the subversive code is designed, the task is to make sure it is hidden on every card produced, undetectable. It is beyond the scope of this article to describe this in detail. However, if third party compilers and library files have less stringent security requirements than the developed SW, and commercial interest prohibits full insight into the source code of them, it could serve as an excellent opportunity for the adversary.

3.3   Exploitation Phase

The success of the attack relies on the adversary or his accomplice placing a receiver in the vicinity of where infected cards are used. The subversive code will be executed during normal use and secret information broadcasted to any receiver in the vicinity.

The range of the covert channel will have a great impact on how difficult this will be. Given a range of several meters, the receiver can be placed somewhere in the room and maybe in an adjacent room. It may also be possible to carry a concealed receiver and stand nearby or be in the line behind the victim. If the range is in order of cm, the probe of the receiver must be placed close to the terminal. This may be possible if the accomplice is the store owner or maintenance personnel with access to the terminal.

The receiver can be optimized to cost, range, channel capacity, probability of error, size etc, but even a cheap commercial receiver used in this experiments gives promising results. Due to the relative long exposure time, when the card is used in a terminal (up to 30 sec) the bit rate does not need to be high. Assuming that the covert channel use only 1% of the processor time, reduces the risk of detection, and still gives 0.3 sec for the attack. Sending 1024 bits in 0.3 sec requires a channel capacity of only 3.5 kbits/s.

4   Experiment

The experiments have been carried out on a modern smart card with several security features against side channel attacks. The identity of the card and the details about the security features are withheld due to a Non Disclosure Agreement (NDA).

In the preparation phase, the electromagnetic signature of 25 instructions were collected. None of the instructions activated the I/O interface of the smart card. Signatures were collected with and without security features against side channel attacks activated. Spectrum analyzer Advantest 3641 was used. Measurements were done from DC to 60 MHz, with 100 averages, providing signatures of 4206 samples. Typical signatures can be seen in figure 2.

The object of the implementation phase is to analyze the 25 signatures collected and to identify frequencies where the emitted energy can be controlled by toggling between two instructions. Therefore, the spectral difference diff(i,j) is of more importance than the shape of the signature, this is shown in figure 3. The maximum amplitude difference for all combinations of instructions, when security features are activated, has been plotted in figure 4.

These are potential carrier frequencies for the covert channel and the corresponding instructions are used to create the subversive code. As an example,

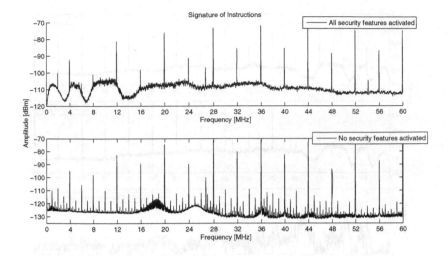

Fig. 2. Average power spectrum density as signatures of instructions. Instructions executed on card with and without security features activated.

using instruction A and B at frequency $f_c=11.5$ MHz provides an amplitude difference of 10.5 dB. It may be interesting to notice that the peaks around 53 to 57 MHz are introduced by one of the security features.

Three different subversive codes have been designed to test the covert channel and serves to illustrate the potential. It is assumed that the highly skilled insider will be able to create more sophisticated codes. The first code was designed to demonstrate that subversive code can manipulate the energy emitted and that the channel is detectable by a receiver. For this purpose two instructions are executed n times alternately, to create a pulse train with fundamental frequency dependent on n. With $1\mu s$ execution time of each instruction, choosing $n = 500, 250$ and 125 results in a fundamental frequency of 1,2 and 4 kHz respectively. This is in the audible range and serves well for a demonstration with an AM receiver. The second code was designed to demonstrate that messages can be transmitted. A short or a long audible tone is used to send morse code (SOS) to the receiver. The third code broadcasts the memory contents of a smart card in an attempt to demonstrate how secret information can be compromised.

Using the ICOM IR-20 receiver with the extendable rod antenna, the audible tones and the morse code are easily detected. On a simple card the tone has been detected 10 meter from the terminal. The modern card is detectable within 1 meter even with security features activated. The covert channel is also detectable on the peaks introduced by one of the security features at 53-57 MHz. The same procedure as with morse code can be used to broadcast the memory content of a smart card to the AM receiver. This is a low rate transmission and work is in progress to improve the transmission rate.

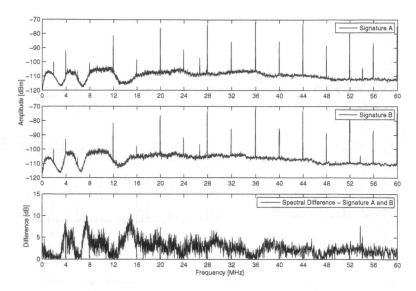

Fig. 3. Individual signatures of two instructions, with all security features activated, are shown above. In a covert channel context the spectral difference between them shown in the lower figure, illustrates our ability to manipulate the emitted energy for various frequencies.

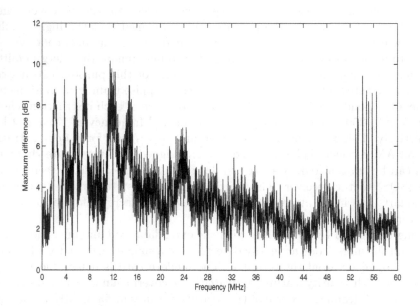

Fig. 4. The largest spectral difference for all combinations of instructions, illustrates the overall covert channel potential

5   Analysis

The feasibility of the attack has been confirmed through the use of a cheap AM receiver. An important issue left is the rate of information leakage from the smart card, the channel capacity of the covert channel.

The source rate, R, how fast the smart card (source) can transmit information, is given by [18]:

$$R = \frac{H}{T} \ bits/sec \qquad (1)$$

where H is the average information (entropy) of the source , given by Shannon [19], and T is the time required to send each message. For a binary system with equal probability of sending zero and one, the entropy is H=1. Since each message, m_1 or m_2, is represented with the waveform resulting from execution of instructions, the execution speed of the microprocessor will set a lower limit on T. Assume a microprocessor architecture that requires multiple of 4 clock cycles per instruction. Choosing two, single cycle, instructions with clock frequency of 4 MHz gives $T = 1\mu s$. Using (1) a source rate of $R = 1 \ Mbit/s$ is found. This is an upper limit and not very realistic as it e.g. does not take into consideration fetching the next message before sending it. By analyzing the flow chart of the test code, designed to read and broadcast the memory contents of a smart card, an average of 37 clock cycles ($T = 9.25 \ \mu s$) is required to send each message. The source rate is then $R = 1/9.25 \ \mu s \approx 108 \ kbit/s$.

The source rate , R, is important when designing a communication channel. Shannon [19] has shown that, for the case of signal plus white gaussian noise, it is theoretically possible to have the probability of error approach zero for a channel capacity of C bits/sec, as long as $R < C$. The equation for C is then

$$C = B \log_2(1 + \frac{S}{N}) \qquad (2)$$

where B is the channel bandwidth in hertz (Hz) and S/N is the signal-to-noise power ratio (watts/watts) at the input to the receiver.

Using the recorded signature we can estimate B and S/N. B should be the lowest bandwidth in the communication chain. In our experiment this is the receiver with B=15 kHz. Using the amplitude difference in dB from diff(i,j) as the value for S/N can be justified since one of the signatures is close to the noise floor at the chosen frequency. The experiment suggested a pair of instructions with 10.5 dB difference. With a receiver bandwidth of 15 kHz this gives C=32 kb/s. This is an upper limit for error free communication that may be approached using efficient coding. The adversary is limited to the waveforms emitted when executing instructions and cannot hope to achieve this capacity. However, a transmission rate of one tenth of C is realistic and can be sufficient. A key of 1024 bits is transmitted in 32 ms at 3,2 kb/s. Assuming 1 % processor load for the covert channel requires the card to be turned on for 32 seconds, which is not unreasonable in e.g. a bank terminal.

Care must be taken if the requirement of $R < C$ is violated. This is not a problem if handled properly, R can be decreased or C increased. Reducing the rate of transmission is not a problem and can be solved with different coding techniques. A simple approach can be to represent each message m_1 and m_2 with n execution of an instruction, where n is chosen such that $R < C$. The drawback is that the risk of exposing the subversive code increases as the size and execution time of the code increases. Increasing C can be done by increasing the bandwidth of the receiver or the S/N ratio at the receiver. An interesting approach would be to exploit differences between signatures at several different frequencies as opposed to one frequency.

The results in this experiment are believed to be moderate, as many improvements are possible. One obvious improvement would be to use a receiver with larger bandwidth. Work is in progress to calculate the potential channel capacity when the transmitter and not the receiver is the limiting factor for bandwidth.

Finally, some remarks about countermeasures. It is beyond the scope of this article to suggest new or improved countermeasures, but maybe it will serve as a reminder that countermeasures should be considered for the entire life cycle of the product and for the entire system, including third party SW, terminals and locations of use. It is also important to remember that in a complex system, introducing new functionality may have unwanted side effects. This has been demonstrated in this experiment as one security measure against side-channel attacks introduced a peak that could be exploited as a covert channel.

6   Conclusion and Future Work

This article presents a new attack on smart cards. The wireless covert channel attack (WCCA) combines theory from subversion and covert channels with side channel attack.

Experiments have shown that by manipulating the energy leakage from a smart card can create a covert channel that will give access to secret information when the card is used and that the attack will work on modern smart cards equipped with countermeasures against side channel attacks. It has been estimated that transmitting secret information at a rate of 108 kb/s is possible from the tested card.

Work in progress include designing a receiver to match this transmission rate by exploiting energy differences in a larger frequency range.

Acknowledgements. We would like to thank Arne Wold, at Gjovik University College, for helpful discussion and guidance related to the analysis of the results.

References

1. D. C. Giancoli. *Physics for Scientists and Engineers.* Prentice Hall, 1989.
2. W. van Eck. Electromagnetic radiation from video display units: An eavesdropping risk. *Computers & Security*, 4:269–286, 1985.
3. R. Anderson and M. Kuhn. Tamper resistance-a cautionary note. In *USENIX E-Commerce Workshop*, USENIX Press, pages 1–11, 1996. ISBN 1-880446-83-9.

4. P. Kocher. Timing attacks on implementations of diffie-hellman, rsa, dss, and other systems. In *Advances in Cryptology-Crypto 96*, volume 1109 of *Lecture Notes in Computer Science*, pages 104–113. Springer-Verlag, 1996.
5. P. Kocher, J. Jaffe, and B. Jun. Differential power analysis. In *Advances in Cryptography - Crypto 99*, volume 1666 of *Lecture Notes in Computer Science*, pages 388–397. Springer-Verlag, 1999.
6. J-J. Quisquater and D. Samyde. A new tool for non-intrusive analysis of smart cards based on electromagnetic emissions:the sema and dema methods. *Eurocrypt rump session*, 2000.
7. J-J. Quisquater and D. Samyde. Electromagnetic analysis (ema): Measures and counter-measures for smart cards. In *Esmart 01*, volume 2140 of *Lecture Notes in Computer Science*, pages 200–210. Springer-Verlag, 2001.
8. S. Chari, J.R. Rao, and P. Rohatgi. Template attack. In *CHES'02*, volume 2523 of *Lecture Notes in Computer Science*, pages 13–28. Springer-Verlag, 2003.
9. D. Agrawal, B. Archambeault, J.R. Rao, , and P. Rohatgi. The em side-channel(s):attacks and assessment methodologies. In *CHES'03*, Lecture Notes in Computer Science. Springer-Verlag, 2003.
10. D. Agrawal, B. Archambeault, J.R. Rao, and P. Rohatgi. The em side-channel(s). In *Cryptographic Hardware and Embedded Systems - CHES'02*, volume 2523 of *Lecture Notes in Computer Science*, pages 29–45. Springer-Verlag, 2003.
11. D. Agrawal, B. Archambeault, S. Chari, J.R. Rao, and P. Rohatgi. Advances in side-channel cryptanalysis, electromagnetic analysis and template attacks. *CryptoBytes*, 6(1):20–32, Spring 2003.
12. D. Agrawal, J.R. Rao, and P. Rohatgi. Multi-channel attack. In *CHES'03*, volume 2779 of *Lecture Notes in Computer Science*, pages 2–16. Springer-Verlag, 2003.
13. J.R. Rao and P. Rohatgi. Empowering side-channel attacks. volume 037 of *IACR ePrint*, 2001.
14. J-J. Quisquater and D. Samyde. Automatic code recognition for smart cards using a kohonen neural network. In *5th Smart Card Research and Advanced Application Conference*. USENIX, 2002.
15. R. Anderson and M. Kuhn. Soft tempest: Hidden data transmission using electromagnetic emanations. In *2nd Workshop on Information Hiding*, volume 1525 of *Lecture Notes in Computer Science*, pages 124–142. Springer-Verlag, 1998.
16. P.A. Myers. Subversion: The neglected aspect of computer security. Master's thesis, Naval Postgraduate School, 1980.
17. Jr. P.Z. Peebles. *Digital Communication Systems*. Prentice Hall, 1987.
18. L.W. Couch II. *Digital and Analog Communication Systems*. Macmillan, 1993.
19. C.E. Shannon and W. Weaver. *The Mathematical Theory of Communication*. University of Illinois Press, 1998.

From Proxy Encryption Primitives to a Deployable Secure-Mailing-List Solution

Himanshu Khurana, Jin Heo, and Meenal Pant

National Center for Supercomputing Applications (NCSA),
University of Illinois, Urbana-Champaign
{hkhurana, jinheo, mpant}@ncsa.uiuc.edu

Abstract. Proxy encryption schemes transform cipher-text from one key to another without revealing the plain-text. Agents that execute such transformations are therefore minimally trusted in distributed systems leading to their usefulness in many applications. However, till date no application of proxy encryption has been deployed and used in practice. In this work we describe our efforts in developing a deployable secure mailing list solution based on proxy encryption techniques. Securing emails exchanged on mailing lists requires that confidentiality, integrity, and authentication of the emails be provided. This includes ensuring their confidentiality while in transit at the list server; a functionality that is uniquely supported by proxy encryption. In developing this solution we addressed the challenges of identifying requirements for deployability, defining a component architecture that maximizes the use of COTS components to help in deployment, developing the proxy encryption protocol to satisfy requirements and to fit within the component architecture, implementing and testing the solution, and packaging the release. As evidence of its deployability, the resulting secure mailing list solution is compatible with common email clients including Outlook, Thunderbird, Mac Mail, Emacs, and Mutt.

1 Introduction

Proxy encryption techniques enable the transformation of cipher-text from one public key to another without revealing the plain-text to the transforming agent. These techniques have been developed and studied for almost a decade since they were proposed by Mambo and Okamoto [25] and Blaze *et al.* [4]. Since then researchers have identified useful properties of proxy encryption schemes and developed several protocols that satisfy these properties [2], [18], [19], [33]. An important consequence of this cipher-text transformation capability of proxy encryption is that the transformation agent can participate in distributed protocols with minimal trust as it never gets access to the plain-text while still providing useful processing capabilities. Centered around this consequence of trust minimization several applications have been identified including simplification of key distribution [4], key escrow [18], file sharing [2], security in publish/subscribe systems [22], multicast encryption [10], and secure and certified email mailing lists [20], [21]. Furthermore, [2], [20] demonstrate practical feasibility of proxy encryption via prototype development and testing.

In this work we take on the task of building a deployable application that requires proxy encryption. Doing so for any new cryptographic technique in general, and proxy

P. Ning, S. Qing, and N. Li (Eds.): ICICS 2006, LNCS 4307, pp. 260–281, 2006.

encryption in particular, requires that several challenges be addressed. First, there is the need to identify requirements of the security application geared towards deployability. This involves a requirement analysis and an in-depth study of both the application domain (e.g., file systems, mailing lists) and, if available, the lessons learned from successful security applications deployed in the domain. Second, the system design task must be undertaken to satisfy these requirements. This effort should attempt to maximize the use of COTS (Common-Off-The-Shelf) components in order to make deployment easier. Third, the proxy encryption based protocol must be designed and implemented using available cryptographic libraries. The protocol design must address the needs of the security application and it is often the case that protocol and system design steps are inter-linked and iterative. Fourth, the implemented components must be integrated with the application and then tested for performance and presence of vulnerabilities and errors. Finally, the integrated security application must be packaged and released along with an identified maintenance process. The security application that we develop by addressing these challenges is secure email mailing lists.

As more and more user communities are engaging in collaborative tasks, use of Email List Services (or simply *Mailing Lists* - MLs) is becoming common; i.e., emails exchanged with the help of a list server (examples of commonly used list server software include Mailman (http://list.org) and Majordomo (http://www.greatcircle.com/majordomo/)). Many tasks where MLs are used require exchange of private information. For example, a ML of security administrators that manage critical infrastructure would not want their emails publicly disclosed to prevent hackers from getting that information. Specific instances of this include the LHC Grid (http://lcg.web.cern.ch/LCG/) and TeraGrid (http://security.teragrid.org/) systems where the Incident Handling and Response policies recommend the use of encrypted and signed mailing lists. In general, use of encrypted and signed lists is recommended for incident response by IETF [7] and CERT [29]. Additional examples include a list of (1) healthcare and pharmaceutical researchers would not the want their emails publicly disclosed to protect patient privacy, and (2) corporate executives would not want their emails disclosed to protect proprietary information. For such lists cryptographic solutions are needed that provide adequate protection (i.e., confidentiality, integrity, and authentication) for the private content from threats at the client side, at the network paths where the emails arc in transit, and at the server side where the emails are processed for distribution to the list. That is, there is a need to develop Secure Mailing Lists (SMLs). Threats to the server side are an important concern in practice and lack of good solutions today has forced users to develop their own clunky ones; e.g., distribution of passwords to list members out-of-band and requiring members to use password-based-encryption so that the list server does not have access to email plain-text[1]. It is in addressing this threat that proxy encryption provides a good solution by allowing the list server to transform email cipher-text between list members without gaining access to the plain-text.

By addressing the outlined challenges for mailing lists we developed PSELS − a Practical Secure Email List Service. Looking at the history of secure email development and deployment as well as the needs of mailing lists, we identified requirements in

---

[1] This particular approach has been adopted by several critical infrastructure security protection groups today.

the categories of security properties (i.e., confidentiality, integrity, and authentication), infrastructure compatibility, key management and performance. A primary requirement here is the minimization of trust in the list server. We then designed the architecture to include several COTS components that minimize development effort and maximize ease of deployment. In particular, we were able to use the OpenPGP message format [8] and standard GnuPG plugins at the client side to eliminate the need for developing email client-specific plugins. We then developed the PSELS protocol to satisfy the identified requirements and to fit with the system architecture and design. In particular, PSELS uses proxy encryption to minimize trust in the list server. This proxy encryption protocol is a modified version of that proposed in [20], however, unlike [20] it focuses on deployment and practical use. We then implemented the protocol and the system using the Mailman list server, GnuPG and BouncyCastle cryptographic libraries, and standard GnuPG plugins and APIs. We then tested our implementation in a test-bed environment for functionality, email client compatibility, and performance. Our results show the viability of PSELS in enterprise settings, compatibility with Microsoft Outlook, Emacs, Mac Mail, Mutt and Thunderbird, and satisfactory performance that scales to support enterprise mail servers that process hundreds of thousands of emails per day.

An initial version of the software has been packaged and released for community evaluation and is available at http://sels.ncsa.uiuc.edu. We plan to support the release in terms of software patching and update as well as enhancing the software with additional features.

The rest of this paper is organized as follows. In Section 2 we identify the requirements. In Section 3 we present the PSELS component architecture. In Section 4 we present the PSELS protocol. In Section 5 we discuss the implementation and testing efforts. In Section 6 we analyze the security of our design, protocol, and implementation. In Section 7 we discuss related work and conclude in Section 8.

2   Requirements

In this relatively new area of Secure Mailing Lists (SMLs) there is both a need and an opportunity to define a set of technical requirements such that the resulting tools and solutions that satisfy these requirements have a high likelihood of being deployed and used in practice. Fortunately, this area can benefit from the long history of solutions for secure two-party email exchange (or simply, secure email). Though secure email is not used nearly as commonly as the security research community would like, availability of inexpensive tools and solutions based on the S/MIME [26] and OpenPGP [8] standards bring us closer to this vision of ubiquitous secure email use with every passing year. We identify three important lessons for SMLs from the history of secure email (i.e., history of standards and tools such as S/MIME and OpenPGP). First, a secure email solution must provide the necessary security properties, namely, confidentiality, integrity, and authentication. Second, a secure email solution will be adopted by users only if it comes with support for easily obtaining, trusting, and managing public and private keys. Third, a secure email solution is deployable only if it is compatible with existing email infrastructure and if its hardware, software and administrative costs are reasonable. These lessons form the basis of our design and implementation efforts geared towards deployability. We now define the various entities in SMLs and the technical requirements for PSELS.

2.1 SML Entities

- *List Moderator (LM)*. *LM* is a user (or process) that creates a list to be maintained at the list server, authenticates users, and helps them subscribe to and unsubscribe from the list.
- *List Server (LS)*. *LS* creates lists, maintains membership information (e-mail addresses and key material), adds and removes subscribers based on information received from *LM*, and forwards e-mails sent by a valid list subscriber to all current subscribers of that list.
- *Users/Subscribers*. Users subscribe to lists by sending join requests to *LM*, and send emails to the list with the help of *LS*.

2.2 Technical Requirements

Security Properties. A SML solution must provide *confidentiality*, *integrity*, and *authentication* for all emails exchanged on the list. Confidentiality of emails means that only authorized users (i.e. subscribers of the list) should be able to access the plain-text contents. Note that this definition excludes the list server from being able to read emails as it is not a valid subscriber. Example scenarios where the list server is not trusted to have access to cleartext contents include: (1) when protecting a distributed critical infrastructure the system administrators may not trust the list server as it may be located in a part of the network where most of the administrators have no control but, at the same time, its compromise will affect the security of their own networks, and (2) in military settings, the list server administrator may have a lower security clearance than the list subscribers and, therefore, should preferably not have access to the cleartext contents. In addition, this requirement also protects email content from an adversary that compromises the list server. Arguably, an adversary can more easily compromise a list subscriber to get access to email contents; however, if the email contents are available at the list server then its compromise would allow the adversary access to all messages on all lists managed by the server. Integrity of emails ensures that they cannot be modified in transit without such modifications being detected. Authentication of emails means that recipients can verify the identity of the sender.

Conceptually, by requiring a list server that provides message processing and forwarding functions but does not have access to message contents, we essentially deem it to be a semi-trusted third party. Such an approach minimizes trust liabilities in essential services for multi-party protocols and is often used; e.g., in fair exchange of digital goods [15].

Infrastructure Compatibility. In order to enable the deployment and use of SMLs, the protocols and tools must be compatible with existing email infrastructure. This includes the existing email servers, list servers, and email clients. All of this infrastructure will typically comply with a subset of existing email standards (http://www.imc.org/rfcs.html). While it is challenging to support all possible infrastructure systems and configurations, the choice of supported ones greatly influences the spread of SML use.

Key Management. To adopt SML solutions, users need to obtain, trust and manage cryptographic keys. These key management functions should either be built into the SML solutions or must be accessible through easily available, inexpensive means. In contrast, consider the fact that subscribers of a ML can come from a large number of domains. If, in order to use an SML solution, they need to obtain and trust CA certificates of all the domains then the key management becomes too complex.

Performance. Busy mail servers in medium-sized organizations today process more than 50,000 emails a day on average. Since SMLs will depend on existing mail servers for their delivery, it is essential that their performance not overburden them. Requiring additional servers for SMLs would significantly increase their infrastructure deployment costs.

3   Component Architecture

In Figure 1 we illustrate the component architecture of PSELS. We identify components on the server, the list moderator, and subscribers. Where appropriate we identify

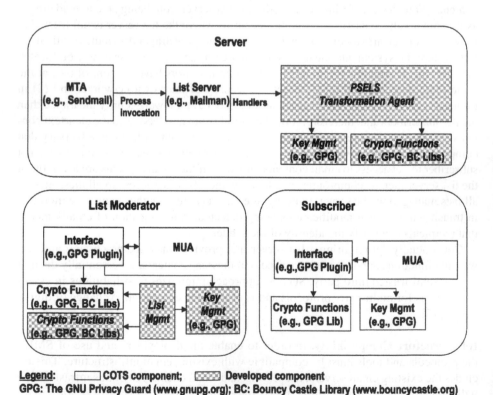

Fig. 1. Component Architecture

examples of COTS tools that can be used for the component functionality as is or with suitable modifications. This architecture is based on the requirements identified earlier, namely, security properties, infrastructure compatibility, key management, and performance.

Server Components

We envisioned the use of public-key based proxy encryption schemes to address the confidentiality requirements and the PSELS Transformation Agent provides that functionality. The Agent needs to include Crypto Functions that execute proxy encryptions as well as Key Management functions that provide generation, storage, and use of cryptographic keying material. Standard libraries such as GPG and BC can be used to develop the necessary crypto functions while for key management the use of COTS tools such as GPG is appropriate. For infrastructure compatibility we envisioned the use of COTS list servers and mail servers with a commonly used example of each being Mailman and Sendmail respectively. It is at the server side that performance is a major concern (as opposed to list moderator or subscriber side) because of a potentially large number of proxy encryption operations that may need to be executed. We study this performance via extensive experimentation but as a design parameter we envisioned the use of appropriate message passing interfaces (e.g., Mailman handlers) to connect the transformation agent with the list server so that, if needed, the agent can run on a separate machine or on multiple machines.

Subscriber Components

We observed that the development of new components on the client-side will greatly impact the infrastructure compatibility requirement because (1) users have preference for email clients (or, MUAs- Mail User Agents) so the new components must be compatible with their existing MUAs and (2) users are reluctant to install new software as well as updates to the software. At the same time, subscribers will need Key management and Crypto Functions to use PSELS; e.g., to store encryption and signature verification keys and to encrypt, decrypt, sign, and verify emails. To address this requirement we envisioned the use of a COTS Interface component that (1) provides the necessary key management and crypto functions for commonly used email clients and (2) complies with standardized messaging formats to ensure interoperability. Two examples of such a component are S/MIME tools for the S/MIME messaging format [26] and GPG tools for the OpenPGP messaging format [8]. These components are available today either as easy-to-install plugins or provided natively for many MUAs. S/MIME standards and tools are RSA based and since our proxy encryption protocol is El Gamal based these standards and tools cannot be used. Therefore, we chose to go with OpenPGP message formats and GPG tools. Furthermore, we argue in later sections that developing RSA based proxy encryption schemes for PSELS is especially challenging because it can result in sharing of the RSA modulus, which is considered insecure. As a result of the design choice of using a COTS Interface component, we require no development on the client side and yet ensure compatibility with a large number of commonly used email clients.

List Moderator Components

LM helps in creating lists and subscribing users with capabilities provided by the List Management and Key Management components. Since user subscription will require generation and distribution of proxy keys, *LM* will need to access crypto functions that are developed using appropriate crypto libraries (such as GPG and BC). Other *LM* components include a MUA and an Interface that provides access to basic crypto and key management functions for which tools such as GPG will suffice.

4   PSELS Protocol

For developing a protocol for PSELS that satisfies the outlined requirements and the component architecture, we evaluated existing protocols for multi-recipient email encryption and encrypted mailing lists [20], [28], and [32]. Of these SELS [20] offered a good starting point. However, the protocol required several modifications for satisfying the infrastructure compatibility and key management requirements. For example, SELS requires modifications to messaging formats and special processing capabilities on the client-side making it impossible to satisfy our client-side infrastructure compatibility requirements as well as the client-side component architecture. In this section, we present the PSELS protocol, which is a modified version of SELS. After we present the PSELS protocol we discuss the specific differences and improvements over SELS.

4.1   Proxy Encryption Scheme

We present the ElGamal public-key encryption scheme $\mathcal{E}_{eg}$ and the PSELS public-key encryption scheme, $\mathcal{E}$, which is based on the discrete log problem like El Gamal. $\mathcal{E}$ specifies an encryption transformation function that enables *LS* to transform an e-mail message encrypted with the list public-key into messages encrypted with the receivers' public keys.

Let $\mathcal{E}_{eg} = (Gen, Enc, Dec)$ be the notation for standard ElGamal encryption [16]. *Gen* is the key generating function. Hence $Gen(1^k)$ outputs parameters (g, p, q, a, g^a) where g, p and q are group parameters, (p being k bits), a is the private key, and $y = g^a$ mod p is the public key. The *Enc* algorithm is the standard El Gamal encryption algorithm and is defined as $e = (mg^{ar}$ mod p, g^r mod $p)$, where r is chosen at random from Z_q. To denote the action of encrypting message m with public key y, we write $Enc_{PK_y}(m)$. *Dec* is the standard El Gamal decryption algorithm and requires dividing mg^{ar} (obtained from e) by $(g^r)^a$ mod p. We assume all arithmetic to be *modulo p* unless stated otherwise.

We denote the PSELS encryption scheme by $\mathcal{E} = (IGen, UGen, AEnc, ADec, \Gamma)$. Here *IGen* is a distributed protocol executed by *LM* and *LS* to generate group parameters g, p and q, private decryption keys K_{LM} and K_{LS} and public encryption keys $PK_{LM} = g^{K_{LM}}$, $PK_{LS} = g^{K_{LS}}$, and $PK_{LK} = g^{K_{LM}} \cdot g^{K_{LS}}$. K_{LM} is simply a random number in Z_q chosen by *LM*, and K_{LS} is a random number chosen by *LS*. *UGen* is a distributed protocol executed by user U_i, *LM*, and *LS* to generate private keys for U_i and *LS*. $UGen(K_{LM}, K_{LS})$ outputs private keys K_{U_i}, K'_{U_i} and the public keys $PK_{U_i} = g^{K_{U_i}}$, $PK'_{U_i} = g^{K'_{U_i}}$. K'_{U_i} is called user U_i's *proxy key* and is held by *LS*. Furthermore, it is guaranteed that $K_{U_i} + K'_{U_i} = K_{LM} + K_{LS} \bmod q$. This protocol requires LM, and LS to generate random numbers and add/subtract them from K_{LM} and K_{LS}. $AEnc$ and $ADec$ are identical to Enc and Dec defined above for $\mathcal{E}_{eg}$. $\Gamma_{K'_{U_i}}$ is a transformation function that uses user U_i's proxy key to transform messages encrypted with PK_{LK} into messages encrypted with user U_i's public key. It takes as input an encrypted message of the form $(g^{rK_{LK}}M, g^r)$ and outputs $(g^{rK_{U_i}}M, g^r) = ((g^{rK'_{U_i}})^{(-1)} g^{rK_{LK}}M, g^r)$. Once $UGen$ has been executed for users U_i and U_j, then sending a message between the users requires user U_i calling $AEnc_{PK_{LK}}$, LS calling $\Gamma_{K'_{U_j}}$, and user U_j calling $ADec_{K_{U_j}}$. The encryption scheme $\mathcal{E}$ is correct because $ADec_{K_{U_j}}(\Gamma_{K'_{U_j}}(AEnc_{PK_{LK}}(m))) = m$. In practice, hybrid encryption is used for efficiency as illustrated in Figure 2.

The encryption scheme $\mathcal{E}$ is secure if it retains the same level of security as the standard El Gamal scheme against all adversaries $\mathcal{A}$, and if LS cannot distinguish between encryptions of two messages even with access to multiple proxy keys. The formal theorem and proof of $\mathcal{E}$'s security is provided in [21].

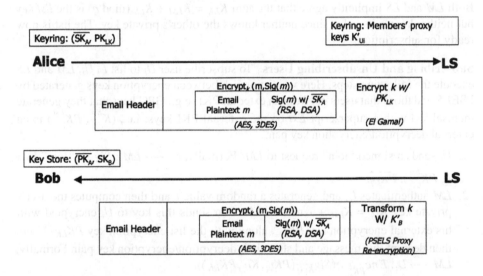

Fig. 2. Sending Emails in PSELS

4.2 Protocol Steps

We now present the protocol steps for creating a list, subscribing users, sending e-mails, and unsubscribing users. The step for sending emails is illustrated in Figure 2, which follows standard secure email messaging formats of S/MIME and OpenPGP. In the protocol description, $Enc_{PK_i}(m)$ denotes the encryption of message m with public-key PK_i, and $Sig_{\overline{K_i}}(m)$ denotes the message m along with its signature with private key $\overline{K_i}$. We distinguish between encryption/decryption keys and signature/verification keys by placing a *bar* on top of signature/verification keys; i.e., $(\overline{K_i}, \overline{PK_i})$ represents a signature and verification key pair and (K_i, PK_i) represents a decryption and encryption key pair. As illustrated in the figure, hybrid encryption is used in standard email message formats as using bulk encryption with public key technologies is expensive. However, to simplify the protocol description we do not include details of the hybrid encryption. Therefore, $Enc_{PK_i}(m)$ is actually $\{Enc_k(m), Enc_{PK_i}(k)\}$ where k is a symmetric key and Enc_k is a symmetric encryption function such as AES. That is, for simplicity of representation we just use $Enc_{PK_i}(m)$.

Creating a List. To create a new list L, LM and LS execute the following steps:

1. LM begins the execution of $IGen$ and generates parameters $(g, p, q, K_{LM}, g^{K_{LM}})$, and associates the key pair (K_{LM}, PK_{LM}) with the list.
2. LM then sends LS a message with the values g, p, and q, and the new list ID L. Formally, $LM \longrightarrow LS$: $Sig_{\overline{K_{LM}}}$("Create" List L, g, p, q).
3. LS then completes the execution of $IGen$ by choosing a new private key K_{LS} using the group parameters sent by LM, computing public key $PK_{LS} = g^{K_{LS}}$ and associating the key pair with the list. LS then sends the computed public key back to LM. Formally, $LS \longrightarrow LM$: $Sig_{\overline{K_{LS}}}(L, PK_{LS})$.

Both LM and LS implicitly agree that the sum $K_{LK} = K_{LM} + K_{LS}$ (mod q) is the *list key* but neither knows its value since neither knows the other's private key. The list is now ready for subscription.

Subscribing and Unsubscribing Users. To subscribe user U_i to list L, U_i, LM and LS execute the following steps. Here we distinguish between encryption keys generated by PSELS and those that users get from an external PKI (e.g., GPG keys that they generate themselves) with a superscript Ext on the external PKI keys; i.e., (K_i^{Ext}, PK_i^{Ext}) is an external decryption/encryption key pair.

1. U_i sends a signed "join" request to LM. Formally, $U_i \longrightarrow LM$: $Sig_{\overline{K_{U_i}}}$("Join" List L, $PK_{U_i}^{Ext}$), $\overline{PK_{U_i}}$.
2. LM authenticates U_i and generates a random value r and then computes the user's private key $K_{U_i} = K_{LM} + r$ mod q. LM then sends this key to U_i encrypted with his external encryption key $PK_{U_i}^{Ext}$, along with the list encryption key PK_{LK}. Users then decrypt this message and store their decryption/encryption key pair. Formally, $LM \longrightarrow U_i$: $Enc_{PK_{U_i}^{Ext}}(Sig_{\overline{K_{LM}}}(PK_{U_i}, K_{U_i}, PK_{LK}))$.
3. LM sends the value r to LS. Formally, $LM \longrightarrow LS$: $Enc_{PK_{LS}}(Sig_{\overline{K_{LM}}}$("Join" L, U_i, $PK_{U_i}, r))$.
4. LS obtains r from LM, and computes and stores the proxy key $K'_{U_i} = K_{LS} - r$ mod q.

To unsubscribe from list L, user U_i, LM, and LS execute the following steps:

1. U_i sends a signed "leave" request to LM. Formally, $U_i \longrightarrow LM$: $Sig_{\overline{K_{U_i}}}$("Leave" List L).
2. LM authenticates U_i and, deletes U_i's signature verification and external encryption keys from its key ring, and sends a request to LS to delete the user's proxy keys. Formally, $LM \longrightarrow LS$: $Sig_{\overline{K_{LM}}}$("Leave" L, U_i, PK_{U_i}).
3. LS verifies LM's signature on the message and deletes users U_i's proxy key K'_{U_i} from its keyring.

Sending E-mails. To send an e-mail to the list L, sender U_i, LS, and all receivers U_b ($b \neq i$) execute the following steps:

1. U_i first signs the e-mail m with his private key $\overline{K_{U_i}}$ and then encrypts it with the list public key PK_{LK}. U_i then sends to LS the encrypted e-mail message: Formally,
   $U_i \longrightarrow LS : (X = Enc_{PK_{LK}} (Sig_{\overline{K_{U_i}}}(m))$

2. To forward the e-mail to every user U_b who is subscribed to list L, LS computes and sends to U_b a transformation of X with U_b's proxy key K'_{U_b}. Formally, $LS \longrightarrow U_b$:
   $(Y_b = \Gamma_{K'_{U_b}} (X))$.

3. Each recipient decrypts the e-mail message Y_b from LS using his private key K_{U_b} with algorithm $ADec$. The receiver can then verify the sender's signature on the decrypted e-mail.

4.3 Differences with the SELS protocol [20]

The PSELS protocol specified above differs from the one presented in [20] in three ways and all of these changes were needed to enable satisfaction of the infrastructure compatibility and key management requirements. First, the proxy encryption scheme is modified to encrypt outgoing emails with the list public key, PK_{LK}, as opposed to the sender's public-key. This simplifies the proxy re-encryption step and is also more aligned with the manner in which email encryption is used today with standard crypto interface components (like GPG); i.e., associating the list encryption key with the list email address. Second, we simplify user subscription by allowing LM to compute and send users' decryption keys. In SELS a distributed protocol is used so that LM does not have access to users' decryption keys. We argue that this is not needed in practice because LM anyway has access to all emails exchanged on the list and our simplification allows us to satisfy the infrastructure compatibility requirement by not developing any new software on the client side. Third, as opposed to SELS, we do not use keyed MACs on email messages for authentication at LS. Such MACing capabilities will require modifications on the client side and, therefore, were excluded from PSELS.

5   Implementation, Testing, and Experiments

5.1   Component Design and Development

Server Components
On the server side we were able to use COTS components for the Mail Server and the List Server and then had to develop components for the PSELS Transformation Agent along with the needed Crypto Functions and Key Management components. For the List Server we chose the open source Mailman tool, which has extensible features and is widely deployed today. Mailman works with most SMTP servers and we chose Send-Mail in keeping with our open source approach. To connect the Transformation Agent with Mailman we used Mailman handlers to allow for easy installation of developed server components on new and existing Mailman setups. The handlers also allow for the Transformation Agent to run on a different machine if needed; e.g., for reasons of performance or security. The Transformation Agent was developed in C, Python and

Java leveraging the GPG and BC crypto libraries for proxy key generation and encryption functions, the GPG key management component for key storage and access, and the Python GnuPGInterface (http://py-gnupg.sourceforge.net/) for the interface between Mailman and GPG functions. Since the PSELS proxy encryption scheme is based on El Gamal we decided to go with GPG tools and the standardized OpenPGP message format. Both GPG and BC crypto libraries are open source and provide suitable capabilities to implement the proxy key generation and encryption functions while the GPG key management functions provide suitable capabilities for storing and accessing proxy keys.

For each of the four protocol steps, namely, list creation, list subscription, email sending, and list unsubscription, we define a unique Mailman handler that leads to an execution of that step at LS. Most of the operations in executing these steps involve the use of standard GPG functions with the following two exceptions: creating a proxy key on user join and proxy transformation on email forwarding. To generate a proxy key on user join the Agent uses a specialized crypto function developed using BC to extract the random value r from the LM's message and the private key, K_{LS}, and compute the user's proxy key as specified in the protocol.

To send an email to list L, a user first signs the email and then encrypts it with the list public key all using any email client that works with a GPG plugin. The resulting email message is a standard OpenPGP message, which consists of one or more packets. Each encrypted message has a Public-Key Encrypted Session Key Packet followed by a Symmetrically Encrypted Data Packet. The Public-Key Encrypted Session Key packet contains the randomly generated session key (symmetric key) used to encrypt a message and key IDs of public keys used to encrypt the session key. The Symmetrically Encrypted Data Packet contains email contents encrypted with the session key. The data can further be compressed or signed. A handler at LS, extracts the Public-Key Encrypted Session Key Packet and uses specialized crypto functions developed using GPG libraries to parse the incoming GPG messages into packets. After correctly locating Public-Key Encrypted Session Key Packet, the functions apply proxy transformation to this packet. This process is repeated for every recipient and the resulting messages are passed to MTA for delivery to list members.

Subscriber Components

On the Subscriber side we were able to use COTS tools for the MUA, Key Management, Crypto Functions, and Interface components. In keeping with the approach discussed above, we use GPG tools and ensure compatibility with all MUA's for which GPG plugins are available. Among others this includes popular MUAs like Outlook, Thunderbird, Eudora, Emacs, Mac Mail, and Mutt. GPG plugins provide all the necessary key management and crypto functions needed by subscribers to use PSELS.

For subscribing to lists, users send signed GPG messages to LM and receive back a set of necessary GPG keys and certificates. That is, users receive the list encryption key, their individual decryption keys (encrypted with their external GPG public keys), LM's signature verification key, and their own signature verification key signed by LM. Depending on the features of their GPG plugin they either automatically or manually add all these keys and certificates to their GPG keyring. To send an email to the list, subscribers sign the email with their GPG signature keys and encrypt it with the list public key (which is again a standard GPG key in their keyring). Since the list encryption key is associated it with the list email address, the GPG plugin automatically finds and encrypts the email with this key. On receiving an email on the list, subscribers simply use their GPG plugins to automatically find the appropriate keys and decrypt and verify the message.

List Moderator Components
For the List Moderator we were able to use COTS tools for the MUA, Key Management, Crypto Function and Interface components, and had to develop the List Management component. Similar to the reasons discussed above, we chose to use GPG tools for the Interface component along with the provided crypto and key management functions. The List Management component was developed in Python and Java using the GPG and BC libraries. For storing and accessing keys, the standard GPG key management functions were used.

To create lists, the List Management component uses standard GPG functions (via the command-line interface) to generate an ElGamal key pair and then sends the public key to LS via email in a GPG signed message. When LM receives LS's public key back via email, a special crypto function developed using BC computes the list public key, PK_{LK}, by multiplying LM's and LS's public keys.

To subscribe users, the List Management component executes the following steps after receiving the user's subscription request: (1) verify the user's signature on the request, (2) use a special crypto function developed using BC to generate a private key for the user as specified in the protocol, and (3) send signed and encrypted emails to the user and to LS with the appropriate keying material. Once the emails have been sent, LM deletes the user's decryption keys for security reasons.

Additional Functions: Trust Management and Key Update
In addition to implementing the protocol steps as described above, PSELS components also implement two additional features: Trust Management and Key Update. Trust management involves distribution of signature verification keys to allow subscribers to verify signatures on emails sent to the list. Key Update involves the distribution of an updated set of decryption and proxy keys.

Subscribers in a mailing list may belong to different organizations, which make it difficult for them to distribute and trust their signature verification keys. In PSELS we address this problem by using LM as the trust anchor for the lists. Since LM is trusted to distribute decryption keys and to help in generation of proxy keys at LS, it is an appropriate entity to enable the establishment of trust in subscribers' signature verification keys. To do so, LM signs every subscriber's signature verification key in list subscription step and stores this signed key in the list key ring (as noted above, LM also sends the signed key back to the subscriber). Since subscribers already have LM's signature key in their key rings and trust this key, they can place transitive trust in other subscribers' signature verification keys. Furthermore, LM can also distribute the signed verification keys to subscribers on request by extracting them from the list key ring and sending it to the subscribers as an email attachment.

The PSELS solution works on the assumption that an adversary cannot get access to the decryption key K_{LK} by simultaneously compromising either LM and LS (as $K_{LK} = K_{LM} + K_{LS} \bmod q$) or any user U_i and LS (as $K_{LK} = K_{U_i} + K'_{U_i} \bmod q$). Though unlikely, such compromise is possible. To address this concern, the protocol includes a key update step that allows LM to easily initiate and complete the process of changing all list encryption/decryption keys. This key update step would be executed either on a periodic basis for proactive security or when a compromise is detected. Key update can also be used to change the LM for a given list. To initiate a key update, LM sends a "Update L" message to LS, which includes a new key PK_{LM}. On receiving this message, LS (via a handler 'UpdateL') computes a new key pair (K_{LS}, PK_{LS}) and a new list key PK_{LK}. LS also deletes all proxy keys for this list. LM then generates a new encryption/decryption key pair for each subscriber and sends it encrypted with the subscriber's GPG encryption key stored in LM's key ring (this is the external encryption key referred to as $PK_{U_i}^{Ext}$ in the protocol described in Section 4.2.2). On receiving the message from LM, a subscriber simply adds the new certificates to his key ring and associates them with the list. LM also sends a "U_i JOIN LIST L" message to LS for each subscriber, which is processed as usual. The list has now been re-keyed.

5.2   Testing

We have tested the PSELS implementation for correct functionality and for compatibility with multiple platforms and MUAs. To do so, we have set up a test-bed that includes a linux Debian server (which includes Sendmail and Mailman) and a set of client machines each of which have a different platform (including Windows, Mac, and different flavors of *-nix). Since Mailman only works on *-nix platforms, which are similar in nature, we felt that for initial testing on the server side using any one *-nix platform is sufficient. (In the future, we will test other *-nix server platforms as well.) For the List Moderator and Subscriber side, however, we needed to test compatibility with a variety of platforms.

Functional Testing. We wrote scripts that automate all of the protocol steps, namely, list creation, list subscription, email sending, and list unsubscription. We ran these scripts on the test-bed to verify that the implementation works correctly. The scripts use both correct and incorrect inputs and check whether the results are correspondingly correct or incorrect. This process helped us identify several useful checks that were then included in the implementation. For example, the scripts used incorrect list public keys for encrypting emails. Initially, this resulted in undecipherable messages being delivered to the subscribers. To address this we included a check at LS to ensure that only emails encrypted with the correct public key are delivered to subscribers.

Compatibility Testing. We've tested the combination of the COTS and developed List Moderator components on three platforms successfully: *-nix (in particular, Debian, Fedora, and Red Hat Linux), Mac, and Windows (XP). In each case a configuration file is generated to allow the developed components access to installed GPG tools.

For the client side, we've successfully tested PSELS with five commonly used email clients each of which has its own GPG plugin (http://www.gnupg.org/(en)/related_software/frontends.html): (1) Thunderbird with Enigmail, (2) Microsoft

Outloook with gpg4win, (3) Emacs with Mailcrypt, (4) Mutt with built-in GPG support, and (5) Mac Mail with MacGPG. Testing efforts resulted in a few changes at *LS* to accommodate slight differences in email encryption between the various GPG plugins (e.g., the gpg4win plugin adds an additional attachment to encrypted html messages). We've documented the steps necessary to ensure correct configuration and setup with each email client.

5.3 Experiments

In this section we evaluate the performance of the PSELS implementation. In most organizations the ML software is co-located with the MTA in the mail server. The main goal of the experiments is to observe how the addition of our security solution affects the overall performance of the mail server. To evaluate the performance of these solutions we use an insecure ML setup as a common baseline.

Experimental Setup
For all experiments shown in this paper, we run both Mailman and Sendmail on the same machine. The mail server machine we use for our experiments is equipped with two 3GHZ Dual Core Intel Xeon processors and 3GB RAM. The machine runs Debian Linux with kernel version 2.6.8 (compiled with SMP option turned on). We use version 2.1.5 of Mailman, which was the most recent version when we started this research. For the MTA, we use the Debian linux distribution of Sendmail version 8.13.4. For PSELS, we have developed Mailman handlers and crypto functions using GPG 1.4.2 to perform proxy transformations.

To gauge the overhead of PSELS we use *throughput* as our performance metric; i.e., the maximum number of emails per unit time that the mail server can process and deliver. We focus exclusively on MLs so we assume that the mail server does not process any two-party email exchange. Since we are only interested in the throughput of the mail server, we ignore networking delays by placing list subscribers on the same server machine. In our setup the emails for the subscribers are delivered to /var/spool/mail/userid. To estimate the throughput we measure the average delay for processing one email message sent from a list subscriber and delivered to all list subscribers. We then compute the normalized *throughput* $= \frac{1}{delay} * list\ size$ where *list size* represents the number of subscribers in the list. Here *list size* is the normalization factor and is important for our experiments because PSELS executes cryptographic operations per email per recipient. For a more detailed analysis of the results we measure the delay in two cases: (1) for Mailman alone, and (2) for Mailman and Sendmail combined; i.e., from receiving the message at Sendmail, its processing at Mailman via handlers, to completing delivery for all subscribers. In the first case we use the Mailman log entries to measure the delay. In the second case we use the wall clock time when the email is sent by our test client as the start time and the log entry of Sendmail when it finishes delivering the email to all subscriber inboxes as the end time.

Measurements
In order to get an idea of how PSELS affects throughput we vary both the list size (number of subscribers) as well as the size of the email message. We use 10, 25, 50, 100, and 200 as the different list sizes and 1KB, 10KB, and 100KB as the different email sizes.

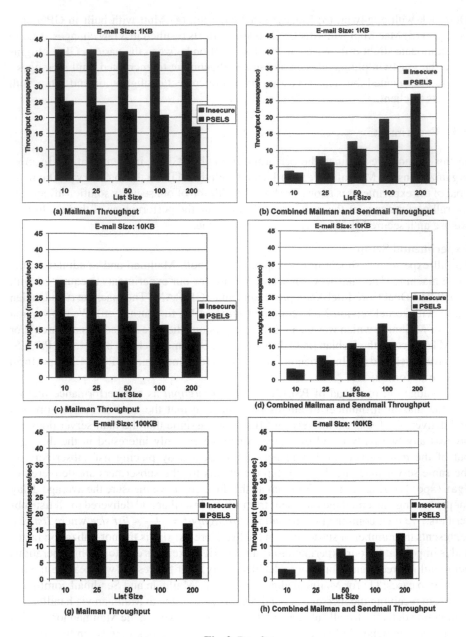

Fig. 3. Results

We limit the list size to 200 because we argue that any sensitive message that needs to be encrypted is unlikely to be sent to a large number of recipients. (If the list has only signed but otherwise cleartext contents then the list server need not do any additional work.) Since in MLs subscribers usually do not send large attachments and most of the posted messages are text (including HTML, RTF formats), we believe that 100KB is a reasonable maximum size.

To run the experiments we first populate the lists by generating user keys (stored in GPG key rings) and subscribing users. The subscription process in PSELS also results in generation of proxy keys for *LS*, which are stored using a GPG key ring. We also pre-generate the signed and encrypted messages of the different sizes to be sent on the lists. We then run the experiments as follows. For each of the two setups (Insecure baseline and PSELS) we first fix the list size as well as the email size. We then execute a script at the sender to send 20 emails (one at a time waiting for complete processing and delivery) and measure the delays for Mailman as well as for Mailman and Sendmail combined for email processing and delivery. We average the result over these 20 runs. We then vary the email size and the list size and measure the delays similarly.

Figure 3 (a), (c), and (e) shows the measured throughput using Mailman, and Figure 3 (b), (d), and (f) shows the measured throughput using Mailman and Sendmail combined. In all of the figures, the *x* axis represents list size and the *y* axis shows the throughput in terms of messages per second (processed and delivered). Figures 3 (a), (c), and (e) show the expected result of the baseline case having the better performance with the throughput reaching up to 40 messages/sec regardless of list size. PSELS has lower performance that degrades as the list size increases. Figures 3 (b), (d), and (f) are similar in that the baseline case has better performance with one big difference being that here the throughput of the two setups increases with list size and varies greatly.

Analysis

In all experiments the baseline insecure setup show the better performance, as expected, since there are no cryptographic operations involved. Also, the performance of the base case is not affected by list size because besides delivery to individual subscriber inboxes there is no additional processing of an email message per recipient.

Mailman Throughput. We first discuss the throughput for Mailman, which is shown in figures 3 (a), (c), and (e). In PSELS, across all measurements, throughput decreases as the list size increases. This is because increase in list size leads to large key ring files and our measurements indicate that the overhead of searching and reading through the key ring files begins to dominate. A general observation for these set of experiments is that as the email message size increases, the throughput decreases. The difference is significant and owes to the overhead of managing larger sized buffers for the email messages.

Combined Mailman and Sendmail throughput. Figures 3 (b), (d), and (f) indicate that the throughput increases with list size and varies greatly. This is because Sendmail has a constant overhead in processing an incoming mail message — about 3 sec in our setup. The effect of this overhead reduces as the list size increases and, therefore, the throughput increases with list size. This is true for both setups and the performance of PSELS lags behind the Insecure case. Similar to the case above, as we increase the email message size the throughput decreases.

Average throughput. In the case of Mailman, PSELS shows a 42.2% average throughput degradation against the baseline. For combined Mailman and Sendmail throughput, PSELS shows a 28.8% average throughput degradation. Overall, we see that even the worst throughput of 2.5 messages/sec for PSELS with list size 10 and message size 100KB corresponds to a throughput of more than 200,000 messages per day. Since most mail servers in small and medium-sized organizations do not typically process more than 100,000 messages per day (of which only a subset are ML messages) we conclude that adding security to MLs will not impose an undue overhead on the mail servers.

6 Security Analysis

After the functional, compatibility, and performance testing of the PSELS implementation, we analyzed the design and implementation and identified the following security concerns.

List Key Compromise

If an adversary compromises either LM and LS or any user U_i and LS then he can compute the list decryption key K_{LK}. This is because $K_{LK} = K_{LM} + K_{LS} \bmod q = K_{U_i} + K'_{U_i} \bmod q$. This would allow the adversary to read all emails encrypted with PK_{LK}. Furthermore, it would also allow him to compute every list subscribers decryption keys as $\forall_j K_{U_j} = K_{LK} - K'_{U_j} \bmod q$. This latter capability is a known property of proxy encryption schemes sometimes referred to as the "collusion" property [2]. The consequence of this attack is that recovery requires re-keying of the entire list rather than revoking one member. However, note that this would not allow the adversary to arbitrarily impersonate a list subscribers because all emails are signed with the subscribers' signature keys that are not compromised in this attack. In [2] they develop signcryption schemes that provide combined signing and proxy encryption capability and provide similar protection against impersonation by ensuring that compromise of decryption key does not imply compromise of signing capability.

To resolve this problem one can consider both a theoretical and a practical approach. Theoretically, the design of collusion-resistant proxy encryption schemes is an open problem. Designing such schemes to work with COTS components in a deployable architecture compounds this problem further. In practice, one can argue that simultaneous compromise of LS and LM (or U_i) is very unlikely. Furthermore, the provided key update functionality provides a mechanism to (1) prevent K_{LK} compromise by executing it as soon any one entity is compromised and (2) limit the adversary's access to email contents in case of successful K_{LK} compromise by executing it periodically to change list encryption keys. However, there are cases where this risk may be unacceptable. In such cases, additional security can be provided by splitting the list key, K_{LK}, three or more ways with the additional splits being hosted in different servers or by using threshold cryptographic approaches such as the one proposed by Jakobsson [19]. Now, the adversary would have to compromise multiple servers in order to get access to K_{LK}. However, this security comes at significant infrastructure costs of managing multiple servers that execute appropriate distributed protocols for proxy transformation. We argue that these costs would be unacceptable in most enterprises today, however, in the future world of virtual machines it may be possible to split the key across multiple virtual machines on the same physical server with lower costs.

Denial of Service Against *LS*

A potential attack against our design that was also observed in initial testing efforts is denial-of-service against *LS*. This attack would involve an adversary composing a large number of encrypted messages and sending them to valid list aliases from valid subscriber email addresses (which can be spoofed). In the PSELS protocol *LS* does not cryptographically verify authenticity of emails sent by subscribers because the senders' signatures are enveloped by the encryption. Consequently, *LS* may end up executing a large number of cryptographic proxy transformation operations leading to a potential denial-of-service attack.

In our current implementation we mitigate this attack by requiring *LS* to check whether incoming emails are encrypted with the list encryption key, PK_{LK}, using the encrypted session key packet of OpenPGP. Though the adversary can spoof this packet, it imposes an additional hurdle in the adversary's path. SELS [20] addresses this problem by using HMAC based authentication at *LS*, which unfortunately requires fundamental changes to email message formats and is therefore not a deployable solution. Fortunately, the S/MIME Extended Security Services [17] (ESS) include an additional signature wrapping around encrypted envelopes that would enable *LS* to verify sender signatures prior to the transformation. Since RSA signature verification is much cheaper that proxy transformation, the denial-of-service threat would get significantly mitigated. As these ESS services are deployed we will look at integrating them with PSELS.

LM **Generated Decryption Keys**

In the PSELS protocol and implementation *LM* generates every user's decryption key, K_{U_i}, and sends it to the user. As part of the protocol, *LM* then deletes the key. This can be viewed as a weak security design because ideally only the true owner of the decryption key (in this case user U_i) should generate and have access to the key. In fact, in the original SELS protocol, users added a random number in the proxy key generation process to ensure a strong security design.

In PSELS *LM* generates the decryption keys so as to avoid the need for developing new client-side software and achieve our deployability goals. We see three potential consequences of this design choice: (1) a corrupt *LM* can choose to retain K_{U_i} and decrypt messages intended for the user, (2) a corrupt *LM* can share K_{U_i} with users outside of the list, and (3) a corrupt *LM* can retain K_{U_i} and attempt to avoid revocation at a later point in time. For the first two consequences we argue that *LM* already has his own decryption key, K_{LM}, that allows him to decrypt all emails sent on the list and one that he can share with adversaries if he chooses to do so. For the third consequence, the key update protocol can be used whenever the list moderator changes to ensure that the previous list moderator cannot continue to be a part of the list.

7 Related Work

Proxy Encryption. Previous proxy encryption schemes enable unidirectional and bidirectional proxy transformations by first setting up a transformation agent that is given the proxy key and then sending messages to the agent for transformation [4], [18] and [25]. Unidirectional schemes only allow transformations from some entity *A* to another entity *B* with a given proxy key while bidirectional schemes additionally allow transformations from B to A with the same proxy key. For PSELS we need a proxy encryption scheme that allows for the transformation from one entity, LS, to many subscriber entities (i.e., to all list subscribers). The El Gamal based unidirectional proxy encryption scheme of Ivan and Dodis [18] is closest in nature to PSELS with the additional relationship between the proxy keys (i.e., $\forall_i\ K'_{U_i} + K_{U_i} = K_{LK}$) imposed to allow for a single list encryption key, PK_{LK}, to suffice. Extending the RSA based unidirectional scheme of [18] in a similar manner will not work because it would require the sharing of the modulus across all list subscribers. Jakobsson [19] and Zhou et al. [33] allow for proxy transformation without the need for distributing proxy keys but use costly threshold crypto-systems to ensure the necessary security. Ateniese et al. [2] extend proxy encryption schemes with useful properties such as non-interactiveness, which for PSELS might allow for generation of proxy keys without involving both LM's and LS's decryption keys; however, their scheme uses proprietary message formats and bilinear maps that are not easily available in standard cryptographic libraries or tools with interfaces to email systems making deployability very challenging.

Multi-recipient Email Encryption. The problem of sending confidential messages to multiple recipients has been addressed in past via multi-recipient email encryption [28], multi-party certified email [32], secure group communication and broadcast encryption. A major difference between these approaches and ours is that by using a mailing list we remove the user's burden of managing recipient addresses and public keys while still satisfying the confidentiality requirement. In these approaches the sender must manage the sender list and address all of the intended recipient's directly. In multi-recipient email encryption, Wei et al. [28] combine techniques from identity-based mediated RSA and re-encryption mixnets to enable a sender to encrypt messages to multiple recipients with only two encryptions (as opposed to one encryption for each recipient in the trivial case). To do so, they use a partially trusted demultiplexer that is akin to LS in terms of its security properties but also use an additional fully trusted CA. Their scheme is not intended for mailing lists and, furthermore, requires development of client-specific plugins. In PSELS the sender needs to execute only one encryption allowing compatibility with existing messaging formats and tools thereby avoiding the need to develop client-specific plugins. In multi-party certified email [32], the sender must maintain each recipient's public key and encrypt the message individually to each recipient. This overhead is avoided in PSELS via the use of mailing lists while still providing confidentiality.

In secure group communication either a trusted group controller (e.g., LKH [30]) distributes session keys to group members or the group members generate session keys in a distributed manner (e.g., TGDH [23]). In either case, list subscribers would have to maintain state on current session keys and update them on every membership change (in PSELS existing subscribers are not affected by the joins and leaves of other members). This makes the use of secure group communication techniques impractical for secure mailing lists as it goes against the nature of the largely offline email use. So-called "stateless" broadcast encryption schemes (e.g., [14], [6]) allow for encryption of messages to a dynamic set of group members without the members requiring to maintain state and executing key updates on membership changes. However, they vary the encryption key and cipher-text sizes depending on the group membership. This variation cannot be supported by today's mailing lists making such solutions difficult to implement. PSELS, on the other hand, addresses the confidentiality and deployability requirements of secure mailing lists in a practical way.

Secure Mailing Lists. Simple approaches that extend security solutions for two-party email to mailing lists have already been developed; e.g., (http://non-gnu.uvt.nl/mailman-ssls). In these solutions, subscribers send emails to the list server encrypted with the list server's public key. The list server decrypts the emails and then re-encrypts them for every subscriber using their registered public keys. Clearly, these solutions do not satisfy the confidentiality requirement as they allow the list server access to decrypted emails. Previously we have developed a Secure Email List Service solution that satisfies the confidentiality problem in mailing lists by using proxy encryption [20]. However, as we discussed in Section 4 this work is not practical for deployment in today's email systems. We have also developed a Certified Mailing List protocol that uses proxy encryption techniques to provide certified delivery in mailing lists [21]. This protocol provides confidentiality using proxy encryption similar to that in PSELS. However, since the primary motivation is a protocol for certified delivery, the protocol results in modifications of messaging formats and special processing at client-side making it impractical for deployment in today's email systems.

8   Conclusions and Future Work

In this work we have described the process of going from the new cryptographic primitive of proxy encryption to a deployable application that secures mailing lists. We chose mailing lists because there is a need to secure sensitive messages in multi-party settings for which email is a convenient, default method. In designing secure mailing lists we identify the need to minimize trust liabilities in the list server for which proxy encryption provides the necessary capabilities. We then defined a component architecture and a protocol geared towards deployability taking into account available COTS tools and configurations of deployed email infrastructures. The resulting PSELS implementation was then tested for functionality, compatibility, and performance.

The PSELS software is now available for community evaluation. We look forward to supporting the software in terms of software patching and update as well enhancing it with new features that the community desires. In addition, we will undertake usability studies to understand the effectiveness of the solution and report the results back to the community.

Acknowledgements

We would like to thank Jim Basney and Von Welch for their comments and suggestions, which greatly improved the design and development of PSELS. We would like to thank Rakesh Bobba for help in development and testing of the software. This material is based upon work supported by the Office of Naval Research (ONR) grant N0001404-1-0562. Any opinions, findings, and conclusions or recommendations expressed in this publication are those of the authors and do not necessarily reflect the view of ONR.

References

1. B. Adida, S. Hohenberger, and R. L. Rivest, "Lightweight Encryption for Email", Proceedings of Usenix's Symposium on Reducing Unwanted Traffic on the Internet (SRUTI 2005), July 2005.
2. G. Ateniese, K. Fu, M. Green and S. Hohenberger, "Improved proxy re-encryption schemes with applications to secure distributed storage," in Proceedings of the 12th Annual Network and Distributed System Security Symposium (NDSS), San Diego, CA, February 3-4, 2005.
3. D. Bentley, G. G. Rose and T. Whalen, "ssmail: Opportunistic Encryption in sendmail", in Proceedings of the 13th Usenix Systems Administration Conference (LISA), 1999.
4. M. Blaze, G. Bleumer, and M. Strauss, "Divertible protocols and atomic proxy cryptography", in Eurocrypt'98, LNCS 1403, Springer-Verlag, 1998.
5. D. Boneh and M. Franklin, "Identity based encryption from the Weil pairing", *SIAM Journal of Computing*, Vol. 32, No. 3, pp. 586-615, 2003.
6. D. Boneh, C. Gentry, and Brent Waters, "Collusion Resistant Broadcast Encryption with Short Ciphertexts and Private Keys", Annual International Cryptology Conference (CRYPTO), Santa Barbara, California, USA, August 14-18, 2005, Lecture Notes in Computer Science 3621 Springer pp 258-275.
7. N. Brownlee and E. Guttman, "Expectations for Computer Security Incident Response", IETF Network Working Group, RFC 2350, June 1998.
8. J. Callas, L. Donnerhacke, H. Finney, R. Thayer, "OpenPGP Message Format", IETF Network Working Group, Request for Comments, RFC 2440, November 1998.
9. J. Callas, "Identity-Based Encryption with Conventional Public-Key Infrastructure", in Proceedings of the 4th Annual PKI R&D Workshop, 2005.
10. Y-P. Chiu, C-L. Lei, and C-Y. Huang, "Secure Multicast Using Proxy Encryption", Proceedings of the 7th International Conference on Information and Communications Security (ICICS '05), LNCS 3783, December 2005.
11. S. Crocker, N. Freed, J. Galvin, and S. Murphy, "MIME Object Security Services", IETF Network Working Group, Request for Comments, 1848, October 1995.
12. M. Delaney, Editor, "Domain-based Email Authentication Using Public-Keys Domain-based Email Authentication Using Public-Keys", IETF Internet Draft, September 2005.
13. X. Ding and G. Tsudik, "Simple Identity-Based Cryptography with Mediated RSA", in Proceedings of the RSA Conference, Cryptographer's Track, 2003.
14. Y. Dodis and N. Fazio, "Public Key Broadcast Encryption for Stateless Receivers", ACM Workshop on Digital Rights Management (DRM), November 2002.
15. M. Franklin and G. Tsudik, "Secure group barter: multi-party fair exchange with semi-trusted neutral parties", in Financial Cryptography, 1998.
16. T. E. Gamal, "A Public Key Cryptosystem and a Signature Scheme Based on the Discrete Logarithm", *IEEE Transactions of Information Theory*, pages 31(4): 469-472, 1985.
17. P. Hoffman (Editor), "Enhanced Security Services for S/MIME", IETF Network Working Group, RFC 2634, June 1999.
18. A. Ivan and Y. Dodis, "Proxy Cryptography Revisited", in Proceedings of the Network and Distributed System Security Symposium (NDSS), February 2003.
19. M. Jakobsson, "On quorum controlled asymmetric proxy re-encryption", in Proceedings of the Second International Workshop on Practice and Theory in Public Key Cryptography (PKC'99), volume 1560 of Lecture Notes in Computer Science, pages 112–121, Berlin, Germany, 1999.
20. H. Khurana, A. Slagell, and R. Bonilla, "SELS: A Secure E-mail List Service", in the Security Track of the ACM Symposium on Applied Computing (SAC), March 2005.

21. H. Khurana and H-S. Hahm, "Certified Mailing Lists", in n Proceedings of the ACM Symposium on Communication, Information, Computer and Communication Security (ASIACCS'06), Taipei, Taiwan, March 2006.
22. H. Khurana and R. Koleva, "Scalable Security and Accounting Services for Content-Based Publish Subscribe Systems", in the *International Journal of E-Business Research*, Vol. 2, Number 3, 2006.
23. Y. Kim, A. Perrig and G. Tsudik, "Simple and Fault-Tolerant Key Agreement for Dynamic Collaborative Groups", in Proceedings of 7th ACM Conference on Computer and Communication Security (CCS), 2000.
24. J. Linn, "Privacy Enhancement for Internet Electronic Mail: Part I: Message Encryption and Authentication Procedures", IETF PEM WG RFC 21, 1993.
25. M. Mambo and E. Okamoto, "Proxy Cryptosystems: Delegation of the Power to Decrypt Ciphertexts", *IEICE Transactions on Fundamentals*, vol. E80-A, No. 1, 1997.
26. B. Ramsdell, Editor, "Secure/Multipurpose Internet Mail Extensions (S/MIME) Version 3.1 Message Specification", IETF Network Working Group, Request for Comments, RFC 3851, July 2004.
27. D. K. Smetters and G. Durfee, "Domain-based authentication of identity-based cryptosystems for secure email and IPsec," in Proceedings of the 12th Usenix Security Symposium, August 4-8, 2003, Washington, D. C..
28. W. Wei, X. Ding, and K. Chen," Multiplex Encryption: A Practical Approach to Encrypting Multi-Recipient Emails", International Conference on Information and Communications Security (ICICS), 2005.
29. M. J. West-Brown, D. Stikvoort, K-P. Kossakowski, G. Killcrece, R. Ruefle, and M. Zajicek, "Handbook for Computer Security Incident Response Teams (CSIRTs)", CERT Handbook, CMU/SEI-2003-HB-002, April 2003. Available at http://www.cert.org/archive/pdf/csirt-handbook.pdf.
30. C. K. Wong, M. G. Gouda, S. S. Lam, "Secure group communications using key graphs", *IEEE/ACM Transactions on Networking* 8(1): 16-30, 2000.
31. P. Zimmerman, *The Official PGP User's Guide*, MIT Press, ISBN: 0-262-74017-6, 1995.
32. J. Zhou, "On the Security of a Multi-Party Certified Email Protocol", in proceedings of the International Conference on Information and Communications Security, Malaga, Spain, October 2004.
33. L. Zhou, M. A. Marsh, F. B. Schneider, and A. Redz, "Distributed Blinding for Distributed ElGamal Re-Encryption", International Conference on Distributed Computing Systems (ICDCS), 2005, pp. 815-824.

Mathematical Foundations for the Design of a Low-Rate DoS Attack to Iterative Servers (Short Paper)

Gabriel Maciá-Fernández, Jesús E. Díaz-Verdejo, and Pedro García-Teodoro

Dpt. of Signal Theory, Telematics and Communications - University of Granada
c/ Daniel Saucedo Aranda, s/n - 18071 - Granada, Spain
gmacia@ugr.es, jedv@ugr.es, pgteodor@ugr.es

Abstract. A low-rate DoS attack to iterative servers has recently appeared as a new approach for defeating services using rates of traffic that could be adjusted to bypass security detection mechanisms. Although the fundamentals and effectiveness of these kind of attacks are known, it is not clear how to design the attack to achieve specific constraints based on the used rate and the efficiency in denial of service obtained. In this paper[1], a comprehensive mathematical framework that models the behaviour of the attack is presented. The main contribution of this model is to give a better understanding of the dynamics of these kind of attacks, in order to facilitate the development of detection and defense mechanisms.

1 Introduction

Recently, one of the most important problems in security are denial of service (DoS) attacks. The primary goal of these attacks is to deny legitimate users the access to specific resources [1]. This goal has been traditionally achieved by following several possible strategies. One of them is to exploit some vulnerability in a protocol or a service in such a way that an attacker, using a few resources, can defeat a machine with much more capacity. Another strategy consists in flooding the target service with a traffic that exhaust either the connectivity or some resources of the server.

So important are these kind of attacks that many big companies have suffered from their effects [2], reason for which much research has focused its activity on the development of detection and defense mechanisms. This way, several approaches have been proposed in the field of prevention, like egress [3] or ingress filtering [4], disabling unused services [5], honeypots [6], and others, while many efforts have been made in the field of detection through intrusion detection paradigms (IDS) [7].

A low-rate DoS attack to iterative servers has been recently presented in [8] as an attack capable of defeating an iterative server by using an adaptable traffic

---

[1] This work has been partially supported by the Spanish Government through MYCT (Project TSI2005-08145-C02-02, FEDER funds 70%).

P. Ning, S. Qing, and N. Li (Eds.): ICICS 2006, LNCS 4307, pp. 282–291, 2006.

rate according to the desired level of denial that the attacker wants to afflict to the server.

For other recently presented attacks, like the low-rate TCP targeted attack [9], some solutions in the field of detection and response [10] [11] have appeared. However, until now, neither defense nor prevention mechanisms have been proposed for [8], mainly due its novelty. In this line, there is a necessity for a more comprehensive analysis of the mechanisms that the intruder could use to carry out the attack in order to facilitate the development of detection and prevention measures. The goal of this study is to present such analysis, based on the development of a mathematical framework. The proposed model establishes the relation between the design parameters for the attack and the efficiency and rate values obtained.

The rest of this paper is organized as follows. Section 2 recapitulates the fundamentals of the attack introduced in [8]. In Section 3, some indicators to measure the effectiveness of the attack are proposed. Section 4 presents the mathematical models that support the design of the attack. Section 5 shows some experimental results for the validation of the models. Finally, some conclusions and future work are given.

2   Fundamentals of the Low-Rate DoS Attack

The scenario where the low-rate DoS attack [8] to iterative servers is analyzed consists of a generic client-server configuration in which an iterative server is going to receive aggregated traffic coming from both legitimate users and intruders. The server receives requests from the clients and responds to them after doing some processing. The low-rate DoS attack focuses the effort in the task of maintaining the destination service queue occupied with malicious requests for as long a period as possible. Due to the functioning of an iterative server, each time that a response or output to a request is generated, a position in the queue is freed. So, to achieve the goal, when an output is given, the intruder should occupy the new position in the queue as soon as possible. A vulnerability present in iterative servers, that allows to forecast the instant at which the next output is going to happen, is exploited for that purpose.

The fundamentals of the vulnerability and the attack are simple. By sending the requests in such a way that all of them ask for the same resource at the server, the time between consecutive answers or outputs, called the *inter-output time* τ, will be determined by the required service time, t_s, and so easily obtained. However, despite the solicited resource being always the same, the inter-output time is observed by the intruder as a random process, τ_{int}, because there are some variations in the service time caused by the round trip time (RTT), and the fact that each request is processed in a multitasking operating system. This random process is modelled by the authors in [8] as a normal variable with a mean value $\overline{t_s}$ and a variance of $var[t_s] + var[RTT]$.

The intruder sends the requests in such a way that they arrive at the server in the minimum possible time after a position is freed. Moreover, the traffic generated by the intruder should be low-rate. For the attainment of these two objectives, an ON/OFF attack waveform, synchronized with the outputs from the server, is used.

The attack waveform is characterized by the following parameters: (a) An *interval* (Δ) that is the time elapsed between the sending of two consecutive packets during the interval of activity; (b) an *ontime interval* (t_{ontime}) that consists on an activity interval during which an attempt to seizure a freed position in the service queue is made by emitting request packets at a rate given by $1/\Delta$; and also by (c) an *offtime interval* ($t_{offtime}$), that is, an inactivity interval previous to *ontime* in the period of attack, during which no attack packets are transmitted.

The selection of different values for these defined parameters of the attack yields in a variety of combinations between the denial efficiency achieved by the attack, and the traffic rate generated against the server. Intuitively, a higher rate will result in more denial efficiency and vice versa. However, this intuitive conclusion does not fit the need of quantitative tools for the evaluation of the effects of the attack.

To address this problem, a main task has to be afforded: that of defining a formal model which allows to relate the performance of the attack (in terms of efficiency and rate) with its operational parameters (Δ, $t_{offtime}$, t_{ontime}) and the target server and network characteristics. The following sections will deal with this objective.

3   Indicators for Evaluating the Attack

The evaluation of the attack in terms of the efficiency obtained and the rate of traffic involved leads, as a preliminary task, to the definition of some indicators to measure these features.

The following indicators are defined:

- *Effort* (E): it is the ratio between the traffic rate generated by the intruder and the maximum traffic rate accepted by the server (server capacity).
- *User perceived performance* (UPP): it is the ratio between the number of legitimate users requests processed by the server, and the total number of requests sent by them.
- *Mean idle time* ($\overline{T}_{idle}$): this indicator is defined for a scenario where legitimate users send no traffic. In this environment, $\overline{T}_{idle}$ is the percentage of time during which the system has any free positions in the service queue, related to the total duration of the attack.

As defined, the *effort* gives an idea about the traffic rate that the intruder needs to generate for the attack to succeed. On the other hand, both *UPP* and $\overline{T}_{idle}$ specify how to measure the efficiency of the attack. The value of *UPP* points out the DoS degree experienced by the legitimate users. Although it may be a good indicator to compare attack configurations, it is dependent on the characteristics of the legitimate users traffic. Because of this, the indicator $\overline{T}_{idle}$

is also defined to measure the efficiency of the attack; by using it the probability of seizure a position for a legitimate user can be deducted. As it is referred to a scenario free of legitimate users traffic, there is no dependence on it.

The aim of the attack is thus to minimize *UPP*. This will be similar to minimize $\overline{T}_{idle}$, because doing this, the probability of a legitimate user to seize a free position in the queue is reduced. On the other hand, the intruder will also try to minimize the *effort* needed to carry out the attack by choosing optimized settings for the parameters. In this way, the attack will become less detectable by intrusion detection systems based on high-rate detection.

Despite it seems that a reduction in the *UPP* value implies a higher *effort* as an expense and vice versa, it is desirable to find a quantitative relation between the setting of the parameters of the attack and the values obtained for the indicators previously defined. In the following section, some mathematical models that addresses this problem are discussed.

4   Mathematical Modelling for the Attack Behaviour

To address the issue of finding a quantitative relationship between a specific setting of the parameters of the attack and the values for the indicators that evaluate it, a mathematical framework is proposed in the following.

4.1   Mathematical Model for the Mean Idle Time

The *mean idle time* is defined as the percentage of the time during which at least a free position is available. In the evaluation of this indicator, a period of an attack, that is, an *offtime* interval followed by an activity interval (*ontime*) is taken as the observation period.

Fig. 1 represents the observed attack period (ON/OFF pattern), along with the curve of probability (normal distribution as proposed in [8]) for the generation of an output at the server. The instants for the arrival of attack packets (during the *ontime interval*) are represented by vertical arrows. These arrivals occur at the instants $a_i (i \geq 1)$. We will refer, henceforth, to the instants a_i at which an attack packet arrives at the server as *calculation points* in the model. A special calculation point, a_0, which does not correspond to the instant of a packet arrival is also defined. The position of this point is, by definition, at a time $\overline{RTT}$ before the reception of the first attack packet in the observation period, that is, $a_0 = a_1 - \overline{RTT}$.

Although in the example shown in Fig. 1 there are only three attack packets due to the chosen value for the *interval* Δ, it could be generically defined a set of calculation points $\mathcal{A} = \{a_0, a_1, \ldots, a_n\}$, where $n = floor[t_{ontime}/\Delta]$. These calculations points will be used by the model as references for the mathematical expressions.

The calculation points delimit a set of intervals at which we will calculate the instantaneous values of *idle time*, T_i. Following, the values of T_i are specified for each interval delimited by the calculation points.

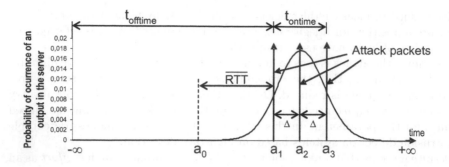

Fig. 1. Diagram of occurrence for an output: probability function and associated calculation points

If the output occurs within the interval $(-\infty, a_0)$, the value of T_i will be $\overline{RTT}$. In effect, when an answer is given by the server, it travels to the intruder and just then a new request is generated as a response to the reception of the output. This new request has to reach the server again. The whole process implies a time equal to $\overline{RTT}$. When the output rises at an instant t situated within the interval (a_{i-1}, a_i), for all the possible values of a_i in $\mathcal{A}$, and assuming that the intervals between two consecutive calculation points are short enough to keep the condition $\Delta = a_i - a_{i-1} \leq \overline{RTT}$, the *idle time* will take the value $(a_i - t)$. Finally, when the output occurs during the interval (a_n, ∞), we have the same case as in the first interval, and thus the value of the originated *idle time* is $\overline{RTT}$.

Thus, for the case in which $\Delta \leq \overline{RTT}$ is assumed, the *mean idle time* in a period of attack can be obtained from the instantaneous values previously deducted as:

$$\overline{T}_{idle_{(\Delta \leq \overline{RTT})}} = \frac{1}{T_p} \cdot \left[\int_{-\infty}^{a_0} \overline{RTT} \cdot f(t)dt + \int_{a_0}^{a_1} (a_1 - t) \cdot f(t)dt + \right.$$

$$\left. + \ldots + \int_{a_{n-1}}^{a_n} (a_n - t) \cdot f(t)dt + \int_{a_n}^{\infty} \overline{RTT} \cdot f(t)dt \right] \quad (1)$$

where $f(t)$ is the probability function for the generation of an output at the instant t and T_p is the duration of an attack period, that is, $T_p = t_{offtime} + t_{ontime}$. As it can be seen, the model is independent of the proposed distribution. If a normal distribution is taken and, for the sake of simplicity, a temporal translation is considered to get a mean value for the distribution equal to zero, the resolution of the equation leads to

$$\overline{T}_{idle_{(\Delta \leq \overline{RTT})}} = \frac{1}{T_p} \cdot \left[\overline{RTT} \cdot \left(F(a_0) + 1 - F(a_n) \right) + \right. \quad (2)$$

$$\left. + \sum_{i=1}^{n} a_i \cdot \left(F(a_i) - F(a_{i-1}) \right) + \frac{\sigma}{\sqrt{2\pi}} \cdot (e^{-\frac{a_n^2}{2\sigma^2}} - e^{-\frac{a_0^2}{2\sigma^2}}) \right]$$

where the operator $F(t)$ means the value of the distribution function associated to $f(t)$ at the instant t.

In a common design of the attack, the value of Δ is low enough to accomplish the condition $\Delta \leq \overline{RTT}$. However, although expression (2) provides the value of $\overline{T}_{idle}$ for the previous condition, the model could be easily adapted to the opposite condition, that is, $\Delta > \overline{RTT}$, considering that the intervals for which the instantaneous *idle time* varies are only those within (a_1, a_n). In effect, each one of these intervals are now split into two parts where the value for T_i is different.

This value is:

$$T_{i_{(\Delta > \overline{RTT})}}^{(a_{i-1}, a_i)} = \begin{cases} a_i - t & \text{if} \quad a_i - \overline{RTT} < t < a_i \\ \overline{RTT} & \text{if} \quad a_{i-1} < t < a_i - \overline{RTT} \end{cases} \tag{3}$$

And, as a consequence, a new expression for the evaluation of the *mean idle time* is yielded:

$$\overline{T}_{idle_{(\Delta > \overline{RTT})}} = \frac{1}{T_p} \cdot \left[\int_{-\infty}^{a_0} \overline{RTT} \cdot f(t)dt + \sum_{i=1}^{n} \left(\int_{a_{i-1}}^{a_i - \overline{RTT}} \overline{RTT} \cdot f(t)dt + \right. \right.$$
$$\left. \left. + \int_{a_i - \overline{RTT}}^{a_i} (a_i - t) \cdot f(t)dt \right) + \int_{a_n}^{\infty} \overline{RTT} \cdot f(t)dt \right] \tag{4}$$

In the proposed model, the server characteristics are considered in the $f(t)$ term. Besides, the main network factor that affects the attack is the round trip time, which is also included in the model through the mean value $\overline{RTT}$, and its variance, $var[RTT]$ (included in the distribution $f(t)$). Finally, the setting of the attack is reflected on the calculation points of the expression. In effect, their positions depend on the parameters of the attack, that is, $t_{offtime}$, t_{ontime}, and the considered value for Δ.

4.2   Mathematical Model for the User Perceived Performance

The legitimate users packet arrivals are modelled in [8] by a Poisson distribution. This implies that the probability of packet reception from a legitimate user during a period of time is given by the exponential distribution function of mean value λ: $F(T) = 1 - e^{-\lambda T}$, that represents the arrival rate of packets from the legitimate users.

The calculation of *UPP* implies the evaluation of the probability for a legitimate user to capture a position in the service queue during a period of the attack. Intuitively, this probability is derived from the originated *mean idle time*, that is, an user will capture a position in the queue with more probability as the position is free during more time. As $\overline{T}_{idle}$ is given by the summing up of contributions from the different intervals delimited by the calculation points (see Fig. 1), the probability for the k-th interval, that is (a_{k-1}, a_k), is affected by the *idle time* originated during this interval, T_{idle}^k, that is

$$T_{idle}^k = \frac{1}{a_k - a_{k-1}} \int_{a_{k-1}}^{a_k} T_i^{(a_{k-1}, a_k)} f(t) dt \tag{5}$$

However, these terms, as defined above, does not consider the presence of traffic coming from legitimate users. In effect, the *mean idle time* will take different values depending whether the considered output corresponds to either a user or the intruder. When the output is sent to a legitimate user, the intruder will not receive it and consequently a new attack packet will not generated. Therefore, the maximum value of T_i will not be $\overline{RTT}$.

In considering the above effect, and for the sake of simplicity, two approximations are made. First, the condition $\Delta \leq \overline{RTT}$ is retained, as discussed in the previous section, with the expression (1) being used to calculate the *mean idle time*. Second, the effect of the variation of the *mean idle time* is not considered when the packets coming from legitimate users arrive at the server in the intervals within a_0 and a_n. This is not an unreasonable approximation, due to the fact that the variation in the originated *idle time* for these intervals is up to Δ, if the intervals (a_1, a_n) are considered, and $\overline{RTT}$ for the interval (a_0, a_1). However, the experimental results shown later in Section 5 confirm the goodness of these approximations.

Thus, only the first interval $(-\infty, a_0)$ and the last one (a_n, ∞) are going to be affected by the above effect, thus their expressions being:

$$T_{idle}^0 = F(a_0) \left[\overline{RTT} \cdot (1 - P_u) + min \left[\frac{1}{\lambda}, \overline{t_s} - t_{ontime} \right] \cdot P_u \right]$$

$$T_{idle}^{n+1} = (1 - F(a_n)) \left[\overline{RTT}(1 - P_u) + min \left[\frac{1}{\lambda}, \overline{t_s} - t_{ontime} \right] P_u \right] \tag{6}$$

where P_u is the probability for a legitimate user to seizure a position in the service queue during a complete period of the attack. It will be given by the sum of the corresponding terms from the different intervals:

$$P_u = \sum_{k=0}^{n+1} \left(1 - e^{-\lambda T_{idle}^k} \right) \tag{7}$$

where n is the index of the last calculation point.

It is important to notice that the calculation of the expressions for T_{idle}^k and P_u should be made recursively, due to the fact that there is a crossed dependency between them. In all the experiments made, the value of P_u converges in a reduced number of iterations.

Once the value for P_u is obtained, the final expression for the *UPP*, for an attack of duration T, with C seizures, is given by:

$$UPP = \frac{P_u \cdot C}{T/\lambda} \tag{8}$$

4.3   Mathematical Model for the Effort of the Attack

The *effort* is determined by the number of packets sent to the server during the attack. Two factors contribute to the generation of attack packets. First, the activity period, *ontime*, during which these packets are generated at a rate $1/\Delta$. Second, the new packet sent as a response to the reception of an output by the intruder.

For the calculation of the *effort* an assumption will be made: the intruder will receive the answers from the server after the sending of all the packets corresponding to the *ontime* interval. This is similar to suppose that the attack period is not going to be restarted during *ontime*, being the number of packets generated $floor(t_{ontime}/\Delta) + 1$.

As previously discussed, not all the outputs are received by the intruder, and so no new attack packets are always sent. The percentage of attack periods at which an output is not received from the server is given by *UPP*. Thus, in these attack periods no additional attack packet is generated as a response to the output.

Considering that during the observation period, that is, an attack period, only one request is accepted by the server, the final expression for the *effort* is:

$$E = \left(floor(\frac{t_{ontime}}{\Delta}) + 1 \right) + (1 - UPP) \tag{9}$$

5   Conformance Analysis for the Mathematical Models

The purpose at this point is to validate the theoretical framework presented in the above Sections with experimental results obtained from simulations made within Network Simulator 2 (NS2) [12]. The values obtained from the proposed mathematical models are contrasted with those obtained through some experimental simulations to check their validity.

To check how accurate and precise are the expressions proposed for *mean idle time*, *effort* and *user perceived performance* in the mathematical models, we have evaluated the behaviour in a set of scenarios with different configurations for both the attack and server parameters. The results from these experiments have been compared to the values derived from the mathematical model, obtaining a very good approximation between them. Fig. 2 shows the corresponding values of *mean idle time*, *UPP* and *effort* for 13 simulations. The maximum variation in $\overline{T}_{idle}$ (see Fig. 2.a) given by the model is 3,77%, with a mean value of 1,71%, what is a very good approximation. The results for *UPP* are showed in absolute values (Fig. 2.b). The obtained values from the model approximate well to the simulated ones, with a mean variation of 0,4% and a maximum of 1,46%. Finally, it can be observed in the comparison for the effort (Fig. 2.c) that the model approximates well the simulated values, with a mean variation of 1,42% and a maximum of 4,02%.

As a conclusion, the approximations made in the mathematical model are accurate enough to consider it as a tool to evaluate the potential effect of an attack starting from the knowledge of its design parameters.

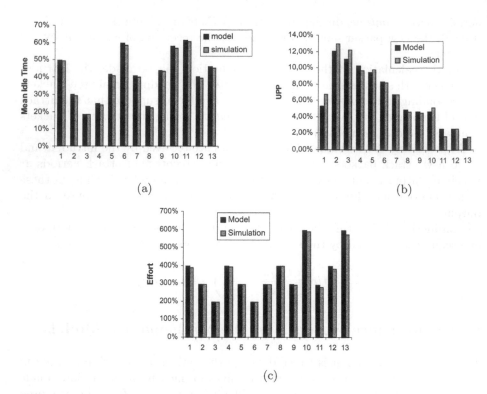

(a)   (b)

(c)

Fig. 2. Comparison between the values of (a) *mean idle time*, and (b) *UPP* from simulation and mathematical models, for 13 different scenarios

6   Conclusions and Future Work

This study is oriented to find the relationship between the design parameters of the low-rate DoS attack to monoprocess servers in [8], and the results obtained from this attack. A comprehensive study over the attack is made and some indicators to measure both the efficiency and the rate involved in a specific setting of the attack have been defined. But the main contribution of this work concerns the mathematical models that allow to quantitatively obtain the values for these defined indicators starting from a specific setting of the design parameters of the attack.

As a consequence of this study, a deeper understanding of the fundamentals of the attack is achieved. It should lead to the development of defense and response mechanisms that protect the target systems. As a future work, we plan to extend the mathematical models to concurrent systems attacked by the same mechanisms. The preliminary results we have obtained in this field show that it is possible not only to attack these systems with a similar mechanism but also it is likely to find a mathematical framework to analyze these attacks.

References

1. CERT coordination Center. Denial of Service Attacks. Available from <http://www.cert.org/tech_tips/denial_of_service.html>
2. M. Williams. Ebay, Amazon, Buy.com hit by attacks, 02/09/00. IDG News Service, 02/09/2000. http://www.nwfusion.com/news/2000/0209attack.html
3. Global Incident Analysis Center - Special Notice - Egress filtering. Available from <http://www.sans.org/y2k/egress.htm>.
4. P. Ferguson, D. Senie, Network ingress filtering: defeating Denial of Service attacks which employ IP source address spoofing, RFC 2827, 2001.
5. X.Geng, A.B.Whinston, Defeating Distributed Denial of Service attacks, IEEE IT Professional 2(4)(2000) 36-42.
6. N.Weiler, Honeypots for Distributed Denial of Service, in: Proceedings of the Eleventh IEEE International Workshops Enabling Technologies: Infrastructure for Collaborative Enterprises 2002, Pittsburgh, PA, USA, June 2002, pp. 109-114.
7. Axelsson S. Intrusion detection systems: a survey and taxonomy. Department of Computer Engineering, Chalmers University, Goteborg, Sweden. Technical Report 99-15; March 2000.
8. G. Maciá-Fernández, J. E. Díaz-Verdejo, P. García-Teodoro, Low Rate DoS Attack to Monoprocess Servers; LNCS Vol. 3934, pp. 43-57. 3rd Conf. on Security in Pervasive Computing, March 2006.
9. A. Kuzmanovic and E. Knightly, Low Rate TCP-targeted Denial of Service Attacks (The Shrew vs. the Mice and Elephants), in Proc. ACM SIGCOMM 2003, Aug. 2003, pp. 75-86.
10. H.Sun, J.C.S. Lui, and D.K.Y.Yau, Defending Against Low-Rate TCP Attacks: Dynamic Detection and Protection, in Proc. IEEE Conference on Network Protocols (ICNP2004), Oct. 2004, pp. 196-205.
11. A. Shevtekar, K. Anantharam and N. Ansari, Low Rate TCP Denial-of-Service Attack Detection at Edge Routers, in IEEE Communications Letters, vol 9, no. 4, pp. 363-365, April 2005.
12. Network Simulator 2. Available at: http://www.isi.edu/nsnam/ns/

An Independent Function-Parallel Firewall Architecture for High-Speed Networks (Short Paper)

Errin W. Fulp

Wake Forest University, Department of Computer Science,
Winston-Salem NC 27109, USA
fulp@wfu.edu
http://nsg.cs.wfu.edu

Abstract. A function-parallel network firewall is a scalable architecture that consists of multiple firewalls. Rules are distributed across the array such that each firewall implements a portion of the original policy. This resutls in significantly lower delays than other parallel designs; however, the design requires firewall intercommunication to coordinate the array which is difficult to implement and introduces additional delay.

This paper describes how the performance of a function-parallel firewall array can be increased if the individual firewalls can operate independently, without firewall intercommunication. By distributing rules using accept sets, the independent firewall array and a traditional single firewall will always arrive at the same decision (integrity is maintained). Simulation results will show the system is significantly faster than other designs and has the unique ability to provide service differentiation.

1 Introduction

Parallelization has been increasingly used as an approach for inspecting network packets in a high speed environment [1,2,3]. As seen in figure 2(a), a parallel firewall system consists of an array of firewalls connected in parallel. However as depicted in the figure, the systems differ based on what is distributed, packets (data-parallel) or policy rules (function-parallel).

Each firewall in a data-parallel system implements the complete security policy and arriving packets are distributed across the firewalls such that only one firewall processes any given packet [1]. Although the data-parallel firewall design achieves a higher throughput than traditional firewalls [1], the performance benefit is only evident under high traffic loads. Furthermore, stateful inspection requires all traffic from a certain connection or exchange to traverse the same firewall to maintain state information, which is difficult at high speeds [3].

As depicted in 2(b), a function-parallel design also consists of an array firewalls, however each firewall implements only a portion of the security policy [4]. When a packet arrives to the function-parallel system it is processed by every firewall in parallel, thus the processing time required per packet is reduced. Furthermore, maintaining state information is possible since a packet is inspected

P. Ning, S. Qing, and N. Li (Eds.): ICICS 2006, LNCS 4307, pp. 292–301, 2006.

by every firewall. Once processing is complete for a packet, results from the individual firewalls are sent to a *gate* device that stores the packet and determines the final action (accept or drop). The system can perform better than an equivalent data-parallel firewall [4]; however, the gate device implementation requires specialized hardware and introduces an additional delay.

This paper describes how function-parallel firewall array can operate independently (without a gate device) which will yield better performance. Independence can be achieved if firewall rules are distributed based on the security policy *accept set*, which describes the set of packets that will be accepted. Distribution must be done such that the union of each local accept set equals the original accept set (original and distributed policies accept the same packets), while the intersection of the local accept sets is the empty set (a packet will be accepted by only one firewall). By meeting these two requirements, it will be proven that policy integrity is maintained. Simulation results will show the independent function-parallel firewalls perform better under various conditions. In addition, accept sets can be designed such that certain types of packets are only processed on specific firewalls, yielding the ability to provide service differentiation which is a key component for maintaining network QoS. Thus, the function-parallel design has the most potential for successfully inspecting packets in a high-speed environment.

The remainder of this paper is structured as follows. Section 2 reviews firewall policy models that are used for rule distribution in the proposed parallel system. Parallel firewall designs are described in section 3, including the independent function-parallel design and rule distribution methods. Then section 4 will demonstrate the experimental performance of the parallel design. Section 5 reviews the parallel firewall design and discusses some open questions.

No.	Proto.	Source IP	Port	Destination IP	Port	Action
1	UDP	190.1.1.*	*	*	80	deny
2	UDP	210.1.*	*	*	90	accept
3	TCP	180.*	*	180.*	90	accept
4	TCP	210.*	*	220.*	80	accept
5	UDP	190.*	*	*	*	accept
6	*	*	*	*	*	deny

Fig. 1. Example security policy consisting of multiple ordered rules

2   Firewall Security Policies

A firewall rule r can be modeled as an ordered tuple, $r = (r[1], r[2], ..., r[k])$, where each tuple $r[l]$ is a set that can be fully specified, given as a range, or contain wildcards '*' in standard prefix format. For the Internet, firewall rules are commonly represented as a 5-tuple consisting of: protocol type, source IP address, source port number, destination IP address, and destination port number

[5]. In addition to the prefixes, each filter rule has an action, which is to accept or deny. Security can be enhanced with connection state and packet audit information [5].

Using the rule definition, a security policy can be modeled as an ordered set (list) of n rules, denoted as $R = \{r_1, r_2, ..., r_n\}$. State can be viewed as a preliminary extension of the policy that contains a set of rules for established connections [5]. Starting with the first rule, a packet p is sequentially compared against each rule r_i until a match is found, then the associated action is performed. This type of packet processing is referred to as a *first-match* policy and is typically the default for the majority of firewall systems including the Linux firewall implementation `iptables` [6].

When designing or verifying a firewall security policy it is important to determine the packets that will be accepted, denied, or not match any rule. Given a policy R, let A be the set of packets that will be accepted, let D be the set of packets that will be denied, and let U be the set of packets that do not match any rule. If the set of all possible packets is C, then a policy R is comprehensive if $U = \emptyset$ (i.e. $A \cup D = C$). Therefore, policy R is comprehensive if for every possible packet a match is found, which is an important objective. Furthermore, assume R does not necessarily equal R' in terms of the policy rules.

There are many ways to implement a given policy (e.g. using a single or parallel firewall) or even modify it (e.g. reorder, combine, add, or remove rules); therefore, it is important to determine equivalence and policy integrity. Consider two comprehensive policies R and R' that have accept sets A and A' respectively. The two policies are considered equivalent if $A = A'$. Therefore, if policy R is replaced by an equivalent policy R' then the **integrity** of R is maintained. Therefore, it is important to maintain the precedence constraints with implementing a firewall security policy.

3   Parallel Firewalls

As described in the introduction, parallelization offers a scalable technique for improving the performance of network firewalls. Using this approach an array of m firewalls processes packets in parallel, as seen in figure 2. However, the designs depicted in the figure differ based on what is distributed: packets or rules. Using terminology from parallel computing, distributing packets can be considered *data-parallel* since the data (packets) is distributed across the firewall [7]. In contrast, *function-parallel* designs distribute policy rules across the firewalls.

3.1   Data-Parallel Architecture

As shown in figure 2(a), data-parallel firewall architecture consists of an array of identically configured firewalls [1]. Each firewall j in the system implements a local policy R_j, where $R_j = R$. Arriving packets are distributed across the firewalls for processing (one packet is sent to one firewall), allowing different packets to be processed in parallel. Since the accept set for each firewall j equals the accept set of the original policy, $A_j = A$, policy integrity is maintained.

Distributing packets across the array allows a data-parallel firewall to increase system throughput as compared to a traditional (single machine) firewall [1]. However the data-parallel approach has three major disadvantages. First, stateful inspection requires all traffic from a certain connection or exchange to traverse the same firewall (where the stateful rule resides) or the constant distribution and management of stateful rules. As a result, successful connection tracking is difficult to perform at high speeds using the data-parallel approach [1,3]. Second, distributing packets is only beneficial when each firewall in the array has a significant amount of traffic to process (firewalls are never idle). The performance benefit (higher throughput) only occurs under high traffic loads. Finally, the design does not differentiate between traffic classes only load balancing. Therefore efficiently maintaining different QoS requirements is not possible.

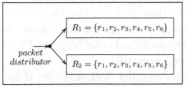

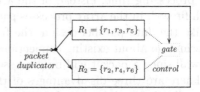

(a) Data-parallel, packets distributed across equal firewalls.

(b) Function-parallel with gate, rules distributed across firewalls.

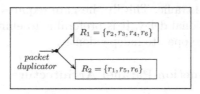

(c) Function-parallel, rules distributed across independent firewalls.

Fig. 2. Various parallel designs for network firewalls. The original security policy consists of six rules $R = \{r_1, ..., r_6\}$ and each design consists of two firewalls (depicted as solid rectangles, where local policies are given within each rectangle).

3.2   Function-Parallel Architecture

Unlike the data-parallel model which distributes packets, the function-parallel design distributes policy rules across the firewall array [4]. The function-parallel design consists of multiple firewalls connected in parallel and a *gate* device. As seen in figure 2(b), when a packet arrives to the function-parallel system it is forwarded to every firewall and the gate. Each firewall processes the packet using its local policy, including any state information. Since the local policies are smaller than the original, the processing delay is reduced as compared to a traditional firewall. Once the firewall finishes processing a packet, it then signals the gate indicating either no match was found, or provides the rule number and action if a match was found. The gate stores the results for the packet and determines the final action to perform.

Since firewalls only implement a portion of the original policy, it is critical that rule distribution is done to maintain integrity. The integrity of a policy R is maintained if the rules are distributed such that every rule in R exists in the system and if the precedence constraints of R are observed in each local policy R_j. As a result, the accept set of the gate equals the accept set of the original policy [4]. Several different distributions are possible that adhere the described guidelines. Essentially the rule numbers (indexes from the original policy) in each local policy must be in ascending order, as seen in figure 2(b).

The function-parallel design has several significant advantages over traditional and data-parallel firewalls. First, the function-parallel design results in faster processing since every firewall is utilized to process a single packet. Reducing the processing time, instead of the arrival rate, yields better performance since each firewall in the array processes packets regardless of the traffic load. Second, unlike the data-parallel design, the function-parallel design can maintain state information about existing connections. The new state rule can be placed in any firewall since a packet will be processed by every firewall.

There are three disadvantages of the function-parallel design. First, there is a possible limitation on scalability, since the system cannot have more firewalls than rules. However, given the size of most firewall policies range in the thousands of rules [8], the scalability limit is not an important concern. Second, the system is unable to differentiate traffic. Thirdly the gate requires specialized hardware and introduces an additional delay. It is preferable to eliminate the gate device and allow the firewalls to operate independently.

3.3 Independent Function-Parallel Architecture

As described in the previous subsection, a function-parallel system consists of an array of firewalls where arriving packets are duplicated and policy rules are distributed. Each firewall processes an arriving packet using its local policy and a gate device is required to ensure integrity is maintained. However, it is possible to allow the firewalls to operate independently, thus eliminating the gate device and any need for inter-firewall communications.

Consider a function-parallel system consisting of m firewalls that enforces a comprehensive security policy R. Each firewall j in the array has a local comprehensive policy R_j that is a portion of the security policy R. Therefore, each firewall has a local accept set A_j and a deny set D_j. Integrity will maintained without a gate device if rules are distributed such that a packet $d \in D$ is dropped by all firewalls, while a packet $a \in A$ is accepted by only one firewall. This is more formally stated in the following theorem.

Theorem 1. *An array of m firewalls arranged in a function-parallel fashion enforcing a comprehensive policy R can operate independently and maintain integrity if policy rules are distributed such that: each local policy is comprehensive,* $\bigcup_{j=1}^{m} A_j = A$, *and* $\bigcap_{j=1}^{m} A_j = \emptyset$.

Proof. The first requirement, comprehensiveness, ensures each local policy will either accept or deny a packet ($\bigcup_{j=1}^{m} U_j = \emptyset$). The second requirement $\bigcup_{j=1}^{m} A_j = A$ indicates that collectively the system will accept only the packets accepted by the policy R. The last requirement, $\bigcap_{j=1}^{m} A_j = \emptyset$, ensures multiple firewalls will never accept the same packet (no overlaps in the local accept sets), therefore only one copy of a packet will be accepted. As such, the integrity of the policy R is maintained by the parallel firewall.

An example distribution of the policy given in figure 1 across an array of two independent firewalls is shown in figure 2(c). In this case, the local policy of the upper firewall will accept only packets from the 210 and 180 address range, while the lower firewall will only accept packets from the 190 address range. Duplicating the deny all rule, r_6, is required to make the local-policies comprehensive. Other distributions are possible, such as distributing rules based on the protocol ($R_1 = \{r_1, r_2, r_5, r_6\}$ and $R_2 = \{r_3, r_4, r_6\}$) or destination ports ($R_1 = \{r_1, r_4, r_5, r_6\}$ and $R_2 = \{r_2, r_3, r_6\}$). Policy distribution can be done to balance the packet load (distribute popular rules across the array) or to achieve a certain QoS objective. Of course the number of distributions will depend on the original security policy, where fewer precedence edges allow more distributions.

Like the function-parallel system that relies on a gate device, the independent function-parallel system can manage state information since a packet is sent to every firewall. However, allowing the firewalls to operate independently has several important unique advantages. First, the elimination of the gate device causes the function-parallel design to be compatible with a variety of firewall devices since specialized equipment is not needed. Second, the independent function-parallel system will have lower processing delays than an equivalent data-parallel system or a function-parallel system with a gate device. Third, local-policies can be designed to process certain types of traffic on certain firewalls, yielding the ability to provide service differentiation which is an important component for maintaining QoS requirements.

Although the system has many significant advantages, it is not redundant. Integrity will be lost if a firewall fails since a portion of the policy (local accept set) will not be available. Fortunately, loss of a firewall will only result in a more conservative policy (fewer packets accepted), which is better than the previous function-parallel design with gate device. Redundancy can be provided by duplicating the local policy to another firewall. As done in [1], firewalls can be interconnected to determine if redundant rules should be processed.

4   Experimental Results

The performance of a traditional single firewall, the data-parallel firewall, and the function-parallel firewall (with gate device and independent) was measured under realistic conditions using simulation. Firewalls were simulated to process 6×10^7 rules per second, which is comparable to current technology.

For each experiment the parallel designs always consisted of the same number of firewalls. The gate device delay was equivalent to processing three firewall rules. Short-circuit evaluation was simulated for the gated design, where the firewalls in the array are notified to stop processing a packet once the appropriate match was determined. No additional delay was added to the data-parallel system for packet distribution (load balancing); therefore, the results observed for the data-parallel design are better than what should be expected.

Packets lengths were uniformly distributed between 40 and 1500 bytes, while all legal IP addresses were equally probable. Firewall rules were generated such that the rule match probability was given by a Zipf distribution [9,8]. Rules were distributed for the function-parallel design such that no inter-firewall dependency edges existed, and if possible, more popular rules were located at the top of the local-policies. This distribution ensures integrity is maintained.

Three sets of experiments were performed to determine the effect of increasing arrival rates, increasing policy size, and increasing number of firewalls. For each experiment 1000 simulations were performed, then the average and maximum packet delay were recorded.

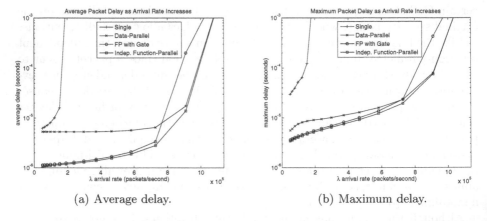

(a) Average delay.   (b) Maximum delay.

Fig. 3. Packet delay as arrival rate increases. Parallel designs consisted of five firewalls.

The impact of increasing arrival rates on the four firewall designs is shown in figure 3. In this experiment, each system implemented the same 1024 rule firewall policy [8] and both parallel designs consisted of five firewalls. The arrival rate ranged from 5×10^3 to 1×10^6 packets per second (6 Gbps of traffic on average).

As seen in figure 3, the parallel designs performed considerable better than the traditional single firewall. As the arrival rate increased, the parallel designs were able to handle larger volumes to traffic due to the distributed design. As seen in figure 3(a), the function-parallel firewall had an average delay that was consistently 4.0 times lower than the data-parallel design, while the independent function-parallel design average delay was 4.3 times lower. This is expected because each firewall in the function-parallel design is used to inspect arriving packets regardless of the arrival rate. The impact of the gate delay is more prominent as the arrival rate increases. Similar to the average delay results, the function-parallel design had a maximum delay 34% lower than the data-parallel design, while the independent function-parallel design was 38% lower.

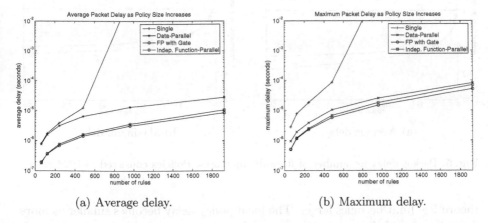

(a) Average delay.

(b) Maximum delay.

Fig. 4. Packet delay as rule number increases. Parallel designs consisted of five firewalls.

The effect of increasing the policy size (number of rules) for the four firewall designs is given in figure 4. In this experiment, the arrival rate was again 1×10^5 packets per second (yielding more than 0.5 Gbps of traffic on average) and both parallel designs consisted of five firewalls. Policies ranged from 60 to 3840 rules.

As seen in figure 4(a), the parallel designs performed considerable better than the traditional single firewall once the policy contained more than 1000 rules. The function-parallel firewall had an average delay that was 4.12 times lower than the data-parallel design, while the independent firewall was 3.79 times lower. This slight difference is primarily due to short-circuit evaluation, where the gate informs firewalls to stop processing a packet once the appropriate match is found. However this is only a marginal gain given the inter-firewall communication and specialized hardware required for short-circuit evaluation.

Figure 5 shows the effect of increasing number of firewalls for the two parallel firewall designs. The number of firewalls ranged from 2 to 256, the number of rules was 1024, and arrival rate was 2×10^5 packets per second (again, yielding more than 1 Gbps of traffic).

As firewalls were added, the function-parallel system always observed a reduction in the delay. This delay reduction trend is expected until the number of firewalls equals the number of rules. In contrast, the delay for data-parallel design quickly stabilizes and the addition of more firewalls has no impact. This is because after a certain point any additional firewalls will remain idle, thus these additional firewalls are unable to reduce the delay. As additional firewalls are added the performance difference between the function-parallel firewall and

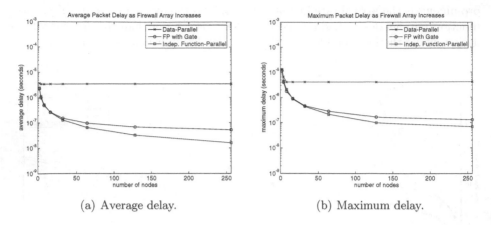

(a) Average delay.   (b) Maximum delay.

Fig. 5. Packet delay as number of firewalls increases. Policies consisted of 1024 rules.

theoretical limit becomes larger. The local policy delay becomes smaller as more firewalls are added; however, the gate delay remains constant, thus more prominent in the total delay experienced.

5   Conclusions

It is important that a network firewall acts transparently to legitimate users, with little or no effect on the perceived network performance. This is especially true in a high-speed environment or if traffic requires specific network Quality of Service (QoS). Unfortunately, the firewall can quickly become a bottleneck given increasing traffic loads and network speeds. Therefore, new firewall designs are needed to meet the challenges associated with the next generation of high-speed networks.

This paper introduced a scalable firewall architecture consisting of multiple independent firewalls, where each firewall implements a portion of the security policy. When a packet arrives to the system it is processed by every firewall simultaneously, which significantly reduces the processing time per packet. In addition, rule distribution guidelines that maintain policy integrity (the parallel design and a traditional single firewall always reach the same decision for any packet) and independence (no inter-firewall communication required) were introduced. Simulation results showed the architecture achieved a processing delay significantly lower than previous parallel firewall designs. Furthermore unlike other designs, the proposed architecture can provide stateful inspections since a packet is processed by every firewall and can be implemented with currently available technology. Therefore, the function-parallel firewall architecture is a scalable solution that can provide better performance and more capabilities.

While the function-parallel firewall architecture is very promising, several open questions exists. For example given the need for QoS in future networks, it is important to develop methods for distributing rules such that traffic flows are isolated. In this case a certain type of traffic would be processed by a certain firewall. Another open question is the optimization of local firewall policies, including redundant policies. However, optimization can only be done if policy integrity is maintained.

Acknowledgment

This work was supported by the U.S. Department of Energy MICS (grant DE-FG02-03ER25581). The views and conclusions contained herein are those of the authors and should not be interpreted as necessarily representing the official policies or endorsements, either expressed or implied, of the DOE or the U.S. Government.

References

1. Benecke, C.: A parallel packet screen for high speed networks. In: Proceedings of the 15th Annual Computer Security Applications Conference. (1999)
2. Goddard, S., Kieckhafer, R., Zhang, Y.: An unavailability analysis of firewall sandwich configurations. In: Proceedings of the 6th IEEE Symposium on High Assurance Systems Engineering. (2001)
3. Paul, O., Laurent, M.: A full bandwidth ATM firewall. In: Proceedings of the 6th European Symposium on Research in Computer Security ESORICS'2000. (2000)
4. Fulp, E.W., Farley, R.J.: A function-parallel architecture for high-speed firewalls. In: Proceedings of the IEEE International Conference on Communications. (2006)
5. Ziegler, R.L.: Linux Firewalls. second edn. New Riders (2002)
6. Ranganath, V.P., Andresen, D.: A set-based approach to packet classification. In: Proceedings of the IASTED International Conference on Parallel and Distributed Computing and Systems. (2003) 889–894
7. Culler, D.E., Singh, J.P.: Parallel Computer Architecture: A Hardware/Software Approach. Morgan Kaufman (1999)
8. Wool, A.: A quantitative study of firewall configuration errors. IEEE Computer 37(6) (2004) 62 –67
9. Leland, W.E., Taqqu, M.S., Willinger, W., Wilson, D.V.: On the self-similar nature of ethernet traffic. IEEE Transactions on Networking 2 (1994) 1 – 15

Estimating Accuracy of Mobile-Masquerader Detection Using Worst-Case and Best-Case Scenario

Oleksiy Mazhelis[1], Seppo Puuronen[1], and Mika Raento[2]

[1] University of Jyväskylä, Finland
{mazhelis, sepi}@it.jyu.fi
[2] University of Helsinki and Helsinki Institute for Information Technology, Finland
Mika.Raento@cs.Helsinki.FI

Abstract. In order to resist an unauthorized use of the resources accessible through mobile terminals, masquerader detection means can be employed. In this paper, the problem of mobile-masquerader detection is approached as a classification problem, and the detection is performed by an ensemble of one-class classifiers. Each classifier compares a measure describing user behavior or environment with the profile accumulating the information about past behavior and environment. The accuracy of classification is empirically estimated by experimenting with a dataset describing the behavior and environment of two groups of mobile users, where the users within groups are affiliated with each other. It is assumed that users within a group have similarities in their behavior and environment and hence are more difficult to differentiate, as compared with distinguishing between the users of different groups. From the practical detection perspective, the former case corresponds to the "worst-case" scenario where the masquerader has a rich knowledge of the user behavior and environment and is able to mimic them, while the latter case corresponds to the "best-case" scenario, where the masquerader makes little or no attempt to mimic the behavior and environment of the user. The classification accuracies are also evaluated for different levels of false rejection errors. The obtained results indicate that, when smaller values of false rejection errors are required, ensembles of few best-performing classifiers are preferable, while a five-classifier ensemble achieves better accuracy when higher levels of false rejection errors are tolerated.

1 Introduction

Nowadays, mobile terminals are often used to store and access sensitive private and corporate information. The survey of Pointsec [1] reveals that smartphones and PDAs are used to store personal and business names and addresses (respectively 86% and 81% of users); to receive and view emails (45% of users), and to store corporate information on them (27% of users), among other purposes. Meanwhile, small-size terminals carried along are susceptible to loss or theft; for instance, according to another survey by Pointsec [2], 24% of respondents have experienced a loss or theft of their PDAs.

P. Ning, S. Qing, and N. Li (Eds.): ICICS 2006, LNCS 4307, pp. 302–321, 2006.

Impersonating the legitimate user in order to obtain an unauthorized access to sensitive data or services is referred to as the masquerade attack. In order to spot this attack, the means of masquerader detection are employed. A number of efforts have been devoted to the problem of detecting masquerade attacks (e.g. [3,4,5,6,7,8]). These works are mainly targeted on networked laptops and workstations as well as servers. The peculiarities of mobile terminals, such as the limited battery power, memory and processing capabilities, the mobility of the terminals and their personal use, are not taken into account in these works. Some approaches assume a specific user interface, e.g. UNIX command-line interface [3,6], which is not available on a majority of mobile terminals.

Some works also focus on resisting masquerader attacks in the context of mobile terminals [9,10,11]. For instance, Sun et al. [11] study the applicability of mobility patterns for detecting masqueraders; their results, however, lack empirical evidence. In [9] and [10], respectively the keystroke dynamics and the gait patterns are used to differentiate mobile-handset users from masqueraders. However, these characteristics are available during a limited portion of time (e.g. keystrokes can be monitored only when the user is typing), and the detection accuracy achieved with these characteristics used alone may be insufficient (the best reported average equal error rates are 12.8% and 7% respectively). Besides, some of the solutions to the problem of fraud detection in telecommunication networks address the problem of mobile-masquerader detection, too [12,13,14,15]. Meanwhile, these approaches are focused on the use of services, and therefore, are not able to detect masquerade attacks if the services are not used, e.g. while the terminal is disconnected from the telecommunication network.

In this paper, the problem of mobile-masquerader detection is approached as an anomaly detection problem [16] based on the assumption that the behavior and environment of a masquerader is anomalous compared with those of the legitimate user. In turn, the problem of anomaly detection is formulated in the paper as a one-class classification problem [17], where the behavior and environment of a claimant (the person interacting with the terminal) is classified as belonging to the legitimate user or not.

In order to improve the detection accuracy, multiple behavioral and environmental features are monitored and analyzed by an ensemble of base (one-class) classifiers. Each classifier learns the norm of user behavior or environment as manifested in previously observed values of these features, and then classifies currently observed values as normal or anomalous. The final classification is produced by fusing the classifications of base classifiers using a combining rule.

Different characteristics have been proposed as potentially useful in masquerader detection. Among them are the peculiarities of typing rhythms [18,19,9], the patterns of user mobility and calling activity [13,11], and the regularities in the application usage [6]. A list of characteristics potentially useful in mobile-masquerader detection has been suggested in [20]. In our earlier work [21], the classification accuracies of several one-class classifiers based on these characteristics were experimentally evaluated. The evaluation was based on the dataset describing the behavior and environment of two groups of mobile users, where the users within groups were affiliated with each other. It can be assumed that users within a group have similarities in their behavior and environment and hence are more difficult to differentiate, as compared with distinguishing between the users of different groups. From the practical detection perspective, the former case can be seen as *the "worst-case" scenario* where the masquerader has a rich knowledge of the user behavior and environment and is able to mimic them, while the latter case can be seen as *the "best-case" scenario*, where the masquerader has little or no knowledge to attempt mimicking the user behavior and environment. In [21], the classification accuracy was estimated only for the worst-case scenario by letting the classifiers distinguish the legitimate user from other users within these groups. Assuming that distinguishing between the users inside the groups was challenging for the classifiers, the obtained accuracy estimations can be seen as *pessimistic*.

This paper builds on earlier work in [21] and extends it in several ways. First, the classification accuracy is estimated for the best-case scenario, i.e. by letting the classifiers distinguish the legitimate user from the users of the other group. Assuming that the classification task is easier in this scenario, the produced accuracy estimates are referred to as *optimistic*. According to the obtained results, indeed, the users from different groups can be distinguished with a significantly higher accuracy than the users within one group.

Second, the classification accuracies are estimated for different levels of false rejection (FR) errors indicating how likely the legitimate user is mistakenly classified as a masquerader. As a result, classifier ensembles are identified which produce superior accuracy for different levels of the FR errors. The obtained results indicate that, when smaller values of the FR errors are required, ensembles of few best-performing classifiers are preferable, while a five-classifier ensemble achieves better accuracy when higher levels of the FR errors are tolerated.

Finally, the design of one of the base classifiers in [21] was found inappropriate for the case when the users of distinct groups were distinguished. Therefore, the design of this classifier had to be improved, and as a result, also the pessimistic estimation of accuracy for this classifier and for the ensembles which include this classifier have improved as compared with the results reported in [21].

The paper is organized as follows. In the next section, our approach to mobile-masquerader detection based on combining one-class classifiers is described. The design of individual classifiers and the employed combining rule are specified in section 3. In section 4, the results of experiments are reported. Section 5 discusses the resource consumption imposed by the proposed approach, and considers how vulnerable to subversions the approach is. Finally, conclusions from the study are provided in section 6.

2   Mobile-Masquerader Detection Based on Combining One-Class Classifiers

An anomaly is often defined in intrusion detection in a probabilistic sense, i.e. as the observations with a low probability to be invoked by the legitimate user.

Various methods based on statistical probability modeling [22,23,3,24,5], outlier detection [25], clustering [4,26], etc. have been proposed to estimate how probable the current behavior and environment is for the legitimate user. Most of these techniques analyze the whole set of features simultaneously. However, substantial disadvantages are inherited into this approach including difficulties with learning when the features are lumped into a single high-dimensional vector [25,27]; and difficulties with the normalization of features having different physical meaning [27]. Besides, it may happen that the values of some features are not available at the time the classification is performed. All these arguments justify the use of an alternative approach based on decision fusion and combining classifiers [28,27]. Following this approach, the features can be divided into subgroups processed by individual one-class classifiers referred to as base classifiers. Each of them is aimed at classifying the current values of features as belonging to either the user class, or the impostor class. By employing a *combining rule*, the final classification is produced based on the classifications of the base classifiers.

In this approach, a set of R base classifiers are employed to classify the object Z (claimant) represented by the values of n_f features $\{x_1, \ldots, x_{n_f}\}$ from the feature space $\mathcal{X}$. The available feature values are used to initialize the observation vector of each base classifier. For this, a sliding window $[\tau_1, \tau_2]$ of the length $l_\tau = \tau_2 - \tau_1$ (determining the time interval, within which the feature values are collected) and the increment for the window δ_τ is used. Classifier i takes as input the observation vector $\mathbf{x}_i \equiv (x_1^{(i)}, \ldots, x_{n_{f_i}}^{(i)}) \subset \{x_1, \ldots, x_{n_f}\}$, $x_j^{(i)} \in \mathcal{X}_i \subset \mathcal{X}$.

The classification process consists of the learning phase and the classification phase. In the learning phase, using the training set $\mathcal{DS}_T$, the classifier i learns to differentiate the user and the impostors by estimating the set of parameters Θ_i constituting the model of the classifier. The training data-set $\mathcal{DS}_T$ includes the vectors of feature values of the user: $\mathcal{DS}_T = \{((x_1, \ldots, x_{n_f})_j, y_j) | j = 1, \ldots, |\mathcal{DS}_T|\}$, where $y_j = C_U$ is the class label.

In the classification phase, the learnt model is used to classify an unlabeled observation vector from the unlabeled dataset $\mathcal{DS}_C = \{((x_1, \ldots, x_{n_f})_j) | j = 1, \ldots, |\mathcal{DS}_C|\}$ into the user class or the impostor class. Given an unlabeled observation vector $(x_1, \ldots, x_{n_f})_j$, each classifier for which the values of needed features are available initializes and processes its vector $\mathbf{x}_i$, and outputs its individual classification $u_i = u_i(\mathbf{x}_i, \Theta_i)$ indicating how likely the claimant is the user $(Z \in C_U)$. Finally, once the outputs of base classifiers are available, the final classification is produced by combining these classifications, using a functional mapping $\gamma(\mathbf{u}, \Theta) : \mathbf{u} \mapsto \{C_U, C_I\}$. Due to unavailability of some of the feature values, classifications of some base classifiers may not be available, and hence the final classification needs to be made using a subset of base classifiers.

The accuracy of the final classification is described by the probability of correct detection P_D and false rejection (FR) error rate P_{FR}. The probability of correct detection is the probability of an impostor being correctly classified as belonging to the impostors; it can be defined as $P_D = P(\gamma = C_I | Z \in C_I)$, where $P(\cdot)$ denotes probability. In turn, the FR error rate reflects the probability of the legitimate user being classified as an impostor; it is defined as $P_{FR} = P(\gamma = $

$C_I|Z \in C_U$). Besides, another related characteristic is the false acceptance (FA) error rate which can be defined as $P_{FA} = P(\gamma = C_U|Z \in C_I) = 1 - P_D$.

3   Individual Classifiers and Combining Scheme

In [20], human personality was assumed to be reflected in different aspects of user *behavior* and *environment*, and a number of characteristics describing such aspects were suggested. It was hypothesized that the superposition of these characteristics is individual, and can be used to distinguish between the user and masqueraders. To measure quantitatively these characteristics, appropriate observable variables, or *measures*, should be assigned to each of them. A list of tentative measures has been proposed in [20]. Some of these measures are employed in the experiments reported in the paper; the choice of the measures to use is based on the information available in the dataset which is described below.

3.1   Dataset

The dataset used in this work was obtained within the Context project at the University of Helsinki and was gathered using the ContextPhone software platform [29]. The data describes the users' movements (GSM cell changes), phone usage (phone profile, application use, idle and active time, charger), physical social interaction (bluetooth environment) and mobile phone communication (phone calls and text messages).

The data comes from two field studies conducted to test ContextContacts, a social awareness service [30]. The first field study was done with a family of four: mother and three children aged 10 to 16. The second group consisted of five high-school students, aged 16 to 18, who ran a small company together. Both studies lasted approximately three months. All subjects were Finns living in the greater Helsinki area. The anonymized version of the dataset is available from http://www.cs.helsinki.fi/group/context/data/.

The data was collected with the ContextLogger application of the Context-Phone platform. The software runs in the background on Nokia Series 60 smartphones, collects data and sends it to a server automatically, and does not normally interfere with the user's actions (some crashes of the software may result in user-visible alerts). The data was collected throughout the daily activities, not limited to certain times, locations, or settings. Coverage of the data over the full study periods ranges from 55 to 95%. Although the data collection software is fairly reliable, the whole process may leave gaps as users may switch off the phone or disable the software. The gaps are not random in respect to the phenomena studied: since missing data is often the result of user behavior, it correlates with the usual/unusual distinction. On the other hand there are long periods, where the data gathering has been continuous, and it can be reliably claimed that the data covers also atypical behavior.

The data collection was done in a setting where the users were testing a novel application on the phone. Additionally, for most users the phone was different from their previous one. Some anomalies in the data related to this should be visible. On the other hand the length of the studies means that the behavior should exhibit a stationary pattern fairly quickly, compared to the full time period.

3.2   Design of Individual Classifiers

Values of some of the measures proposed in [20] are available in the dataset. These measures are assigned as features to individual classifiers; to each type of measures, an individual classifier is assigned. The design of these classifiers is described below. It should be noted that similar classifiers were employed in [21].

Type of program or service evoked. Active applications evoked by the user are registered in the dataset. This measure is referred to as *active applications* (ACT_APP). The assigned classifier estimates the probability of an application j being evoked out of m applications as $\hat{P}(\mathrm{app}_j|U) = (a_{\mathrm{app}_j}+1)/(\sum_m a_{\mathrm{app}_m}+1)$, where a_{app_j} is the number of times the user evokes the application. Assuming the independence of consequent application evocations, the probability of application evocations within a time window $[\tau_1, \tau_2]$ is approximated as

$$\hat{P}(\mathrm{app}_{i-n_{app}+1}, \ldots, \mathrm{app}_i|U) = \prod_{j=i-n_{app}+1}^{i} \hat{P}(\mathrm{app}_j|U), \tag{1}$$

where app_i is the last application evoked within the time window, and n_{app} is the average number of applications evoked within the window. The application evocations within previous window(s) can be taken into account if needed (the same is valid for the other classifiers, too). Given the current active applications to be classified, the classifier outputs the classification $u_i = \hat{P}(\mathrm{app}_{i-n_{app}+1}, \ldots, \mathrm{app}_i|U)$.

Sequence of cells traversed. The dataset records the identifiers of the cells (Cell IDs) wherein the mobile terminal is registered. The information about consecutive Cell IDs can be utilized in order to create the *sequences of cells traversed* measure ($MOVE$). The model of the assigned classifier includes a matrix, where each element $a_{\mathrm{cell}_i\,\mathrm{cell}_j}$ is a counter that stores the number of times the terminal's Cell ID changed from cell i to cell j. The matrix values are used in approximating the probability $\hat{P}(\mathrm{cell}_j|\mathrm{cell}_i, U)$ of a handover:

$$\hat{P}(\mathrm{cell}_j|\mathrm{cell}_i, U) = \frac{a_{\mathrm{cell}_i\,\mathrm{cell}_j} + 1}{\sum_m a_{\mathrm{cell}_i\,\mathrm{cell}_m} + n_{neighbor\ i}}, \tag{2}$$

where cell_m are the cells to which traversals from cell_i were registered, and $n_{neighbor\ i}$ is the number of such cells. Given the parameters l_τ and δ_τ of sliding windows, the average number of handovers n_{ho} within a window is estimated. Assuming the independence of consequent handovers, the probability of a sequence of cell changes within a time window $[\tau_1, \tau_2]$ is approximated as $\hat{P}(\mathrm{cell}_{i-n_{ho}}, \ldots, \mathrm{cell}_i|U) = \prod_{j=i-n_{ho}}^{i-1} \hat{P}(\mathrm{cell}_{j+1}|\mathrm{cell}_j, U)$, where cell_i is the last cell registered within the time window. In the classification phase, given the current route to be classified, the classifier outputs the classification $u_i = \hat{P}(\mathrm{cell}_{i-n_{ho}}, \ldots, \mathrm{cell}_i|U)$.

For the experiments reported in this paper, $n_{neighbor\ i}$ was assigned the value of 40 whenever the number of cells to which traversals from $cell_i$ were registered is less than 40 (in [21], $n_{neighbor\ i}$ was set to 4). This decreases the value of estimated probability of handovers between previously unseen cells. Due to this slight modification, a substantial improvement in the accuracy of the $MOVE$ classifier is achieved, as will be reported in section 4.

Speed of move. Though the speed of move is not available in the dataset, the timestamps of the Cell ID records can be used to estimate the time the terminal spends in a cell, which, in turn, can be used to roughly estimate the terminal's speed in terms of "cell per second" referred as *speed ($SPEED$)* measure.

For each cell, the user speed is modeled separately by the assigned classifier based on the empirical distribution of the user speed in this cell. The value of the speed can be approximated as a ratio of the length of the user's path within the cell to the time the user spent in the cell. The time spent in the cell τ^{stay} is estimated as the length of time interval $[\tau_{ho1}, \tau_{ho2}]$ between consequent handovers. Assuming that the user follows the same path within the cell, the length of the path is omitted from speed calculation, i.e. the speed in the cell is estimated as $v_{\mathrm{cell}_i} = 1/\tau^{stay}$ (in "cell per second"). Only smaller values of τ^{stay} (< 11 minutes) are processed by the speed-based classifier, while greater values are assumed to indicate that the terminal is not moving. Using the accumulated empirical distribution function (EDF) of v_{cell_i}, the probability density $p(v_{\mathrm{cell}_i})$ of the current speed for cell i is evaluated by using k-nearest neighbors method [31]. Assuming independence of the speed in subsequent cells, the likelihood of a user speed within a time window $[\tau_1, \tau_2]$ is approximated as

$$L_{speed}(\mathrm{cell}_{i-n_c+1}, \ldots, \mathrm{cell}_i|U) = \prod_{j=i-n_c+1}^{i} p(v_{\mathrm{cell}_j}), \qquad (3)$$

where $cell_i$ is the last cell registered within the time window, and n_c is the average number of cell changes within a window. Given the current speed values, the classifier outputs the classification $u_i = L_{speed}(\mathrm{cell}_{i-n_c+1}, \ldots, \mathrm{cell}_i|U)$.

Locations where prolonged stops were made. The information about the Cell IDs and the time spent in cells can be used to identify those locations (in terms of Cell IDs) where the terminal stays for a relatively long period of time. This measure is named *places visited ($PLACES$)*. The design of the classifier based on this measure is similar to the design of the classifier based on active applications. The difference is that the locations (Cell IDs) of prolonged stops, as defined in the description of the speed-based classifier, are taken as input instead of the application identifiers.

Temporal lengths of actions. In the dataset, the durations of calls are recorded; they are used as a *call duration (DUR_CALL)* measure. The classifier analyses the mean duration time $\overline{\tau}^{dur}$ within a window $[\tau_1, \tau_2]$. The value of $\overline{\tau}^{dur}$ is calculated as $\overline{\tau}^{dur} = \frac{1}{n_{dur}} \sum_{j=i-n_{dur}+1}^{i} \tau_j^{dur}$, where τ_i^{dur} is the last call duration registered within the window, and n_{dur} is the average number of calls finished within a window. Using the accumulated EDF of the $\overline{\tau}^{dur}$ values, the probability density $p(\overline{\tau}^{dur})$ of the current mean inter-arrival time is evaluated using k-nearest neighbors method. Given the current inter-arrival time values, the classifier outputs the classification $u_i = p(\overline{\tau}^{dur})$.

Address information of the people contacted. Phone numbers contacted via calls or SMS are available in the dataset. This measure is referred to as *contact numbers (CONT_NUM)*. Besides, the identifiers (MAC-addresses) of neighboring Bluetooth-devices are logged in the dataset and are employed as *neighboring Bluetooth devices (BT_DEV)* measure. The classifier based on the phone numbers of contacted people, and the classifier based on the MAC-addresses of neighboring Bluetooth devices are designed similarly to the classifier based on active applications. The difference is that contact numbers or MAC-addresses, respectively, are taken as input instead of the application identifiers.

In addition to the measures described above, the intervals between evocations of calls (*arrival of calls* measure) and SMSs (*arrival of SMS* measure) are available in the dataset. However, according to [21], the classifiers built on these measures, provide poor accuracy indicating that these two measures are poor differentiators between mobile-terminal users. Therefore, these measures and corresponding classifiers are excluded from consideration in this paper.

3.3   Combining Classifiers

Combining the classifications produced by several classifiers is often used as a means to compensate the weaknesses of individual classifiers. Different combining rules have been investigated [27,32,33], and it has been shown that combining may result in a significant reduction of classification errors [32,34]. However, for combining one-class classifiers, where only the knowledge regarding one class is available, relatively few rules can be used. Among them are different modifications of voting rules as investigated by Xu et al. [27]. Tax [17] reported the applicability of the mean vote, the mean weighted vote, the product of weighted votes, the mean of the estimated probabilities, and the product combination of probabilities as combining rules for one-class classifiers. In [35], the mean of the estimated probabilities (MP) rule was justified to be among the most suitable ones in the context of mobile masquerader detection, and an improved version of it (modified MP rule) was proposed. This modified MP rule is used in the experiments in this paper as a scheme for combining individual classifications. Below, the details of this rule are provided.

The modified MP rule assumes that each classifier i outputs its classification as an estimation of the probability density function (pdf) for the user class $p(\mathbf{x}_i|C_U)$. Given R classifiers to be combined, the rule represents the average of the classifier confidences u_i^c:

$$u_{mc}(\mathbf{x}_1, \ldots, \mathbf{x}_R) = R^{-1} \sum_{i=1}^{R} u_i^c(p(\mathbf{x}_i|C_U)), \tag{4}$$

where u_i^c reflects the degree of the classifier confidence in the hypothesis that an object Z belongs to the user class. The confidence values can be calculated as [35]:

$$u_i^c(p(\mathbf{x}_i|C_U)) = \frac{1}{1 + \exp\left(-\ln\frac{p(\mathbf{x}_i|C_U)}{\overline{p}(\mathbf{x}_i|C_U)}\right)} = \frac{p(\mathbf{x}_i|C_U)}{p(\mathbf{x}_i|C_U) + \overline{p}(\mathbf{x}_i|C_U)}, \qquad (5)$$

where $\overline{p}(\mathbf{x}_i|C_U)$ is the mean value of the estimated probability $p(\mathbf{x}_i|C_U)$. This mean value is equal to the probability of a random variable uniformly distributed in the feature space $\mathcal{X}_i$.

The final classification result is made by comparing the obtained u_{mc} value with a threshold t_{mc}:

$$\text{Decide} \quad Z \in C_U \quad \text{if} \quad u_{mc} \geq t_{mc},$$
$$\text{otherwise decide} \quad Z \in C_I. \qquad (6)$$

4   Experimental Results

In this section, the results of experiments are presented. These experiments pursue two goals. First, the classification accuracy of different ensembles of classifiers is estimated, for both the worst-case and the best-case scenario. The obtained pessimistic and optimistic estimates should provide respectively the estimates of the lower and the upper boundary of the classification accuracy which can be achieved with the available ensembles for the dataset used in the study. Second, the classification accuracies are estimated for different levels of false rejection errors. It is hypothesized that for different levels of FR errors, different ensembles may provide better results. In order to test this hypothesis, the ensembles of one, two, three, four, five, and seven classifiers were compared with respect to their accuracy achieved at distinct levels of FR errors.

4.1   Experimental Settings and Evaluation Criteria

In order to evaluate the classification accuracy, the holdout cross-validation [36] was used in the experiments. The model of each classifier was learnt using the training data-set $\mathcal{DS}_T$, and was subsequently used to classify the instances of a classification data-set $\mathcal{DS}_{C_1}$ or $\mathcal{DS}_{C_2}$. In general, a classification data-set should include both the instances originated from the user and the instances originated from masqueraders. However, since the data originated from masqueraders were not available, the data from other users were employed as the masquerader data.

For each user, the data were split into two parts in the relation $2:1$ commonly used in classifier evaluation [36]. The first part formed the training data-set $\mathcal{DS}_{T_i}$ employed for learning the model for user i only. The second part was included into a classification data-set $\mathcal{DS}_{C_1}$ or $\mathcal{DS}_{C_2}$. $\mathcal{DS}_{C_1}$ included the data of users of the first group (users 11 through 14 in the dataset), and $\mathcal{DS}_{C_2}$ included the data of users of the second group (users 21 through 25 in the dataset). The length and the increment of sliding window were set to $l_\tau = 1800$ seconds and $\delta_\tau = 900$ seconds respectively.

The classification datasets $\mathcal{DS}_{C_1}$ and $\mathcal{DS}_{C_2}$ originated from distinct user groups, and were employed in the experiments to estimate the pessimistic and optimistic classification accuracies. The users within groups were acquainted with each other, had common interests, and therefore shared some of the characteristics, such as visited places. As a result, at least for some classifiers and ensembles, the task of distinguishing the users within groups is assumed to be more difficult, thus representing the worst-case scenario from the detection viewpoint. Therefore the obtained estimation of classification accuracy is referred to as a pessimistic one. On the contrary, the task of distinguishing the users of distinct groups is assumed to be less challenging for classifiers, and the obtained accuracy estimation is referred to as an optimistic one.

The pessimistic accuracy is estimated by letting the classifiers distinguish the legitimate user from other users of the same group, for example by letting the classifiers of users 11 through 14 trained on $\mathcal{DS}_{T_{11}}, \ldots, \mathcal{DS}_{T_{14}}$ distinguish these users from other users within the same group represented by $\mathcal{DS}_{C_1}$. On the contrary, the optimistic accuracy is estimated by letting the classifiers distinguish the legitimate user from the users of the other group, for example by letting the classifiers of users 11 through 14 distinguish these users from the users of the second group represented by $\mathcal{DS}_{C_2}$.

In order to evaluate the accuracy of a classifier distinguishing between a user and impostors, the values of the probability of correct detection P_D and FR error rates P_{FR} are usually employed. Since the ideal accuracy, corresponding to the values $P_D = 1$ and $P_{FR} = 0$ is extremely difficult, if at all possible, to achieve, in practice, a trade-off between P_{FR} and P_D is set as a goal. The dependence between P_D and P_{FR} values is represented by the so-called Receiver Operating Characteristic (ROC) curve depicting the P_D values as a function of P_{FR}. The area under the curve (AUC) [37] was employed in the experiments, as it reflects the classifier accuracy; the greater area in general corresponds to the classifier with the better accuracy.

Base ROC-curves, along with the corresponding AUCs, can be employed to assess how accurate single classifications are, provided that these classifications can be delivered by the base classifiers. However, they do not take into account the observation vectors, for which no classification is made by the classifiers, due to the absence of values of the features in a particular window. The number of such non-classifications differs among base classifiers; therefore, their classification accuracy cannot be compared using such base ROC-curves and AUCs.

Therefore, along with the base ROC-curve, a normalized ROC-curve (Figure 1) and normalized AUC were used in the experiments. A normalized ROC-curve depicts P_D^{norm} as a function of P_{FR}^{norm}, where P_D^{norm} and P_{FR}^{norm} represent respectively the normalizations of P_D and P_{FR}, wherein the cases of non-classifications are taken into account [21]. For classifier i, the values of P_D^{norm} and P_{FR}^{norm} are calculated as:

$$P_{D_i}^{norm} = \frac{P_{D_i}\, n_{C_i}}{n_{C\ max}}, \quad P_{FR_i}^{norm} = \frac{P_{FR_i}\, n_{C_i}}{n_{C\ max}}, \tag{7}$$

where n_{C_i} denotes the number of classifications made by classifier i, and $n_{C\ max}$ is the maximum number of classifications that can be made by individual classifiers or combinations thereof. $n_{C\ max}$ is defined as the number of windows, for

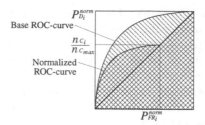

Fig. 1. Example of a base and normalized ROC-curve

which at least one base classifier is able to make a classification (in other words, the number of windows, for which feature values are available for at least one classifier).

In case a base classifier is required to deliver the classifications for the windows, where the feature values are unavailable, the classifier may output classifications for these windows randomly, thus making true detections and false rejections equally likely, i.e. $P_{D_i}^{norm} = P_{FR_i}^{norm}$. The behaviour of such a classifier, randomly guessing whenever it is unable to make a lassification, is represented in the normalized ROC-curve by the diagonal line for the values of $P_{D_i}^{norm}$ and $P_{FR_i}^{norm}$ greater than $n_{C_i}/n_{C\ max}$ (as shown in the upper right part of Figure 1).

An example of the normalized AUC is shown in Figure 1 as a cross-hatched area. Given the value of base AUC (AUC_i), the normalized AUC (AUC_i^{norm}) can be calculated as:

$$AUC_i^{norm} = 0.5 + \frac{(n_{C_i})^2}{(n_{C\ max})^2}(AUC_i - 0.5) \tag{8}$$

Thus, the base AUC reflects how accurate a single classification is provided that the classification can be made, while the normalized AUC reflects how many accurate classifications can be made in general, taking into account both classifications based on available features and random classifications.

Besides total AUC values, the values of a partial area under the curve, referred to as the partial AUC or p-AUC [38], are as well employed. A partial AUC reflects the classification accuracy for lower FR error values (lower than p), and is evaluated as the area under a partial ROC-curve restricted by the values of false rejections lower than p.

4.2 Pessimistic and Optimistic Estimation of Classification Accuracy

In this subsection, for different ensembles, the pessimistic and optimistic accuracy estimations are compared. Both base AUCs and normalized AUCs are calculated for each user, and the produced values are averaged. The classification accuracy has been estimated for a number of ensembles having different number of base classifiers ($R = 1, 2, 3, 4, 5, 7$). For each number of classifiers R, the ensembles providing the best classification accuracy are reported in Table 1.

Table 1. Averaged total AUCs estimated within groups (the worst-case scenario, pessimistic estimations) and across groups (the best-case scenario, optimistic estimations)

Classifier ensemble	Within groups (pessimistic)	Across groups (optimistic)
Base AUC		
MOVE	0.685	0.867
MOVE+BT_DEV	0.709	0.876
MOVE+BT_DEV+CONT_NUM	0.685	0.804
MOVE+BT_DEV+CONT_NUM+PLACES	0.693	0.780
MOVE+BT_DEV+CONT_NUM+PLACES+ACT_APP	0.685	0.771
MOVE+BT_DEV+CONT_NUM+PLACES+ACT_APP+DUR_CALL+SPEED	0.667	0.741
Normalized AUC		
MOVE	0.615	0.728
MOVE+BT_DEV	0.661	0.795
MOVE+BT_DEV+CONT_NUM	0.664	0.774
MOVE+BT_DEV+CONT_NUM+PLACES	0.671	0.753
MOVE+BT_DEV+CONT_NUM+PLACES+ACT_APP	0.685	0.770
MOVE+BT_DEV+CONT_NUM+PLACES+ACT_APP+DUR_CALL+SPEED	0.667	0.741

In the upper half of the table, the averaged base AUCs are shown. As could be seen, estimated accuracy is significantly higher when the ensembles are distinguishing between the users of distinct groups, as compared with the accuracy estimation for the ensembles distinguishing between the users within the groups. Thus, indeed, the accuracy estimation in the former case is the optimistic estimation obtained for the best-case scenario, while in the latter case the accuracy is estimated for the worst-case scenario and the produced estimation is pessimistic.

It should be noted that, in the optimistic accuracy estimation, the inclusion of the $SPEED$ classifier into the seven-classifier ensemble had no effect on the final classifications. This classifier, when distinguishing users from distinct groups, was not able to produce any classifications because little or no CellIDs in common were registered for the users of different groups, even though they lived in the same area.

As can be seen in the bottom part of the table, the difference between pessimistic and optimistic estimations of accuracy is less substantial when normalized AUCs are considered. The difference between the estimations evens-out due to the fact that the cases of non-classification are taken into account in the calculation of normalized AUCs.

As reflected in the normalized AUCs presented in the table, different trends can be found in pessimistic and optimistic estimations of classification accuracy. The pessimistic accuracy grows when the ensemble is produced by including into it sequentially $MOVE$, BT_DEV, $CONT\_NUM$, $PLACES$, and ACT_APP classifiers, and decreases when further classifiers are included. Thus, the best pessimistic accuracy estimation is achieved by the ensemble of five classifiers. Meanwhile, the optimistic accuracy improves when $MOVE$ classifier is combined with the BT_DEV, but deteriorates when further classifiers are added to the ensemble. Furthermore, as will be shown in the next subsection, other ensembles may provide superior results, when lower levels of FR error are considered.

The pessimistic estimations of accuracy were also reported in [21]. However, the pessimistic estimations in Table 1 differ from the values reported in [21], due to the fact that the design of the $MOVE$ classifier is improved. As a result, its normalized AUC has increased from 0.549 to 0.615; consequently, the accuracies of the ensembles that include this classifier have improved, too.

4.3   Evaluating Accuracy for Different Values of FR Rate

Total AUC values describe the classification accuracy of classifiers or classifier ensembles integrated over the range of all values of the FR error. However, in many applications, the FR error rate needs to be kept low, or restricted to predefined limit. Therefore, in this subsection, the classification accuracy is evaluated in terms of partial AUCs (p-AUC) which reflect the classification accuracy for the FR error lower than p. Four levels of p are investigated: 0.1, 0.2, 0.4, and 1.0 (in fact, for $p = 1.0$, p-AUC is identical to the total AUC). Similarly to the experiments in the above subsection, for a variety of ensembles having different number of classifiers, the pessimistic and optimistic accuracy estimations have been calculated. The normalized partial AUCs have been calculated for each user, and the produced values have been averaged. The best results (according to pessimistic estimations) for each number of classifiers R are shown in Figure 2.

The four histograms in the figure illustrate the pessimistic and optimistic accuracy estimations for four different levels of the FR error (as reflected in values of p). Both the pessimistic and optimistic estimations indicate that the best classification accuracy is achieved when a subset of available classifiers is employed in the ensemble. Which ensemble provides the best accuracy, however, depends on the value of p, as well as on whether the pessimistic or optimistic estimation of accuracy is taken into account.

As could be seen, different ensembles provide superior results for different levels of the FR error. In particular, in the case of the pessimistic accuracy estimation, the $MOVE + BT\_DEV$ ensemble gives the best accuracy for $p = 0.1$ and $p = 0.2$, while the accuracy of a three-classifier ensemble ($PLACES + BT\_DEV + CONT\_NUM$) is superior for $p = 0.4$, and the accuracy of a five-classifier ensemble is superior for $p = 1.0$. In the case of the optimistic estimation, the two-classifier ensemble $MOVE + BT\_DEV$ achieves the best accuracy in most cases (namely, for the values of $p \geq 0.2$). Besides, a three-classifier ensemble ($MOVE + BT\_DEV + CONT\_NUM$) achieves the best accuracy for $p = 0.1$; yet, the achieved accuracy comes close to the accuracy of the $MOVE + BT\_DEV$ ensemble.

The selection of the most accurate ensemble as well depends on whether the pessimistic or optimistic accuracy estimation is considered. Only for $p = 0.2$, the $MOVE + BT\_DEV$ ensemble provides the best accuracy when estimated both pessimistically and optimistically. For $p \neq 0.2$, the best optimistic accuracy is achieved more often with the same two-classifier ensemble $MOVE + BT\_DEV$, while the best pessimistic accuracy is more often achieved by the ensembles with greater numbers of classifiers.

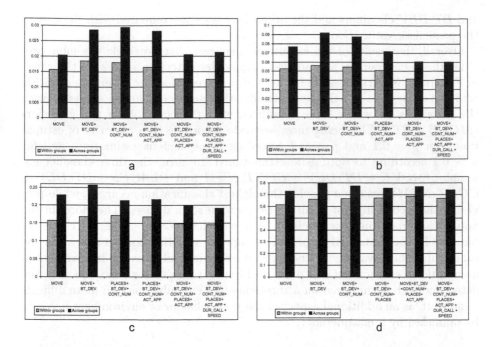

Fig. 2. Averaged normalized p-AUC values for individual classifiers estimated within and across the user groups for different classifier ensembles: a) $p = 0.1$; b) $p = 0.2$; c) $p = 0.4$; and d) $p = 1.0$

According to the optimistic estimations, the best accuracy is obtained when the $MOVE$ classifier is involved, in ensemble with BT_DEV (for $p = 0.2, p = 0.4$ and $p = 1.0$) or in ensemble with BT_DEV and $CONT\_NUM$ ($p = 0.1$). The $MOVE$ classifier is also present in the most accurate ensembles according to the pessimistic estimations (except $p = 0.4$). This contradicts the fact that the individual classifications of the $MOVE$ classifier have rather poor accuracy – in terms of base AUC, its accuracy is lower than the accuracy of $PLACES, CONT\_NUM$, or BT_DEV, both when estimated within and across user groups. However, this classifier produces a significantly greater number of classifications than the other classifiers [21], and consequently, achieves the highest value of the normalized AUC. As a result, the ensembles including this classifier are able to produce more accurate classifications than others.

The better accuracy of the $MOVE+BT\_DEV$ ensemble, especially in the case of optimistic estimation, may be attributed to the facts that i) these classifiers deliver more accurate classifications than the others, and ii) the outputs of these classifiers, even when normalized by the modified MP combining rule, are in average smaller than the outputs of the other classifiers. As a result, in the process of combining, other less accurate classifications may distort the outputs of these two classifiers. Such distortion becomes more influential in the case of an optimistic estimation, since the difference between the accuracy of the $MOVE$

and BT_DEV classifiers and the others increases, as compared with the case of the pessimistic estimation.

Overall, the results of the experiments suggest that no single ensemble provides the best accuracy for mobile-masquerader detection across all the range of FR errors. Nevertheless, the results also suggest that for lower values of FR errors (i.e. for $p < 1$), the best classification accuracy can be achieved with the ensembles of two or three classifiers, with the ensemble of two classifiers $(MOVE + BT\_DEV)$ being most accurate according to a majority of estimations (for $p = 0.1$ and $p = 0.2$ according to pessimistic estimations and for $p > 0.1$ according to optimistic estimations). In turn, the three-classifier ensembles $(MOVE + BT\_DEV + CONT\_NUM$ and $PLACES + BT\_DEV + CONT\_NUM)$ less often provide the highest classification accuracy, while providing the second-highest accuracy estimate in several cases. Therefore, in the applications requiring low levels of FR error, the $MOVE + BT\_DEV$ ensemble may be recommended as providing superior classification accuracy. On the other hand, the advantage of the three-classifier ensembles is the involvement of an additional characteristic into the decision-making process. Consequently, the detection mechanism based on a three-classifier ensemble may be more difficult to subvert, as an additional aspect of the user behavior or environment needs to be mimicked by a masquerader.

5   Discussion

In section 2 above, our approach to mobile-masquerader detection based on combining one-class classifiers was introduced, and in the previous section, some of the classifier ensembles to be used for mobile-masquerader detection were evaluated. In this section, the susceptibility of the proposed approach to subversions is discussed, and the imposed resource consumption is analyzed.

5.1   Resisting Subversions

In the proposed mobile-masquerader detection approach, a limited number of measures are monitored, and a situation can be envisioned, in which this approach would be subverted. It is possible, for instance, that none of the measures will be available when the masquerader uses the terminal, and therefore, no alert will be triggered. In the experiments, the best results were achieved with the monitoring of the terminal's moves, the neighboring Bluetooth devices, and possibly the dialed numbers. If the masquerader's goal is the disclosure of the information stored locally on the terminal (contact numbers, notes, etc.), this goal can be achieved without triggering any of the abovementioned actions. Therefore, the proposed approach can be said to be susceptible to the mimicry attack, consisting in a modification of a traditional attack so that it would become undetectable by the intrusion detection mechanism [39].

On the other hand, the involvement of several measures into the process of masquerader detection makes the detection more difficult to subvert, since several aspects of the legitimate user's environment need to be mimicked simultaneously by a masquerader. As indicated by the experimental results presented in section 4, the superiority of ensembles (in terms of accuracy) depends on the FR error level, and according to the pessimistic estimation, the $MOVE + BT\_DEV$ or $PLACES + BT\_DEV + CONT\_NUM$ are superior when lower levels of the FR errors are required. However, the latter is more difficult to subvert, as three characteristics are involved in the detection; therefore, the $PLACES + BT\_DEV + CONT\_NUM$ ensemble might be prefered.

In order to avoid detection, a masquerader in principle can disable the masquerader detection software. In addition, the masquerader might gradually train the detection mechanism to accept the masquerader's behavior as normal. These arguments suggest that the proposed detection mechanism does not represent a comprehensive security solution, and should be used together with other security mechanisms.

5.2 Resource Consumption

Several types of resources have to be taken into account when running a system on a mobile terminal: storage, CPU usage, local I/O capacity, network capacity, and battery consumption. In the case of collecting the above mentioned data and running an on-line analysis algorithm on it, CPU usage as such tends not to be the problem, but its effect on battery consumption may be. If the algorithm is run on the terminal, network resources are not needed. The smartphone operating system has been carefully built to allow concurrent file-system access without adverse effects on other I/O resources; thus, I/O is not a real concern. Therefore, the storage and the battery consumption represent the main constraints for the deployment of the masquerader detection software.

The software involved in the masquerader detection can be divided into the part responsible for monitoring and data collection (sensors), and the part responsible for processing collected data (classifiers and combining schemes). Furthermore, the storage includes the code and data constituents.

The classifiers and combinations thereof, if implemented in Java, require approximately 120–190kB, depending on the classifiers used. The sizes of user profiles vary between 163kB and 252kB (if the three-classifier ensemble $PLACES + BT\_DEV + CONT\_NUM$ is used). The generalized data collection software requires about 1 megabyte of disk for installation and 1 MB (heap) + 0.75 MB (code) = 1.75 MB of memory to run. Additional data stored on disk needs about 200k. This on its own fits even in the lowest-end smartphones, although it does restrict the ability to run other applications on the first generation devices (Nokia 7650) with around 3.5 MB of user memory and 3 MB of disk (the word 'disk' here is used to denote non-volatile memory, normally Flash). On second generation devices (Nokia 6600) the user memory has been increased to about 12MB and disk to 6MB, which basically means that running the software does not inhibit other use of the device. The amount of disk and memory capacity for the code can be reduced to about half of these figures, if a less generic framework is employed.

The battery consumption for data collection and analysis is difficult to estimate analytically. Mobile phones have complex power management schemes, with chips and buses running in different power modes depending on activity, dynamically adjusted core voltages and heavy assumptions on typical use cases. Adding constantly running background tasks evidently will adversely affect the perceived battery consumption, the question is: how much?

Although the battery consumption is hard to calculate, it can be measured. In actual use, the data collection, including Bluetooth scanning, and analysis will reduce the stand-by time of a Series 60 phone to about three days (from 7-8 days without). The Bluetooth scanning is the single most energy-consuming task in this case. Changing the scanning frequency will affect the battery consumption.

In the experiments, the software implementing classifiers and ensembles was run on a standalone PC, not on a smartphone. Therefore, the estimations above exclude the battery consumption due to the classification routines. However, the experience from running similar algorithms on a smartphone indicate that slight additional processing after an event occurrence does not have a measurable impact on battery life.

Based on the discussion above, the conclusion can be made that it is feasible to deploy and run the proposed masquerader detection mechanism on available smartphones, with the main limiting factor being the battery capacity.

6   Concluding Remarks

Due to the small size of mobile-terminals, they are easily subject to a loss or a theft. As a result, the resources available through these terminals may be accessed by an unauthorized person masquerading as a legitimate user of the terminal.

In this study, the problem of mobile-masquerader detection is approached as an anomaly detection problem, where the anomalies in user behavior and environment are detected by an ensemble of one-class classifiers whose individual classifications are subsequently combined. Some of the classifier ensembles to be used for mobile-masquerader detection were experimentally evaluated on a dataset describing the behavior of nine mobile users.

The accuracy was estimated by distinguishing between the users within the groups of affiliated people, as well as by distinguishing the users not acquainted with each other. In the former, worst-case scenario, the classification task was more challenging for the classifiers, and the produced accuracy estimation is rather pessimistic. On the other hand, in the latter, best-case scenario, the classification task was easier for the classifiers, since little or no commonalities in the behavior and environment was registered for the users not acquainted with each other. Consequently, the produced accuracy estimation is rather optimistic. Therefore, the classification accuracy of the explored ensembles in real-world masquerader detection scenarios may be usually expected to lie between the boundaries represented by the pessimistic and the optimistic estimations above.

The classification accuracy was also evaluated for different levels of FR errors. According to the obtained pessimistic accuracy estimation, for lower values of the FR error, superior accuracy is achieved with the two-classifier ensemble $MOVE + BT\_DEV$ or (for $p = 0.4$) with the three-classifier ensemble $PLACES + BT\_DEV + CONT\_NUM$. The two-classifier ensemble above has been also found superior according to the optimistic accuracy estimations. On the other hand, the three-classifier ensemble above grounds its classifications on three characteristics of user environment, and hence is more resistant to subversions than the two-classifier ensemble. Therefore, while the $PLACES + BT\_DEV + CONT\_NUM$ ensemble yields slightly to the two-classifier ensemble in accuracy, the use of the former ensemble may be more reasonable from the resistance to subversions point of view.

Due to the use of real data in the experiments, the results are likely to be generalizable. On the other hand, the behavior of a limited number of users was recorded in the dataset, and these users may reflect the behavior of mobile users in general imperfectly. Therefore, the reported results may need to be refined in further research, using larger datasets that account the behavior of a larger population of mobile users.

Further work is needed also in other directions. First, the design of some of the base classifiers may be subject to improvement. Second, in further work, additional classifiers based on other characteristics and measures may be investigated. Finally, in the experiments, it was assumed that the behavior of impostors may be approximated by the behavior of other users. Whether such approximation is accurate enough remains a question for further study.

Acknowledgments. This work was partly supported by the COMAS Graduate School and the Information Technology Research Institute of the University of Jyväskylä. The Context project was funded by the Academy of Finland under the PROACT research program. The authors would like to thank anonymous reviewers for valuable comments and suggestions.

References

1. Pointsec Mobile Technologies: IT professionals turn blind eye to mobile security as survey reveals sloppy handheld habits. Pointsec news releases, Available from http://www.pointsec.com/news/release.cfm?PressId=108 (read 09.02.2006) (2005)
2. Pointsec Mobile Technologies: Half of all corporate PDAs unprotected despite employer risk. Pointsec News Letter 2, Available from http://www.pointsec.com/news/mediakit/ (read 09.02.2006) (2004)
3. Schonlau, M., DuMouchel, W., Ju, W., Karr, A., Theus, M., Vardi, Y.: Computer intrusion: Detecting masquerades. Statistical Science **16**(1) (2001) 58–74
4. Sequeira, K., Zaki, M.: ADMIT: anomaly-based data mining for intrusions. In Hand, D., Keim, D., Ng, R., eds.: Proceedings of the eighth ACM SIGKDD international conference on Knowledge discovery and data mining, Edmonton, Alberta, Canada, ACM Press (2002) 386–395
5. Maxion, R.A., Townsend, T.N.: Masquerade detection using truncated command lines. In: Proceedings of the International Conference on Dependable Systems and Networks, Los Alamitos, California, IEEE Computer Society Press (2002) 219–228

6. Lane, T., Brodley, C.E.: An empirical study of two approaches to sequence learning for anomaly detection. Machine Learning **51**(1) (2003) 73–107
7. Shavlik, J., Shavlik, M.: Selection, combination, and evaluation of effective software sensors for detecting abnormal computer usage. In: Proceedings of the 2004 ACM SIGKDD international conference on Knowledge discovery and data mining, ACM Press (2004) 276–285
8. Ray, I., Poolsapassit, N.: Using attack trees to identify malicious attacks from authorized insiders. In de Capitani di Vimercati, S., Syverson, P., Gollmann, D., eds.: Proceedings of ESORICS 2005. Volume 3679 of Lecture Notes in Computer Science., Springer-Verlag GmbH (2005) 231–246
9. Clarke, N.L., Furnell, S.M.: Authenticating mobile phone users using keystroke analysis. International Journal of Information Security (2006) 1–14
10. Mäntyjärvi, J., Lindholm, M., Vildjiounaite, E., Mäkelä, S.M., Ailisto, H.: Identifying users of portable devices from gait pattern with accelerometers. In: Proc. Of IEEE International Conference on Acoustics, Speech, and Signal Processing. Volume II. (2005) 973–976
11. Sun, B., Yu, F., Wu, K., Leung, V.C.M.: Mobility-based anomaly detection in cellular mobile networks. In Jakobsson, M., Perrig, A., eds.: Proceedings of the 2004 ACM workshop on Wireless security, ACM Press (2004) 61–69
12. Fawcett, T., Provost, F.J.: Adaptive fraud detection. Data Mining and Knowledge Discovery **1**(3) (1997) 291–316
13. Samfat, D., Molva, R.: IDAMN: An intrusion detection architecture for mobile networks. IEEE Journal on Selected Areas in Communications **15**(7) (1997) 1373–1380
14. Howard, P., Gosset, P.: D20 - Project final report and results of trials. AS-PeCT: Advanced security for personal communications technologies. Final report AC095/VOD/W31/DS/P/20/E (1998)
15. Hollmen, J.: User Profiling and Classification for Fraud Detection in Mobile Communications Networks. PhD thesis, Helsinki University of Technology (2000)
16. Kumar, S.: Classification and Detection of Computer Intrusions. Ph.D. thesis, Purdue University, West Lafayette, USA (1995)
17. Tax, D.: One-class classification. Ph.D. thesis, Delft University of Technology (2001)
18. Obaidat, M.S., Sadoun, B.: Verification of computer users using keystroke dynamics. IEEE Trans. Syst. Man, and Cybernet. Part B: Cybernet. **27**(2) (1997) 261–269
19. Gunetti, D., Picardi, C.: Keystroke analysis of free text. ACM Trans. Inf. Syst. Secur. **8**(3) (2005) 312–347
20. Mazhelis, O., Puuronen, S.: Characteristics and measures for mobile-masquerader detection. In Dowland, P., Furnell, S., Thuraisingham, B., Wang, X.S., eds.: Proc. IFIP TC-11 WG 11.1 & WG 11.5 Joint Working Conference on Security Management, Integrity, and Internal Control in Information Systems, Springer Science+Business Media (2005) 303–318
21. Mazhelis, O., Puuronen, S., Raento, M.: Evaluating classifiers for mobile-masquerader detection. In Fischer-Hübner, S., Rannenberg, K., Yngström, L., Lindskog, S., eds.: Security and Privacy in Dynamic Environments. Volume 201 of IFIP International Federation for Information Processing., Boston, Springer (2006) 271–283

22. Anderson, D., Lunt, T., Javitz, H., Tamaru, A., Valdes, A.: Detecting unusual program behavior using the statistical components of NIDES. SRI Technical Report SRI-CRL-95-06, Computer Science Laboratory, SRI International, Menlo Park, California (1995)

23. Burge, P., Shawe-Taylor, J.: Detecting cellular fraud using adaptive prototypes. In Fawcett, T., ed.: Technical Report of AAAI-97 Workshop on AI Approaches to Fraud Detection and Risk Management, WS-97-07, AAAI Press (1997) 1–8

24. Ye, N., Chen, Q.: An anomaly detection technique based on a chi-square statistic for detecting intrusions into information systems. Quality and Reliability Engineering International 17(2) (2001) 105–112

25. Aggarwal, C.C., Yu, P.S.: Outlier detection for high dimensional data. In: Proceedings of the 2001 ACM SIGMOD international conference on Management of data, ACM Press (2001) 37–46

26. Eskin, E., Arnold, A., Prerau, M., Portnoy, L., Stolfo, S.: A Geometric Framework for Unsupervised Anomaly Detection: Detecting Intrusions in Unlabeled Data. In: Data Mining for Security Applications. Kluwer (2002)

27. Xu, L., Krzyzak, A., Suen, C.Y.: Methods for combining multiple classifiers and their applications to handwriting recognition. IEEE Transactions on Systems, Man, and Cybernetics 22(3) (1992) 418–435

28. Dasarathy, B.V.: Decision Fusion. IEEE Computer Society Press (1994)

29. Raento, M., Oulasvirta, A., Petit, R., Toivonen, H.: Contextphone, a prototyping platform for context-aware mobile applications. IEEE Pervasive Computing 4(2) (2005)

30. Oulasvirta, A., Raento, M., Tiitta, S.: Contextcontacts: Re-designing smartphone's contact book to support mobile awareness and collaboration. In: Proceedings of the 7th International Conference on Human Computer Interaction with Mobile Devices and Services, MOBILEHCI'05, ACM (2005) 167–174

31. Duda, R.O., Hart, P.E., Stork, D.G.: Pattern Classification. Second edn. John Wily & Sons, Inc., New York (2000)

32. Kittler, J., Hatef, M., Duin, R.P., Matas, J.: On combining classifiers. IEEE Transactions on Pattern Analysis and Machine Intelligence 20(3) (1998) 226–239

33. Puuronen, S., Tsymbal, A.: Local feature selection with dynamic integration of classifiers. Fundamenta Informaticae, Special Issue "Intelligent Information Systems" 47(1-2) (2001) 91–117

34. Kuncheva, L.: A theoretical study on six classifier fusion strategies. IEEE Transactions on Pattern Analysis and Machine Intelligence 24(2) (2002) 281–286

35. Mazhelis, O., Puuronen, S.: Combining one-class classifiers for mobile-user substitution detection. In Seruca, I., Filipe, J., Hammoudi, S., Cordeiro, J., eds.: Proceedings of the 6th International Conference on Enterprise Information Systems (ICEIS 2004). Volume 4., Portugal, INSTICC Press (2004) 130–137

36. Witten, I.H., Frank, E.: Data Mining: Practical Machine Learning Tools and Techniques. Morgan Kaufmann Publishers (2000)

37. Hanley, J.A., McNeil, B.J.: The meaning and use of the area under a receiver operating characteristic (ROC) curve. Radiology 143 (1982) 29–36

38. Maxion, R.A., Roberts, R.R.: Proper use of roc curves in intrusion/anomaly detection. Technical Report Series CS-TR-871, School of Computing Science, University of Newcastle (2004)

39. Wagner, D., Soto, P.: Mimicry attacks on host-based intrusion detection systems. In Atluri, V., ed.: CCS '02: Proceedings of the 9th ACM conference on Computer and communications security, New York, NY, USA, ACM Press (2002) 255–264 General Chair-Sushil Jajodia and Program Chair-Ravi Sandhu.

An Enhanced N-Way Exchange-Based Incentive Scheme for P2P File Sharing (Short Paper)*

Lingli Deng[1,2], Yeping He[1], Ziyao Xu[1,2], and Chunyang Yuan[1,2]

[1] Institute of Software, Chinese Academy of Sciences, Beijing 100080, PRC
[2] Graduate School of the Chinese Academy of Sciences, Beijing 100049, PRC
{denglingli, yphe, ccxu}@ercist.iscas.ac.cn, chunyang03@ios.cn

Abstract. Cooperation between participants is essential to P2P applications' viability. Due to obscure possibility to match peers' needs and supplies in pairs, the widely used pair-wise exchange-based incentive schemes perform poorly. The N-way exchange-based incentive scheme enlarges the matching possibility by introducing n person exchanges. But some old problems remain and some new ones emerge with the N-way design. In this paper we present an enhanced n-way exchange-based incentive scheme for P2P file sharing systems. By distributing extra tasks to all the peers involved in an n-way exchange, the proposed scheme eliminates prohibitive computation and communication cost on the cooperators, resulting in greater efficiency, effectiveness, and security.

Keywords: Peer-to-Peer Security, Incentives for Cooperation, Incentives for Enforcement, Exchange-Based Incentive Schemes, Fake Object Attacks.

1 Introduction

As other distributed systems, peer-to-peer file sharing systems rely on the cooperation of autonomous self-interested peers to achieve their global goals. The symmetric relationship between these so-called servents (i.e. the combination of server and client) dictates the traditional cooperative mode, in which the server are motivated and trusted to provide the expected service to its clients, is not applicable any more. Instead, there is an inherent tension between individual rationality and collective welfare[1]. "Free-riders", users who attempt to use the resources of others without contributing their own, manifest to be a severe problem: it was found in 2000, that in the Gnutella, approximately 70% of peers were free-riding[2]; five years later, the number has increased to 85%[3]. Similar problems caused by the lack of incentive for cooperation pervade nearly all the popular P2P file-sharing networks[4][5][6]. And the characteristics of P2P

---

* Supported by National High-Tech Research and Development Program of China (863) under Grant No. 2002AA141080; National Natural Science Foundation of China under Grant No.60073022 and 60373054; Graduate Student Innovation Grant of Chinese Academy of Sciences.

P. Ning, S. Qing, and N. Li (Eds.): ICICS 2006, LNCS 4307, pp. 322–331, 2006.

systems (e.g. large population and high turnover, asymmetry of interest, collusion, zero-cost identity, and traitors[7]) call for an effective, efficient and secure incentive mechanism to alleviate or overcome the free-rider problem.

The term "incentive" can be seen as remuneration for peers' transactional behaviors[8]. According to remuneration type, existing incentive schemes fall into three major categories: exchange-based, reputation-based and monetary schemes. Exchange-based incentive scheme possesses several elegant features, making it the most desirable alternative in a distributed environment without a centralized authority[9]: It's simple, no centralized authority or dedicated infrastructure is needed like the monetary schemes do; and it's safer than the reputation-based schemes for its immunity to collusion through direct object exchanging. However, primitive pair-wise exchange schemes with the simple tit-for-tat strategy[10][11], are performing unsatisfactorily[12], due to the difficulty for the serving peer to predict which one he is serving to would be serving him in the future. Thus he has to be unnecessarily generous in giving. And this extra generosity can be exploited by tactful free-riders. The problem can be conquered by extending the pair-wise exchange to an n-way pattern[13], where every cooperator gets from its directly upstream peer and gives to its directly downstream peer along a n-way exchange ring. However, the burden of locating and verifying candidate exchange rings, which is put entirely onto the responding peers' shoulders, weakens the incentive for these serving but also rational peers to enforce the n-way scheme, and ultimately erodes its effectiveness in suppressing free-riding. Moreover, in exchange-based schemes there's no explicit incentive for rich peers not currently in need to cooperate.

In this paper we present an enhanced n-way exchange-based incentive scheme for P2P file sharing systems. By distributing extra tasks to all the peers involved in an n-way exchange, the proposed scheme eliminates prohibitive computation and communication cost on the cooperators, resulting in greater efficiency, effectiveness, and security.

The rest of the paper is organized as follows. In Section 2 we describe related work on incentive mechanisms for P2P systems. In Section 3 we present the existing design of exchange-based incentive scheme by[13], and analyze the complexities of its locating procedure and the limited effectiveness of incentive it provides. In Section 4 we describe the Distributed Exchange Ring Locating(DERL) procedure for our enhanced n-way exchange-based incentive scheme in detail, highlighting several key design issues in terms of efficiency and security. Finally, a conclusion is given in Section 5.

2 Related Work

In monetary schemes, the service consumer pays (real money or virtual currency) to the service provider[14][15]. Despite their flexibility and fine-grained control, monetary schemes are the most expensive to deploy, for they require some underlying accounting and micropayments infrastructure.

Under exchange-based or monetary schemes, peers tend to be short-sighted, for they require an immediate reward in return. If not currently in need, a rich peer has little incentive to cooperate. While reputation-based schemes, featured with delayed reward in return for the serving peer, are naturally immune to this problem.

Under a reputation-based scheme, peers maintain records of the transactional behavior history for others, and base their decision of cooperating or not on these records. Two kinds of reputations are currently in use: private reputation and shared reputation. Private reputation is recorded by individuals, often not shared with others. Private history-based schemes provide ample opportunities for reciprocation between peer-pairs in applications with long session durations and relatively small population; e.g. the Tit-for-tat incentive mechanism in BitTorrent[10]and eMule[11]. Private reputation scheme is cheat-proof, since there is no incentive for a peer to modify its own private records of others. But it does not scale well with the system population. In open file-sharing P2P networks, it is likely that most of time, an individual would be dealing with a total stranger, and their relationship does not last long enough for the server to gain its benefit from the client[16]. Shared reputation addresses these problems through a global reputation propagation procedure, either distributed ([16][18]) or centralized [17][19]. Besides the considerable computation and communication overhead introduced, the sharing of reputation data leaves the hole for collusion[7][20].

3   Exchange-Based Incentive Schemes

Pair-wise exchange incentive schemes based on tit-for-tat strategy have been adopted by real-world P2P file-sharing systems[10][11]. But their performance is limited in systems with large population and great diversity of interest, for it's relatively rare to match users in pairs. In [13], the authors conquer this limit by extending exchanges into an n-way pattern. Incentive for cooperation here is the priority given by the system to exchange over non-exchange transfers. If the peer does not providing anything in return, it will not be included in any exchange transfer.

The n-way scheme's improved effectiveness comes at the expense of the prohibitive ring locating procedure. Each peer maintains a Request Tree (RT) and sends it along with the object request to another peer. A's RT_A consists of itself, as the root, and the set of RTs as the first-level sub-trees, each corresponds to an entry in A's Incoming Request Queue (IRQ). Then, A can initiate an n-way exchange if any peer in the RT_A owns an object desired by A. More specifically, to locate a exchange ring including itself, A has to: 1) before issuing a request for object o_e, inspect the entire RT_A to see if any peer provides o_e; 2) when receiving a request r, inspect its RT_r, for any object that A still wants. If a ring is located, A must also circulate a token along the ring to determine whether everyone is still willing to serve.

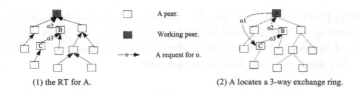

(1) the RT for A.   (2) A locates a 3-way exchange ring.

Fig. 1. Ring location in N-way Exchange [13]

For example, in Fig.1, peer A's RT_A is illustrated in (1). If C possesses o_1 wanted by A, then there exists a candidate exchange ring of A, B and C, by which A would get o_1 from C, B gets o_2 from A, and C gets o_3 from A. To locate a potential ring, before A ask others for o_1, first, it will use the resource locating mechanism provided by the system to find out a set of peers, $S(o_1)$, in possession of o_1; then, it inspects its RT_A for any $p \in S(o_1)$, if at this point the RT_B is included in RT_A, it can find C and locate the ring; otherwise if nobody in A's RT_A owns o_1, A will put $(o_1, S(o_1))$ in its wanted list, W_A, and sends a request $Req(A, o_1, RT'_A)$ to others. When the incoming request $Req(B, o_2, RT'_B)$ to A arrives, A will search in its RT_B for every entry in W_A, and finds out that $C \in S(o_1)$, and locates the exchange ring.

While remaining the inherent weak incentive for non-exchange cooperation, this extension from pair-wise to n-way exchange brings forward new issues on efficiency and security. Despite that the authors have empirically determined that it is sufficient to limit the search for cycles to chains of up to 5 predecessors, the cost of communicating the full RT may still be prohibitive for peers with a large number of incoming requests and their neighborhood in the request graph[21]. To make things worse, the above ring locating procedure puts all the burden of searching and checking for exchange rings on the serving peer (i.e. the responding peer). This design can be improved in the following aspects:

1. **Efficiency.** It is expensive, with the worst case overhead of $O(N)$, in which N represents the population of the system. In large open systems, this scale of overhead for a single transaction is unbearable for a single peer. Since for each ring locating operation, a resource locating operation (to find out who owns the one you need)is required. There is additional communication overhead weighing from $O(N)$(flooding) to $O(logN)$ (DHT).

2. **Effectiveness.** It is ineffective as an incentive scheme. And it deduces another kind of free-riding behavior. The more file it shares, the more extra computation and communication tasks a peer has to fulfill. Thus, it is reasonable to believe that it is irrational for the sharing peers to blindly enforce the proposed n-way scheme. Being patient enough, a self-interested peer may prefer to directly forward any incoming request with its RT, in the hope of free-riding on its successor to perform all the task. The disincentive against free-riding if ever provided will be very limited if most cooperative peers behave rationally and refusing to follow the scheme.

3. **Security.** It is insecure because the computation and communication burden on the serving peers can easily be exploited by malicious peers to launch DOS (Denial of Service) attacks against them, or even against the whole system if most behaved peers do follow the scheme.

4   Enhancing the N-Way Scheme with DERL

In this section we present our enhanced exchange-based incentive scheme, based upon the work of[13], for a file sharing system where every request is in the form of a single object (a relatively large and fixed-size block), and peers can download different parts of the same file concurrently. A candidate exchange ring to be used by peers are located during a Distributed Exchange Ring Locating procedure (DERL) by the cooperation of all the peers involved. The fact that no one could depend on others to locate or search for exchange rings strengthens the incentive for the peers to strictly enforce the proposed scheme.

4.1   DERL: The Basic Idea

A pair-wise DERL is straightforward (See Fig. 2) The requestor Bob issues a request for object o_2, $req(Bob, o_2)$, to the responder $Alice$. Receiving $req(Bob, o_2)$, $Alice$ makes sure that she does own o_2 at the moment, decides the object o_1 she wants currently in exchange for o_2 and then acknowledges Bob's request with $ack(o_1 : Alice|o_2 : Bob)$. If Bob owns o_1, he then locates a pair-wise exchange ring $Ring(Alice : o_2|Bob : o_1)$.

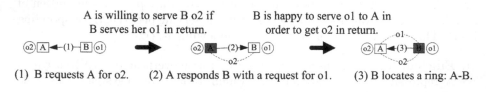

A is willing to serve B o2 if   B is happy to serve o1 to A in
B serves her o1 in return.   order to get o2 in return.

(1) B requests A for o2.   (2) A responds B with a request for o1.   (3) B locates a ring: A-B.

Fig. 2. DERL: A 2-way Example

If Bob does not have o_1 (see the first row in Fig. 3), he checks with his IRQ_B, picks up a request $req(Cindy, o_3)$. After checking he has o_3, Bob includes a forwarded request for o_1 on behalf of $Alice$ in acknowledging $Cindy$, by sending $ack(o_1 : Alice|o_2 : Bob|o_3 : Cindy)$ to her. This message informs $Cindy$ that Bob agrees to give her o_3, if she delivers o_1 to $Alice$. If $Cindy$ owns o_1, she locates a 3-way exchange ring, $Ring(Alice : o_2|Bob : o_3|Cindy : o_1)$. Otherwise, $Cindy$ chooses some of its incoming requestors, and forwards them the acknowledge message from Bob appended with some extra information about itself. And so the recursive procedure goes on and on until some pre-set limit is reached (e.g. the total number of participants in a single ring preset by the system designer), or a candidate exchange ring is located.

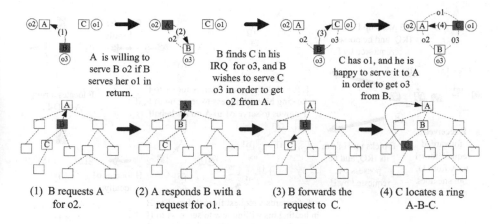

(1) B requests A   (2) A responds B with a   (3) B forwards the   (4) C locates a ring
    for o2.   request for o1.   request to C.   A-B-C.

Fig. 3. Understanding DERL with VRTs: A 3-way Example

We argue that DERL covers every valid candidate exchange rings that the Request Tree mechanism proposed in[13]can locate, except those invalid ones whose participants are no longer in need. This fact is better understood if we review DERL in the context of a "virtual RT" (VRT) of the serving peer (see Fig. 3).

4.2 DERL with Object Sets

Several candidate rings rooted at one peer can be located simultaneously by DERL. For example, although in Fig. 3, a 3-way ring has been located already, the DERL procedure on other independent branches of the "virtual request tree" rooted at *Alice* continues, and two more rings $r2 = Ring(Alice : o_2|David : o_3|Emily : o_4|Fred : o_1)$,$r3 = Ring(Alice : o_2|David : o_3|Emily : o_4|Harry : o_1)$ are located as well. These two rings share common edges from *Alice* to *Emily* via *David*, and they are both independent (sharing no common edges) to the previously $r1 = Ring(Alice : o_2|Bob : o_3|Cindy : o_1)$. DERL's ability of locating multiple rings can be used in two ways:

1. Provided with several candidate rings for a single object, *Alice* can choose the best of them based on several carefully chosen metrics, e.g. the trustworthiness of peers involved, the length of the exchange ring, etc.
2. *Alice* can benefit further by issuing a object set $O_A(o_2)$ including all the objects she wants in exchange of o_2. This modification can be fruitful for three reasons.
   (a) It enables *Alice* to evaluate its cost of delivering o_2 to *Bob* when forming $O_A(o_2)$, and maximize the benefit she could get in return by choosing to participate in the exchange ring from which she gets the most desirable one in $O_A(o_2)$.

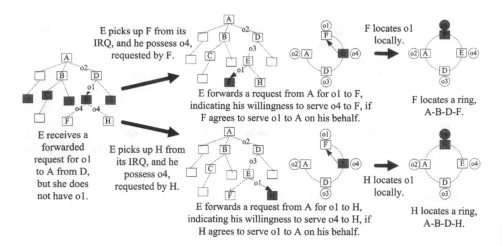

Fig. 4. Multiple Rings Located in a Single Instance of DERL: An Example

(b) *Bob* now has much greater chance of locating an ring with *Alice* since he would succeeds if he owns any $o_x \in O_A(o_2)$, and so does all his successors (the peers located under *Bob* in its *VRT*). If *Bob* owns several objects in $O_A(o_2)$, he can bargain with her by delivering the one with the least cost.

(c) Different exchange rings can be located simultaneously for different objects in $O_A(o_2)$, further benefiting *Alice*.

The pseudo-code description of DERL with object sets is given as follows:(For any peer p_i in the system, we use p_{ic} and p_{is} to denote its dual identities participating DERL, as the requestor and the server, respectively.)

1. **As the requestor in a transaction:** (p_{ic})

   (a) p_{ic} locates the desired object o_{ic} to its current provider p_s, sends $req(p_{ic}, o_{ic})$ to p_s, and waits for the response.

   (b) Upon receiving $ack(O_{p_1}(o_2) : p_1|o_2 : p_2| \cdots |o_{n-2} : p_{n-2}|o_s : p_s|o_{ic} : p_{ic})$ from p_s, p_{ic} searches locally for any $o_{ix} \in O_{p_1}(o_2)$.

   i. If p_{ic} finds a set of objects, it locates a set of candidate n-way exchange ring in the form of $Ring(p_1 : o_2|p_2 : o_3| \cdots |p_s : o_{ic}|p_{ic} : o_{1x})$. p_{ic} exits.

   ii. Otherwise, p_{ic} searches its *IRQ* for any request from p_1. If he finds a local request set $S_{o_i}(p_1)$, P_{ic} locates a set of candidate n-way exchange ring in the form of $Ring(p_1 : o_2|p_2 : o_3| \cdots |p_s : o_{ic}|p_{ic} : o_{1y})$ for each $o_{1y} \in S_{oi}(p_1)$. p_{ic} exits.

   iii. Otherwise, p_{ic} selects a subset of requestors from its own *IRQ*, $S_{p_i}(O_{p_1}(o_2), p_1)$. To each $p_{ix} \in S_{p_i}(O_{p_1}(o_2), p_1)$ requesting for o_x, if p_{ic} currently owns o_x, p_{ic} sends $ack(O_{p_1}(o_2) : p_1|o_2 : p_2| \cdots |o_{n-2} : p_{n-2}|o_s : p_s|o_{ic} : p_{ic}|o_x : p_{ix})$. p_{ic} exits.

2. **As the responder in a transaction:** (p_{is}) Receiving $req(p_x, o_x)$ from p_x, p_{is} checks locally for o_x. If it succeeds and is willing to exchange o_x with p_x for any $o_{sx} \in O_{p_{is}}(o_x)$, p_{is} acknowledges p_x with $ack(O_{p_{is}}(o_x) : p_{is}|o_x : p_x)$.

4.3 Selecting Compatible Rings After DERL

Although three exchange rings have been located during the DERL procedure in Fig. 4, only one of them will be put into real use, since normally $Alice$ wouldn't want to download o_1 more than once. In other words, these three are mutually incompatible. We can define the compatibility relationship on $\mathbb{R}$ as follows:

Definition 1. *Upon the set of candidate exchange rings $\mathbb{R}$, the set of peers in the system $\mathbb{P}$, and the total set of exchangeable objects in the system $\mathbb{O}$, We define the function $o : \mathbb{R} \times \mathbb{P} \mapsto \mathbb{O} \cup \{null\}$ as follows:*

$$\forall r \in \mathbb{R}, \forall p \in \mathbb{P}: \qquad o(r,p) = \begin{cases} o_x & , \text{if } p \text{ participates } r \text{ to get } o_x \\ null & , \text{otherwise} \end{cases}.$$

Definition 2. *The compatibility relationship between any two candidate rings:*

$$\forall r_i, r_j \in \mathbb{R}, ri \neq r_j :$$
$$Com(r_i, rj) = False \quad iff \quad \exists p \in \mathbb{P} : o(r_i, p) = o(r_j, p) \neq null.$$

For example, the three rings illustrated in Fig. 3 and Fig. 4, r_1, r_2 and r_3 are mutually incompatible, since they all provides o_1 to $Alice$ if put to use.

Note that we assume a rational peer will never download an object twice. Therefore, at any point of time, any two rings currently in use in the system must be compatible. The compatibility relationship can be used by participants when making decision in the exchange ring validating procedure following DERL with candidate exchange rings. e.g. if $Alice$ has chosen r_1, then she would refuse to participate r_2 or r_3.

4.4 Comparison and Analysis

First of all, DERL is a distributed procedure, involving all the peers along the candidate ring. By distributing the burdensome locating task to the requestor and its requestors recursively, DERL overcomes the prohibitive overhead on a single peer of the original locating procedure in[13], without losing the capacity to locate every possible candidate ring. DERL further improves its efficiency by eliminating outdated braches (request made earlier but has become invalid by the time the locating procedure is executed) in the VRT automatically since a rational peer never submit a request to another peer for what he has already obtained from a third peer.

Second, in [13]'s design, to locate an exchange ring, the requestor's entire RT tree (or a large part of it) is transferred along with every outgoing request. This incurs a huge communication overhead for both parties involved. In our design, this information is reduced to minimum as each peer only maintains its own Incoming Request Queue (IRQ) locally. However, during the DERL, the responder's request message as forwarded by the requestors recursively is growing continuously until the preset ring length limit is reached. The average communication overhead has been reduced from $O(2^{\mathcal{L}})$ to $O(\mathcal{L})$, where $\mathcal{L}$ denotes the average or preset ring length.

Third, DERL provides much stronger incentive for resource-sharing since the requestor can no longer free-ride on the responder forring locating. On one hand, it becomes more convenient for responders to share, encouraging more peers to cooperate or the cooperating peers to cooperate more. On the other hand, since DERL requires a consistent interaction for the requestors with others, it becomes more energy-consuming to submit a request and participate into a exchange transfer, discouraging lavish misbehavior.

Finally, DERL is more robust and efficient, for several rings rooted at one peer can be located simultaneously during a single instance of DERL's execution. While in the previous work, due to the prohibitive cost for full RT tree searching, root peer exits searching for an given object as soon as one candidate exchange ring is located. In a dynamic environment like P2P networks, where peers come and go frequently, DERL's capacity to locate more candidates may be the key to succeed. And more candidates indicates more flexibility for the requestor in choosing the provider for a given object, which allows room for more sophisticated security enhancement. For example, integrated with a proper-designed reputation system, DERL can also be used to mitigate the impact of fake object attacks, where dishonest peers try to spoof others into exchanging with fake objects.

5   Conclusion

We presented our enhanced version of n-way exchange-based incentive scheme for P2P file-sharing systems in this paper. Using the Distributed Exchange Ring Locating procedure (DERL), the scheme distributes extra tasks to all the peers in an exchange, eliminates the prohibitive cost on the cooperators, and results in greater efficiency and effectiveness in terms of providing strong incentive to rational peers both for cooperating and enforcing the proposed scheme.

References

1. M. Feldman and J. Chuang. Overcoming Free-Riding Behavior in Peer-to-Peer Systems. In ACM SIGecon Exchanges, Vol. 5, No.4, 2005, pp. 41-50.
2. E. Adar and B. Huberman. Free Riding on Gnutella. FirstMonday, 2000.
3. D. Hughes, G. Coulson, and J. Walkerdine. Freeriding. on Gnutella Revisited: the Bell Tolls? IEEE. Distributed Systems Online, 6(6), 2005.
4. S. Saroiu, P. Krishna Gummadi, and S. D. Gribble. A Measurement Study of Peer-to-Peer File Sharing Systems. In Proc. of the 9th Annual Multimedia Computing and Networking (MMCN), 2002.

5. M. Yang, Z. Zhang, X. Li, et al. An Empirical Study of Free-Riding Behavior in the Maze P2P File-Sharing System. In Proc. of the 4th Int'l. Workshop on Peer-To-Peer Systems (IPTPS), 2005.
6. J. Pouwelse, P. Garbacki, D. Epema, et al. The BitTorrent P2P File-sharing System: Measurements and Analysis. In Proc. of the 4th Int'l. Workshop on Peer-To-Peer Systems (IPTPS), 2005.
7. M. Feldman, K. Lai, I. Stoica, et al., Robust Incentive Techniques for Peer-to-Peer Networks. In Proc. of the 6th ACM conference on Electronic Commerce, 2004.
8. P. Obreiter, B. Konig-Ries, M. Klein. Stimulating Cooperative Behavior of Autonomous Devices - An Analysis of Requirements and Existing Approaches. In Proc. of the 2nd Int'l. Workshop on Wireless Information Systems (WIS), 2003, pp.71-82.
9. P. Obreiter, J. Nimis. A Taxonomy of Incentive Patterns-The Design Space of Incentives for Cooperation. In Proc. of the 2nd Int'l. Workshop on Agents and P2P Computing, Melbourne, Australia, Springer-Verlag, LNCS 2872, 2003, pp.678-685.
10. B. Cohen. Incentives Build Robustness in BitTorrent. In Proc. of the 1st Workshop on Economics of Peer-to-Peer Systems (P2PECON), 2003.
11. The EMule Project. http://www.emule-project.net
12. S. Jun and M. Ahamad. Incentives in BitTorrent Induce Free Riding. In Proc. of the ACM Symposium on Communications Architectures and Protocols (SIGCOMM), 2005.
13. Kostas G. Anagnostakis and Michael B. Greenwald, Exchange-based Incentive Mechanisms for Peer-to-Peer File Sharing. In Proc. of the 24th int'l. Conference on Distributed Computing Systems (ICDCS), 2004, pp. 524-533.
14. P. Golle and K. Leyton-Brown. Incentives for Sharing in Peer-to-Peer Networks. In Proc. of the 3rd ACM Conference on Electronic Commerce (EC), 2001.
15. Ioannidis, J., Ioannidis, S., Keromytis, A., et al. Fileteller: Paying and Getting Paid for File Storage. In Proc. of the 6th Int'l. Conference on Financial Cryptography (FC),2002.
16. Ernesto Damiani, Sabrina De Capitani di Vimercati, Stefano Paraboschi, Pierangela Samarati: Managing and Sharing Servents' Reputations in P2P Systems. IEEE Trans. Knowl. Data Eng. 15(4): 840-854,2003.
17. M. Gupta, P. Judge, and MH Ammar. A Reputation System for Peer-to-Peer Networks, in Proc. of the 13th Int'l. Workshop on Network and Operating Systems Support for Digital Audio and Video (NOSSDAV), 2003.
18. Kamvar, Schlosser, Garcia-Molina. The EigenTrust Algorithm for Reputation Management in P2P Networks. In: Proc. of the 12th. Int'l Conference on World Wide Web (WWW), 2003.
19. M. Yang, H. Chen, BY Zhao, et al. Deployment of a Large-scale Peer-to-Peer Social Network. In Proc. of WORLDS, San Francisco, CA, 2004.
20. Q. Lian, Z. Zhang, M. Yang, et al. An Empirical Study of Collusion Behavior in the Maze P2P File-Sharing System. Microsoft Research Technical Report, MSR-TR-2006-14, 2006.
21. Kostas G. Anagnostakis. Exchange Mechanism and Cooperative Computing Systems Design. Doctoral Dissertation, University of Pennsylvania, 2005.

Provably Correct Runtime Enforcement of Non-interference Properties*

V.N. Venkatakrishnan[1], Wei Xu[2], Daniel C. DuVarney[2], and R. Sekar[2]

[1] Department of Computer Science, University of Illinois at Chicago,
Chicago, IL 60607
venkat@cs.uic.edu
[2] Department of Computer Science, Stony Brook University,
Stony Brook, NY 11794-4400
{weixu, dand, sekar}@cs.sunysb.edu

Abstract. *Non-interference* has become the standard criterion for ensuring confidentiality of sensitive data in the information flow literature. However, application of non-interference to practical software systems has been limited. This is partly due to the imprecision that is inherent in static analyses that have formed the basis of previous non-interference based techniques. Runtime approaches can be significantly more accurate than static analysis, and have often been more successful in practice. However, they can only reason about explicit information flows that take place via assignments in a program. Implicit flows that take place without involving assignments, and can be inferred from the structure and/or semantics of the program, are missed by runtime techniques. This paper seeks to bridge the gap between the accuracy provided by runtime techniques and the completeness provided by static analysis techniques. In particular, we develop a hybrid technique that relies primarily on runtime information-flow tracking, but augments it with static analysis to reason about implicit flows that arise due to unexecuted paths in a program. We prove that the resulting technique preserves non-interference, while providing some of the traditional benefits of dynamic analysis such as improved accuracy.

1 Introduction

Protecting the privacy of personal information has become one of the main challenges facing the Internet today. Although traditional access control mechanisms can prevent information from being given to unauthorized principals, they don't address the central problem in privacy, namely, *information flow control*. The domain of information flow control begins at the point where sensitive information is handed to a piece of software, and governs the manner in which this software uses this information. The primary concern is whether sensitive information may

---

* This research was supported in part by NSF grants CCR-0098154, CCR-0208877 and CNS-0551660, and an ONR grant N000140110967.

P. Ning, S. Qing, and N. Li (Eds.): ICICS 2006, LNCS 4307, pp. 332–351, 2006.

flow into (or influence) data that may be read by unauthorized principals. In addition to privacy, information flow techniques can also address integrity concerns. The term "taint" is used in place of "information flow" in the context of integrity, and the techniques are concerned with ensuring that untrustworthy data does not influence data whose trustworthiness needs to be preserved.

There are two basic approaches for dealing with information flows in a program: static analysis and runtime-tracking. A static analysis technique has an advantage over runtime-tracking in terms of runtime performance. However, static analysis techniques need to reason about all possible executions of a program, and reject programs that can potentially leak sensitive information in some runs. In particular, the following weaknesses of static analysis techniques make it significantly less accurate than runtime techniques:

- *Approximations needed to ensure termination of static analysis.* Like most problems in program analysis, it is in general undecidable whether a program contains a prohibited information flow. Approximations need to be made in order to produce a decidable procedure, and these approximation will negatively impact accuracy. In contrast, runtime techniques concern themselves only with the execution path that was actually taken at runtime, and hence can remain decidable without having to resort to approximations.
- *Inability to support programs that occasionally leak information.* Consider a program that sends a crash report to its developer, and assume that this report contains sensitive information. Under normal conditions, there may not be any leak. Such a program can be supported by a runtime-tracking technique by simply suppressing unacceptable flows at runtime, i.e., by disallowing the crash report from being sent. A purely static analysis technique would have to altogether disallow any use of such programs.
- *Inability to support applications where data sensitivity is dynamically determined.* Consider a web browser that interacts with a number of web sites, some of which handle sensitive data and the others don't. Thus, the sensitivity of a piece of information received on a communication channel is determined at runtime, based on the identity of the web site providing the information. Naturally, purely static analysis techniques require sensitivity information to be specified statically, and hence have a hard time coping with such applications.

In fact, these precision issues are sufficiently problematic in the related domain of access control so that static analysis is seldom used in these systems. Within the domain of information flow, runtime techniques [7,26,22,8,34] have also enjoyed more practical applications as compared to their static analysis counterparts.

In spite of these precision issues, static analysis has been the predominant technique in recent information flow literature [20,23,2,31]. This is because runtime techniques aren't able to capture so-called *implicit flows* that do not involve explicit assignments, but can be inferred from the structure of the program. For instance, consider the following program, where h contains sensitive data but l should not, since the latter is being printed to a public channel.

```
1  l := 1;
2  if (h == 1) then l := 0;
3  print l;
```

Assume that h take only two values: 0 or 1. In this case, the value of h can be determined from the value of l printed by the program. However, a runtime tracking technique will not be able to infer this dependency, since there were no explicit actions that transfer information from h to l. Consequently, runtime techniques are incomplete with respect to the notion of *noninterference* [14], which formed the basis of all the above static information flow analysis techniques. Noninterference states that the public outputs of a program should not be changed in any way by changes to its sensitive inputs.

It has often been stated that runtime techniques cannot be expected to preserve noninterference since the presence of information flow is dependent on program paths *not taken* during an execution [24]. It seems natural to conclude that runtime techniques, which make their decisions based on the actual execution trace taken at runtime, cannot detect such flows. We present a result in this paper that, on the surface, seems to contradict this "conventional wisdom." In particular, *we present a runtime information-flow tracking technique that preserves non-interference.* Our technique first employs a program transformation approach to encode information flows that take place due to unexecuted paths into other paths that are, in fact, executed. This transformation itself is guided by a static analysis. This transformation contains additional instructions in the program that perform runtime information-flow tracking. In this paper, we present the rules for such a transformation and formally establish that this transformation technique preserves non-interference, i.e., it ensures that no information about the sensitive variables used by a program can be inferred from public outputs of the program.

The nature of programs handled by this approach are those that are single-threaded and deterministic. In this work, we do not address information leaks resulting from timing, storage and termination channels [24]. The rest of the paper is organized as follows. In Section 2, the details of the analysis and transformation are presented, including a small example of its use. In Section 3 the proof of correctness with respect to the non-interference property is presented. Section 4 discusses practical issues in adoption of the runtime enforcement technique. Section 5 discusses related work. Finally, Section 6 provides a summary of our results.

2   The Transformation

The Language. We use a simple imperative language with procedures for our discussion. The syntax of expressions and statements in the language appear in Figure 1. The language has basic arithmetic and logical expressions (composed using binary operators *(bop)* and unary operators *(uop)*), assignments, conditionals, loops, procedure call, sequencing and skip statements. For procedures, a call-by-value semantics is assumed. Otherwise, the semantics of this language

[expr] $\qquad\qquad e ::= c \mid x \mid e_1 \; bop \; e_2 \mid uop \; e_1$

[stmt] $\quad S ::= x := e \mid \text{if } e \text{ then } S_1 \text{ else } S_2 \text{ endif} \mid \text{while } e \text{ do } S_1 \text{ done} \mid$
$\qquad\qquad\quad \text{call } f(e) \mid S_1; S_2 \mid \text{skip}$

Fig. 1. The syntax of expressions and statements in the language

is standard. Also, we focus on a simple presentation where the results of the transformation are un-optimized; optimizations are discussed later.

The variables in the language can have security types *high* and *low*. For instance, a high security variable can represent a sensitive channel from which sensitive information is read by the program. A low security variable can represent a public input or output channel (such as an insecure network read or a print statement), and hence any assignment of sensitive information to these variables constitutes illegal flow of information. For the variables that are not assigned with *high* or *low* security types based on the security policies, they represent intermediate variables and can hold values from high or low security variables because they are not publicly visible. Constants are always of type *low*.

Basic Idea. In our approach, information flow is tracked through the use of *label* variables. The idea is simple: for each variable in the program, a new boolean label variable is created. At runtime, this label variable records the flow of sensitive information into this variable. When execution reaches an assignment statement that assigns to a low security variable, the corresponding label variable is examined for the presence of sensitive data. If such sensitive data is indeed present, the execution of the program is terminated.

For any variable x, let $\mathcal{L}(x)$ denote the label variable that tracks flows to x at any program point. The label variable is a boolean variable and the value stored in a label variable reflects whether a variable contains sensitive information (in which case it is 1), or not. A label value that is 0 denotes the absence of sensitive information. For example, the execution of the statement $x := y + z$ results in updating $\mathcal{L}(x)$ to $\mathcal{L}(y) \vee \mathcal{L}(z)$. Furthermore, if either y or z contain sensitive data read from a high security variable, then their corresponding label variable ($\mathcal{L}(y)$ or $\mathcal{L}(z)$) is set to *true*, and consequently, $\mathcal{L}(x)$ will be *true* after the assignment. In addition, to simplify the notation, for any expression e, we also use $\mathcal{L}(e)$ to denote the label value obtained by the disjunction of all the label variables corresponding to variables appearing in the expression e. So, for the expression $x * z + y$, $\mathcal{L}(x * z + y)$ is $\mathcal{L}(x) \vee \mathcal{L}(z) \vee \mathcal{L}(y)$.

The Analysis. The simple idea illustrated above would work only for explicit flows through assignments. On entering a conditional branch, there is an implicit flow of information from the conditional to all the variables assigned in both the branches. To compute this set of variables a static analysis is used. The results of this analysis (described below) are present in an environment, denoted by Ψ. The transformation then makes use of the results of this analysis. (Our transformation mechanism can make use of a variety of analysis mechanisms, and hence here

$$[\text{ASSIGN1}] \quad \frac{\Gamma \vdash x : \tau \text{ where } \tau \neq low}{x := e \rightarrow_{\Gamma,\Psi} \mathcal{L}(x) := \mathcal{L}(e) \vee \mathcal{L}(pc);}{x := e}$$

$$[\text{ASSIGN2}] \quad \frac{\Gamma \vdash x : \tau \text{ where } \tau = low}{x := e \rightarrow_{\Gamma,\Psi} \mathcal{L}(x) := \mathcal{L}(e) \vee \mathcal{L}(pc);}{\text{call } policy\_check(\mathcal{L}(x));}{x := e}$$

$$[\text{IF}] \quad \frac{pc_1 \text{ is a fresh temporary variable}}{\Psi \vdash x_1, x_2, \ldots, x_n \in Upd(S_1) \cup Upd(S_2) \quad S_1 \rightarrow_{\Gamma,\Psi} S_1^* \quad S_2 \rightarrow_{\Gamma,\Psi} S_2^*}{\text{if } e \text{ then } S_1 \text{ else } S_2 \text{ endif } \rightarrow_{\Gamma,\Psi} \mathcal{L}(pc_1) := \mathcal{L}(pc);}$$
$$\mathcal{L}(pc) := \mathcal{L}(pc) \vee \mathcal{L}(e);$$
$$\text{if } e \text{ then } S_1^* \text{ else } S_2^* \text{ endif};$$
$$\mathcal{L}(x_i) := \mathcal{L}(x_i) \vee \mathcal{L}(pc); \ (1 \leq i \leq n)$$
$$\mathcal{L}(pc) := \mathcal{L}(pc_1)$$

$$[\text{WHILE}] \quad \frac{pc_1 \text{ is a fresh temporary variable}}{\Psi \vdash x_1, x_2, \ldots, x_n \in Upd(S) \quad S \rightarrow_{\Gamma,\Psi} S^*}{\text{while } e \text{ do } S \text{ done } \rightarrow_{\Gamma,\Psi} \mathcal{L}(pc_1) := \mathcal{L}(pc);}$$
$$\mathcal{L}(pc) := \mathcal{L}(pc) \vee \mathcal{L}(e);$$
$$\text{while } e \text{ do}$$
$$S^*;$$
$$\mathcal{L}(pc) := \mathcal{L}(pc) \vee \mathcal{L}(e);$$
$$\text{done};$$
$$\mathcal{L}(x_i) := \mathcal{L}(x_i) \vee \mathcal{L}(pc); \ (1 \leq i \leq n)$$
$$\mathcal{L}(pc) := \mathcal{L}(pc_1)$$

$$[\text{CALL}] \quad \frac{x_1 \text{ is a fresh temporary variable}}{\text{call } f(e) \rightarrow_{\Gamma,\Psi} \mathcal{L}(x_1) := \mathcal{L}(e) \vee \mathcal{L}(pc);}{\text{call } f(e, \mathcal{L}(x_1))}$$

$$[\text{SEQ}] \quad \frac{S_1 \rightarrow_{\Gamma,\Psi} S_1^* \quad S_2 \rightarrow_{\Gamma,\Psi} S_2^*}{S_1; S_2 \rightarrow_{\Gamma,\Psi} S_1^*; S_2^*} \qquad [\text{SKIP}] \quad \frac{}{\text{skip} \rightarrow_{\Gamma,\Psi} \text{skip}}$$

Fig. 2. Transformation $\rightarrow_{\Gamma,\Psi}$, parameterized by Γ (initial type environment that encodes the security policy) and Ψ (results of the static analysis that are used to account for implicit flows)

we only discuss the results that are required from the static analysis; we discuss possible strategies for performing these analysis in a later section.)

The analysis computes the following: If S denotes a (possibly compound) statement, the set $Upd(S)$ denotes all the variables that get assigned in the statement S. The analysis computes a conservative upper bound in case a precise estimation of the set of variables that are updated is not possible.

Using the results of the analysis, the program is transformed such that, on entering a conditional branch, the value of the label variable corresponding to the condition expression (associated with enclosing nested conditionals), is stored in a global variable called $\mathcal{L}(pc)$ that is used to track implicit flows. For all the assignments that happen inside both branches, the label variables of the left-hand side expressions are updated with the value of the implicit flows. This is done by a disjunction with $\mathcal{L}(pc)$. Thus, $\mathcal{L}(pc)$ includes the combined effect of the enclosing conditionals and loops. When a conditional branch is exited, the value of $\mathcal{L}(pc)$ is restored to its previous value that existed before entering the branch.

The type environment Γ represents the initial type assignment of high and low security variables. This environment is directly initialized from the security policy. For all the variables that are typed *high* the label variables are initialized to true. All the other label variables are initialized to false. When a procedure is invoked, the local variables are initialized in a similar fashion.

The transformation. Figure 2 presents the transformation rules in an inference style formalism. The transformation is denoted by the symbol $\rightarrow_{\Gamma,\Psi}$, as it takes as inputs the security-type environment Γ and the results from the static analysis Ψ.

The transformation rules update the label variables to reflect the sensitivity of the information that is contained in the corresponding program variables. In the transformation rules, updates to the label variables according to the kind of the statement are shown. These updates are present in the transformed program and are executed at run-time. We point out that the *policy_check* procedure checks whether the current assignment (to be performed) is legal. It does so by checking the sensitivity of the data being assigned to a low security variable (by checking whether the boolean value corresponding to its argument is true). If so, then the execution is terminated before the actual information leak occurs. This procedure may be defined as follows:

policy_check(var *lab*) { if (*lab*) then **halt** else **skip**; }

Below, we briefly explain the transformation rules.

The transformation rule SKIP for the **skip** statement is obvious. The rule SEQ for the sequential composition statement of statements S_1 and S_2 defines that the individual statements are transformed to S_1^* and S_2^* respectively.

ASSIGN1 involves assignment to a non-low security variable (which is not observable). For this rule, the effect of all label variables of the expression is computed and assigned to the label variable for the variable on the LHS. The label variable $\mathcal{L}(pc)$ is used to account for implicit flows.

For the assignment rule ASSIGN2, the LHS is a low security variable. In addition to performing actions similar to ASSIGN1, care should be exercised to check whether there is an information leak from the expression in the RHS. For this purpose, the procedure *policy_check* is called, which checks the value of the label of the RHS. If it is *true*, then there is a potential information leak, and the program is halted.

The transformation rule IF for the `if-then-else` statement is more complicated. We explain each of the five steps in this transformation. First, the current value of $\mathcal{L}(pc)$ is recorded in a fresh variable $\mathcal{L}(pc_1)$ (for recovering and restoring it after this statement). Secondly, the value of $\mathcal{L}(pc)$ is updated with the value of the label variables of the variables involved in the condition. This is done to account for implicit flows to any assignments to the body of the `then` or `else` branches. In the third step, the transformation is applied further to both branches of the statement. This is done by transforming the individual statements S_1 and S_2 to S_1^* and S_2^* respectively. In the fourth step, the transformation accounts for implicit flows through assignments in both branches. This is done by consulting the results of the analysis for the update sets of statements S_1 and S_2. The union of these sets, represented by $Upd(S_1) \cup Upd(S_2)$, denotes the set of variables that will carry information about the condition expression as a result of implicit flows. We update their label variables with the current value of $\mathcal{L}(pc)$ to account for implicit flows. (The transformation does this for all the variables in the set, $Upd(S_1) \cup Upd(S_2)$. This is shown in the transform rule for variables $x_1, x_2, \ldots, x_n$ in this set.) Finally, in the fifth step, the value of $\mathcal{L}(pc)$ is restored to the value it originally had before entering the conditional (through the use of $\mathcal{L}(pc_1)$).

Notice that the transformation rule WHILE for the `while` statement is similar to the `if-then-else` statement. To account for implicit flows into variables from the expression in the condition, the value of $\mathcal{L}(pc)$ is augmented with the value of the expression e, before and during each iteration of the loop. (The loop may modify the variables in the expression, and therefore the expression's label value may change). The labels of variables assigned in the loop (such as x_i), are updated after the loop to account for implicit flows from e. (Inside the body, the labels of such variables are updated in the corresponding assignment statements). The body of the `while` statement is then transformed. Note that $\mathcal{L}(pc)$ is restored after the execution of the *while* statement to its original value. (Note that, for an external observer who could observe the timing/termination effects of programs, this could leak one bit of information about the condition. However, we do not address timing/termination channels in this work.)

As shown in the transformation rule CALL, a `call` statement is transformed as follows: A fresh label variable corresponding to the call argument expression is created. Then the flows for each of the individual variables in the expression is accounted for through $\mathcal{L}(e)$. Finally, a call to the transformed procedure (which is explained below) is made with this additional argument.

The transformation of procedure definitions is done in a similar fashion (not shown in figure). The procedure is modified to include an additional label variable for the argument to the procedure. Further, label variables corresponding to local variables are created. The statement body is then transformed according to the above mentioned rules.

Figure 3 (a) & (b) show a program fragment and its transformed version respectively. In the transformed program, a label variable $\mathcal{L}(x)$ is denoted by x'.

1 $x := 1;$	1 $x' := pc';$ $x := 1;$
2 $y := 1;$	2 $y' := pc';$ $y := 1;$
3 if $(h == 0)$ then	3 $pc_1' := pc';$
4 $x := y - 1;$	4 $pc' := pc' \lor h';$
5 else skip;	5 if $(h == 0)$ then
6 endif;	6 $x' := y' \lor pc';$ $x := y - 1;$
7 $l := x;$	7 else skip;
	8 endif;
	9 $x' := x' \lor pc';$
	10 $pc' := pc_1';$
	11 $l' := x' \lor pc';$
	12 $policy\_check(l');$
	13 $l := x;$
(a)	(b)

Fig. 3. (a) Example program and (b) its transformation

3 Formalization of Correctness Criteria

First, we claim the simple result that the transformation is semantics preserving, providing that the call to *policy_check* does not halt. This is clear as the transformation only makes updates to the label variables (such as $\mathcal{L}(x)$ and $\mathcal{L}(pc)$). The only construct in our transformation that has the ability to alter the execution is *policy_check*. Specifically, *policy_check* acts as a *halt* instruction if the condition check succeeds, and acts as a *skip* instruction if the check fails. All the additional instructions in our transformation only make updates to label variables. Hence, the following theorem is true.

Theorem 1 (Semantics preservation). *Let P be any program, and P* the transformed program obtained applying the transformation $\to_{\Gamma,\Psi}$ on P. Then, P and P* are semantically equivalent on all executions in which policy_check never halts P*.*

Next, we show the correctness of the transformation with respect to the non-interference property, which ensures that an attacker cannot learn confidential information by observing only low security variables.

Definition 1 (Non-interference). *A program is said to be non-interfering if for any two sets of input values that differ only on their high security values, their corresponding low security output values are the same.*

To effectively compare two execution traces, the simple notion of program counter (source line number) is not sufficient as the length of the traces will differ due to the effect of loops and branches. To illustrate this point, consider the program fragment given below (assuming it is defined in a procedure named foo). Let h = 1 in the first trace, and h = 2 in the second. Then, at program location 3, we cannot compare the trace elements obtained in the first iteration (when h = 1 in the first trace), and second iteration in the second trace (when h = 1 in the second trace).

```
1   l := 0;
2   while (h > 0) do
3       l := l + 1;
4       h := h − 1;
5   done;
```

By the following definitions, we factor out the effect of loops by including the loop counter in the value of the label variable of the program location.

Definition 2. *A program counter is defined as a finite sequence* $\langle pname, \ell_0 : \langle \ell_1, i_1 \rangle : \langle \ell_2, i_2 \rangle : \ldots : \langle \ell n, i_n \rangle \rangle$.

- *pname is the name of the procedure that is currently being executed.*
- ℓ_0 *is the location (source line number) of the next statement to be executed.*
- *For all k such that $1 \leq k \leq n$, ℓ_k is the location of the* while *statement immediately enclosing ℓ_{k-1}.*
- *For the* while *statement at location ℓ_k ($1 \leq k \leq n$), i_k is the current iteration number (e.g., 1 the first time through the loop, 2 the second, and so on).*

Here, ℓ_1 is the location of the most immediate (i.e., innermost) while statement enclosing the statement at ℓ_0. Note that there may be no enclosing while, in which case the entire program counter value is simply $\langle pname, \ell_0 \rangle$.

Definition 3. *An* extended program counter *within a program P is defined as a sequence of program counters.*
$\langle pname_1, \ell_0^1 : \langle \ell_1^1, i_1^1 \rangle : \langle \ell_2^1, i_2^1 \rangle : \ldots : \langle \ell^1 \rangle_{m_1}, i_{m_1}^1 \rangle \rangle, \langle pname_2, \ell_0^2 : \langle \ell_1^2, i_1^2 \rangle : \langle \ell_2^2, i_2^2 \rangle : \ldots : \langle \ell_{m_2}^2, i_{m_2}^2 \rangle \rangle, \ldots, \langle pname_n, \ell_0^n : \langle \ell_1^n, i_1^n \rangle : \langle \ell_2^n, i_2^n \rangle : \ldots : \langle \ell_{m_n}^n, i_{m_n}^n \rangle \rangle$

In this definition, ℓ_0^2 refers to the location (in procedure $pname_2$) from which the call to procedure $pname_1$ was made. In general, ℓ_0^n refers to the location in procedure $pname_n$ from which a call was made to procedure $pname_{n-1}$.

Example: Using the definition of extended program counter, in the first trace, at source line number 3 for the first (and only) iteration of the loop, the extended program counter is $pc_1 = \langle foo, 3 : (2, 1) \rangle$. (program source line 3, and first iteration of the loop rooted at program line 2). In the second trace, the program location for the first iteration is $pc_2 = \langle foo, 3 : (2, 1) \rangle$ and that for second iteration of the loop is $pc_3 = \langle foo, 3 : (2, 2) \rangle$. Since pc_1 and pc_2 are same for the first iterations, the two trace elements can be compared, whereas the pc_1 and pc_3 cannot be compared since they belong to different iterations of the loop.

Note that extended program counter values are unique within the same execution (due to the fact that we capture iteration counts and procedure in program counters). Equality of extended program counters is defined as the equality of the individual sequences. A trace itself is obtained by collecting program states at various program points in an execution sequence of a program.

Definition 4. *A program state is a pair $\langle pc, env \rangle$ where pc is an extended program counter, and env : $(Var \cup \mathcal{L}(Var) \cup \{\mathcal{L}(pc)\}) \rightarrow \mathbf{Z}$ is an environment mapping all program variables and label variables to values.*

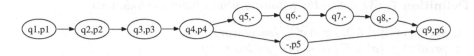

Fig. 4. Example of an execution trace pair

We use the following notation in conjunction with a program state q:

- pc_q the extended program counter value of q;
- env_q the environment of q;
- $stmt_q$ the statement at location pc_q.

Definition 5. *A program execution trace is a sequence of program states $q_0\ q_1\ q_2\ldots q_n$, where q_i is the result of executing $stmt_{q_{i-1}}$ in state q_{i-1}. Given two traces $T_1 = q_0\ q_1\ q_2\ldots q_n$ and $T_2 = p_0\ p_1\ p_2\ldots p_m$ of the same program P with different high security input values, the set of trace pairs, denoted by Σ_{T_1,T_2} is a subset of $T_1 \times T_2$ and is the union of three sets:*

- $\{\langle q_i, p_j\rangle\}$ *when* $pc_{q_i} = pc_{p_j}$
- $\{\langle q_i, -\rangle\}$ *when for all* $p \in T_2, pc_{q_i} \neq pc_p$
- $\{\langle -, p_j\rangle\}$ *when for all* $q \in T_1, pc_{p_j} \neq pc_q$

Note that, for every $q \in T_1$ there is exactly one trace pair involving q and possibly one state from T_2. A symmetric property holds true for all $p \in T_2$.

Definition 6. *Given a set Σ_{T_1,T_2} of trace pairs from traces $T_1 = q_0\ q_1\ q_2\ldots q_n$ and $T_2 = p_0\ p_1\ p_2\ldots p_m$, the stepwise ordering relation $\lhd \subseteq \Sigma \times \Sigma$ is defined by the following rules:*

- *if* $\langle q_i, X\rangle \in \Sigma_{T_1,T_2}$ *and* $\langle q_{i+1}, Y\rangle \in \Sigma_{T_1,T_2}$ *then* $\langle q_i, X\rangle \lhd \langle q_{i+1}, Y\rangle$ *iff* $X = -$ *or* $Y = -$ *or* $X = p_j$ *for some* j *and* $Y = p_{j+1}$
- *if* $\langle Z, p_k\rangle \in \Sigma_{T_1,T_2}$ *and* $\langle W, p_{k+1}\rangle \in \Sigma_{T_1,T_2}$ *then* $\langle Z, p_k\rangle \lhd \langle W, p_{k+1}\rangle$ *iff* $Z = -$ *or* $W = -$ *or* $Z = q_l$ *for some* l *and* $W = q_{l+1}$

By the above definition, the following trace pairs (if they are valid pairs) are related by the stepwise relation: $\langle q_i, p_j\rangle \lhd \langle q_{i+1}, -\rangle$, $\langle q_i, -\rangle \lhd \langle q_{i+1}, -\rangle$, $\langle -, p_j\rangle \lhd \langle -, p_{j+1}\rangle$, $\langle -, p_j\rangle \lhd \langle q_i, p_{j+1}\rangle$.

Note that for every element σ of Σ, there are at most two successors (corresponding to branch entry points), and at most two predecessors (corresponding to merge points). Also, the structure imposed on Σ by $\lhd$ is a linear sequence of trace pairs, interrupted by diverging regions where there are exactly two parallel trace pair sequences. At every point (defined by starting with σ_0, and following $\lhd$) there are one or two active trace pairs, up until the point where (possibly) both traces halt. Figure 4 shows a typical trace pair.

Definition 7. *We define the following utility functions/relations:*

1. $succ(\sigma) = \{\sigma' \in \Sigma \mid \sigma \lhd \sigma'\}$, *(successor)*
2. $pred(\sigma) = \{\sigma' \in \Sigma \mid \sigma' \lhd \sigma\}$, *(predecessor)*
3. $\lhd^+ = $ *the transitive closure of* $\lhd$,
4. $gcai(i,j) = $ *the largest* k *such that* $\sigma_k \lhd^* \sigma_i$ *and* $\sigma_k \lhd^* \sigma_j$,
5. $lcdi(i,j) = $ *the least* k *such that* $\sigma_i \lhd^* \sigma_k$ *and* $\sigma_j \lhd^* \sigma_k$,
6. $gca(\sigma_i, \sigma_j) = \sigma_{gcai(i,j)}$ *(greatest common ancestor)*,
7. $lcd(\sigma_i, \sigma_j) = \sigma_{lcdi(i,j)}$ *(least common descendant)*.
8. *for any* $\Sigma' \subset \Sigma_{T_1,T_2}$, $prefix\_closed(\Sigma') = true$ *if a)* $\langle q_0, p_0 \rangle \in \Sigma'$, *and b)* $\forall \sigma \in \Sigma' - \{\langle q_0, p_0 \rangle\}, pred(\sigma) \subset \Sigma'$

Note that the set of trace pairs Σ_{T_1,T_2}, satisfies the *prefix_closed* relation, and so does the singleton trace pair $\{\langle q_0, p_0 \rangle\}$.

Lemma 1. *Given two traces T_1 and T_2 of a transformed program P^* with inputs that differ only on high security values, and with trace-pair set Σ, then exactly one of the following properties holds true for every $\sigma \in \Sigma$ (depending on the form of σ):*

(a) *if* $\sigma = \langle q_i, p_j \rangle$ *then* $\forall x \in Var$,
    $env_{q_i}(x) \neq env_{p_j}(x) \Rightarrow [env_{q_i}(\mathcal{L}(x)) = env_{p_j}(\mathcal{L}(x)) = 1]$
(b) *if* $\sigma = \langle q_i, - \rangle$ *then* $env_{q_i}(\mathcal{L}(pc)) = 1$
(c) *if* $\sigma = \langle -, p_j \rangle$ *then* $env_{p_j}(\mathcal{L}(pc)) = 1$

The intuition behind this lemma is as follows. Since the two traces are executing the same code with identical initial values except for one or more high security variables, any divergence in values of variables must be due either to a direct flow from one of the high security variables, or an indirect flow. In the case of a direct flow, the transformation rules for assignment will update the label variables so that the flow is noted by a true-valued label variable. In the case of an indirect flow, the two execution traces must diverge. At the first point of divergence, $env(\mathcal{L}(pc))$ will be set to true, and it will remain true until the point where the two traces converge (which might never happen).

Proof. By induction over the size of sets satisfying the *prefix_closed* relation.

Base: For sets of size one, the only element is $\langle q_0, p_0 \rangle$, which is the initial state of every $\langle \Sigma, \lhd \rangle$ structure and is the start state, where $pc_{q_0} = pc_{p_0}$, and env_{q_0} agrees with env_{p_0} on all low security input values. For all the high security input values that may differ in the two traces, as all their label variables are initialized to 1, branch (a) of lemma 1 is trivially satisfied.

Induction Hypothesis: Assume that for all sets Σ' of size n that satisfy $prefix\_closed(\Sigma')$, for all $\sigma \in \Sigma'$, σ satisfies Lemma 1.

Step: pick any $\sigma \notin \Sigma'$, such that all its immediate predecessors are in Σ' $(pred(\sigma) \cap \Sigma' = pred(\sigma))$. σ either has the form (Case 1) $\langle q_i, p_j \rangle$, or (Case 2) $\langle q_i, - \rangle$, or (Case 3) $\langle -, p_j \rangle$.

Case 1: $\sigma = \langle q_i, p_j \rangle$. Consider $pred(\sigma)$.
Either (Case 1.1) $pred(\sigma) = \{\langle q_{i-1}, p_{j-1} \rangle\}$, or (Case 1.2) $pred(\sigma) = \{\langle q_{i-1}, - \rangle,$ $\langle -, p_{j-1} \rangle\}$.

Case 1.1: $\sigma = \langle q_i, p_j \rangle$ and $pred(\sigma) = \{\langle q_{i-1}, p_{j-1} \rangle\}$.
By the induction hypothesis, $\langle q_{i-1}, p_{j-1} \rangle$ satisfies Lemma 1(a). Consider the form of $stmt_{q_{i-1}} (= stmt_{p_{j-1}})$. If $stmt_{q_{i-1}}$ is not an assignment statement, then the env is the same in both σ and $pred(\sigma)$, so σ satisfies Lemma 1(a).

If $stmt_{q_{i-1}}$ is an assignment statement, then it must have the form $x := e;$. If $env_{q_i}(x) = env_{p_j}(x)$, then σ satisfies Lemma 1(a). If $env_{q_i}(x) \neq env_{p_j}(x)$, then we know that there was some $y \in e$ such that If $env_{q_{i-1}}(y) \neq env_{p_{j-1}}(y)$. By the induction hypothesis, $env_{q_{i-1}}(\mathcal{L}(y)) = env_{p_{j-1}}(\mathcal{L}(y)) = 1$. By the transformation rule for the assignment statement, we know that $\mathcal{L}(x)$ is assigned $\mathcal{L}(pc) \vee (\vee_{y \in e}\mathcal{L}(y))$. This will result in $env(\mathcal{L}(x)) = 1$ in both q_{i-1} and p_{j-1}. In all cases, σ satisfies Lemma 1(a).

Case 1.2: $\sigma = \langle q_i, p_j \rangle$. and $pred(\sigma) = \{\langle q_{i-1}, - \rangle, \langle -, p_{j-1} \rangle\}$.
In this case, $stmt_{q_i}$ must be the exit from a while or if statement. Let $\langle q_l, p_m \rangle = gca(\langle q_{i-1}, - \rangle, \langle -, p_{j-1} \rangle)$. By the induction hypothesis, $\langle q_l, p_m \rangle$ satisfies Lemma 1(a). Also, by the induction hypothesis, in each state along the path from $\langle q_l, p_m \rangle$ to q_i satisfies Lemma 1(b), and each state along the path from $\langle q_l, p_m \rangle$ to to p_j satisfies Lemma 1(c) (i.e., $env(\mathcal{L}(pc))$ is 1 along these paths). Because of the latter two facts, we show that for any variable x, $env(\mathcal{L}(x))$ can only go from 0 to 1 along either path (it can never become 0 from 1).

Pick any $x \in Var$, by the induction hypothesis, if $env_{q_l}(x) \neq env_{p_m}(x)$, then $env_{q_l}(\mathcal{L}(x)) = env_{p_m}(\mathcal{L}(x)) = 1$, and if x is not assigned anywhere between $\langle q_l, p_m \rangle$ to $\langle q_i, p_j \rangle$, then the same value of x and $\mathcal{L}(x)$ will propagate to $\langle q_i, p_j \rangle$, so $\langle q_i, p_j \rangle$ will satisfy $env_{q_i}(x) \neq env_{p_j}(x) \Rightarrow env_{q_i}(\mathcal{L}(x)) = env_{p_j}(\mathcal{L}(x)) = 1$. The same is true if $env_{q_l}(x) = env_{p_m}(x)$, and x is assigned to along both paths (since $env(\mathcal{L}(x))$ will become 1 as $env(\mathcal{L}(pc)) = 1$ at the point of assignment until the merge).

The only remaining case is where $env_{q_l}(x) \neq env_{p_m}(x)$, and x is assigned to along on one path (without loss of generality assume it is the path from q_l to q_i), and x is not assigned to along the other path (p_m to p_j). There are two ways this could happen: a) execution flow follows two different paths of an if or b) execution flow passes once through a while loop on $q_l \ldots q_i$ but not on $p_m \ldots p_j$.

In both these cases, there will be implicit flows from all the variables in the condition plus $\mathcal{L}(pc)$ to $\mathcal{L}(x)$ along the path where x is not modified ($p_m \ldots p_j$). Since, $env(\mathcal{L}(pc)) = 1$, $env(\mathcal{L}(x))$ will become one, (by the transformation rules for assignment) and $env_{p_j}(\mathcal{L}(x)) = 1$. The final result is that in $\langle q_i, p_j \rangle$, $env_{q_i}(x) \neq env_{p_j}(x) \Rightarrow env_{q_i}(\mathcal{L}(x)) = env_{p_j}(\mathcal{L}(x)) = 1$.

In every possible sub-case of case 1.2, for any $x \in Var$, $env_{q_i}(x) \neq env_{p_j}(x) \Rightarrow env_{q_i}(\mathcal{L}(x)) = env_{p_j}(\mathcal{L}(x)) = 1$, hence $\langle q_i, p_j \rangle$ satisfies Lemma 1(a).

Case 2: $\sigma = \langle q_i, - \rangle$.
Consider $pred(\sigma)$. Either (Case 2.1) $pred(\sigma) = \{\langle q_{i-1}, - \rangle\}$, or (Case 2.2) $pred(\sigma) = \{\langle q_{i-1}, p_j \rangle\}$.

Case 2.1: $\sigma = \langle q_i, - \rangle$ and $pred(\sigma) = \{\langle q_{i-1}, - \rangle\}$.

By the induction hypothesis, $env_{q_{i-1}}(\mathcal{L}(pc)) = 1$. Consider If q_{i-1} is not the exit from (i.e., last state in the execution of) an if or while, then $env(\mathcal{L}(pc))$ is preserved in q_i, and σ satisfies Lemma 1(b). If q_{i-1} is the exit from an if or while, then $stmt_{q_{i-1}}$ must be embedded within an enclosing if or while (otherwise, the second trace would reach the same extended program counter location and σ would have the form $\langle q_i, p_{j+1} \rangle$. In the latter case, $env(\mathcal{L}(pc))$ will still be 1 when the if or while exits according to the transformation rules. So, in both cases, σ satisfies Lemma 1(b).

Case 2.2: $\sigma = \langle q_i, - \rangle$ and $pred(\sigma) = \{\langle q_{i-1}, p_j \rangle\}$.

In this case, $pred(\sigma)$ must be the beginning of an if or while with two successors (due to trace divergence). That means that the expression e used to determine the branch outcome evaluated differently in q_{i-1} and p_{j-1}, which must be due to some set of variables X whose values differ in $env_{q_{i-1}}$ and $env_{p_{j-1}}$. By the induction hypothesis, for each $x \in X$, $\mathcal{L}(x)$ evaluates to 1 in both $env_{q_{i-1}}$ and $env_{p_{j-1}}$. According to the transformation rules, $\mathcal{L}(pc)$ will be bound in env_{q_i} to the result of or-ing the $\mathcal{L}(x)$ values together (along with some other values), so the result will be $env_{q_i}(\mathcal{L}(pc)) = 1$. Hence σ satisfies Lemma 1(b).

Case 3: $\sigma = \langle -, p_j \rangle$.

By an argument symmetric to Case 2, σ satisfies Lemma 1(c).

Conclusion: In all cases, Lemma 1 is satisfied. By induction, all $\sigma \in \Sigma$ reachable by traversing $\lhd$ from $\langle q_0, p_0 \rangle$ satisfy Lemma 1.

Theorem 2. *The transformation $\rightarrow_{\Gamma, \Psi}$ respects non-interference, i.e., if the program P has two traces that differ on assignments to low security variables (thus causing differing observable outputs) when only high security input values differ in the program, then the transformed program P^* exits before such an assignment occurs.*

Proof. Consider the differing assignment statement. Depending on whether the assignment to the low security variable happened in both traces, two cases are possible.

Case a) The assignment happens on both the traces with different values assigned to the low security variable x(say). In this case, the trace pair is of the form $\langle q_i, p_j \rangle$ which satisfies Lemma 1(a), since the values assigned to x are different, then $env_{q_i}(\mathcal{L}(x)) = env_{p_j}(\mathcal{L}(x)) = 1$ before the assignment, and the *policy_check* procedure inserted before the assignment halts on inspecting this value of $\mathcal{L}(x)$.

Case b) The assignment happens in only one trace. In this case, the trace pair is of the form $\langle q_i, - \rangle$ or $\langle -, p_j \rangle$. $env_{q_i}(\mathcal{L}(pc)) = env_{p_j}(\mathcal{L}(pc)) = 1$ by Lemma 1(b) (or by Lemma 1(c)). Hence by the transformation rule for the assignment statement, for the variable x that is assigned, $env_{q_i}(\mathcal{L}(x))$ and $env_{p_j}(\mathcal{L}(x))$ will become 1. The *policy_check* procedure will halt the execution in a similar fashion. Hence the proof.

4   Practical Issues in Runtime Information Flow Enforcement

Any approach for dealing with information flow must deal with several practical issues involved with general purpose programs. We discuss the key issues related to static analysis for the transformation, optimizations, variable aliasing, and information declassification in this section.

4.1   Static Analysis for Transformation

Our transformation is parameterized by a static analysis that can compute the set of variables $Upd(S)$ that are updated in a compound statement S. For statements that do not involve procedural calls, this analysis can simply collect all the LHS variables of assignments in the compound statement S and return the results as $Upd(S)$. When procedural calls are involved, an inter-procedural side effect analysis is needed to compute $Upd(S)$. Many such analysis algorithms (e.g. [9]) are found in the literature.

The precision of the static analysis for computing update sets will affect the precision of runtime monitoring of the transformed program. When such a static analysis is imprecise and conservative, the variables that never get assigned in the statement S may be included in $Upd(S)$. Updating the label variable of such a variable with $\mathcal{L}(pc)$ can lead to false alarms on information leaks because the implicit flows from the branch condition in S to the variable in question actually do not present in the program. We note that our approach is conservative yet sound in these cases and will not fail to detect the actual information leaks happened in the program.

4.2   Optimizations

The transformation presented in Section 2 was kept simple, avoiding all possible optimizations, for the sake of readability and clarity. In this section, we discuss techniques to optimize the performance of the run-time approach.

– **Optimizations to transformation rules (if-then-else and while).** We first note that the transformation for the if-then-else and while statements include updates to all the variables in the update set (denoted in the figure as $Upd(S_1) \cup Upd(S_2)$), Note that it adds updates to label variables after executing either branch. This is clearly redundant, as we need to only update the label variables corresponding to the branch not taken (to account for implicit flows). This simple optimization reduces the number of instructions added for tracking implicit flows directly to one half of the original number. A similar optimization can be done for the while statement to reduce the number of instructions needed to track implicit flows.
– **Optimizations based on information type inference results.** As noted earlier in the introduction, we note that our approach can be used to maintain

safe information flows when the static type analysis checks do not declare the program as safe. We can leverage on the results of such as type analysis to further optimize the number of instructions added for runtime tracking. We can first use static information flow analysis/inference to propagate the sensitive types (only the high values) across the program. This propagation of sensitive types will result in partitioning the set of program variables into two pools: the *sensitive* pool, that denote potentially sensitive variables, and the *non-sensitive* pool, that denote variables that do not receive sensitive information. A key insight here is that variables from the non-sensitive pool do not ever receive sensitive information throughout their lifetime in any execution of the program. Hence runtime tracking is unnecessary for these variables. With this information, label variables are not added for these variables, and no updates are made (either for implicit or explicit flows) for these variables. This second step further reduces the number of instructions added to the original program. In addition, if the program counter label $\mathcal{L}(pc)$ is ever augmented with this label variable (if the original variable is used in a condition), then this update to $\mathcal{L}(pc)$ need not be performed at all. This will also mean that $\mathcal{L}(pc)$ does not require to be saved and restored before and after the body of this statement.

- **Use of standard compiler optimizations for eliminating dead assignments to label variables.** Modern compilers have several intra-procedural optimizations that are built-in. These assignments optimize the original program code. We note that when such optimizations happen, the same optimizations can also be performed on the corresponding label variables, thereby reducing the number of additional instructions to the original program. For instance, every dead assignment in the original program has a corresponding dead label variable assignment and this can be eliminated. This can be performed by a standard compiler that supports live variable analysis followed by dead assignment elimination of the program, resulting in code that is further optimized on label assignments. In a similar fashion, other compiler optimizations such as copy propagation, constant folding and loop optimizations can be applied to label variables as well, resulting in reducing the number of such label assignments.

Analysis of the number of additional instructions introduced due to the transformation. We now briefly discuss the additional number of instructions (label variable updates) introduced by the transformation. The transformation introduces label assignments for two cases (i) explicit flows and (ii) implicit flows. In the case of explicit flows, there is exactly one assignment for each assignment to a program variable. For the case of implicit flows, it may seem as if the number of added assignments is equal to the number of branch assignment statements in both branches. However, this is not true. The transformation adds only one assignment for every updated variable in the branch not taken. Hence the number of added label assignments is bounded by the number of unique variables updated in both branches. The effect of the above optimizations due to results from the type analysis and standard compiler optimizations reduces the number of such label variable assignments even further.

4.3 Handling Aliasing

An alias of a variable refers to the same storage location of the variable through a different name. Writes to the storage location through an alias variable will affect the accesses through all other aliases. Variable aliasing is common in modern program languages such as Java and C++. An alias to a variable can be generated by creating a pointer or reference to the variable (e.g. by passing an object to another method in Java, or by using the reference operator & in C++).

In order to correctly track how the sensitive information flows in a program in the presence of aliasing, our transformation should ensure that the label variables of the aliased variables are also similarly aliased each other. However, it is rather difficult to synchronize such an aliasing relationship of label variables with that of program variables.

To solve this problem, we can use a pointer alias analysis (e.g. [33,11]) to partition variables in a program into different sets, each of which contains only the variables that are aliased each other. We then assign one single label variable to each of such variable sets in the transformed program. This ensures that the label variable for each set of aliased variables gets updated properly for both explicit and implicit information flows into these variables.

4.4 Declassification

Declassification of information is required to downgrade sensitive information intentionally to a low security value, when dictated by certain situations. A classic example is a password program that accepts input (low) from a user, and compares it to the stored (high) password. Such comparison is bound to leak information, such leaks are generally considered acceptable for programs that have to deal with disclosure of such small amounts of sensitive information. Recent works in information flow analysis have looked at issues in safe uses of such declassifications [19,17].

Declassification can be introduced either as part of the original language through a special declassify operator, or as external specifications to the program. The declassify operator takes an expression as parameter. The use of an operator needs changes to the compiler framework for the language, as well as changes to existing programs, while making the intent explicit in the source code. The use of an external specification does not require both, but may have readability issues for someone reading the program. Regardless of how the declassification is specified, it is provided as input to our transformation framework, and associated static analysis mechanisms.

The process of tracking flows with the presence of declassification is straightforward. On the instance of a declassify operator, say, the label value arising out of the expression that is declassified is set to false. This has the net effect of downgrading, and no additional changes to the transformation rules are necessary. On the other hand, static analysis mechanism used may benefit from such specifications. As described earlier, they may possibly eliminate any variables assigned out of such declassified expressions from the update sets.

5 Related Work

Approaches addressing the information flow problem broadly fall into three categories: runtime analysis approaches, static analysis approaches, and theorem proving based approaches.

Runtime analysis approaches. Early work on protecting confidentiality of data involved the use of runtime monitoring. This was mainly started with the development of mandatory access control model in the context of multi-level security by Bell and LaPadula [5]. Subsequent models, such as Fenton [13], followed this approach in the context of programs, in which the sensitivity of the output of a computation was calculated along with the computation. However, this approach fails to protect implicit flows due to paths that are not taken. Since then, most approaches started focusing on using static analysis techniques.

The scripting language Perl has a taint mode [32] that tracks data that arrives from untrusted sources (such as the network). Perl also supports implicit downgrading data from "tainted" to "untainted" through pattern matching. However, Perl does not track implicit flows. Recently, several taint mechanisms have appeared in the context of protecting system integrity [22,8,26,6] Similar to Perl, none of these mechanisms handle implicit flows. The taint mechanism described in [34] has some limited support for implicit flow. However, there are no guarantees about non-interference properties.

Static analysis checks have been considered out of EM enforcement mechanisms [25]. While EM-enforceable properties are those over traces, information flow properties are not EM- enforceable, as they are properties of trace sets[30]. Hence, a purely runtime mechanism will not be able to enforce information flow policies. In this paper, we augment the execution trace with information about other possible executions that relate to the current execution. By doing this, we gain the ability to enforce information flow policies on programs.

Two other works use dynamic approaches in the context of the information flow analysis problem to address some of the limitations that were discussed in the introduction. The first is due to Zheng et al [35], which provides support for dynamically providing the values of labels for data items (such as a file whose access permission is not known). The second work by Tse et al [28] provides similar support for unknown principals (that are only available at runtime) that interact with the system. In both these works, the use of dynamic techniques is to expand the scope of the static analysis based policy enforcement mechanism. However, they still do not support programs that may occasionally leak information such as the crash example discussed in the introduction.

Guernic and Jensen [15] have independently developed a similar approach that provides non-interferences guarantees based on a single run of a program. They present their approach through an operational semantics, but do not provide a proof. Our work [29] precedes their work.

Static analysis approaches. Various static analysis based approaches have been used for information flow analysis. (We only discuss most representative work here, a detailed survey article on various language based techniques for tracking information flow is available [24]).

Denning's approach [12] based on program certification was the first work that used an augmented compiler to track information flows. Andrews and Reitman [1] used an extended axiomatic logic with the secure flow certification of Denning. The work of Volpano et al [31], is based on the use of type-analysis for detecting information flows, and the approach is provably secure in handling implicit flows.

Myers presents a *decentralized label model* [21] for information flow where the owner specifies the access rights of data owned by her and the language, Jif, uses a type-analysis combined with runtime checks to detect illegal flows [20]. This is the first work that addressed the problem of information flow in a real programming language realm. Flow Caml [23], developed by Simonet and Pottier, is also a high-level, realistic programming language aiming at support information-flow controls. More recently, a certifying compiler for information flow policies was described in Barthe [4]. Banerjee and Naumann [2] connect information-flow policies and stack inspection (an access control mechanism) for static checking of information flow policies in a Java-like language. Mclean [18] presents a specification of a program using trace semantics and develops a systematic theory to enable reasoning about non-interference for such specifications.

As we pointed out in the introduction, static analysis based approaches have drawbacks that may result in rejection of safe programs. Information leaks in certain unusual cases are common in many useful programs. Static analysis based approaches will reject such programs, while our runtime analysis based approach will permit the execution of such programs and halt them only when the actual information leak happens.

Theorem proving based approaches. Precise characterization of information flow is inherently an undecidable problem. Static analysis based mechanisms guarantee termination by providing a sound solution to the problem, with the possibility of rejecting safe programs. The approach taken originally in Joshi et al [16], and more recently by Darvas et al [10] and Barthe et al [3] use theorem proving as a technique to make improve the precision of static analysis. This is done by characterizing information flow as a safety problem (using a technique called self-composition, summarized in a formulation by [27]) and using theorem proving technology to certify programs as safe. Theorem proving certainly has the ability to provide more precise results. However, in the case of all theorem proving techniques, there is a risk of non-termination as exemplified by a simple example discussed in [27]. Static analysis mechanisms, by definition, always terminate. Our focus in this work is to occupy a position that is midway between static analysis and theorem proving. We try to support execution of programs that are rejected by static analysis by improving precision, and also by providing a transformation approach that always terminates.

6   Conclusion

As we have shown, runtime detection of implicit information flows are possible when information from a simple static analysis are combined with program instrumentation which performs runtime flow tracking. Furthermore, we have established the soundness of such an approach with respect to the non-interference property. The contributions of this paper is mainly theoretical in nature. In future work, we plan to implement this technique and evaluate its effectiveness and performance in practice.

Although the presented approach ensures confidentiality of secure data, it can easily be changed to ensure integrity as well. In this case, the objective is to prevent the flow of information from untrusted variables to trusted ones. The primary change that is required is in the initial labeling of variables; otherwise, the propagation rules for labels are similar.

References

1. G. R. Andrews and R. P. Reitman. An axiomatic approach to information flow in programs. *ACM Transactions on Programming Languages and Systems (TOPLAS)*, 2(1):56–75, 1980.
2. A. Banerjee and D. A. Naumann. Using access control for secure information flow in a java-like language. In *Proc. IEEE Computer Security Foundations Workshop*, 2003.
3. G. Barthe, P. D'Argenio, and T. Rezk. Secure information flow by self-composition. In *Proc. IEEE Computer Security Foundations Workshop*, 2004.
4. G. Barthe, T. Rezk, and D. Naumann. Deriving an information flow checker and certifying compiler for java. In *IEEE Symposium on Security and Privacy*, 2006.
5. D. E. Bell and L. J. LaPadula. Secure computer systems: Mathematical foundations. Technical Report MTR-2547, Vol. 1, MITRE Corp., 1973.
6. Y. Beres and C. Dalton. Dynamic label binding at run-time. In *New Security Paradigms Workshop*, 2003.
7. P. Broadwell, M. Harren, and N. Sastry. Scrash: A system for generating security crash information. In *USENIX Security Symposium*, 2003.
8. S. Chen, J. Xu, N. Nakka, Z. Kalbarczyk, and R. K. Iyer. Defeating memory corruption attacks via pointer taintedness detection. In *IEEE International Conference on Dependable Systems and Networks (DSN)*, 2005.
9. K. D. Cooper and K. Kennedy. Interprocedural side-effect analysis in linear time. In *Programming Languages Design and Implementation (PLDI)*, 1988.
10. A. Darvas, R. Hähnle, and D. Sands. A theorem proving approach to analysis of secure information flow. In D. Hutter and M. Ullmann, editors, *Proc. 2nd International Conference on Security in Pervasive Computing*, volume 3450 of *LNCS*, pages 193–209. Springer-Verlag, 2005.
11. M. Das. Unification-based pointer analysis with directional assignments. In *Programming Languages Design and Implementation (PLDI)*, 2000.
12. D. E. Denning and P. J. Denning. Certification of programs for secure information flow. *Comm. of the ACM*, 20(7):504–513, 1977.
13. J. S. Fenton. Memoryless subsystems. *Computing J.*, 17(2):143–147, 1974.

14. J. A. Goguen and J. Meseguer. Security policies and security models. In *IEEE Symposium on Security and Privacy*, pages 11–20, 1982.
15. G. L. Guernic and T. Jensen. Monitoring information flow. In *Workshop on Foundations of Computer Security*, 2005.
16. R. Joshi and K. R. M. Leino. A semantic approach to secure information flow. *Science of Computer Programming*, 37(1–3):113–138, 2000.
17. P. Li and S. Zdancewic. Downgrading policies and relaxed noninterference. In *ACM Symposium on Principles of Programming Languages (POPL)*, 2005.
18. J. McLean. Proving noninterference and functional correctness using traces. *Journal of Computer Security*, 1(1), 1992.
19. A. Myers, A. Sabelfeld, and S. Zdancewic. Enforcing robust declassification. In *Proc. IEEE Computer Security Foundations Workshop*, 2004.
20. A. C. Myers. JFlow: Practical mostly-static information flow control. In *ACM Symposium on Principles of Programming Languages (POPL)*, pages 228–241, 1999.
21. A. C. Myers and B. Liskov. Complete, safe information flow with decentralized labels. In *IEEE Symposium on Security and Privacy*, pages 186–197, 1998.
22. J. Newsome and D. Song. Dynamic taint analysis for automatic detection, analysis, and signature generation of exploits on commodity software. In *Network and Distributed System Security Symposium (NDSS)*, 2005.
23. F. Pottier and V. Simonet. Information flow inference for ml. In *ACM Symposium on Principles of Programming Languages (POPL)*, 2002.
24. A. Sabelfeld and A. C. Myers. Language-based information-flow security. *IEEE J. Selected Areas in Communications*, 21(1), 2003.
25. F. B. Schneider. Enforceable security policies. *ACM Transactions on Information and System Security (TISSEC)*, 3(1), 2001.
26. G. E. Suh, J. W. Lee, D. Zhang, and S. Devadas. Secure program execution via dynamic information flow tracking. In *International Conference on Architectural Support for Programming Languages and Operating Systems*, pages 85–96, 2004.
27. T. Terauchi and A. Aiken. Secure information flow as a safety problem. In *Static Analysis Symposium (SAS)*, 2005.
28. S. Tse and S. Zdancewic. Run-time principals in information-flow type systems. In *IEEE Symposium on Security and Privacy.*, 2004.
29. V. N. Venkatakrishnan, D. C. DuVarney, W. Xu, and R. Sekar. A program transformation technique for enforcement of information flow properties. Technical Report SECLAB-04-01, Department of Computer Science, Stony Brook University, 2004.
30. D. Volpano. Safety versus secrecy. In *Static Analysis Symposium (SAS)*, volume 1694 of *Lecture Notes in Computer Science*, pages 303–311, 1999.
31. D. Volpano, G. Smith, and C. Irvine. A sound type system for secure flow analysis. *Journal of Computer Security (JCS)*, 4(3):167–187, 1996.
32. L. Wall, T. Christiansen, and R. Schwartz. *Programming Perl*. O'Reilly, 1996.
33. J. Whaley and M. S. Lam. Cloning-based context-sensitive pointer alias analysis using binary decision diagrams. In *Programming Languages Design and Implementation (PLDI)*, 2004.
34. W. Xu, S. Bhatkar, and R. Sekar. Taint-enhanced policy enforcement: A practical approach to defeat a wide range of attacks. In *USENIX Security Symposium*, 2006.
35. L. Zheng and A. Myers. Dynamic security labels and noninterference. In *Workshop on Formal Aspects in Security and Trust (FAST)*, 2004.

An Attack on SMC-Based Software Protection

Yongdong Wu, Zhigang Zhao, and Tian Wei Chui

Institute for Infocomm Research
21, Heng Mui Keng Terrace, Singapore, 119613
{wydong, zzhao, twchui}@i2r.a-star.edu.sg

Abstract. Self-modifying codes (SMC) refer to programs that intentionally modify themselves at runtime, causing the runtime code to differ from the static binary representation of the code before execution. Hence SMC is an effective method to obstruct software disassembling. This paper presents a method which circumvents the SMC protection, thus improving the performance of disassembling. By disabling the write privilege to the code section, an access violation exception occurs when an SMC attempts to execute. Intercepting this exception allows the attacker to determine and thus compromise the SMC and generate equivalent static code. Our experiments demonstrate that it is viable and efficient.

1 Introduction

Currently, most commercial software (e.g., Microsoft^{TM} Office, Adobe^{TM} Acrobat) are distributed in binary form to protect the software implementation, particularly mechanisms preventing unauthorized distribution of the software. However, attackers are able to reverse engineer the code in order to analyze and circumvent these protection schemes. For example, the encryption mechanism in Microsoft's Windows Media Player was cracked [1] by reverse engineering, allowing access to protected content in unauthorized environments. Such reverse engineering is heavily dependent on the use of disassembling techniques.

1.1 Disassembly Technology

Disassembling aims to produce a higher-level representation of a program to enable comprehension and possible modification to the software. A disassembler enables a cracker to easily translate binary code into human-readable code. For instance, IDAPro [2] translates a binary code into assembly code while Relogix^{TM} [3] further converts an assembly source into readable, structured, commented C source - in a truly natural C style.

Disassembly methods can be distinguished as either static or dynamic disassembly. Static techniques, including linear sweep and recursive traversal, analyze the binary structure statically, parsing the instructions as they are found in the binary image.

Linear sweeping (e.g. objdump [4]) scans the static code from start to end, and decodes the instructions sequentially. Therefore linear sweep disassemblers

P. Ning, S. Qing, and N. Li (Eds.): ICICS 2006, LNCS 4307, pp. 352–368, 2006.

are easy to implement but prone to errors resulting from data bytes that have been interleaved with the code bytes, misleading the disassembler.

Recursive traversal (e.g., `IDApro` [2], and [5]) follows the control flow of the program, thus avoiding incorrect disassembly of data bytes. However, certain code sections may not be part of the control flow, particularly if the target address is produced in real time (e.g., pointer functions). Hence, the recursive disassembler will not reach and disassemble these regions. To overcome this weakness, a linear sweep algorithm is typically used to analyze these sections.

Dynamic techniques (e.g., `rordbg` [6]) create a debug environment to run the application. By monitoring the program's execution, a dynamic disassembler is able to identify the executed instructions and recover a disassembled version of the binary. Nonetheless, dynamic techniques have several weaknesses: (1) they only operate on the instructions that were executed in a particular set of runs. Therefore, only partial codes are disassembled; (2) program execution in a debug environment is slow and vulnerable to time-sensitive codes; (3) some instructions (e.g., exception handling) can not be analyzed correctly.

1.2 Protection Method

As it is believed to be impossible to completely prevent software cracking, software protection methods aim to make it sufficiently hard to understand the structure of a program. Hence, it is a practical challenge to protect the software from analysis and tampering to protect the proprietary algorithms and/or security critical codes. Presently, obfuscation, integrity verification and self-modifying codes (SMC) are the major anti-disassembly means.

Obfuscation technology [7] converts an original software into an equivalent form that crackers cannot easily understand. There are several software obfuscation methods such as fingerprinting [8], instruction occurrence [9], instruction re-ordering [10] and class transform [11]. Particularly, in [12], with a one-way tamper-proof permutation, a point-function/boolean function such as password checking is obfuscated. These obfuscation technologies produce obfuscated software that is equivalent to the original software for all input. Nonetheless, based on control flow graph information and statistical methods, Kruegel *et al.* [13] presented binary analysis techniques which can identify a large fraction of the program's instructions. These analysis techniques substantially improve the success of the disassembly process when confronted with obfuscated binaries.

Integrity protection methods [14][15] verify the code in real-time so as to prevent a tampered software from successfully running. Unfortunately, a substitution attack [16] [17] is applicable to all the integrity protections by modifying the underlying operating system. Although Giffin *et al.* [18] strengthened the checksum method with SMC code, they acknowledge that their improvement is vulnerable improvements in substitution attacks. Although control-flow integrity [19] is a way to enforce security, it is also naturally vulnerable to substitution attacks.

As a third protection method, SMC technology [21] alters software codes at the target addresses to produce the dynamic codes. As a special case of SMC, code encryption [22] - [25] scrambles the software, protecting the software from disassembling/tampering. Since the dynamic code generated by SMC technology is unknown in advance, a static disassembler cannot output a good assembly code. Thus it is difficult for the cracker to analyze and tamper the SMC-protected binary. Maebe *et al.* [26] has previously proposed to detect memory pages where SMCs occur utilizing the page protection mechanism of modern processors. However their implementation works for code run by a just-in-time compiler in a Linux environment, and hence reduces the performance of target software dramatically.

1.3 Our Contribution

Since the SMC-enabled static code structure is different from the dynamic code, the disassembled code may be incorrect if a static disassembler is used to analyze the static binary file. In order to produce a correct disassembly, the static disassembler should have access to static code which is the same as the runtime code. To this end, we remove the SMC protection using an exception mechanism that may occur during the execution of a Windows program. The attack disables the code modification attribute, triggering access violation exceptions each time a code modification is attempted. By intercepting the exception, we can obtain the modification's target address and codes, allowing us to perform the code modification. As a result, we can produce a static representation of the runtime code, in effect enhancing a static disassembler with some functions of a dynamic disassembler.

The outline of the present paper is as follows. Section 2 introduces the structure of the executable file and its mapping in the memory. Section 3 introduces SMC technology. Section 4 elaborates our proposal of removing the SMC. Section 5 proposes two implementations. Section 6 describes our experiments and results. We conclude in Section 7.

2   Primitives

In this paper, we denote $[X]$ as the value stored in the address X and Y_h as the value Y in hexadecimal.

2.1 PE Structure

The Portable Executable (PE) format [27] is a standard format under Microsoft Windows operating system. As a flat space structure, a PE-format executable is segmented into sections. Each section is a continuous structure of unlimited size but aligned along page[1] boundaries. The PE header includes important information such as the address of the program entry point and the code section starting address. Each section header includes section attributes, e.g., READ

---

[1] A page is a continuous space of fixed size. For example, in Microsoft Windows XP, a page is of 4K bytes in memory and 200 bytes in file.

(40000000_h), WRITE (80000000_h), EXECUTE (20000000_h).When a PE file is loaded into memory by a program loader, it is mapped into a real-time executable format. The structure in the memory is shown in Fig.1, where the sections are

- .text: codes generated by the compiler or assembler.
- .rdata: read-only data in run time.
- .data: initialization data.
- .idata: import table which includes other DLL (Dynamic Link Library) functions and re-localization information.
- .rsrc: resource data such as icons, menus, bitmaps etc.

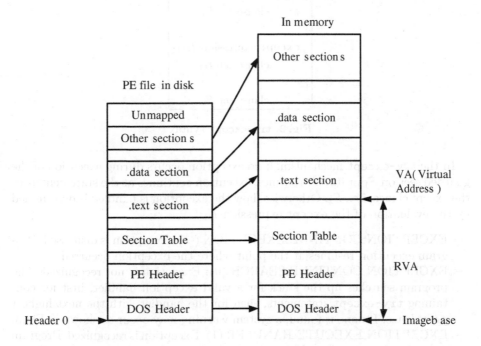

Fig. 1. PE file structure and mapping in memory

With regard to Fig.1, each section in the memory maps to one section in the file. Suppose the base address of code section is B_f in the file and B_m in memory, then for any memory address A_m, its disk file location A_f is

$$A_f = B_f + (A_m - B_m) \tag{1}$$

in the specific section. For the Microsoft Windows platform, the default base address is $B_m = 400000_h$ for the code section.

2.2 try-except Mechanism

The **try-except** statement is a Microsoft extension to the C and C++ languages. It is a structured exception handler enabling 32-bit target applications to gain control when there are events that would normally terminate program execution. Such events are called exceptions which can be either hardware-based (e.g., access violation) or software-based (e.g., **throw** command). Exception handlers which process these exceptions as they occur are declared in the syntax shown in Fig.2, where the clause set S_1 is the body or guarded section where an exception might occur, and clause set H_1 is the exception handler.

```
__try{
        clause set S₁
}
__except(expression E₁){
        clause set H₁
}
        clause set S₂
```

Fig. 2. try-except syntax

In the **try-except** mechanism, if no exception occurs during execution of the guarded section S_1 or its sub-routines, execution continues at the statement after the except clause, i.e., S_2. Otherwise, how the exception is handled is determined by the evaluation of the **except** expression E_1:

- EXCEPTION_CONTINUE_EXECUTION (-1): Exception is dismissed. Program execution resumes at the point where the exception occurred.
- EXCEPTION_CONTINUE_SEARCH (0): Exception is not recognized. The program searches up the stack for a valid exception handler, first for containing **try-except** statements, then for the handler with the next highest precedence. If none is found, a system warning may occur as shown in Fig.3.
- EXCEPTION_EXECUTE_HANDLER (1): Exception is recognized. Program control is transferred to the exception handler and the instructions in H_1 are executed to handle the exception. Thereafter program execution continues at S_2.

3 Self-modifying Code

3.1 SMC Instruction Syntax

In the following sections, we will illustrate the instructions with the x86 assembler language. For simplicity, we will focus on memory-write SMC instructions such as

$$A_1 : \texttt{opCode}\ [A_2], \texttt{src}$$

Fig. 3. Access Violation warning without a proper handler, where $C0000005_h$ identifies the access violation exception

where `opCode` is the instruction code, A_1 is the address of the instruction, A_2 is the target address whose value will be changed by the SMC, and `src` is the target code to be written to address A_2. A list of possible SMC instructions is given in the Appendix. In this paper, we will use SMC to refer to the instruction which modifies the software code, and to refer to the whole code if there is no ambiguity.

Fig.4 illustrates an example where an instruction at address A_1 changes the code at address A_2 at run-time. Since the SMC modifies the code section, the instruction bytes present in the original executable is different from the actual instruction bytes executed at run-time.

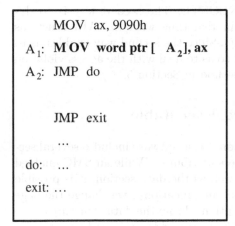

Fig. 4. Self-modifying code and its equivalent. The left side is the original program code, while the right side is the actual run-time code. Both sides are equal in function, where 90_h means "NOP"(no operation).

3.2 Violation by SMC

To generate an executable, the compiler transforms source code (e.g., C/C++ code test1.cpp) into an object file (e.g., text1.obj). Following that, an executable (e.g., test1.exe) is generated with a linker. If the executable code is an SMC-enabled program without the required write permission, an access violation warning will occur as shown in Fig.5. Therefore, it is necessary to assign WRITE privilege to the target address to allow the SMC instruction to execute without exception.

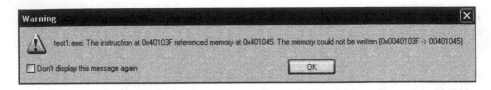

Fig. 5. Access violation warning when attempting a write to a non-writable code section in IDAPro environment, where $A_1 = 40103F_h$ and $A_2 = 401045_h$

3.3 Assigning WRITE Attribute

In the Windows system, there are two ways to assign the WRITE attribute to the code in memory. One is to statically enable the whole code section to be writable with a linker. For instance, to generate a binary executable test1.exe from a text1.obj, perform

```
c>link /nologo /section.text, RWE test1.obj
```

where RWE means READ| WRITE| EXECUTE. The second way is to dynamically assign the WRITE attribute in real time with the API functions VirtualProtect() or VirtualProtectEX(). Since the second way enables us to change the WRITE attribute dynamically so as to deal with the access violation exception, we will elaborate the second method in Section 5.

4   Disassembling SMC-Enabled Executable

According to the PE structure in Subsection 2.1, a software includes several sections which may be assigned different access attributes. While an SMC-enabled software may modify the code section as well as the data section, it is possible to differentiate data modification from code modification if we change the page attributes to produce access violation exceptions. From the data structure of the resulting exception, we are able to obtain the target address A_2 and target codes in an SMC-enabled code so as to disassemble the original software.

4.1 Wrapping Original Software

To obtain the target address of an SMC instruction, we control the execution of the target program **P**. To this end, we produced a monitoring software **M** whose structure is as Fig.6, where the program entry point (i.e., the address of the first executed instruction) of **P** is `oldEntry`. Hence, program **M** wraps up the original program **P** such that the original program **P** is the guarded code of `try-except` syntax in **M**.

Denote the entire program as M_P which includes **M** and **P**. Then the program entry point of M_P is the program entry point of **M**. When M_P executes, **M** will call **P** with `call oldEntry`. Since program **M** and **P** are in the same address space, **M** can access the data/code of **P** such as the target address A_2 and value SMC.

Merged program M_P	
Monitoring program **M**	Original program **P**

__**try**{   call `OldEntry`
 	
 }
 __**except**(E_1){
 	
      exception handler H_1
 	
 }
	`OldEntry:`
	
	 $\vdots$
	
	 A_1 : `opCode` $[A_2]$, `src` (SMC)
	
	 $\vdots$

Fig. 6. Wrapping the original program

4.2 Locating the SMC Code

As SMCs essentially perform write operations to a location in memory, an access violation will occur if the SMC attempts to write bytes to a non-writable address A_2. Therefore if an adversary alters the entire code section to be non-writable, access violation exceptions will occur whenever SMCs in M_P are executed. From the exception structure, the adversary can obtain the address where the violation occurs and thus the target address and code, defeating the SMC protection. Specifically, after program M_P is started,

1. Program control is transferred to the guarded section, i.e., the program entry point `oldEntry`. Program **P** will execute normally until an exception occurs.
2. If the exception is handled by **P** itself, execution continues without control being transferred to **M**.
3. Otherwise, exception handling is passed to **M**. If the exception that occurred is an EXCEPTION_ACCESS_VIOLATION exception, **M** will record the SMC that attempted to execute, perform the SMC, then allow **P** to resume at the next instruction.

4.3 Disassembling Target Code

After locating the SMC codes, the adversary obtains a log file containing the SMC codes that **P** attempted to execute and their address in memory. Based on the mapping rule between memory and file locations, the adversary can modify the executable file with Eq.(1) to generate an equivalent executable with the modifications that would have been performed by the SMC. From this executable, a disassembler such as IDAPro can obtain an accurate static disassembly.

5   Implementations

This section describes two implementations using the Windows XP platform with C++ programming language. The first implementation wraps the target software to form a merged program, while the second one debugs the target software. Both methods are able to extract the necessary data: the target address and target code of the SMC. The following Subsections 5.1-5.5 elaborate the first implementation, and Subsection 5.6 describes the second implementation.

5.1   Creating Program M

As shown in Fig.7, program **M** includes two modules: filter(·) which determines the SMC and clearWR(·) which performs the SMC so that **P** executes properly.

```
__try{
        call OldEntry
}
__except(filter(GetExceptionInformation())){}
```

Fig. 7. Structure of program **M**

filter   When an exception occurs, filter receives an exception structure from the OS which includes the exception code, exception address A_1, etc. If the exception code is EXCEPTION_ACCESS_VIOLATION ($C0000005_h$), the filter routine will:

- Extract the SMC address A_1 from the exception structure, and read several (e.g., 128) code bytes starting from A_1 into a string S.
- Parse S to obtain the SMC instruction according to Table 1.
- Assign the pages including $[A_1, A_1 + n)$ with the WRITE attribute, where n is the size of of the SMC instruction.
- Save S into a buffer $\mathbb{B}$.
- Replace the bytes in address $[A_1, A_1 + n)$ with instruction code "call clearWR", filling any excess bytes with NOP instructions.
- Return the value -1, instructing the program to resume execution at the point where the exception occurred.

For all other exception codes, filter returns the value 0 to instruct the program to continue searching up the stack for an appropriate handler. We assume n is at least the size of the call instruction. If not, we can always parse the instruction following the SMC and save that instruction to $\mathbb{B}$ as well.

clearWR clearWR operates as follows.

- Obtain the SMC from the saved buffer $\mathbb{B}$ and re-write it back to its original location
- Parse the SMC instruction. Assume the region $[A_2, A_2 + m)$ will be written by SMC, where m is the size of written region.
- Assign WRITE attribute to the pages that cover address region $[A_2, A_2 + m)$ exactly.
- Execute the SMC code in the address space of $\mathbf{M}$.
- Disable the WRITE attribute of all the pages that cover address region $[A_1, A_1 + n) \cup [A_2, A_2 + m)$ exactly.
- Record A_2 and the new bytes in the region $[A_2, A_2 + m)$ into a log file.
- Return program control to $\mathbf{P}$.

filter cannot perform the SMC directly since by the exception handling mechanism, program execution will either continue at where the exception occurred, i.e., the SMC code, or after the except clause, i.e., the end of the program $\mathbf{M}$. Thus by inserting the instruction call clearWR at the address A_1, clearWR will be performed instead of the SMC after filter returns. Subsequently after clearWR returns, the instruction pointer can move to the next instruction.

In clearWR, the SMC is restored to its original location so that program $\mathbf{P}$ can be run correctly even if the SMC is included in an iterative structure or protected by a checksum-like mechanism.

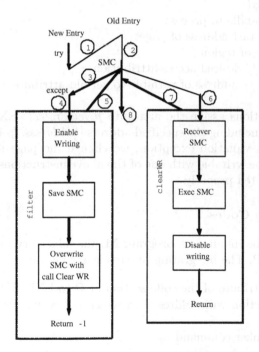

Fig. 8. Program control flow when an SMC occurs

5.2   Designing Program Structure

As mentioned in Section 4, we modify the original program **P** such that the monitoring program **M** can control **P**. We generate the new program structure as Fig.7. When an exception handling is passed to **M**, the program control will be passed to the exception filter, and GetExceptionInformation(.) returns the exception structure. The new program control flow will occur as shown in Fig.8.

5.3   Modifying WRITE Attribute

In a protected software, there may be several SMC instructions randomly located in the program **P**. In order to detect all the SMC instructions, an adversary will remove the WRITE attribute of the code section, but assign the WRITE attribute to the target address so that the program **P** runs correctly. To this end, the adversary adopts the attribute assignment functions:

VirtualProtect(
      lpAddress, // start address of pages
      dwSize, // size of the region
      flNewProtect, // desired access attribution
      lpflOldProtect // address of variable to get old attribution
);
or
VirtualProtectEx(
      hProcess, // handle to process
      lpAddress, // start address of pages
      dwSize, // size of region
      flNewProtect, // desired access attribution
      lpflOldProtect // address of variable to get old attribute
);

These two functions assign the attribute *flNewProtect*=EXECUTE_READ_WRITE to pages including the specified address [*lpAddress*, *lpAddress*+dwSize).

For each access violation exception, we change the page that includes the target address to be writable with one of the above instructions. As a result, the SMC can be executed properly.

5.4   Integrating Codes

After producing the monitoring program **M**, the adversary merges it with the original program **P**. The integrating process is as follows.

- Change the attribute of the code section of **P** to EXECUTE_READ only.
- Add a new section with address rva which is beyond the address space of **P**.
- Execute the linker command as

```
c>link /base:rva M
```

- Copy the code section of the monitoring program **M** into the new blank section.
- Change the program entry `AddressofEntryPoint` to that of the new program **M**.
- Insert functions such as `VirtualProtect`, `VirtualQuery` and `RaiseException` into the import table.

5.5 Detecting Craft Code

If the original program **P** uses the same method to enable SMC, the present method may not work since access violation exceptions are handled by program **P** itself. To overcome this weakness, we can detect the function `VirtualProtect` from the import table, and change the attribute parameter *flNewProtect* back to non-writable such that **P** will not respond to access violation exceptions.

Additionally, in the Subsection 4.3, we only considered cases that SMC replaces dummy code in region $[A_2, A_2+m)$. If the code in the region is useful, (i.e., the same address is used for two more instructions, for example encrypted code), we should enable the disassembler to disassemble both the old code and the target code. That is to say, the present method can be extended to disassemble encrypted codes.

5.6 Alternative Implementation

Following Section 4, the task of the monitoring program includes the steps: disabling WRITE attribute of the SMC's target address, intercepting the SMC instruction, restoring the WRITE attribute, and finally executing SMC. Hence, if we build a debugging environment such that SMC can be executed by Single-Step, we are able to find the target address and target code too. Fig.9 illustrates this debugger-like implementation. In this alternative implementation, the monitor program **T**

(1) Disables the WRITE attribute of the code section of **P**, then loads and runs **P**.
(2) Wait for an access violation from **P**. When an access violation exception occurs, the exception handler in **T** will parse the SMC and obtain the target address.
(3) Enable the WRITE attribute of the target address, and initiate SINGLE_STEP interruption.
(4) Execute SMC in Single-step mode, and activate single-step exception.
(5) Remove WRITE attribute of target address via the EXCEPTION_SINGLE_STEP exception handler.
(6) Recode the target address and target code.

In comparison with the previous wrapper implementation, this method can process the craft code in Subsection 5.5 by intercepting access violation exceptions before the program's own exception handling routine. However, this method takes more computation time since an EXCEPTION_SINGLE_STEP exception and debugging operation are processed for each SMC execution.

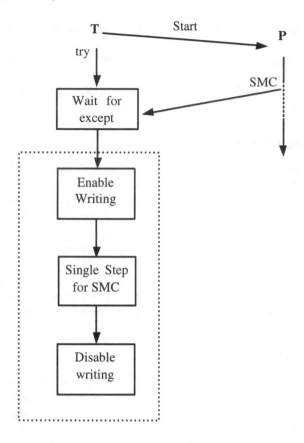

Fig. 9. Debugger-like implementation

6   Experiments

6.1   Improvement on Disassembler

In this experiment, we create a sample binary executable and used the disassembler **IDAPro** for test tool. Fig.10(a) is the disassembly code generated with **IDAPro** directly. With the proposed method, the monitoring program outputs the target address and target code in the SMC instructions, and records them. After modifying the SMC-enabled code with the recorded data, we disassemble the modified code with **IDAPro.exe** again, the new disassembly code is shown in Fig.10(b). Clearly, the wrapper-assisted disassembler outputs a better assembly code in case of SMC.

6.2   Time Overhead

In our scheme, since the exception of **P** is processed in the monitoring program **M**, the run time of **P** will be increased. To evaluate the time cost, the freeware gzip

```
.text:0040820A mov ds:byte_408221, 75h
             ⋮
.text:00408221 db 74h
.text:00408222 adc al, 83h
.text:00408224 sti
.text:00408225 add [esi+0Fh], edi
```

(a) Output of original disassembler.

```
.text:0040820A nop
             ⋮
.text:00408210 nop
             ⋮
.text:00408221 jnz short loc_408237
.text:00408223 cmp ebx, 1
.text:00408226 jle short loc_408237
```

(b) Output of enhanced disassembler.

Fig. 10. Output difference between original disassembler and enhanced disassembler. After detecting and accounting for the code modification performed at $A_1 = 40820A$, we can obtain an accurate disassembly shown in (b).

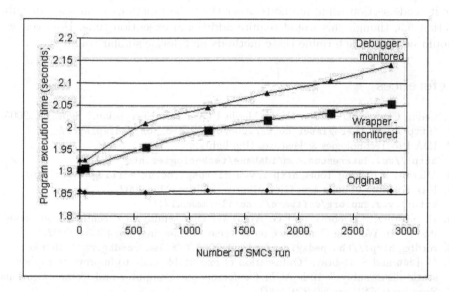

Fig. 11. Overhead of Execution time. The lower, middle and upper curves describe the time used in original `gzip`, wrapper-monitored `gzip` and debugger-monitored `gzip` respectively.

package [28] is used as a tested sample. We inserted a number of SMC instructions into the protected program `gzip`, and calculated the time taken to compress a 16MB collection of text files. Fig.11 shows the time cost with regard to the number of SMC instructions executed. Generally, the time cost is only increased 10%, or $35\mu s$ per SMC instruction using a Pentium IV 2.2GHz system. Analysis can also be restricted to a targeted code subsection by disabling the WRITE attribute only for that subsection. Hence, the proposed scheme can detect the SMC easily with little time cost. According to Fig.11, the debugger-like implementation consumes more time. In fact, this observation is sound since an extra interruption and single-step exception are executed for each SMC in a debug environment.

7   Conclusion and Future Work

SMC changes the software in real-time such that the dynamic code is different from the static code, and hence provides an effective way to defeat static disassembler. However, if a monitoring program identifies the target address of the SMC codes and replaces the bytes in the target addresses with target bytes, it will produce a corrected static code which is identical to dynamic code. This paper presents a method which employs exception mechanism, and implements the method in two implementations. Our experiments demonstrate that the proposed method is effective in defeating SMC protection.

The program can counter this attack by regularly enabling the write privilege for its code section using methods other than the functions mentioned in Subsection 5.3, though this would require additional execution time. However, we should be able to determine these methods and devise similar counters.

References

1. Gavin Clarke, "DVD Jon Hacks Media Player File Encryption," Sept. 02, 2005, (http://www.theregister.co.uk/2005/09/02/dvd_jon_mediaplayer/
2. IDA Pro Technologies & Features Highlights, http://www.datarescue.com/idabase/technologies.htm
3. MicroAPL Porting Tools, http://www.microapl.co.uk/Porting/index.html
4. Free Software Foundation. GNU Binary Utilities, Mar 2002. http://www.gnu.org/software/binutils/manual/.
5. B. Schwarz, S. Debray, and G. Andrews,"Disassembly of executable code revisited.," 9th Working Conference on Reverse Engineering, pp. 45C54, 2002.
6. rordbg, http://bbs.pediy.com/upload/2006/8/files/rordbg.rar_116.rar
7. C. Linn and S. Debray, "Obfuscation of executable code to improve resistance to static disassembly.," 10th ACM Conference on Computer and Communications Security (CCS), pp.290-299, 2003.
8. R. L. Davidson, N. Myhrvold, "Method and System for Generating and Auditing a Signature for a Computer Program," US Patent 5,559,884, Assignee: Microsoft Corp, 1996.
9. J.P. Stern, G. Hachez, F. Koeune, J.-J. Quisquater, "Robust Object Watermarking: Application to Code," 3rd Workshop on Information Hiding, LNCS 1768, pp.368-378, 1999
10. Masahiro Mambo, Takanori Murayama, Eiji Okamoto, "A Tentative Approach to Constructing Tamper-Resistant Software," 1997 New Security Paradigms Workshop, pp.23-33.
11. Mikhail Sosonkin, Gleb Naumovich, Nasir Memon, "Obfuscation of Design Intent in Object-oriented Applications," ACM Workshop On Digital Rights Management, pp.142-153, 2003.
12. Hoeteck Wee, "On Obfuscating Point Functions," Annual ACM symposium on Theory of computing (STOC), pp. 523-532 2005.

13. Christopher Kruegel, William Robertson, Fredrik Valeur, and Giovanni Vigna, "Static Disassembly of Obfuscated Binaries," USENIX security Symposium, pp.255-270, 2005.
14. H. Chang and M. Atallah, "Protecting Software Code by Guards," Security and Privacy in Digital Rights Management, LNCS 2320, pp.160-175, 2001.
15. Bill Horne, Lesley R. Matheson, Casey Sheehan, Robert Endre Tarjan, "Dynamic Self-Checking Techniques for Improved Tamper Resistance," Digital Rights Management, LNCS 2320, pp.141-159, 2001.
16. G.Wurster, P. C. van Oorschot, and A. Somayaji, "A Generic Attack on Checksumming-based Software Tamper Resistance," IEEE Symposium on Security and Privacy, pp.127-138, 2005.
17. P. C. van Oorschot, A. Somayaji, and G.Wurster, "Hardware assisted circumvention of self-hashing software tamper resistance," IEEE Transactions on Dependable and Secure Computing, 2(2):82-92, 2005.
18. Jonathon T. Giffin, Mihai Christodorescu, Louis Kruger, "Strengthening Software Self-Checksumming via Self-Modifying Code," pp.23-32, 21st Annual Computer Security Applications Conference, 2005.
   http://www.cs.wisc.edu/wisa/papers/acsac05/GCK05.pdf
19. Martin Abadi, Mihai Budiu, Ulfar Erlingsson, and Jay Ligatti, "Control-flow integrity: Principles, Implementations, and Applications," ACM conference on Computer and communications security, pp.340-353, 2005.
20. M. Christodorescu, and Somesh Jha, "Static Analysis of Executables to Detect Malicious Patterns," USENIX Security Symposium, pp.169-186, 2003.
21. Yuichiro Kanzaki, Akito Monden, Masahide Nakamura, Ken-ichi Matsumoto, "Exploiting Self-Modification Mechanism for Program Protection," International Computer Software and Applications Conference (COMPSAC), pp.170-179, 2003
22. D. J. Albert and S. P. Morse, "Combating Software Piracy by Encryption and Key Management," Computer, Apr. 1984.
23. D. W. Aucsmith, "Tamper Resistant Software: An Implementation," Information Hiding Workshop, LNCS 1174, pp.317-333, 1996.
24. Ping Wang, *Tamper Resistance for Software Protection*, Master Thesis, Information and Communications University, Korea, 2005.
25. Jaewon Lee, Heeyoul Kim, and Hyunsoo Yoon, "Tamper Resistant Software by Integrity-Based Encryption," PDCAT 2004, LNCS 3320, pp. 608C612, 2004.
26. Jonas Maebe, Koen De Bosschere, "Instrumenting Self-Modifying Code," Fifth Intl. Workshop on Automated and Algorithmic Debugging, pp. 103-113, Sep. 2003.
27. Microsoft Corporation, "Microsoft Portable Executable and Common Object File Format Specification", Revision 6.0, February 1999,
   http://www.microsoft.com/whdc/system/platform/firmware/PECOFF.mspx.
28. The gzip compression program, http://www.gzip.org/

A   SMC Instructions

Table 1 lists possible SMC instructions where A_2 and/or src may be stated implicitly in some instructions.

Table 1. SMC instructions

Instruction	opCode	semantics	size
ADD(ADC) mem, reg	01(11) /r	Add (with CF) r32 to r/m32	6
ADD mem, imm	81 /0(2) id	Add (with CF) imm32 to r/m32	10
SUB mem, reg	29 /r	Subtract r32 from r/m32	6
SUB mem, imm	81 /5 id	Subtract imm32 from r/m32	10
DEC(INC) mem	FF /1(0)	Decrement(increment) r/m32	6
AND mem, reg	21 /r	AND r32 to r/m32	6
AND mem, imm	81 /4 id	AND imm32 to r/m32	10
OR(XOR) mem, reg	09(31) /r	OR(XOR) r32 to r/m32	6
OR(XOR) mem, imm	81 /1(6) id	OR(XOR) imm32 to r/m32	10
NEG mem	F7 /3	2's complement negate r/m32	6
NOT mem	F7 /2	Reverse each bit of r/m32	6
POP mem	8F /0	Pop stack into mem32	6
MOV mem, reg	89 /r	Move r32 to r/m32	6
MOV mem, imm	C7 /0	Move imm32 to r/m32	10
MOV mem16, segreg	8C /r	Move segment reg to r/m16	2
MOVS/ /B/W/D	A4(5)	Move from DS:ESI to ES:EDI	1
STOS mem	AB	Store EAX at ES:EDI	1
XADD mem, reg	0F C1 /r	Exchange r32 and r/m32 Store sum in r/m32	7
XCHG mem, reg	87 /r	Exchange r32 with r/m32	6
RCL(RCR) mem, imm8	C1 /2(3) ib	Rotate(CF) left(right) imm8 times	7
RCL(RCR) mem, CL	D3 /2(3)	Rotate(CF) left(right) imm8 times	6
ROL(ROR) mem, imm8	C1 /0(1)	Rotate left(right) imm8 times	7
ROL(ROR) mem, CL	D3 /0(1)	Rotate left(right) imm8 times	6
SHL(SHR) mem, imm8	C1 /4(5)	Mult(div) by 2, imm8 times	7
SHL(SHR) mem, CL	D3 /4(5)	Mult(div) by 2, imm8 times	6
SAL/SAR mem, imm8	C1 /4(7)	Signed mult(div) by 2, imm8 times	7
SAL/SAR mem, CL	D3 /4(7)	Signed mult(div) by 2, imm8 times	6
SHLD(SHRD) mem, reg, CL	0F A5(D)	Shift r/m32 CL places left(right) and shift bits in from r32	7
SHLD(SHRD) mem, reg, imm8	0F A4(C)	Shift r/m32 imm8 places left(right) and shift bits in from r32	7

Modular Behavior Profiles in Systems with Shared Libraries (Short Paper)

Carla Marceau and Matt Stillerman

ATC-NY, 33 Thornwood Drive, Ithaca NY 14850, USA
{carla, matt}@atc-nycorp.com

Abstract. Modern computing environments depend on extensive shared libraries. In this paper, we propose monitoring the calls between those libraries as a new source of data for host-based anomaly detection. That is, we characterize an application by its use of shared library functions and characterize each shared library function by its use of (lower-level) shared libraries. This approach to intrusion detection offers significant benefits, especially in systems such as Windows, much of which is implemented above the kernel as dynamically linked libraries (DLLs). It localizes anomalies to particular code modules, facilitating anomaly analysis and assessment and discouraging mimicry attacks. It reduces retraining after system updates and enables training concurrent with detection. The proposed approach can be used with various techniques for modeling call sequences, including N-grams, automata, and techniques that consider parameter values. To demonstrate its potential, we have studied how a DLL-level profiling IDS would detect two recent attacks on Windows systems.

Keywords: Anomaly detection, intrusion detection, behavior profile, shared libraries, dynamic link libraries.

1 Introduction

After ten years of research on host-based anomaly detection systems, anomaly detection is still a remote dream for applications that run on most desk-top systems. One reason for this is that modern applications, especially Windows applications, are huge and exhibit a very wide range of behaviors; as the set of legitimate behaviors grows, the probability of false negatives increases, as does the time needed to train a behavior profile. This problem is exacerbated by mimicry attacks [1], which imitate normal application behavior as seen by a given detector in order to defeat that detector. Second, as applications grow, training the anomaly detector takes longer. Worse, Windows systems are subject to frequent patches and updates, any one of which can invalidate the current behavior profile of an application and provoke retraining. Third, anomaly detectors indicate that something might be wrong, but they typically provide very little information for anomaly assessment and response. In particular, they cannot localize the anomaly to a specific program module, which might provide further information for assessment. For these reasons, most current approaches to application anomaly detection are unlikely to succeed for Windows applications.

P. Ning, S. Qing, and N. Li (Eds.): ICICS 2006, LNCS 4307, pp. 369–378, 2006.

In this paper, we propose a novel approach to application anomaly detection that addresses these difficulties. The basic idea is to exploit the use of shared libraries by applications to create profiles for the exported functions of each shared library. We model the behavior of the application by its calls to DLLs and the behavior of each DLL function by its calls to other DLLs. The result is a localized profile of each module (application binary or DLL). Figure 1 schematically represents this key idea. In the system of Figure 1, Application 1 is characterized by its calls to Kernel32.dll, AAA.dll, and BBB.dll. BBB.dll is characterized by its calls to CCC.dll, kernel32.dll, and DDD.dll.

It might seem that the use of shared libraries is too limited to profile applications. However, modern computing systems include extensive shared libraries that implement GUI components, display pictures, enable access to networks and databases, manage mail and other higher level protocols, and provide other reusable functionality. Much of the Windows operating system is implemented in well over a thousand DLLs that execute in user space and mediate access to the kernel. As one example, opening Outlook to open a single email exercises well over one hundred DLLs, of which up to five may be represented on the call stack at any one time. Furthermore, many vulnerabilities in Windows systems are located in DLLs, including a recently discovered vulnerability in the graphics rendering engine (gdi32.dll) that affects every Windows system shipped between 1990 and January 2006 [2, 3]. It is not surprising that most published Windows system vulnerabilities occur in DLLs, since DLLs are available for attackers to study and the payoff for cracking them (a large number of potential victims) is high.

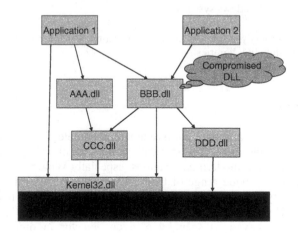

Fig. 1. Structure of a Windows application

This paper makes the following novel contributions:

- It defines DLL profiles and a class of intrusion detection systems based on DLL profiles
- It demonstrates that DLL profiles associate suspicious behavior with specific code modules

- It shows that identifying the locus of suspicious behavior opens new sources of data for analyzing anomalies
- It provides evidence that DLL profiles reduce false negatives and resist mimicry attacks
- It argues that DLL profiles can be used to minimize the burden of training and enable detection to proceed concurrently with retraining after updates

The paper is organized as follows. In Section 2, we review the structure of Windows processes and explain how DLL profiles can be used to detect anomalous program execution. In Section 3, we discuss related work. In Section 4, we briefly describe our experiments detecting two recent exploits on a small application. In Section 5, we substantiate the claimed benefits of DLL profiles. We conclude with suggestions for further research.

2 An Intrusion Detection Model Based on DLL Profiles

A Windows process comprises multiple (kernel-supported) threads, some of which are dedicated to GUI or system functions. Windows applications make extensive use of DLLs that implement the operating system and supply additional functionality. The Windows kernel API is defined by ntdll.dll. However, Windows applications rarely call ntdll.dll directly. Indeed, the Microsoft Visual Studio development environment does not support calls to ntdll.dll. Instead, kernel32.dll[1] defines the standard interface to the operating system, although a few DLLs call ntdll directly. Many calls to kernel32 are mediated through higher-level DLLs. As a result, the typical application cascades through layers of DLLs and results in multiple calls to ntdll and the kernel.

Ground-breaking work by Forrest, et al. [4, 5] showed that kernel-call traces capture application behavior. However, in systems and applications dominated by DLLs, much of the information in kernel-call traces characterizes the internal behavior of DLLs. Therefore, a single N-gram in such a trace often reflects the behavior of multiple DLLs. In the short execution of Outlook mentioned above, up to five DLLs at a time were represented on the call stack. Other characterizations of the behavior of the application as a whole also describe the combined behavior of many shared libraries.

In DLL profiling, we characterize each module (the application and the DLLs) by the calls it makes to other DLLs—not to the kernel. When one DLL calls another, their combined state can be represented with a *stack* of traces of calls between modules, one for each current invocation of a module. Figure 2 represents a snapshot of the stack. Each box represents a separate sequence that is *currently* being accumulated. In Figure 2, the most recent inter-module call by the application is to function f() in AAA, which in turn has called function c() in CCC. When function c returns, the current inter-DLL sequence for function c() is complete. If function f()

---

[1] The name "Kernel32" suggests that this DLL defines an interface to the kernel. Kernel32 provides very basic operating system functionality, but it accesses the kernel only through ntdll, which implements the kernel API. In this paper, we will commonly write DLL names without the .dll extension.

calls some other function in another DLL, a sequence for that function is pushed onto the stack. Note that since DLLs are reentrant, the stack may include multiple instantiations of a single module.

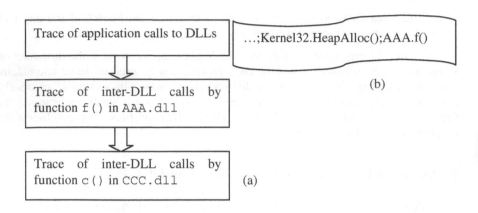

Fig. 2. (a) The stack of inter-DLL-call sequences in a thread. Each stack element is a trace (b) of calls from an exported function of a DLL (or the application main) to other DLLs.

DLL profiles support a new class of intrusion detection methods, depending on what information is recorded in the traces and the profile for each exported DLL function. For example, if the profile focuses on control flow, training traces record the identity of the called functions. N-grams, automata, or other methods may be used to represent the set of traces, as for kernel-call traces [4-11]. Alternatively, if the profile focuses on dataflow, the training traces can record not only the functions called, but also relations among the arguments to the function being profiled and the arguments of the functions it calls. The experiments described in this paper used N-grams, with N=6,[2] but most of our results are more generally applicable.

An IDS that uses the DLL stack model for intrusion detection can be realized in a straightforward way. We posit that the IDS maintains a profile of each function exported by a Windows system DLL, in addition to a profile of each application module (binary or DLL) to be protected. At run time, calls to each profiled DLL are captured, for example by mediating connectors [12, 13], and sent to the IDS. For each thread, the IDS maintains a stack of currently executing modules (DLLs or the main application). For each function in the stack, it records information about the external calls made by the function, as in Figure 2. When an exported function of a DLL is called from another DLL, the instrumentation informs the IDS of the call. The IDS notes the call in the trace at the top of the DLL stack for that thread, checks for anomalies against the profile of the calling function, and pushes a trace for the called function onto the stack. When the DLL function returns, its trace is popped off the DLL stack.

---

[2] Although Forrest's group used N=6 to model UNIX and Linux processes, a smaller value for N may be more appropriate for tracking behavior in terms of inter-DLL calls.

After an update to a DLL, the IDS continues to function but switches to training mode for the updated DLL. When an exported function from the newly updated DLL is called, the IDS pushes the DLL onto the stack, but instead of comparing the trace of the DLL function to the old profile, it collects the trace for input into a new profile. When the DLL function returns, the completed trace is added to the collection of traces for that function, and the profile creation module of the IDS processes it. At some point, the profile is deemed sufficiently mature to be used for detection. At that point, the IDS switches back into detection mode for that DLL function. Note that function profiles mature at different rates, depending on each function's range of behavior and on how frequently it is exercised.

3 Related Work

Much work has been done on profiling programs by sequences of calls, analyzing such sequences, and evading detection based on such sequences. The VtPath model of Feng et al. [14], who use much the same information as the process characterization of Figure 2. They exploit the call stack at each system call to record calls and returns between successive system calls. Like the VtPath model, DLL profiles are used to detect anomalies above the kernel-interface level. Our model differs from theirs in that (1) it records the thread history per calling DLL, rather than for the application as a whole, and (2) it is sparser in that it includes only calls between modules. At any one time, the expected number of functions on the DLL stack is much smaller than the number of functions on the call stack, because functions exported by a DLL are gateways to the DLL's entire functionality, much of which may be implemented in other functions. The exported function may make several calls within the DLL before some function makes a call to another DLL.

We note the difference between our approach and that of Sekar [15]; that approach characterizes an application as a whole by the sequence of its kernel calls augmented by a notation of the origin of the kernel call in the application itself. With Sekar's approach, it is possible to avoid characterizing library functions and focus on the behavior of the application itself; our approach also characterizes the application per se. However, by characterizing the intermediate shared library functions, we are able to identify attacks aimed precisely at these libraries. Indeed, this accounts for a very large number of attacks on Windows systems. Note that both [14] and [15] employ stack tracing in Linux to obtain data for the analysis. In Windows systems, stack tracing is often infeasible because of stack optimization, in which the compiler may use idiosyncratic stack structures within a DLL.

4 Experiments with DLL Profiles

To investigate DLL profiles, we created a DLL profile for a small Windows application and used it to detect two recent exploits. In this section, we describe the experiment.

The first exploit, introduced in the Fall of 2004, exploits a vulnerability present in most versions of gdiplus [3] up to Windows XP, Service Pack 1. It causes a heap overflow when gdiplus is used to display a malicious JPEG image. To study the exploit, we instrumented ImgViewer/32 [16], a freeware application for viewing pictures in GIF, JPEG, and other formats. Like many image viewing applications, ImgViewer/32 relies on Microsoft's graphics processing DLLs, gdi32 and gdiplus, and hence is vulnerable to the attack.

The gdiplus attack, as described in [17], occurs in two stages. In the first stage, a specially-crafted JPEG image header causes function GdipGetPropertyCount() to overwrite the heap with code contained in the "comments" section of the header. Later, during execution of the function GdiplusShutdown(), the overwritten code is executed. The version of the exploit that we used [18] takes advantage of the heap overflow to create a new user with administrative privileges.

Our experiment was conducted as follows. We created a profile of normal behavior by exercising the ImgViewer application on harmless JPEG images in thirty training runs. We then ran the application with a malicious image. The exploit traces were compared with the profiles to find anomalies, and the anomalies were analyzed. We obtained examples of harmless anomalies by exercising the ImgViewer application with JPEG comments against a profile that excluded images with comments.

The ImgViewer application exercises the application binary and 24 DLLs in several threads; we monitored only threads that were governed by the application, which used 14 DLLs. Using those threads, we constructed profiles as described in Section 2. Individual profiles were expressed as sets of N-grams.

We also profiled the effect of the recently discovered WMF exploit [19]. In January 2006, a vulnerability in gdi32.dll was discovered that had existed in all Windows systems since 1990. The vulnerability, which lies in the part of gdi32 that displays WMF pictures, enables a picture to specify arbitrary code to be executed when the picture is displayed. To exercise the vulnerability, we created a small WMF exploit that simply halts the process when invoked. We then used DLL profiles based on a short training period to detect the WMF exploit. Training consisted of the previous thirty executions of ImgViewer on JPEG images, followed by three executions of ImgViewer on benign WMF images.

We discuss the first example in some detail in Section 5. Results from the second example were similar.

We used two types of instrumentation in our experiments. Our first efforts were performed using mediating connectors [12, 13], which are wrappers placed at the point of entry into functions exported by a DLL. These connectors are ideal for intercepting calls into ntdll, but using them to capture calls from modules requires that the signature of each exported function of each DLL be known in advance. An alternative is to start with an application and automatically instrument each DLL as it is invoked; the result is a cascade of wrappers. We have implemented such a cascade and used it for our experiments. When the application or a DLL is linked, the instrumentation modifies its import table so that when a call is made, the instrumentation obtains control and writes a log entry.

5   Benefits of DLL Profiles

In this section, we claim several benefits for DLL profiles and illustrate them with experimental evidence from the gdiplus experiment.

Localization of anomalous behavior to code modules. The gdiplus exploit manifested in anomalies in traces of five exported DLL functions. First, GdipGetPropertyCount, in which the heap overflows, exhibited many calls to five functions that were not in its profile. Second, GdiplusShutdown, which executes the attack code, exhibited four anomalies—all to novel functions—as shown in Table 1. Third, during the execution of GdipGetPropertyCount, the HeapAlloc() function of kernel32 exhibited a call to RtlUnwind, which unwinds the stack after an exception. RtlUnwind() did not appear in the RtlUnwind's profile.

Table 1. Anomalous calls from GdiplusShutdown during the attack

DLL	Function	Comment
kernel32	LoadLibraryA	Loads netapi32
netapi32	NetUserAdd	Adds a new user for the machine
netapi32	NetLocalGroupAddMembers	Gives the new user privilege
kernel32	ExitProcess	End application

Two other functions—CoCreateInstance() in ole32.dll and NdrClientCall2() in rpcrt4.dll—also exhibited anomalies with respect to the available profiles. However, the profiles of those functions had not converged by the end of training. An IDS based on DLL profiles as described above would still be accumulating these two profiles. Thus, it would not (yet) be using them for detection.

False negatives and resistance to mimicry attacks. The DLL functions we have profiled typically have a narrow range of behavior. 90% of all traces are of length 6 or less, and half call just one other function. This dramatically reduces the chances of a false negative, since it is unlikely that attack behavior happens to fall into the narrow range of the function's normal behavior. For example, GdiplusShutdown() normally executes 10 functions in 2 DLLs, as shown in Table 2.

The narrow range of normal behavior reduces the probability of false negatives and makes mimicry attacks infeasible by making the target much smaller: 2 DLLs instead of 14 and 10 functions instead of over 800. Consider the gdiplus exploit, for example. Our exploit payload created a new user through calls to the netapi32 DLL. A clever attacker will avoid such blatantly malicious behavior, but will find himself constrained by the normal profile of the vulnerable function, in our case GdiplusShutdown. A mimicry attacker has to find a function that is not only vulnerable but also enables the desired functionality. In the case of GdiplusShutdown, it is hard to imagine any malicious behavior (other than crashing the application) that an attacker could accomplish using the functions in Table 2.

Anomaly analysis. Localizing anomalies to one or more DLLs makes it possible to draw on knowledge about the DLLs to analyze anomalies. Anomaly analysis in real time helps the IDS decide whether to treat the anomaly as novel application behavior or an attack. For example, the WMF exploit, described earlier, was in operating system code that had been stable for fifteen years. Suppose that an IDS based on

DLL behavior, as described here, had been in use for that whole time. The behavior profiles for that DLL would have been stable for much of that time. Thus, the anomalous behavior, when it appeared, would be very suspicious, in contrast with anomalies from a DLL whose profile has only recently converged.

Table 2. Functions invoked by GdiplusShutdown

DLL	Function	Comment
Kernel32	EnterCriticalSection	Wait for mutex object
	LeaveCriticalSection	Release mutex object
	SetEvent	Signal on (parameter) event
	WaitForSingleObject	Wait on locked object
	CloseHandle	Release object
	DeleteCriticalSection	Release resources for mutex
	HeapFree	Free block in heap
	HeapDestroy	Destroy user-created heap
Gdi32	DeleteObject	Delete object created by gdiplus
	DeleteDC	Delete gdi32 device context

Anomaly analysis can also consider the distance of the anomaly from the profile. For example, the gdiplus exploit called two functions in netapi32, which creates new users; netapi32 does not appear in the profile. Other factors of interest are the provenance and change history of the DLL.

Anomaly analysis can sometimes use information about functions to estimate their potential harm. A call to NetUserAdd() in the context of gdiplus is highly suspicious. We obtained examples of harmless anomalies by exercising the ImgViewer on JPEG images with comments against a profile based on images without comments. This resulted in three anomalous calls to the two functions of Table 3. An IDS armed with knowledge about common functions could guess that these two functions, which collect information about a device (the screen), are probably benign.

Table 3. Harmless anomalies

DLL	Function	Description
user32	GetDC	Retrieves a handle to a display device context (DC) for the client area of a specified window or for the entire screen.
gdi32	GetDeviceCaps	Retrieves device-specific information for the specified device, specified by a handle.

Easing the burden of training (and retraining). In a system whose architecture is dominated by DLLs, when one DLL is updated the system-call profiles of all applications that use that DLL are invalidated, and must be retrained. In contrast, an IDS based on DLL profiles can retrain just the profile of the one changed DLL, and can continue to use all other profiles mature profiles for detection. Retraining a given DLL occurs less frequently and is quicker than training an entire application; it also allows detection of anomalies in other DLLs to continue while the updated DLL is being trained.

The rate at which profiles converge is apt to vary from one DLL function to another. In our experiments, the profiles for two functions never converged; we were nevertheless able to feel quite confident about anomalies detected in other functions whose profiles had converged quickly and unambiguously.

6 Conclusion and Future Work

We have presented a novel approach to host-based anomaly detection that relies on profiles of functions exported by shared libraries. We have argued and shown evidence that such profiles reduce false negatives, localize anomalies to code modules and provide opportunities analyze them, and reduce the burden of training.

Much research remains to be done to realize the potential benefits of DLL profiles. A major question is the performance cost of deploying various types of profiles and how to minimize that cost. Our preliminary measurements with Outlook suggest a performance penalty of 5-10%. This number assumes an IDS in which most anomaly checks are simple (like a table lookup) and the remainder represent state changes.

In addition, an IDS system based on DLL profiles faces non-trivial "bookkeeping" and security challenges. To make retraining practical, ways to base updated function profiles on the profiles for the previous version must be developed.

Finally, DLL profiles open new possibilities for anomaly analysis. Additional information about shared libraries and their functions, as well about connections between libraries (including static analysis of binaries) may lead to algorithms and heuristics for estimating the potential harmfulness of a large class of program anomalies.

Acknowledgements

This work was supported by the Army Research Office under contract DAAD 19-03-C-0060. We are grateful to Matthew Donovan and Ian Lenz for technical assistance. Mediating connectors used in the experiments were provided by Teknowledge Corporation.

References

1. Wagner, D. and P. Soto. "Mimicry Attacks on Host Based Intrusion Detection Systems," in *Proceedings of the Ninth ACM Conference on Computer and Communications Security*. 2002.
2. Allison, K., "Windows PCs Face 'Huge' Virus Threat," in Financial Times, January 2, 2006.

3. Microsoft (TM), "Microsoft Security Bulletin Ms05-053: Vulnerabilities in Graphics Rendering Engine Could Allow Code Execution (896424)," http://www.microsoft.com/technet/security/bulletin/MS05-053.mspx.
4. Forrest, S., S.A. Hofmeyr, and A. Somajayi. "A Sense of Self for UNIX Processes," in *Proceedings of the IEEE Symposium on Computer Security and Privacy*. 1996: IEEE Press.
5. Hofmeyr, S.A., S. Forrest, and A. Somayaji, "Intrusion Detection Using Sequences of System Calls," *Journal of Computer Security*, 1998. **6**(3): p. 151–180.
6. Debar, H., et al. "Fixed vs. Variable-Length Patterns for Detecting Suspicious Process Behavior," in *Proceedings of the ESORICS 98, 5th European Symposium on Research in Computer Security*. 1998. Louvain-la-Neuve, Belgium.
7. Warrender, C., S. Forrest, and B. Pearlmutter. "Detecting Intrusions Using System Calls: Alternative Data Models," in *Proceedings of the IEEE Symposium on Security and Privacy*. 1999, pp. 133-145.
8. Ghosh, A.K., A. Schwatzbard, and M. Shatz. "Learning Program Behavior Profiles for Intrusion Detection," in *Proceedings of the 1st USENIX Workshop on Intrusion Detection and Network Monitoring*. 1999. Santa Clara, California.
9. Marceau, C. "Characterizing the Behavior of a Program Using Multiple-Length N-Grams," in *Proceedings of the New Security Paradigms Workshop*. 2000. Ballycotton, Ireland.
10. Pfleger, K. "On-Line Cumulative Learning of Hierarchical Sparse N-Grams," in *Proceedings of the International Conference on Development and Learning*. 2004.
11. Michael, C.C. and A. Ghosh, "Simple, State-Based Approaches to Program-Based Intrusion Detection," *ACM Transactions on Information and System Security*, 2002. **5**(3): p. 203-237.
12. Balzer, R. and N. Goldman. "Mediating Connectors," in *Proceedings of the ICDCS Workshop on Electronic Commerce and Web-Based Applications*. 1999. Austin, TX, pp. 73-77.
13. Balzer, R. and N. Goldman. "Mediating Connectors: A Non-Bypassable Process Wrapping Technology," in *Proceedings of the 19th IEEE International Conference on Distributed Computing Systems*. 1999.
14. Feng, H., et al. "Anomaly Detection Using Call Stack Information," in *Proceedings of the IEEE Security and Privacy*. 2003. Oakland, CA, USA.
15. Sekar, R., et al. "A Fast Automaton-Based Method for Detecting Anomalous Program Behaviors," in *Proceedings of the IEEE Symposium on Security and Privacy*. 2001. Oakland, CA, pp. 144-155.
16. Arcata Pet, "Imgviewer/32," http://www.arcatapet.net/imgv32.cfm.
17. Ries, C., "Analysis of a Malicious JPEG Attack," http://www.vigilantminds.com/files/jpeg_attack_wp.pdf.
18. French Security Incident Response Team (FSIRT), "Windows JPEG GDI+ Overflow Administrator Exploit (Ms04-028)," http://www.frsirt.com/exploits/09232004.ms04-28-admin.sh.php.
19. Microsoft (TM) TechNet, "Microsoft Security Bulletin Ms06-001: Vulnerability in Graphics Rendering Engine Could Allow Remote Code Execution (912919)," http://www.microsoft.com/technet/security/bulletin/MS06-001.mspx.

Efficient Protection Against Heap-Based Buffer Overflows Without Resorting to Magic

Yves Younan, Wouter Joosen, and Frank Piessens

DistriNet, Dept. of Computer Science, Katholieke Universiteit Leuven
Celestijnenlaan 200A, B-3001 Heverlee, Belgium
{yvesy, wouter, frank}@cs.kuleuven.be

Abstract. Bugs in dynamic memory management, including for instance heap-based buffer overflows and dangling pointers, are an important source of vulnerabilities in C and C++. Overwriting the management information of the memory allocation library is often a source of attack on these vulnerabilities. All existing countermeasures with low performance overhead rely on magic values or canaries. A secret value is placed before a crucial memory location and by monitoring whether the value has changed, overruns can be detected. Hence, if attackers are able to read arbitrary memory locations, they can bypass the countermeasure. In this paper we present an approach that, when applied to a memory allocator, will protect against this attack vector without resorting to magic. We implemented our approach by modifying an existing widely-used memory allocator. Benchmarks show that this implementation has a negligible, sometimes even beneficial, impact on performance.

1 Introduction

Security has become an important concern for all computer users. Worms and hackers are a part of every day Internet life. A particularly dangerous technique that these attackers may employ is the code injection attack, where they are able to insert code into the program's address space and can subsequently execute it. Vulnerabilities that could lead to this kind of attack are still a significant portion of the weaknesses found in modern software systems, especially in programs written in C or C++.

A wide range of vulnerabilities exists that allow an attacker to inject code. The most well-known and most exploited vulnerability is the standard stack-based buffer overflow: attackers write past the boundaries of a stack-based buffer and overwrite the return address of a function so that it points to their injected code. When the function subsequently returns, the code injected by the attackers is executed [1].

However, several other vulnerabilities exist that allow an attacker to inject code into an application. Such vulnerabilities can also occur when dealing with dynamically allocated memory, which we describe in more detail in Section 2. Since no return addresses are available in the heap, an attacker must overwrite other data stored in the heap to inject code. The attacker could overwrite

P. Ning, S. Qing, and N. Li (Eds.): ICICS 2006, LNCS 4307, pp. 379–398, 2006.

a pointer located in this memory, but since these are not always available in heap-allocated memory, attackers often overwrite the management information that the memory allocator stores with heap-allocated data.

Many countermeasures have been devised that try to prevent code injection attacks [2]. Several approaches try and solve the vulnerabilities entirely [3,4,5,6]. These approaches generally suffer from a substantial performance impact. Others with better performance results have mostly focused on stack-based buffer overflows [7,8,9,10,11].

Countermeasures that protect against attacks on dynamically allocated memory can be divided into four categories. The first category tries to protect the management information from being overwritten by using magic values that must remain secret [12,13] . While these are efficient, they can be bypassed if an attacker is able to read or guess the value based on other information the program may leak. Such a leak may occur, for example, if the program has a 'buffer over-read' or a format string vulnerability. A second category focuses on protecting all heap-allocated data by placing guard pages[1] around them [14]. this however results in chunk size which are multiples of page sizes (which is 4 kb on IA32), which results in a large waste of memory and a severe performance loss (because a separate guard page must be allocated every time memory is allocated). A third category protects against code injection attacks by performing sanity checks to ensure that the management information does not contains impossible values[15]. The fourth category separates the memory management information from the data stored in these chunks. In this paper we propose an efficient approach which falls in the fourth category. It does not rely on magic values and can be applied to existing memory allocators.

To illustrate that this separation is practical we have implemented a prototype (which we call dnmalloc), that is publicly available [16]. Measurements of both performance and memory usage overhead show that this separation can be done at a very modest cost. This is surprising: although the approach is straightforward, the cost compared to existing approaches in the first category is comparable or better while security is improved.

Besides increased security, our approach also implies other advantages: because the often-needed memory management information is stored separately, the pages that only hold the program's data, can be swapped out by the operating system as long as the program does not need to access that data [17]. A similar benefit is that, when a program requests memory, our countermeasure will ensure that it has requested enough memory from the operating system to service the request, without writing to this memory. As such, the operating system will defer physical memory allocation until the program actually uses it, rather than allocating immediately (if the operating system uses lazy or optimistic memory allocation for the heap [18]).

The paper is structured as follows: Section 2 describes the vulnerabilities and how these can be used by an attacker to gain control of the execution flow using

---

[1] A guard page is page of memory where no permission to read or to write has been set. Any access to such a page will cause the program to terminate.

a memory allocator's memory management information. Section 3 describes the main design principles of our countermeasure, while Section 4 details our prototype implementation. In Section 5 we evaluate our countermeasure in multiple areas: its performance impact, its memory overhead and its resilience against existing attacks. In Section 6 we describe related work and compare our approach to other countermeasures that focus on protecting the heap. Section 7 contains our conclusion.

2   Heap-Based Vulnerabilities

Exploitation of a buffer overflow on the heap is similar to exploiting a stack-based overflow, except that no return addresses are stored in this segment of memory. Therefore, an attacker must use other techniques to gain control of the execution-flow. An attacker could overwrite a function pointer or perform an indirect pointer overwrite [19] on pointers stored in these memory regions, but these are not always available. Overwriting the memory management information that is generally associated with dynamically allocated memory [20,21,22], is a more general way of exploiting a heap-based overflow.

Memory allocators allocate memory in chunks. These chunks typically contain memory management information (referred to as *chunkinfo*) alongside the actual data (*chunkdata*). Many different allocators can be attacked by overwriting the *chunkinfo*. We will describe how dynamic memory allocators can be attacked by focusing on a specific implementation of a dynamic memory allocator called *dlmalloc* [23] which we feel is representative. *Dlmalloc* is used as the basis for *ptmalloc* [24], which is the allocator used in the GNU/Linux operating system. *Ptmalloc* mainly differs from *dlmalloc* in that it offers better support for multithreading, however this has no direct impact on the way an attacker can abuse the memory allocator's management information to perform code injection attacks. In this section we will briefly describe some important aspects of *dlmalloc* to illustrate how it can be attacked. We will then demonstrate how the application can be manipulated by attackers into overwriting arbitrary memory locations by overwriting the allocator's *chunkinfo* using two different heap-based programming vulnerabilities.

2.1   Doug Lea's Memory Allocator

The *dlmalloc* library is a runtime memory allocator that divides the heap memory at its disposal into contiguous chunks. These chunks vary in size as the various allocation routines (*malloc, free, realloc, ...*) are called. An important property of this allocator is that, after one of these routines completes, a free chunk never borders on another free chunk, as free adjacent chunks are coalesced into one larger free chunk. These free chunks are kept in a doubly linked list, sorted by size. When the memory allocator at a later time requests a chunk of the same size as one of these free chunks, the first chunk of that size is removed from the list and made available for use in the program (i.e. it turns into an allocated chunk).

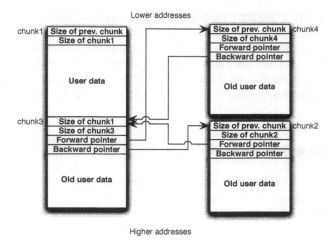

Fig. 1. Heap containing used and free chunks

All memory management information (including this list of free chunks) is stored in-band. That is, the information is stored in the chunks: when a chunk is freed, the memory normally allocated for data is used to store a forward and backward pointer. Figure 1 illustrates what a typical heap of used and unused chunks looks like. *Chunk1* is an allocated chunk containing information about the size of the chunk stored before it and its own size[2]. The rest of the chunk is available for the program to write data in. *Chunk3* is a free chunk that is allocated adjacent to *chunk1*. *Chunk2* and *chunk4* are free chunks located in an arbitrary location on the heap.

Chunk3 is located in a doubly linked list together with *chunk2* and *chunk4*. *Chunk2* is the first chunk in the chain: its forward pointer points to *chunk3* and its backward pointer points to a previous chunk in the list. *Chunk3*'s forward pointer points to *chunk4* and its backward pointer points to *chunk2*. *Chunk4* is the last chunk in our example: its forward pointer points to a next chunk in the list and its backward pointer points to *chunk3*.

2.2   Attacks on Dynamic Memory Allocators

Figure 2 shows what could happen if an array that is located in *chunk1* is overflowed: an attacker overwrites the management information of *chunk3*. The size fields are left unchanged (although these can be modified if an attacker desires). The forward pointer is changed to point to 12 bytes before function f0's return address, and the backward pointer is changed to point to code that will jump over the next few bytes and then execute the injected code. When *chunk1*

---

[2] The size of allocated chunks is always a multiple of eight, so the three least significant bits of the size field are used for management information: a bit to indicate if the previous chunk is in use or not and one to indicate if the memory is mapped or not. The last bit is currently unused.

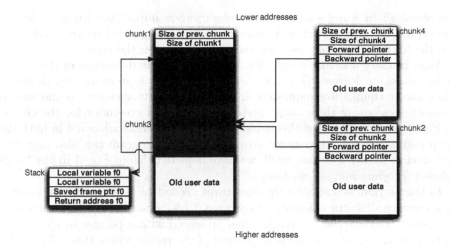

Fig. 2. Heap-based buffer overflow

is subsequently freed, it is coalesced together with *chunk3* into a larger chunk. As *chunk3* is no longer a separate chunk after the coalescing, it must first be removed from the list of free chunks (this is called unlinking). Internally a free chunk is represented by a datastructure containing the fields depicted in *chunk3* in Fig. 2. A chunk is unlinked as follows:

chunk3–>fd –>bk = chunk3–>bk
chunk3–>bk–>fd = chunk3–>fd

As a result, the value of the memory location that is twelve bytes (because of the location of the field in the structure) after the location that *fd* points to will be overwritten with the value of *bk*, and the value of the memory location eight bytes after the location that *bk* points to will be overwritten with the value of *fd*. So in the example in Fig. 2 the return address will be overwritten with a pointer to code that will jump over the place where *fd* will be stored and will execute code that the attacker has injected. This technique can be used to overwrite arbitrary memory locations [20,21].

A similar attack can occur when memory is deallocated twice. This is called a double free vulnerability [25].

3   Countermeasure Design

The main principle used to design this countermeasure is to separate management information (*chunkinfo*) from the data stored by the user (*chunkdata*). This management information is then stored in a separate contiguous memory regions that only contains other management information. To protect these regions from being overwritten by overflows in other memory mapped areas, they are protected by guard pages. This simple design essentially makes overwriting the *chunkinfo* by using a heap-based buffer overflow impossible. Figure 3 depicts the typical memory layout of a program that uses a general memory allocator (on the left) and one that uses our modified design (on the right).

Most memory allocators will allocate memory in the datasegment that could be increased (or decreased) as necessary using the *brk* systemcall [26]. However, when larger chunks are requested, it can also allocate memory in the shared memory area[3] using the *mmap*[4] systemcall to allocate memory for the chunk. In Fig. 3, we have depicted this behavior: there are chunks allocated in both the heap and in the shared memory area. Note that a program can also map files and devices into this region itself, we have depicted this in Fig. 3 in the boxes labeled 'Program mapped memory'.

In this section we describe the structures needed to perform this separation in a memory allocator efficiently. In Section 3.1 we describe the structures that are used to retrieve the *chunkinfo* when presented with a pointer to *chunkdata*. In Section 3.2, we discuss the management of the region where these *chunkinfos* are stored.

3.1   Lookup Table and Lookup Function

To perform the separation of the management information from the actual *chunkdata*, we use a *lookup table*. The entries in the *lookup table* contain pointers to the *chunkinfo* for a particular *chunkdata*. When given such a *chunkdata* address, a lookup function is used to find the correct entry in the *lookup table*.

The table is stored in a map of contiguous memory that is big enough to hold the maximum size of the *lookup table*. This map can be large on 32-bit systems, however it will only use virtual address space rather than physical memory. Physical memory will only be allocated by the operating system when the specific page is written to. To protect this memory from buffer overflows in other memory in the shared memory region, a guard page is placed before it. At the right hand side of Fig. 3 we illustrate what the layout looks like in a typical program that uses this design.

3.2   Chunkinfo Regions

Chunkinfos are also stored in a particular contiguous region of memory (called a *chunkinfo region*), which is protected from other memory by a guard page. This region also needs to be managed, several options are available for doing this. We will discuss the advantages and disadvantages of each.

Our preferred design, which is also the one used in our implementation and the one depicted in Fig. 3, is to map a region of memory large enough to hold a

---

[3] Note that memory in this area is not necessarily shared among applications, it has been allocated by using *mmap*.

[4] mmap is used to map files or devices into memory. However, when passing it the *MAP_ANON* flag or mapping the */dev/zero* file, it can be used to allocate a specific region of contiguous memory for use by the application (however, the granularity is restricted to page size) [26].

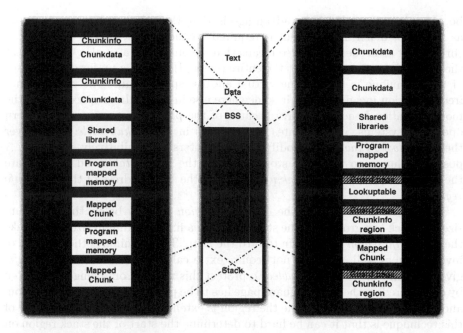

Fig. 3. Original (left) and modified (right) process memory layout

predetermined amount of *chunkinfos*. To protect its contents, we place a guard page at the top of the region. When the region is full, a new region, with its own guard page, is mapped and added to a linked list of *chunkinfo regions*. This region then becomes the active region, meaning that all requests for new *chunkinfos* that can not be satisfied by existing *chunkinfos*, will be allocated in this region. The disadvantage of this technique is that a separate guard page is needed for every *chunkinfo region*, because the allocator or program may have stored data in the same region (as depicted in Fig. 3). Although such a guard page does not need actual memory (it will only use virtual memory), setting the correct permissions for it is an expensive system call.

When a *chunkdata* disappears, either because the associated memory is released back to the system or because two *chunkdatas* are coalesced into one, the *chunkinfo* is stored in a linked list of free *chunkinfos*. In this design, we have a separate list of free *chunkinfos* for every region. This list is contained in one of the fields of the *chunkinfo* that is unused because it is no longer associated with a *chunkdata*. When a new *chunkinfo* is needed, the allocator returns one of these free *chunkinfos*: it goes over the lists of free *chunkinfos* of all existing *chunkinfo regions* (starting at the currently active region) to attempt to find one. If none can be found, it allocates a new *chunkinfo* from the active region. If all *chunkinfos* for a region have been added to its list of free *chunkinfos*, the entire region is released back to the system.

An alternative design is to map a single *chunkinfo region* into memory large enough to hold a specific amount of *chunkinfos*. When the map is full, it can be extended as needed. The advantage is that there is one large region, and as such, not much management is required on the region, except growing and shrinking it as needed. This also means that we only need a single guard page at the top of the region to protect the entire region. However, a major disadvantage of this technique is that, if the virtual address space behind the region is not free, extension means moving it somewhere else in the address space. While the move operation is not expensive because of the paging system used in modern operating systems, it invalidates the pointers in the *lookup table*. Going over the entire *lookup table* and modifying the pointers is prohibitively expensive. A possible solution to this is to store offsets in the *lookup table* and to calculate the actual address of the *chunkinfo* based on the base address of the *chunkinfo region*.

A third design is to store the *chunkinfo region* directly below the maximum size the stack can grow to (if the stack has such a fixed maximum size), and make the *chunkinfo region* grow down toward the heap. This eliminates the problem of invalidation as well, and does not require extra calculations to find a *chunkinfo*, given an entry in the *lookup table*. To protect this region from being overwritten by data stored on the heap, a guard page has to be placed at the top of the region, and has to be moved every time the region is extended. A major disadvantage of this technique is that it can be hard to determine the start of the stack region on systems that use address space layout randomization [27]. It is also incompatible with programs that do not have a fixed maximum stack size.

These last two designs only need a single, but sorted, list of free *chunkinfos*. When a new *chunkinfo* is needed, it can return, respectively, the lowest or highest address from this list. When the free list reaches a predetermined size, the region can be shrunk and the active *chunkinfos* in the shrunk area are copied to free space in the remaining *chunkinfo region*.

4   Prototype Implementation

Our allocator was implemented by modifying *dlmalloc 2.7.2* to incorporate the changes described in Section 3. The ideas used to build this implementation, however, could also be applied to other memory allocators. *Dlmalloc* was chosen because it is very widely used (in its *ptmalloc* incarnation) and is representative for this type of memory allocators. *Dlmalloc* was chosen over *ptmalloc* because it is less complex to modify and because the modifications done to *dlmalloc* to achieve *ptmalloc* do not have a direct impact on the way the memory allocator can be abused by an attacker.

4.1   Lookup Table and Lookup Function

The *lookup table* is in fact a lightweight hashtable: to implement it, we divide every page in 256 possible chunks of 16 bytes (the minimum chunksize), which is the maximum amount of chunks that can be stored on a single page in the heap. These 256 possible chunks are then further divided into 32 groups of 8 elements. For every such group we have 1 entry in the *lookup table* which contains a pointer

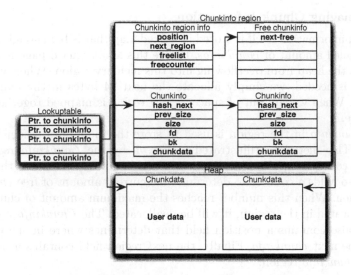

Fig. 4. *Lookup table* and chunkinfo layout

to a linked list of these elements (which has a maximum size of 8 elements). As a result we have a maximum of 32 entries for every page. The *lookup table* is allocated using the memory mapping function, mmap. This allows us to reserve virtual address space for the maximum size that the *lookup table* can become without using physical memory. Whenever a new page in the *lookup table* is accessed, the operating system will allocate physical memory for it.

We find an entry in the table for a particular group from a *chunkdata*'s address in two steps:

1. We subtract the address of the start of the heap from the *chunkdata*'s address.
2. Then we shift the resulting value 7 bits to the right. This will give us the entry of the chunk's group in the *lookup table*.

To find the *chunkinfo* associated with a chunk we now have to go over a linked list that contains a maximum of 8 entries and compare the *chunkdata*'s address with the pointer to the *chunkdata* that is stored in the *chunkinfo*. This linked list is stored in the hashnext field of the *chunkinfo* (illustrated in Fig. 4).

4.2   Chunkinfo

A *chunkinfo* contains all the information that is available in *dlmalloc*, and adds several extra fields to correctly maintain the state. The layout of a *chunkinfo* is illustrated in Fig. 4: the *prev_size*, *size*, *forward* and *backward* pointers serve the same purpose as they do in *dlmalloc*, the *hashnext* field contains the linked list that we mentioned in the previous section and the *chunkdata* field contains a pointer to the actual allocated memory.

4.3   Managing Chunk Information

The chunk information itself is stored in a fixed map that is big enough to hold a predetermined amount of *chunkinfos*. Before this area a guard page is mapped, to prevent the heap from overflowing into this memory region. Whenever a new *chunkinfo* is needed, we simply allocate the next 24 bytes in the map for the *chunkinfo*. When we run out of space, a new region is mapped together with a guard page.

One *chunkinfo* in the region is used to store the meta-data associated with a region. This metadata (illustrated in Fig. 4, by the *Chunkinfo region info* structure) contains a pointer to the start of the list of free chunks in the freelist field. It also holds a counter to determine the current amount of free *chunkinfos* in the region. When this number reaches the maximum amount of chunks that can be allocated in the region, it will be deallocated. The *Chunkinfo region info* structure also contains a position field that determines where in the region to allocate the next *chunkinfo*. Finally, the next_region field contains a pointer to the next *chunkinfo* region.

5   Evaluation

The realization of these extra modifications comes at a cost: both in terms of performance and in terms of memory overhead. To evaluate how high the performance overhead of *dnmalloc* is compared to the original *dlmalloc*, we ran the full SPEC® CPU2000 Integer reportable benchmark [28] which gives us an idea of the overhead associated with general purpose programs. We also evaluated the implementation using a suite of allocator-intensive benchmarks which have been widely used to evaluate the performance of memory managers [29,30,31,32]. While these two suites of benchmarks make up the macrobenchmarks of this section, we also performed microbenchmarks to get a better understanding of which allocator functions are faster or slower when using *dnmalloc*.

Table 1 holds a description of the programs that were used in both the macro- and the microbenchmarks. For all the benchmarked applications we have also included the number of times they call the most important memory allocation functions: *malloc, realloc, calloc*[5] and free (the SPEC® benchmark calls programs multiple times with different inputs for a single run; for these we have taken the average number of calls).

The results of the performance evaluation can be found in Section 5.1. Both macrobenchmarks and the microbenchmarks were also used to measure the memory overhead of our prototype implementation compared to *dlmalloc*. In Section 5.2 we discuss these results. Finally, we also performed an evaluation of the security of *dnmalloc* in Section 5.3 by running a set of exploits against real world programs using both *dlmalloc* and *dnmalloc*.

Dnmalloc and all files needed to reproduce these benchmarks are available publicly [16].

---

[5] This memory allocator call will allocate memory and will then clear it by ensuring that all memory is set to 0.

Table 1. Programs used in the evaluations

SPEC CPU2000 Integer benchmark programs					
Program	Description	malloc	realloc	calloc	free
164.gzip	Data compression utility	87,241	0	0	87,237
175.vpr	FPGA placement routing	53,774	9	48	51,711
176.gcc	C compiler	22,056	2	0	18,799
181.mcf	Network flow solver	2	0	3	5
186.crafty	Chess program	39	0	0	2
197.parser	Natural language processing	147	0	0	145
252.eon	Ray tracing	1,753	0	0	1,373
253.perlbmk	Perl	4,412,493	195,074	0	4,317,092
254.gap	Computational group theory	66	0	1	66
255.vortex	Object Oriented Database	6	0	1,540,780	1,467,029
256.bzip2	Data compression utility	12	0	0	2
300.twolf	Place and route simulator	561,505	4	13,062	492,727
Allocator-intensive benchmarks					
Program	Description	malloc	realloc	calloc	free
boxed-sim	Balls-in-box simulator	3,328,299	63	0	3,312,113
cfrac	Factors numbers	581,336,282	0	0	581,336,281
espresso	Optimizer for PLAs	5,084,290	59,238	0	5,084,225
lindsay	Hypercube simulator	19,257,147	0	0	19,257,147

5.1   Performance

This section evaluates our countermeasure in terms of performance overhead.
All benchmarks were run on 10 identical machines (Pentium 4 2.80 Ghz, 512MB
RAM, no hyperthreading, Redhat 6.2, kernel 2.6.8.1).

Macrobenchmarks. To perform these benchmarks, the SPEC® benchmark
was run 10 times on these PCs for a total of 100 runs for each allocator. The
allocator-intensive benchmarks were run 50 times on the 10 PCs for a total of
500 runs for each allocator.

Table 2 contains the average runtime, including standard error, of the programs in seconds. The results show that the runtime overhead of our allocator are
mostly negligible both for general programs as for allocator-intensive programs.
However, for *perlbmk* and *cfrac* the performance overhead is slightly higher: 4%
and 6%. These show that even for such programs the overhead for the added
security is extremely low. In some cases (*vortex* and *twolf*) the allocator even
improves performance. This is mainly because of improved locality of management information in our approach: in general all the management information
for several chunks will be on the same page, which results in more cache hits
[29]. When running the same tests on a similar system with L1 and L2 cache[6]
disabled, the performance benefit for *vortex* went down from 10% to 4.5%.

---

[6] These are caches that are faster than the actual memory in a computer and are used
to reduce the cost of accessing general memory [33].

Table 2. Average macrobenchmark runtime and memory usage results for *dlmalloc* and *dnmalloc*

SPEC CPU2000 Integer benchmark programs						
Program	DL r/t	DN r/t	R/t overh.	DL mem	DN mem	Mem. overh.
164.gzip	253 ± 0	253 ± 0	0%	180.37	180.37	0%
175.vpr	361 ± 0.15	361.2 ± 0.14	0.05%	20.07	20.82	3.7%
176.gcc	153.9 ± 0.05	154.1 ± 0.04	0.13%	81.02	81.14	0.16%
181.mcf	287.3 ± 0.07	290.1 ± 0.07	1%	94.92	94.92	0%
186.crafty	253 ± 0	252.9 ± 0.03	-0.06%	0.84	0.84	0.12%
197.parser	347 ± 0.01	347 ± 0.01	0%	30.08	30.08	0%
252.eon	770.3 ± 0.17	782.6 ± 0.1	1.6%	0.33	0.34	4.23%
253.perlbmk	243.2 ± 0.04	255 ± 0.01	4.86%	53.80	63.37	17.8%
254.gap	184.1 ± 0.03	184 ± 0	-0.04%	192.07	192.07	0%
255.vortex	250.2 ± 0.04	223.6 ± 0.05	-10.61%	60.17	63.65	5.78%
256.bzip2	361.7 ± 0.05	363 ± 0.01	0.35%	184.92	184.92	0%
300.twolf	522.9 ± 0.44	511.9 ± 0.55	-2.11%	3.22	5.96	84.93%
Allocator-intensive benchmarks						
Program	DL r/t	DN r/t	R/t overh.	DL mem	DN mem	Mem. overh.
boxed-sim	230.6 ± 0.08	232.2 ± 0.12	0.73%	0.78	1.16	49.31%
cfrac	552.9 ± 0.05	587.9 ± 0.01	6.34%	2.14	3.41	59.13%
espresso	60 ± 0.02	60.3 ± 0.01	0.52%	5.11	5.88	15.1%
lindsay	239.1 ± 0.02	242.3 ± 0.02	1.33%	1.52	1.57	2.86%

Microbenchmarks. We have included two microbenchmarks. In the first microbenchmark, the time that the program takes to perform 100,000 *mallocs* of random[7] chunk sizes ranging between 16 and 4096 bytes was measured. Afterwards the time was measured for the same program to *realloc* these chunks to different random size (also ranging between 16 and 4096 bytes). We then measured how long it took the program to *free* those chunks and finally to *calloc* 100,000 new chunks of random sizes. The second benchmark does essentially the same but also performs a *memset*[8] on the memory it allocates (using *malloc*, *realloc* and *calloc*). The microbenchmarks were each run 100 times on a single PC (the same configuration as was used for the macrobenchmarks) for each allocator.

The average of the results (in seconds) of these benchmarks, including the standard error, for *dlmalloc* and *dnmalloc* can be found in Table 3. Although it may seem from the results of the *loop* program that the *malloc* call has an enormous speed benefit when using *dnmalloc*, this is mainly because our implementation does not access the memory it requests from the system. This means that on systems that use optimistic memory allocation (which is the default behavior on Linux) our allocator will only use memory when the program accesses it.

---

[7] Although a fixed seed was set so two runs of the program return the same results.
[8] This call will fill a particular range in memory with a particular byte.

Table 3. Average microbenchmark runtime results for *dlmalloc* and *dnmalloc*

Microbenchmarks			
Program	DL r/t	DL r/t	R/t Overh.
loop: malloc	0.28721 ± 0.00108	0.06488 ± 0.00007	-77.41%
loop: realloc	1.99831 ± 0.00055	1.4608 ± 0.00135	-26.9%
loop: free	0.06737 ± 0.00001	0.03691 ± 0.00001	-45.21%
loop: calloc	0.32744 ± 0.00096	0.2142 ± 0.00009	-34.58%
loop2: malloc	0.32283 ± 0.00085	0.39401 ± 0.00112	22.05%
loop2: realloc	2.11842 ± 0.00076	1.26672 ± 0.00105	-40.2%
loop2: free	0.06754 ± 0.00001	0.03719 ± 0.00005	-44.94%
loop2: calloc	0.36083 ± 0.00111	0.1999 ± 0.00004	-44.6%

To measure the actual overhead of our allocator when the memory is accessed by the application, we also performed the same benchmark in the program *loop2*, but in this case always set all bytes in the acquired memory to a specific value. Again there are some caveats in the measured result: while it may seem that the *calloc* function is much faster, in fact it has the same overhead as the *malloc* function followed by a call to *memset* (because *calloc* will call *malloc* and then set all bytes in the memory to 0). However, the place where it is called in the program is of importance here: it was called after a significant amount of chunks were freed and as a result this call will reuse existing free chunks. Calling *malloc* in this case would have produced similar results.

The main conclusion we can draw from these microbenchmarks is that the performance of our implementation is very close to that of *dlmalloc*: it is faster for some operations, but slower for others.

5.2   Memory Overhead

Our implementation also has an overhead when it comes to memory usage: the original allocator has an overhead of approximately 8 bytes per chunk. Our implementation has an overhead of approximately 24 bytes to store the chunk information and for every 8 chunks, a *lookup table* entry will be used (4 bytes). Depending on whether the chunks that the program uses are large or small, our overhead could be low or high. To test the memory overhead on real world programs, we measured the memory overhead for the benchmarks we used to test performance, the results (in megabytes) can be found in Table 2. They contain

Table 4. Results of exploits against vulnerable programs

Exploit for	Dlmalloc	Dnmalloc
Wu-ftpd 2.6.1 [34]	Shell	Continues
Sudo 1.6.1 [35]	Shell	Crash
Sample heap-based buffer overflow	Shell	Continues
Sample double free	Shell	Continues

the complete overhead of all extra memory the countermeasure uses compared to *dlmalloc*.

In general, the relative memory overhead of our countermeasure is fairly low (generally below 20%), but in some cases the relative overhead can be very high, this is the case for *twolf*, *boxed-sim* and *cfrac*. These applications use many very small chunks, so while the relative overhead may seem high, if we examine the absolute overhead it is fairly low (ranging from 120 KB to 2.8 MB). Applications that use larger chunks have a much smaller relative memory overhead.

5.3   Security Evaluation

In this section we present experimental results when using our memory allocator to protect applications with known vulnerabilities against existing exploits.

Table 4 contains the results of running several exploits against known vulnerabilities when these programs were compiled using *dlmalloc* and *dnmalloc* respectively. When running the exploits against *dlmalloc*, we were able to execute a code injection attack in all cases. However, when attempting to exploit *dnmalloc*, the overflow would write into adjacent chunks, but would not overwrite the management information, as a result the programs kept running.

These kinds of security evaluations can only prove that a particular attack works, but it can not disprove that no variation of this attack exists that does work. Because of the fragility of exploits, a simple modification in which an extra field is added to the memory management information for the program would cause many exploits to fail. While this is useful against automated attacks, it does not provide any real protection from a determined attacker. Testing exploits against a security solution can only be used to prove that it can be bypassed. As such, we provide these evaluations to demonstrate how our countermeasure performs when confronted with a real world attack, but we do not make any claims as to how accurately they evaluate the security benefit of *dnmalloc*.

However, the design in itself of the allocator gives strong security guarantees against buffer overflows, since none of the memory management information is stored with user data. We contend that it is impossible to overwrite it using a heap-based buffer overflow. This will protect from those attacks where the memory management information is used to perform a code injection attack.

Our approach does not *detect* when a buffer overflow has occurred. It is, however, possible to easily and efficiently add such detection as an extension to dnmalloc. A technique similar to the one used in [12,13] could be added to the allocator by placing a random number at the top of a chunk (where the old management information used to be) and by mirroring that number in the management information. Before performing any heap operation on a chunk, the numbers would be compared and if changed, it could report the attempted exploitation of a buffer overflow. A major advantage of this approach over [12] is that it does not rely on a global secret value, but can use a per-chunk secret value. While this approach would improve detection of possible attacks, it does not constitute the underlying security principle, meaning that the security does not rely on keeping values in memory secret.

Finally, our countermeasure (as well as other existing ones [15,12]) focuses on protecting this memory management information, it does not provide strong protection to pointers stored by the program itself in the heap. There are no efficient mechanisms yet to transparently protect these pointers from modification through all possible kinds of heap-based buffer overflows. In order to achieve reasonable performance, countermeasure designers have focused on protecting the most targeted pointers. Extending the protection to more pointers without incurring a substantial performance penalty remains a challenging topic for future research.

6   Related Work

Many countermeasures for code injection attacks exist. In this section, we briefly describe the different approaches that could be applicable to protecting against heap-based buffer overflows, but will focus more on the countermeasures which are designed specifically to protect memory allocators from heap-based buffer overflows.

6.1   Protection from Attacks on Heap-Based Vulnerabilities

Countermeasures that protect against attacks on dynamically allocated memory can be divided into three categories. The first category tries to protect the management information from being overwritten by using magic values that must remain secret. While these are efficient, they can be bypassed if an attacker is able to read or guess the value based on other information the program may leak. Such a leak may occur, for example, if the program has a 'buffer over-read' or a format string vulnerability. A second category focuses on protecting all heap-allocated data by placing guard pages around them. this however results in chunk size which are multiples of page sizes, which results in a large waste of memory and a severe performance loss. A third category protects against code injection attacks by performing sanity checks to ensure that the management information does not contains impossible values.

Robertson et al. [12] designed a countermeasure that attempts to protect against attacks on the *ptmalloc* management information. This is done by changing the layout of both allocated and unallocated memory chunks. To protect the management information a checksum and padding (as chunks must be of double word length) is added to every chunk. The checksum is a checksum of the management information encrypted (XOR) with a global read-only random value, to prevent attackers from generating their own checksum. When a chunk is allocated, the checksum is added and when it is freed, the checksum is verified. Thus, if an attacker overwrites this management information with a buffer overflow, a subsequent free of this chunk will abort the program because the checksum is invalid. However, this countermeasure can be bypassed if an information leak exists in the program that would allow the attacker to read the encryption key (or the management information together with the checksum). The attacker can then modify the chunk information and calculate the correct value of the checksum. The allocator would then be unable to detect that the chunk information has been changed by an attacker.

This countermeasure is efficient, although other benchmarks were used to test the performance overhead in [12], they report similar overhead to ours.

Dlmalloc 2.8.x also contains extra checks to prevent the allocator from writing into memory that lies below the heap (this however does not stop it from writing into memory that lies above the heap, such as the stack). It also offers a slightly modified version of the Robertson countermeasure as a compile-time option.

ContraPolice [13] also attempts to protect memory allocated on the heap from buffer overflows that would overwrite memory management information associated with a chunk of allocated memory. It uses the same technique as proposed by StackGuard [7], i.e. canaries, to protect these memory regions. It places a randomly generated canary both before and after the memory region that it protects. Before exiting from a string or memory copying function, a check is done to ensure that, if the destination region was on the heap, the canary stored before the region matches the canary stored after the region. If it does not, the program is aborted. While this does protect the contents of other chunks from being overwritten using one of these functions, it provides no protection for other buffer overflows. It also does not protect a buffer from overwriting a pointer stored in the same chunk. This countermeasure can also be bypassed if the canary value can be read: the attacker could write past the canary and make sure to replace the canary with the same value it held before.

Although no performance measurements were done by the author, it is reasonable to assume that the performance overhead would be fairly low.

Recent versions of glibc [15] have added an extra sanity check to its allocator: before removing a chunk from the doubly linked list of free chunks, the allocator checks if the backward pointer of the chunk that the unlinking chunk's forward pointer points to is equal to the unlinking chunk. The same is done for the forward pointer of the chunk's backward pointer. It also adds extra sanity checks which make it harder for an attacker to use the previously described technique of attacking the memory allocator. However, recently, several attacks on this countermeasure were published [36]. Although no data is available on the performance impact of adding these lightweight checks, it is reasonable to assume that no performance loss is incurred by performing them.

Electric fence [14] is a debugging library that will detect both underflows and overflows on heap-allocated memory. It operates by placing each chunk in a separate page and by either placing the chunk at the top of the page and placing a guard page before the chunk (underflow) or by placing the chunk at the end of the page and placing a guard page after the chunk (overflow). This is an effective debugging library but it is not realistic to use in a production environment because of the large amount of memory it uses (every chunk is at least as large as a page, which is 4kb on IA32) and because of the large performance overhead associated with creating a guard page for every chunk. To detect dangling pointer references, it can be set to never release memory back to the system. Instead Electric fence will mark it as inaccessible, this will however result in an even higher memory overhead.

6.2 Alternative Approaches

Other approaches that protect against the more general problem of buffer overflows also protect against heap-based buffer overflows. In this section, we give a brief overview of this work. A more extensive survey can be found in [2].

Compiler-based countermeasures. Bounds checking [3,4,5,6] is the ideal solution for buffer overflows, however performing bounds checking in C can have a severe impact on performance or may cause existing object code to become incompatible with bounds checked object code.

Protection of all pointers as provided by PointGuard [37] is an efficient implementation of a countermeasure that will encrypt (using XOR) all pointers stored in memory with a randomly generated key and decrypts the pointer before loading it into a register. To protect the key, it is stored in a register upon generation and is never stored in memory. However, attackers could guess the decryption key if they were able to view several different encrypted pointers. Another attack described in [38] describes how an attacker could bypass PointGuard by partially overwriting a pointer. By only needing a partial overwrite, the randomness can be reduced, making a brute force attack feasible (1 byte: 1 in 256, 2 bytes: 1 in 65536, instead of 1 in 2^{32}).

Operating system-based countermeasures. Non-executable memory [27,39] tries to prevent code injection attacks by ensuring that the operating system does not allow execution of code that is not stored in the text segment of the program. This type of countermeasure can however be bypassed by a return-into-libc attack [40] where an attacker executes existing code (possibly with different parameters).

Address randomization [27,41] is a technique that attempts to provide security by modifying the locations of objects in memory for different runs of a program, however the randomization is limited in 32-bit systems (usually to 16 bits for the heap) and as a result may be inadequate for a determined attacker [42].

Library-based countermeasures. LibsafePlus [43] protects programs from all types of buffer overflows that occur when using unsafe C library functions (e..g *strcpy*). It extracts the sizes of the buffers from the debugging information of a program and as such does not require a recompile of the program if the symbols are available. If the symbols are not available, it will fall back to less accurate bounds checking as provided by the original Libsafe [9] (but extended beyond the stack). The performance of the countermeasure ranges from acceptable for most benchmarks provided to very high for one specific program used in the benchmarks.

Execution monitoring. Program shepherding [44] is a technique that will monitor the execution of a program and will disallow control-flow transfers[9] that

---

[9] Such a control flow transfer occurs when e.g. a *call* or *ret* instruction is executed.

are not considered safe. An example of a use for shepherding is to enforce return instructions to only return to the instruction after the call site. The proposed implementation of this countermeasure is done using a runtime binary interpreter, as a result the performance impact of this countermeasure is significant for some programs, but acceptable for others.

Control-flow integrity [45] determines a program's control flow graph beforehand and ensures that the program adheres to it. It does this by assigning a unique ID to each possible control flow destination of a control flow transfer. Before transferring control flow to such a destination, the ID of the destination is compared to the expected ID, and if they are equal, the program proceeds as normal. Performance overhead may be acceptable for some applications, but may be prohibitive for others.

7   Conclusion

In this paper we presented a design for existing memory allocators that is more resilient to attacks that exploit heap-based vulnerabilities than existing allocator implementations. We implemented this design by modifying an existing memory allocator. This implementation has been made publicly available. We demonstrated that it has a negligible, sometimes even beneficial, impact on performance. The overhead in terms of memory usage is very acceptable. Although our approach is straightforward, surprisingly, it offers stronger security than comparable countermeasures with similar performance overhead because it does not rely on the secrecy of magic values.

References

1. Aleph One: Smashing the stack for fun and profit. Phrack **49** (1996)
2. Younan, Y., Joosen, W., Piessens, F.: Code injection in C and C++ : A survey of vulnerabilities and countermeasures. Technical Report CW386, Departement Computerwetenschappen, Katholieke Universiteit Leuven (2004)
3. Austin, T.M., Breach, S.E., Sohi, G.S.: Efficient detection of all pointer and array access errors. In: Proc. of the ACM '94 Conf. on Programming Language Design and Implementation, Orlando, FL (1994)
4. Jones, R.W.M., Kelly, P.H.J.: Backwards-compatible bounds checking for arrays and pointers in C programs. In: Proc. of the 3rd Int. Workshop on Automatic Debugging, Linköping, Sweden (1997)
5. Ruwase, O., Lam, M.S.: A practical dynamic buffer overflow detector. In: Proc. of the 11th Network and Distributed System Security Symp., San Diego, CA (2004)
6. Xu, W., DuVarney, D.C., Sekar, R.: An Efficient and Backwards-Compatible Transformation to Ensure Memory Safety of C Programs. In: Proc. of the 12th ACM Int. Symp. on Foundations of Software Engineering, Newport Beach, CA (2004)
7. Cowan, C., Pu, C., Maier, D., Hinton, H., Walpole, J., Bakke, P., Beattie, S., Grier, A., Wagle, P., Zhang, Q.: StackGuard: Automatic adaptive detection and prevention of buffer-overflow attacks. In: Proc. of the 7th USENIX Security Symp., San Antonio, TX (1998)

8. Etoh, H., Yoda, K.: Protecting from stack-smashing attacks. Technical report, IBM Research Divison, Tokyo Research Laboratory (2000)

9. Baratloo, A., Singh, N., Tsai, T.: Transparent run-time defense against stack smashing attacks. In: USENIX 2000 Technical Conf. Proc., San Diego, CA (2000)

10. Xu, J., Kalbarczyk, Z., Patel, S., Ravishankar, K.I.: Architecture support for defending against buffer overflow attacks. In: Second Workshop on Evaluating and Architecting System dependabilitY, San Jose, CA (2002)

11. Younan, Y., Pozza, D., Joosen, W., Piessens, F.: Extended protection against stack smashing attacks without performance loss. In: Proc. of the Annual Computer Security Apps. Conf., Miami, FL (2006)

12. Robertson, W., Kruegel, C., Mutz, D., Valeur, F.: Run-time detection of heap-based overflows. In: Proc. of the 17th Large Installation Systems Administrators Conf., San Diego, CA (2003)

13. Krennmair, A.: ContraPolice: a libc extension for protecting applications from heap-smashing attacks. http://www.synflood.at/contrapolice/ (2003)

14. Perens, B.: Electric fence 2.0.5. http://perens.com/FreeSoftware/ (1999)

15. Free Software Foundation: GNU C library. http://www.gnu.org/software/libc (2004)

16. Younan, Y.: Dnmalloc 1.0. http://www.fort-knox.org (2005)

17. Kamp, P.H.: Malloc(3) revisted. In: Proc. of the USENIX 1998 Anual technical conference, New Orleans, LA (1998)

18. Summit, S.: Re: One of your c.l.c faq question. Comp.lang.C newsgroup (2001)

19. Bulba, Kil3r: Bypassing Stackguard and stackshield. Phrack **56** (2000)

20. anonymous: Once upon a free(). Phrack **57** (2001)

21. Kaempf, M.: Vudo - an object superstitiously believed to embody magical powers. Phrack **57** (2001)

22. Solar Designer: JPEG COM marker processing vulnerability in netscape browsers. http://www.openwall.com/advisories/OW-002-netscape-jpeg.txt (2000)

23. Lea, D., Gloger, W.: malloc-2.7.2.c. Comments in source code (2001)

24. Gloger, W.: ptmalloc. http://www.malloc.de/en/ (1999)

25. Dobrovitski, I.: Exploit for CVS double free() for linux pserver. http://seclists.org/lists/bugtraq/2003/Feb/0042.html (2003)

26. Stevens, W.R.: Advanced Programming in the UNIX env. Addison-Wesley (1993)

27. The PaX Team: Documentation for PaX. http://pax.grsecurity.net (2000)

28. Henning, J.L.: Spec cpu2000: Measuring cpu performance in the new millennium. Computer **33**(7) (2000)

29. Grunwald, D., Zorn, B., Henderson, R.: Improving the cache locality of memory allocation. In: Proc. of the ACM 1993 Conf. on Programming Language Design and Implementation, New York, NY (1993)

30. Johnstone, M.S., Wilson, P.R.: The memory fragmentation problem: Solved? In: Proc. of the 1st ACM Int. Symp. on Memory Management, Vancouver, BC (1998)

31. Berger, E.D., Zorn, B.G., McKinley, K.S.: Composing high-performance memory allocators. In: Proc. of the ACM Conf. on Programming Language Design and Implementation, Snowbird, UT (2001)

32. Berger, E.D., Zorn, B.G., McKinley, K.S.: Reconsidering custom memory allocation. In: Proc. of the ACM Conf. on Object-Oriented Programming Systems, Languages and Apps., Seattle, WA (2002)

33. van der Pas, R.: Memory hierarchy in cache-based systems. Technical Report 817-0742-10, Sun Microsystems, Sant a Clara, CA (2002)

34. Zen-parse: Wu-ftpd 2.6.1 exploit. Vuln-dev mailinglist (2001)

35. Kaempf, M.: Sudo exploit. Bugtraq mailinglist (2001)
36. Phantasmagoria, P.: The malloc maleficarum. Bugtraq mailinglist (2005)
37. Cowan, C., Beattie, S., Johansen, J., Wagle, P.: PointGuard: protecting pointers from buffer overflow vulnerabilities. In: Proc. of the 12th USENIX Security Symp., Washington, DC (2003)
38. Alexander, S.: Defeating compiler-level buffer overflow protection. ;login: The USENIX Magazine 30(3) (2005)
39. Solar Designer: Non-executable stack patch. http://www.openwall.com (1998)
40. Wojtczuk, R.: Defeating Solar Designer's Non-executable Stack Patch. Bugtraq mailinglist (1998)
41. Bhatkar, S., DuVarney, D.C., Sekar, R.: Address obfuscation: An efficient approach to combat a broad range of memory error exploits. In: Proc. of the 12th USENIX Security Symp., Washington, DC (2003)
42. Shacham, H., Page, M., Pfaff, B., Goh, E.J., Modadugu, N., Boneh, D.: On the Effectiveness of Address-Space Randomization. In: Proc. of the 11th ACM Conf. on Computer and communications security, Washington, DC (2004)
43. Avijit, K., Gupta, P., Gupta, D.: Tied, libsafeplus: Tools for runtime buffer overflow protection. In: Proc. of the 13th USENIX Security Symp., San Diego, CA (2004)
44. Kiriansky, V., Bruening, D., Amarasinghe, S.: Secure execution via program shepherding. In: Proc. of the 11th USENIX Security Symp., San Francisco, CA (2002)
45. Abadi, M., Budiu, M., Erlingsson, U., Ligatti, J.: Control-flow integrity. In: Proc. of the 12th ACM Conf. on Computer and Communications Security, Alexandria, VA (2005)

Cryptanalysis of Timestamp-Based Password Authentication Schemes Using Smart Cards

Guilin Wang and Feng Bao

Institute for Infocomm Research
21 Heng Mui Keng Terrace, Singapore 119613
{glwang, baofeng}@i2r.a-star.edu.sg

Abstract. Password authentication is an important mechanism for remote login systems, where only authorized users can be authenticated
via using their passwords and/or some similar secrets. In 1999, Yang and
Shieh [14] proposed two password authentication schemes using smart
cards. Their schemes are not only very efficient, but also allow users to
change their passwords freely and the server has no need to maintain
a verification table for authenticating users. However, their schemes are
later identified to be flawed. To overcome those security flaws, Shen et
al. [9] and Yoon et al. [17] proposed further improvements and claimed
their new schemes are secure. In this paper, we first point out that Yang
et al.'s attack [15] against Shen et al.'s scheme is actually *invalid*, since
we can show that in a real implementation it is extremely difficult to
find two hash values such that one is divisible by the other. After that,
we show that both of Shen et al.' scheme and Yoon et al.'s scheme are
insecure by identifying several effective impersonation attacks. Those attacks enable an outsider to be successfully authenticated and then enjoy
the resources and/or services provided by the server.

Keywords: password authentication, smart card, attack, hash function.

1 Introduction

Password authentication is an important mechanism for remote login systems to
implement remote authentication through a public and insecure network, such as
Internet. In such a system, it is required that only authorized users can be authenticated by the server, and then are granted to access the resources and/or services
provided by the server. Since in this environment users usually hold portable but
capability-limited devices such as smart cards with passwords, it is highly desirable that only simple and efficient operations, rather than complicated cryptographic techniques, are exploited to implement the authentication procedure.

The first remote authentication scheme is proposed by Lamport in 1981 [6].
After that, a number of password authentication schemes [14, 5, 3, 4, 9] have
been proposed and analyzed due to the facts that those schemes are both potentially important in practical applications and amazingly attractive in their
simple structures. In 1999, Yang and Shieh [14] proposed two password authentication schemes using smart cards, one is timestamp-based and the other is

P. Ning, S. Qing, and N. Li (Eds.): ICICS 2006, LNCS 4307, pp. 399–409, 2006.
© Springer-Verlag Berlin Heidelberg 2006

nonce-based. Compared with previous schemes, their schemes are very interesting since the following two features are achieved: (a) All legal users are allowed to set and change their passwords freely; and (b) The server has no need to maintain a verification table for authenticating users. Later, Chan and Cheng [3], and Fan et al. [4] pointed out that the Yang-Shieh scheme is vulnerable to impersonation attacks if the users' identities IDs are not carefully formatted or encoded. To thwart those attacks, Shen, Lin, and Hwang [9] improved the Yang-Shieh scheme. However, Yang, Yang and Wang [15] recently presented a simple attack against Shen at al.'s scheme by finding two hash values so that one is a multiple of the other. In another direction, Yang, Wang, and Chang [16] also enhanced the Yang-Shieh scheme. However Yoon et al. [17] showed that Yang et al.'s schemes in [16] are also insecure and further proposed improvements.

In this paper, we present a cryptanalysis of two above mentioned timestamp-based password authentication schemes, i.e., the SLH scheme [9] and the YKY scheme [17]. We show that both of those two authentication schemes are vulnerable to impersonation attacks, and that the YYW attack [15] against the SLH scheme is invalid. In more detail, this paper has the following contributions. We first point out that the YYW attack against the SLH scheme is actually *invalid*, since we can show that in a real implementation it is *extremely difficult* to find two hash values such that one is divisible by the other. Precisely speaking, we prove that if a hash function is modelled as a random function [1], then the probability that one hash value is divisible by another is less than $(1 + k)/2^k$, where k is the fixed output length of the hash function. In real applications, however, k should be set as 128 at least. Then, on the other hand, we show that Shen et al.'s password authentication scheme is indeed *insecure* by successfully identifying two effective impersonation attacks. By exploiting our attacks, the attacker as an outsider can impersonate a legitimate user to access the resources and/or services provided by the server. Finally, we demonstrate that the YKY scheme is also insecure, contrary to the authors' claim in [17], since it suffers a similar impersonation attack.

The rest of the paper is organized as follows. We first review the SLH scheme in Section 2, discuss the invalidity of the YYW attack in Section 3, and present our impersonation attacks against the SLH scheme in Section 4. Then, we turn to review and analyze the YKY scheme in Section 5. Finally, the conclusion is given in Section 6.

2   Review of the SLH Scheme

The SLH timestamp-based password authentication scheme [9] consists of three phases: registration, login, and authentication. We now review each phase as follows.

2.1   Registration Phase

It is assumed that the server has an RSA cryptosystem [8] with key material (n, e, d), where $n = pq$ is the product of two large primes p and q, e is a prime number, and $d = e^{-1} \bmod (p-1)(q-1)$. Furthermore, g is a primitive element in both $GF(p)$ and $GF(q)$, and $f(\cdot)$ is a secure hash function. Except (d, p, q) are kept as secrets, $(n, e, g, f(\cdot))$ are publicly published.

When a user U_i wants to register with the server, he/she first submits his/her identity ID_i and a chosen password PW_i to the server through a secure channel. Then, the server computes three values of (S_i, h_i, CID_i) as follows:

$$S_i = ID_i^d \bmod n, \quad h_i = g^{PW_i \cdot d} \bmod n, \text{ and } CID_i = f(ID_i \oplus d), \quad (1)$$

where $\oplus$ denotes the exclusive operation, and CID_i is treated as the card identity.

Finally, the server writes $(n, e, g, f, ID_i, CID_i, S_i, h_i)$ into a smart card, and then delivers this smart card to the user U_i.

2.2   Login Phase

When the user U_i wants to login into the server, he/she inserts his/her smart card into a card reader and enters his/her identity ID_i and password PW_i. If both ID_i and PW_i are valid, the smart card selects a random number r_i, and then computes values X_i and Y_i by[1]

$$X_i = g^{r_i \cdot PW_i} \bmod n \text{ and } Y_i = S_i \cdot h_i^{r_i \cdot f(CID_i, T_1)} \bmod n, \quad (2)$$

where the timestamp T_1 denotes the current date and time when this login occurs. Finally, the login request message $M = \{ID_i, CID_i, X_i, Y_i, n, e, g, T_1\}$ is sent to the server.

2.3   Authentication Phase

Upon receiving $M = \{ID_i, CID_i, X_i, Y_i, n, e, g, T_1\}$, the server checks the validity of this login request message according to the following procedures:

- $CID_i \equiv f(ID_i \oplus d)$.
- $Y_i^e \equiv ID_i \cdot X_i^{f(CID_i, T_1)} \bmod n$.
- $T_2 - T_1 \leq \Delta T$, where T_2 denotes the date and time when the server received the request M, and ΔT is a predefined time interval to balance the reasonable transmission delay and potential replay attack.

If any of the above verifications fails, the login request is rejected. Otherwise, the server first calculates $R = f(CID_i, T_2)^d \bmod n$, and then sends back message $N = \{R, T_2\}$ to the user U_i. After receiving message N, the user U_i accepts the server's service if and only if both of the following checks hold:

- $R^e \equiv f(CID_i, T_2) \bmod n$.
- $T_3 - T_2 \leq \Delta T$, where T_3 denotes the date and time when U_i received message N.

---

[1] Note that in [15], the value X_i is calculated by $X_i = g^{r_i \cdot f(CID_i, T_1)} \bmod n$. However, this formula is incorrect since it is inconsistent with the original specification of the SLH scheme [9]. Therefore, this typo is corrected here.

3   The YYW Attack and Its Invalidity

Under the assumption that an attacker can find two hash values such that one is a multiple of the other, Yang et al. [15] identified the following attack on the SLH scheme.

1. The attacker first intercepts a login request message $M = \{ID_i, CID_i, X_i, Y_i, n, e, g, T_1\}$ over the communication channel.
2. Then, the attacker finds a value a such that $a \cdot f(CID_i, T_1') = f(CID_i, T_1)$, where T_1' is the attacker's login time.
3. Finally, the attacker sends a forged login request message $M' = \{ID_i, CID_i, X_i', Y_i, n, e, g, T_1'\}$ to the server, where X_i' is computed by

$$X_i' = X_i^a \bmod n \ (= g^{r_i \cdot PW_i \cdot a} \bmod n).$$

It is easy to know that this attack is correct, since both (ID_i, CID_i) and (X_i', Y_i) are valid pairs, i.e.,

$$CID_i = f(CD_i \oplus d) \text{ and } Y_i^e = ID_i \cdot X_i'^{f(CID_i, T_1')} \bmod n.$$

However, we notice that the YYW attack is actually *invalid* in practice, because it is *extremely difficult* to find a login time T_1' such that $f(CID_i, T_1')$ is a factor of $f(CID_i, T_1)$. Formally, we have the following theorem.

Theorem 1. *Let X and Y be two random inputs of a hash function $f(\cdot)$ with k-bit output. Then, under the assumption that the outputs of hash function $f(\cdot)$ can be considered as random numbers, the probability that $f(Y)$ is divisible by $f(X)$ is at most $(k+1)/2^k$. That is, we have*

$$P \triangleq Pr[f(X)|f(Y)] \leq (1+k)/2^k. \tag{3}$$

Proof: Let $x = f(X)$ and $y = f(Y)$. Since the outputs of hash function $f(\cdot)$ are assumed to be random numbers with k bits, x and y can be treated as two random integers independently chosen from interval $[0, 2^k - 1]$. More specifically, pair (x, y) could be any element of set $S = \{(a, b)|\forall a, b \in [0, 2^k - 1]\}$ with equal probability 2^{-2k}.

To compute probability P, we need to count how many pairs (a, b) in set S satisfying $a|b$, i.e., there exists an integer t such that $b = a \cdot t$. That is, we have to compute or estimate the cardinality of subset $T = \{(a, b)|(a, b) \in S \wedge a|b\}$. Actually, we can estimate $|T|$, i.e., the numbers of pairs in subset T, according to the value of a as follows:

- $a = 0$: there is only one pair in T, i.e., $(0, 0)$;
- $a = 1$: there are 2^k pairs in T, i.e., all $(1, b)$ for any $b \in [0, 2^k - 1]$;
- $a = 2$: there are at most $(1 + \frac{2^k}{2})$ pairs in T;
- $a = 3$: there are at most $(1 + \frac{2^k}{3})$ pairs in T;
- ......;

- $a = i$: there are at most $(1 + \frac{2^k}{i})$ pairs in T;
- ......;
- $a = 2^k - 1$: there are at most $(1 + \frac{2^k}{2^k-1})$ pairs in T.

Therefore, we have the following estimate for the upper bound of $|T|$:

$$
\begin{aligned}
|T| &\leq 1 + 2^k + (1 + \tfrac{2^k}{2}) + (1 + \tfrac{2^k}{3}) + \cdots + (1 + \tfrac{2^k}{i}) \\
&\quad + \cdots + (1 + \tfrac{2^k}{2^k-1}) \\
&\leq 2^k + 2^k + \tfrac{2^k}{2} + \tfrac{2^k}{3} + \cdots + \tfrac{2^k}{i} + \cdots + \tfrac{2^k}{2^k-1} \\
&\leq 2^k \cdot [2 + (\tfrac{1}{2} + \tfrac{1}{3}) + (\tfrac{1}{4} + \cdots + \tfrac{1}{7}) + \cdots + (\tfrac{1}{2^j} + \\
&\quad \cdots + \tfrac{1}{2^{j+1}-1}) + \cdots + (\tfrac{1}{2^{k-1}} + \cdots + \tfrac{1}{2^k-1})] \\
&\leq 2^k [2 + \sum_{j=1}^{k-1} 2^j \cdot \tfrac{1}{2^j}] \\
&\leq 2^k [1 + k].
\end{aligned}
$$

As $|S| = 2^{2k}$, we consequently get the following upper bound for probability P:

$$
P = Pr[f(X)|f(Y)] = |T|/|S| \leq (1 + k)/2^k. \tag{4}
$$

This is what we want to prove. □

In a real system, the output length of hash function $f(\cdot)$ is at least 128-bit. In this case ($|f(\cdot)| = 128$), according to Proposition 1 we know that that for any randomly chosen T_1', the probability that $f(CID_i, T_1)$ is a multiple of $f(CID_i, T_1')$ is at most $(1 + 128)/2^{128} < 2^{-120}$, a negligible quantity. As specified in Proposition 1, this statement holds under the assumption that the outputs of hash function $f(\cdot)$ can be treated as random integers with fixed length [1]. Naturally, a real-world hash function cannot be *completely* treated as a random function. However, as one of cryptographic requirements on hash functions they should be *very* close to a random function. In fact, this treatment is a popular method exploited in modern cryptography research, called random oracle model, first introduced by Bellare and Rogaway in [1].

Note that just due to the fact that probability $P = (1 + k)/2^k$ is negligible in security parameter k, i.e., the fixed output length of hash function $f(\cdot)$, an attacker can neither run the YYW attack by polynomial times (in k) to get an successful login with a non-negligible probability. For example, in the case $k = 128$, to get a successful login by using the YYW attack the attacker have to try about 2^{120} times. If one try needs one second to finish, this means the attacker have to cost over than 2^{95} years to succeed one impersonating login. This is the exact reason why we say the YYW attack is invalid or infeasible in practice. However, as shown in next section, the SLH authentication scheme is truly weak and can be attacked by an outsider without much cost.

4   New Attacks Against the SLH Scheme

In this section, we show that the SLH authentication scheme [9] is indeed insecure by presenting two effective attacks, though the YYW attack is invalid as we just discussed. The first attack can be mounted if the RSA public exponent e is a small prime number, while the second attack works without any assumption on the size of public RSA exponent e.

4.1   Impersonation Attack A

The SLH authentication scheme [9] just requires the RSA public exponent e should be a prime number but did not specify the size of e. In other words, one may implement the SLH authentication scheme by selecting a small prime number as the value of e, for example, 3, 7, 13, 17 etc. Actually, this is likely to happen due to two reasons: (1) Some standards, e. g. PKCS #1 [7], recommend to use small exponent e such as 3 to speed up the RSA signature verification; and (2) Small exponent e can reduce the computational cost of smart cards, which are employed in the SLH scheme as the authentication devices for users.

However, if the exponent e is truly set as a small prime number, the SLH authentication scheme is vulnerable to the following impersonation attack A.

1. The attacker first intercepts a login request message $M = \{ID_i, CID_i, X_i, Y_i, n, e, g, T_1\}$ over the communication channel.
2. Then, the attacker checks whether $f(CID_i, T_1)$ is divisible by e or not, i.e., $e|f(CID_i, T_1)$. If not, intercept more login request messages. Otherwise, continue.
3. Let $f(CID_i, T_1) = eb$ for some integer $b \in Z$. Then, compute S_i by

$$S_i = Y_i \cdot X_i^{-b} \bmod n. \tag{5}$$

4. For any timestamp T_1', the attacker selects a random number $r \in Z_n$, and then compute X_i' and Y_i' as follows:

$$X_i' = r^e \bmod n \quad \text{and} \quad Y_i' = S_i \cdot r^{f(CID_i, T_1')} \bmod n. \tag{6}$$

5. Finally, the attacker can impersonate user U_i to access the server by sending out a forged login request message $M' = \{ID_i, CID_i, X_i', Y_i', n, e, g, T_1'\}$.

Note that in the above attack, we have $CID_i \equiv f(ID_i \oplus d)$ and $Y_i'^e \equiv ID_i \cdot X_i'^{f(CID_i, T_1')} \bmod n$. The latter formula is justified by the following equalities:

$$
\begin{aligned}
Y_i'^e &= [S_i \cdot r^{f(CID_i, T_1')}]^e \bmod n \\
&= S_i^e \cdot (r^e)^{f(CID_i, T_1')} \bmod n \\
&= (Y_i \cdot X_i^{-b})^e \cdot X_i'^{f(CID_i, T_1')} \bmod n \\
&= (Y_i^e \cdot X_i^{-be}) \cdot X_i'^{f(CID_i, T_1')} \bmod n \\
&= (Y_i^e \cdot X_i^{-f(CID_i, T_1)}) \cdot X_i'^{f(CID_i, T_1')} \bmod n \\
&= ID_i \cdot X_i'^{f(CID_i, T_1')} \bmod n.
\end{aligned}
\tag{7}
$$

Therefore, our attack A is successful if the forged login request message $M' = \{ID_i, CID_i, X_i', Y_i', n, e, g, T_1'\}$ can be delivered to the server before $T_1' + \Delta T$. This is not a problem for the attacker, since this condition applies to all legal users too. The only concern is the probability of $e|f(CID_i, T_1)$. Under the assumption that the outputs of hash function $f(\cdot)$ are random numbers, it is easy to know $e|f(CID_i, T_1)$ for a random timestamp T_1 with probability of $1/e$. This implies that to successfully amount attack A, the attacker only needs to intercept a dozen of valid login messages on average if e is an odd prime less than 20. Actually, even if $e = 65537 = 2^{16} + 1$ attack A remains feasible in practice if an attacker eavesdrops thousands of valid login messages (not limited to one single legitimate user).

However, note that if $|e| \geq 80$ it seems infeasible to amount attack A since each single run of the attacking algorithm with success probability only about 2^{-80}, a negligible quantity. This is the reason why we have to assume that e should be a small number in attack A. However, attack B described in the next section does not rely on this assumption any more.

4.2   Impersonation Attack B

In this attack, to access the server by impersonating the user U_i an attacker as outsider just needs to know user U_i's identity ID_i and smart card identity CID_i. That is, to mount our attack it is sufficient to intercept one valid login request message $M = \{ID_i, CID_i, X_i, Y_i, n, e, g, T_1\}$, made by user U_i. After that, to login the server at timestamp T_1' the attacker checks whether $\gcd(e, f(CID_i, T_1')) = 1$, i.e., whether the integers e and $f(CID_i, T_1)$ are relatively prime to each other. Note that for two randomly selected integers u and v, $\gcd(u, v) = 1$ happens with probability $6/\pi^2 \approx 0.6$ [10, 11]. Since the hash function $f(\cdot)$ is usually considered as a random function with k-bit outputs, $\gcd(e, f(CID_i, T_1')) = 1$ should occur with a similar probability. However, due to the fact that the RSA public exponent e is required to be a prime number in the SLH scheme, it is not difficult to see that for arbitrary timestamp T_1' $\gcd(e, f(CID_i, T_1')) = 1$ holds with probability $1 - 1/e$, if the outputs of hash function $f(\cdot)$ are assumed to be random numbers with k bits. Therefore, to get a value $f(CID_i, T_1')$ such that $\gcd(e, f(CID_i, T_1')) = 1$, the attacker *only* needs to try one or two timestamps. Once such a timestamp T_1' is obtained, the attacker can complete the following impersonation attack B:

1. Since $\gcd(e, f(CID_i, T_1')) = 1$, the attacker can use the Extended Euclidean algorithm to compute two integers a and b such that

$$a \cdot e + b \cdot f(CID_i, T_1') = 1 \quad (\text{in } \mathbb{Z}). \tag{8}$$

2. Then, the attacker computes X_i' and Y_i' by

$$X_i' = (ID_i)^{-b} \bmod n, \quad Y_i' = (ID_i)^a \bmod n. \tag{9}$$

3. Finally, the attacker sends the forged login request message $M' = \{ID_i, CID_i, X_i', Y_i', n, e, g, T_1'\}$ to the server.

Again, the above attack is successful since we have $CID_i \equiv f(ID_i \oplus d)$ and $Y_i'^e \equiv ID_i \cdot X_i'^{f(CID_i,T_1')} \bmod n$. The latter expression is justified as follows:

$$
\begin{aligned}
Y_i'^e &= [(ID_i)^a]^e \bmod n \\
&= ID_i^{ae} \bmod n \\
&= ID_i^{1-b\cdot f(CID_i,T_1')} \bmod n \\
&= ID_i \cdot (ID_i^{-b})^{f(CID_i,T_1')} \bmod n \\
&= ID_i \cdot X_i'^{f(CID_i,T_1')} \bmod n.
\end{aligned}
\tag{10}
$$

Remark 1: Note that neither of the attacks from Chan and Cheng [3] and Fan et al. [4] can apply to the SLH scheme, since in the SLH scheme user's identity ID_i is validated by checking $CID_i \equiv f(ID_i \oplus d)$. Therefore, without the secret d anybody cannot forge a valid smart card identity CID_i for an identity ID_i. In addition, it is also infeasible to derive the secret d from $CID_i = f(ID_i \oplus d)$ via off-line attacks, since d should be a large number [2]. In the case of $|n| = 1024$, this means we are supposed to select d such that $|d| \geq 300$.

5 The YKY Scheme and Its Security

Since the YKY authentication scheme [17] is also an enhancement of the Yang-Shieh scheme [14], it has a similar structure as the SLH scheme [9]. In this section, we briefly overview the YKY scheme and analyze its security.

5.1 Review of the YKY Scheme

The three phases of the YKY scheme are recalled as follows.

1. Registration Phase: As in the SLH scheme, the server sets an RSA cryptosystem with key material (n, e, d), where $n = pq$ and $ed = 1 \bmod (p-1)(q-1)$, and makes $(n, e, g, f(\cdot))$ public, while keeping d secret. To be registered, a user U_i securely delivers his/her identity ID_i and a chosen password PW_i to the server. After that, the server issues user U_i a smart card which contains information $(n, e, g, f(\cdot), ID_i, CID_i, S_i^*, h_i)$, where

$$
S_i^* = ID_i^{CID_i \cdot d} \bmod n, \quad h_i = g^{PW_i \cdot d} \bmod n, \text{ and } CID_i = f(ID_i \oplus d). \tag{11}
$$

2. Login Phase: To access the server, user U_i inserts his/her smart card into a card reader and types the password PW_i. If the password PW_i is correct, the smart card sends a login request message $M = \{ID_i, CID_i^*, X_i, Y_i^*, n, e, g, T_1\}$ to the server by computing

$$
CID_i^* = CID_i^e \bmod n, \quad X_i = g^{r_i \cdot PW_i} \bmod n, \text{ and } Y_i^* = S_i^* \cdot h_i^{r_i \cdot T_1} \bmod n. \tag{12}
$$

Here, r_i is a randomly chosen number and T_1 is the current date and time.

3. Authentication Phase: Once M is received, the server accepts user U_i's login request if and only if all of the following verifications hold:

- Check the validity of ID_i.
- Check $T_2 - T_1 \leq \Delta T$, where T_2 denotes the date and time when the server received M, and ΔT is a appropriately predefined time interval.
- Compute $CID_i = (CID_i^*)^d \bmod n$, and check that $CID_i \equiv f(ID_i \oplus d)$.
- Check $(Y_i^*)^e \equiv ID_i^{CID_i} \cdot X_i^{T_1} \bmod n$.

In contrast, the values of (S_i^*, CID_i^*, Y_i^*) in the YKY scheme are used to replace (S_i, CID_i, Y_i) in the SLH scheme. Especially, the smart card identifier CID_i contained in M is transferred as a ciphertext CID_i^* rather than plaintext. This reason is that by using a valid smart card identifier CID_i, Yoon et al. [17] launched an impersonation attack against the YWC scheme [16]. So, in their improvemed YKY scheme CID_i is not transferred in plaintext anymore. In addition, note that the YKY scheme only enables the server to authenticate a user, while the SLH scheme provides both directions of authentication service.

5.2 Security of the YKY Scheme

In [17], Yoon et al. claimed that the YKY scheme can resist impersonation attack, password guessing attack, smart card loss attack, and replay attack. They argued that their scheme is immune to impersonation attack, since an attacker without the server's secret d cannot derive CID_i from its RSA ciphertext CID_i^*. Without the card identifier CID_i, however, the attacker cannot forge a pair (X_i', Y_i') such that $(Y_i')^e \equiv ID_i^{CID_i} \cdot X_i'^{T_1} \bmod n$.

We notice that to amount a personation attack in the YKY scheme, an attacker *does not* need to get the value of CID_i at all. The attacking strategy is analogous to Attack B against the SLH scheme. To this end, an attacker first intercepts a valid login request message $M = \{ID_i, CID_i^*, X_i, Y_i^*, n, e, g, T_1\}$, which is sent to the server by some legitimate user U_i. Due to the validity of M, we have $(Y_i^*)^e \equiv ID_i^{CID_i} \cdot X_i^{T_1} \bmod n$. Therefore, the attacker gets the following value A by computing

$$A = (Y_i^*)^e \cdot X_i^{-T_1} \bmod n \ (= ID_i^{CID_i} \bmod n). \tag{13}$$

After that, the attacker computes a timestamp T_1' such that $\gcd(e, T_1') = 1$ (This even happens with probability about $1 - 1/e$, as e is a prime). So, the attacker can use the Extended Euclidean algorithm to compute two integers a and b such that

$$a \cdot e + b \cdot T_1' = 1 \quad (\text{in } \mathbb{Z}). \tag{14}$$

Finally, the attacker sends the forged login request message $M' = \{ID_i, CID_i^*, X_i', Y_i', n, e, g, T_1'\}$ to the server, where

$$X_i' = A^{-b} \bmod n \quad \text{and} \quad Y_i' = A^a \bmod n. \tag{15}$$

It is easy to know that the above attack is successful, since we have $CID_i \equiv f(ID_i \oplus d) \equiv (CID_i^*)^e \bmod n$ and $Y_i'^e \equiv ID_i^{CID_i} \cdot X_i'^{T_1'} \bmod n$. The latter expression is justified by

$$Y_i'^e = A^{ae} \bmod n = A^{1-b \cdot T_1'} \bmod n = A \cdot (A^{-b})^{T_1'} \bmod n = ID_i^{CID_i} \cdot X_i'^{T_1'} \bmod n.$$

Remark 2: Interestingly, we note that similar impersonation attack cannot apply to Yoon et al.'s nonce-based password authentication scheme (See Section 4.2 of [17]). In this scheme, to access the server a user U_i needs to send a request message $M = (X_i, Y_i, n, e, g)$ such that $Y_i^e \equiv ID_i^{CID_i} \cdot X_i^N \bmod n$, where $N = f(CID_i, r_j)$ and r_j is a random number selected by the server. Since both values of CID_i and N are unavailable to an attacker, it seems really hard to amount an impersonation attack.

6 Conclusion

Password authentication is an important mechanism for remote login systems that enables the server to authenticate its users. In this paper, we first pointed out that Yang et al.'s attack [15] against Shen at al.'s timestamp-based password authentication scheme [9] is actually invalid, since we showed that in a real implementation it is extremely difficult to find two hash values such that one is divisible by the other. Then, we showed that Shen et al.'s authentication scheme is really *insecure* by demonstrating two effective impersonation attacks. Finally, we illustrated that Yoon et al.'s timestamp-based authentication scheme [17] is also suffers to a similar personation attack. In our security analysis, we employed the following two facts on hash functions: (1) If the outputs of a hash function can be modelled as random numbers with fixed length k, the probability that one hash value is a multiple of another is less than $(1+k)/2^k$, a negligible quantity in k; and (2) The probability that one hash value is relatively prime with another hash value (or a fixed integer), however, is certainly high, about 0.6. Actually, we notice that those two facts on hash functions are potentially useful in other scenarios, such as analyzing the security of digital signatures [13].

In addition, we notice that our analysis presented in this paper also applies to Wang et al.'s attack [12] against Fan et al.'s password authentication scheme [4]. In other words, Wang et al.'s attack is also *invalid* since they exploited the same attacking strategy as Yang et al. did in [15]; but Fan et al.'s scheme is also insecure because it is vulnerable to similar attacks as we identified in this paper. As the future work, we are considering to design password authentication schemes using smart cards with formal security.

References

1. M. Bellare and P. Rogaway, "Random oracles are practical: A paradigm for designing efficient protocols," *Proc. of the 1st ACM Conference on Computer and Communications Security (CCS'93)*, pp. 62-73. ACM press, 1993.
2. D. Boneh and G. Durfee, "Cryptanalysis of RSA with private key d less than $N^{0.292}$," *IEEE Transactions on Information Theory*, vol. 46, no. 4, pp. 1339-1349, 2000.
3. C.K. Chan and L.M. Cheng, "Cryptanalysis of timestamp-based password authentication scheme," *Computers & Security*, vol. 21, no. 1, pp. 74-76, 2002.
4. L. Fan, J. H. Li, and H. W. Zhu, "An enhancement of timestamp-based password authentication scheme," *Computers & Security*, vol. 21, no. 7, pp. 665-667, 2002.

5. M.S. Hwang and L.H. Li, "A new remote user authentication scheme smart cards," *IEEE Transactions on Consumer Electronics*, vol. 46, pp. 28-30, 2000.
6. L. Lamport, "Password authentication with insecure communication," *Communications of the ACM*, vol. 24, pp. 770-772, 1981.
7. PKCS, "Public key cryptography standards, PKCS #1 v2.1," RSA Cryptography Standard, Draft 2, 2001. http://www.rsasecurity.com/rsalabs/pkcs/
8. R.L. Rivest, A. Shamir, and L.M. Adleman, "A method for obtaining digital signatures and public-key cryptosystems," *Communications of the ACM*, vol. 21, No. 2, pp. 120-126, Feb. 1978.
9. J.J. Shen, C.W. Lin, and M.S. Hwang, "Security enhancement for the timestamp-based password authentication scheme using smart cards," *Computers & Security*, vol. 22, no. 7, pp. 591-595, 2003.
10. G. Tenenbaum. *Introduction to Analytic and Probabilistic Number Theory* (Theorem 5, page 41). Cambridge studies in advanced mathematics, Vol. 46. Cambridge University Press, 1995.
11. http://mathworld.wolfram.com/RelativelyPrime.html
12. B. Wang, J.-H. Li, and Z.-P. Tong, "Cryptanalysis of an enhanced timestamp-based password authentication scheme," *Computers & Security*, vol. 22, no. 7, pp. 643-645, 2003.
13. G. Wang, "On the security of a group signature scheme with forward security," *Proc. of the 6th Annual International Conference on Information Security and Cryptology (ICISC'03)*, LNCS 2971, pp. 27-39. Springer-Verlag, 2004.
14. W.H. Yang and S.P. Shieh, "Password authentication schemes with smart cards," *Computers & Security*, vol. 18, no. 8, pp. 727-733, 1999.
15. C.-C. Yang, H.-W. Yang, and R.-C. Wang, "Cryptanalysis of security enhancement for the timestamp-based password authentication scheme using smart cards," *IEEE Transactions on Consumer Electronics*, vol. 50, No. 2, pp. 578-579, May 2004.
16. C.C. Yang, R.C. Wang, and T.Y. Chang, "An improvement of the Yang-Shieh password authentication schemes," *Applied Mathematics and Computation*, vol. 162, No. 3, pp. 1391-1396, 2005.
17. E.-J. Yoon, W.-H. Kim, and K.-Y. Yoo, "Security enhancement for password authentication schemes with smart cards," *Proc. of Trust and Privacy in Digital Business (TrustBus'05)*, LNCS 3592, pp. 311-320. Springer-Verlag, 2005.

Cryptanalysis of ID-Based Authenticated Key Agreement Protocols from Bilinear Pairings (Short Paper)*

Kyung-Ah Shim[1] and Seung-Hyun Seo[2]

[1] Department of Mathematics,
Ewha Womans University, Seoul, Korea
kashim@ewha.ac.kr
[2] Graduate School of Information Securities,
Center for Information Security Technologies (CIST),
Korea University, Seoul, Korea
seosh@korea.ac.kr

Abstract. Recently, a number of ID-based authenticated key agreement protocols from bilinear pairings have been proposed. In this paper we present security analysis of four ID-based authenticated key agreement protocols from pairings proposed in [11, 12, 7, 18]. These results demonstrate that no more ID-based authenticated key agreement protocols should be constructed with such ad-hoc methods, i.e, the formal design methodology as in [1, 2, 3, 10] should be employed in future design.

1 Introduction

In ID-based cryptography [14], the main idea is to simplify public-key and certificate management by using a user's identity (e.g., its email address) as its public key. For this to be possible, the ID-based system requires a trusted third party, typically called a Private Key Generator, to generate user private keys from its master secret and the user's identity. Such cryptosystems alleviate the certificate overhead and solve the problems of PKI technology: certificate management including storage, distribution and the computational cost of certificate verification. Since Boneh and Franklin's ID-based encryption scheme based on Weil pairing [6], bilinear pairings of algebraic curves have initiated some completely new fields in cryptography, making it possible to realize cryptographic primitives that were previously unknown or impractical.

At first, Joux [9] proposed a one round tripartite Diffie-Hellman key agreement protocol based on Weil pairings. However, like the basic Diffie-Hellman key agreement protocol [8], Joux's protocol also suffers from man-in-the-middle attacks because it does not attempt to authenticate the communicating entities. Smart [15] proposed an ID-based two-party authenticated key agreement (AK)

* This work was supported by the Korea Research Foundation Grant funded by the Korean Government(MOEHRD) (KRF-2005-217-C00002), and by the second Brain Korea 21 Project.

P. Ning, S. Qing, and N. Li (Eds.): ICICS 2006, LNCS 4307, pp. 410–419, 2006.
© Springer-Verlag Berlin Heidelberg 2006

protocol which combines the idea of Boneh and Franklin with that of Joux. But, Shim [16] pointed out that Smart's protocol does not provide full forward secrecy and proposed a new protocol which provides full forward secrecy. However, it turns out the protocol is insecure against man-in-the-middle attacks [17]. Recently, Kim *et al* [11], Kim *et al* [12], Choi *et al* [7] and Xie [18] proposed two-party or three-party ID-based authenticated key agreement protocols from pairings. The authors argued that the protocols satisfy all the required security attributes for authenticated key agreement protocols described in [5]. In this paper we show that the four protocols do not achieve some attributes of them.

The rest of this paper is organized as follows. In the following Section, we introduce admissible pairings and ID-based public key infrastructures. In Section 3, we point out that Kim *et al* [11], Kim *et al* [12], Choi *et al* [7] and Xie [18] protocol are vulnerable to key-compromise impersonation attacks, unknown key-share attacks, signature forgery attacks and impersonation attacks, respectively. A concluding remark is given in Section 4.

2 Preliminaries

ADMISSIBLE PAIRINGS. Let $\mathbb{G}_1$ and $\mathbb{G}_2$ be two cyclic groups of a large prime order q. We write $\mathbb{G}_1$ additively and $\mathbb{G}_2$ multiplicatively. We assume that the discrete logarithm problems in both $\mathbb{G}_1$ and $\mathbb{G}_2$ are hard. We call $\hat{e}$ an *admissible pairing* if $\hat{e} : \mathbb{G}_1 \times \mathbb{G}_1 \to \mathbb{G}_2$ is a map with the following properties:

1. Bilinearity: $\hat{e}(aP, bQ) = \hat{e}(P, Q)^{ab}$ for all $P, Q \in \mathbb{G}_1$ and for all $a, b \in \mathbb{Z}$.
2. Non-degeneracy: There exists $P \in \mathbb{G}_1$ such that $\hat{e}(P, P) \neq 1$. In other words, the map does not send all pair $\mathbb{G}_1 \times \mathbb{G}_1$ to the identity in $\mathbb{G}_2$.
3. Computability: There is an efficient algorithm to compute $\hat{e}(P, Q)$ for any $P, Q \in \mathbb{G}_1$.

The Weil and Tate pairings associated with supersingular elliptic curves or abelian varieties can be modified to create such admissible pairing, as in [6].

ID-BASED PUBLIC KEY INFRASTRUCTURES. An ID-based public key infrastructure involves a Private Key Generatior (PKG) and users. It consists of **Setup** and **Private Key Extraction** algorithms. Let P be a generator of $\mathbb{G}_1$. Let $H : \{0,1\}^* \to \mathbb{Z}_q$ and $H_1 : \{0,1\}^* \to \mathbb{G}_1$ be two cryptographic hash functions.

[**Setup**]: PKG chooses a random $s \in \mathbb{Z}_q^*$ and set $P_{Pub} = sP$. PKG publishes the system parameters $\langle \mathbb{G}_1, \mathbb{G}_2, q, \hat{e}, P, P_{Pub}, H \text{ or } H_1 \rangle$ and keep s as a master secret.

[**Private Key Extraction I**]: For a given string $ID \in \{0,1\}^*$, compute the user's public key as $Q_{ID} = H_1(ID) \in \mathbb{G}_1$ and set the private key S_{ID} to be sQ_{ID}, where s is a master secret.

[**Private Key Extraction II**]: For a given string $ID \in \{0,1\}^*$, compute $\alpha = H(ID) \in \mathbb{Z}_q$ and set the private key d_{ID} to be $\frac{1}{\alpha+s}P$, where $\alpha P + sP$ is the public key corresponding to ID.

In the following section, Kim et al's protocol [11], Kim et al's protocol [12], Choi et al's protocol [7] use the **Private Key Extraction I** algorithm, while Xie's protocol [18] adapts the **Private Key Extraction II** algorithm.

3   Cryptanalysis of Four ID-Based AK Protocols

3.1   Kim et al's Tripartite AK Protocol with Multiple PKGs

Recently, Kim et al [11] proposed ID-based AK protocols among entities whose private keys were issued by different PKGs. We show that the 3PAK-MPE protocol for tripartite key agreement of their protocols is insecure against key-compromise impersonation (K-CI) attacks.

[**Different PKGs Setup**]. Let A, B and C be legitimate entities who have gotten their private keys from PKG_1, PKG_2 and PKG_3, respectively. The three different PKGs do not share the system parameters;

- PKG_i $(1 \leq i \leq 3)$ chooses its system parameters $\langle \mathbb{G}_1^i, \mathbb{G}_2^i, q^i, \hat{e}^i, P^i, P_{Pub}^i, H^i \rangle$, where $\mathbb{G}_1^i$ and $\mathbb{G}_2^i$ are groups with prime order q^i, P^i is a generator of $\mathbb{G}_1^i$, $\hat{e}^i :$ $\mathbb{G}_1^i \times \mathbb{G}_1^i \to \mathbb{G}_2^i$ is the bilinear pairing and $H^i : \{0,1\}^* \to \mathbb{G}_1^i$ is a cryptographic hash function.
- PKG_i chooses a random $s^i \in \mathbb{Z}_{q^i}^*$ and set $P_{Pub}^i = s^i P^i$.
- Assume that all users agree on the hash function $H_3 : \{0,1\}^* \to \{0,1\}^k$ used to compute the resulting session key, where k is the length of the session key.

Consequently, the public/private key pairs of A, B and C are $(Q_A^1 = H^1(ID_A)$, $S_A^1 = s^1 Q_A^1)$, $(Q_B^2 = H^2(ID_B)$, $S_B^2 = s^2 Q_B^2)$, and $(Q_C^3 = H^3(ID_C)$, $S_C^3 = s^3 Q_C^3)$, respectively.

■ 3PAK-MPE Protocol

[**The First Round**]. Users A, B and C choose ephemeral private keys $\{a^i\}_{i=1}^3$, $\{b^i\}_{i=1}^3$ and $\{c^i\}_{i=1}^3$, respectively, where $a_i, b_i, c_i \in \mathbb{Z}_{q^i}^*, 1 \leq i \leq 3$. Then they compute $\{W_A^i = a^i P^i\}_{i=1}^3, \{W_B^i = b^i P^i\}_{i=1}^3$ and $\{W_C^i = c^i P^i\}_{i=1}^3$ and broadcast these values.

$$(1) \quad A \longrightarrow B, C: \quad W_A^1 = a^1 P^1, \quad W_A^2 = a^2 P^2, \quad W_A^3 = a^3 P^3,$$
$$(2) \quad B \longrightarrow A, C: \quad W_B^1 = b^1 P^1, \quad W_B^2 = b^2 P^2, \quad W_B^3 = b^3 P^3,$$
$$(3) \quad C \longrightarrow A, B: \quad W_C^1 = c^1 P^1, \quad W_C^2 = c^2 P^2, \quad W_C^3 = c^3 P^3.$$

After receiving the messages from the other entities, each entity computes the partial session keys. In detail, A computes partial keys K_{AB} and K_{AC} as follows;

$$K_{AB} = H_3(\hat{e}^1(S_A^1, W_B^1) \| a^1 W_B^1 \| \hat{e}^2(Q_B^2, a^2 P_{Pub}^2) \| a^2 W_B^2)),$$

$$K_{AC} = H_3(\hat{e}^1(S_A^1, W_B^1) \| a^1 W_C^1 \| \hat{e}^3(Q_C^3, a^3 P_{Pub}^3) \| a^3 W_C^3)).$$

Similarly, B computes partial keys K_{BA} and K_{BC} as follows;

$$K_{BA} = H_3(\hat{e}^1(Q_A^1, b^1 P_{Pub}^1) \| b^1 W_A^1 \| \hat{e}^2(S_B^2, W_A^2) \| b^2 W_A^2)),$$

$$K_{BC} = H_3(\hat{e}^2(S_B^2, W_C^2)||b^2 W_C^2||\hat{e}^3(Q_C^3, b^3 P_{Pub}^3)||b^3 W_C^3)).$$

C also computes partial keys K_{CA} and K_{CB} as follows;

$$K_{CA} = H_3(\hat{e}^1(Q_A^1, c^1 P_{Pub}^1)||c^1 W_A^1||\hat{e}^3(S_C^3, W_A^3)||c^3 W_A^3),$$

$$K_{CB} = H_3(\hat{e}^2(Q_B^2, c^2 P_{Pub}^2)||c^2 W_B^2||\hat{e}^3(S_C^3, W_B^3)||c^3 W_B^3).$$

Then $K_{AB} = K_{BA}$, $K_{AC} = K_{CA}$ and $K_{BC} = K_{CB}$.

[**The Second Round**]. A, B, and C choose random numbers R_A, R_B, R_C and broadcast $\langle\{R_A\}_{K_{AB}}, \{R_A\}_{K_{AC}}\rangle$, $\langle\{R_B\}_{K_{BA}}, \{R_B\}_{K_{BC}}\rangle$, and $\langle\{R_C\}_{K_{CA}}, \{R_C\}_{K_{CB}}\rangle$, respectively, where $\{M\}_K$ denotes a symmetric encryption under the key K.

(1) $A \longrightarrow B, C : \{R_A\}_{K_{AB}}, \{R_A\}_{K_{AC}},$
(2) $B \longrightarrow A, C : \{R_B\}_{K_{BA}}, \{R_B\}_{K_{BC}},$
(3) $C \longrightarrow A, B : \{R_C\}_{K_{CA}}, \{R_C\}_{K_{CB}}.$

The definition of key-compromise impersonation resilience attribute described in [5] 2 is originally defined on a two-party setting. But, the definition is easily extended to a multi-party setting as follows; Let $\{A_1, \cdots, A_n\}$ ba a set of communicating entities. Suppose that m $(m < n)$ long-term private keys of A_i $(i = 1, \cdots, m)$ are compromised to an adversary. Then the K-CI resilience implies that the adversary can neither impersonate the other entities A_j $(j = m+1, \cdots, n)$ to A_i $(i = 1, \cdots, m)$ nor obtain the session keys computed by A_i $(i = 1, \cdots, m)$. Now, we show that the 3PAK-MPE protocol is insecure against a K-CI attack in the three-party setting.

■ **K-CI Attacks on the 3PAK-MPE Protocol**

Suppose that long-term private keys S_A^1 and S_B^2 of A and B, respectively, are compromised to an adversary E and E wants to impersonate C to A and B.

1. First, E chooses random numbers $c^i, u^i, v^i \in \mathbb{Z}_{q^i}^*$, $i = 1, 2, 3$ and computes $W_C^i = c^i P^i, U_A^i = u^i P^i, V_B^i = v^i P^i$, $i = 1, 2, 3$.
2. When A and B broadcast $\{W_A^i\}_{i=1}^3$ and $\{W_B^i\}_{i=1}^3$, respectively, E replaces them with $\{U_A^i\}_{i=1}^3$ and $\{V_B^i\}_{i=1}^3$, respectively, and simultaneously broadcast $\{W_C^i\}_{i=1}^3$ impersonating C. $E(C)$ denotes E masquerades as C.

(1) $A \longrightarrow B, C$: $W_A^1, W_A^2, W_A^3 \implies U_A^1, U_A^2, U_A^3,$
(2) $B \longrightarrow A, C$: $W_B^1, W_B^2, W_B^3 \implies V_B^1, V_B^2, V_B^3,$
(3) $E(C) \longrightarrow A, B$: $W_C^1, W_C^2, W_C^3.$

After receiving the messages, A computes the partial session keys K_{AB} and K_{AC} from $\{V_B^i\}_{i=1}^3$ and $\{W_C^i\}_{i=1}^3$ as follows;

$$K_{AB} = H_3(e^1(S_A^1, V_B^1)||a^1 V_B^1||e^2(Q_B^2, a^2 P_{Pub}^2)||a^2 V_B^2),$$

$$K_{AC} = H_3(e^1(S_A^1, W_B^1)||a^1 W_C^1||e^3(Q_C^3, a^3 P_{Pub}^3)||a^3 W_C^3)).$$

From S_A^1, S_B^2 and v^i $(i = 1, 2)$, E also computes K'_{AB} as follows;

$$K'_{AB} = H_3(e^1(S_A^1, V_B^1)||v^1 W_A^1||e^2(S_B^2, W_A^2)||v^2 W_A^2).$$

Then, $K_{AB} = K'_{AB}$. However, E cannot obtain K_{AC} since E, who does not know S_C^3, cannot compute the term $e^3(Q_C^3, a^3 P_{Pub}^3)$ of K_{AC} Also, B computes K_{BA} and K_{BC} from $\{U_A^i\}_{i=1}^3$ and $\{W_C^i\}_{i=1}^3$ as follows;

$$K_{BA} = H_3(e^1(Q_A^1, b^1 P_{Pub}^1)||b^1 U_A^1||e^2(S_B^2, U_A^2)||b^2 U_A^2)),$$

$$K_{BC} = H_3(e^2(S_A^2, W_C^2)||b^2 W_C^2||e^3(Q_C^3, b^3 P_{Pub}^3)||b^3 W_C^3)).$$

Similarly, from S_A^1, S_B^2 and u^i ($i = 1, 2$), E can compute K'_{BA} as follows;

$$K_{BA} = H_3(e^1(S_A^1, W_B^1)||u^1 W_B^1||e^2(S_B^2, U_A^2)||u^2 W_B^2)).$$

Then, $K_{BA} = K'_{BA}$. However, E cannot obtain K_{BC} since E, who does not know S_C^3, cannot compute the term $e^3(Q_C^3, b^3 P_{Pub}^3)$ of K_{BC}.

3. In the second round, when A and B broadcast $\langle\{R_A\}_{K_{AB}}, \{R_A\}_{K_{AC}}\rangle$ and $\langle\{R_B\}_{K_{BA}}, \{R_B\}_{K_{BC}}\rangle$, E replaces $\langle\{R_A\}_{K_{AB}}, \{R_A\}_{K_{AC}}\rangle$ and $\langle\{R_B\}_{K_{BA}}, \{R_B\}_{K_{BC}}\rangle$ with $\langle\{R_B\}_{K_{BA}}, \{R_A\}_{K_{AC}}\rangle$ and $\langle\{R_A\}_{K_{AB}}, \{R_B\}_{K_{BC}}\rangle$, respectively, and simultaneously broadcast $\langle\{R_A\}_{K_{AC}}, \{R_B\}_{K_{BC}}\rangle$ to A and B, impersonating C.

(1) $A \longrightarrow B, C: \{R_A\}_{K_{AB}}, \{R_A\}_{K_{AC}} \Longrightarrow \{R_B\}_{K_{BA}}, \{R_A\}_{K_{AC}},$
(2) $B \longrightarrow A, C: \{R_B\}_{K_{BA}}, \{R_B\}_{K_{BC}} \Longrightarrow \{R_A\}_{K_{AB}}, \{R_B\}_{K_{BC}},$
(3) $E(C) \longrightarrow A, B: \qquad \{R_A\}_{K_{AC}}, \{R_B\}_{K_{BC}}.$

4. After receiving $\{R_A\}_{K_{AB}}$ and $\{R_A\}_{K_{AC}}$ intended to A, A can obtain R_A by decrypting $\{R_A\}_{K_{AB}}$ and $\{R_A\}_{K_{AC}}$ under K_{AB} and K_{AC}, respectively. Then A computes the session key $SK_A = H_3(R_A||R_A||R_A)$ from the decrypted messages and its own choice R_A. Similarly, B also obtain R_B by decrypting $\{R_B\}_{K_{BA}}$ and $\{R_B\}_{K_{BC}}$ under K_{BA} and K_{BC}, respectively. Then B computes the session key $SK_B = H_3(R_B||R_B||R_B)$ from the decrypted messages and its own choice R_B. E also obtains R_A and R_B by decrypting $\{R_A\}_{K_{AB}}$ and $\{R_B\}_{K_{BA}}$ under K'_{AB} and K'_{BA}, respectively, because $K_{AB} = K'_{AB}$ and $K_{BA} = K'_{BA}$. Therefore, E can compute the session keys SK_A and SK_B calculated by A and B from R_A and R_B. Finally, E succeeds in impersonating C to both A and B as well as in obtaining the session keys SK_A and SK_B.

In the attack, E, can compute neither $\{R_A\}_{K_{AC}}$ nor $\{R_B\}_{K_{BC}}$ in the second round because E knows neither K_{AC} nor K_{BC}. But, E can obtain $\{R_A\}_{K_{AC}}$ and $\{R_B\}_{K_{BC}}$ from the messages sent by A and B, respectively and so replay them to A and B impersonating C as C's second message. Since the messages themselves cannot contain any information on the receivers, they can be reused as messages intended to other entities. Its weakness against the K-CI attacks are the lack of explicitness in messages transmitted. Thus, the attacks can be prevented by adding the ordered pair of identities in messages being signed, for example, $\{R_A\}_{K_{AB}}$ is replaced with $\{R_A||Q_B||Q_C\}_{K_{BA}}$ as described in [11]. But, in their paper, it is not mandatory but optional. Such a misused optional condition opens the door to the attacks.

3.2   Kim *et al*'s ID-Based Multiple AK Protocol

Kim *et al* [12] proposed an ID-based authenticated multiple-key agreement protocol (KRY protocol) which allows two entities to establish multiple session keys in a protocol run. We show that the KRY protocol is insecure against an unknown key-share (UK-S) attack and does not achieve forward secrecy in the case of the compromise of additional secret information.

■ KRY Protocol

(1) $A \longrightarrow B : P_A = aP,\ P'_A = a'P,\ T_A = H(P_A)H(P'_A)S_A + (a + a')P_{Pub}$,
(2) $B \longrightarrow A : P_B = bP,\ P'_B = b'P,\ T_B = H(P_B)H(P'_B)S_B + (b + b')P_{Pub}$.

Assume that A and B want to agree to four session keys. First, A sends (P_A, P'_A, T_A) to B. On the receipt of the message from A, B verifies

$$\hat{e}(T_A, P) = \hat{e}(H(P_A)H(P'_A)Q_A + P_A + P'_A,\ P_{Pub}).$$

If the equation holds, B sends (P_B, P'_B, T_B) to A and then computes four session keys as $K_B^{(1)} = \hat{e}(P_A,\ P_{Pub})^b, K_B^{(2)} = \hat{e}(P_A,\ P_{Pub})^{b'}, K_B^{(3)} = \hat{e}(P'_A,\ P_{Pub})^b, K_B^{(4)} = \hat{e}(P'_A, P_{Pub})^{b'}$. After receiving the message, A verifies

$$\hat{e}(T_B, P) = \hat{e}(H(P_B)H(P'_B)Q_B + P_B + P'_B,\ P_{Pub}).$$

If the equation holds, A computes the session keys $K_A^{(1)} = \hat{e}(P_B, P_{Pub})^a, K_A^{(2)} = \hat{e}(P'_B, P_{Pub})^a, K_A^{(3)} = \hat{e}(P_B, P_{Pub})^{a'}, K_A^{(4)} = \hat{e}(P'_B, P_{Pub})^{a'}$. Each entity takes the four values $K^i\ (i = 1, \cdots, 4)$ as the final session keys $K^{(1)} = \hat{e}(P,\ P)^{abs}, K^{(2)} = \hat{e}(P,\ P)^{ab's}, K^{(3)} = \hat{e}(P,\ P)^{a'bs}, K^{(4)} = \hat{e}(P,\ P)^{a'b's}$.

■ UK-S Attacks on the KRY Protocol

Suppose that an adversary E, who is a legitimate entity, has gotten her own long-term private key S_E. Then attack on the protocol is mounted as follows;

1. When A sends $\{P_A = aP,\ P'_A = a'P,\ T_A,\ ID_A\}$ to B, an adversary E intercepts it and computes (P_E, P'_E, T_E) as follows;
   - First, E chooses a random $r \in \mathbb{Z}_q^*$ and let $r = a + r'$. Then E can obtain $r'P$ by computing $rP - aP$.
   - Next, E takes P_E and P'_E as aP and $r'P$, respectively and computes her own signature on $\{P_E, P_{E'}\}$ as $T_E = H(P_A)H(P'_E)S_E + rP_{Pub}$. Note that E knows neither a nor r', while she knows aP, $r'P$ and r.
   Next, E sends (P_E, P'_E, T_E) together with her identity ID_E to B.
2. On the receipt of the message, B thinks that the protocol run is initiated by E. Then B verifies E's signature. In fact, the verification always holds, because T_E is E's valid signature on $\{P_E,\ P'_E\}$. B sends $\{P_B, P'_B, T_B, ID_B\}$ to E which forwards to A. Next, B computes four session keys as follows;

$$K_B^{(1)} = \hat{e}(P_E,\ P_{Pub})^b = \hat{e}(P,P)^{abs},\ K_B^{(2)} = \hat{e}(P_E,\ P_{Pub})^{b'} = \hat{e}(P,P)^{ab's},$$
$$K_B^{(3)} = \hat{e}(P'_E,\ P_{Pub})^b = \hat{e}(P,P)^{r'bs},\ K_B^{(4)} = \hat{e}(P'_E, P_{Pub})^{b'} = \hat{e}(P,P)^{r'b's}.$$

3. After receiving the message, A verifies B's signature and computes

$$K_A^{(1)} = \hat{e}(P_B, \ P_{Pub})^a = \hat{e}(P, P)^{abs}, \ K_A^{(2)} = \hat{e}(P_B', \ P_{Pub})^a = \hat{e}(P, P)^{ab's},$$
$$K_A^{(3)} = \hat{e}(P_B, \ P_{Pub})^{a'} = \hat{e}(P, P)^{a'bs}, \ K_A^{(4)} = \hat{e}(P_B', P_{Pub})^{a'} = \hat{e}(P, P)^{a'b's}.$$

4. Finally, A and B share the same two of four session keys, $K^{(1)} = \hat{e}(P, P)^{abs}$, $K^{(2)} = \hat{e}(P, P)^{ab's}$. A thinks that the session keys are shared with B, while B mistakenly believes that he shares the keys with E.

Finally, the UK-S attack on two of four session keys is successfully mounted. If A and B use the former two session keys for a subsequent encryption, serious consequences stated in [4] will be happened. Its weakness against the UK-S attack is due to the fact that an adversary E, who knows neither a and r', can generate its signature on $\{P_E = aP, P_{E'} = r'P\}$. In fact, it is known that all types of UK-S attacks can be prevented by adding identities of the communicating entities in inputs of a key derivation function [4]. However, to avoid the attack without using additional functions such as a key derivation function, the adapted signature should be designed so that only one, who knows both a and a', can generate its signature on $\{aP, a'P\}$.

■ Forward Secrecy of the KRY Protocol

Now, we show that the KRY protocol does not satisfy forward secrecy in the case of the compromise of additional secret information. Suppose that the long-term private keys, S_A and S_B of A and B, respectively, are compromised to an adversary E. Then E can obtain some equations related to each user's ephemeral private keys. Indeed, E, who knows S_A, can compute $(a + a')P_{Pub}$ from $T_A = H(P_A)H(P_A')S_A + (a + a')P_{Pub}$ by computing $T_A - H(P_A)H(P_A')S_A$. Similarly, E, who knows S_A, can compute $(b + b')P_{Pub}$ from $T_B = H(P_B)H(P_B')S_B + (b + b')P_{Pub}$ by computing $T_B - H(P_B)H(P_B')S_B$. Finally, E can compute the following equations;

$$\hat{e}((a + a')P_{Pub}, bP) = \hat{e}(P, P)^{(a+a')bs} \quad (1)$$
$$\hat{e}((a + a')P_{Pub}, b'P) = \hat{e}(P, P)^{(a+a')b's} \quad (2)$$
$$\hat{e}((b + b')P_{Pub}, aP) = \hat{e}(P, P)^{(b+b')as} \quad (3)$$
$$\hat{e}((b + b')P_{Pub}, a'P) = \hat{e}(P, P)^{(b+b')a's} \quad (4).$$

These relationships lead to serious consequences in the case of the compromise of additional secret information. If one session key of the past session, say $K^{(1)} = \hat{e}(P, P)^{abs}$, is compromised then the other three session keys, $K^{(2)}$, $K^{(3)}$ and $K^{(4)}$ are revealed, i.e., E can recover $K^{(2)} = \hat{e}(P, P)^{ab's}$ from the equation (3) by calculating $(3) \times K_1^{-1} = \hat{e}(P, P)^{ab's}$, $K^{(3)} = \hat{e}(P, P)^{a'bs}$ from the equation (1) by calculating $(1) \times K_1^{-1} = \hat{e}(P, P)^{a'bs}$, and $K^{(4)} = \hat{e}(P, P)^{a'b's}$ from the equation (2) by calculating $(2) \times K_2^{-1} = \hat{e}(P, P)^{a'b's}$. Thus, it does not satisfy forward secrecy in the case of the compromise of additional secret information.

In general, we note the compromise of long-term secret keys does not necessarily mean that they are obtained via an inversion of the long-term public key. Long-term secrets are in practice vulnerable secrets in the system; in a typical setting, they are stored on disk, perhaps protected by a password. Since users must store their secret keys for use in key computation, the secret keys may also be obtained through lack of suitable physical measures. An adversary is also able to obtain the session key used in any sufficiently old previous run of the protocol. In some environments (e.g., due to implementation and engineering decisions), the probability of compromise of session keys may be greater than that of long-term keys. In particular, when using cryptographic techniques of only moderate strength, the possibility exists that over time extensive cryptanalytic effort may uncover past session keys. These properties may be attractive for the robustness of the security in most commercial applications where customers does not always protect their key sufficiently. Thus, a secure protocol design will minimize the effects of such events.

3.3   Choi *at al*'s ID-Based AK Protocol

Choi *et al* [7] proposed two ID-based AK protocols satisfying the forward secrecy. Their protocol I uses a signature scheme to provide authentication; the authenticity of the ephemeral public keys in the protocol is assured by each user's signature. We show that the protocol I does not achieve authentication as intended, i.e., anyone can forge each user's signature.

■ **Protocol I**

$$(1)\ A \longrightarrow B\ :\ U_A = aP_{Pub},\ V_A = aS_A$$
$$(2)\ B \longrightarrow A\ :\ U_B = bP_{Pub},\ V_B = bS_B.$$

First, A sends (U_A, V_A) to B. On the receipt of the message from A, B verifies $\hat{e}(V_A, P) = \hat{e}(Q_A, U_A)$. If the equation holds, B sends $(U_B V_B)$ to A and computes $K_B = bU_A$. After receiving the message from B, A verifies $\hat{e}(V_B, P) = \hat{e}(Q_B, U_B)$. If the equation holds, A computes $K_A = aU_B$. The resulting session key is $K = kdf(K_A, Q_A, Q_B) = kdf(K_B, Q_A, Q_B) = kdf(absP, Q_A, Q_B)$, where kdf is a key derivation function.

■ **Signature Forgery Attack on the Protocol I**

In the protocol I, anyone can generate a valid pair (U_A, V_A) satisfying $\hat{e}(V_A, P) = \hat{e}(Q_A, U_A)$ as follows; an adversary chooses a at random and then computes $U_A = aP$ and $V_A = aQ_A$. Then the pair satisfies the verification equation;

$$\hat{e}(V_A, P) = \hat{e}(aQ_A, P) = \hat{e}(Q_A, aP) = \hat{e}(Q_A, U_A).$$

Therefore, an adversary, who does not know the corresponding long-term private key, can forge each user's signature on the ephemeral public key. In fact, the adversary cannot obtain the session key established in this session involved in this forgery attack. However, the signature scheme adapted to the cryptographic protocols should be secure against forgery attacks.

3.4   Xie's ID-Based AK Protocol with Escrow

Recently, Xie [18] showed that McCullagh and Barreto's AK protocol [13] is insecure against impersonation attacks. Then he proposed an improved protocol to defeat the attacks and argued that its protocol satisfies all the security attributes. We show that the protocol satisfies neither the implicit key authentication nor the K-CI resilience.

■ **Xie's Protocol**
This protocol uses the **Private Key Extraction II** algorithm. Let $H_1(ID_A) = a$ and $H_1(ID_B) = b$. First, A and B exchange the ephemeral public keys A_{KA} and B_{KA}.

$$(1)\ \ A \longrightarrow B\ :\ A_{KA} = x(bP + sP)$$
$$(2)\ \ B \longrightarrow A\ :\ B_{KA} = y(aP + sP).$$

Then, A and B compute $K_A = \hat{e}(B_{KA}, d_A)^{x+1}\hat{e}(P, P)^x$ and $K_B = \hat{e}(A_{KA}, d_B)^{y+1}\hat{e}(P, P)^y$, respectively. The resulting session key is $K = K_A = K_B = e(P, P)^{xy+x+y}$.

Now we show that Xie's protocol is insecure against impersonation attacks, i.e., an adversary can impersonate A to B at any time. The attack on the protocol is mounted as follows;

■ **Impersonation Attacks on Xie's Protocol**

Suppose that an adversary E wants to impersonate A to B. $E(A)$ denotes E masquerade as A. First, $E(A)$ sends $A_{KA} = -(bP + sP)$ to B impersonating A. After receiving the message, B sends $B_{KA} = y(aP + sP)$ and computes the session key

$$K_B = \hat{e}(-(bP + sP), d_B)^{y+1}\hat{e}(P, P)^y = \hat{e}(P, P)^{-y-1}\hat{e}(P, P)^y = \hat{e}(P, P)^{-1}.$$

By bilinearity of $\hat{e}$, the value $\hat{e}(P, P)^y$ disappears in the resulting session key. Thus, E is able to compute $K_B = \hat{e}(P, P)^{-1}$ from known value. Finally, E succeeds in impersonating A to B as well as in obtaining the session key K_B.

In above attack, an adversary can generate an ephemeral public key to confine the shared secret to a predictable value. Thus, Xie's protocol does not provide implicit key authentication attribute. From the attack, we can easily see that it is insecure against man-in-the-middle attacks and key-compromise impersonation attacks. The same attacks can be applied to Xie's ID-based AK protocol without escrow and AK protocol between members of distinct domains.

4   Conclusion

We have shown that four ID-based AK protocols are insecure against several active attacks including unknown key-share attacks and key-compromise impersonation attacks. Our results demonstrate that no more ID-based AK protocols should be constructed with such ad-hoc methods and the formal design methodology in [1, 2, 3, 10] should be employed in future design.

References

1. M. Bellare, R. Canetti, and H. Krawczyk, A modular approach to the design and analysis of authentication and key exchange protocols, Proc. 30th Annual Symposium on the Theory of Computing, ACM, pp. 419-428, 1998.
2. M. Bellare and P. Rogaway, Provably secure session key distribution; the three party case, Proc. 27th Annual Sym. on the Theory of Computing, ACM, pp. 57-66, 1995.
3. M. Bellare and P. Rogaway, Entity autentication and key distribution, Advances in Cryptology; Crypto'93, LNCS 773, Springer-Verlag, pp. 232-249, 1994.
4. S. Blake-Wilson, D. Johnson and A. Menezes, Unknown key-share attacks on the station-to-station (STS) protocol, PKC'99, LNCS 1560, Springer-Verlag, pp. 154-170, 1999.
5. S. Blake-Wilson and A. Menezes, Authenticated Diffie-Hellman key agreement protocols, Proc. of the 5th Annual Workshop on Selected Areas in Cryptography, SAC'98, LNCS 1556, Springer-Verlag, pp. 339-361, 1999.
6. D. Boneh and M. Franklin, Identity-based encryption from the Weil pairing, Advances in cryptology; Crypto'01, LNCS 2139, Springer-Verlag, pp. 213-229, 2001.
7. Y. J. Choie, E. Jeong and E. Lee, Efficient identity-based authenticated key agreement protocol from pairings, Applied Mathematics and Computation, 162(1), pp. 179-188, 2005.
8. W. Diffie, and M. Hellman, New directions in cryptography, IEEE Transactions on Information Theory, 22(6), pp. 644-654, 1976.
9. A. Joux, A one round protocol for tripartite Diffie-Hellman, ANTS IV, LNCS 1838, Springer-Verlag, pp. 385-394, 2000.
10. J. Katz and M. Yung, Scalable protocols for authenticated group key exchange, Advances in Cryptology; Crypto'03, LNCS 1807, Springer-Verlag, 2004.
11. K. Kim, H. Lee, and H. Oh, Enhanced ID-based authenticated key agreement protocols for a multiple independent PKG environment, ICICS'05, LNCS 3783, Springer-Verlag, pp. 323-335, 2004.
12. K. Kim, E. Ryu, and K. Yoo, ID-based authenticated multiple-key agreement protocol from pairing, International Conference on Computational Science and Its Applications, ICCSA'04, LNCS 3046, Springer-Verlag, pp. 672-680, 2004.
13. N. McCullagh, P. S. L. M. Barreto, A new two-party identity-based authenticated key agreement, CT-RSA'05, LNCS 3376, Springer-Verlag, pp. 262-274, 2005.
14. A. Shamir, Identity-based cryptosystems and signature schemes, Advances in Cryptology; Crypto'84, LNCS 196, Springer-Verlag, pp. 47-53, 1884.
15. N. Smart, An ID-based authenticated key agreement protocol based on the Weil pairing, Elec. Lett., vol. 38(13), pp. 630-632, 2002.
16. K. Shim, Efficient one round authenticated tripartite key agreement protocol from Weil pairing, Elec. Lett., vol. 39(8), pp. 653-654, 2003.
17. H. Sun and B. Hsieh, Security analysis of Shim's authenticated key agreement protocols from pairings, Cryptogarphy ePrint Archive, Report 2003/113, available at http://eprint.iacr.org/2003/113/.
18. G. Xie, An ID-based key agreement scheme from pairing, Cryptology ePrint Archive: Report 2005/093, available at http://eprint.iacr.org/2005/093, 2005.

Seifert's RSA Fault Attack: Simplified Analysis and Generalizations

James A. Muir*

School of Computer Science
Carleton University, Ottawa, Canada
http://www.scs.carleton.ca/~jamuir

Abstract. Seifert (ACM CCS 2005) recently described a new fault attack against an implementation of RSA signature *verification*. Seifert's attack differs from the seminal work of Boneh, DeMillo and Lipton (EUROCRYPT 1997) in that it targets a public-key rather than a private-key operation. Here we give a simplified analysis of Seifert's attack and gauge its practicality against RSA moduli of practical sizes. Our intent is to give practice-oriented work estimates rather than asymptotic results. We also suggest an improvement to Seifert's attack which has the following consequences: If an adversary is able to cause random faults in only 4 bits of a 1024-bit RSA modulus stored in a device, then there is a greater than 50% chance that they will be able to make that device accept a signature on a message of their choice. For 2048-bit RSA, 6 bits suffice.

Keywords: hardware faults, fault analysis, signature verification, RSA signatures.

1 Introduction

Recently, Seifert described a novel attack against an implementation of the RSA signature verification operation [8]. His attack is based on the following assumptions:

- An adversary has a device which contains an RSA public key, (N, e), stored in protected read-only memory (e.g., in EEPROM).
- The values N and e are known to the adversary.
- On input m, s, the device transfers the values N and e from protected memory to working memory, and then proceeds to check if s is a valid signature for m.
- As the device transfers the value N from protected memory, *the adversary can induce data faults.*

The attacker's goal is to create a message-signature pair which the device will accept as valid. Seifert describes a probabilistic algorithm which does this. Moreover, Seifert's attack is a *selective forgery*; that is, an adversary is able to select

---

* J.A. Muir is supported by a Natural Sciences and Engineering Research Council of Canada Postdoctoral Fellowship.

P. Ning, S. Qing, and N. Li (Eds.): ICICS 2006, LNCS 4307, pp. 420–434, 2006.

an arbitrary message, compute a "signature" on it and have the device accept these as a valid message-signature pair. This is all done without factoring N and without learning the private key, d.

Seifert's attack uses an incredibly simple strategy: If forging RSA signatures using the modulus N is too difficult, then modify some bits of N and create a new modulus, $\widehat{N}$, where it is easy to forge signatures. Seifert points out that it is very easy to create signatures when $\widehat{N}$ is prime, since then we can simply compute the private exponent, $\widehat{d}$, as $e^{-1} \bmod (\widehat{N} - 1)$, assuming that e is relatively prime to $\widehat{N} - 1$. In the off-line part of Seifert's attack, the adversary modifies some of the least significant bits of N to create $\widehat{N}$. In the on-line part of the attack, the adversary repeatedly queries the device with a specially constructed message-signature pair and causes data faults until this particular $\widehat{N}$ is used as the modulus in the signature verification algorithm.

To put a practical perspective on Seifert's attack, imagine that the device is a "locked" computer that will only execute code if it can validate a signature on that code. This is exactly what Microsoft had hoped to implement in its Xbox game-console [10]. Microsoft attempted to design the Xbox so that only software signed by Microsoft would run on it. However, a number of Xbox enthusiasts found ways to circumvent Microsoft's software authentication techniques [5]. In fact, Seifert credits Andy Green and Franz Lehner's Xbox "hack" [5, page 143] as the inspiration for his attack. However, there is an important distinction between the two techniques. Green and Lehner's attack involves a *deterministic* change to an internal parameter; Seifert's attack involves a *random* change to an internal parameter. If an attacker has the ability to change bits of (N, e) deterministically, then it is much easier to unlock the device. In this case, it is possible to defeat the authentication procedure by just setting e to equal 1.

After the publication of Seifert's attack, one of the most pressing questions concerning it involved its practical consequences (e.g., What is the estimated work factor and success probability for an adversary who mounts the attack against a 1024-bit public RSA key?). The analysis provided in [8] gives a number of asymptotic expressions for the work factor and success probability of the attack, but extracting practical information from them is nontrivial. For example, the main result (Thm. 1) in [8] says that if an adversary can cause faults in the least significant $O(\lg \lg N)$ bits of N, then, assuming that the Riemann Hypothesis is true, they can make the device accept a signature on an arbitrary message with probability $\Theta(1/\lg N)$ in $\lg^{O(1)} N$ time. Clearly, the real-world implications of this result for 1024-bit RSA depend on the constants hidden in the asymptotic terms. It turns out that it is possible to give a more precise and straightforward analysis of Seifert's attack. With this analysis it is possible to make statements like the following: If an adversary can cause faults in only 4 bits of an RSA modulus, then there is a greater than 50% chance that they will be able to make the device accept a signature on an arbitrary message after 2^4 on-line queries.

Our contributions. Our main contribution is a simplified analysis of Seifert's attack. The work estimates we present are practice-oriented and can be easily interpreted. We verify our analysis against some computational trials which use RSA public keys of practical sizes (i.e., 1024 bits and 2048 bits). In addition, we offer two straightforward generalizations to Seifert's attack. We demonstrate that we do not need to restrict ourselves to errors only in the least significant bits of the modulus. Also, we show that we do not need to limit ourselves to moduli, $\widehat{N}$, that are prime – what we really want is moduli that have easily computed factorizations.

Outline. In §2 we describe the fault model which we use throughout the paper. In §3 we review Seifert's attack and adapt it to our fault model. An analysis and some computational results are presented in §3.1 and §3.2. In §4 we give an improvement to Seifert's attack; analysis and computational results are provided in §4.1 and §4.2. We briefly discuss some open problems related to fault attacks on discrete log based signature schemes in §5. We end with some remarks in §6.

2   Fault Model

Suppose that the target device (i.e., the locked computer) implements Algorithm 1. In this algorithm, the operator "↞" denotes an assignment operation

---

Algorithm 1. Faulty RSA Signature Verification

Input: $m \in \{0,1\}^*$, $s \in \mathbb{Z}_N$.
Output: "accept" or "reject".

1: $(\widehat{N}, \widehat{e}) \twoheadleftarrow (N, e)$
2: $h \leftarrow H(m)$
3: $h' \leftarrow s^{\widehat{e}} \bmod \widehat{N}$
4: **if** $h = h'$ **then return** "accept"
5: **else return** "reject"

---

that is subject to bit-faults; we will make this more precise in a moment. The function H denotes a message encoding function which typically incorporates some cryptographic hash function. For example, H might be a full-domain hash function constructed from a concatenation of SHA-256 hashes [2].

The bit-faults which affect the public key are instigated by the adversary. In our model, *we only consider bit-faults in the RSA modulus, N*. These faults change N to $\widehat{N}$ non-deterministically while e remains unchanged. This assumption – that faults can be localized to a particular parameter of a cryptographic computation – is commonly used in the theory of fault analysis (cf. [3]).

Recently, Naccache, Nguyen, Tunstall and Whelan [7] presented a key recovery attack on DSA which requires that an adversary zeroize some of the least-significant bits of the nonce k used in signature generation. What's more, they successfully implemented their attack against a smartcard and demonstrated that it is possible for an adversary to engineer the required data faults. However, despite the physical experiments conducted by Naccache et al., the practicality of the assumption that bit-faults will affect N but not e depends upon the characteristics of a specific target device and the tools and skills of a specific adversary (the fact that the bit-length of e is much shorter than N may be of some help). So let us state plainly that the validity of our assumptions for any particular target device are untested; however, experience shows that often attacks can be modified minorly to adapt to different situations, and thus we believe this fault model is important to consider as a starting point. For example, if an adversary can localize faults to N only 20% of the time, this may suffice to carry out the attack.

Concerning bit-faults in e, it seems unlikely that an adversary would be able to take advantage of such errors. But, if by randomly flipping bits of e, we could obtain a value $\hat{e}$ for which it is easy to compute $\hat{e}$-th roots modulo N, then this type of attack would certainly be worth exploring. However, unless the adversary has a way to set $\hat{e} = 1$ with high probability, this would seem to happen very rarely. In practice, e is usually taken to be 3 or 65537 since these values help make signature verification more efficient.

An excellent survey of techniques for inducing computational faults in a device is presented in [1]. For example, a *random-data fixed-location* fault (i.e., random data appears at a fixed location within N) can be induced by illuminating one of the device's registers or data buses with a strong light source. Alternately, a *fixed-data random-location* fault (i.e., constant data appears at a random location within the modulus) can be initiated by varying the device's supply voltage.

We model the effect of faults on the modulus using an *error function*, ξ. This function takes two parameters: the first is N and the second is a nonce, Δ. Both ξ and Δ determine how N is transformed. One possible definition of ξ is the following

$$\xi(N, \Delta) = N \oplus 0^{n-b-c} \| \Delta \| 0^c, \quad \text{where} \quad \Delta \in \{0,1\}^b. \tag{1}$$

Here, N is considered as an n-bit array; its value is changed by xoring it with a b-bit string, Δ, which is offset according to the value c. The values b and c are fixed non-negative integers that satisfy $0 \le b+c \le n$. This error function models random-data fixed-location faults.

Another possible definition of ξ is

$$\xi(N, \Delta) = N \ \& \ 1^{n-b-\Delta} \| 0^b \| 1^\Delta, \quad \text{where} \quad \Delta \in \{0, 1, 2, \ldots n - b\}. \tag{2}$$

The symbol "&" denotes a bit-wise "and". Now, the bits of N are changed by zeroing a block of b bits offset according to the parameter Δ (which is now an integer). This error function models fixed-data random-location faults.

In general, we can consider

$$\xi : \{0,1\}^n \times S \to \{0,1\}^n$$

where S is a finite set. The nonce Δ is drawn uniformly from S (we denote this as $\Delta \in_R S$). In Algorithm 1, after the operation $(\widehat{N}, \hat{e}) \rightsquigarrow (N, e)$, we have that

$$\widehat{N} = \xi(N, \Delta), \text{ for some } \Delta \in_R S, \quad \text{and} \quad \hat{e} = e.$$

When Algorithm 1 is executed, the adversary initiates faults but they *cannot* control the value of Δ.

For the sake of clarity, we continue our exposition assuming that ξ is defined as in (1). Thus, we have

$$\widehat{N} = N \oplus 0^{n-b-c} \| \Delta \| 0^c, \text{ for some } \Delta \in_R \{0,1\}^b.$$

Δ is b-bits wide; we sometimes refer to Δ as an *error vector*. The value of b might be influenced by the size of the device's data-bus or registers; for example, many smart cards have 8-bit registers while typical desktop PCs have 32-bit registers. The bit-length of the modulus is n, so we have $n = \lfloor \lg N \rfloor + 1$.

Using the parameters b, c, Δ, we can rewrite the signature verification operation like so:

Algorithm 2. Faulty RSA Signature Verification

Input: $m \in \{0,1\}^*$, $s \in \mathbb{Z}_N$.
Output: "accept" or "reject".

1: $\Delta \in_R \{0,1\}^b$
2: $\widehat{N} \leftarrow N \oplus 0^{n-b-c} \| \Delta \| 0^c$
3: $\widehat{e} \leftarrow e$
4: $h \leftarrow H(m)$
5: $h' \leftarrow s^{\widehat{e}} \bmod \widehat{N}$
6: **if** $h = h'$ **then return** "accept"
7: **else return** "reject"

---

3   Seifert's Attack

In Algorithm 3 we present a simplified description of Seifert's attack which is adapted according to our fault model. Note that the title "Algorithm" is applied loosely. To turn the description into a true algorithm, we would need to bound the number of times that the second iterative loop (lines 11-13) is executed.

Essentially, what is happening in Algorithm 3 is that we randomly flip bits of N until we find a value $\widehat{N}$ such that $\widehat{N}$ is prime and e^{-1} exists modulo $\widehat{N} - 1$. If we find such a value, then we use it to construct a new private exponent $\widehat{d}$ by computing the inverse of e modulo $\widehat{N} - 1$. This can be done efficiently using the extended Euclidean algorithm or Fermat's Theorem. Next, we generate a signature for m, using $\widehat{d}$, which will verify against the public key $(\widehat{N}, e)$. All of this work so far is done *off-line* (i.e., it does not require any interaction with the device). The attack finishes with an *on-line* phase where we repeatedly query the device with our selected message and the signature we constructed for it. Each time we query the device, we hope that the bit-faults we initiate will cause the device to use the modulus $\widehat{N}$ when it checks our message and signature.

Algorithm 3. Seifert's Fault Attack

Input: An arbitrary message $m \in \{0,1\}^*$, the device's RSA public key (N, e).
Output: "success" or "fail".

1: $S \leftarrow \{0,1\}^b \setminus \{0^b\}$
2: **repeat**
3:      $\Delta \in_R S$
4:      $S \leftarrow S \setminus \{\Delta\}$
5:      $\widehat{N} \leftarrow N \oplus 0^{n-b-c} \| \Delta \| 0^c$
6: **until** ($\widehat{N}$ is prime **and** $\gcd(e, \widehat{N} - 1) = 1$) **or** ($S = \varnothing$)
7: **if** $S = \varnothing$ **then return** "fail"
8: $\widehat{d} \leftarrow e^{-1} \bmod (\widehat{N} - 1)$
9: $h \leftarrow H(m)$
10: $s \leftarrow h^{\widehat{d}} \bmod \widehat{N}$
11: **repeat**
12:      output $\leftarrow$ the output of Algorithm 2 on input m, s.
13: **until** output = "accept"
14: **return** "success"

Note that Algorithm 3 generalizes Seifert's original attack model in an obvious way. The original model did not consider the parameter c as bit-faults were always restricted to the b least-significant bits of N. We will see that the value of c has no effect on the running time or success probability of the attack; however, the value of b does.

3.1 Analysis

Algorithm 3 contains two iterative loops. The first loop (lines 2-6) is executed during the off-line portion of the attack:

repeat
    $\Delta \in_R S$
    $S \leftarrow S \setminus \{\Delta\}$
    $\widehat{N} \leftarrow N \oplus 0^{n-b-c} \| \Delta \| 0^c$
until ($\widehat{N}$ is prime **and** $\gcd(e, \widehat{N} - 1) = 1$) **or** ($S = \varnothing$)

Note that the error space $S = \{0,1\}^b \setminus \{0^b\}$ may be traversed in other ways (e.g., it might be more convenient to enumerate the elements of S in lexicographic order).

The off-line portion of the attack succeeds if we can find a value of $\widehat{N}$ that causes the loop to exit before we exhaust the error space. The probability of this happening for a particular value of $\widehat{N}$ is

$$\Pr(\widehat{N} \text{ is prime}) \cdot \Pr(\gcd(e, \widehat{N} - 1) = 1).$$

In practice, e is usually equal to 3 or 65537 which are both prime numbers. We will make the simplifying assumption that e is prime. Thus,

$$\Pr(\gcd(e, \widehat{N} - 1) = 1) = \Pr(e \nmid \widehat{N} - 1) = \frac{e-1}{e}.$$

A consequence of the Prime Number Theorem is that the probability that a random *odd* positive integer x is prime is roughly $2/\ln x$. Using this fact, and the bound $2^{n-1} \le \widehat{N} < 2^n$, we have

$$\Pr(\widehat{N} \text{ is prime}) \approx \frac{2}{\ln \widehat{N}} > \frac{2}{\ln 2^n} = \frac{2}{n \ln 2}.$$

The reader who carefully examines the definition of Algorithm 3 may notice that there are some values of $\widehat{N}$ that are *not* necessarily odd. This happens only when $c = 0$. However, in the off-line phase of the attack, since we are searching for $\widehat{N}$ that are prime, when carrying out our search we would simply modify the error space, S, so that $\widehat{N}$ is always odd.

Now we can estimate the probability that $\widehat{N}$ meets our criteria as

$$\frac{2(e-1)}{e \cdot n \ln 2}.$$

Thus, the expected number of $\widehat{N}$ values we need to consider before we find one that suits our needs is $\frac{e \cdot n \ln 2}{2(e-1)}$. The probability that there is *no* good value of $\widehat{N}$ inside our search space can be estimated as

$$\left(1 - \frac{2(e-1)}{e \cdot n \ln 2}\right)^{2^b - 1}.$$

This represents the probability that the off-line stage of the attack *fails*.

The *on-line* portion of the attack is described in the second iterative loop (lines 11-13):

> **repeat**
>   output ← the output of Algorithm 2 on input $m, s, (N, e)$.
> **until** output = "accept"

This portion of the attack is much simpler to analysis. We want the RSA verification algorithm to be affected by a particular error vector; assuming that each error vector from $\{0, 1\}^b$ is equiprobable, this happens with probability $\frac{1}{2^b}$. Thus, the expected number of faulted signature verification operations needed before the desired error occurs is 2^b.

Some of the important characteristics of Algorithm 3 are summarized in Figure 1. Notice how the parameter b affects the success probability and running time of the attack. By increasing b we can increase the probability that the

off-line stage	worst case running time	$O(2^b - 1)$
	expected running time	$O\left(\frac{e \cdot n \ln 2}{2(e-1)}\right)$
	probability of success	$1 - \left(1 - \frac{2(e-1)}{en \ln 2}\right)^{2^b - 1}$
on-line stage	expected running time	$O(2^b)$

Fig. 1. Characteristics of Algorithm 3

off-line stage of the attack succeeds. However, this also increases the expected number of steps in the on-line stage of the attack. Depending on how quickly the target device processes and responds to on-line queries, the expected number of on-line queries required can present a major obstacle to attack implementors.

3.2   The Off-Line Search in Practice

We constructed two RSA public keys by pairing the RSA challenge numbers RSA-1024 and RSA-2048 [12] with the exponent $e = 65537$. For each public key, we examined the search space used in the off-line stage of Algorithm 3 for various values of b and c (recall that b is the error-width and c is its offset). All our numerical computations (i.e., probabilistic primality testing and gcd's) were done using the C++ library NTL [9].

For each public key, we took $b \in \{4, 6, 8, 10, 12, 14, 16\}$. For each value of b, we set c to equal each multiple of b in the interval $0 \ldots n - b - 1$; so, c takes on $1 + \lfloor \frac{n-b-1}{b} \rfloor$ different values. In theory, the offset, c, could take any value in the interval $0 \ldots n - b$; our reason for limiting c to multiples of b was that we wanted the c values to define disjoint search spaces.

We illustrate our experiments with an example. Suppose $b = 4$ and $n = 1024$. For these parameters, the error offset c takes on 255 different values; namely, $0, 4, 8, 12, \ldots, 1016$. Each value of c defines a search space which is disjoint from all the others. We found that 3 of the 255 search spaces contained $\widehat{N}$ values for which the off-line stage of the attack succeeds. The ratio $3/255$ can be compared to our estimate of the probability that the off-line stage of the attack succeeds when $b = 4$ (see below). Across the 255 search spaces, we examined $255 \cdot (2^4 - 1) = 3825$ values of $\widehat{N}$. Of these 3825 values, 3 had the desired properties. The ratio $3/3825$ can be compared to our estimate of the probability that $\widehat{N}$ is prime and $\widehat{N} - 1$ is relatively prime to $e = 65537$. The same methodology was used for the other values of b. Our experimental results are summarized in Figure 2.

From our analysis in the previous section, for the 1024-bit public key, we estimate the probability that a value of $\widehat{N}$ has the desired properties as

$$\frac{2 \cdot 65536}{65537 \cdot 1024 \cdot \ln 2} \approx 0.00282.$$

The empirical values listed for RSA-1024 in column 5 of Figure 2 appear to converge toward this estimate. From the probability above, we see that the expected number of values of $\widehat{N}$ we must examine before we find one that meets our criteria is $1/0.00282 = 355$. If the architecture of a device permits the attacker some control over the size of b, then they might choose b so that their search space contains at least 355 values (but, of course, this does not guarantee that the search space will contain a good value of $\widehat{N}$). In practice, it would seem prudent to first find lots of good values of $\widehat{N}$, for various values of b and c, and then pick one that has a short error-width which is easy to instantiate in the device.

	b	good $\widehat{N}$'s	total # of $\widehat{N}$'s	ratio	good c's	total # of c's	ratio
RSA-1024	4	3	3825	0.00078	3	255	0.0118
$e = 65537$	6	24	10710	0.00224	23	170	0.135
	8	68	32385	0.00210	53	127	0.417
	10	264	104346	0.00253	97	102	0.951
	12	969	348075	0.00278	85	85	1
	14	3354	1195959	0.00280	73	73	1
	16	11658	4128705	0.00282	63	63	1
RSA-2048	4	11	7665	0.00144	11	511	0.0215
$e = 65537$	6	44	21483	0.00205	41	341	0.120
	8	106	65025	0.00163	80	255	0.314
	10	332	208692	0.00159	164	204	0.804
	12	1018	696150	0.00146	169	170	0.994
	14	3433	2391918	0.00144	146	146	1
	16	11601	8322945	0.00139	127	127	1

Fig. 2. Experimental results for the off-line stage of Algorithm 3

Using the probability above, we can estimate the probability that the off-line stage of the attack will succeed for different values of b:

$$b = 4, \quad 1 - (1 - 0.00282)^{2^4 - 1} \approx 0.0415$$
$$b = 6, \quad 1 - (1 - 0.00282)^{2^6 - 1} \approx 0.163$$
$$b = 8, \quad 1 - (1 - 0.00282)^{2^8 - 1} \approx 0.513$$
$$b = 10, 1 - (1 - 0.00282)^{2^{10} - 1} \approx 0.944.$$

These estimates are quite close to the empirical values listed for RSA-1024 in column 8 of Figure 2.

Similar comparisons can be made for RSA-2048. We estimate the probability that a 2048-bit value of $\widehat{N}$ has the desired properties as

$$\frac{2 \cdot 65536}{65537 \cdot 2048 \cdot \ln 2} \approx 0.00141.$$

And, we estimate the probability that the off-line stage of the attack will succeed for different values of b as:

$$b = 4, \quad 1 - (1 - 0.00141)^{2^4 - 1} \approx 0.0209$$
$$b = 6, \quad 1 - (1 - 0.00141)^{2^6 - 1} \approx 0.0851$$
$$b = 8, \quad 1 - (1 - 0.00141)^{2^8 - 1} \approx 0.302$$
$$b = 10, 1 - (1 - 0.00141)^{2^{10} - 1} \approx 0.764.$$

These estimates are quite close to our empirical results.

Although our fault model and method of analysis greatly simplify many of the arguments from Seifert's paper, these experiments demonstrate that our analysis does give an accurate picture of what can be expected in practice.

4   Improving Seifert's Attack

The criteria that Seifert uses for his off-line search can be relaxed. When we examine various values of $\widehat{N}$, what we really want is an integer that has an *easily computed prime factorization*. If $\widehat{N}$ is prime, then this is certainly true. However, there are many other integers which have this property. If we know the prime factorization of $\widehat{N}$, then we can easily compute $\varphi(\widehat{N})$ and then use the extended Euclidean algorithm to obtain $\widehat{d} = e^{-1} \bmod \varphi(\widehat{N})$.

Deciding whether or not the prime factorization of a random integer can be easily computed is a subjective task. It depends upon what factorization method you are using, how efficiently it is implemented and how much time you are willing to invest. The strategy we used was this: given $\widehat{N}$, divide out any prime factors $\leq 2^{10}$, and then check whether the quotient is equal to 1 or is prime. We chose a small bound of 2^{10} since we did not want to invest much time in attempting to factor each $\widehat{N}$ in our simulations. Adversaries who are willing to invest more time into attempting to factorize a few values of $\widehat{N}$ might utilize, say, the elliptic curve factoring method since it tends to find small prime factors of $\widehat{N}$ first.

The off-line stage of the attack now becomes

$S \leftarrow \{0,1\}^b \setminus \{0^b\}$
repeat
$\quad \Delta \in_R S$
$\quad S \leftarrow S \setminus \{\Delta\}$
$\quad \widehat{N} \leftarrow N \oplus 0^{n-b-c}\|\Delta\|0^c$
$\quad \widehat{N}_0 \leftarrow \widehat{N}$ with any prime factors $\leq 2^{10}$ divided out.
until ($\widehat{N}_0$ is prime or equal to 1 **and** $\gcd(e, \varphi(\widehat{N})) = 1$) **or** ($S = \varnothing$)

Obviously, the bound 2^{10} can be replaced with one larger or smaller according to the preference of the implementor. There is a convenient data structure in NTL which can be used to generate all primes less than 2^{30} in sequence[1].

4.1   Analysis

The probability that a value of $\widehat{N}$ causes the loop above to exit is

$$\Pr(\widehat{N}_0 \text{ is prime or equal to 1}) \cdot \Pr(\gcd(e, \varphi(\widehat{N})) = 1) \quad =$$

$$\Pr(\text{the second-largest prime factor of } \widehat{N} \text{ is } \leq 2^{10}) \cdot \Pr(\gcd(e, \varphi(\widehat{N})) = 1).$$

The distribution of the second-largest prime factor of random integers $\leq x$ as $x \to \infty$ was investigated by Knuth and Trabb Pardo [6]. Following their discussion, we define

---

[1] Actually, during our experiments, we found that the largest prime generated by NTL's `PrimeSeq` class to be $2^{30} - 2^{16} - 1$ which is not the greatest prime $\leq 2^{30}$; there are 3184 more primes which are larger.

$F_2(\beta) := \lim_{x \to \infty} \Pr(\text{a random integer} \leq x \text{ has its 2nd-largest prime factor} \leq x^\beta)$.

Knuth and Trabb Pardo showed that this limit exists, and also presented a method for approximating its value. Over the interval $0 \leq \beta \leq 1/2$, $F_2(\beta)$ increases monotonically from 0 to 1; for $\beta \geq 1/2$, $F_2(\beta) = 1$. Since n is the bit-length of the modulus, N, we have $\widehat{N} \leq 2^n$. Setting x and β equal to 2^n and $10/n$, respectively, we obtain

$F_2(10/n) \approx \Pr(\text{a random integer} \leq 2^n \text{ has its 2nd-largest prime factor} \leq 2^{10})$.

Assuming $\widehat{N}$ behaves like a random integer $\leq 2^n$, this is the probability that we want to approximate. Using our assumption that e is prime, we estimate the probability that $\widehat{N}$ meets our criteria as

$$\frac{(e-1)F_2(10/n)}{e}.$$

Unfortunately, $F_2(\beta)$ does not have a simple closed form so it is not immediate what sort of improvement this achieves. However, we can quantify the difference by plugging in some numbers.

A table of values for $F_2(\beta)$ is provided in [6]. From this table, we build a polynomial approximation to $F_2(\beta)$ in the interval $0 \leq \beta \leq 1/2$. This gives us

$$F_2(10/1024) \approx 0.0175, \quad F_2(10/2048) \approx 0.00872,$$
$$F_2(30/1024) \approx 0.0538, \quad F_2(30/2048) \approx 0.0264.$$

Now, for a 1024-bit public key with $e = 65537$, the probability that a random value of $\widehat{N}$ ends our search when we cast out prime factors $\leq 2^{10}$ is roughly

$$\frac{65536 \cdot 0.0175}{65537} \approx 0.0175.$$

So, our chances, which we calculated in §2.4, have increased from 0.282% to 1.75%. If we cast out primes less than 2^{30}, we get 5.38%. Some more comparisons are made in Figure 3. The most dramatic difference appears in the number of values of $\widehat{N}$ we expect to consider before the search ends.

4.2   The Improved Off-Line Search in Practice

We repeated the experiments from §2.4 using our new on-line search criteria. For various error widths and offsets, we exhausted the resulting search spaces and determined which $\widehat{N}$'s could be easily factorized after casting out prime factors $\leq 2^{10}$. Our results are summarized in Figure 4. Our empirical results are close to what our analysis predicts.

Although we have considered only random-data fixed-location faults in our experiments, it is just as easy to treat fixed-data random-location faults. An interesting demonstration of this is presented in Appendix A.

		Seifert's off-line search		off-line search using primes $\leq 2^{10}$		off-line search using primes $\leq 2^{30}$	
	b	expected iterations	probability of success	expected iterations	probability of success	expected iterations	probability of success
RSA-1024	4	355	0.041	57	0.233	19	0.564
$e = 65537$	6	355	0.084	57	0.421	19	0.820
	8	355	0.513	57	0.989	19	0.999
RSA-2048	4	710	0.021	115	0.123	38	0.331
$e = 65537$	6	710	0.043	115	0.238	38	0.564
	8	710	0.302	115	0.893	38	0.999

Fig. 3. Comparison of off-line search strategies

	b	good $\widehat{N}$'s	total # of $\widehat{N}$'s	ratio	good c's	total # of c's	ratio
RSA-1024	4	63	3825	0.0165	54	255	0.212
$e = 65537$	6	191	10710	0.0178	111	170	0.653
	8	545	32385	0.0168	126	127	0.992
	10	1843	104346	0.0177	102	102	1
	12	6018	348075	0.0173	85	85	1
	14	20861	1195959	0.0174	73	73	1
	16	72711	4128705	0.0176	63	63	1
RSA-2048	4	63	7665	0.00822	60	511	0.117
$e = 65537$	6	203	21483	0.00945	155	341	0.455
	8	598	65025	0.00920	228	255	0.894
	10	1863	208692	0.00893	204	204	1
	12	6259	696150	0.00899	170	170	1
	14	20910	2391918	0.00874	146	146	1
	16	72968	8322945	0.00877	127	127	1

Fig. 4. Experimental results of searching for easily factorable $\widehat{N}$'s

5   Further Work

An interesting lesson that can be taken from Seifert's attack is that public-key authentication systems based on the integer factorization problem are somewhat fragile with respect to bit-faults; that is, if you randomly flip a few bits of the public-key then there is a non-negligible probability that you end up with an integer that is easy to factor. It would be interesting to determine if similar fault attacks exist for discrete log based authentication systems. We briefly consider some problems related to the ElGamal signature scheme [4].

In the ElGamal signature scheme

- the *private key* is $x \in_R [1, p - 2]$.
- the *public key* is (y, g, p) where $y = g^x \mod p$, p is a large prime (say, 1024 bits) and g is a generator of $\mathbb{Z}_p^*$.

The signature verification algorithm is presented in Algorithm 4.

Algorithm 4. ElGamal Signature Verification

Input: $m, (r, s), (y, g, p)$
Output: "accept" or "reject"

1: **if** $r \notin [0, p-1]$ **or** $s \notin [0, p-2]$ **then**
2:         **return** "reject"
3: $h \leftarrow H(m)$
4: $u \leftarrow g^h \bmod p$
5: $u' \leftarrow r^s y^r \bmod p$
6: **if** $u = u'$ **then return** "accept"
7: **else return** "reject"

To forge a signature on a message m, we must find (r, s) such that

$$g^{H(m)} \equiv r^s y^r \pmod{p}. \tag{3}$$

It is well-known that the forgery problem is no harder than computing discrete logs in $\mathbb{Z}_p^*$ (to see this, choose r at random and then solve a discrete log to obtain s). Now, if we are able to randomly flip bits in one of p, y, g, it may be that the forgery problem becomes tractable.

For example, if we change p to $\widehat{p}$, where $\widehat{p}$ is easily factorable, then we can apply the CRT to $\mathbb{Z}_{\widehat{p}}$ which may reduce our work in solving $g^{H(m)} \equiv r^s y^r$ $(\bmod \ \widehat{p})$ using, say, an index-calculus method. Also, if $\varphi(\widehat{p})$ is smooth, then the Pohlig-Hellman algorithm can be utilized; however, we ideally want an attack that has a high probability of success.

One tempting possibility to consider is replacing g with $\widehat{g}$ where the order of $\widehat{g}$ is small (as in a small subgroup attack). However, the probability that randomly flipping bits of g moves us into a small subgroup of $\mathbb{Z}_p^*$ seems to be negligible.

It is possible that computing $\log_g \widehat{y}$ might be easier than computing $\log_g y$. This motivates the following relaxation of the discrete log problem: given y, find $\widehat{y}$ and $\widehat{x}$ such that $\widehat{y} = g^{\widehat{x}}$ and $y \oplus \widehat{y}$ has low weight.

6 Remarks

Our analysis and computational trials show that if an adversary is able to cause random faults in *only 4 bits* of a 1024-bit RSA modulus stored in a device, then there is a greater than 50% chance that they will be able to make that device accept a signature on a message of their choice; for 2048-bit RSA, *6 bits* suffice.

These percentages do not take into account any of the practical difficulties that might be involved in a real-world implementation of the attack. For example, it might be difficult to limit the effect of faults to a particular block of bits within the modulus. Our examination was limited to a mathematical model and so we did not deal with these issues. Presently, there is no record of anyone successfully or unsuccessfully carrying out this attack in the open literature. Whether this is because the assumptions of the attack are too strong or that simply no one has yet attempted to implement it remains to be seen.

One way to defend against this attack is to have the device check the integrity of its public key. This might be done by computing a cryptographic hash of the public key and then comparing it to some stored value. However, care must be taken in when this comparison is done. If an integrity check is done before a signature is verified, this will not stop attackers who cause bit-faults in the public key after the check. Other countermeasures, against fault analysis attacks in general, are discussed in [1].

Acknowledgements

The author thanks Paul Van Oorschot for providing helpful comments on an earlier version of this paper.

References

1. H. BAR-EL, H. CHOUKRI, D. NACCACHE, M. TUNSTALL AND C. WHELAN. The sorcerer's apprentice guide to fault attacks. *Proceedings of the IEEE* **94** (2006), 370–382.
2. M. BELLARE AND P. ROGAWAY. The exact security of digital signatures: How to sign with RSA and Rabin. In "Advances in Cryptology – Eurocrypt '96", *Lecture Notes in Computer Science* **1070** (1996), 399–416.
3. D. BONEH, R. DEMILLO, AND R. LIPTON. On the importance of checking cryptographic protocols for faults. *Journal of Cryptology* **14** (2001), 101–119.
4. T. ELGAMAL. A public key cryptosystem and a signature scheme based on discrete logarithms. *IEEE Transactions on Information Theory* **31** (1985), 469–472.
5. A. HUANG. *Hacking the Xbox: An Introduction to Reverse Engineering*, No Starch Press, 2003.
6. D. KNUTH AND L. TRABB PARDO. Analysis of a simple factorization algorithm. *Theoretical Computer Science* **3** (1976), 321–348.
7. D. NACCACHE, P. NGUYEN, M. TUNSTALL, C. WHELAN. Experimenting with faults, lattices and the DSA. In "Public Key Cryptography – PKC 2005", *Lecture Notes in Computer Science* **3386** (2005), 16–28.
8. J. SEIFERT. On authenticated computing and RSA-based authentication. In *Proceedings of the 12th ACM Conference on Computer and Communications Security (CCS 2005)*, November 2005, pp. 122–127.
9. V. SHOUP. NTL: A library for doing number theory (version 5.4). http://shoup.net/ntl/
10. Microsoft Xbox, http://www.microsoft.com/xbox/
11. Operation X, http://sourceforge.net/projects/opx/
12. RSA Challenge Numbers, http://www.rsasecurity.com/rsalabs/node.asp?id=2093

A   Fixed-Data Faults

Some of the techniques for inducing faults explained in [1] can be used to zeroize bytes of data. An off-line search for an easily factorable modulus with respect to this fault model is easy carry out. Here, we present an interesting example of this.

The 2048-bit modulus from the public RSA key that Microsoft stores inside the Xbox can be found in publicly available source code [11]. Here is the modulus in hexadecimal:

```
A44B1BBD7EDA72C7143CD5C2D4BA880C7681832D5198F75FCAB1618598E2B3E4
8D9A47B0BFF6BC967CAE88F198266E535A6CB41B470C0A38A19D8F57CB11F568
DB52CF69E49F604EEA52F4EB9D37E80C60BD70A5CF5A67EC05AA6B3E8C80C116
819A14892BFA7603BECE39F09C42724EE9F371C473AAA09FEDA34F9EA1019827
BD07CA52A80013BE9471E46FCF1CA4D915FB9DF95E9344330B6AAE0B90526AD1
BE475D10797526075C9206FF758A3EB3BAF7C0A22E51645BB9F13FE129A22F2E
1BEDDA95D68AFC6D46585B01FBB5737273C6AEE399148C5B8E77B479DE8B05BD
EEC27FEFFF7B349C64F51002D2F6522ED43617F2A1A3D4C2E6D73D66E54ED7D3
```

This modulus consists of 256 bytes. If we index the bytes from least significant (byte $0 = $ D3) to most significant (byte $255 = $ A4), then the smallest index, i, such that when we zeroize byte i we obtain an easily factorable number is $i = 16$. The method of factorization we used was to cast out all prime factors $\leq 2^{30}$ and then apply a probabilistic primality test. The factorization is $3 \cdot 13 \cdot 199 \cdot 856469 \cdot p_0$ where p_0 is a large prime. The smallest index, j, such that when we zeroize byte j we obtain a prime number is $j = 104$.

The Fairness of Perfect Concurrent Signatures

Guilin Wang, Feng Bao, and Jianying Zhou

Institute for Infocomm Research
21 Heng Mui Keng Terrace, Singapore 119613
{glwang, baofeng, jyzhou}@i2r.a-star.edu.sg

Abstract. In Eurocrypt 2004, Chen, Kudla and Paterson introduced the concept of *concurrent signatures*, which allow two parties to produce two ambiguous signatures until the initial signer releases an extra piece of information (called *keystone*). Once the keystone is publicly known, both signatures are bound to their true signers *concurrently*. In ICICS 2004, Susilo, Mu and Zhang further proposed *perfect concurrent signatures* to strengthen the ambiguity of concurrent signatures. That is, even if the both signers are known having issued one of the two ambiguous signatures, any third party is still unable to deduce who signed which signature, different from Chen et al.'s scheme. In this paper, we point out that Susilo et al.'s two perfect concurrent signature schemes are actually *not* concurrent signatures. Specifically, we identify an attack that enables the initial signer to release a carefully prepared keystone that binds the matching signer's signature, but not the initial signer's. Therefore, their schemes are *unfair* for the matching signer. Moreover, we present an effective way to avoid this attack so that the improved schemes are truly perfect concurrent signatures.

Keywords: Concurrent signature, fair exchange, security protocol.

1 Introduction

The concept of *concurrent signatures* was introduced by Chen, Kudla and Paterson in Eurocrypt 2004 [11]. Such signature schemes allow two parties to produce and exchange two ambiguous signatures until an extra piece of information (called *keystone*) is released by one of the parties. More specifically, before the keystone is released, those two signatures are *ambiguous* with respect to the identity of the signing party, i.e., they may be issued either by two parties together or just by one party alone; after the keystone is publicly known, however, both signatures are bound to their true signers *concurrently*, i.e., any third party can validate who signed which signature.

As explained below, concurrent signatures contribute a novel approach for the traditional problem of fair exchange of signatures: Two mutually mistrustful parties want to exchange their signatures in a *fair* way, i.e., after the completion of exchange, either each party gets the other's signature or neither party does. Fair exchange of signatures is widely useful in electronic commerce, like contract signing and e-payment.

P. Ning, S. Qing, and N. Li (Eds.): ICICS 2006, LNCS 4307, pp. 435–451, 2006.

According to whether a trusted third party (TTP) is needed in the exchange procedure, there are two essentially different approaches in the literature for the problem of fair exchanging signatures: (a) Gradual exchange without TTP; and (b) Optimal exchange with TTP. Though without the help of a TTP, the first type solutions (e.g., [21,15,13]) impractically assume that both parties have equivalent computation resources, and inefficiently exchange signatures "bit-by-bit" for many interactive rounds. There are many efficient implementations belonging to the second approach, such as verifiably encrypted signatures [6,5,9], escrowed signatures [3,4], convertible signatures [8], and verifiable confirmation of signatures [10] etc. However, all those schemes require a dispute-resolving TTP whose functions are beyond that of a CA (certification authority) in PKI (public key infrastructure). The point is that such an appropriate TTP may be costly or even unavailable to the parties involved.

In [11], Chen et al. remarkably observed that the *full* power of fair exchange is *not necessary* in many applications, since there exist some mechanisms that provide a more natural dispute resolution than the reliance on a TTP. In particular, concurrent signatures can be used as a weak tool to realize practical exchanges, if one of the two parties would like to complete such an exchange. Chen et al. presented several such applications, including one party needing the service of the other, credit card payment transactions, secret information releasing, and fair tendering of contracts. In the following, we only review a concrete example of the first kind application.

Consider a situation where a customer Alice would like to purchase a laptop from a computer shop owned by Bob. For this purpose, Alice and Bob can first exchange their ambiguous signatures via the Internet as follows. As the initial signer, Alice first chooses a keystone, and signs her payment instruction ambiguously to pay Bob the price of a laptop. Upon receiving Alice's signature, Bob as the matching signer agrees this order by signing a receipt ambiguously that authorizes Alice to pick one up from Bob's shop. However, to get the laptop from the shop physically, Alice has to show both Bob's signature and the keystone, because Bob's ambiguous signature alone can be forged by Alice easily. But the point is that once the keystone is released, both of the two ambiguous signatures become bound concurrently to Alice and Bob respectively. Therefore, Bob can present Alice's signature together with the corresponding keystone to get money from bank.

In the above example, Alice indeed has a degree of extra power over Bob, since she controls whether to release the keystone. Actually, this is the exact reason why concurrent signatures can only provide a somewhat weak solution for fair exchange of signatures. In the common real life, however, if Alice does not want to buy a laptop (by releasing the keystone), why she wastes her time to order it. At the same time, by adding a time limit in the receipt, Bob could cancel Alice's order conveniently like the practice in booking air-tickets nowadays. The advantage is that those solutions using concurrent signatures [11,27] can be implemented very efficiently in both aspects of computation and communication, and do not rely on any TTP. Therefore, the shortcomings in traditional solutions for fair exchange of signatures are overcome in a relatively simple and natural way.

In ICICS 2004, Susilo, Mu and Zhang [27] pointed out that in Chen et al.'s concurrent signatures, if the two parties are known to be trustworthy any third party can identify who is the true signer of both ambiguous signatures *before* the keystone is released. To strengthen the ambiguity of concurrent signatures, Susilo et al. further proposed a strong notion called *perfect concurrent signatures*, and presented two concrete constructions from Schnorr signature and bilinear pairing. That is, in their schemes even a third party knows or believes both parties indeed issued one of the two signatures, he/she still cannot deduce who signed which signature, different from Chen et al.'s scheme.

In this paper, we shall point out that Susilo et al.'s perfect concurrent signatures are actually *not* concurrent signatures. Specifically, we identify an attack against their two schemes that enables the initial signer Alice to release a carefully prepared keystone such that the matching signer Bob's signature is binding, but not her. Therefore, both of their two perfect concurrent signature schemes are *unfair* for the matching signer Bob. At the same time, we also address another weakness in their keystone generation algorithm. To avoid those flaws, we present an effective way to improve Susilo et al.'s schemes [27] so that the results are truly perfect concurrent signatures. Moreover, our improvement from Schnorr signature obtains about 50% performance enhancement over their original scheme. In addition, we notice that a similar attack applies to a generic construction of identity-based perfect concurrent signatures, which is proposed by Chow and Susilo in ICICS 2005 [12].

For simplicity, we call PCS1 and PCS2 for Susilo et al.'s two perfect concurrent signatures from Schnorr and bilinear pairing, respectively. Sections 2 presents the security model for perfect concurrent signatures. In Section 3, we review PCS1 and analyze its security. In Section 4, we discuss PCS2 and its security. In Section 5, we present and analyze the improved schemes. Finally, Section 6 concludes the paper.

2   Security Model and Definitions

This section presents a formal model for perfect concurrent signatures, which is adapted from [11,27]. Specifically, a perfect concurrent signature (PCS) scheme works just as a usual concurrent signature scheme but achieves stronger security. That is, besides the requirements of unforgeability and fairness for standard concurrent signatures, a PCS scheme is supposed to satisfy perfect ambiguity (see below) rather than (usual) ambiguity specified in [11].

Definition 1 (Syntax of Concurrent Signatures). *A concurrent signature scheme consists of the following five algorithms.*

SETUP: *On input a security parameter ℓ, this probabilistic algorithm outputs the descriptions of a tuple $(\mathcal{U}, \mathcal{M}, \mathcal{S}, \mathcal{K}, \mathcal{F})$, where $\mathcal{U}$ is the set of users, $\mathcal{M}$ the* *message space, $\mathcal{S}$ the signature space, $\mathcal{K}$ the keystone space, $\mathcal{F}$ the keystone fix space. The algorithm also outputs the public keys $\{X_i\}$ of all users, while each user keeps the corresponding private key x_i.*

KGEN: *This is a mapping from $\mathcal{K}$ to $\mathcal{F}$, which is called the keystone generation algorithm. Note that KGEN should be a one-way function, i.e., it is difficult to derive k from KGEN(k).*

ASIGN: *On inputs (X_i, X_j, x, f, m), where X_i and X_j are two distinct public keys, x is the private key corresponding to X_i or X_j (i.e. $x = x_i$ or $x = x_j$), $f \in \mathcal{F}$, and $m \in \mathcal{M}$, this probabilistic algorithm outputs an ambiguous signature $\sigma = (c, s_1, s_2) \in \mathcal{S} \times \mathcal{F} \times \mathcal{F}$ on message m, where $s_1 = f$ or $s_2 = f$.*

AVERIFY: *On input $S = (\sigma, X_i, X_j, m)$, where $\sigma = (c, s_1, s_2) \in \mathcal{S} \times \mathcal{F} \times \mathcal{F}$, X_i and X_j are two different public keys, and $m \in \mathcal{M}$, this deterministic algorithm outputs accept or reject. We also require AVERIFY should have the symmetry property, i.e., AVERIFY(σ, X_i, X_j, m) $\equiv$ AVERIFY(σ', X_j, X_i, m), where $\sigma' = (c, s_2, s_1)$ is derived from $\sigma = (c, s_1, s_2)$.*

VERIFY: *On inputs (k, S), where $k \in \mathcal{K}$ and $S = (\sigma, X_i, X_j, m)$, this deterministic algorithm outputs accept if AVERIFY(S)=accept and the keystone k is valid. Otherwise, it outputs reject.*

Please refer to Section 2.2 of [11] for a framework how the concurrent signatures can be generated and exchanged between two mutually mistrustful parties, i.e., their general concurrent signature protocol.

Now, we describe the security requirements for perfect concurrent signatures, i.e., correctness, unforgeability, perfect ambiguity, and fairness. *Correctness* requires that (a) every anonymous signature σ properly generated by ASIGN will be accepted by AVERIFY, and every pair (k, σ) properly generated by KGEN and ASIGN will be accepted by VERIFY. Since this is just a simple and basic requirement, we do not mention it any more. The other three security requirements should be considered under a chosen message attack in the multi-party setting, extended from the existential unforgeability given in [22]. The purpose is to capture an adversary who can simulate and/or observe concurrent signature protocol runs between any pair of users, as noticed in [11]. Informally, *unforgeability* requires any efficient adversary with neither of the corresponding two secret keys cannot forge a valid concurrent signature with non-negligible probability under chosen message attacks. Since this paper focuses on the fairness and perfect ambiguity of concurrent signatures, we just mention the following formal definition of unforgeability without specifying the details of the game between a challenger and an adversary.

Definition 2 (Unforgeability). *A concurrent signature scheme is* `existentially unforgeable` *under a chosen message attack in the multi-party model, if the success probability of any polynomially bounded adversary in the game specified in Section 3.2 of [11] is a negligible function of the security parameter ℓ.*

In [11], *ambiguity* means that given a concurrent signature without the keystone, any adversary cannot distinguish who of the two signers issued this signature. This notion is strengthened by Susilo et al. (See Definition 5 in [27]) to capture that there are four cases (not only three cases) for the issuers of two signatures. We call this strengthened notion *perfect ambiguity*, and refine its definition here by providing a full formal specification. That is, the perfect ambiguity of a concurrent signature scheme is formally defined via the following game between an adversary E and a challenger C.

Setup: For a given security parameter ℓ, C runs SETUP to obtain all descriptions of the user set $\mathcal{U}$, the message space $\mathcal{M}$, the signature space $\mathcal{S}$, the keystone space $\mathcal{K}$, the keystone fix space $\mathcal{F}$, and the keystone generation algorithm KGEN : $\mathcal{K} \to \mathcal{F}$. SETUP also outputs the public and private key pairs $\{(X_i, x_i)\}$ for all users. Then, E is given all the public parameters and the public keys $\{X_i\}$, while C retains the private keys $\{x_i\}$.

Phase 1: E makes a sequence of KGen, KReveal, ASign and Private Key Extract queries. These are answered by C as in the unforgeability game (Refer to Section 3.2 of [11]).

Challenge: E selects a challenge tuple (X_i, X_j, m_1, m_2) where X_i and X_j are public keys, and $m_1, m_2 \in \mathcal{M}$ are two messages to be signed. In response, C first selects keystones $k, k' \in_R \mathcal{K}$, computes $f_1 = \text{KGEN}(k)$ and $f_2 = \text{KGEN}(k) + \text{KGEN}(k') \mod q$. Then, by randomly selecting $b \in \{1, 2, 3, 4\}$, C outputs ambiguous signatures $\sigma_1 = (c, s_1, s_2)$ and $\sigma_2 = (c', s_1', s_2')$ as follows:
 - If $b = 1$, $\sigma_1 \leftarrow \text{ASIGN}(X_i, X_j, x_i, f_1, m_1)$, $\sigma_2 \leftarrow \text{ASIGN}(X_i, X_j, x_i, f_2, m_2)$;
 - If $b = 2$, $\sigma_1 \leftarrow \text{ASIGN}(X_i, X_j, x_j, f_1, m_1)$, $\sigma_2 \leftarrow \text{ASIGN}(X_i, X_j, x_j, f_2, m_2)$;
 - If $b = 3$, $\sigma_1 \leftarrow \text{ASIGN}(X_i, X_j, x_i, f_1, m_1)$, $\sigma_2 \leftarrow \text{ASIGN}(X_i, X_j, x_j, f_2, m_2)$;
 - If $b = 4$, $\sigma_1 \leftarrow \text{ASIGN}(X_i, X_j, x_j, f_1, m_1)$, $\sigma_2 \leftarrow \text{ASIGN}(X_i, X_j, x_i, f_2, m_2)$.

Phase 2: E may continue to make another sequence of queries as in Phase 1; these are handled by C as before.

Output: E finally outputs a value $b' \in \{1, 2, 3, 4\}$ as its guess for b. We say E *wins* the game if $b' = b$ and E has not made a KReveal query on any of the following values: $s_1, s_2, s_1' - f_1$, and $s_2' - f_1$.

Definition 3 (Perfect Ambiguity). *A concurrent signature scheme is called* **perfectly ambiguous** *if no polynomially bounded adversary can win the above game with a probability that is non-negligibly greater than $1/4$.*

Fairness intuitively requires that (1) a concurrent signature scheme should be fair for the initial signer Alice, i.e., only Alice can reveal the keystone; and (2) a concurrent signature scheme should be fair for the matching signer Bob, i.e., once the keystone is released, both signatures are bound to their signers concurrently. This concept is formally defined via the following game (adapted from [11]) between an adversary E and a challenger C:

Setup: This is the same as in the game for perfect ambiguity.

Queries: KGen, KReveal, ASign and Private Key Extract queries are answered by C as in the unforgeability game (Section 3.2 of [11]).

Output: E finally chooses the challenge public keys X_c and X_d, outputs a keystone $k \in \mathcal{K}$ and $S = (\sigma, X_c, X_d, m)$ such that $\text{AVERIFY}(S) = \text{accept}$, where $m \in \mathcal{M}$ and $\sigma = (c, s_1, s_2) \in \mathcal{S} \times \mathcal{F} \times \mathcal{F}$. The adversary *wins* the game if either of the following two cases holds:

1. (k, S) is accepted by VERIFY so that $s_2 = \mathsf{KGEN}(k)$ is a previous output from a KGen query but no KReveal query on input s_2 was made.
2. E additionally produces $S' = (\sigma', X_c, X_d, m')$ along with another key-stone $k' \in \mathcal{K}$, where $m' \in \mathcal{M}$ and $\sigma' = (c', s'_1, s'_2) \in \mathcal{S} \times \mathcal{F} \times \mathcal{F}$, such that $\mathsf{AVERIFY}(S') = \text{accept}$ and $s'_1 = s_2 + H_1(k')$. Furthermore, (k, k', S') is accepted by VERIFY, but (k, S) is not accepted by VERIFY.

Definition 4 (Fairness). *A concurrent signature scheme is* **fair** *if the success probability of any polynomially bounded adversary in the above game is negligible.*

Definition 5. *We say that a correct concurrent signature scheme is* **secure***, if it is existentially unforgeable, perfectly ambiguous, and fair under a chosen message attack in the multi-party setting.*

3   PSC1 and Its Security

3.1   Review of PSC1

We now review PCS1 [27], which is a concurrent signature scheme derived from Schnorr signature [26]. Susilo et al. constructed PCS1 by using some techniques from ring signatures [24,1], as did by Chen et al. in [11].

- SETUP. On input a security parameter ℓ, the SETUP algorithm first randomly generates two large prime numbers p and q such that $q|(p-1)$, and a generator $g \in \mathbb{Z}_p$ of order q, where q is exponential in ℓ. Then, the SETUP algorithm sets the message space $\mathcal{M}$, the keystone space $\mathcal{K}$, the signature space $\mathcal{S}$, and the keystone fix space $\mathcal{F}$ as follows: $\mathcal{M} = \mathcal{K} = \{0,1\}^*$, and $\mathcal{S} = \mathcal{F} = \mathbb{Z}_q$. It also selects a cryptographic hash function $H_1 : \{0,1\}^* \rightarrow \mathbb{Z}_q$, which is used as the message digest function and the keystone generation algorithm. In addition, we assume that $(x_A, y_A = g^{x_A} \bmod p)$ and $(x_B, y_B = g^{x_B} \bmod p)$ are the private/public key pairs of Alice and Bob, respectively.
- ASIGN. The algorithm ASIGN takes input (y_i, y_j, x, s, m), where y_i and y_j are two public keys $(y_i \neq y_j)$, x is the private key corresponding to y_i or y_j (i.e. $x = x_i$ or $x = x_j$), $s \in \mathcal{F}$ is a keystone fix, and $m \in \mathcal{M}$ is the message to be signed. By picking a random number $\alpha \in_R \mathbb{Z}_q$, the algorithm outputs an ambiguous signature $\sigma = (c, s_1, s_2)$ as follows:
  - If $x = x_i$: $c = H_1(m, g^\alpha y_j^s \bmod p)$, $s_1 = (\alpha - c) \cdot x_i^{-1} \bmod q$, $s_2 = s$;
  - If $x = x_j$, $c = H_1(m, g^\alpha y_i^s \bmod p)$, $s_1 = s$, $s_2 = (\alpha - c) \cdot x_j^{-1} \bmod q$.
- AVERIFY. Given an ambiguous signature-message pair (σ, y_i, y_j, m), where $\sigma = (c, s_1, s_2)$, y_i and y_j are two public keys, the AVERIFY algorithm outputs accept or reject according to whether the following equality holds:

$$c \equiv H_1(m, g^c y_i^{s_1} y_j^{s_2} \bmod p). \tag{1}$$

- VERIFY. The algorithm takes input (k, S), where $k \in \mathcal{K}$ is the keystone and $S = (\sigma, y_i, y_j, m)$, and $\sigma = (c, s_1, s_2)$. The algorithm VERIFY outputs accept if $\mathsf{AVERIFY}(S) = \text{accept}$ and the keystone k is *valid* by running a *keystone verification algorithm*. Otherwise, VERIFY outputs reject.

Note that the above are just the basic algorithms for generating and verifying concurrent signatures. In the following concrete concurrent signature protocol, it explicitly describes how to generate and verify keystones, and how to exchange concurrent signatures between two parties without the help of any TTP.

PCS1 Protocol: Before running the protocol, we assume that the SETUP algorithm is executed and the public keys y_A and y_B are published. Here we also assume that Alice is the initial signer and Bob is the matching signer and they want to exchange their signatures on messages m_A and m_B. Symmetrically, one can get the protocol description for the case where the roles of Alice and Bob are changed.

1. Alice sends Bob $(\sigma_A, \hat{t}, m_A)$, which are computed as follows.
   - Choose a random keystone $k \in_R \mathcal{K}$ and set $s_2 = H_1(k)$.
   - Run $\sigma_A = (c, s_1, s_2) \leftarrow \mathsf{ASIGN}(y_A, y_B, x_A, s_2, m_A)$.
   - Pick a random $t \in_R \mathbb{Z}_q$ and compute $\hat{t} = y_A^t \bmod p$.
2. Upon receiving $(\sigma_A, \hat{t}, m_A)$, where $\sigma_A = (c, s_1, s_2)$, Bob checks whether $\mathsf{AVERIFY}(\sigma_A, y_A, y_B, m_A) \equiv \mathsf{accept}$. If not, then Bob aborts. Otherwise, he sends (σ_B, m_B) to Alice by performing as follows.
   - Compute $r = \hat{t}^{x_B} \bmod p$, $r' = r \bmod q$, and set $s_1' = s_2 + r' \bmod q$.
   - Run $\sigma_B = (c', s_1', s_2') \leftarrow \mathsf{ASIGN}(y_A, y_B, x_B, s_1', m_B)$.
3. After (σ_B, m_B) is received, where $\sigma_B = (c', s_1', s_2')$, Alice performs as follows.
   - Check whether $\mathsf{AVERIFY}(\sigma_B, y_A, y_B, m_B) = \mathsf{accept}$. If not, Alice aborts. Otherwise, continue.
   - Compute $r' = s_1' - s_2 \bmod q$, $r = y_B^{x_A t} \bmod p$, and check whether $r' \equiv r \bmod q$. If not, then Alice aborts. Otherwise, continue.
   - Issue the following signature proof Γ to show that r and $\hat{t}$ are properly generated by using the knowledge of his private key x_A (Refer to Section 2.2 in [27] for details):

$$\Gamma \leftarrow SPKEQ(\gamma : r = y_B^{t\gamma} \wedge \hat{t} = g^{t\gamma} \wedge y_A = g^\gamma)(k). \tag{2}$$

   - Release the keystone $\kappa = \{k, r, t, \hat{t}, \Gamma\}$ publicly to bind both signatures σ_A and σ_B concurrently.
4. VERIFY Algorithm. After the keystone $\kappa = \{k, r, t, \hat{t}, \Gamma\}$ is released publicly, $\sigma_A = (c, s_1, s_2)$ and $\sigma_B = (c', s_1', s_2')$ are validated as Alice's and Bob's signature w.r.t. messages m_A and m_B respectively, iff all the following verifications hold.
   - Check whether $H_1(k) \equiv s_2$;
   - Check whether $r' = r \bmod q$, where $r' = s_1' - s_2 \bmod q$;
   - Check whether Γ is a valid signature proof;
   - Check $\mathsf{AVERIFY}(\sigma_A, y_A, y_B, m_A) \equiv \mathsf{accept}$ and $\mathsf{AVERIFY}(\sigma_B, y_A, y_B, m_B) \equiv \mathsf{accept}$.

In a summary, by using two pieces of keystone Susilo et al. strengthened the ambiguity of concurrent signatures so that there are four cases of authorship for two ambiguous signatures σ_A and σ_B. Due to this reason, their schemes achieves *perfect ambiguity*. As pointed in [27], in such schemes even an outsider knows (or believes) that Alice and Bob signed exactly one of two signatures σ_A and σ_B, he/she still cannot deduce whether Alice signed σ_A or σ_B. In Chen et al.'s scheme, however, this is very easy for an outsider. Based on the similarity of PCS1 and Chen et al.'s scheme, the unforgeability of PCS1 can be established in the random oracle model under the discrete logarithm assumption in subgroup $\langle g \rangle$, as stated in [27]. This reason is that one can incorporate the forking lemma [23] to provide a proof as did by Chen et al. in [11]. For the fairness, however, it is a different story.

3.2   On the Fairness

The authors of [27] argued the fairness of PCS1 protocol by the following two claims:

Claim 1. Before $\kappa = \{k, r, t, \hat{t}, \Gamma\}$ is released, both signatures σ_A and σ_B are ambiguous (Theorem 1 in [27]).

Claim 2. After $\kappa = \{k, r, t, \hat{t}, \Gamma\}$ is released, both signatures σ_A and σ_B are bound to the two signers concurrently (Theorem 2 in [27]).

Claim 1 is correct, but Claim 2 may be false if the initial signer Alice is dishonest. To illustrate this point, we now present a concrete attack against PCS1 protocol such that once κ is released, (σ_A, m_A) is not binding to Alice, but (σ_B, m_B) is indeed binding to Bob. Moreover, if necessary Alice can issue another signature-message $(\bar{\sigma}_A, \bar{m}_A)$ to binding herself, where message $\bar{m}_A$ is chosen at her will. From the view point of Bob, he is cheated by Alice, because what he expected is to exchange his signature on message m_B with Alice's signature on message m_A. But the result is that Alice indeed obtained his signature on message m_B, while Bob did not get Alice's signature on message m_A (though he may get Alice's signature on a different message $\bar{m}_A$). Naturally, this is *unfair* for the matching signer Bob. Because fairness implies that the matching signer Bob cannot be left in a position where a keystone binds his signature to him while the initial signer Alice's signature is not bound to Alice (See the last paragraph of page 296 in [11]). In the example of purchasing laptop given in Section 1, due to this attack Bob may be unable to get money from Alice, but Alice can pick up one laptop from Bob's shop.

The following is the basic idea of this attack. It is truly a natural and interesting method to construct perfect concurrent signatures by exploiting two keystones instead of one. However, we notice that in step 2 of PCS1 protocol no mechanism is provided for Bob to check the validity of the keystone fix s_2. Based on this observation, dishonest initial signer Alice can set $s_2 = H_1(k) + r' - \tilde{r}' \bmod q$, i.e., $s_2 + \tilde{r}' = H_1(k) + r' \bmod q$, where r' and $\tilde{r}'$ are some properly generated values. Then, Alice generates an ambiguous signature on m_A by using value s_2 (though she does not know the keystone for s_2). After receiving Bob's ambiguous signature on m_B, Alice can issue her signature on $\bar{m}_A$ by using the value $\bar{s}_2 = H_1(k)$ at her will. The detail follows.

Attack 1 on PCS1 Protocol. In this attack, we assume that the initial signer Alice is dishonest, but the matching signer Bob is honest, i.e., he follows each step of PCS1 protocol properly.

1. The dishonest initial signer Alice performs in the following way.
   1.1) Pick $t, \tilde{t} \in_R \mathbb{Z}_q$, and compute values $\hat{t}, r, r', \hat{t}', \tilde{r},$ and $\tilde{r}'$ by

$$\begin{aligned}
\hat{t} &= y_A^t \bmod p, & r &= y_B^{x_A t} \bmod p \ (= \hat{t}^{x_B} \bmod p), & r' &= r \bmod q, \\
\hat{t}' &= y_A^{\tilde{t}} \bmod p, & \tilde{r} &= y_B^{x_A \tilde{t}} \bmod p \ (= \hat{t}'^{x_B} \bmod p), & \tilde{r}' &= \tilde{r} \bmod q.
\end{aligned} \tag{3}$$

   1.2) Choose a keystone $k \in_R \mathcal{K}$ and set $s_2 = H_1(k) + r' - \tilde{r}' \bmod q$. So Alice has the following equality

$$s_2 + \tilde{r}' = H_1(k) + r' \bmod q. \tag{4}$$

   1.3) Run $\sigma_A = (c, s_1, s_2) \leftarrow \mathsf{ASIGN}(y_A, y_B, x_A, s_2, m_A)$.
   1.4) Send $(\sigma_A, \hat{t}', m_A)$ to the matching signer Bob.
2. Since $\mathsf{AVERIFY}(\sigma_A, y_A, y_B, m_A) \equiv$ accept, honest Bob sends Alice (σ_B, m_B) by
   2.1) Compute $\tilde{r} = \hat{t}'^{x_B} \bmod p$, and $\tilde{r}' = \tilde{r} \bmod q$;
   2.2) Set $s_1' = s_2 + \tilde{r}' \bmod q$;
   2.3) Run $\sigma_B = (c', s_1', s_2') \leftarrow \mathsf{ASIGN}(y_A, y_B, x_B, s_1', m_B)$.
3. Since (σ_B, m_B) is properly generated by honest Bob, it is easy to know that $\mathsf{AVERIFY}(\sigma_B, y_A, y_B, m_B) \equiv$ accept and that $\tilde{r}' \equiv s_1' - s_2 \bmod q$. That is, (σ_B, m_B) is Bob's valid signature. Now, Alice selects a message $\bar{m}_A$ at her choice and performs as follows.
   3.1) Set $\bar{s}_2 = H_1(k)$.
   3.2) Run $\bar{\sigma}_A = (\bar{c}, \bar{s}_1, \bar{s}_2) \leftarrow \mathsf{ASIGN}(y_A, y_B, x_A, \bar{s}_2, \bar{m}_A)$.
   3.3) Retrieve $(t, \hat{t}, r, r')$ from Step 1.1 (recall Eq. (3)).
   3.4) Issue a proof $\Gamma \leftarrow SPKEQ(\gamma : r = y_B^{t\gamma} \wedge \hat{t} = g^{t\gamma} \wedge y_A = g^\gamma)(k)$.
   3.5) Output $(\bar{\sigma}_A, \bar{m}_A), (\sigma_B, m_B)$, and the keystone $\kappa = \{k, r, t, \hat{t}, \Gamma\}$.

On the validity of attack 1, we have the following proposition:

Proposition 1. *After the keystone information $\kappa = \{k, r, t, \hat{t}, \Gamma\}$ is released, the two signature-message pairs $(\bar{\sigma}_A, \bar{m}_A)$ and (σ_B, m_B) are bound to Alice and Bob, respectively. However, (σ_A, m_A) is not bound to Alice.*

Proof: This proof is almost self-evident, so we just mention the following main facts:

- $H_1(k) \equiv \bar{s}_2$ (recall Step 3.1).
- $r' \equiv s_1' - \bar{s}_2 \bmod q \equiv r \bmod q$ (recall Eqs. (3), (4)).
- Γ is a valid signature proof for $SPKEQ(\gamma : r = y_B^{t\gamma} \wedge \hat{t} = g^{t\gamma} \wedge y_A = g^\gamma)(k)$, since it is properly generated by Alice in Step 3.4.
- $\mathsf{AVERIFY}(\sigma_A, y_A, y_B, m_A) \equiv$ accept and $\mathsf{AVERIFY}(\sigma_B, y_A, y_B, m_B) \equiv$ accept, since both $\sigma_B = (c', s_1', s_2')$ and $\bar{\sigma}_A = (\bar{c}, \bar{s}_1, \bar{s}_2)$ are properly generated by running algorithm ASIGN in Steps 3.2 and 2.3, respectively.

Therefore, according to the specification of algorithm VERIFY reviewed in Section 2, $(\bar{\sigma}_A, \bar{m}_A)$ and (σ_B, m_B) are truly binding to Alice and Bob. However, the same keystone information $\kappa = \{k, r, t, \hat{t}, \Gamma\}$ cannot be used to bind (σ_A, m_A) to Alice. In fact, even Alice is unable to reveal a keystone k' such that $s_2 = H_1(k')$. Otherwise, this implies Alice can find a pre-image of hash value $s_2 = H_1(k) + r' - \tilde{r}' \bmod q$. □

3.3   On the Keystone Generation

In PCS1 protocol, a variant of Diffie-Hellman key exchange technique [14] is used to derive keystone fix r'. In summary, r' is generated as follows. By selecting a random number $t \in \mathbb{Z}_q$, Alice first sets $\hat{t} = y_A^t \bmod p$ and sends $\hat{t}$ to Bob. Then, Bob computes $r = \hat{t}^{x_B} \bmod p$, $r' = r \bmod q$, and sets $s'_1 = s_2 + r' \bmod q$. Finally, Alice issues a signature proof $\Gamma \leftarrow SPKEQ(\gamma : r = y_B^{t\gamma} \wedge \hat{t} = g^{t\gamma} \wedge y_A = g^\gamma)(k)$, and releases keystone information $\kappa = \{k, r, t, \hat{t}, \Gamma\}$. Hence, from the public information κ any third party can derive the value $y_{AB} \overset{\triangle}{=} g^{x_A x_B} \bmod p$ by calculating

$$y_{AB} = r^{t^*} \bmod p, \quad \text{where } t^* = t^{-1} \bmod q. \tag{5}$$

A problem is that the value of y_{AB} is the crux for some other cryptosystems, such as the strong designated verifier signature (SDVS) of Saeednia et al. [25], and the signcryption scheme of Huang and Cheng [19]. That is, if y_{AB} is available to an adversary those cryptosystems are broken (Check [18] for more discussions on SDVS). This implies that one user *cannot* use the same key pair to run PCS1 protocol and those cryptosystems, even though all of them work in the discrete logarithm setting with the same parameters. In other words, this is an example showing that the simultaneous use of related keys for two cryptosystems is insecure (See [17] for some positive results).

4   PCS2 and Its Fairness

This section briefly reviews and analyzes PCS2, which is a perfect concurrent signature constructed from bilinear pairing.

- SETUP: This algorithm first selects an *admissible bilinear pairing* (Sec 2.1 of [27]) $e : \mathbb{G}_1 \times \mathbb{G}_1 \to \mathbb{G}_2$, where $\mathbb{G}_1$ and $\mathbb{G}_2$ are two cyclic (additive and multiplicative, respectively) groups with the same prime order q. It also selects two cryptographic hash functions $H_0 : \{0,1\}^* \to \mathbb{G}_1$ and $H_1 : \{0,1\}^* \to \mathbb{Z}_q$. Alice and Bob have private/public key pairs $(x_A, P_A = x_A P)$ and $(x_B, P_B = x_B P)$, where $x_A, x_B \in \mathbb{Z}_q^*$, and P is a generator of group $\mathbb{G}_1$. System parameters $\{\mathbb{G}_1, \mathbb{G}_2, e, q, P, H_0, H_1\}$ are publicly known.
- ASIGN: The ASIGN algorithm takes inputs (P_i, P_j, x, f, m), where x is the secret key associated with public keys P_i or P_j (i.e., $x = x_i$ or $x = x_j$), $f \in \mathcal{F}$ is a keystone fix, and $m \in \mathcal{M}$ is the message to be signed. By selecting a random number $a \in_R \mathbb{Z}_q$, the algorithm outputs an ambiguous signature $\sigma = (c, s_1, s_2)$ as follows:

- If $x = x_i$: $c = H_1(P_i||P_j||e(aH_0(m), P) \cdot e(fH_0(m), P_j))$, $s_1 = (a - c)x_i^{-1} \bmod q$, $s_2 = f$;
- If $x = x_j$: $c = H_1(P_i||P_j||e(aH_0(m), P) \cdot e(fH_0(m), P_i))$, $s_1 = f$, $s_2 = (a - c)x_j^{-1} \bmod q$.

- AVERIFY: Given $\sigma = (c, s_1, s_2)$, AVERIFY$(\sigma, P_i, P_j, m) = $ accept iff the following equality holds.

$$c \equiv H_1(P_i||P_j||e(H_0(m), P)^c \cdot e(H_0(m), P_i)^{s_1} \cdot e(H_0(m), P_j)^{s_2}).$$

- VERIFY: Given a concurrent signature (k, S), where $k \in \mathcal{K}$ and $S = (\sigma = (c, s_1, s_2)$, $P_i, P_j, m)$, VERIFY$(k, S) = $ accept iff k is a valid keystone by executing the keystone verification algorithm, and AVERIFY$(S) = $ accept.

PCS2 Protocol. Without losing generality, we assume that the initial signer Alice and the matching signer Bob want to exchange their signatures on messages m_A and m_B, respectively.

1. Alice first sends (σ_A, Z) to Bob by performing as follows
   - Select a random keystone $k \in_R \mathcal{K}$ and set $s_2 = H_1(k)$;
   - Pick a randomness $\alpha \in \mathbb{Z}_q^*$ and compute $Z = \alpha P$;
   - Run $\sigma_A = (c, s_1, s_2) \leftarrow$ ASIGN$(P_A, P_B, x_A, s_2, m_A)$.
2. Upon receiving (σ_A, Z), Bob checks whether AVERIFY$(\sigma_A, P_A, P_B, m_A) \equiv$ accept. If not, Bob aborts. Otherwise, he returns the following value σ_B to Alice.
   - Compute $r = e(P_A, Z)^{x_B}$, and set $s_1' = s_2 + r \bmod q$;
   - Run $\sigma_B = (c', s_1', s_2') \leftarrow$ ASIGN$(P_A, P_B, x_B, s_1', m_B)$.
3. Once $\sigma_B = (c', s_1', s_2')$ is received, Alice first computes $r = e(P_B, Z)^{x_A}$, then checks whether both AVERIFY$(\sigma_B, P_A, P_B, m_B) \equiv$ accept and $s_1' \equiv s_2 + r \bmod q$. If any of those two verifications fails, Alice aborts. Otherwise, she releases the keystone (k, α) so that both signatures σ_A and σ_B are binding concurrently. With (k, α), the validity of σ_A and σ_B is validated if all the following verifications hold:
   - $s_2 \equiv H_1(k)$ and $s_1' \equiv s_2 + r \bmod q$, where $r = e(P_A, P_B)^{\alpha}$;
   - AVERIFY$(\sigma_A, P_A, P_B, m_A) \equiv$ accept;
   - AVERIFY$(\sigma_B, P_A, P_B, m_B) \equiv$ accept.

Attack 2 on PCS2 Protocol. Compared with PCS1, PCS2 protocol is more efficient since the 2nd keystone fix r is exchanged between Alice and Bob in a more effective way (thanks to the bilinear pairing). However, PCS2 protocol is also *unfair* for the matching signer Bob, since a dishonest initial signer Alice can cheat Bob in an analogous way as in PCS1. More precisely, dishonest Alice can first select three random numbers $k, \alpha, \alpha' \in_R \mathbb{Z}_q^*$, and compute $Z = \alpha P$, $Z' = \alpha' P$, $r = e(P_A, P_B)^{\alpha}$, and $r' = e(P_A, P_B)^{\alpha'}$. Then, Alice further sets $s_2 = H_1(k) + r - r' \bmod q$, i.e., the following equality holds:

$$s_2 + r' \equiv H_1(k) + r \bmod q \qquad (6)$$

After that, Alice runs $\sigma_A \leftarrow$ ASIGN$(P_A, P_B, x_A, s_2, m_A)$, and sends (σ_A, Z') to Bob. Once getting Bob's valid signature $\sigma_B = (c', s_1', s_2')$ on message m_B, where

$s_1' = s_2 + r'$ mod q and $r' = e(P_A, Z')^{x_B}$, Alice releases (k, α) so that (σ_B, m_B) is bound to Bob. However, the same keystone information (k, α) does not bind (σ_A, m_A) to Alice. Moreover, if needed Alice can generate her signature $\bar{\sigma}_A$ on a different message $\bar{m}_A$ of her choice by using value $\bar{s}_2 = H_1(k)$. Due to Eq. (6), the keystone (k, α) shall bind $(\bar{\sigma}_A, \bar{m}_A)$ to Alice as well as (σ_B, m_B) to Bob.

5   The Improved Schemes

5.1   Description of the Improved Schemes

We observe that the attacks against the fairness of PCS1 and PCS2 result from the following fact: The initial signer Alice sets both two pieces of keystone alone. This privilege allows Alice to choose two pairs of keystone fixes so that the sums of them have the same value (recall Eqs. (4) and (6)). However, this sum determines the matching signer Bob's signature. Therefore, to avoid this attack we shall improve PCS1 and PCS2 as iPCS1 and iPCS2 by letting Bob choose the second keystone. At the same time, our improved protocols are designed to achieve a symmetry for both keystones. That is, both keystones can be values in the same domain and have the same verification algorithm. Moreover, the signature proof Γ is totaly removed in our iPCS1 to get a more efficient concurrent signature protocol (Check Table 1). The reason is that in the iPCS1 protocol (see below), the authenticity of $H_1(k')$ can be checked by Alice in Step 3 as follows: $s_1' \equiv s_2 + H_1(k')$ mod q, where $k' = (\hat{t}^{x_A}$ mod $p)$ mod q and $(\hat{t}, s_1')$ is received from Bob.

In the following description, we just specify the two improved concurrent signature protocols iPCS1 and iPCS2, while the corresponding algorithms are the same as in PCS1 and PCS2, respectively. In addition, note that iPCS1 protocol also works well for Chen et al.'s concurrent signature scheme [11].

iPCS1 Protocol: As in PCS1, we assume that the SETUP algorithm is already executed, and that the initial signer Alice and the matching signer Bob want to exchange their signatures on messages m_A and m_B, respectively.

1. Alice sends Bob (σ_A, m_A), where $\sigma_A = (c, s_1, s_2)$ is calculated as follows:
   - Choose a random keystone $k \in_R \mathcal{K}$ and set $s_2 = H_1(k)$;
   - Run $\sigma_A = (c, s_1, s_2) \leftarrow \mathsf{ASIGN}(y_A, y_B, x_A, s_2, m_A)$.
2. Upon receiving (σ_A, m_A), Bob checks whether $\mathsf{AVERIFY}(\sigma_A, y_A, y_B, m_A) \equiv$ accept. If not, Bob aborts. Otherwise, Bob returns back $(\sigma_B, m_B, \hat{t})$ to Alice by
   - Pick a random $t \in_R \mathbb{Z}_q$ and compute $\hat{t} = y_B^t$ mod p;
   - Compute $r = y_A^{x_B t}$ mod p, and $k' = r$ mod q;
   - Set $s_1' = s_2 + H_1(k')$ mod q;
   - Run $\sigma_B = (c', s_1', s_2') \leftarrow \mathsf{ASIGN}(y_A, y_B, x_B, s_1', m_B)$.
3. Upon receiving $(\sigma_B, m_B, \hat{t})$, where $\sigma_B = (c', s_1', s_2')$, Alice performs as follows:
   - Compute $r = \hat{t}^{x_A}$ mod p, and $k' = r$ mod q;
   - Test whether $s_1' \equiv s_2 + H_1(k')$ mod q;

- Check whether $\mathsf{AVERIFY}(\sigma_B, y_A, y_B, m_B) \equiv \mathsf{accept}$;
- If σ_B is invalid, abort. Otherwise, release the keystone (k, k') publicly to bind both signatures σ_A and σ_B concurrently.

4. VERIFY Algorithm. With the keystone (k, k'), anybody can check the validity of $\sigma_A = (c, s_1, s_2)$ and $\sigma_B = (c', s'_1, s'_2)$ as follows.
   - Alice signs σ_A iff $s_2 \equiv H_1(k)$ and $\mathsf{AVERIFY}(\sigma_A, y_A, y_B, m_A) \equiv \mathsf{accept}$.
   - Bob signs σ_B iff $s'_1 \equiv H_1(k) + H_1(k') \bmod q$ and $\mathsf{AVERIFY}(\sigma_B, y_A, y_B, m_B) \equiv \mathsf{accept}$.

iPCS2 Protocol: Again, we assume that the initial signer Alice and the matching signer Bob want to exchange their signatures on messages m_A and m_B, respectively.

1. Alice first sends Bob (σ_A, m_A), where σ_A is computed as follows.
   - Select a random keystone $k \in_R \mathcal{K}$ and sets $s_2 = H_1(k)$;
   - Run $\sigma_A = (c, s_1, s_2) \leftarrow \mathsf{ASIGN}(P_A, P_B, x_A, s_2, m_A)$.

2. Upon receiving (σ_A, m_A), Bob checks that $\mathsf{AVERIFY}\ (\sigma_A, P_A, P_B, m_A) \equiv \mathsf{accept}$. If not, Bob aborts. Otherwise, he returns back (σ_B, Z) to Alice by performing below.
   - Pick a random $\alpha \in \mathbb{Z}_q^*$, compute $Z = \alpha P$ and $r = e(P_A, P_B)^\alpha$;
   - Set the second keystone $k' = r \bmod q$;
   - Compute $s'_1 = s_2 + H_1(k') \bmod q$;
   - Run $\sigma_B = (c', s'_1, s'_2) \leftarrow \mathsf{ASIGN}(P_A, P_B, x_B, s'_1, m_B)$.

3. Once $\sigma_B = (c', s'_1, s'_2)$ is received, Alice acts in the following way:
   - Compute $r = e(Z, P_B)^{x_A}$, and $k' = r \bmod q$.
   - Test whether $s'_1 \equiv s_2 + H_1(k') \bmod q$. If not, abort. Otherwise, continue.
   - Check whether $\mathsf{AVERIFY}(\sigma_B, P_A, P_B, m_B) \equiv \mathsf{accept}$.
   - If σ_B is invalid, Alice aborts. Otherwise, Alice releases the keystone (k, k') to bind both signatures σ_A and σ_B concurrently.

4. VERIFY Algorithm. With the keystone (k, k'), anybody can check the validity of $\sigma_A = (c, s_1, s_2)$ and $\sigma_B = (c', s'_1, s'_2)$ as follows.
   - Alice signs σ_A iff $s_2 \equiv H_1(k)$ and $\mathsf{AVERIFY}(\sigma_A, y_A, y_B, m_A) \equiv \mathsf{accept}$.
   - Bob signs σ_B iff $s'_1 \equiv H_1(k) + H_1(k') \bmod q$ and $\mathsf{AVERIFY}(\sigma_B, y_A, y_B, m_B) \equiv \mathsf{accept}$.

Table 1 gives the efficiency comparison for all concurrent signature protocols discussed in this paper. As the main computational overheads, we only consider multi-exponentiations (denote by E), scalar multiplications (denote by M), and bilinear mappings (denote by e). As in [5], we assume that simultaneous exponentiations are efficiently carried out by means of an exponent array. Namely, the costs for $a_1^{x_1} a_2^{x_2}$ and $a_1^{x_1} a_2^{x_2} a_3^{x_3}$ are only equivalent to 1.16 and 1.25 single exponentiation, respectively. Note that our iPCS1 outperforms the original PCS1 by about 50%, while iPCS2 is a little more efficient than PCS2.

Table 1. Efficiency Comparison

Protocol	Comp. Cost of Alice	Comp. Cost of Bob	Comp. Cost of Verifier	Signature Size	Keystone Size
CS [11]	2.41E	2.41E	2.5E	$3|q|$	$|q|$
CPS1 [27]	9.41E	3.41E	7.98E	$3|q|$	$4|q| + 2|p|$
iCPS1	3.41E	4.41E	2.5E	$3|q|$	$2|q|$
CPS2 [27]	6e+3.41E+1M	6e+3.41E	7e+3.5E	$3|q|$	$2|q|$
iCPS2	6e+3.41E	6e+3.41E+1M	6e+2.5E	$3|q|$	$2|q|$

5.2 Security Analysis of the Improved Schemes

Based on the results in [11,27] and the discussions previously provided, it is not difficult to see that both iPCS1 and iPCS2 are truly perfect concurrent signature protocols. Formally, we have the following theorem.

Theorem 1. *The above iPCS1 is a secure perfect concurrent signature protocol in the random oracle model under the discrete logarithm assumption. That is, iPCS1 is perfectly ambiguous, fair, and existentially unforgeable under a chosen message attack in the multi-party setting.*

Proof. First of all, *unforgeability* holds due to the facts that all basic algorithms in our iPCS are the same as in PCS1, and PCS1 is unforgeable (Theorem 4 in [27]). Second, *perfect ambiguity* is almost evident. The reason is that in the game of perfect ambiguity, to guess the signer of $\sigma_1 = (c, s_1, s_2)$ the adversary E has to distinguish whether either s_1 or s_2 is a random number from $\mathbb{Z}_q$ or an output of $H_1(\cdot)$ for some keystone k. However, this is impossible in the random oracle model, since the hash function $H_1(\cdot)$ is treated as a truly random function with the range of $\mathbb{Z}_q$. Similarly, E cannot determine the authorship of σ_2 better than guessing. Therefore, the adversary E cannot guess correctly the value $b \in \{1, 2, 3, 4\}$ selected by the challenger C at random with an advantage that is non-negligibly greater than $1/4$. Now, we turn to prove *fairness* in detail.

We suppose that there exists an algorithm E that with non-negligible probability wins the fairness game, under the assumption that $H_1(\cdot)$ is a random oracle. Then, based on E's output we derive some contradictions.

To initialize the fairness game for a given security parameter ℓ, the challenger C runs the SETUP algorithm to generate the public parameters (p, q, g) as usual, where q is exponential in ℓ, choose all the private keys $x_i \in_R \mathbb{Z}_q$, set the public keys as $y_i = g^{x_i} \bmod p$, and give these public keys to the adversary E. Then, C responds to E's different kinds of queries as follows.

H_1-Queries: E can query the random oracle H_1 at any time. C simulates the random oracle by keeping a list of pairs (m_i, r_i), which is called the H_1-List. When an input $m \in \{0, 1\}^*$ as H_1-query is received, C responds as follows:
1. If the query m is the first component for some pair (m_i, r_i) in the H_1-List, then C outputs r_i.

2. Otherwise, C selects a random number $r \in_R \mathbb{Z}_q$, outputs r as the value of $H_1(m)$, and adds the pair (m, r) to the H_1-List.

KGen Queries: E can request that the challenger C properly generate a keystone fix. To this end, C maintains a K-List of pairs (k_i, f_i), and answers such a query by choosing a random keystone $k \in_R \mathcal{K}$ and computing $f = H_1(k)$. C outputs f and adds the tuple (k, f) to the K-List. Note that K-List is a sublist of H_1-List, but is required to answer KReveal queries later.

KReveal Queries: E can request that the challenger C reveal the keystone k for any keystone fix f which is produced for answering a previous KGen Query. If there exists a pair (k, f) on the K-List, then C returns k, otherwise it outputs invalid.

ASign Queries: E can also make any signature query of the form (y_i, y_j, s, m), where $s \in \mathbb{Z}_q$, y_i and y_j $(y_i \neq y_j)$ are two public keys, and $m \in \{0, 1\}^*$ is the message to be signed. To answer E's query, C computes the signature as normal and outputs $\sigma = (c, s_1, s_2) = \mathsf{ASIGN}(y_i, y_j, x_i, s, m)$.

Private Key Extract Queries: E can request the private key for any public key y_i. Since it is C that sets up all the private keys, C just returns the appropriate private key x_i as its answer.

In the final stage, E finally outputs $S = (\sigma, y_A, y_B, m)$ and a keystone $k \in \mathcal{K}$ with non-negligible probability η, where y_A and y_B are two public keys, $m \in \mathcal{M}$, and $\sigma = (c, s_1, s_2) \in \mathcal{S} \times \mathcal{F} \times \mathcal{F}$, such that $\mathsf{AVERIFY}(S) = \mathsf{accept}$ and either of the following two cases holds:

1. (k, S) is accepted by VERIFY so that $s_2 = \mathsf{KGEN}(k)$ is a previous output from a KGen query but no KReveal query on input s_2 was made.
2. E additionally produces $S' = (\sigma', y_A, y_B, m')$ along with another keystone $k' \in \mathcal{K}$, where $m' \in \mathcal{M}$ and $\sigma' = (c', s_1', s_2') \in \mathcal{S} \times \mathcal{F} \times \mathcal{F}$, such that $\mathsf{AVERIFY}(S') = \mathsf{accept}$ and $s_1' = s_2 + H_1(k')$. Furthermore, (k, k', S') is accepted by VERIFY, but (k, S) is not accepted by VERIFY.

Since the adversary E produces the above output with non-negligible probability η, either case 1 or case 2 must occur with non-negligible probability. We now analyze those two cases separately and then derive contradictions.

Case 1. Suppose E's outputs satisfy the conditions in case 1 with non-negligible probability. Namely, E has found a keystone k and an output of a KGen query s_2 such that $s_2 = H_1(k)$, but without making a KReveal query on input s_2. Since $H_1(\cdot)$ is a random oracle, E's probability of producing such a k is at most $\mu_1 \mu_2 / q$, where μ_1 is the number of H_1 queries made by E and μ_2 is the number of KGen queries made by E. Both μ_1 and μ_2 are polynomially bounded in the security parameter ℓ and q is exponential in ℓ, so this probability is negligible. This contradicts our assumption that case 1 occurs with non-negligible probability.

Case 2. Suppose case 2 occurs with non-negligible probability, i.e., the adversary E's outputs satisfy all conditions in case 2. Since $S' = (\sigma', y_A, y_B, m')$ is accepted by AVERIFY, $s_1' = s_2 + H_1(k')$, and (k, k', S') is accepted by VERIFY, we must have $s_2 = \mathsf{KGEN}(k) = H_1(k)$. At the same time, since $S = (\sigma, y_A, y_B, m)$ is also accepted by AVERIFY and we already have $s_2 = \mathsf{KGEN}(k) = H_1(k)$, this implies that (k, S) is also accepted by VERIFY. This contradicts to the condition in case 2 that (k, S) is not accepted by VERIFY. □

Theorem 2. *The above iPCS2 is a secure perfect concurrent signature protocol in the random oracle model under bilinear Diffie-Hellman assumption. That is, iPCS2 is perfectly ambiguous, fair, and existentially unforgeable under a chosen message attack in the multi-party setting.*

Theorem 2 can be proved analogously as Theorem 1. That is, unforgeability and perfect ambiguity essentially follow from the results in [27] since all basic algorithms in iPCS2 are the same as in PCS2, while fairness can be obtained in a similar way as we do in Theorem 1.

6 Conclusion

For the applications with somewhat weak requirement of fairness, concurrent signatures [11] provide very simple and natural solutions for the traditional problem of fair exchange signatures without involving any trusted third party. To strengthen the ambiguity of concurrent signatures, two perfect concurrent signatures are proposed in [27]. This paper successfully identified an attack against those two perfect concurrent signatures by showing that they are actually *not* concurrent signatures. Consequently, those two schemes are *unfair* in fact. To avoid this attack, we presented effective improvements to achieve truly perfect concurrent signatures. Moreover, our improvement from Schnorr signature obtains about 50% performance enhancement over the original scheme in [27]. We also addressed another weakness in their keystone generation algorithm. In addition, we remarked that a similar attack can apply to an identity-based perfect concurrent signature scheme proposed in [12]. As the future work, it is interesting to consider how to improve the efficiency of perfect concurrent signatures, and how to construct concurrent signature schemes in multi-party setting.

References

1. M. Abe, M. Ohkubo, and K. Suzuki. 1-out-of-n signatures from a variety of keys. In: *Asiacrypt '02*, LNCS 2501, pap. 415-432. Spriger-Verlag, 2002.
2. N. Asokan, M. Schunter, and M. Waidner. Optimistic protocols for fair exchange. In: *Proc. 4th ACM Conf. on Comp. and Comm. Security*, pp. 8-17. ACM Press, 1997.
3. N. Asokan, V. Shoup, and M. Waidner. Optimistic fair exchange of digital signatures. In: *Eurocrypt '98*, LNCS 1403, pp. 591-606. Springer-Verlag, 1998.
4. N. Asokan, V. Shoup, and M. Waidner. Optimistic fair exchange of digital signatures. *IEEE Journal on Selected Areas in Communications*, 18(4): 591-606, 2000.
5. G. Ateniese. Efficient verifiable encryption (and fair exchange) of digital signature. In: *Proc. of AMC Conference on Computer and Communications Security (CCS'99)*, pp. 138-146. ACM Press, 1999.
6. F. Bao, R.H. Deng, and W. Mao. Efficient and practical fair exchange protocols with off-line TTP. In: *Proc. of IEEE Symposium on Security and Privacy*, pp. 77-85, 1998.

7. M. Ben-Or, O. Goldreich, S. Micali, and R. L. Rivest. A fair protocol for signing contracts. *IEEE Trans. on Inform. Theory*, 36(1): 40-46, 1990.
8. C. Boyd and E. Foo. Off-line fair payment protocols using convertible signatures. In: *Asiacrypt '98*, LNCS 1514, pp. 271-285. Springer-Verlag, 1998.
9. J. Camenisch and V. Shoup. Practical verifiable encryption and decryption of discrete logarithms. In: *Crypto '03*, LNCS 2729, pp. 126-144. Springer-Verlag, 2003.
10. L. Chen. Efficient fair exchange with verifiable confirmation of signatures. In: *Asiacrypt '98*, LNCS 1514, pp. 286-299. Springer-Verlag, 1998.
11. L. Chen, C. Kudla, and K. G. Paterson. Concurrent signatures. In: *Eurocrypt '04*, LNCS 3027, pp. 287-305. Spriger-Verlag, 2004.
12. S.S.M. Chow and W. Susilo. Generic construction of (identity-based) perfect concurrent signatures. In: *Information and Communications Security ICICS '05*, LNCS 3783, pp. 194-206. Spriger-Verlag, 2005.
13. I. B. Damgård. Practical and provably secure release of a secret and exchange of signatures. *Journal of Cryptology*, 8(4): 201-222, 1995.
14. W. Diffie, and M.E. Hellman. New directions in cryptography. *IEEE Trans. on Inform. Theory*, 22: 644-654, 1976.
15. S. Even, O. Goldreich, and A. Lempel. A randomized protocol for signing contracts. *Communications of the ACM*, 28(6): 637-647, 1985.
16. S. Even and Y. Yacobi. Relations among public key signature schemes. *Technical Report 175*, Computer Science Dept., Technion, Israel, 1980.
17. S. Haber and B. Pinkas. Securely combining public-key cryptosystems. In: *Proc. of the 8th ACM Conf. on Computer and Communications Security*, pp. 215-224. ACM Press, 2001.
18. H. Lipmaa, G. Wang, and F. Bao. Designated verifier signature schemes: Attacks, new security notions and a new construction. In: *Proc. of the 32nd International Colloquium on Automata, Languages and Programming (ICALP'05)*, LNCS 3580, pp. 459-471. Springer-Verlag, 2005.
19. H.-F. Huang and C.-C. Chang. An efficient convertible authenticated encryption scheme and its variant. In: *Information and Communications Security (ICICS'03)*, LNCS 2836, pages 382-392. Springer-Verlag, 2003.
20. J. Garay, M. Jakobsson, and P. MacKenzie. Abuse-free optimistic contract signing. In: *Crypto '99*, LNCS 1666, pp. 449-466. Sprnger-Verlage, 1999.
21. O. Goldreich. A simple protocol for signing contracts. In: *Crypto '83*, pp. 133-136. Plenum Press, 1984.
22. S. Goldwasser, S. Micali, and R. Rivest. A digital signature scheme secure against adaptive chosen-message attack. *SIAM Journal of Computing*, 17(2): 281-308, 1988.
23. D. Pointcheval and J. Stern. Security arguments for digital signatures and blind signatures. *Journal of Cryptology*, 13(3): 361-396, 2000.
24. R. L. Rivest, A. Shamir, and Y. Tauman. How to Leak a Secret. *Asiacrypt '01*, LNCS 2248, pp. 552-565. Spriger-Verlag, 2001.
25. S. Saeednia, S. Kremer, and O. Markowitch. An efficient strong designated verifier signature scheme. In: *Information Security and Cryptology - ICISC 2003*, LNCS 2971, pp. 40-54. Springer-Verlag, 2004.
26. C.P. Schnorr. Efficient signature generation by smart cards. *Journal of Cryptology*, 4(3): 161-174, 1991.
27. W. Susilo, Y. Mu, and F. Zhang. Perfect concurrent signature schemes. In: *Information and Communications Security (ICICS '04)*, LNCS 3269, pp. 14-26. Spriger-Verlag, 2004.

Secure Set Membership Using 3SAT*
(Extended Abstract)

Michael de Mare and Rebecca N. Wright

Department of Computer Science
Stevens Institute of Technology
Hoboken, NJ 07030, USA

Abstract. A wide variety of powerful cryptographic tools have been built using RSA, Diffie-Hellman, and other similar assumptions as their basis. Computational security has been achieved relative to complexity assumptions about the computational difficulty of a variety of number theoretic problems. However, these problems are closely related, and it is likely that if any one of them turns out to be efficiently solvable with new mathematical advances or new kinds of computational devices, then similar techniques could be applicable to all of them. To provide greater diversity of security assumptions so that a break of one of them is less likely to yield a break of many or all of them, it is important to expand the body of computational problems on which security systems are based. Specifically, we suggest the use of hardness assumptions based on the complexity of logic problems, and in particular, we consider the well known Boolean 3SAT problem.

In this paper, we consider the use of the 3SAT problem to provide a cryptographic primitive, *secure set membership*. Secure set membership is a general problem for participants holding set elements to generate a representation of their set that can then be used to prove knowledge of set elements to others. Set membership protocols can be used, for example, for authentication problems such as digital credentials and some signature problems such as timestamping.

1 Introduction

The most popular computational foundation for cryptographic security is based on number-theoretic problems such as factoring, discrete logarithm, and elliptic logarithm [12,26,7]. These problems are all related, so if one is broken it is likely that they all will be broken [11]. Their security is not proven and is likely to either remain unproven or be broken. They are also vulnerable to quantum attacks [27]. It would be desirable to have many kinds of cryptographic primitives whose security is based on a wide array of unrelated assumptions. This would mean that if one system is compromised, they are not necessarily all compromised. In this paper, we present a system based on an alternative logic-based assumption that does not appear to be closely related to these other assumptions.

---

* This work was supported in part by the National Science Foundation under grant number CCR-0331584.

P. Ning, S. Qing, and N. Li (Eds.): ICICS 2006, LNCS 4307, pp. 452–468, 2006.

Specifically, we consider the use of the well known Boolean satisfiability problem to provide a very general cryptographic primitive, *secure set membership*. Secure set membership can be used to provide digital credentials, with or without identification, as well as for some signature problems such as timestamping. For example, consider a system for maintaining encrypted PINs for credit cards. Each credit card may have multiple PINs (for multiple users); any solution should hide the PINs in such a way that the system accepts valid PINs, but nobody can determine any valid PIN that he does not already know. If the system is used in a setting in which it is reasonable for the system to be able to determine which user it is talking to, then it is possible for the system to simply store hashes of all the valid PINs and compare a received hashed PIN with this list to determine if it is valid. This is an example of *credentials with identification*. However, if the users of the credit card do not want to identify themselves, or if the credit card issuer prefers to have users not identify themselves, except as a valid user of the credit card in question, when they make a purchase, then this results in the goal of *anonymous credentials*. For anonymous credentials, the user wants to prove that he has valid credentials without giving the credentials away.

In this paper, we provide a means for constructing a secure set membership system that can be used both for credentials with identification and for anonymous credentials. Secure set membership can be used as an alternative to digital signatures for some applications including timestamping [6]. We note that our system has the desirable property that each participant can choose her own set elements. In the setting of digital credentials, this allows participants to choose their credential values (rather than having them determined by a third party or as an output of a distributed credential generation algorithm), thus making the system suitable for use with credentials that are determined by user-chosen passwords or biometrics.

Our solution is based on the Boolean satisfiability problem (SAT), which has not previously been used for digital credentials. We are aware that the use of the problem of finding witnesses for 3SAT instances as a security assumption is unusual and the practice of basing cryptographic hardness on *NP*-completeness is shaky in general, because the worst case hardness required for *NP*-completeness does not say anything about most cases or the expected case. However, we think it is of interest nonetheless. First, algorithmic advances and new computing models threaten many of the commonly used cryptographic assumptions, such as the hardness of factoring. Secondly, SAT is perhaps one of the most studied *NP*-complete problems, and a fair bit is known about how to choose instances that appear to be hard. We discuss this further in Section 3.4 and Section 5 in the context of our proposed solution.

1.1 Related Work

The set membership problem was first addressed by Benaloh and de Mare with one-way accumulators in 1993 [6]. A number of schemes based on one-way accumulators were developed including schemes for digital credentials [10,3]. The schemes for credentials typically differ from the other schemes, which tend to concentrate on the idea of a distributed signature, in several ways. These include central authorities in the credential scheme, as well as support of additional properties such as revocation. All these schemes depend on the difficulty of the RSA problem for their security.

Another approach to set membership is to use Merkle trees or similar tree-based methods to store the elements of the set [23,24,5]. In these methods, each participant retains a certificate and her own set element. In effect, each element of the set is signed by a central authority. However, these methods are either not storage-efficient or require more than a constant amount of time to check relative to the number of entries [28].

In a credential system, members of the credentialed group have, or are given, credentials that they can use to prove their membership in the set of authorized persons, without revealing which of the members they are. Biometric data may be used to prevent transferability of credentials, together with zero knowledge proofs of knowledge, for a group member to prove to a verifier that she holds a valid credential without revealing it. Anonymous credentials have been widely studied and solutions based on various cryptographic assumptions have been given (e.g. [9,10,1,21]).

Several approaches have been taken to digital credentials. Most of these approaches require a central authority (such as [6,10]), though some approaches based on one-way accumulators do not require a central authority. In contrast, our approach can work with or without a central authority. The combination of one-way accumulators and zero-knowledge proofs was introduced by Camenisch and Lysyanskaya [10]. Other credential systems allow revocation of anonymity such as a different system by Camenisch and Lysyanskaya [9].

Our work makes use of the assumed computational difficulty of finding satisfying assignments to certain kinds of satisfiable 3SAT instances. A related use of the hardness of SAT for achieving security has been recently proposed for hiding information in anomaly detection applications [14,15,16,13]. Their work is concerned with maintaining lists of information that, if compromised, will not compromise the larger system for applications such as intrusion detection. The central idea of our system is to represent an element of a set by an assignment to a set of variables, and the set of elements by a 3SAT instance that is satisfied by the corresponding assignments. In comparison, the work of Esponda et al. uses a SAT instance to represent a database; in their case, they represent the values *not* in the database by satisfying assignments.

We note that both our use of 3SAT and Esponda et al.'s use of SAT do not have the same difficulties as with earlier use of *NP*-complete problems for cryptography, such as the knapsack problem [25], because it is not necessary to embed a trapdoor to be used for operations such as decryption.

1.2   Our Contribution

Our contribution includes three protocols with applications to anonymous credentials, credentials with identification, accounts with multiple users, and digital timestamping.

Our protocols propose a solution to the set membership problem. Specifically, we provide a method for generating representations of sets of provided elements. We also provide a method of using a resulting representation to prove a particular element was in the set at the time the representation was generated, and a method of using the representation to show a party holds a valid set element without revealing the element itself. Our representations are random 3SAT instances of a particular form which accept the chosen witnesses. Theorem 1 shows that among 3SAT instances that accept the selected witnesses and have the selected number of clauses, the algorithm chooses one uniformly at random. The security of the scheme relies on the computational difficulty of finding satisfying assignments to such 3SAT instances. Our system has the following properties:

- It generates instances of 3SAT that are satisfied by a given set of strings.
- It generates any suitable instance of 3SAT with equal probability. This is shown in Theorem 1.
- In combination with zero knowledge proofs for 3SAT, it provides interactive proofs that can be used for anonymous credentials.
- Assuming the 3SAT instances generated are appropriately hard, it provides security against an attacker either finding a participant's element from the information needed to verify set membership or finding other bit strings that satisfy the set membership problem.

We define the set membership problem in Section 2. We present our system in Section 3. In Section 4, we discuss applications, including anonymous credentials and digital timestamping. We conclude with further discussion in Section 5.

2   Preliminaries

In this section, we define the secure set membership problem. A *secure set membership system* consists of two parts. First, the set must be established. Later, holders of set elements can prove their elements' set membership to others. Depending on the application, it may be desirable for the proof to reveal the set element or to keep it secret. Specifically, we have the following definitions.

Definition 1. *A* set establishment protocol *is a protocol carried out by some number m of participants $P_1, \ldots, P_m$. Each P_i holds as input set element w_i. The output of the protocol is a set representation $T = T(w_1, \ldots, w_m)$.*

Definition 2. *A* set membership protocol *is a protocol carried out by a participant P holding a set element w and a verifier V holding a set representation T. An honest verifier accepts if and only if the representation T was generated from a set of elements including w, even if P is cheating. The verifier learns w.*

Obviously, the set membership protocol is unsuitable for credential systems in which the set elements are reusable credentials, because it allows both V (and possibly eavesdroppers) to learn w and thereby to masquerade as P in the future to others. The protocol is also unsuitable for anonymous credential systems unless further measures are taken because it allows V to distinguish between different provers because they have differing credentials. Fortunately, both of these difficulties can be eliminated by using a proof of possession protocol, defined below, instead of a set membership protocol.

Definition 3. *A proof of possession protocol is a protocol carried out by a participant P holding a set element w and a verifier V holding a set representation T. An honest verifier accepts if and only if the representation T was generated from a set of elements including w, even if P is cheating. The verifier V does not learn w, even if V is cheating.*

These definitions can be formalized according to the standard definitions of zero knowledge and simulatability.

In the sequel, we assume all participants are computationally bounded. In particular, our solutions depend on the computational infeasibility of finding witnesses for certain 3SAT expressions (also called *instances*). We discuss the validity of this assumption further in Section 3.4.

When we discuss a 3SAT instance, we pay attention to two parameters. These are the number, ℓ, of variables and the number, n, of clauses, also called the *size* of the instance. We also consider the *clause density* $\alpha = \frac{n}{\ell}$, which is an important parameter for determining the difficulty of a 3SAT instance [2].

In our solution, the elements of the set are interpreted as assignments to a set of variables, also called *witnesses*. We refer to a 3SAT instance that represents the set of elements as a *set representation* or, when clear from context, simply as a *set*.

3   Secure Set Membership

In this section, we describe our secure set membership protocols. We first describe in Section 3.1 a centralized process for a trusted party to establish a set representation for a set of given elements. In Section 3.2, we describe a distributed version of the set establishment protocol, which can be carried out by the participants holding set elements and does not require a centralized trusted party. In Section 3.3, we describe how to show set membership for elements of the established set. We discuss the security of our solutions in Section 3.4.

3.1   Centralized Set Establishment Protocol

Let $W = \{w_1, w_2, \cdots, w_m\}$ be a set of assignments to ℓ variables $V = \{v_1, \ldots, v_\ell\}$. Each w_i represents an individual element. The trusted party, say $\mathcal{T}$, generates a set representation for W—that is, a 3SAT instance satisfied by each $w_i \in W$. To do this, $\mathcal{T}$ repeatedly generates random clauses that are the conjunction of 3 literals over variables in V. He checks each clause he generates to determine whether it is satisfied by every $w_i \in W$. If there is some $w_i \in W$ that does not satisfy the clause, then $\mathcal{T}$ discards the clause and randomly selects a replacement clause which goes through the same test. Once n satisfied clauses are found, where n is a security parameter representing the desired size of the expression,

Input: A set of variable assignments $W = \{w_1, w_2, \cdots, w_m\}$, the number ℓ of variables to be used, and the target number n of clauses.
Output: A 3SAT instance satisfied by all $w \in W$.

While there are fewer than n clauses do:

1. Select three different random numbers $\{v_1, v_2, v_3\} \in \{1, \ldots, \ell\}$.
2. Select three random bits n_1, n_2, n_3. For each bit, if the bit is set, the corresponding random number is considered to be a negation of the variable.
3. If another clause has the same three numbers and corresponding negations discard v_1, v_2, v_3 and n_1, n_2, n_3 and return to Step 1.
4. For each w_j do
    If, for all $i \in \{1, 2, 3\}$ ((n_i is true and v_i is set in w_j) or (n_i is false and v_i is not set in w_j)) then delete $v_1, v_2, v_3, n_1, n_2, n_3$ and goto Step 1.
5. Add the clause represented by $\{(n_1, v_1), (n_2, v_2), (n_3, v_3)\}$ to the instance.

Algorithm 1. A centralized protocol for establishing a set

their conjunction forms the desired set representation T, which is output by $\mathcal{T}$. The complete algorithm is given in Algorithm 1.

Note that the output T is an instance of the 3SAT problem satisfied by the assignments that the participants have specified as elements. It may also be satisfied by some other unknown assignments. However, even if there are such spurious witnesses, that does not mean they are easy for an attacker to find. Nonetheless, it seems desirable to avoid having many such spurious witnesses. One can reduce the number of spurious witnesses by choosing a large n, because the probability of a given assignment satisfying a 3SAT instance decreases exponentially with the size of the instance. Specifically, n should be chosen to be large enough to satisfy three security criteria:

- The conjunction of the clauses should be satisfied by very few assignments that are not valid elements.
- The size of the conjunctive normal form (CNF) expression that is made by the clauses should be large enough that there is high probability that it is not an instance of SAT for which an efficient solution is known.
- The size of the CNF expression should be large enough that it can potentially be computationally infeasible to find satisfying assignments.

In general, this can be accomplished by choosing a suitably large number of variables and setting the clause density to a suitable value. The security of the scheme is discussed further in Section 3.4.

We now turn our attention to the computational complexity of this algorithm. We note that there is some chance that the algorithm might not even terminate, if there are not a sufficient number of available clauses that satisfy the given witnesses. However, if ℓ is chosen relatively large in comparison to m, and ℓ is sufficiently large compared to m and n, there should be a sufficient number of clauses that satisfy the witnesses. Further analysis or experiments are needed in order to determine appropriate values to use.

Assuming that there is a large number of clauses that satisfy the given witnesses, consider a particular witness representing one set element and consider a single randomly chosen 3SAT clause. There are three variables in a clause, all of which are given some assignment in the witness. Each variable in the clause can appear as a literal in either positive or negative form, so there are eight possible cases. Of these, seven are satisfied by the witness; it is only not satisfied (and therefore not accepted) in the case where none of the three literals is satisfied. Thus, the probability of a clause satisfying one witness is $\frac{7}{8}$. If there are m witnesses, then the probability of a clause satisfying all of them is $(\frac{7}{8})^m$. It follows that the expected number of tries required to generate a clause in the set representation is $(\frac{8}{7})^m$. It takes $O(\log \ell)$ bits to represent a clause and the clause must be checked against m witnesses, each of which can be done in constant time. Therefore, it takes $O(m \log \ell)$ time to test a clause to determine whether it is satisfied by all the witnesses.

In order to generate n clauses, it is necessary to find n distinct clauses that are satisfied by W. As each clause is found, it becomes slightly harder to find the next clause, as duplicates will sometimes be chosen. However, as long as n is very small relative to the total number of clauses that satisfy W, this has a negligible effect. If the probability that a random chosen clause passes both tests (satisfies W and is not a duplicate) were fixed at $(\frac{7}{8})^m$, then the expected running time to generate a set representation would be $O(n((\frac{8}{7})^m)m \log \ell)$. We note that in cases where n is a significant fraction of the total number of clauses that satisfy W, then this would not be the case.

In practice, this means that it is only computationally efficient to generate an instance for at most up to around a hundred witnesses. A hundred witnesses leads to an expectation of 629,788 rejected clauses per accepted clause, easily doable with current computers. When the number of witnesses reaches a hundred and fifty, there is an expectation of about five hundred million rejected clauses for each accepted clause, probably infeasible for a typical modern computer when the number of clauses is considered.

3.2   Distributed Set Establishment Protocol

We now discuss the distributed protocol for establishing T, which is given in Algorithm 2. This algorithm works for *honest-but-curious* participants, who are assumed to follow their specified protocols. It also has some resilience against cheating participants; for example, cheating parties can cause an easy instance of 3SAT to be chosen, but in some cases the other participants can detect that this may be happening. At a high level, the protocol executes as follows: the participants locally generate local copies of the same random clause. Each determines if the clause is satisfied by her own witness and communicates this information to the others. If the clause is satisfied by all the witnesses, it is kept. Otherwise, it is discarded.

In order to protect the participants' witnesses from being disclosed, we use a verifiable secret-ballot election scheme by Benaloh [4]. The scheme is based on *homomorphic encryption* and *secret sharing*. It operates by designating some participants as *tellers*. Participants give secret shares of their votes to the tellers. The tellers then use the homomorphic properties of the secret-sharing scheme to compute shares of the tally. They then collaborate to compute the actual tally and provide a proof to the participants that the tally was computed correctly.

In order to detect cheating of individual participants in our scheme, the tellers count the number of times that any participant votes "no" for any given clause. This can be accomplished without revealing the votes to the tellers by using the homomorphic property of the election scheme. The tellers maintain a running sum of each participant's votes and collaborate to determine that sum after a clause is chosen. If this sum exceeds a threshold value *maxreject*, then the instance is discarded and the protocol restarted from the beginning. Depending on the application setting for the protocol, it may be desirable to exclude participants who have exceeded the *maxreject* threshold some number of times from further participation. We note that even if a cheating participant succeeds in influencing the outcome of the protocol, she can neither learn another participant's witness nor cause another participant's witness to not satisfy the resulting 3SAT instance.

The goal is to choose *maxreject* high enough so that it detects cheating at levels that could lead to malicious participants being able to break the security of the result, but low enough so that it does not unnecessarily restart the protocol when no participants are cheating. As a somewhat arbitrary threshold, we suggest:

$$maxreject = \frac{\left(\frac{8}{7}\right)^m}{8} - \frac{n}{\log\frac{7}{8}} - \frac{2}{\log\frac{7}{8}},$$

which is derived as follows. As mentioned previously, the probability of a random clause satisfying a given witness is $\frac{7}{8}$. The first term of the formula for *maxreject* is the inverse of the probability of all the witnesses being satisfied for a single clause divided by the number of them that a single witness rejects. This is not sufficient to give a useful probability of an honest run not being rejected because there are n clauses yielding a probability that all n is satisfied of 2^{-n}. The second term of the formula for *maxreject* brings the probability of an honest run being rejected to $1/2$ by being the solution to the equation: $\left(\frac{7}{8}\right)^{f(n)} = 2^{-n}$. By adding $f(n)$ to the number of elections, we are dividing the probability by 2^{-n} for probabilities not approaching one. The third term further increases the probability that all terms are satisfied to $\frac{7}{8}$ by dividing the probability by $\frac{1}{4}$. Further analysis or experiments are needed in order to determine how effective this or any choice of *maxreject* is.

To ensure termination and also to provide some protection against multiple cheating participants colluding and "spreading out" their "no" votes in order not to individually exceed the *maxreject* threshold, it would also be a good idea to have a check in each iteration of the while loop that the loop has not been executed too many times, and to abort the protocol if this occurs.

In our set establishment protocol, the participants have a public shared source R of random or pseudorandom numbers. Using R, each participant generates a clause as the disjunction of three elements. Since the same random source is

Input: A set of variable assignments $W = \{w_1, w_2, \cdots, w_m\}$. Each w_i is known to participant P_i. All participants also know the number ℓ of variables to be used and the target number n of clauses, as well as a sufficiently long random string R.
Output: An instance of 3SAT that is satisfied by all participants' witnesses.

− set
$$maxreject = \frac{\left(\frac{8}{7}\right)^m}{8} - \frac{n}{\log\frac{7}{8}} - \frac{2}{\log\frac{7}{8}}$$

− While there are fewer than n clauses do:
1. Using R, select three different variables v_1, v_2, v_3 and three flags n_1, n_2, n_3.
2. Construct the clause where the flags denote the negation of variables.
3. If the clause is equivalent to a clause already generated, discard it and return to Step 1.
4. Hold a verifiable secret-ballot election (see [4]) using "yes" if the clause is satisfied by the witness and "no" otherwise. If the tally is unanimously "yes", then add the clause to the instance. Otherwise, delete it. Each teller should maintain a running sum of each participant's shares of votes.
5. return to Step 1.
− Use the homomorphic property to compute the number of "no" votes for each participant. If one exceeds *maxreject*, discard all the clauses.

Algorithm 2. A distributed algorithm

used, all the participants generate the same clause. The participants hold a verifiable secret-ballot election. If the tally is unanimously "yes", the clause is kept; otherwise, it is rejected. If a participant votes "no", then the clause is discarded. This process is repeated until the target number n of clauses has been generated.

It is easy to verify that the output T is satisfied by all the inputs $w_1, \ldots, w_m$, so Algorithm 2 meets the definition of a set establishment protocol. Assuming that parties behave honestly, the expected number of tries to find a clause is $(\frac{8}{7})^m$ as in the centralized protocol of Section 3.1.

3.3   Set Membership

Our set representations lend themselves easily to both set membership and proof of possession protocols.

Set membership involves a participant P, who knows his element w, and a verifier V, who knows T. P wants to convince V that T was generated as a set representation that included the element w. In our case, then, P wants to convince V that w satisfies T.

A straightforward set membership protocol (in which V is allowed to communicate w to P, as per the definitions in Section 2), is for P to communicate w to V, who can then easily check in polynomial time whether w satisfies T. If it does, V accepts; otherwise, V rejects.

For proof of possession, it is important that the verifier never learns the credentials and cannot impersonate the prover. Fortunately, in our solution, it is not necessary to present the element to show set membership, but rather it is sufficient to show that one knows a satisfying string. This can be done with a zero knowledge proof. Assuming trapdoor one-way functions exist, then such zero knowledge proofs are possible for 3SAT using a generic construction that applies to any NP-complete problem [17]. Additionally, this can be made secure against quantum computers [29], in keeping with our motivation to avoid reliance on number-theoretic assumptions. If one is willing to rely on such assumptions, there are also simple examples of zero knowledge proofs for 3SAT that rely on factoring [8,4].

3.4 Security

The security of the set membership protocol and the proof of possession protocol depends on the difficulty of finding witnesses that satisfy a set representation T constructed by the set establishment protocol. We show below in Theorem 1 that the representation T is random among all instances of 3SAT with n clauses and ℓ variables satisfied by the specified assignments $W = \{w_1, \ldots, w_m\}$. The instance T may possibly be satisfied by some other assignments. That is, given a set of witnesses and a specified number of clauses, there is an equal probability that our algorithm produces any instance that is satisfied by the witnesses and has the proper number of variables and clauses. The probability that T is hard is the same as the probability that it is hard to find a witness for a random such instance of 3SAT. Unfortunately, it is not known what this probability is. (In fact, if $P = NP$, then the probability is zero.)

Our system rests on the assumption that a sufficiently large random instance of 3SAT satisfying a given set of witnesses and having an appropriately chosen clause density has a high probability of being hard to solve. If this assumption holds, then it is hard for anyone to find a witness which is not an element. It is also hard for a party who does not already know an element of T to find one. These two properties provide the security for both the set membership protocol and the proof of possession protocol. In particular, for the set membership protocol, the ability for an adversary to succeed in forging a witness without overhearing one is precisely the adversary's ability to determine a satisfying assignment to T, because this property can be exactly checked by the verifier. In the case of the proof of possession protocol, the security additionally relies on the soundness of the zero knowledge proof. An adversary who cannot find a valid witness has only negligible probability of convincing the verifier to accept.

Theorem 1. *Algorithms 1 and 2 generate with equal probability any 3SAT instance consisting of n different clauses that is satisfied by all the assignments in W.*

Proof (sketch). The same argument applies to both Algorithm 1 and Algorithm 2. This is because Algorithms 1 and 2 save or reject clauses for the same reasons. The only difference is whether the checking is handled by the participants or by a centralized authority.

Consider the "random algorithm," which simply has a list of all the possible instances consisting of n distinct 3-literal clauses over ℓ variables that are satisfied by all $w \in W$ and selects one instance uniformly at random.

First, we show that our algorithm generates the same set of instances as the random algorithm. Suppose a possible 3SAT instance (in the random algorithm's list) cannot be generated by our algorithm. Then a clause in it must be rejected by our algorithm either because it is a duplicate or because some assignment does not satisfy the clause. It cannot be a duplicate, as this violates the requirement for the random algorithm's list that the clauses be distinct. If some assignment does not satisfy the clause, then no instance including that clause is satisfied by the assignment. Therefore, including it would violate the condition for the random algorithm's list that it must be satisfied by W. Hence, all instances in the list drawn on by the random algorithm are candidates for generation by our algorithm.

Conversely, suppose a 3SAT instance generated by our algorithm cannot be generated by the random algorithm. Then there are two possible reasons. The first is that there is a duplicate clause resulting in the number of unique clauses being less than n. This instance cannot be generated by our algorithm because the duplicate clause will be suppressed. The other possible reason is that it is not satisfied by one of the witnesses. In this case, one of the clauses is not satisfied by that witness (as the instance is a conjunction of the clauses). This clause will be rejected by our algorithm, so this instance cannot be generated. Therefore, the set of instances selected by the random algorithm is exactly the set of instances that our algorithm can generate. Call the size of this set N.

Finally, we show that our algorithm generates each instance with the same probability as the random algorithm. The random algorithm has probability $1/N$ of choosing each of the N instances that it can generate. Our algorithm also generates each of these instances with equal probability. To see this, note that in our algorithm, each clause has a constant probability depending on how many clauses have already been chosen. The product of a fixed number of constants is a constant. Therefore all of the instances have the same probability. It follows that, for our algorithm, each clause has probability $\frac{1}{N}$, as desired.   ∎

Theorem 1 states that, given ℓ and n, the system can generate any 3SAT instance of ℓ variables with n clauses that is satisfied by the specified witnesses. We make some observations and propose some heuristic recommendations for selecting the security parameters:

- Beyond a certain threshold, increasing the number of variables without increasing the number of clauses actually reduces security because there are not enough instantiations of the variables.
- Recall that the clause density of an instance is defined as $\alpha = \frac{n}{\ell}$. Alekhnovich and Ben-Sasson [2] show that if $\alpha \leq 1.63$, then the instance can be solved in linear time. They also demonstrate empirically that $\alpha < 2.5$ seems to be easy

to solve. We recommend taking $\alpha \geq 8$ (i.e., choosing $n \geq 8\ell$) for security. For example, $\ell = 128$ and $n = 1024$. If one is concerned about quantum attacks, then we suggest $\ell = 256$ and $n = 2048$ due to the quadratic advantage given by Grover's algorithm [18].

- A certain number of variables are trivial in any particular instance (i.e., because they either do not appear in positive form or in negative form, and therefore it is clear how to set them in a satisfying assignment). This can reduce the security of the system, by making it easier for an adversary to find satisfying assignments. Additionally, once the trivial variables are assigned, an adversary can then "remove" those clauses, potentially resulting in more trivial variables.

  If our instances were random among all 3SAT instances with n clauses and ℓ variables, then the expected number of trivial variables could be limited by taking the clause density sufficiently large. However, as noted before, our instances are random only among those 3SAT instances that are actually satisfied by the set W of witnesses. Further study is needed to determine how many trivial variables our instances are likely to have and whether this can be reduced.

The *phase boundary* of 3SAT is the clause density at which instances go abruptly from being mostly satisfiable to mostly unsatisfiable. The 3SAT decision problem—determining whether a 3SAT instance is satisfiable or not—is believed to be hardest when instances are just above the phase boundary [20]. However, our problem is a little different. Our set representation instances are always satisfiable (since they are specifically chosen to satisfy a particular set of witnesses). The problem at hand for an attacker is to find a satisfying assignment. We conjecture that the problem of finding satisfying assignments for instances that are known to be satisfiable gets harder as the probability of a random instance of the same parameter being satisfiable gets smaller—i.e., well above the phase boundary.

SATLIB contains resources for experimental research on SAT and 3SAT, including the results of competitions in solving random SAT instances. The literature on SATLIB suggests that progress has not been made on high clause density instances [20]. We also note that there is an optimization variant of the SAT problem called MAXSAT [20,19,22]. Specifically, it is possible to approximate 3SAT by finding assignments that satisfy most, but not all clauses. Known algorithms are polynomial time for finding a 7/8 assignment, but become exponential in the worst case when trying to do a full assignment.

Multiple cheating participants might collude to try to "spread out" their cheating rejections so that they can influence the outcome without exceeding *maxreject*. This can be compensated for by decreasing *maxreject* or by limiting the total number of rejections allowed cumulatively for all participants rather than for individual participants. However, this also increases the chance of "false positives," in which the protocol is restarted even without cheating behavior, so it is only likely to work well for a small number of colluding participants. It remains open to address other types of cheating and collusions.

4   Applications

There are a number of applications of the set membership problem, including credentials and document timestamping.

4.1   Digital Credentials

Our system applies to anonymous credentials in a fairly straightforward manner. The credentials are the elements. They are generated using either the centralized protocol or the distributed protocol and they are verified using the proof of possession protocol. In this way, the credentials are all generated at once and then the instance is distributed to the verifiers. Verifiers use the instance to anonymously determine whether a member is credentialed. If credentials with identification are desired, then the member can present his witness; the verifier can check that the witness satisfies the instance.

4.2   Accounts with Multiple Users

The system is also useful in situations where there need to be multiple authentication strings for a single account. An example is accounts with multiple users. Suppose there are three debit cards issued on one bank account and they all have the same number but each has a different PIN. The PINs can then be used as witnesses in constructing an instance. When a user wants to demonstrate that she is an authorized user of the account, she runs the proof of possession protocol using her PIN. This way, joint holders of an account can access the account without giving away their PINs (which might also be used for other accounts that are not shared).

Other applications of multiple user accounts include the use of RFID tags as witnesses in an access control system based on proximity sensors and other access control situations where it is not desirable to uniquely identify the user.

4.3   Document Timestamping

Document timestamping [5,6] may require a little more explanation. In document timestamping applications, we think of the distributed protocol as a distributed signature. All the parties participating in the protocol are attesting that one of their number knew each witness at the time the protocol was run by accepting the set that results from the protocol. It would not be possible for the protocol participant to execute the protocol and then choose a satisfying witness at some later date.

The timestamping system proceeds in rounds. All documents submitted during the same round are considered to be simultaneous, like patent applications arriving at the patent office on the same day. Each participant's witness is a hash of the document(s) she would like to timestamp. The distributed protocol is run, and everyone remembers the round's set, which is the timestamp. The parties may jointly publish it if they wish to allow anyone to verify a timestamp.

To verify that a document was submitted during a given round, the verifier merely needs to run the set membership protocol. The security of this system does not depend on computational security, in that if a cheating prover wishes to make his specific document appear to be timestamped and it does not satisfy the 3SAT instance, there is nothing he can do to change that. (We note, though, that in most practical settings, the adversary may be able to change his document in ways that do not affect its meaning, but do affect its encoding into a bit string, so this guarantee is not absolute.)

Digital timestamping can be used for intellectual property disputes, among other applications. In the intellectual property application, a consortium generates a timestamp with each company using a hash of the hashes of all of its documents. Each company retains the daily timestamp and publishes it for other interested parties. In a patent dispute, for instance, a party can get all the other honest participants to attest to its possession of a document on or before a certain date. This could also be used to prevent backdating in stock or other business transactions.

5 Discussion

We have presented a general solution to the set membership problem whose security depends on the difficulty of finding witnesses to random 3SAT instances satisfying a given set of witnesses. We have also presented applications to access control, digital credentials, and timestamping. We have shown a distributed protocol for establishing a set.

A strong justification for considering security based on 3SAT is the increased worry that advances in conventional or quantum computing may one day yield efficient algorithms for problems such as factoring and discrete logarithms typically used as a source of hardness in cryptography. It is therefore important to investigate cryptographic algorithms based on alternate (plausible) hardness assumptions to provide resilience against "breaking" of any one assumption or class of assumptions.

Further work includes analysis and experiments to determine the probability distribution of the output of our set establishment protocol with respect to all 3SAT instances. In particular, it should be investigated experimentally whether a randomly generated instance of 3SAT of size n that is satisfied by the chosen witnesses falls into one of the patterns whose solution is known to be easy, as well as determining whether all such instances can be specifically avoided.

Our protocol can be used for digital credentials including anonymous credentials, timestamping, and other set membership applications. It can also be used for applications where multiple users share an account. These include some access control and financial applications. For set membership applications like timestamping, the set representation can be thought of as a distributed signature. It can be proven to any honest participant or observer using the set membership protocol that a document was used for inclusion in the set. These applications have broad applicability to problems in cryptography and security.

The advantages of this method over one-way accumulators include not needing to remember a second string and not being dependent on the factoring problem [6].

As previously discussed, the expected number of clauses that must be tried to generate a clause in the set representation is $(\frac{8}{7})^m$, where m is the number of witnesses to be represented. We note that this probability depends on the number of elements and is independent of n and ℓ. In contrast, the security of the system is based on the adversary's difficulty of finding an element as a function of n and ℓ, so it may be possible to limit m so as to have efficient solutions for the participants without making the adversary's task solvable. As described earlier in Section 3.1, we believe that one hundred witnesses can be dealt with easily, but that as the number of witnesses begins to reach one hundred fifty, it becomes infeasible to generate an instance. For the distributed protocol, the limits may be slightly lower to compensate for communication overhead. This can be countered by replacing 3SAT with k-SAT where k is $\Theta(m)$. This eliminates the exponential complexity for the participants. However, in this case, it is necessary to make α significantly greater than the phase boundary for k-SAT. It is an open problem to determine the phase boundary of k-SAT for $k > 3$.

The space complexity for a set based on 3SAT is $\Theta(\ell \log \ell)$. For instance, a system with 128 variables requires 1024 clauses. Altogether, this requires three kilobytes of storage. This space complexity is independent of the number of set elements. However, if k-SAT is used instead of 3SAT, then the space complexity grows both in the number of bits required to represent a clause and in the number of clauses required to be above the phase boundary.

Directions for future research include developing a better understanding of the expected hardness of the 3SAT instances generated by our algorithm and extending the distributed set establishment protocol to efficiently handle general malicious behavior.

Acknowledgements

We thank David Evans and the anonymous reviewers for their helpful comments.

References

1. Alessandro Acquisiti. Anonymous credentials through acid mixing, 2003. Unpublished manuscript.
2. Mikhail Alekhnovich and Eli Ben-Sasson. Linear upper bounds for random walk on small density random 3-CNFs. In *Proceedings of the 44th Annual IEEE Symposium on the Foundations of Computer Science*, 2003.
3. Niko Baric and Birgit Pfitzmann. Collision-free accumulators and fail-stop signature schemes without trees. In *Advances in Cryptology – Eurocrypt '97*, volume 1233 of *Lecture Notes in Computer Science*. Springer, 1997.
4. Josh Benaloh. *Verifiable Secret-Ballot Elections*. PhD thesis, Yale University Department of Computer Science, September 1987.
5. Josh Benaloh and Michael de Mare. Efficient broadcast time-stamping. Technical Report TR-MCS-91-1, Clarkson University Department of Mathematics and Computer Science, 1991.

6. Josh Benaloh and Michael de Mare. One-way accumulators: A decentralized approach to digital signatures. In *Advances In Cryptology – Eurocrypt '93*, volume 765 of *Lecture Notes in Computer Science*, pages 274–285. Springer, 1994.

7. Dan Boneh and Matthew Franklin. Identity-based encryption from the Weil pairing. *SIAM Journal of Computing*, 32(3):586–615, 2003.

8. G. Brassard and C. Crepeau. Zero-knowledge simulation of boolean circuits. In *Advances in Cryptography – Crypto '86*, volume 263 of *Lecture Notes in Computer Science*, pages 223–233. Springer, 1987.

9. Jan Camenisch and Anna Lysyanskaya. An efficient system for non-transferable anonymous credentials with optional anonymity revocation. In *Advances in Cryptology – Eurocrypt 2001*, volume 2045 of *Lecture Notes in Computer Science*. Springer, 2001.

10. Jan Camenisch and Anna Lysyanskaya. Dynamic accumulators and application to efficient revocation of anonymous credentials. In *Advances in Cryptology – Crypto 2002*, volume 2442 of *Lecture Notes in Computer Science*. Springer, 2002.

11. Michael de Mare. An analysis of certain cryptosystems and related mathematics. Master's thesis, State University of New York Institute of Technology, Dec. 2004.

12. W. Diffie and M. Hellman. New directions in cryptography. *IEEE Transactions on Information Theory*, 22(6):644–654, Nov. 1976.

13. F. Esponda. *Negative Representations of Information*. PhD thesis, University of New Mexico, 2005.

14. Fernando Esponda, Elena S. Ackley, Stephanie Forrest, and Paul Helman. On-line negative databases. In *Proceedings of the 3rd International Conference on Artificial Immune Systems (ICARIS)*, pages 175–188. Springer-Verlag, Sep. 2004.

15. Fernando Esponda, Stephanie Forrest, and Paul Helman. Enhancing privacy through negative representations of data. Technical report, University of New Mexico, 2004.

16. Fernando Esponda, Stephanie Forrest, and Paul Helman. Information hiding through negative representations of data. Technical report, University of New Mexico, 2004.

17. Oded Goldreich, Silvio Micali, and Avi Wigderson. How to prove all NP statements in zero-knowledge and a methodology of cryptographic protocol design. In *Advances in Cryptology – Crypto '86*, volume 263 of *Lecture Notes in Computer Science*, pages 171–185. Springer, 1987.

18. Lov Grover. A fast quantum mechanical algorithm for database search. In *Proceedings of the Twenty-Eighth Annual ACM Symposium on Theory of Computing*, pages 212–219. ACM Press, 1996.

19. Johan Håstad. Some optimal inapproximability results. *J. ACM*, 48(4):798–859, 2001.

20. Holger H. Hoos and Thomas Stützle. SATLIB: An online resource for research on SAT. In *SAT 2000*, pages 283–292. IOS Press, 2000. http://www.satlib.org.

21. Russell Impagliazzo and Sara Miner. Anonymous credentials with biometrically-enforced non-transferability. In *Proceedings of the 2003 ACM Workshop on Privacy in the Electronic Society*, pages 60–71. ACM, 2003.

22. Howard J. Karloff and Uri Zwick. A 7/8-approximation algorithm for MAX 3SAT? In *Proceedings of the 38th Annual Symposium on Foundations of Computer Science*, pages 406–415. IEEE Computer Society, 1997.

23. Ralph C. Merkle. *Secrecy, authentication, and public key systems*. UMI Research Press, 1982.

24. Ralph C. Merkle. A digital signature based on a conventional encryption function. In *Advances in Cryptology – Crypto '87*, volume 293 of *Lecture Notes in Computer Science*. Springer, 1988.
25. A. M. Odlyzko. The rise and fall of the knapsack cryptosystems. In *PSAM: Proceedings of the 42nd Symposium in Applied Mathematics*, pages 75–88, 1990.
26. R. Rivest, A. Shamir, and L. Adleman. A method for obtaining digital signatures and public key cryptosystems. *Communications of the ACM*, 21(2):120–126, Feb. 1978.
27. P. Shor. Algorithms for quantum computation: discrete logarithms and factoring. In *Proceedings of the 35th Annual Symposium on Foundations of Computer Science*, pages 124–134. IEEE, 1994.
28. Michael Szydlo. Merkle tree traversal in log space and time. In *Advances in Cryptology – Eurocrypt 2004*, volume 3027 of *Lecture Notes in Computer Science*, pages 541–554, 2004.
29. John Watrous. Zero knowledge against quantum attacks. In *STOC '06 – 38th Annual ACM Symposium on Theory of Computing*, pages 296–315. ACM, 2006.

Left-to-Right Signed-Bit τ-Adic Representations of n Integers (Short Paper)*

Billy Bob Brumley

Helsinki University of Technology,
Laboratory for Theoretical Computer Science,
P.O.Box 5400, FI-02015 TKK, Finland
billy.brumley@hut.fi

Abstract. Koblitz curves are often used in digital signature schemes where signature verifications need to be computed efficiently. Simultaneous elliptic scalar multiplication is a useful method of carrying out such verifications. This paper presents an efficient alternative to τ-adic Joint Sparse Form that moves left-to-right for computations involving two points. A generalization of this algorithm is then presented for generating a low joint weight representation of an arbitrary number of integers.

Keywords: Koblitz curves, elliptic curve cryptography, digital signatures, joint sparse form, simultaneous elliptic scalar multiplication.

1 Introduction

Elliptic curve digital signatures are attractive due to the reduced size of keys and signatures. The main group operation is *elliptic scalar multiplication* and is generally considered to be the most efficient on Koblitz curves. This paper deals only with these types of curves, particularly with speeding up *simultaneous* scalar multiplication on these curves involving two or more points. This is a common computation for signature verification.

RELATED WORK. Solinas [1] showed that scalar multiplication on Koblitz curves is very efficient. He also developed [2] a representation for a pair of integers with minimal joint weight called Joint Sparse Form (JSF). Ciet [3], et. al developed a τ-adic JSF for use with Koblitz curves. A generalization of JSF to an arbitrary number of integers has been developed [4,5]. There is also an alternative [6] to the generalized JSF.

CONTRIBUTIONS. An efficient alternative to τ-adic JSF is presented in Sect. 3, which works left-to-right, in-line with Shamir's Trick, and requires less memory.

* This work was supported by the project "Packet Level Authentication" funded by TEKES. Thanks to Prof. Kaisa Nyberg for suggestions, comments, and generous support. Additionally, the author gratefully acknowledges those involved in the PLA project.

P. Ning, S. Qing, and N. Li (Eds.): ICICS 2006, LNCS 4307, pp. 469–478, 2006.
© Springer-Verlag Berlin Heidelberg 2006

A generalization of this algorithm to an arbitrary number of integers is presented in Sect. 4, based on the algorithm in [6].

APPLICATIONS. These contributions make simultaneous scalar multiplication on Koblitz curves more efficient. This is a common method for signature verifications (sum of two terms), as well as self-certified signature verifications (three terms [7]). Scalar multiplication using *combing* [4,8] can also be improved using these results.

2   Background

2.1   Elliptic Scalar Multiplication

Elliptic scalar multiplication computes k multiples of the point $P = (x, y)$. A binary signed-digit representation known as *Non-Adjacent Form* (NAF) [8] of the ℓ-bit integer $k = \langle k_{\ell-1} \ldots k_0 \rangle$, $k_i \in \{1, -1, 0\}$ is commonly used, as point addition has the same cost as point subtraction (as opposed to multiplicative groups where multiplication is much cheaper than inversion). NAF is generated by repeatedly dividing k by 2, choosing a remainder such that the quotient is divisible by 2. Then k multiples of P can be computed as

$$kP = \sum_{i=0}^{\ell-1} k_i 2^i P. \tag{1}$$

The average number of non-zero digits in ℓ-bit k is $\ell/3$, so (1) is executed at the average cost of $(\ell/3)\mathsf{A} + \ell\mathsf{D}$ operations, where A and D denote point additions and doublings, respectively.

2.2   Koblitz Curves

Koblitz curves [9] are anomalous binary curves of the form

$$E_a : y^2 + xy = x^3 + ax^2 + 1 \text{ where } a \in \{0, 1\} \tag{2}$$

The *Frobenius map* $\tau : E_a(\mathbb{F}_{2^m}) \to E_a(\mathbb{F}_{2^m})$ is a mapping such that $(x, y) \mapsto (x^2, y^2)$. Squaring a binary field element is a very cheap operation[1]. It can be shown from the point addition formula that for all $(x, y) \in E_a$

$$(x^4, y^4) + 2(x, y) = \mu(x^2, y^2) \text{ , where } \mu = (-1)^{1-a} \text{ , or,}$$
$$(\tau^2 + 2)P = \mu\tau P \text{ , from where}$$
$$\tau^2 + 2 = \mu\tau. \tag{3}$$

Using elliptic scalar multiplication along with the Frobenius map, it is possible to obtain multiples of a point by using complex multiplication by an element

---

[1] The cost depends on the representation of the field elements of $\mathbb{F}_{2^m}$. When using a normal-basis representation, squaring a field element is only a rotation of the bits.

of the ring $\mathbb{Z}[\tau]$. More specifically, instead of representing integer k as distinct powers of 2 as in (1), k is represented as the sum of distinct powers of τ, called a τ-adic expansion of k. Analogous to NAF, τ-adic NAF is generated by repeatedly dividing k by τ, choosing a remainder such that the quotient is divisible by τ [1]. Analogous to (1), multiples of the point P are then computed as

$$kP = \sum_{i=0}^{\ell-1} k_i \tau^i P \, . \tag{4}$$

Since no point doublings are required, it is executed at the cost of $(\ell/3)$A operations, which is a large improvement over the binary NAF case.

2.3 Joint Sparse Form

Given n integers in a joint representation, the *joint weight* (JW) is defined as the number of columns with at least one non-zero entry. *Joint Sparse Form* (JSF) [2] is a generalization of NAF for a pair of integers used to speed up the computation of a sum of integer multiples of two points. JSF has minimal JW among all joint signed-binary digit representations for a pair of integers, yielding an average of $\ell/2$ non-zero columns.

A τ-adic analogue of JSF [3] exists, which moves right-to-left (as does the original JSF). Table 1 continues the example provided therein. The first entry demonstrates that simply using τ-adic NAF on both integers is not optimal with regards to the JW. The second entry is the τ-adic JSF representation with lower JW. The third entry is related to Alg. 1 and will be explained in Sect. 3. Note that these are all different representations of the same integers.

Table 1. τ-adic JSF representations

Form	Representation	JW	Length
τ-NAF [1]	$\langle 10\bar{1}0\bar{1}0101 \rangle$		
	$\langle 0\bar{1}0\bar{1}00010 \rangle$	8	9
τ-JSF [3]	$\langle 100110011 \rangle$		
	$\langle 0\bar{1}0\bar{1}00010 \rangle$	6	9
Alg. 1	$\langle 0110\bar{1}0011 \rangle$		
	$\langle 0\bar{1}0\bar{1}00010 \rangle$	6	8

2.4 Shamir's Trick

Shamir's Trick [10] or *Straus's Algorithm* [11] is useful for speeding up computations of the form $k_0 P + k_1 Q$, which a common computation for elliptic curve signature verification primitives. It works by precomputing all possible values of a column in a joint representation, then moves left-to-right as in the elliptic

	computing: **13P + 7Q**
	precomp: $(P + Q), (P - Q)$
	$\text{NAF}(13) = 10\bar{1}01 \ (2^4 - 2^2 + 2^0 = 13)$
	$\text{NAF}(7) \ \ = 0100\bar{1} \ (2^3 - 2^0 = 7)$
	$R \leftarrow \infty$
$i = 4$	$R \leftarrow 2R = \infty$
	$R \leftarrow \infty + P = P$
$i = 3$	$R \leftarrow 2P$
	$R \leftarrow 2P + Q$
$i = 2$	$R \leftarrow 2(2P + Q) = 4P + 2Q$
	$R \leftarrow 4P + 2Q - P = 3P + 2Q$
$i = 1$	$R \leftarrow 2(3P + 2Q) = 6P + 4Q$
	$R \leftarrow 6P + 4Q + \infty = 6P + 4Q$
$i = 0$	$R \leftarrow 2(6P + 4Q) = 12P + 8Q$
	$R \leftarrow 12P + 8Q + (P - Q) = \mathbf{13P + 7Q}$

Fig. 1. Small example of Shamir's Trick, computing $13P + 7Q$ ($\bar{1} = -1$)

scalar multiplication methods shown previously. A small example appears in Fig.1.

Given the average density of JSF as $\ell/2$, Shamir's Trick (for two points) requires on average $(\ell/2+2)\text{A}+\ell\text{D}$ operations (including precomputation), whereas processing these computations separately then adding the results requires on average $(2\ell/3 + 1)\text{A} + 2\ell\text{D}$ operations. The same method can be used with τ-adic JSF by simply replacing the point doublings with applications of τ. However, the gains are less as there are no point doublings to be performed (as shown with the NAF and τ-NAF case).

3   An Efficient Alternative to τ-Adic Joint Sparse Form

As shown, Shamir's Trick moves left-to-right through the expansions of (k_0, k_1). Therefore, a method of generating a low-weight joint τ-adic representation that moves left-to-right would work in-line with Shamir's Trick and also be more memory efficient, as separate storage for the joint representation would not longer be needed. This is presented as Alg. 1[2]. The strategy is to create more zero-columns given the fact that $\tau^2 + 1 = \tau - 1$. The first **for** loop generates the digits and the bottom **while** loop performs he elliptic curve arithmetic. It is known that τ-adic JSF lacks optimality; the optimality (or lack thereof) of Alg. 1 has not been examined.

The third entry in Table 1 is the output from Alg. 1, which happens to demonstrate how moving left-to-right can also decrease the length of the representation by one if substitutions can be made in the first column (meaning up to one point addition and one application of τ can be saved).

---

[2] Assumes $\mu = 1$. For $\mu = -1$, only small modifications are needed.

Algorithm 1. Left-to-right τ-adic simultaneous scalar multiplication

---

Input: ℓ-bit integers k_0, k_1 in τ-NAF, points $P, Q \in E(\mathbb{F}_{2^m})$
Output: $k_0 P + k_1 Q$
Precompute $xP + yQ \ \forall \ x, y \in \{0, -1, 1\}$
$R \leftarrow \infty, \ i \leftarrow \ell - 1$
while $i \geq 0$ do
    $j \leftarrow 1$ /* number of columns to process */
    for $n \leftarrow 0$ to 1 do
        if $i > 1$ and $k_{n,i} + k_{n,i-2} = \pm 2$ and $k_{1-n,i} = 0$ then
            $k_{n,i-1} \leftarrow k_{n,i} \, , \ k_{n,i-2} \leftarrow -k_{n,i} \, , \ k_{n,i} \leftarrow 0$ /* replace the bits */
            $j \leftarrow 2$ /* two columns can be processed */
        end
    end
    while $j > 0$ do
        $R \leftarrow \tau R$ /* square the coordinates of R */
        $R \leftarrow R + (k_{0,i} P + k_{1,i} Q)$
        $i \leftarrow i - 1 \, , \ j \leftarrow j - 1$
    end
end
return R

---

4 Generalizing to n Integers

A generalization of JSF [4,5] provides a method for generating a representation of n different integers with low joint weight. One alternative [6] to these methods moves left-to-right and is based on the fact that for all $n > 0$

$$2^n - 1 = \sum_{i=0}^{n-1} 2^i \ . \tag{5}$$

However, when using τ-adic representations each digit represents a power of τ, not a power of 2. Hence, the same replacements cannot be made. τ-adic analogues are usually constructed by finding the equivalent operation when working with powers of τ, as demonstrated previously with NAF and τ-adic NAF.

Unfortunately, when working with powers of τ the τ-adic analogue of (5) is not immediately apparent as opposed to the NAF case. To produce a τ-adic analogue of the algorithm in [6], for all $n > 1$ the task is to find a solution to one of

$$\tau^n \pm 1 = \sum_{i=0}^{n-1} x_i \tau^i \text{ where } x_i \in \{1, -1, 0\}. \tag{6}$$

It turns out that one has four different cases to consider with respect to the value of n (mod 4). Given (3) and assuming $\mu = 1$, the following solutions are obtained to (6) for the initial cases of $n = 2, 3, 4$, or 5, leading to Theorem 1. Appendix A.1 contains solutions when $\mu = -1$.

$$\tau^2 + 1 = \tau - 2 + 1 = \tau - 1$$
$$\tau^3 + 1 = \tau(\tau^2) + 1 = \tau^2 - 2\tau + 1 = \tau - 2 - 2\tau + 1 = -\tau - 1$$
$$\tau^4 - 1 = (\tau^2 + 1)(\tau^2 - 1) = (\tau - 1)(\tau^2 - 1) = \tau^3 - \tau^2 - \tau + 1$$
$$\tau^5 - 1 = \tau(\tau^4) - 1 = \tau^4 - \tau^3 - \tau^2 + 2\tau - 1 = \tau^4 - \tau^3 + \tau + 1$$

Theorem 1. *Given an arbitrary $n > 1$ and assuming $\mu = 1$, one of $\tau^n \pm 1$ can be expressed by the equation below depending on the value $k = n$ (mod 4)*

$$\tau^n + S_k = \sum_{I_k}^{n-1} \tau^i - \sum_{J_k}^{n-2} \tau^i \, , \ where \tag{7}$$

k	S_k	I_k	J_k
0	-1	$i = 0 \mid i \equiv 0, 3 \pmod 4$	$i = 0 \mid i \equiv 1, 2 \pmod 4$
1	-1	$i = 0 \mid i \equiv 0, 1 \pmod 4$	$i = 3 \mid i \equiv 2, 3 \pmod 4$
2	1	$i = 0 \mid i \equiv 1, 2 \pmod 4$	$i = 0 \mid i \equiv 0, 3 \pmod 4$
3	1	$i = 3 \mid i \equiv 2, 3 \pmod 4$	$i = 0 \mid i \equiv 0, 1 \pmod 4$

Proof. Only the case $n \equiv 0$ (mod 4) is proved here, as the other cases are similar. The proof will be by induction. The base case of $n = 4$ holds as

$$\tau^4 - 1 = \tau^3 - \tau^2 - \tau + 1 \, .$$

Assume that, for an arbitrary $k > 1$ satisfying $k \equiv 0$ (mod 4), the following formula holds:

$$\tau^k = \left(\sum_{i=0 \mid i \equiv 0,3 \pmod 4}^{k-1} \tau^i \right) - \left(\sum_{i=0 \mid i \equiv 1,2 \pmod 4}^{k-2} \tau^i \right) + 1$$

Then the inductive step of $k + 4$ yields

$$\left(\sum_{i=0 \mid i \equiv 0,3 \pmod 4}^{k+3} \tau^i \right) - \left(\sum_{i=0 \mid i \equiv 1,2 \pmod 4}^{k+2} \tau^i \right) + 1$$
$$= \left(\sum_{i=0 \mid i \equiv 0,3 \pmod 4}^{k-1} \tau^i \right) - \left(\sum_{i=0 \mid i \equiv 1,2 \pmod 4}^{k-2} \tau^i \right) + 1 + \tau^{k+3} - \tau^{k+2} - \tau^{k+1} + \tau^k$$
$$= \tau^k + \tau^{k+3} - \tau^{k+2} - \tau^{k+1} + \tau^k$$
$$= \tau^k (\tau^3 - \tau^2 - \tau + 2) = \tau^k (\tau^4) = \tau^{k+4} \, .$$

Therefore, the inductive step also holds. Since the base case and the inductive step are both true, the theorem holds.   □

Now that solutions are known for (6), a generalized left-to-right algorithm for generating a low-weight signed-bit τ-adic joint representation of n integers is presented as Alg. 2. Note that Alg. 1 is the explicit case of $n = 2$. This algorithm assumes $\mu = 1$. For the $\mu = -1$ case, modifications to steps 1c, 2b, and 2c should be made corresponding to Theorem 2 in Appendix A.1.

Algorithm 2. Generating a τ-adic joint representation of n integers

---

Input: n ℓ-bit integers k_n in τ-NAF expansion
Output: Low-weight signed-bit τ-adic joint representation of k_n

1. Scan the ℓ columns $\times$ n rows from left to right. For each non-zero entry in the column, determine if that row is reducible.
   (a) Count the number of consecutive zeros (denoted C) rightward from the non-zero entry (x). Examine at most n bits. Since all k_n are n τ-NAF, note that $C \geq 1$. If $C \geq n$, then the row **is not** reducible.
   (b) Check the C columns of the n rows rightward from x. If there already exists at least one all-zero column in the next C columns, then the current non-zero column **is not** reducible.
   (c) Determine reducibility as follows:
      i. $C + 1 \equiv 2, 3 \pmod 4$. If the bits from x to the next non-zero entry (x') are of the form $x0...0x$ (same sign), the row **is** reducible.
      ii. $C + 1 \equiv 0, 1 \pmod 4$. If the bits from x to x' are of the form $x0...0\overline{x}$ (opposite sign), the row **is** reducible.
2. If all rows with non-zero entries are determined to be reducible, then perform the replacement in each of the rows to zero-out the column as follows.
   (a) Replace x with 0.
   (b) Replace the bit to the right of x with x.
   (c) For the next C bits (meaning up to and including x'), repeat the pattern $\overline{x}\overline{x}xx\overline{x}\overline{x}xx...\overline{x}\overline{x}xx$ (two x of opposite sign, two x of same sign, two x of opposite sign ...).
   (d) If C is even, replace the bit two to the left of x' with 0 (e.g., $x\overline{x}\overline{x} \rightarrow 0\overline{x}\overline{x}$).
3. If replacements were made, continue scanning again from step 1 after skipping $C + 1$ columns (start scanning again from bit x'). All of the column between are not reducible due to the consecutive bits inserted above. If replacements were not made, check the next column (rows in the current column were not reducible or already zero).

---

5   Results and Conclusions

In this section, estimated efficiency gains when using Alg. 2 are given. A comparison of the probabilities of a non-zero column given n different integers is presented in Table 2. These values correspond to the number of point additions needed (not including precomputation). Values in the Alg. 2 column are estimates from [4]; values for $n = 1, 2, 3$ have been verified by simulation, while simulation results for $n > 3$ are forthcoming.

Table 2. Probabilities of a non-zero column given n terms

n	τ-adic	τ-NAF	Alg. 2
1	.5	.3333	.3333
2	.75	.5555	.5
3	.875	.7037	.5897
4	.9375	.8025	.6425
5	.9688	.8683	.6727
6	.9844	.9122	.6999

Table 3 shows a comparison of the number of operations needed[3] for the common 163-bit standardized Koblitz curve K-163 [12] for computing the sum of n scalar multiplications using simultaneous and separate scalar multiplications (including precomputation). There are also methods for speeding up this precomputation [13].

Table 3. Average operations needed for K-163

n	Method	A	Field Mult.	Gain
2	τ-NAF (separate)	111	888	
2	Alg. 2 (simul)	84	672	**24.3 %**
3	τ-NAF (separate)	167	1336	
3	Alg. 2 (simul)	107	856	**35.9 %**

These figures suggest that using Alg. 2 leads to much lower joint weight than other hybrid methods. Because of the lower joint weight, when using simultaneous scalar multiplication the number of point additions is significantly reduced. The lower joint weight will also lead to less point additions for popular single fixed-point combing methods [4,8].

5.1 Future Work

The properties of the representation that Alg. 2 generates need to be well-defined. The average joint weights need to be proved, and the question of optimality needs to be explored. A straight analogue of the generalized JSF [4] would be nice, but it is not immediately clear if such an analogue can be constructed. In the signed-binary case, it is easy to "push up" ones. In the τ-adic case, Theorems 1 and 2 show that the same strategy is not always possible.

As Solinas mentioned [2], looking at coefficients other than $\pm1, 0$ could also be future work in this area. It is unclear what coefficients could lead to the most efficient method.

---

[3] The number of field multiplications is an estimate based on the usage of mixed coordinates (affine and López-Dahab), where the cost of one point addition is eight field multiplications.

References

1. Solinas, J.A.: Efficient arithmetic on Koblitz curves. Designs, Codes, and Cryptography **19**(2–3) (2000) 195–249
2. Solinas, J.A.: Low-weight binary representations for pairs of integers. Technical Report CORR 2001-41, Centre for Applied Cryptographic Research, University of Waterloo, Canada (2001)
3. Ciet, M., Lange, T., Sica, F., Quisquater, J.J.: Improved algorithms for efficient arithmetic on elliptic curves using fast endomorphisms. Advances in Cryptology-Eurocrypt 2003 **2656** (2003) 388–400
4. Proos, J.: Joint sparse forms and generating zero columns when combing. Technical Report CORR 2003-23, Centre for Applied Cryptographic Research, University of Waterloo, Canada (2003)
5. Grabner, P.J., Heuberger, C., Prodinger, H.: Distribution results for low-weight binary representations for pairs of integers. Theoretical Computer Science **319**(1-3) (2004) 307–331
6. Ruan, X., Katti, R.S.: Low-weight left-to-right binary signed-digit representation of n integers. In: 2004 IEEE International Symposium on Information Theory. (2004)
7. Brumley, B.B.: Efficient three-term simultaneous elliptic scalar multiplication with applications. In: Proceedings of the 11th Nordic Workshop on Secure IT Systems (NordSec 2006), Linköping, Sweden (2006) to appear.
8. Hankerson, D., Menezes, A., Vanstone, S.: Guide to elliptic curve cryptography. Springer, New York (2004)
9. Koblitz, N.: Cm-curves with good cryptographic properties. In: CRYPTO '91: Proceedings of the 11th Annual International Cryptology Conference on Advances in Cryptology, London, UK, Springer-Verlag (1992) 279–287
10. ElGamal, T.: A Public-Key Cryptosystem and a Signature Scheme Based on Discrete Logarithms. IEEE Transactions on Information Theory **IT-31**(4) (1985) 469–472
11. Straus, E.G.: Addition chains of vectors (problem 5125). American Mathematical Monthly **71** (1964) 806–808
12. NIST: Recommended elliptic curves for federal government use. Technical report, National Institute of Standards and Technology (NIST) (1999)
13. Järvinen, K.: Unified elliptic curve point addition and subtraction algorithm. Technical report, Packet Level Authentication Project, Signal Processing Laboratory, Helsinki University of Technology, Espoo, Finland (2006) Internal.

A   Appendix

A.1   The $\mu = -1$ Case

Given (3) and assuming $\mu = -1$, the following solutions to (6) are obtained for the initial cases of $n = 2, 3, 4$, or 5, leading to Theorem 2.

$$\tau^2 + 1 = -\tau - 2 + 1 = -\tau - 1$$

$$\tau^3 - 1 = \tau(\tau^2) - 1 = -\tau^2 - 2\tau - 1 = -(-\tau - 2) - 2\tau - 1 = -\tau + 1$$

$$\tau^4 - 1 = (\tau^2 + 1)(\tau^2 - 1) = (-\tau - 1)(\tau^2 - 1) = -\tau^3 - \tau^2 + \tau + 1$$

$$\tau^5 + 1 = \tau(\tau^4) + 1 = -\tau^4 - \tau^3 + \tau^2 + 2\tau + 1 = -\tau^4 - \tau^3 + \tau - 1$$

Theorem 2. *Given an arbitrary $n > 1$ and assuming $\mu = -1$, one of $\tau^n \pm 1$ can be expressed by the equation below depending on the value $k = n \pmod 4$*

$$\tau^n + S_k = \sum_{I_k}^{n-3} \tau^i - \sum_{J_k}^{n-1} \tau^i + T_k \;, \; where \tag{8}$$

k	S_k	T_k	I_k		J_k	
0	-1	0	$i = 0$	$i \equiv 0, 1 \pmod 4$	$i = 2$	$i \equiv 2, 3 \pmod 4$
1	1	$-\tau^2$	$i = 1$	$i \equiv 1, 2 \pmod 4$	$i = 0$	$i \equiv 0, 3 \pmod 4$
2	1	0	$i = 2$	$i \equiv 2, 3 \pmod 4$	$i = 0$	$i \equiv 0, 1 \pmod 4$
3	-1	τ^2	$i = 0$	$i \equiv 0, 3 \pmod 4$	$i = 1$	$i \equiv 1, 2 \pmod 4$

The proofs are similar to those of Theorem 1.

Universal Designated Verifier Signature Without Delegatability

Xinyi Huang, Willy Susilo, Yi Mu, and Wei Wu

Center for Information Security Research
School of Information Technology and Computer Science
University of Wollongong
Wollongong 2522, Australia
{xh068, wsusilo, ymu}@uow.edu.au

Abstract. In Asiacrypt 2003, the notion of the universal designated verifier signature (UDVS) was put forth by Steinfeld, Bull, Wang and Pieprzyk. In the new paradigm, *any* signature holder (not necessarily the signer) can designate the standard signature to any desired designated verifier (using the verifier's public key), such that *only* the designated verifier will believe that the signature holder holds a valid standard signature, and hence, believe that the signer has indeed signed the message. When the signature holder is the *signer* himself, the UDVS scheme can be considered as a designated verifier signature (DVS) which was proposed by Jakobsson, Sako and Impagliazzo in Eurocrypt 1996. In the recent paper published in ICALP 2005, Lipmaa, Wang and Bao introduced a new security property, called "non-delegatability", as an essential property of (universal) designated verifier signature. Subsequently, Li, Lipmaa and Pei used this new property to "attack" four designated verifier signatures in ICICS 2005 and showed that *none* of them satisfy the required property. To date, there is no UDVS scheme that does not suffer from the delegatability problem. In this paper, we propose the *first* provably secure UDVS without delegatability, which can also be regarded as another DVS scheme *without* delegatability. We also refine the models of the UDVS schemes and introduce the notion of the strong universal designated verifier signature (SUDVS). We believe that the model itself is of an independent interest.

Keywords: Universal Designated Verifier Signatures, Designated Verifier Signatures, Non-delegatability, Bilinear Pairings.

1 Introduction

Digital signatures, introduced in the pioneering paper of Diffie and Hellman [3], allow a signer with a secret key to sign messages such that anyone with access to the corresponding public key can verify the authenticity of the message. A signature verifier can convince any third party about this fact by presenting a digital signature on a message. The ease of copying and transmitting digital signatures in some implementations is of great convenience, but it is unsuitable for many other applications in the real world where a verifier does not want to

P. Ning, S. Qing, and N. Li (Eds.): ICICS 2006, LNCS 4307, pp. 479–498, 2006.

present the publicly verifiable signatures to other parties, such as certificates for hospital records, income summary, etc.

The notion of the *designated verifier signature* (DVS) was proposed by Jakobsson, Sako and Impagliazzo in [4]. In a DVS, the signature provides authentication of a message *without* providing a non-repudiation property of traditional signatures. A DVS can be used to convince a single third party, i.e. the designated verifier, and *only* the designated verifier who can be convinced about its validity or invalidity. This is due to the fact that the designated verifier can always create a signature intended for himself that is indistinguishable from an original signature. In the same paper, Jakobsson, Sako and Impagliazzo also introduced a stronger version of designated verifier signatures called *strong designated verifier signatures* (SDVS). In this concept, *no third party* can even verify the designated verifier signature as the designated verifier's secret key is *required* during the verification phase. Saeednia, Kremer and Markowitch firstly formalized the notion of strong DVS [15] and proposed an efficient scheme in the same paper. Some other recent papers discussing both DVS and SDVS include [5,6,8,9,10].

Universal designated verifier signature, which was introduced by Steinfeld, Bull, Wang and Pieprzyk [16] in Asiacrypt 2003, is a variant of DVS, in the sense that, given a standard signature from the signer, a signature holder (not necessarily the signer) can convert it to a UDVS which is designated to a verifier, such that only this designated verifier can believe that the message has been signed by the signer. However, any other third party cannot believe it since this verifier can use his secret key to create a valid UDVS which is designated to himself. Thus, one cannot distinguish whether a UDVS is created by the signature holder or the designated verifier himself. When the signature holder and the signer are the same user, a universal designated signature will form a designated verifier signature. Therefore, UDVS can be viewed as an application of general designated verifier signatures where the signer designates a non-interactive proof statement to a designated verifier.

From BLS short signature[2], Steinfeld, Bull, Wang and Pieprzyk [16] proposed the first UDVS scheme in Asiacrypt 2003. Steinfeld, Wang and Pieprzyk continued to show how to obtain a UDVS scheme from the Schnorr/RSA signature scheme in PKC 2004 [17]. Zhang, Susilo, Mu and Chen [21] extended this notion to the Identity-based setting and proposed two Identity-based UDVS schemes. The first UDVS scheme without random oracle was proposed by Zhang, Furukawa and Imai [20] in ACNS 2005, where a variant of BB's [1] short signature scheme without random oracle is used as the building block. Very recently, Vergnaud proposed two extensions of pairing-based signatures into universal designated verifier signatures [19].

Recently, Lipmaa, Wang and Bao introduced a new security notion for DVS schemes called *non-delegatability* [10]. They argued that this notion is necessary in many applications such as hypothetical e-voting protocol provided in [10]. They also showed that Saeednia-Kremer-Markowitch's scheme [15], Steinfeld-Bull-Wang-Pieprzyk's scheme [16] and Steinfeld-Wang-Pieprzyk's [17] are delegatable. In ICICS 2005, Li, Lipmaa and Pei presented an "attack" to another four schemes, namely Susilo-Zhang-Mu's scheme [18], Ng-Susilo-Mu's scheme [11], Laguillaumie-Vergnaud's scheme [6] and Zhang-Furukawa-Imai's scheme [20], and show that they are delegatable [9]. Together with the analysis in [10] and [9], there are only two known provably secure DVS schemes without delegatability: one is the scheme proposed in [4] and the other one is in [10]. Nonetheless, there is *no* provably secure UDVS without delegatability. Therefore, whether the delegatability is an inherent problem of UDVS is an open research problem.

Our Contribution

In this paper, we firstly show that the two UDVS schemes which are very recently proposed by Vergnaud in ICALP 2006 [19] are delegatable. Then we refine the definitions of the UDVS and introduce the notion of the strong universal designated verifier signature (SUDVS). We proceed by proposing the *first* construction of non-delegatable UDVS scheme with formal security analysis in the random oracle model.

Organization of The Paper

In the next section, we will review some preliminaries required throughout the paper. In Section 3, we review the definition of the delegatability by analyzing two UDVS schemes which are very recently proposed in ICALP 2006. We provide the security models of UDVS in Section 4. In Section 5, we propose the *first* construction of UDVS without delegatabiity together with its security analysis. Finally, Section 6 concludes this paper.

2   Preliminaries

In this section, we will review some fundamental backgrounds used throughout this paper, namely bilinear pairing, complexity assumptions and the formal models of the universal designated verifier signature.

2.1   Bilinear Pairing

Let $\mathbb{G}_1$ and $\mathbb{G}_T$ be two groups of prime order p and let g be a generator of $\mathbb{G}_1$. The map $e : \mathbb{G}_1 \times \mathbb{G}_1 \to \mathbb{G}_T$ is said to be an admissible bilinear pairing if the following three conditions hold true:

- e is bilinear, i.e. $e(g^a, g^b) = e(g, g)^{ab}$ for all $a, b \in \mathbb{Z}_p$.
- e is non-degenerate, i.e. $e(g, g) \neq 1_{\mathbb{G}_T}$.
- e is efficiently computable.

We say that $(\mathbb{G}_1, \mathbb{G}_T)$ are bilinear groups if there exists the bilinear pairing $e : \mathbb{G}_1 \times \mathbb{G}_1 \to \mathbb{G}_T$ as above, and e, and the group action in $\mathbb{G}_1$ and $\mathbb{G}_T$ can be computed efficiently. See [2] for more details on the construction of such pairings.

2.2   Complexity Assumptions

Definition 1. Computational Diffie Hellman(CDH) Problem in $\mathbb{G}_1$
Given $g, g^a, g^b \in \mathbb{G}_1$ for some unknown $a, b \in \mathbb{Z}_p$, compute $g^{ab} \in \mathbb{G}_1$.

The probability that a polynomially bounded algorithm $\mathcal{A}$ can solve the CDH problem is defined as:

$$Succ_{\mathcal{A},\mathbb{G}_1}^{CDH} = \Pr[g^{ab} \leftarrow \mathcal{A}(\mathbb{G}_1, g, g^a, g^b)].$$

Definition 2. Computational Diffie-Hellman(CDH) Assumption in $\mathbb{G}_1$
Given $g, g^a, g^b \in \mathbb{G}_1$ for some unknown $a, b \in \mathbb{Z}_p$, $Succ_{\mathcal{A},\mathbb{G}_1}^{CDH}$ is negligible.

2.3   Formal Model of Universal Designated Verifier Signature

There are three parties in the universal designated verifier signature: the Signer S, the Signature Holder SH and the Verifier V where

1. S is the one who uses his/her secret key to generate a standard signature σ_{SS} on the message m.
2. SH is the one who owns S's standard signature σ_{SS} on the message m and will generate a universal designated verifier signature σ_{DV} to convince V that S has signed the message m and he owns σ_{SS}.
3. V is the designated verifier of the signature σ_{DV} and is convinced that S has signed the message m. However, V cannot convince anyone else that S has signed the message m, even V sharing his secret key with the one who wants to be convinced.

The universal designated verifier signature scheme UDVS consists of the following algorithms: (CPG, KG, SS, SV,DS, $\overline{DS}$, DV)

1. Common Parameter Generation CPG: a probabilistic algorithm, on input a security parameter k, outputs a string $cp \leftarrow CPG(k)$ which denotes the common scheme parameters.
2. Key Generation KG: a probabilistic algorithm, on input a common parameter cp, outputs a secret/public key-pair $(sk, pk) \leftarrow KG(cp)$ for the signer S and verifier V, respectively.
3. Standard Signing SS: a probabilistic (deterministic) algorithm, on input the common parameter cp, S's secret key sk_s and the message m, outputs S's standard signature $\sigma_{SS} \leftarrow SS(cp, sk_s, m)$.
4. Standard Verification SV: a deterministic algorithm, on input the common parameter cp, S's public key pk_s, the signed message m and S's standard signature σ_{SS}, outputs verification decision $d \in \{Acc, Rej\}$ where $\{Acc, Rej\} \leftarrow SV(cp, pk_s, m, \sigma_{SS})$.
5. Designation by Signature Holder DS: a probabilistic (deterministic) algorithm, on input the common parameters cp, S's public key pk_s, V's public key pk_v, S's standard signature σ_{SS} of the message m, outputs the designated verifier (DV) signature $\sigma_{DV} \leftarrow DS(cp, pk_s, pk_v, \sigma_{SS}, m)$.
6. Simulation by Verifier $\overline{DS}$: a probabilistic (deterministic) algorithm, on input the common parameter cp, S's public key pk_s, V's secret key sk_v and the message m, outputs the designated verifier(DV) signature $\overline{\sigma_{DV}} \leftarrow \overline{DS}(cp, pk_s, sk_v, m)$ which is designated to himself.

7. Designation Verification DV: a deterministic algorithm, on input the common parameter cp, S's public key pk_s, V's secret/public key pair (sk_v, pk_v), the signed message m and the DV signature σ_{DV}, outputs the verification decision $d \in \{Acc, Rej\}$ where $\{Acc, Rej\} \leftarrow DV(cp, pk_s, sk_v, pk_v, m, \sigma_{DV})$.

Consistency:

In addition to the above algorithms, we also require three obvious consistency of the **UDVS** schemes.

1. SV Consistency: this property requires that the standard signature produced by the SS algorithm is accepted as a valid signature by the SV algorithm, i.e. $\Pr[SV(cp, pk_s, m, SS(cp, sk_s, m)) = Acc] = 1$
2. DV Consistency of DS: this property requires that the DV signature produced by the DS algorithm is accepted as a valid signature by the DV algorithm, i.e.

$$\Pr[DV(cp, pk_s, sk_v, pk_v, m, DS(cp, pk_s, pk_v, \sigma_{SS}, m)) = Acc] = 1.$$

3. DV Consistency of $\overline{DS}$: this property requires that the DV signature produced by the $\overline{DS}$ algorithm is accepted as a valid signature by the DV algorithm, i.e.

$$\Pr[DV(cp, pk_s, sk_v, pk_v, m, \overline{DS}(cp, pk_s, sk_v, m)) = Acc] = 1.$$

3 Delegatability of Universal Designated Verifier Signature Schemes

Let $(sk_s, pk_s), (sk_v, pk_v)$ denote the secret/public key pairs of the signer and the designated verifier, respectively. Delegatability of a UDVS [10] refers the case where the signer *delegates* the UDVS signing rights to $\mathcal{A}$ by disclosing some side information $y_{sv} = f_s(sk_s, pk_v)$ that will help $\mathcal{A}$ to generate valid signatures. Analogously, the designated verifier might delegate this signing rights by simulating capability by disclosing some side information $y_{sv'} = f_v(sk_v, pk_s)$. The implication of the delegatability of UDVS schemes will confuse the designated verifier, when he/she sees a valid universal designated verifier signature that is not generated by himself/herself, then he/she can only conclude that the signature is generated by someone who knows either y_{sv} or $y_{sv'}$. To explain the delegatability more clearly, we analyze the following two UDVS schemes which are recently proposed by Vergnaud [19] in ICALP 2006. For the delegatability of other UDVS schemes [11,16,17,20], please refer to [9,10].

3.1 Vergnaud's UDVS-BB [19]

In [19], the author proposed two UDVS schemes which are designed for the devices with constrained computation capabilities since the SS and DS algorithms are pairing-free. The first UDVS scheme in [19] combines the BB short signature scheme without random oracle [1] to obtain a UDVS scheme without random oracle. The UDVS-BB [19] consists of the following algorithms. (We rewrite their scheme with different notations in order to keep the consistence of the whole paper)

CPG: Let $(\mathbb{G}_1, \mathbb{G}_T)$ be a bilinear groups where $|\mathbb{G}_1| = |\mathbb{G}_T| = p$, k be the system security number and g be the generator of $\mathbb{G}_1$. e denotes the bilinear pairing $\mathbb{G}_1 \times \mathbb{G}_1 \rightarrow \mathbb{G}_T$. The message space $D_{\mathcal{M}} = \mathbb{Z}_p^*$. The system parameter $cp = \{\mathbb{G}_1, \mathbb{G}_T, p, k, e, g, D_{\mathcal{M}}\}$ which is shared by all the users in the system.

KG: The Signer S picks two secret numbers $u_a, v_a \in_R \mathbb{Z}_p^*$ and sets the secret key $sk_s = (u_a, v_a)$. Then S computes the public key $pk_s = (U_a, V_a) = (g^{u_a}, g^{v_a})$. Similarly, the verifier V's secret/public key-pair is $sk_v = (u_b, v_b), pk_v = (U_b, V_b) = (g^{u_b}, g^{v_b})$ where u_b, v_b are randomly chosen in $\mathbb{Z}_q^*$.

SS: For a message $m \in D_{\mathcal{M}}$ to be signed, S chooses $r \in \mathbb{Z}_p^*$ and computes the standard signature $\sigma_{\mathsf{SS}} = (\sigma_{\mathsf{SS}_1}, \sigma_{\mathsf{SS}_2}) = (r, g^{\frac{1}{u_a + m + v_a r}})$.

SV: Given a message m, the standard signature $\sigma_{\mathsf{SS}} = (\sigma_{\mathsf{SS}_1}, \sigma_{\mathsf{SS}_2})$ and S's public key pk_s, one can check whether $e(\sigma_{\mathsf{SS}_2}, U_a \cdot g^m \cdot V_a^{\sigma_{\mathsf{SS}_1}}) \overset{?}{=} e(g, g)$. If the equality holds, outputs Acc, otherwise, Rej.

DS: Given the standard signature signature $\sigma_{\mathsf{SS}} = (\sigma_{\mathsf{SS}_1}, \sigma_{\mathsf{SS}_2}) = (r, g^{\frac{1}{u_a + m + v_a r}})$ and the verifier's public key pk_v, the signature holder SH selects $t \in_R \mathbb{Z}_p^*$ and computes $Q_1 = g^{\frac{t}{u_a + m + v_a r}}$, $Q_2 = (U_b)^t$ and $Q_3 = g^t$. The signature holder sends the universal designated verifier signature $\sigma_{DV} = (r, Q_1, Q_2, Q_3)$ to the verifier V.

$\overline{\mathrm{DS}}$: Given the signer's public key pk_s and the message m, the verifier V chooses $t, r \in_R \mathbb{Z}_p^*$ and computes $R = (U_a \cdot g^m \cdot V_a^r)^t$. The universal designated verifier signature generated by the verifier is $\overline{\sigma_{DV}} = (r, Q_1, Q_2, Q_3)$ where $Q_1 = g^t$, $Q_2 = R^{u_b}$ and $Q_3 = R$.

DV: Given the designated verifier signature (r, Q_1, Q_2, Q_3), the verifier checks whether $e(Q_1, U_a \cdot g^m \cdot V_a^r) \overset{?}{=} e(Q_3, g)$ and $e(Q_3, g^{u_b}) \overset{?}{=} e(Q_2, g)$. If both equalities hold, output Acc, otherwise, Rej.

Delegatability:

We will show that the knowledge of $y_{sv} := (g^{u_b u_a}, g^{u_b v_a})$ is sufficient to generate a valid signature of Vergnaud's UDVS-BB scheme. Given a message m and y_{sv}, anyone can choose $t, r \in_R \mathbb{Z}_q^*$ and compute $R = (U_a \cdot g^m \cdot V_a^r)^t$. Then he computes $Q_1 = g^t$, $Q_2 = (g^{u_b u_a} \cdot U_b^m \cdot (g^{u_b v_a})^r)^t$ and $Q_3 = R$. Note that (r, Q_1, Q_2, Q_3) is a valid signature of Vergnaud's UDVS-BB since

$$
\begin{aligned}
e(Q_1, U_a \cdot g^m \cdot V_a^r) &= e(g^t, U_a \cdot g^m \cdot V_a^r) \\
&= e(g^{t(u_a + m + rv_a)}, g) = e((U_a \cdot g^m \cdot V_a^r)^t, g) \\
&= e(R, g) = e(Q_3, g).
\end{aligned}
$$

and

$$
\begin{aligned}
e(Q_3, g^{u_b}) &= e(R, g^{u_b}) = e(R^{u_b}, g) \\
&= e((U_a \cdot g^m \cdot V_a^r)^{tu_b}, g) \\
&= e((g^{u_a u_b} \cdot U_b^m \cdot (g^{u_b v_a})^r)^t, g) = e(Q_2, g).
\end{aligned}
$$

Note that both the signer and the verifier can compute y_{sv}. The signer can use his secret key u_a, v_a to compute $y_{sv} = ((U_b)^{u_a}, U_b^{v_a})$ where U_b is a part of the verifier's public key $pk_v = (U_b, V_b)$. Similarly, the verifier also can use his secret key (u_b, v_b) to compute $y_{sv} = (U_a^{u_b}, V_a^{u_b})$ where (U_a, V_a) is the public key of the signer. Therefore, a valid message signature pair $(m, \sigma_{\mathsf{DV}})$ of UDVS-BB can not convince the verifier that S has signed this message.

3.2   Vergnaud's UDVS-BLS [19]

The seconde UDVS scheme UDVS-BLS in [19] combines the BLS short signature [2] to obtain a UDVS with shorter signature length compared with UDVS-BB. It consists of the following algorithms. (We rewrite their scheme with different notations in order to keep the consistence of the whole paper)

CPG: Let $(\mathbb{G}_1, \mathbb{G}_T)$ be a bilinear groups where $|\mathbb{G}_1| = |\mathbb{G}_T| = p$, k be the system security number and g be the generator of $\mathbb{G}_1$. e denotes the bilinear pairing $\mathbb{G}_1 \times \mathbb{G}_1 \to \mathbb{G}_T$. Let $h : \{0,1\}^* \to \mathbb{G}_1^*$ be a secure cryptographic hash function. The message space $D_{\mathcal{M}} = \{0,1\}^*$. The system parameter $cp = \{\mathbb{G}_1, \mathbb{G}_T, p, k, e, h, D_{\mathcal{M}}\}$ which is shared by all the users in the system.

KG: The Signer S picks a secret value $x_s \in_R \mathbb{Z}_p^*$ and sets the secret key $sk_s = x_s$. Then, S computes the public key $pk_s = g^{x_s}$. Similarly, the verifier V's secret/public key-pair is $(sk_v, pk_v) = (x_v, g^{x_v})$ where x_v is randomly chosen in $\mathbb{Z}_p^*$.

SS: For a message m to be signed, S computes the standard signature $\sigma_{\mathsf{SS}} = h(m)^{sk_s} \in \mathbb{G}_1$.

SV: Given a message m, the standard signature σ_{SS} and S's public key pk_s, one can check the equation $e(\sigma_{\mathsf{SS}}, g) \stackrel{?}{=} e(h(m), pk_s)$. If the equality holds, outputs Acc, otherwise, Rej.

DS: Given the standard signature signature σ_{SS} and the verifier's public key pk_v, the signature holder SH selects $t \in_R \mathbb{Z}_p^*$ and computes $Q_1 = \sigma_{\mathsf{SS}}^t$ and $Q_2 = pk_v^{t^{-1}}$. Then SH sends the universal designated verifier signature $\sigma_{DV} = (Q_1, Q_2)$ to the verifier V.

$\overline{\mathrm{DS}}$: Given the signer's public key pk_s and the message m, the verifier V chooses $t \in_R \mathbb{Z}_p^*$ and computes $Q_1 = h(m)^{t^{-1}}$ and $Q_2 = (pk_s^{sk_v})^t$ The universal designated verifier signature generated by the verifier is $\overline{\sigma_{DV}} = (Q_1, Q_2)$.

DV: Given the designated verifier signature (Q_1, Q_2), the verifier checks whether $e(Q_1, Q_2) \stackrel{?}{=} e(h(m), pk_s^{sk_v})$. If the equality holds, outputs Acc, otherwise, Rej.

Delegatability:

We will show that the knowledge of $y_{sv} := g^{sk_s sk_v}$ is sufficient to generate a valid signature of Vergnaud's UDVS-BLS. Given a message m and y_{sv}, anyone can choose $t \in_R \mathbb{Z}_p^*$ and compute $Q_1 = h(m)^t, Q_2 = y_{sv}^{t^{-1}}$. Note that (Q_1, Q_2) is a valid signature of Vergnaud's UDVS-BLS since $e(Q_1, Q_2) = e(h(m)^t, y_{sv}^{t^{-1}}) = e(h(m), g^{sk_s sk_v}) = e(h(m), pk_s^{sk_v})$.

Note that both the signer and the verifier can compute y_{sv}. The signer can use his secret key sk_s to compute $y_{sv} = pk_v^{sk_s}$. Similarly, the verifier also can use his secret key sk_v to compute $y_{sv} = pk_s^{sk_v}$. Therefore, a valid message signature pair (m, σ_{DV}) of UDVS-BLS can not convince the verifier that the signature holder holds the signer S's signature on this message.

4   Security Models of Universal Designated Verifier Signature

In this section, we will define the security models of our UDVS scheme. Compared with the known security models of UDVS defined in [16,17,20], an important refinement of our model is that we allow the adversaries to adaptively corrupt the users in the system and adaptively choose the target signer and the designated verifier. In the defined models, we allow adversaries to adaptively submit Key Register (KR) queries to register the users in the system and obtain all the public keys he has registered. He can also submit the SS queries to obtain the standard signature of the message under the signer he chooses. In addition, the adversary can choose the message m, the signer S and the verifier V and submit (m, S, V) as DS or $\overline{\text{DS}}$ query to obtain the designated verifier signature. If necessary, the adversary can also submit DV queries to decide whether σ_{DV} is a valid designated verifier signature under the signer S and the verifier V^1. We also allow the adversary to submit SecretKey (SK) queries adaptively to obtain the secret keys of some users, thus the adversaries can corrupt some users and adaptively choose the target signer and designated verifier, which reflects more essence of real world adversaries.

Unforgeability
Actually, there are two types of unforgeability properties that can be used [16]. The first property, *standard signature unforgeability* (SS-Unforgeability), is just the usual existential unforgeability notion under chosen message attacker [7] for the standard signature scheme SS, which states that no one should be able to forge a standard signature of the signer S. The second property, *designated verifier signature unforgeability* (DV-Unforgeability), requires that it is difficult for an attacker to forge a DV signature σ_{DV}^* on a new message m^*, such that the pair (M^*, σ_{DV}^*) passes the DV algorithm with respect to a signer's public key pk_s^* and a designated verifier's public key pk_v^*, which states that for any message, an adversary without the standard signature should not be able to convince a designated verifier of holding such a standard signature. DV-Unforgeability always implies the SS-Unforgeability [16]. Thus, it is enough to consider only DV-Unforgeability. The existential unforgeability of UDVS is defined via the following game between the simulator S and the adaptively chosen message and chosen public key adversary $\mathcal{F}_{EUF,\ UDVS}^{CMA,\ CPKA}$:

---

[1] Such queries are only needed when the execution of DV algorithm needs the secret key of the verifier. Otherwise, $\mathcal{F}$ can use the public keys of signer S and the verifier V to verify whether a σ_{DV} is valid.

- Setup: The simulator S runs the CPG to generate the common parameter cp. He then returns cp to $\mathcal{F}$.
- Key Register (KR) queries: $\mathcal{F}$ can register for the users in the system. In response. S runs the KG algorithm to generate the secret/public key pair for this user. S returns the public key to $\mathcal{F}$.
- SS queries: $\mathcal{F}$ can ask the standard signature of the message m under the public key pk_s he chooses. In response, S runs the SS algorithm to generate the signature σ_{SS} and returns to $\mathcal{F}$ as the answer.
- DS queries: $\mathcal{F}$ can ask the universal designated verifier signature σ_{DV} which is generated by the algorithm DS on the message m under the public keys (pk_s, pk_v), where pk_s denotes the signer and pk_v denotes the verifier chosen by $\mathcal{F}$. In response, S firstly runs SS to generate the standard signature σ_{SS} on this message. Then S runs DS algorithm to generate the universal designated verifier signature σ_{DV}. S returns σ_{DV} to $\mathcal{F}$ as the answer.
- $\overline{DS}$ queries: $\mathcal{F}$ can ask the designated verifier signature $\overline{\sigma_{DV}}$ which is generated by the algorithm $\overline{DS}$ on the message m and under the public keys (pk_s, pk_v), where pk_s denotes the signer and pk_v denotes the verifier chosen by $\mathcal{F}$. In response, S runs $\overline{DS}$ algorithm to obtain the designated verifier signature $\overline{\sigma_{DV}}$. S then returns $\overline{\sigma_{DV}}$ to $\mathcal{F}$ as the answer.
- DV queries: $\mathcal{F}$ can ask whether σ_{DV} is a valid universal designated verifier signature on the message m under the public keys (pk_s, pk_v), where pk_s denotes the signer and pk_v denotes the verifier chosen by $\mathcal{F}$. In response, S will run DV algorithm and return the decision $d \in \{Acc, Rej\}$ to $\mathcal{F}$.
- SK queries: $\mathcal{F}$ can request the secret key of the public key pk. In response, S returns corresponding secret key sk to $\mathcal{F}$.

We say $\mathcal{F}$ wins the game if $\mathcal{F}$ outputs a forged messgae/signature pair(m^*, σ_{DV}^*) under the public keys (pk_s^*, pk_v^*) if:

1. $Acc \leftarrow DV(cp, pk_s^*, sk_v^*, pk_v^*, m^*, \sigma_{DV}^*)$.
2. (m^*, pk_s^*) has never been submitted as one of the SS queries.
3. (m^*, pk_s^*, pk_v^*) has never been submitted as one of the DS or $\overline{DS}$ queries.
4. Neither pk_s^* nor pk_v^* has been submitted as one of the SK queries.

The success probability of an adaptively chosen message and chosen public key attacker $\mathcal{F}$ wins the above game is defined as Succ $\mathcal{F}_{EUF, \ UDVS}^{CMA, \ CPKA}$.

Definition 3. *We say* $\mathcal{F}_{EUF, \ UDVS}^{CMA, \ CPKA}$ *can* $(t, q_H, q_{KR}, q_{SS}, q_{DS}, q_{\overline{DS}}, q_{DV}, q_{SK}, \varepsilon)$-*break the* **UDVS** *scheme if* $\mathcal{F}_{EUF, \ DVS}^{CMA, \ CPKA}$ *runs in time at most* t, *makes at most* q_H *queries to the random oracle,* q_{KR} *key registration queries,* q_{SS} SS *queries,* q_{DS} DS *queries,* $q_{\overline{DS}}$ $\overline{DS}$ *queries,* q_{DV} DV *queries,* q_{SK} SK *queries and* Succ $\mathcal{F}_{EUF, \ UDVS}^{CMA, \ CPKA}$ *is at least* ε.

Non-delegatability

A universal designated verifier signature can be regarded as a kind of non-interactive system of proofs of knowledge of the signer S's standard signature

σ_{SS} or the verifier's secret key sk_v. Thus, both the signature holder and the designated verifier can generate this proof. However, as pointed out by Lipmaa, Wang and Bao in [10], the definition of the unforgeability does not cover the case when the signer (the verifier) is dishonest. Namely, without disclosing $sk_s(sk_v)$, the signer(verifier) can delegate the signing rights to some party $\mathcal{A}$ by disclosing some "side information" which helps the latter to produce valid universal designated verifier signatures on any message, as we have shown in Section 3. One can see a lot of concrete instances in [9,10].

Definition 4. *Let* $(sk_s, pk_s), (sk_v, pk_v)$ *be the secret/public key-pair of signer* S *and verifier* V. *Let* $\mathcal{A}$ *be an algorithm, who does not necessarily know the signer's* SS *signature* σ_{SS} *of the message* m *or the secret key* sk_v, *can produce a valid UDVS on the message* m *with non-negligible probability* ε, *we say that a* **UDVS** *scheme is* (τ, κ) *non-delegatable if in time* τ, *there exists a knowledge extractor* $\mathcal{K}$ *who can use* $\mathcal{A}$ *to obtain* σ_{SS} *or* sk_v *with probability greater than* κ.

Non-transferability

Roughly speaking, the Non-Transferability of UDVS requires that: (1) Only the designated verifier can be convinced by the UDVS, even if he shares all the secret information with entities that want get convinced. (2) Even an entity can see many universal designated verifier signatures σ_{DV}'s on the same message m but with different designated verifiers, which is generated by the signature holder using the same standard signature σ_{SS}, he can not be convinced that the signer has signed on this message. In other words, universal designated verifier signatures of the message m with different designated verifiers must be independent. We define the existential Non-Transferability of the UDVS against adaptively chosen message and chosen public key distinguisher $\mathcal{D}_{TRANS,\ UDVS}^{CMA,\ CPKA}$ via the game with the simulator $\mathcal{S}$. The model is divided into two phases.

- Phase 1: $\mathcal{D}$ can submit KR, SS, DS, $\overline{DS}$, DV and SK queries as defined in the model of **Unforgeability**, the simulator $\mathcal{S}$ responses to these queries as same as defined in the **Unforgeability** model.
- Challenge: When the distinguisher $\mathcal{D}$ decides the first phase is over, he submits m^*, pk_s^*, pk_v^* to $\mathcal{S}$ as the challenge with the constraints that
  1. pk_s^* can not be submitted as one of the SK queries during Phase 1.
  2. (m^*, pk_s^*) can not be submitted as one of the SS queries during Phase 1.
  3. (m^*, pk_s^*, pk_v^*) has never been submitted as one of the DS during Phase 1.
  As response, the simulator $\mathcal{S}$ chooses a random bit $b \in \{0, 1\}$. If $b = 0$, $\mathcal{S}$ runs DS algorithm and returns σ_{DV} to $\mathcal{D}$. Otherwise $b = 1$, $\mathcal{S}$ runs $\overline{DS}$ algorithm and returns $\overline{\sigma_{DV}}$ to $\mathcal{D}$.
- Phase 2: On receiving the challenging signature, the distinguisher can submit more queries except that:
  1. pk_s^* can not be submitted as one of the SK queries during Phase 1.
  2. (m^*, pk_s^*) can not be submitted as one of the SS queries during Phase 1.
  3. (m^*, pk_s^*, pk_v^*) has never been submitted as one of the DS during Phase 1.

– Guessing: Finally, the distinguisher $\mathcal{D}$ outputs a guess b'. The adversary wins the game if $b = b'$.

The advantage of an adaptively chosen message and chosen public key distinguisher $\mathcal{D}$ has in the above game is defined as $\mathsf{Adv}\ \mathcal{D}_{TRANS,\ UDVS}^{CMA,\ CPKA} = |\Pr[b' = b] - 1/2|$.

Definition 5. *We say a* **UDVS** *scheme is Non-Transferable against a* $(t, q_H, q_{KR}, q_{SS}, q_{DS}, q_{\overline{DS}}, q_{DV}, q_{SK})$ *adaptively chosen message and chosen public key distinguisher* $\mathcal{D}_{TRANS,\ UDVS}^{CMA,\ CPKA}$ *if* $\mathsf{Adv}\ \mathcal{D}_{TRANS,\ UDVS}^{CMA,\ CPKA}$ *is negligible after making at most* q_H *queries to the random oracle,* q_{KR} *key registration queries,* q_{SS} SS *queries,* q_{DS} DS *queries,* $q_{\overline{DS}}$ $\overline{DS}$ *queries,* q_{DV} DV *queries and* q_{SK} SK *queries in time* t.

4.1 Strong Universal Designated Verifier Signature: Privacy of Signer

Given a UDVS scheme satisfies the security requirements defined above, one can not decide who generates the universal designated verifier signature. Both the signature holder SH and the designated verifier V can generate valid universal designated verifier signatures. However, in order to protect the privacy of the signer S in some cases as described in [4], the algorithm DV cannot be executed publicly. Therefore, an additional strong notion: **Privacy of Signer** is introduced into the universal designated verifier signature.

Informally speaking, this property requires that given a message m and a V designated UDVS σ_{DV}, without the secret keys of the designated verifier V and the possible two original signers S_0, S_1, one can not decide which original signer S_0 or S_1 generates the standard signature σ_{SS}. It is defined using the following games between the distinguisher $\mathcal{D}_{Privacy, SUDVS}^{CMA, CPKA}$ and the simulator $\mathcal{S}$:

– Phase 1: $\mathcal{D}$ can submit KR, SS, DS, $\overline{DS}$, DV and SK queries as defined in the model of **Unforgeability**, the simulator $\mathcal{S}$ responds to these queries in the same way as defined in the model of **Unforgeability**.
– Challenge: When the distinguisher $\mathcal{D}$ decides the first phase is over, he submits $(m^*, pk_{s_0}^*, pk_{s_1}^*, pk_v^*)$ to $\mathcal{S}$ as the challenge with the constraints that
  1. Neither $pk_{s_0}^*, pk_{s_1}^*$ nor pk_v^* has been submitted as one of the SK queries during Phase 1.
  2. Neither $(m^*, pk_{s_0}^*)$ nor $(m^*, pk_{s_1}^*)$ has been submitted as one of the SS queries during Phase 1.
  3. Neither $(m^*, pk_{s_0}^*, pk_v^*)$ nor $(m^*, pk_{s_1}^*, pk_v^*)$ has been submitted as one of DS and $\overline{DS}$ queries during Phase 1.

  In response, the simulator $\mathcal{S}$ chooses a random bit $b \in \{0, 1\}$. If $b = 0$, $\mathcal{S}$ firstly runs $SS(m, sk_{s_0}^*)$ to obtain S_0's standard signature σ_{SS_0} on message m^*, then he runs DS algorithm and sets $\sigma_{DV}^* = \sigma_{DV_0}$. Otherwise $b = 1$, $\mathcal{S}$ runs $SS(m, sk_{s_1}^*)$ to obtain S_1's standard signature σ_{SS_1} on message m^*, then he runs $\overline{DS}$ algorithm and sets $\sigma_{DV}^* = \sigma_{DV_1}$.

- **Phase 2:** On receiving the challenging signature σ_{DV}^*, the distinguisher can submit more queries except that:
  1. $pk_{s_0}^*, pk_{s_1}^*$ and pk_v^* can not be submitted as one of the SK queries during Phase 2.
  2. $(m^*, pk_{s_0}^*)$ and $(m^*, pk_{s_1}^*)$ can not be submitted as one of the SS queries during Phase 2.
  3. $(m^*, pk_{s_0}^*, pk_v^*)$ and $(m^*, pk_{s_1}^*, pk_v^*)$ can not be submitted as one of the DS or $\overline{\mathsf{DS}}$ queries during Phase 2.
  4. $(m^*, \sigma_{\mathsf{DV}}^*, pk_{s_0}^*, pk_v^*)$ and $(m^*, \sigma_{\mathsf{DV}}^*, pk_{s_1}^*, pk_v^*)$ can not be submitted as one of the DV queries during Phase 2.
- **Guessing:** Finally, the distinguisher $\mathcal{D}$ outputs a guess b'. The adversary wins the game if $b = b'$.

The advantage of an adaptively chosen message and chosen public key distinguisher $\mathcal{D}$ has in the above game is defined as $\mathsf{Adv}\ \mathcal{D}_{Privacy,\ UDVS}^{CMA,\ CPKA} = |\Pr[b' = b] - 1/2|$.

Definition 6. *We say a* **UDVS** *scheme satisfies the property: privacy of signer against a* $(t, q_H, q_{KR}, q_{SS}, q_{DS}, q_{\overline{DS}}, q_{DV}, q_{SK})$ *adaptively chosen message and chosen public key distinguisher* $\mathcal{D}_{Privacy,\ UDVS}^{CMA,\ CPKA}$ *if* $\mathsf{Adv}\ \mathcal{D}_{Privacy,\ UDVS}^{CMA,\ CPKA}$ *is negligible after making at most* q_H *queries to the random oracle,* q_{KR} *key registration queries,* q_{SS} SS *queries,* q_{DS} DS *queries,* $q_{\overline{DS}}$ $\overline{DS}$ *queries,* q_{DV} DV *queries and* q_{SK} SK *queries in time* t.

As we call DVS with Privacy of Signer as Strong DVS (SDVS), we call that UDVS with this property as Strong UDVS (SUDVS).

5   Proposed Scheme

In this section, we will firstly describe our universal designated verifier signature scheme without delegatability. Then we provide the formal security analysis of our scheme in the random oracle model. Our scheme consists of the following algorithms:

CPG: Let $(\mathbb{G}_1, \mathbb{G}_T)$ be a bilinear groups where $|\mathbb{G}_1| = |\mathbb{G}_T| = p$, for some prime number $p \geq 2^k$, k be the system security number and g be the generator of $\mathbb{G}_1$. e denotes the bilinear pairing $\mathbb{G}_1 \times \mathbb{G}_1 \to \mathbb{G}_T$. Let $h_0 : \{0,1\}^* \to \mathbb{G}_1^*, h_1 : \{0,1\}^* \to \mathbb{Z}_p$ be two secure cryptographic hash functions.

KG: The Signer S picks a secret value $x_s \in_R \mathbb{Z}_p^*$ and sets the secret key $sk_s := x_s$. Then S computes the public key $pk_s = g^{x_s}$. Similarly, the verifier V's secret/public key-pair is $(sk_v, pk_v) = (x_v, g^{x_v})$ where x_v is randomly chosen in $\mathbb{Z}_p^*$.

SS: For a message m to be signed, S computes the standard signature $\sigma_{\mathsf{SS}} = h_0(m)^{sk_s}$.

SV: Given a message m, the standard signature σ_{SS} and S's public key pk_s, one can check the equation $e(\sigma_{\mathsf{SS}}, g) \stackrel{?}{=} e(h_0(m), pk_s)$. If the equality holds, output Acc, otherwise, Rej.

DS: Given the standard signature σ_{SS} and the verifier's public key pk_v, the signature holder SH selects $r, c_v, d_v \in_R \mathbb{Z}_p$ and computes

1. $z_s = e(g,g)^r, z_v = g^{d_v} pk_v{}^{c_v}$
2. $c = h_1(m, pk_s, pk_v, z_s, z_v)$
3. $c_s = c - c_v \pmod{p}, d_s = \frac{g^r}{(\sigma_{SS})^{c_s}}$

Then, SH sends the universal designated verifier signature $\sigma_{DV} = (c_s, c_v, d_s, d_v)$ to the verifier V.

$\overline{\text{DS}}$: Given the signer's public key pk_s and the message m, the verifier V selects $r, c_s \in_R \mathbb{Z}_p, d_s \in \mathbb{G}_1$ and computes

1. $z_s = e(d_s, g) e(h_0(m), pk_s)^{c_s}, z_v = g^r$
2. $c = h_1(m, pk_s, pk_v, z_s, z_v)$
3. $c_v = c - c_s \pmod{p}, d_v = r - c_v sk_v \pmod{p}$

The universal designated verifier generated by the verifier is $\overline{\sigma_{DV}} = (c_s, c_v, d_s, d_v)$.

DV: Given the designated verifier signature (c_s, c_v, d_s, d_v), anyone can check whether

$$c_s + c_v \stackrel{?}{=} h_1(m, pk_s, pk_v, e(d_s, g) e(h_0(m), pk_s)^{c_s}, g^{d_v} pk_v{}^{c_v}) \pmod{p}$$

If the equality holds, output *Acc*, otherwise, *Rej*.

Consistency:

- SV Consistency: If σ_{SS} is generated by the algorithm SS, then $\sigma_{SS} = h_0(m)^{sk_s}$. Therefore $e(\sigma_{SS}, g) = e(h_0(m)^{sk_s}, g) = e(h_0(m), pk_s)$. That is: $\Pr[\text{SV}(cp, pk_s, m, \text{SS}(cp, sk_s, m)) = Acc] = 1$
- DV Consistency of DS: If σ_{DS} is generated by the algorithm DS, then $\sigma_{DV} = (c_s, c_v, d_s, d_v)$ where $c_v, d_v \in_R \mathbb{Z}_p$ and

$$c_s = h_1(m, pk_s, pk_v, e(g,g)^r, g^{d_v} pk_v{}^{c_v}) - c_v \pmod{p}, r \in \mathbb{Z}_p \text{ and } d_s = \frac{g^r}{(\sigma_{SS})^{c_s}}.$$

Therefore,

$$h_1(m, pk_s, pk_v, e(d_s, g) e(h_0(m), pk_s)^{c_s}, g^{d_v} pk_v{}^{c_v})$$
$$= h_1(m, pk_s, pk_v, e(g,g)^r, g^{d_v} pk_v{}^{c_v}) = c_s + c_v \pmod{p}$$

That is: $\Pr[\text{DV}(cp, pk_s, pk_v, m, \text{DS}(cp, pk_s, pk_v, \sigma_{SS}, m)) = Acc] = 1$.

- DV Consistency of $\overline{\text{DS}}$: If $\overline{\sigma_{DS}}$ is generated by the algorithm $\overline{\text{DS}}$, then $\sigma_{DV} = (c_s, c_v, d_s, d_v)$ where $c_s \in_R \mathbb{Z}_p, d_s \in_R \mathbb{G}_1$ and

$$c_v = h_1(m, pk_s, pk_v, e(d_s, g) e(h_0(m), pk_s)^{c_s}, g^r) - c_s \pmod{p}, r \in \mathbb{Z}_p$$

and $d_v = r - c_v sk_v \pmod{p}$. Therefore,

$$h_1(m, pk_s, pk_v, e(d_s, g) e(h_0(m), pk_s)^{c_s}, g^{d_v} pk_v{}^{c_v})$$
$$= h_1(m, pk_s, pk_v, e(d_s, g) e(h_0(m), pk_s)^{c_s}, g^r) = c_s + c_v \pmod{p}$$

That is: $\Pr[\text{DV}(cp, pk_s, pk_v, m, \overline{\text{DS}}(cp, pk_s, sk_v, m)) = Acc] = 1$

5.1   Security Analysis

Theorem 1. *If there exists an algorithm $\mathcal{F}_{EUF,\ DVS}^{CMA,\ CPKA}$ can $(t, q_{h_0}, q_{h_1}, q_{KR}, q_{SS}, q_{DS}, q_{\overline{DS}}, q_{DV}, q_{SK}, \varepsilon)$-break our UDVS scheme, then there exists a simulator $\mathcal{S}$ who can solve a random instance of the Computational Diffie Hellman problem on $\mathbb{G}_1$ with probability $Succ_{\mathcal{S}, \mathbb{G}_1}^{CDH} \geq \frac{1}{9} \frac{1}{(q_{SS}+q_{SK})^2}$, after running $\mathcal{F}$ by $\frac{12}{\varepsilon} + \frac{56 q_{h_1}}{\varepsilon}$ times with assumption $\varepsilon \geq 56 q_{h_1} \frac{1}{2^k}(q_{DS} + q_{\overline{DS}})(q_{h_1} + q_{DS} + q_{\overline{DS}}) + 1$, where k is the system security number.*

Proof: See Appendix.

Theorem 2. *Let $(pk_s, sk_s) \leftarrow \mathsf{KG}(k)$, $(pk_v, sk_v) \leftarrow \mathsf{KG}(k)$. If $\mathcal{A}$ is an algorithm, who can produce a valid UDVS on the message m with probability ϵ in time t, then our scheme UDVS scheme is (τ, κ) non-delegatable in the random oracle where $\kappa \geq \frac{1}{9}, \tau \leq \frac{16 t q_{h_1}}{\varepsilon}$ if h_1 is regarded as the random oracle, $\mathcal{A}$ asks at most q_{h_1} queries to the random oracle and $\epsilon \geq \frac{7 q_{h_1}}{2^k}$, where k is the system security number.*

Proof: See Appendix.

Theorem 3. *The proposed* **UDVS** *scheme is non-transferable against a $(t, q_{h_0}, q_{h_1}, q_{KR}, q_{SS}, q_{DS}, q_{\overline{DS}}, q_{DV}, q_{SK})$ adaptively chosen message and chosen public key distinguisher $\mathcal{D}_{TRANS,\ UDVS}^{CMA,\ CPKA}$.*

Proof: See Appendix.

6   Conclusion

Non-delegatability is a property recently introduced by Lipmaa, Wang and Bao as an essential property of (universal) designated verifier signature. In this paper, we propose the first universal designated verifier signature scheme without delegatability. Additionally, we refine the security models of the universal designated verifier signature and introduce the notion of the strong universal designated verifier signature. However, as there is no secure non-delegatable strong designated verifier signature, the scheme proposed in this paper is not a strong universal designated verifier signature. How to construct a non-delegatable strong (universal) designated verifier signature remains as an open research problem.

Acknowledgement. The authors would like to thank the anonymous referees of International Conference on Information and Communications Security (ICICS 2006) for the suggestions to improve this paper.

References

1. D. Boneh and X. Boyen. Short signatures without random oracles. EUROCRYPT 2004. Lectue Notes in Computer Science 3027, pp. 56-73, Springer–Verlag, Berlin, 2004.

2. D. Boneh, B. Lynn, and H. Shacham. Short signatures from the Weil pairing. ASIACRYPT 2001, Lectue Notes in Computer Science 2248, pp. 514-532, Springer–Verlag, Berlin, 2001.
3. W. Diffie and M. Hellman. New directions in cryptography. IEEE IT, 22: 644-654, 1976.
4. M. Jakobsson, K. Sako, and R. Impagliazzo. Designated Verifier Proofs and Their Applications. Advances in Cryptology - Eurocrypt '96, Lecture Notes in Computer Science 1070, pp. 143 - 154, Springer-Verlag, Berlin, 1996.
5. F. Laguillaumie and D. Vergnaud. Designated Verifiers Signature: Anonymity and Efficient Construction from *any* Bilinear Map. Fourth Conference on Security in Communication Networks'04 (SCN 04), Lecture Notes in Computer Science 3352, pp. 107 - 121, Springer-Verlag, Berlin, 2004.
6. F. Laguillaumie and D. Vergnaud. Multi-Designated Verifiers Signatures. Information and Communications Security (ICICS 2004), Lecture Notes in Computer Science 3269, pp. 495 - 507, Springer-Verlag, Berlin, 2004.
7. S. Goldwasser, S. Micali and R. Rivest. A Digital signature scheme secure against adaptively chosen message attacks. SIAM Journal on Computing, 17(2):281-308, 1988
8. X. Huang, Y. Mu, W. Susilo, and F. Zhang. Short Designated Verifier Proxy Signature from Pairings. The First International Workshop on Security in Ubiquitous Computing Systems (SecUbiq'05), Lecture Notes in Computer Science 3823, pp. 835 - 844, Springer-Verlag, Berlin, 2005.
9. Y. Li, H. Lipmaa and Dingyi Pei. On Delegatability of Four Desiganted Verifier Signatures. ICICS 2005, Lecture Notes in Computer Science 3783, pp. 61 - 71, Springer-Verlag, Berlin, 2005.
10. H. Lipmaa, G. Wang and F. Bao. Designated Verifier Signature Schemes: Attacks, New Security Notions and A New Construction. The 32nd International Colloquium on Automata, Languages and Programming, ICALP 2005, Lecture Notes in Computer Science 3580, pp. 459 - 471, Springer-Verlag, Berlin, 2004.
11. C. N. g, W. Susilo and Y. Mu. Universal Designated Multi Verifier Signature Schemes. The First International Workshop on Security in Networks and Distributed Systems (SNDS2005), IEEE Press, pp. 305 - 309, 2005.
12. W. Ogata, K. Kurosawa, and S.-H. Heng. The Security of the FDH Variant of Chaums Undeniable Signature Scheme. Public Key Cryptography - PKC 2005: 8th International Workshop on Theory and Practice in Public Key Cryptography, Lecture Notes in Computer Science 3385, pp. 328 - 345, Springer-Verlag, Berlin, 2005.
13. D. Pointcheval and J. Stern. Security arguments for digital signatures and blind signatures. Journal of Cryptology, Volume 13 - Number 3, pp. 361-396, Springer–Verlag, Berlin, 2000.
14. R. L. Rivest, A. Shamir, Y. Tauman. How to Leak a Secret. Proceedings of Asiacrypt 2001, Lecture Notes in Computer Science 2248, pp. 552 - 565, Springer–Verlag, Berlin, 2001.
15. S. Saeednia, S. Kramer, and O. Markovitch. An Efficient Strong Designated Verifier Signature Scheme. The 6th International Conference on Information Security and Cryptology (ICISC 2003), pp. 40 - 54, Springer-Verlag, Berlin, 2003.
16. R. Steinfeld, L. Bull, H. Wang, and J. Pieprzyk. Universal Designated-Verifier Signatures. Proceedings of Asiacrypt 2003, Lecture Notes in Computer Science 2894, pp. 523 - 543, Springer-Verlag, Berlin, 2003.

17. R. Steinfeld, H. Wang, and J. Pieprzyk. Efficient Extension of Standard Schnorr/RSA Signatures into Universal Designated-Verifier Signatures. Proceedings of PKC 2004, Lecture Notes in Computer Science 2947, pp. 86 - 100, Springer-Verlag, Berlin, 2004.
18. W. Susilo, F. Zhang, and Y. Mu. Identity-based Strong Designated Verifier Signature Schemes. Information Security and Privacy, 9th Australasian Conference, ACISP 2004, Lecture Notes in Computer Science 3108, pp. 313 - 324, Springer-Verlag, Berlin, 2004.
19. D. Vergnaud. New Extensions of Pairing-based Signatures into Universal Designated Verifier Signatures. Automata, Languages and Programming: 33rd International Colloquium, ICALP 2006. Lecture Notes in Computer Science 4052, pp. 58-69, Springer-Verlag, Berlin, 2006. Also available at http://www.math.unicaen.fr/~vergnaud/publications.php
20. R. Zhang, J. Furukawa and H. Imai. Short signature and universal designated verifier signature without random oracles. Applied Cryptography and Network Security (ACNS 2005), Lecture Notes in Computer Science 3531, pp. 483 - 498, Springer-Verlag, Berlin, 2005.
21. F. Zhang, W. Susilo, Y. Mu and X. Chen. Identity-based Universal Designated Verifier Signatures. The First International Workshop on Security in Ubiquitous Computing Systems (SecUbiq'05), Nagasaki, Japan, Lecture Notes in Computer Science 3823, pp. 825-834, Springer-Verlag, Berlin, 2005.

Appendix

Proof of Theorem 1: Suppose there exists a forger $\mathcal{F}$ who can $(t, q_{\mathsf{KR}}, q_{h_0}, q_{h_1}, q_{\mathsf{SS}}, q_{\mathsf{DS}}, q_{\overline{\mathsf{DS}}}, q_{\mathsf{DV}}, q_{\mathsf{SK}}, \varepsilon)$ break our UDVS scheme. We will show there exists a simulator $\mathcal{S}$ who can use $\mathcal{F}$ to solve the Computational Diffie Hellman problem. In the proof, we assume that when $\mathcal{F}$ requests the signature of the signer pk or asks the secret key corresponding to the public key pk, $\mathcal{F}$ has obtained the public key pk from KR queries. We will regard hash functions h_0, h_1 as the random oracles.

Let $(\mathbb{G}_1, \mathbb{G}_T)$ be a bilinear groups where $|\mathbb{G}_1| = |\mathbb{G}_T| = p$, for some prime number $p \geq 2^k$, k be the system security number, g be the generator of $\mathbb{G}_1$ and e denote the bilinear pairing $\mathbb{G}_1 \times \mathbb{G}_1 \to \mathbb{G}_T$. Let (g, g^a, g^b) be a random instance of the computational diffie hellman problem on $\mathbb{G}_1$.

- Setup: $\mathcal{S}$ returns $cp = (\mathbb{G}_1, \mathbb{G}_T, g, p, e)$ to the forger $\mathcal{F}$.
- KR queries: At any time, $\mathcal{F}$ can regisrer for the ith user. In response, $\mathcal{S}$ will maintain a *pk-list* which stores his responses to such queries. For a new query, $\mathcal{S}$ chooses a number $e_i \in \{0,1\}$ such that $\Pr[e_i = 1] = \frac{1}{q_{\mathsf{SS}}+q_{\mathsf{SK}}}$. If $e_i = 0$, $\mathcal{S}$ sets $sk_i = f_i \in_R \mathbb{Z}_p^*, pk_i = g^{sk_i}$. Otherwise, $e_i = 1$ and $\mathcal{S}$ sets $pk_i = (g^a)^{f_i}$, where $f_i \in_R \mathbb{Z}_p^*$. For either case, $\mathcal{S}$ adds (pk_i, e_i, f_i) into the *pk-list* and returns pk_i to $\mathcal{F}$ as the answer.
- h_0 queries: $\mathcal{F}$ can issue h_0 queries for the message m_i. In response, $\mathcal{S}$ will maintain an *h_0-list* which stores his responses to such queries. For a new query, $\mathcal{S}$ chooses a number $x_i \in \{0,1\}$ such that $\Pr[x_i = 1] = \frac{1}{q_{\mathsf{SS}}+q_{\mathsf{SK}}}$. Firstly, $\mathcal{S}$ chooses $y_i \in_R \mathbb{Z}_p^*$. If $x_i = 0$, sets $h_0(m_i) = w_i = g^{y_i}$. Otherwise,

$\mathcal{S}$ sets $h_0(m_i) = w_i = (g^b)^{y_i}$. $\mathcal{S}$ then adds (m_i, x_i, y_i, w_i) to the h_0-$list$ and returns w_i to $\mathcal{F}$.

- h_1 queries: $\mathcal{F}$ can issue h_1 queries with the query $Q_i = (m_i, pk_s, pk_v, z_s, z_v)$. In response, $\mathcal{S}$ will maintain an h_1-$list$ which stores his responses to such queries. For a new query Q_i, $\mathcal{S}$ chooses $u_i \in \mathbb{Z}_p$ and adds (Q_i, u_i) to h_1-$list$. Then $\mathcal{S}$ returns u_i to $\mathcal{F}$ as the answer.

- SS queries: On a standard sign query (m_i, pk_j), $\mathcal{S}$ firstly checks h_0-$list$ to obtain $w_i = h_0(m_i)$. If m_i has not been submitted by $\mathcal{F}$ as one of the h_0 queries, $\mathcal{S}$ generates the value of $h_0(m_i)$ as he responds to h_0 queries and adds (m_i, x_i, y_i, w_i) into the h_0-$list$. By assumption, (pk_j, e_j, f_j) has been in the pk-$list$. (1) If $e_j = 1, x_i = 1$, $\mathcal{S}$ reports failure and aborts. (2) Else $e_j = 1, x_i = 0$, $\mathcal{S}$ can compute the standard signature $\sigma_{SS} = (pk_j)^{y_i}$. (3) Else $e_j = 0$, $\mathcal{S}$ can compute the standard signature $\sigma_{SS} = (w_i)^{f_j}$.

- DS queries: $\mathcal{F}$ can request a designated verifier signature σ_{DV} of the message m_i under the public key (pk_s, pk_v), where pk_s denotes the signer and pk_v denotes the designated verifier. $\mathcal{S}$ firstly tries to compute σ_{SS} of this message m. If m_i has not been submitted by $\mathcal{F}$ as one of the h_0 queries, $\mathcal{S}$ generates $w_i = h_0(m_i)$ as its response to h_0 queries and adds (m_i, x_i, y_i, w_i) into the h_0-$list$. By assumption, $(pk_s, e_s, f_s), (pk_v, e_v, f_v)$ have been in the pk-$list$. If $x_i \neq 1$ or $e_s \neq 1$, $\mathcal{B}$ can generate the signature σ_{SS} as its response to the SS queries, then he runs DS algorithm as defined in Section 5. If $x_i = 1, e_s = 1$, $\mathcal{S}$ chooses $c_s, c_v, d_v \in_R \mathbb{Z}_p$ and $d_s \in_R \mathbb{G}_1$ and computes $z_s = e(d_s, g)e(w_i, pk_s)^{c_s}, z_v = g^{d_v}(pk_v)^{c_v}$. Then $\mathcal{S}$ sets $Q_i = (m_i, pk_s, pk_v, z_s, z_v)$ and adds $(Q_i, c_s + c_v)$ into the h_1-$list$. If query Q_i has been requested by $\mathcal{F}$, $\mathcal{S}$ reports failure and aborts.

- $\overline{\text{DS}}$ queries: $\mathcal{F}$ can request designated verifier signature $\overline{\sigma_{DS}}$ of the message m_i under the public key (pk_s, pk_v), where pk_s denotes the signer and pk_v denotes the designated verifier. In response, $\mathcal{S}$ firstly generates the value of $h_0(m_i)$ as its response to h_0 queries and adds (m_i, x_i, y_i, w_i) into the h_0-$list$. By assumption, $(pk_s, e_s, f_s), (pk_v, e_v, f_v)$ have been in the pk-$list$. If $e_v = 0$, then $sk_v = f_v$. $\mathcal{S}$ can run the $\overline{\text{DS}}$ algorithm as defined in the Section 5. Otherwise, $e_v = 1$. In this case, $pk_v = (g^a)^{f_v}$ and $\mathcal{S}$ does not know the secret key sk_v. Similarly as its response to DS queries, $\mathcal{S}$ chooses $c_s, c_v, d_v \in_R \mathbb{Z}_p$ and $d_s \in_R \mathbb{G}_1$ and computes $z_s = e(d_s, g)e(w_i, pk_s)^{c_s}, z_v = g^{d_v}(pk_v)^{c_v}$. Then, $\mathcal{S}$ sets $Q_i = (m_i, pk_s, pk_v, z_s, z_v)$ and adds $(Q_i, c_s + c_v)$ into the h_1-$list$. Similarly, if query Q_i has been requested by $\mathcal{F}$, $\mathcal{S}$ reports failure and aborts.

- DV queries: $\mathcal{F}$ can execute the DV algorithm by himself since DV algorithm does not need the secret keys of the signer and the designated verifier.

- SK queries: $\mathcal{F}$ can request the secret key corresponding to the public key pk_i. By assumption, (pk_i, e_i, f_i) has been in the the pk-$list$. If $e_i = 0$, $\mathcal{S}$ returns f_i to $\mathcal{F}$. Otherwise, if $e_i = 1$, $\mathcal{B}$ reports failure and aborts.

Finally, $\mathcal{F}$ outputs a forged messgae/signature pair (m^*, σ_{DV}^*) $(\sigma_{DV}^* = (c_s^*, c_v^*, d_s^*, d_v^*))$ under the public keys (pk_s^*, pk_v^*) such that:

1. $Acc \leftarrow \text{DV}(cp, pk_s^*, pk_v^*, m^*, \sigma_{DV}^*)$.
2. (m^*, pk_S^*) has never been submitted as one of the SS queries.

3. (m^*, pk_s^*, pk_v^*) has never been submitted as one of the DS or $\overline{\text{DS}}$ queries.
4. Neither pk_s^* nor pk_v^* has been submitted as one of the SK queries.

Therefore, if $\mathcal{S}$ does not abort during the simulation, $\mathcal{F}$ can output a valid forgery with probability greater than ε. Now it remains to compute the probability that $\mathcal{S}$ does not abort:

1. The probability $\mathcal{S}$ does not abort during the SS queries is greater than $(1 - (\frac{1}{q_{SS}+q_{SK}})^2)^{q_{SS}}$.
2. The probability $\mathcal{S}$ does not abort during the SK queries is greater than $(1 - \frac{1}{q_{SS}+q_{SK}})^{q_{SK}}$.
3. The probability that there is no collision happens during the DS or $\overline{\text{DS}}$ queries is greater than $(1 - \frac{q_{h_1}+q_{DS}+q_{\overline{DS}}}{2^k})^{q_{DS}+q_{\overline{DS}}}$.

Therefore, the probability $\mathcal{S}$ does not abort during the simulation is

$$(1 - (\frac{1}{q_{SS}+q_{SK}})^2)^{q_{SS}}(1 - \frac{1}{q_{SS}+q_{SK}})^{q_{SK}}(1 - \frac{q_{h_1}+q_{DS}+q_{\overline{DS}}}{2^k})^{q_{DS}+q_{\overline{DS}}}$$

$$\geq (1 - \frac{1}{q_{SS}+q_{SK}})^{q_{SS}+q_{SK}}(1 - \frac{(q_{DS}+q_{\overline{DS}})(q_{h_1}+q_{DS}+q_{\overline{DS}})}{2^k})$$

Since h_1 is regarded as a random oracle, the probability that $\mathcal{F}$ succeeds and has not submitted $Q^* = (m^*, pk_s^*, pk_v^*, z_s^*, z_v^*)$ ($z_s^* = e(d_s^*, g)e(w^*, pk_s^*)^{c_s^*}$, $z_v^* = g^{d_v^*}(pk_v^*)^{c_v^*}$) to the random oracle h_1 is less than $\frac{1}{2^k}$. Therefore, $\mathcal{F}$ can output a valid forgery $(m^*, pk_s^*, pk_v^*, \sigma_{DV}^*)$ such that Q^* has been submitted to the random oracle with probability $\varepsilon' \geq \varepsilon(1 - \frac{1}{q_{SS}+q_{SK}})^{q_{SS}+q_{SK}}(1 - \frac{(q_{DS}+q_{\overline{DS}})(q_{h_1}+q_{DS}+q_{\overline{DS}})}{2^k}) - \frac{1}{2^k} \geq \varepsilon(1 - \frac{1}{q_{SS}+q_{SK}})^{q_{SS}+q_{SK}} - \frac{(q_{DS}+q_{\overline{DS}})(q_{h_1}+q_{DS}+q_{\overline{DS}})+1}{2^k} \geq \frac{\varepsilon}{7}$. (with assumption $\varepsilon \geq 56q_{h_1}\frac{(q_{DS}+q_{\overline{DS}})(q_{h_1}+q_{DS}+q_{\overline{DS}})+1}{2^k}$). Therefore, the probability $\mathcal{F}$ succeeds with no collision happens is more than $\frac{\varepsilon}{7}$. Now, we apply the forking lemma [13]. Let $\mathcal{F}$ begins with the the random tape Ω and h_1 is regarded as the random oracle Θ. If $\mathcal{S}$ runs $\mathcal{F}$ $12/\varepsilon$ times with the random oracle Ω and Θ, $\mathcal{S}$ gets a least one pair (Ω, Θ) with success probability $1 - e^{-12/7} \geq \frac{4}{5}$ such that Q^* has been requested as one of the h_1 queries. Let the βth queries $Q_\beta = Q^*$ and the response is $u_{\beta1}^*$. If $\mathcal{S}$ replays forger $\mathcal{F}$ with different response $u_{\beta2}^*$ to Q_β and the same responses to $Q_i, i \leq \beta$, $\mathcal{S}$ can obtain another forged signature on the same message with probability more than $\frac{\varepsilon'}{4q_{h_1}} - 1/2^k \geq \frac{\varepsilon}{56q_{h_1}}$ (with assumption $\varepsilon \geq 56q_{h_1}\frac{(q_{DS}+q_{\overline{DS}})(q_{h_1}+q_{DS}+q_{\overline{DS}})+1}{2^k}$).

Due to the forking lemma, after running $\mathcal{F}$ $\frac{12}{\varepsilon} + \frac{56q_{h_1}}{\varepsilon}$ times, $\mathcal{S}$ can obtain two valid universal designated verifier signatures $(m^*, c_{s1}^*, c_{v1}^*, d_{s1}^*, d_{v1}*)$ and $(m^*, c_{s2}^*, c_{v2}^*, d_{s2}^*, d_{v2}^*)$ with probability greater than $1/9$ and

$$e(d_{s1}^*, g)e(w^*, pk_s^*)^{c_{s1}^*} = e(d_{s2}^*, g)e(w^*, pk_s^*)^{c_{s2}^*} \tag{1}$$

$$g^{d_{v1}^*}(pk_v^*)^{c_{v1}^*} = g^{d_{v2}^*}(pk_v^*)^{c_{v2}^*} \tag{2}$$

but $c_{s1}^* + c_{v1}^* \neq c_{s2}^* + c_{v2}^* \pmod{p}$.

1. If $c_{s1}^* \neq c_{s2}^*$ (mod p), with probability $\frac{1}{q_{SS}+q_{SK}}$, $w^* = (g^b)^{y^*}$. Additionally, with probability $\frac{1}{q_{SS}+q_{SK}}$, $pk_s^* = (g^a)^{f_s^*}$. Therefore, with probability $(\frac{1}{q_{SS}+q_{SK}})^2$, the following equation holds from equation (1): $d_{s1}^*(g^{ab})^{f_s^* y^* c_{s1}^*} = d_{s2}^*(g^{ab})^{f_s^* y^* c_{s2}^*}$. Therefore $g^{ab} = (d_{s1}^*/d_{s2}^*)^{(f_s^* y^*)^{-1}(c_{s2}^* - c_{s1}^*)^{-1}}$

2. Otherwise, $c_{v1}^* \neq c_{v2}^*$ (mod p), then $sk_v^* = (c_{v2}^* - c_{v1}^*)^{-1}(d_{v1}^* - d_{v2}^*)$ (due to the equation (2)). With probability $\frac{1}{q_{SS}+q_{SK}}$, $pk_v^* = (g^a)^{f_v^*}$, therefore, $a = (f_v^*)^{-1}(c_{v2}^* - c_{v1}^*)^{-1}(d_{v1}^* - d_{v2}^*)$ and $g^{ab} = (g^b)^{(f_v^*)^{-1}(c_{v2}^* - c_{v1}^*)^{-1}(d_{v1}^* - d_{v2}^*)}$.

In either way, $\mathcal{S}$ can compute g^{ab} with probability $\frac{1}{9}(\frac{1}{q_{SS}+q_{SK}})^2$ after running $\mathcal{F}$ by $\frac{12}{\varepsilon} + \frac{56q_{h_1}}{\varepsilon}$ times.   □

Proof of Theorem 2: In the extraction, $\mathcal{K}$ will act as the random oracle to reply $\mathcal{A}$'s q_{h_1} h_1 queries. Let $pk_s = g^{sk_s}, pk_v = g^{sk_v}$ be the public keys of the signer and the verifier. For each h_1 query $Q_i = (m_i, pk_s, pk_v, z_s, z_v)$, $\mathcal{K}$ chooses a random number $u_i \in \mathbb{Z}_p^*$ and sets $h_1(Q_i) = u_i$. If $\mathcal{A}$ can produce a valid universal designated verifier signature with probability $\varepsilon \geq \frac{7q_{h_1}}{2^k}$, due to the forking lemma, $\mathcal{K}$ can use $\mathcal{A}$ to obtain two valid signatures on the same message m with probability $\kappa \geq \frac{1}{9}$ after running $\mathcal{A}$ by $\frac{2}{\varepsilon} + \frac{14q_{h_1}}{\varepsilon}$ times. Let (m, c_s, c_v, d_s, d_v) and $(m, c_s', c_v', d_s', d_v')$ be these two valid signatures, then $e(d_s, g)e(h_0(m), pk_s)^{c_s} = e(d_s', g)e(h_0(m), pk_s)^{c_s'}$, $g^{d_v}pk_v^{c_v} = g^{d_v'}pk_v^{c_v'}$ but $c_s + c_v \neq c_s' + c_v'$ (mod q). Then the following two equations hold:

$$e(h_0(m), pk_s)^{c_s - c_s'} = e(\frac{d_s}{d_s'}, g), sk_v(c_v - c_v') = d_v' - d_v.$$

If $c_s \neq c_s'$, then $e(h_0(m), pk_s) = e(\frac{d_s}{d_s'}, g)^{(c_s - c_s')^{-1}}$. Therefore $\mathcal{K}$ can compute $\sigma_{SS} = (\frac{d_s}{d_s'})^{(c_s - c_s')^{-1}}$. Otherwise, $c_s = c_s', c_v \neq c_v'$. $\mathcal{K}$ can compute $sk_v = (d_v' - d_v)(c_v - c_v')^{-1}$. Therefore, $\mathcal{K}$ can extract σ_{SS} or sk_v with probability $\kappa \geq \frac{1}{9}$ in time $\tau \leq \frac{16tq_{h_1}}{\varepsilon}$.   □

Proof of Theorem 3: In the proof, the simulator $\mathcal{S}$ runs KG algorithm to generate all the secret/public keys. He then sends the public keys to the distinguisher $\mathcal{D}$ and keep the secret keys only known to himself. Because $\mathcal{S}$ has the knowledge of all secret keys, he can run SS, DS and $\overline{DS}$ to response $\mathcal{D}$'s queries. Neither will he abort during $\mathcal{D}$'s SK queries. For each h_0 queries, $\mathcal{S}$ chooses a random element in $\mathbb{G}_1^*$ as the response. Similarly, $\mathcal{S}$ chooses a random number in $\mathbb{Z}_p$ as the response to each h_1 queries. Therefore, $\mathcal{S}$ will not abort during the simulations.

Firstly we show that the distribution of signature σ_{DV} generated by the algorithm DS is uniform in $\mathbb{Z}_p \times \mathbb{Z}_p \times \mathbb{G}_1 \times \mathbb{Z}_p$. Let $\sigma_{DV} = (c_s, c_v, d_s, d_v)$ is the universal designated verifier signature generated by the DS algorithm,

$$\sigma_{DV} = (c_s, c_v, d_s, d_v) : \begin{cases} c_s = h_1(m, pk_s, pk_v, e(g, g)^r, g^{d_v}pk_v^{c_v}) - c_v \pmod{p}, \\ \text{where } r, c_v, d_v \in_R \mathbb{Z}_p \text{ and} \\ d_s = \frac{g^r}{(\sigma_{SS})^{c_s}}, r \in_R \mathbb{Z}_p \end{cases}$$

Therefore, for a randomly chosen signature $\sigma^* = (c_s^*, c_v^*, d_s^*, d_v^*)$, the probability $\Pr[\sigma_{\mathsf{DV}} = \sigma^*] = \frac{1}{p^4}$.

Then we show that the distribution of signature simulated by the algorithm $\overline{\mathsf{DS}}$ is also uniform $\mathbb{Z}_p \times \mathbb{Z}_p \times \mathbb{G}_1 \times \mathbb{Z}_p$.

$$\overline{\sigma_{\mathsf{DV}}} = (c_s, c_v, d_s, d_v) : \begin{cases} c_v = h_1(m, pk_s, pk_v, e(d_s, g)e(h_0(m), pk_s)^{c_s}, g^r) - c_s \\ \quad (\mathrm{mod}\ p), \text{where } r, c_s \in_R \mathbb{Z}_p, d_s \in_R \mathbb{G}_1 \text{ and} \\ d_v = r - c_v sk_v \quad (\mathrm{mod}\ p), r \in_R \mathbb{Z}_p \end{cases}$$

Therefore, for a randomly chosen signature $\sigma^* = (c_s^*, c_v^*, d_s^*, d_v^*)$, the probability $\Pr[\overline{\sigma_{\mathsf{DV}}} = \sigma^*] = \frac{1}{p^4}$.

Therefore, given a valid universal designated verifier signature, one can not distinguish whether it is generated by DS algorithm or $\overline{\mathsf{DS}}$ algorithm. Hence, our proposed scheme satisfies the untransferability property.

Tracing HTTP Activity Through Non-cooperating HTTP Proxies (Short Paper)*

Richard J. Edell, Peter Kruus, and Uri Meth

SPARTA, Inc.
7110 Samuel Morse Drive
Columbia, MD 21046
{Richard.Edell, Peter.Kruus, umeth}@sparta.com

Abstract. Tracing nefarious HTTP activity to its source is sometimes extremely difficult when HTTP (and/or SOCKS) proxies are used for origin obfuscation. This paper describes a technique for tracing HTTP traffic through one or more non-cooperating HTTP (and/or SOCKS) proxies. The technique uses only passive observations of TCP/IP headers. Furthermore, the technique need only observe a single direction of the underlying TCP flows, i.e. the technique is asymmetric-route-robust. The technique represents a set of HTTP transactions as an activity profile. These profiles may be either distilled from passive network observations, or logged by a cooperating web server. Using statistical correlation techniques, we can trace both end-to-end SSL-encrypted HTTP, and unencrypted HTTP despite the source obfuscation methods employed by many contemporary proxies. The technique may be used to narrow the search space before applying other more resource intensive traceback techniques.

1 Introduction

Identifying the origin of Hypertext Transfer Protocol (HTTP) activity is sometimes extremely important. HTTP activity may be the direct transport mechanism of a network-borne attack. For example, an attacker may attempt a brute force password cracking attack against a web server; or, attempt to exploit vulnerabilities within a web server's software. Other times the HTTP activity is a client accessing an otherwise legitimate web service, but for illegitimate purposes. For example, a spy may exchange stolen data through a web-based file sharing service; a terrorist may communicate using a web-based email service; or, a criminal may fraudulently access a banking web site.

Identifying the origin of HTTP activity can be difficult when technologies designed to obscure the source are employed. Among these technologies are HTTP proxies. HTTP proxies can be configured to obfuscate the origin of HTTP activity by removing easily traceable information such as IP source addresses. Furthermore, HTTP proxies can be "chained" together effectively creating multiple layers of origin obfuscation. There are thousands of publicly available HTTP proxies on the Internet (see, for example, http://www.proxy.org). Furthermore, remotely compromised hosts

---

* Approved for Public Release; distribution unlimited.

P. Ning, S. Qing, and N. Li (Eds.): ICICS 2006, LNCS 4307, pp. 499–506, 2006.
© Springer-Verlag Berlin Heidelberg 2006

can be configured to operate as private HTTP proxies that can then be used to obfuscate the origin of nefarious activity.

This paper describes our HTTP traceback technique for tracing HTTP activity backwards, from the destination server, through some non-cooperating HTTP proxies, and toward the origin of the activity. Our technique requires only passive network observations of TCP/IP headers. Furthermore, the technique requires only unidirectional observations and as such is robust in the presence of asymmetric routing. The technique works with end-to-end SSL-encrypted HTTP. The technique also works with unencrypted HTTP traffic that is transformed by some HTTP proxies. The technique relies upon the variability of message sizes and timing within HTTP sessions. The technique further relies upon proxies applying repeatable transformations to the HTTP messages. Generally, aspects of the technique can be applied to traceback of other remote procedure call (RPC)-like protocols such as Common Object Request Broker Architecture (CORBA), Microsoft RPC/Distributed Component Object Model (MSRPC/DCOM), Lightweight Directory Access Protocol (LDAP), etc.

Several studies [1], [2], [3], [6] have explored a related problem – the weaknesses of using SSL for cloaking the content of HTTP communication. In general, these studies suppose a prior catalog of fingerprinted web content; SSL-encrypted HTTP traffic is observed and fingerprinted; by correlating the traffic and cataloged fingerprints, the observer can infer the web pages accessed. In these studies, HTTP session-specific variable factors such as browser software, browser cache state, web content changes, etc. partially confound the comparison of observed traffic with the separately cataloged web content. Detection thresholds are adjusted appropriately. Consequently, false-positives and false-negatives are a recurring issue.

Our approach utilizes similar methods for extracting features from HTTP connections, it relies partially upon the same variability of object sizes documented in those studies, and it is sensitive to many of the same countermeasures. However, because we have different objectives, we frame our problem differently and make different assumptions. We seek to trace HTTP activity backward from the HTTP server, past non-cooperating proxies, and toward the client. We suppose multiple simultaneous network traffic observations from various points within the Internet. Our approach functions in both online-distributed traceback [4], [5] and offline-centralized traceback environments. When we compare traffic observations, we are trying to find the same HTTP session. And so the same session-specific variation that confounds the alternative perspective (matching traffic to web pages) tends to assist us in distinguishing HTTP sessions.

In this paper, we first describe the HTTP traceback problem in abstract terms. Next, we outline the traceback technique, noting two key observations about HTTP traffic and proxy behavior, and commenting on the correlation method. We then present an initial evaluation where we confirm our key observations.

2   Problem Statement

Fig. 1, below, depicts a reference network topology. The figure shows three web servers (S_1, S_2, and S_3), two proxies (P_1, and P_2), and two clients (C_1, and C_2). The lines connecting clients, proxies, and web servers indicate who communicates directly with whom. The lines hide the complexity of network switches, routers, and links; in other words, the lines are like the typical "network cloud". While this communication often occurs over multiple parallel TCP connections, this figure does not show that detail. Each HTTP transaction consists of a request sent by a client to a server, and a response sent by the server back to the client. A single TCP connection carries one or more HTTP transactions. Discrete HTTP transactions are indicated in the figure by v_i, w_j, and x_k with various accent marks. When a transaction has been transformed by a proxy, its indication is changed by changing the accent mark ("‾", "^", or "~").

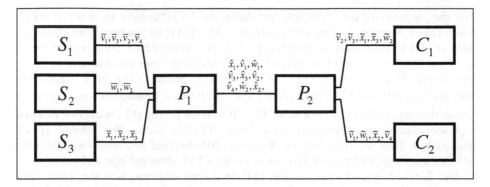

Fig. 1. Reference Network Topology. Targeted servers (S_1, S_2, and S_3), HTTP proxies (P_1, and P_2), and HTTP clients (C_1, and C_2) are shown.

The reference network figure shows client-server communication paths via two proxies in tandem, i.e. proxy chaining. This may occur either by proxy configuration, or by a client tunneling requests through proxies. A client can tunnel requests by using an HTTP proxy's "CONNECT" method, or by using a SOCKS proxy.

We now offer some concrete examples using **Fig. 1**. We first frame these examples as if there were an omniscient traceback oracle to illustrate the types of traceback requests that can be answered positively. Suppose S_3 determined HTTP traceback was needed for a transaction set $\{\bar{x}_1, \bar{x}_3\}$. It would describe that transaction set in some way, and query the oracle. The oracle would respond positively and indicate the path $C_1 \leftrightarrow P_2 \leftrightarrow P_1 \leftrightarrow S_3$. Had S_3 instead requested traceback of $\{\bar{x}_1, \bar{x}_2, \bar{x}_3\}$ (i.e., transactions mixed from different clients), the oracle would respond negatively as there is no single client-server path that contains that entire transaction set. Alternatively, S_3 could request traceback of $\{\bar{v}_1, \bar{v}_4\}$ or $\{\bar{v}_2, \bar{v}_3\}$ and receive positive responses. Other combinations of $\bar{v}_i$, $\bar{w}_j$, and $\bar{x}_k$ would not yield positive responses either because they would mix client transactions, or represent too small of a transaction set.

We now reframe the preceding examples by replacing the omniscient oracle with more realistic passive network listening posts. These listening posts are deployed at discrete points within the network. A listening post can only detect similar transaction sets that happen to appear at its discrete observation point; furthermore, when it does detect a similar transaction set, it can only identify the immediate transport layer endpoints within the proxy chain. For example, listening posts that happen to observe the $C_1 \leftrightarrow P_2$ segment of the $C_1 \leftrightarrow P_2 \leftrightarrow P_1 \leftrightarrow S_3$ path can detect the $\{\overline{x}_1, \overline{x}_3\}$ transaction set (appearing on that segment as $\{\widetilde{x}_1, \widetilde{x}_3\}$) and identify C_1 and P_2 as endpoints of a segment of the path. Listening posts that do not observe any segment of the $C_1 \leftrightarrow P_2 \leftrightarrow P_1 \leftrightarrow S_3$ path cannot detect the $\{\overline{x}_1, \overline{x}_3\}$ transaction set.

3   HTTP Traceback Technique

For the purposes of this technique, we define an HTTP session as a set of HTTP transactions between a client and a server. An HTTP transaction is an operation such as "GET /pathname/objectname.type." It is communicated by a request message sent from a client to a server and the resulting response message sent by the server back to the client. A transaction profile (TP) is a three-tuple $(requestSize, responseSize, requestTime)$ that represents a transaction's messages. A transaction set profile (TSP) is a set of TPs. A session profile (SP) is a set of TPs that represent transaction messages from a single HTTP session. We redefine HTTP traceback in these terms as follows: Given an SP observed near a server, determine whether a corresponding set of TPs exists within a TSP observed near a client.

Fig. 2, below, shows some sample TSP data[1], and diagrams how the source data was collected, processed into TSPs, and then correlated. The plot in the left side shows the *requestSize* and *responseSize* components of selected TSPs; the schematic

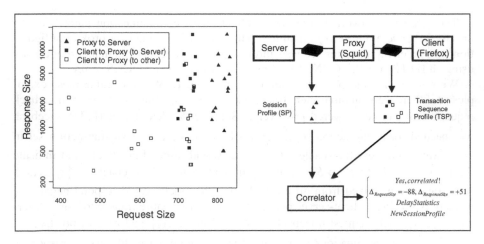

Fig. 2. Example Transaction Set Profile and Session Profile. Note, the filled vs. empty box indications within the Transaction Set Profile (TSP) are not actually indicated within the TSP. We have indicated them here to show how the Session Profile (SP) and TSP correlate.

---

[1] The data shown here is from an initial evaluation of our traceback technique. Later in this paper, we will discuss that evaluation further.

in the top-right diagrams how the data was collected. We configured an HTTP client (Firefox) to use an HTTP proxy (Squid, see http://www.squid-cache.org), and then browsed an HTTP server. Simultaneously, we captured packets using tcpdump at two points depicted in the figure by magnifying glasses. The TCP/IP headers going from "Proxy" to "Server" were processed to create a TSP, and that TSP is presumed to be an SP (triangles) because there was only one proxy client. Similarly the TCP/IP headers going from the "Client" to "Proxy" were processed to create another TSP (filled and empty boxes). The plot within the figure shows seven seconds of this data.

Our traceback technique is based on two key observations:

1. Non-trivial HTTP sessions can be fingerprinted by their SPs. In **Fig. 2**, the pattern of triangles is an example fingerprint. Previous studies [3], [6] have established the variability in object lengths, across large sets of web pages. Our SPs include additional information from the HTTP session (*requestSize* and *requestTime*) thus yielding even greater variability.

2. Today's common HTTP proxies transform request and response messages in predicable ways. Within an HTTP session, these transformations share common properties. Therefore, a session's SPs as observed on opposite sides of a proxy share distinctive characteristics. In **Fig. 2** the TSP subset indicated with filled-boxes has the same pattern as the SP indicated with triangles. In this example, each filled-box is offset by -88 bytes in the *requestSize* dimension, and +51 bytes in the *responseSize* dimension from its corresponding triangle. In other words, in this example the proxy added 88 bytes to the client's HTTP requests before forwarding them to the server, and the proxy added 51 bytes to the server's HTTP responses before forwarding them to the client.[2]

Note that the plot in **Fig. 2** does not represent the *requestTime* components of either the SP or TSP. That temporal component does contribute to the uniqueness of any given SP. Additionally, HTTP proxies are expected to slightly delay HTTP requests and that delay is expected to vary slightly. Therefore, the temporal component can be used when correlating SPs against TSPs. Elements of the figure's triangular SP and filled-box TSP can be paired in a way that yields a constant *requestSize* and *responseSize* difference. That pairing yields a small *requestTime* difference and that difference varies slightly.

4   Initial Evaluation

We have begun evaluating this traceback technique using a limited dataset. **Fig. 2**, introduced above, diagrams the data collection arrangement. Network traffic was recorded at two points: (1) between the proxy and the far-end web servers, and (2) between the client and the proxy. The client and proxy were specifically setup for this evaluation; the network and far-end servers were uncontrived. We recorded approximately 8 minutes of

---

[2] More precisely, the proxy server added/removed/modified headers having the net effect of changing the request/response message sizes. In this example, the net effect of the changes added bytes.

network traffic. Five different web-based services were accessed and eight different web sites were identified as providing those five services.

Working only from TCP/IP headers in the "forward" direction, 734 transactions were identified and profiled between the client and the proxy (i.e., a TSP); similarly, 520 transactions were identified and profiled between the proxy and the eight web servers (i.e., eight SPs). Therefore, for each of the eight SPs, we expect to find *the entire* SP within the TSP with some constant difference in *requestSize* and *responseSize*, and a small slightly varying difference in *requestTime*. However, in the course of attempting to correlate those eight SPs against the TSP, we discovered two minor difficulties.[3] These difficulties are a direct consequence of our limited perspective (unidirectional TCP/IP headers), and are limited to the last transaction of each TCP connection. Therefore, we have excluded the last transaction of each TCP connection from our SPs. We call the remaining transactions the "Non-FIN" transactions.

Table 1, below, lists the eight websites, the length of their SPs, and data showing how well their SPs correlated with the TSP. The correlation method considers hypothetical offsets in *requestSize* and *responseSize*, seeking to identify the "best" hypothesis. We define the best hypothesis as one that matches the largest portion of the SP within the TSP. The first four servers' SPs were found entirely within the TSP. That is, all Non-FIN SP elements were found within the TSP by applying a fixed offset to *requestSize* and *responseSize*. The next two servers' SPs were only partially

Table 1. Initial Evaluation Data. Eight SPs and correlation with TSP are shown.

Web Server	Number of Transactions		Number of Matching Transactions		Best Hypoth. Delay	
	All	Non-FIN	Best Hypothesis	Next Best Hypothesis	Avg. (ms)	S.D. (ms)
www.washingtonpost.com	58	50	50	2	14	46
media.washingtonpost.com	47	44	44	3	22	79
mail.google.com	88	62	62	3	12	15
cdn.mapquest.com	117	113	113	10	18	64
www.box.net	140	127	117	11	14	79
www.mapquest.com	20	17	11	5	45	85
web.mapquest.com	6	0	N/A (no non-FIN transactions)			
x.y.hotmail.msn.com	7	0	N/A (no non-FIN transactions)			

---

[3] First, we use TCP acknowledgement numbers to infer data flow in the unobserved direction. That works well except for the ambiguous connection close sequence. That ambiguity leads to an occasional off-by-one error in the inferred *responseSize* for that last transaction over each TCP connection. Second, an HTTP server usually signals within a transaction's headers that it intends to close the TCP connection after completing that connection. We have observed, however, that the presence of such signaling is sometimes dependent on the HTTP response message body's content-type. Since the header size is based upon something we do not observe, we can't easily correlate the last transaction of a TCP connection observed between a proxy and a web server.

found within the TSP. In all cases, the "next best" hypothesis matched a significantly smaller portion of the SP. Considering the first server, all SP subsets of three or more elements will correlate with precisely the correct elements of the TSP. This precision gives us hope that the traceback technique will have a low false-positive rate.

Each of the "best" hypothetical offsets implies a *particular* pairing of most (and sometimes all) SP elements to TSP elements. From those implied pairings we can evaluate the differences in *requestTime*, i.e. the implied transit delays. **Table 1** shows the average and standard deviation of the delays implied by the best hypotheses. Note that these hypothetical matches were formed without regard to time, yet the resulting delays implied are all small in average and with small standard deviation. Evidently, the correlation method's best hypotheses did not mismatch SP elements with TSP elements.

Note, we expected to find, but did not find, all elements of each SP within the TSP. In the case of the www.box.net, ten SP elements were inconsistent with the best hypothesis. Those ten elements, however, were all consistent with the next best hypothesis. That is, the entire SP can be found within the TSP by applying one of two offsets to each SP element. In the case of www.mapquest.com, six SP elements were inconsistent with the best hypothesis. However, in this case two additional hypotheses are necessary to locate all SP elements within the TSP. By inspecting the packet contents, we have determined why these additional hypotheses are necessary. For www.box.net, a particular hop-by-hop header in the server response messages ("keep-alive") had one length in 117 transactions, and another length in ten transactions. For www.mapquest.net, the client included an atypical cache-control directive in five requests, and the server added extraneous whitespace to the "content-length" header in one response. Evidently, a small number of intra-session behavioral variations, by both clients and servers, do sometimes occur. We will consider enhancing our correlation method to consider a small set of hypothetical offsets that match the largest portion (or the entirety) of the SP within the TSP.

5 Conclusion

Our initial evaluation is intended to motivate design, and to validate the observations underlying the traceback technique. From that evaluation, we believe that the traceback technique shows promise. We have noted some difficulties and will explore the enhancement we suggested. Furthermore, we are planning a more comprehensive evaluation that involves a greater variety of websites accessed, simultaneous users accessing the same websites, and considers additional proxy implementations. That more comprehensive evaluation is expected to reveal instances of false-positives, i.e. of TSPs incorrectly identified as bearing an SP's fingerprint. Hopefully the uniqueness of HTTP activity profiles will result in low false-positive rates. The characteristics of those false-positives may yet motivate new traceback techniques.

The widespread availability of HTTP proxies (both publicly available with many users, and privately setup on compromised hosts) offers hackers, spies, terrorists, and even rote criminals opportunities to hide their true location while using the Internet. The HTTP traceback technique outlined in this paper is a valuable tool in tracking their location.

References

1. Cheng, H.; Avnur, R., "Traffic Analysis of SSL Encrypted Web Browsing," 1998.
2. Danezis, D., "Traffic Analysis of the HTTP Protocol over TLS," unpublished paper.
3. Hintz, A., "Fingerprinting websites using traffic analysis," In Workshop on Privacy Enhancing Technologies, San Francisco, CA, April 2002.
4. Kindred, D.; Reid, T.; Wilson, B., "Phase I Final Technical Report: Tracing Attacks through Non-Cooperating Networks," SPARTA Technical Report, April 2005.
5. Schnackenberg, D.; Holliday, H.; Smith, R.; Djahandari, K.; Sterne, D., "Cooperative Intrusion Traceback and Response Architecture (CITRA)," *DARPA Information Survivability Conference & Exposition II, 2001. DISCEX '01. Proceedings*, vol.1, no.pp.56-68 vol.1, 2001.
6. Sun, Q.; Simon, D. R.; Wang, Y.; Russell, W.; Padmanabhan, V. N.; and Qiu, L., "Statistical identification of encrypted web browsing traffic." In Proceedings of IEEE Symposium on Security and Privacy, Oakland, CA, USA, May 2002.

A Fast RSA Implementation on Itanium 2 Processor

Kazuyoshi Furukawa, Masahiko Takenaka, and Kouichi Itoh

FUJITSU LABORATORIES LTD.,
4-1-1, Kamikodanaka, Nakahara-ku, Kawasaki, 211-8588, Japan
{kazful, takenaka, kito}@labs.fujitsu.com

Abstract. We show the fastest implementation result of RSA on Itanium 2. For realizing the fast implementation, we improved the implementation algorithm of Montgomery multiplication proposed by Itoh et al. By using our implementation algorithm, pilepine delay is decreased than previous one on Itanium 2. And we implemented this algorithm with highly optimized for parallel processing. Our code can execute 4 instructions per cycle (At maximum, 6 instructions are executed per cycle on Itanium 2), and its probability of pipeline stalling is just only 5%. Our RSA implementation using this code performs 32 times per second of 4096-bit RSA decryption with CRT on Itanium 2 at 900MHz. As a result, our implementation of RSA is the fastest on Itanium2. This is 3.1 times faster than IPP, a software library developed by Intel, in the best case.

Keywords: RSA, Montgomery multiplication, software implementation, Itanium 2.

1 Introduction

The RSA [13] is one of the standard public-key cryptosystems. The security of RSA relies on a fact that factoring huge integers, which is used as a public-key in RSA, is infeasible. Thus the key-length of RSA is chosen so as to avoid such factorization. In the past, 1024-bit was enough. However, with a remarkable development of semiconductor technologies, we need longer RSA keys in the near future. For example, NIST recommends using 2048-bit or 3072-bit RSA keys after the year 2010 [16] [17]. If the key-length of RSA becomes longer, its computational cost grows with the cube of the bit length. Therefore, realizing a high-speed RSA with longer-keys is more important than ever.

Most of the RSA processing time is spent in modular multiplications. For performing modular multiplication effectively, several types of primitive algorithms was proposed by Montgomery [1], Barrett [14], Kaihara-Takagi [15] and so on. Currently, the most popular algorithm is the Montgomery's one (Montgomery multiplication). In addition, many improvements on this algorithm have been proposed. Dusse and Kaliski transformed a multiplication and reduction for long bit integers into an effective integration of multiplication and reduction for small bit integers [18]. Related with hardware architecture for scalable Montgomery multiplication, many results are known [7] [8] [9] [10] [11] [12]. Related with software implementation, Koc et al. [2] presented several effective software implementation algorithms of the Montgomery multiplication (e.g. SOS, CIOS, FIOS and more), and evaluated the required resources of these implementation algorithms. Furthermore, FIOS, one of the improvement by Koc et al. [2], was

P. Ning, S. Qing, and N. Li (Eds.): ICICS 2006, LNCS 4307, pp. 507–518, 2006.
© Springer-Verlag Berlin Heidelberg 2006

improved by Itoh et al [3]. This improved algorithm (Itoh's algorithm) is very suitable for pipelining, and allows high-performance RSA implementation on a DSP [3].

Our objective of this paper is to realize a fast implementation of RSA on Itanium 2, because it has attractive features for establishing high-performance RSA. That is, it can operate a 64-bit × 64-bit multiply instruction with very low latency (4 cycles) and low delay (1 cycle), and can execute 6 instructions in parallel at 1 cycle. Our strategy has 2 steps as follows.

In the first step, we analyzed the dependency between data calculations in a Montgomery multiplication in the Itoh's algorithm. By considering the specific conditions for Itanium 2 pipeline scheduling, the pipeline delays are evaluated. However, we found that a naive application of the Itoh's algorithm causes heavy overheads on Itanium 2. Thus we enhanced the Itoh's algorithm so as to avoid such overheads, which is one of our contributions of this paper.

In the second step, based on the pipeline scheduling found in the first step, we established an optimized code in parallel processing in assembly language of Itanium 2 by trial and errors. Our code can execute 4 instructions per cycle, while Itanium 2 can execute at maximum 6 instructions. Since the probability of pipeline stalling of our code is just only 5%, we think our code is optimal. These results show the high-performance in parallel processing for software implementation. In fact, our code performs 32 times 4096-bit RSA decryptions with CRT per second on Itanium 2 at 900MHz. Compared with IPP, an RSA software library developed by Intel, our code is 3.1 times faster in the best case.

As far as the authors know, this is the first paper which analyzes the optimizing process and presents performance results for RSA software implementation specified for Itanium 2.

The rest of this paper is organized as follows. We describe primitives of the Montgomery multiplication and previous implementation algorithms in chapter 2, our proposed algorithm in chapter 3, implementational results of our proposed algorithm in chapter 4 and a conclusion in chapter 5.

2   Montgomery Multiplication and Itoh's Algorithm

In this chapter, we briefly introduce the Montgomery multiplication method for modular multiplications and its implementation algorithm.

The Montgomery method allows efficient modular multiplications [1]. The most crucial part of this method is the Montgomery multiplication (REDC) shown in Algorithm 1. Let N be an integer is greater than 1, and R be an integer greater than N and relatively prime to N. Also let N' be an integer such that $0 < N' < R$ and $N' = -N^{-1}$ (mod R). Under these notations, Algorithm 1 calculates a Montgomery multiplication $REDC(A, B) = A \times B \times R^{-1}$ (mod N) for integers A and B with $0 \le A \times B \le R \times N$.

To compute a modular multiplication $A \times B$ (mod N) with the Montgomery multiplication, we covert A and B to so-called the Montgomery domain in which the Montgomery multiplications are effectively computed (this conversion is done by applying an appropriate constant R). After a Montgomery multiplication, a result is re-converted to the previous domain and output. An outline is shown in Algorithm 2.

```
·input: A, B, R, N.
·output: REDC(A,B) = A×B×R⁻¹ (mod N)
·algorithm
    N' := -N⁻¹ (mod R)
    Y := AB
    M := ( Y (mod R) ) × N' (mod R)
    Y := Y + MN
    Y := Y/R
    if Y ≥ N then Y := Y - N
    return Y
```

Alg. 1. Montgomery Multiplication (REDC)

```
·input: A, B, R, N.
·output: A×B (mod N)
·algorithm

    A' = A×R (mod N)

    B' = B×R (mod N)

    C' = REDC(A',B') = A×B×R×R×R⁻¹ (mod N) = A×B×R (mod N)

    C  = REDC(C', 1) = A×B×R×R⁻¹ (mod N) = A×B (mod N)

    return C
```

Alg. 2. Structure of "CORE loop of REDC" in Algorithm 3

In typical implementations of REDC, input integers A, B and output integer Y are represented with multi-precision, namely an $s \times w$-bit integer A is represented as $(a_{s-1}, a_{s-2}, \ldots, a_0)$ where every $a_i (0 \leq i \leq s - 1)$ is a w-bit word data. (Here, $R = 2^{s \times w}$ is used). So, in these implementations, all integers are represented with multi-precision and looped calculations for every word data are required. Thus such implementations are not efficient.

In 1996, Koc et al. presented some implementation algorithms of REDC [2]. FIOS (Finely Integrated Operand Scanning) algorithm was among these implementations and further improved by Itoh et al [3] so as to suitable for pipelining [3]. We focus on this algorithm (Itoh's algorithm) in the rest of this paper. An outline of the Itoh's algorithm is shown in Algorithm 3. And "Core loop of REDC" structure in Algorithm 3 is shown in Fig 1. Here, "Upper Computation" in Fig 1 is corresponding to the first equation of "Core loop of REDC" in Algorithm 3. And "Lower Computation" is corresponding to the second equation. To handle carries of each equation to the next loop, the first equation in the $(i + 1)$-th loop does not refer to a result of the second equation in the i-th loop. Thus Itoh's algorithm can compute the first and second equations in parallel, which is an improvement in comparison with the original FIOS algorithm. This is why the Itoh's algorithm is suitable for pipelining.

3   Enhancement on the Itoh's Algorithm

Our objective of this paper is to realize a fast implementation of RSA on Itanium 2. To do so, our strategy has 2 steps. As the first step, we analyze the dependency between data

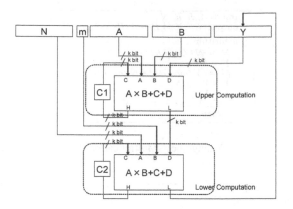

Fig. 1. Structure of "CORE loop of REDC" in Algorithm 3

calculations in the Itoh's algorithm in this chapter. Also, an enhanced Itoh's algorithm, which avoids heavy overheads on Itanium 2 are proposed in this chapter.

3.1   Analysis of "Core Loop of REDC" in the Itoh's Algorithm

For improving the Itoh's algorithm, analyzing "Core loop of REDC" part in Algorithm 1 is required. Figure 2 shows our dependency analysis of "Core loop of REDC" in which the i-th and the $(i + 1)$-th loops are discussed. Here "Upper MAA" corresponds to "Upper Computation" in Fig. 1 and "Lower MAA" to "Lower Computation" in Fig. 1 (MAA means one multiplication and two additions).

In Fig.2, "Lower MAA" needs a temporal result of "Upper MAA" before starting its computation. We call this relation "dependency" and represent as directions in Fig.2. Similarly, three following dependencies can be found Fig.2. Here a representation $X \rightarrow Y$ means that Y needs a result of X to start its computation. We call this relation as "Y depends to X".

> (1-i) Upper $MAA \rightarrow$ Lower MAA
> (1-ii) i-th Upper $MAA \rightarrow (i + 1)$-th Upper MAA
> (1-iii) i-th Lower $MAA \rightarrow (i + 1)$-th Lower MAA

REDC implementations with FIOS cannot avoid a dependency between the i-th Lower MAA and the $(i + 1)$-th Upper MAA. On the other hand, the Itoh's algorithm computes i-th Lower MAA and $(i + 1)$-th Upper MAA in parallel, because there is no dependency between them. Thus, the Itoh's algorithm is very suitable for pipelining.

For implementing the Itoh's algorithm on Itanium 2, some specific conditions for Itanium 2 pipeline scheduling shold be considered. As the first condition, Itanium 2 cannot operate one multiplication and two additions (multiply-add-add) within 1 instruction, but can operate one multiplication and one addtion (multiply-add) within 1 instruction. By taking this restriction into account, a pipeline scheduling of the Itoh's algrithm is modified as in Fig.3, where a symbol MA represents a multiply-add operation and a symbol A' represents an add operation. Note that MA can be operated within 1 instruction, while A' cannot within 1 instruction.

```
·input: A, B, R, N.
·output: REDC(A,B) = A×B×R⁻¹ (mod N)
·Multi-precision integers
A=(a_{s-1}, ..., a_0)
B=(b_{s-1}, ..., b_0)
N=(n_{s-1}, ..., n_0)
Y=(y_s, ..., y_0)
N'=(n'_{s-1}, ..., n'_0)
·w-bit word data.
tmp, C1, C2, m

· algorithm
   Y := 0
   for j=0 to s-1
   (C1, tmp) := y_0 + a_0 × b_j
   m := tmp × n'_0 (mod r)        /* r is 2^w */
   (C2, tmp) := tmp + m × n_0
      for i=0 to s-1
      (C1, tmp) := y_i + C1 + a_i × b_j       ⎫
      (C2, y_{i-1}) := tmp + C2 + m × n_i      ⎬ Core loop of REDC
      next i                                   ⎭
      (C2, C1) := C1 + C2 + y_s
      y_{s-1} := C1
      y_s := C2
   next j
   if Y >= N then Y := Y - N
   return Y
```

Alg. 3. Itoh's algorithm for REDC

In the pipeline scheduling of Fig.3, there are three dependencies shown in the following (2-i)–(2-iii).

(2-i) Upper $A' \rightarrow$ Lower MA

(2-ii) i-th Upper $MA \rightarrow (i+1)$-th Upper MA

(2-iii) i-th Lower $A \rightarrow (i+1)$-th Lower A'

In Fig.3, MA can be operated within 1 instruction (XMA instruction of Itanium 2). However, there is another specific condition of Itanium 2 that XMA instructions are executed only to floating-point registers for input and output data. Since Upper A' (integer addition) is executed to general registers, not to floating-point registers, we require a trick like follows:

(a1) One idea is to operate an Upper A' by an XMA instruction. This can be done by substituting integers in general registers to floating-point registers and by executing an XMA instruction with a dummy multiplication (namely, a multiplication with 1). In total, two XMA instructions are required, which cause overheads because XMA instructions are heavy operations compared to integer addition instructions to general registers.

(a2) Another idea is to operate an Upper A' as integer addition. This can be done by converting from general registers to floating-point registers before an XMA instruction, and by converting floating-point registers to general registers after the instruction. Again, this idea causes performance overheads due to two data-conversion instructions, which are much heavier than XMA instructions on Itanium 2.

In the next section, we enhance the Itoh's algorithm and propose an efficient algorithm for "Core loop of REDC" based on (a2) rather than (a1). This is because integer additions are very light instructions on Itanium 2.

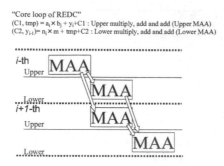

Fig. 2. Pipeline scheduling of "Core loop of REDC" in the Itoh's algorithm (not optimized to Itanium 2)

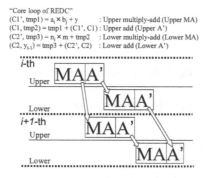

Fig. 3. Pipeline scheduling of "Core loop of REDC" in the Itoh's algorithm (optimized to Itanium 2)

3.2   Proposed Algorithm

As described in the previous section, two approaches (a1) and (a2) have heavy overheads. A main reason of these overheads is a pipeline delay of Lower MA by the dependency (2-i). Especially in (a2), a pipeline delay caused by Upper A' is large enough, because it consists of 1 conversion instruction (floating-point registers to general registers), 1 addition instruction for general registers and another 1 conversion instruction (general registers to floating-point registers).

Our approach for this problem is to break the dependency between Upper A' and Lower MA. Since this dependency is a result of the Itoh's algorithm, we go back to the Itoh's algorithm and enhance it so as to break the dependency. In fact, we established an enhanced version of the Itoh's algorithm in Fig.4 and Fig.5, in which Lower MA does not depend on Upper A' anymore but Lower MA depends on that of the previous loop. By this enhancement, overheads by the pipeline delay are eliminated.

In Fig.4, two symbols MA and A'' are used, where a symbol MA is same as in Fig.3 while a symbol A'' represents an addition of 4 values, the carry (C3), data stored on

"Core loop of REDC"
(C1, tmp1) = C1 + a$_i$ × b$_j$: Upper multiply-add (Upper MA)
(C2, tmp2) = C2 + m × n$_i$: Lower multiply-add (Lower MA)
(C3, y$_{i-1}$) = y$_i$ + C3 + tmp1 + tmp2 : Sum of results (Lower A")

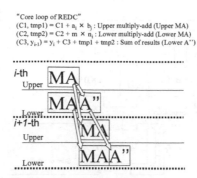

Fig. 4. Pipeline scheduling of "Core loop of REDC" in our enhanced Itoh's algorithm (optimized to Itanium 2)

memory (yi) and calculated results by Upper and Lower *MA* (tmp1 and tmp2). The dependencies of Fig.4 are shown in the following (3-i)–(3-iv).

(3-i) i-th Upper *MA* → i-th Lower *A"*
(3-ii) i-th Upper *MA* → (i + 1)-th Upper *MA*
(3-iii) i-th Lower *MA* → (i + 1)-th Lower *MA*
(3-iv) i-th Lower *A"* → (i + 1)-th Lower *A"*

By changing the dependency (2-i) to the dependency (3-iii), we succeeded to cancel the pipeline delay by Upper *A'* in Fig.3.

4 Implementation of Our New Algorithm on Itanium 2

In this chapter, as the second step for realizing fast RSA implementation, we describe implementational aspects of our new algorithm proposed in section 3.2 including the experimental performance results of RSA decryptions on Itanium 2.

4.1 Characteristics of Itanium 2

Itanium 2 belongs to a processor family called IPF (Itanium Processor Family), which is developed by Intel and Hewlett Packard, and its architecture is based on that of IA-64. The greatest characteristic of IPF is the EPIC (Explicitly Parallel Instruction Computing) technology, which does not support out-of-order executions unlike IA-32 architecture processors. In the out-of-order executions, instruction scheduling was dynamically done by a processor. But in IPF, instruction scheduling is done by the compiler. So the effectiveness of the compiler is directly reflected to the performance of software implementation. Other characteristics of Itanium 2 are listed in followings:

- Executes 6 instructions within 1 cycle at maximum. In other words, maximum IPC (Instruction Per Cycle) is 6.
- Provides many ports for executing various types of instructions (4 ports for memory, 2 ports for general, 2 ports for floating-point and 3 ports for blanch)

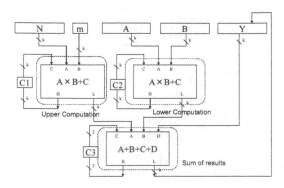

Fig. 5. New structure of "CORE loop of REDC" in our enhanced Itoh's algorithm

- Has 128 of 64-bit general registers.
- Has 128 of 82-bit floating-point registers.
- Provides software pipelining by CPU (MSL, Modulo Schedule Loop).
- Provides instructions for 64-bit fixed-point multiply-add instructions with 4 cycles latency and 1 cycle delay.

4.2 Implementation Environment

We used an hp workstation zx 2000 for implementation, whose specifications are summarized in the followings:

- CPU and frequency: Itanium 2 at 900 MHz
- Size of DRAM : 2 Gigabytes of memory
- Size of L1 cache: 16 K byte (Instruction) / 16K byte (Data)
- Size of L2 cache: 256 K byte
- Size of L3 cache: 1.5 M byte
- OS: Red Hat Enterprise Linux 4
- Compiler: gcc 3.4 and icc 9.0

In the following sections, we implemented REDC and RSA based on our enhanced Itoh's algorithm described in the previous sections. At the optimization, the performance of 1-time calculation of 4096-bit REDC is mainly considered. Our analys is used three factors, namely the number of total instructions, the probability of pipeline stalling and averaged IPC of total instructions. These factors are measured by the "performance monitoring counter" provided for Itanium 2. In this counter, the number of total instructions does not include NOP instructions, and averaged IPC of total instructions are obtained with dividing the number of total instructions by total cycles. We did not consider cache hit-miss here because its occasion is hard to be monitored.

4.3 Implementation and Optimization of REDC

In this section, we describe implementation aspects of REDC with C language and assembly language.

Implementation with C language. At the first step of the optimization, we implemented our new algorithm with C language. Here, instructions to operate multiply-add (XMA instruction) cannot be directly used with C language. So we used intrinsic function of Intel C Compiler 9.0 (icc 9.0) to operate XMA instruction. Grammar of the intrinsic function is represented as follows:

```
__int64 _m64_xmalu(__int64 a, __int64 b, __int64 c)
__int64 _m64_xmahu(__int64 a, __int64 b, __int64 c)
```

We show the evaluation result for optimization of our C language code in table 2. We obtained probability of pipeline stalling comes up to 14, most of which are waiting cycles to execute XMA instrutions. We found we can eliminate some instructions of assemble codes output by icc 9.0. An example of this elimination is shown in Table 1 which shows the assemble code of D=_m64_xmalu(A,B,C); by icc 9.0 and its eliminated result by hand-assembled code. We note grA, grB and grC represent the interger registers and frA, frB and frC represents the floating-point registers.

Table 1. Assembly list output by icc 9.0 (left column) and result of elimination by hand-assembled code (right column)

ld8 grA = [&A];
ld8 grB = [&B];
ld8 grC = [&C];
setf.sig.frA = grA;
setf.sig.frB = grB;
setf.sig.frC = grC;
xma.lu.frD=frA,frB,frC;
getf.sig.grD=frD;
st8[&D]=grD;
	ldf8 frA=[&A];
	ldf8 frB=[&B];
	ldf8 frC=[&C];
	xma.lu.frD=frA,frB,frC;
	stf8[&D] = frD;

Implementation with hand-assembled code. In section 4.3.1, we implemented our new REDC algorithm with C language and found out we can eliminate some instructions. So we optimized the code with extreme technique of hand-assembling by eliminating the total number of instructions, tuning the software pipeline schedule based on the instruction latencies. Finally, we attained the result that average IPC of REDC is 4.02. Especially, average IPC in the "Core loop of REDC" of is 5.25 which is extremely good result because maximum IPC of Itanium 2 is 6. In table 2, we show the result of the evaluation for optimization of the hand-assembled code with comparison that of C language for 4096-bit our REDC algorithm.

4.4 Implementation of RSA

We measured the performance of RSA decryption with CRT by using the hand-assembled optimized code of our new REDC algorithm described in section 4.3.2. At the implementation of RSA modular exponentiation, we used the technique of sliding-window method with 5-bit window size. Our result showed very fast performance, that

Table 2. Comparison of evaluation results for two types of implemented code for 4096-bit REDC of our proposal, one is with C language and another is with hand-assembled code

	C language	Hand-assembled code
Total cycles	65,111	18,801
Total instructions (NOT including NOP instruction)	177,199	75,560
Probability of pipeline stalling	14%	5%
Average IPC of total instructions	2.57	4.02

Table 3. Measured total time of the 1-time execution of our REDC algorithm in our environment

Bit length	Total time on our environment (μ sec)
512	0.62
768	1.15
1024	1.81
2048	5.88
3072	12.24
4096	20.87

is, our implementation attained 1,090 times of 1024-bit RSA CRT decryptions on Itanium 2 at 900MHz.

We compared our result of performance measurement with that of Intel Performance Primitive (IPP) which is software RSA library developed by Intel. This library is well known as fast library on Intel processors series. Especially, it is the fastest RSA library of marketed products on Itanium 2. We show the comparison in Table 4. In this table, results of IPP are obtained by our measurement. Our results are $1.19 - 3.1$ times faster than IPP, and are the fastest on Itanium 2.

Table 4. Measured total time of the 1-time execution of our REDC algorithm in our environment

Bit length	INTEL (μ sec)	Our Implementation	Ratio
4096	95,482	30,829	3.09
3072	44,383	14,277	3.10
2048	5,984	4,759	1.25
1024	1,099	917	1.19
768	659	512	1.28
512	313	237	1.32

5   Concluding Remarks

In this paper, we proposed new implementation algorithm of the primitive of Montgomery multiplication (REDC) by improving the Itoh's algorithm. Our new algorithm is suitable for pipeline scheduling on Itanium 2 which has an instruction to operate multiply-add (XMA instruction). And we implemented our new algorithm on Itanium 2. In the implementation, we optimized for parallel processing of REDC with extremely technique of hand-assembled code. By using our optimized code, average IPC of REDC is 4.02. Especially, average IPC in the "Core loop of REDC" is 5.25, which is an extremely good result because maximum IPC of Itanium 2 is 6, and its probability of pipeline stalling of our implementation is just only 5%. We also implemented RSA decryption with CRT based on our optimized code of REDC and technique of sliding-window method with 5-bit window size. Our implementation result attained 32 times of 4096-bit RSA decryption of CRT on Itanium 2 at 900MHz. Our REDC and RSA implementation can process variable bit length of RSA. And our RSA implementation performs 3.1 times faster than Intel's library in the best case.

A motivation of this paper is to realize fast implementation of RSA with long (say 4096-bit) keys. For such keys, Karatsuba and/or FFT algorithms may work better than conventional Montgomery's approach. Comparing such implementations (especially on Itanium 2) will be our future work.

Acknowledgement. The authors would like to thank to Kouichi Kumon for his technical advice of code optimazation on Itanium 2, and Tetsuya Izu for his editorial suggestions of the paper. We also thank anonymous referees of this paper for their comments.

References

[1] P.L.Montgomery, "Modular Multiplication without Trial Division", Mathematics of Computation, Vol.44, No.170, pp.519-521, 1985.

[2] C.K.Koc, T.Acar and B.S.Kaliski Jr., "Analyzing and Comparing Montgomery Multiplication Algorithms", IEEE Macro, Vol.16, No.3, pp.26-33, June 1996.

[3] K.Itoh, M.Takenaka, N.Torii, S.Temma and Y. Kurihara, "Fast Implementation of Public-Key Cryptography on a DSP TMS320C6201", Cryptographic Hardware and Embedded Systems -CHES '99,(LNCS1717), pp.61-72, 1999.

[4] Itanium 2 Processor Reference Manual for Software Development and Optimization, Intel, 2002.6

[5] Intel Itanium Architecture Software Developer's Manuals, Intel, 2005

[6] Intel C++ Compiler for Linux Reference, Intel, 2005

[7] A.F.Tenca, G.Todorov and C.K.Koc, "High-Radix Design of a Scrable Modular Muitiplier", Cryptographic Hardware and Embedded Systems - CHES 2001, (LNCS 2162), pp. 185-201, 2001.

[8] C.D.Walter, "Systolic Modular Multiplication", IEEE Trans. Computers, vol.42, no.3, pp. 376-378, Mar, 1993.

[9] G.Orlando and C.Paar, "A Scalable GF(p) Elliptic Curve Processor Archtechture for Programable Hardware" Cryptographic Hardware and Embedded Systems - CHES 2001 (LNCS 2162), pp. 348-363, 2001.

[10] S.E.Eldridge and C.D.Walter, "Hardware Implementation of Montgomery's Modular Multiplication Algorithm", IEEE Transactions on Computers, vol. 42, no. 6, July 1993, pp. 693699.

[11] C.D.Walter, "Montgomery's Multiplication Technique: How to Make It Smaller and Faster", Cryptographic Hardware and Embedded Systems - CHES'99 (LNCS 1717), pp. 80-93, 1999.

[12] A.F.Tenca and C.K.Koc, "A Scalable Archtecture for Montgomery Multiplication", Cryptographic Hardware and Embedded Systems - CHES '99 (LNCS 1717), pp. 94-108, 1999.

[13] R.L.Rivest, A.Shamir and L.Adleman, "A Method of obtaining digital signature and public key cryptosystems", Comm.of ACM, Vol.21, No.2, pp.120-126, Feb.1978.

[14] Paul Barrett, "Implementing the Rivest, Shamir, and Adleman Public-Key Encryption Algorithm on a Standard Digital Signal Processor", Advances in Cryptology-CRYPTO'86(LNCS263), pp.311-323, 1987.

[15] M.E.Kaihara and N.Takagi, "Bipartile Modular Multiplication", Cryptographic Hardware and Embedded Systems - CHES 2005 (LNCS 3659), pp. 185-210, 2005.

[16] National Institute for Standards and Technology (NIST), SP 800-57: Recommendation on Key Management, 2005.

[17] National Institute for Standards and Technology (NIST), SP 800-78: Cryptographic Algorithms and Key Sizes for Personal Identity Verification, 2005.

[18] S.R.Dusse and B.S.Kaliski Jr., "A Crytographic Library for the Motorola DSP56000", Advances in Cryptology - EUROCRYPTO '90 (LNCS 473), pp.230-244, 1990.

Efficient Implementation of Public Key Cryptosystems on Mote Sensors (Short Paper)

Haodong Wang and Qun Li

Department of Computer Science
College of William and Mary
{wanghd, liqun}@cs.wm.edu

Abstract. We report our implementation of the RSA and ECC public-key cryptosystem on Berkeley Motes. We detail the implementation of 1024-bit RSA and 160-bit ECC cryptosystems on MICA mote sensors. We have achieved the performance of 0.79s for RSA public key operation and 21.5s for private operation, and 1.3s for ECC signature generation and 2.8s for verification. For comparison, we also show our new ECC implementation on TelosB motes with a signature time 1.60s and a verification time 3.30s. For the detailed description of the implementation, we refer to our technical report[13].

1 Introduction

Public-key cryptography has been used extensively in data encryption, digital signature, user authentication, access control[12,14], etc. Compared with the symmetric key based schemes proposed for sensor networks, public-key cryptography is more flexible requiring no complicated key pre-distribution and no pairwise key sharing negotiation. It is a popular belief, however, in sensor network research community that public-key cryptography, such as RSA and Elliptic Curve Cryptography (ECC), is not practical because the required computational intensity is prohibitive for sensors with limited computation capability and extremely constrained memory space. The nascent exploration has already disabused of this misconception. The recent progress in ECC and RSA implementation on Atmel ATmega128[3], a CPU of 8Hz and 8 bits, shows that public-key cryptography is feasible for sensor network security related applications. This paper describes our implementation of 1024-bit RSA cryptosystem and 160-bit ECC cryptosystem on Motes of MICA2 family with a comparison of our new ECC implementation on TelosB motes.

The major operations in RSA and ECC cryptosystems are large integer arithmetics over the finite field. To efficiently perform RSA and ECC exponentiations on the low-power CPU of sensor motes, it is essential to optimize the expensive large integer operations, especially multiplication and reduction. Since most CPU cycles are consumed in these two integer operations, the efficiency of these two integer operation modules directly determines the performance of the encryption and decryption. Low-power sensor microcontroller usually has a very limited number of registers (32 8-bit registers in ATmega 128). Thus the time

P. Ning, S. Qing, and N. Li (Eds.): ICICS 2006, LNCS 4307, pp. 519–528, 2006.

for long integers to be loaded from or stored to memory is not negligible and the memory accesses have to be optimized for better performance. In this paper, we adopt the hybrid multiplication method [4], which is a very effective way to reduce the number of memory accesses. To precisely control the register and memory operations, we implement this module in assembly language. Our experiments demonstrate that the hybrid multiplication is at least 7 times faster than the conventional multi-precision multiplication programmed in C language. The modular reduction can also be optimized under certain conditions. For example, when the modulus is a pseudo-Mersenne number, the reduction can be greatly optimized and be finished more than 10 times faster than the classic long division method.

In addition to the optimization of the big integer operations, RSA and ECC can be further optimized. In RSA, Montgomery reduction can be applied to efficiently calculate the RSA exponentiation, and Chinese Remainder Theorem (CRT) can be used to reduce the exponent sizes and speed up the RSA exponentiation for up to 4 times. In ECC, we apply a mixed coordinate, the combination of Affine coordinate and Jacobian coordinate, to accelerate ECC exponentiation by avoiding operations such as inversions or reducing the amount of operations such as multiplication and squaring.

Our experiments show that both RSA and ECC can efficiently run on MICAz motes. For RSA, it takes 0.79 second to do a public key operation, and 21.5 seconds to perform a private key operation. For ECC, it takes 1.3 seconds to generate a signature, and 2.8 seconds to perform a signature verification. For our new ECC implementation on TelosB, the signature time and verification time are 1.60s and 3.30s respectively. It is possible to further reduce the computation time by using extended instruction set adopted in [4]. Our experiment results demonstrate that most operations in RSA and ECC are feasible for sensor network security applications.

2   Implementation

We have implemented RSA and ECC cryptosystems on MICAz motes, powered by ATmega128 microcontroller. The ATmega128 incorporates an 8MHz, 8-bit RISC CPU, 128K bytes programmable flash memory (ROM) and 4K bytes SRAM. This architecture provides 133 powerful instructions and 32×8 general purpose registers. Besides, ATmega128 also features an on-chip multiplier. In this section, we first describe the optimized large integer operation modules, which can be used for both RSA and ECC cryptosystems. Then we focus on the protocol related optimizations specifically for RSA and ECC, respectively. For ECC implementation, without further clarification, we concentrate on SECG recommended 160-bit elliptic curve: secp160r1.

2.1   Large Integer Operations

We have implemented a suite of large integer arithmetic operations, including addition, subtraction, shift, multiplication, division and modular reduction.

Among three different multiplication implementations [4,8,7], we have chosen to use Hybrid Multiplication proposed in [4]. We have implemented Hybrid multiplication in assembly language with column width $d = 4$, which requires 9 accumulator registers, 5 operand registers, 6 pointer registers, and others for temporary storage and loop control. For the comparison purpose, we also implement a standard multi-precision multiplication program in C language. Our experiments show the standard C program needs $122.2ms$ to finish the multiplication between two 128-byte integers, while it only takes $17.6ms$ for our Hybrid multiplication to do the same computation, which is more than 7 times faster.

Squaring is a special case of the multiplication, which has the same the multiplicand and the multiplier. Given an m-bit large integer $A = (A_1, A_0)$, where A_1, A_0 are two halves, $A^2 = A_1A_1 \times 2^m + 2A_1A_0 \times 2^{m/2} + A_0A_0$. Therefore, we can take advantage of the fact that A_1A_0 only needs to be calculated once. Compared with the multiplication, the optimized squaring can reduce the computational complexity up to 25%.

For Modular Reduction, We choose the classic long division method to implement this operation. Fortunately, the number of this type of modular reduction is very limited, it does not affect the overall performance much. The long division producer reduces the remainder by one byte in each iteration. In ECC cryptosystem, we choose to use pseudo-Mersenne primes as specified in NIST/SECG curves, the modular reduction can be optimized by conducting a fixed number of integer additions.

Modular inversion is used in both ECC and RSA. For ECC operation, we adopt an efficient Great Divide scheme [11]. For RSA operation, we use the classic Extended Euclidean Algorithm.

2.2 RSA Operations

In our first RSA implementation, it takes 4.6 seconds to finish the public key operation and 389 seconds to do a private key operation. To reduce the computational time, we have implemented the following two optimizations.

Montgomery Reduction. Montgomery reduction [9] is a method to efficiently perform the modular reduction without doing expensive division. For example, suppose we want to compute T modulo N, the algorithm says it is easy to compute $TR^{-1} \pmod N$ (without any division), where R is a radix ($R > N$) and co-prime to N. We do not validate this algorithm in this paper. Interested reader may refer to [9] for details. Having implemented the Montgomery reduction module, the performance of RSA public key and private key operations have been improved significantly to 1.2s and 82.2s, respectively.

Chinese Remainder Theorem (CRT). The complexity of the exponentiation in RSA largely depends on the the size of modulus n and the exponent (either public key or private key). Chinese Remainder Theorem (CRT) can be used to effectively reduce the computational complexity of exponentiation by reducing the size of both n and the exponent. With CRT implemented, the public key operation has been reduce to 0.79s. Correspondingly, the private key operation is reduced to 21.5s, approximately 1/4 of the time before doing CRT.

2.3 ECC Operations

Here we briefly discuss our optimizations for ECC operations.

ECC Addition and Doubling. The fundamental ECC operation is point addition and point doubling. The point multiplication can be decomposed to a series of addition and doubling operations. As discussed in previous section, point addition and doubling in Affine coordinate require integer inversion, which is considered much slower than integer multiplication. Cohen *et al.* showed that these operations in Projective coordinate and Jacobian coordinate yield better performance [1]. They further found addition and doubling in mixed coordinate, with the combination of Modified Jacobian coordinate and Affine coordinate, lead to the best performance [2]. As the result, point doubling operation reduces to 4 multiplications and 4 squaring, and the computational complexity of the point addition reduces to 8 multiplications and 3 squaring. Our experiments show that the performance of point multiplication improves around 6% compared with our previous implementation in Jacobian coordinate.

Modular Reduction on ECC Curve. Recall that modular reduction has to be applied after every large integer multiplication, it is also a performance critical operation. By taking advantage of pseudo-Mersenne primes specified in SECG curves, the complexity of the modular reduction operation can be reduced to a negligible amount.

Further Optimization. Examining the computational complexity, we notice that point addition is more expensive than point doubling. We adopt Non-adjacent forms (NAFs) [10] and sliding window method [5] in our implementation. According to our experiments, point multiplication with NAFs contributes at least 5% performance improvement. For sliding window, we select window size $s = 4$. Correspondingly, there are 16 entries in the partial result table. Our experiments show sliding window method is more effective than NAFs for fixed point multiplication, the performance of sliding window method is more than 10% better than that of NAFs.

3   Experiments and Performance Evaluation

We have implemented the 1024-bit RSA and the 160-bit ECC security primitive on MICAz motes, the latest sensor motes of the MICA family from Crossbow. Our experiments show that the public key operation (17-bit public key) only takes 0.79s and private key operation takes 21.5s. For the ECC operations, it takes 1.3 seconds to generate a signature and 2.8 second to do a signature verification. Considering that RSA verification normally happens at sensor side, and expensive signature generation is done by powerful devices, such as PDAs, we conclude both RSA and ECC are practical for small sensor nodes.

3.1   RSA Evaluation

In this subsection, we describe the experimental performance of 1024-bit RSA on our MICAz motes. We first present our experimental results and related issues during the implementation. We then give the performance analysis to quantify the computational complexity.

Experimental Results and Implementation Challenge. In the experiment, we randomly select two 512-bit prime number as p and q. For the public key operation, we choose a small exponent of $e = 2^{16} + 1$, which is commonly used value for e. Our program uses 15,832 byte code size and 3,224 byte data size. Compared with RSA implementation in [4], our code size is much larger because of the assignments of precomputation values during initialization stage. Our implementation spends 0.79s to finish a publick key operation and 21.5s to do a private key operation.

The biggest challenge in implementing 1024-bit RSA on MICAz motes is the memory constraint. MICAz mote only has 4KB RAM, which is the total space for data and program stack. Since the operands in 1024-bit RSA are mostly 128 integers, the subroutines, such as modular reduction, Extended Euclidean Algorithm and Montgomery reduction, have to reserve considerable amount of memory space for storing temporary results. In addition, for optimization purpose, a number of pre-computations are required. In our program, 1152 bytes of memory are used for storing system parameters, such as p, q and n, and precomputation results, such as R_p, R_q in CRT. Therefore, attentions need to be paid not to waste any memory usage. In practice, we have adopted two methods to save the memory space. First, we declare more global variables. The idea is to share the memory space among different subroutines in each module. Note this method is only good for those subroutines do not call each other. Otherwise the intermediate data will be lost. Second, we conduct every possible precomputation so that some modules may not be required during the RSA operation in the real time. For example, the Extended Euclidean algorithm is only used to find the public/private key pairs and to precompute the parameters used in Montgomery reduction. Removing this module saves us 1K data space.

Performance Analysis. To analyze the computational complexity distribution among the components in RSA exponentiation, we profile the execution time of multiplication, squaring, and modular reduction modules, the three most time consuming operations in RSA exponentiation. The profiling information is shown in Table 1.

Our analysis assumes that all optimization schemes have been applied in RSA exponentiation. To simplify the presentation, we denote "MUL" as, large integer multiplication, and let "SQR" be large integer squaring, and let "MOD" be large integer modular reduction. An "m/n" MOD means a MOD operation for a m-byte integer over a modulus with n-bytes. For example, 128/64 MOD denotes a modular reduction of a 128 byte integer with a 64 byte modulus.

Table 1. Execution time profiles of some important modules

Module	Operand Sizes (bytes)	Execution Time (ms)
MUL.	128 by 128	17.1
MUL.	64 by 64	4.48
SQR.	128 by 128	14.1
SQR.	64 by 64	3.87
MOD.	256/128	132
MOD.	192/128	74
MOD.	128/64	40

Let us consider an example of RSA operation to calculate $M = C^x \pmod{n}$, where x can be either public key or private key. Following the CRT algorithm, we first do two MODs to calculate C_p and C_q. Then, we conduct two Montgomery reductions to get M_p and M_q. Finally, two MULs, one MODs and one addition are required to compute M. Note the last two steps in CRT, which requires 2 MODs, can be simplified by doing addition first and then only one MOD. Except the Montgomery reduction, both public key and private key operation need to do two 128/64 MODs, two 128 × 128 MULs, one 192/128 MODs operations, which totally account for $2 \times 40 + 2 \times 17.1 + 74 = 188.2ms$.

The difference of execution time between public key and private key operations is at exponentiation part. Each Montgomery reduction requires two 64 × 64 MULs, one 128-byte addition and possible another 128-byte subtraction. The cost of addition and subtraction can be ignored. Therefore, the execution time of each Montgomery reduction is $2 \times 4.48 = 8.96ms$. Since we choose the public key to be $2^{16} + 1$, there are totally 16 64 × 64 SQRs and 1 64 × 64 MUL in the exponentiation. According to Table 1, the total time for SQRs and MUL with Montgomery reduction should be $16 \times 3.87 + 4.48 + 17 \times 8.96 = 218.7ms$. In addition, two 128/64 MODs are needed to convert operands between integer and N-residue before and after each exponentiation. For CRT optimization, we need to do two 512-bit exponentiations. Therefore, the exponentiation execution time for public key operation is $2 \times (218.7 + 2 \times 40) = 597.4ms$. Combined with the rest operations in CRT, the public key operation consumes $594.4 + 188.2 = 782.6ms$, which matches our test result very well.

For the private key operation, the number of SQRs is 511 (after CRT) in each reduced exponentiation. The number of MULs depends on the Hamming weight of the exponent. Our experiment shows the average Hamming weight of D_p and D_q of our private key is 278. Hence, there are 277 MULs required in each exponentiation. Therefore, the execution time for each exponentiation is $511 \times 3.87 + 277 \times 4.48 + 788 \times 8.96 = 10279ms$. Since the exponentiation execution time in private key operation overwhelmingly dominates other operations, we only need to consider the execution time of exponentiations only. Two such exponentiations consumes 20.5 seconds, closely matching our experiment result of 21.5s.

3.2 ECC Evaluation

In this subsection, we first present the performance of our implementation. Then we give an overall analysis to quantify the computation complexity.

The Performance of ECC Implementation. In experiments, we measure execution time and code size of our implementation. We choose secp160r1 as the elliptic curve in all experiments. We use the embedded system timer (921.6kHz) to measure the execution time of major operations in ECC, such as point multiplication, point addition and point doubling.

We first test point multiplication operation, which is comprised of point addition and doubling. We consider two cases in point multiplication. One is multiplying large integer with a fixed point(base point), and the other one is with a random point. Fixed point multiplication allows for optimization by precomputing. We apply sliding window technique[6] and set window size to 4, i.e., precomputing $2^4 - 1 = 15$ points. In experiments, we randomly generate 20 large integers to multiply with the point and take the average execution time as the result.

Since ECC point multiplication consists of addition and doubling operations, we further evaluate these two operations separately. We generate random points and large integers for tests. Since a single operation takes very little time, to reduce the error of clock inaccuracy, we measure 100 operations every round and take the average value.

Table 3 shows the experimental results of execution time. Point addition and doubling of our implementation is superior to the other two implementations, which results in a faster point multiplication.

Next, we implement ECDSA signature scheme. The experimental results are shown in Table 3. In fact, signing a message is mainly a fixed point multiplication. As we can see, the signature time is very close to the time consumed in fixed point multiplication. On the other hand, verification of ECDSA consists of one fixed point multiplication and one random point multiplication. Therefore, the performance of the verification is roughly the summation of one fixed point multiplication and one random point multiplication.

Table 2 presents the code size of the ECC implementation. The ECC library itself only uses 18.8KB ROM and 1.36KB RAM. However, ECDSA consumes 56.4KB ROM and 1.7KB RAM. The reason is that we add SHA1 hash function and radio communication module in the ECDSA package, where SHA-1, occupying more than 30KB memory space, takes a large portion of the code size.

Table 2. ECC implementation code sizes

	ECC library		ECDSA	
	ROM	RAM	ROM	RAM
ECC	18.8k	1.36k	56.4k	1.7k

A Performance Anatomy of ECC Point Multiplication on MICAz.
Since ECC point multiplication dominates the computational complexity in ECC
signature and verification, we are curious to learn the performance anatomy in
ECC point multiplication.

This analysis is based on 160-bit ECC curves. We use secp160r1 as the example. We also assume 4-bit sliding window method is used, and partial results are
precomputed. The computational cost for each window unit is 4 point doubling
and 1 point addition. Given a 161 bit private key, there are 41 window units.
Totally , 164 point doubling and 41 point additions are required to finish 1 point
multiplication.

Large (160-bit) integer multiplication, squaring and reduction are the most expensive operations in point doubling and point addition. To learn the amount of
time contributed by the above three operations in a fix point multiplication. We
first individually test the performance of large integer multiplication, squaring
and reduction. Our results show that it takes $0.47ms, 0.44ms$ and $0.07ms$ to perform a 160×160 multiplication, squaring and reduction, respectively. Next, we
count the the number of each operation required in a point multiplication. Since
we adopt the mixed coordination (the combination of Jacobian coordinate and
Affine coordinate), each point addition requires 8 large integer multiplications
and 3 large integer squaring, and each point doubling requires 4 large integer
multiplications and 4 large integer squaring. In addition, each multiplication,
squaring or shifting operation has to be followed by a modular reduction. Our
program shows the point addition requires 12 modular reductions, and the point
doubling requires 11 modular reductions. In total, each point multiplication costs
$164 \times 4 + 41 \times 8 = 984$ large integer multiplications, $164 \times 4 + 41 \times 3 = 779$ large
integer squaring and $164 \times 11 + 41 \times 12 = 2,296$ large integer modular reductions. Plugging in the results of the individual tests, we get the total amount
of time consumed on the three operations is 0.97s, roughly 78.2% of the total
time to do a fix point multiplication. The rest of 21.8% of the time is spent on
various operations, including inversion operation (to convert the Jacobian coordinate to Affine), addition, subtraction, shifting and memory copy, etc. Based
on above analysis, we believe the performance of ECC operations on MICAz can
be further improved by more refined and careful programming.

Performance Comparison. In the last part of the evaluation, we first investigate the performance difference of our cryptosystem implementation on different
sensor platforms. Then we compare the performance of our implementation with
existing research result [4] and give the possible explanation of the performance
gap.

To learn the performance of the public key cryptosystems on different sensor platforms, we have revamped our previous ECC implementation on TelosB
mote[14]. We summarize the performance comparison in Table 3. It clearly shows
that the performance of ECC operation on MICAz is slightly better than that on
TelosB, even though TelosB is equipped with a 8MHz, 16-bit CPU. After a careful and tedious investigation, we found the performance degradation on TelosB
is due to the following two reasons. First, the 8MHz CPU (MSP430) frequency

Table 3. The comparison of ECC execution Time on both mote platform operations, including fixed point multiplication (FPM), random point multiplication (RPM), point addition (PAdd) and point doubling (PDbl) and ECDSA signature generation (SIGN), verification (VERIFY) time

	FPM	RPM	PAdd	PDbl	SIGN	VERIFY
MICAz	1.24s	1.35s	6.2ms	5.8ms	1.35s	2.85s
TelosB	1.44s	1.60s	7.3ms	7.0ms	1.60s	3.32s

on TelosB is just a nominal value. In reality, the maximum CPU clock rate is actually 4MHz. Second, the hardware multiplier in MSP430 CPU uses a group of special peripheral registers which are located outside of MSP430 CPU. As the result, it takes MSP430 eight CPU cycles to perform an unsigned multiplication, while it at most takes four cycles to do the same operation in Atmega CPU. The above two reasons explain why TelosB cannot perform better than MICAz.

We also compare our ECC performance with the result in [4]. Gura *et al.* implemented the ECC (the same curve) on Atmega128 CPU, which is the same CPU used on MICAz mote. Their result, 0.81s for a random point multiplication, is about 40% faster than 1.35s of our result. We notice that the time for their 160×160 multiplication is 0.39ms, roughly 17% faster than our 0.47ms. In general, we believe their code is more polished and optimized in many aspects than our code. Furthermore, Our code is implemented in TinyOS, and mostly written with NesC (except several critical large integer operations), which could introduce additional CPU cycles.

4   Conclusion

In this paper, we present a number of optimization schemes to efficiently implement the public key cryptosystems in small, less-powerful sensor devices. We implement 1024-bit RSA and 160-bit ECC on Mica motes. Our experiments demonstrate that the public key cryptography is promising for sensors. Our experiments show that the times for ECC signature generation and verification are 1.3s and 2.8s respective for Mica motes, and 1.6s and 3.3s for TelosB motes. For RSA implementation, we have achieved 0.79s for public key operation and 21.5s for private operation on Mica motes. We believe the performance can be improved by more careful programming or using more powerful sensors.

References

1. H. Cohen, A. Miyaji, and T. Ono. Efficient elliptic curve exponentiation. In *ICICS'97*, pages 282–290, Springer-Verlag, 1997.
2. H. Cohen, A. Miyaji, and T. Ono. Efficient elliptic curve exponentiation using mixed coordinates. In *ASIACRYPT*, 1998.
3. V. Gupta, M. Millard, S. Fung, Y. Zhu, N. Gura, H. Eberle, and S. Shantz. Sizzle: A standards-based end-to-end security architecture for the embedded internet. In *PerCom*, Kauai, Mar. 2005.

4. N. Gura, A .Patel, A. Wander, H. Eberle, and S. C. Shantz. Comparing elliptic curve cryptography and rsa on 8-bit cpus. In *CHES*, Boston, Aug. 2004.
5. C. K. Koc. High-speed rsa implementation, rsa laboratories technical report tr-201, version 2.0. Nov 22 1994.
6. C. K. Koc. High-speed rsa implementation. In *RSA Lab TR201*, Nov. 1994.
7. A. Liu and P. Ning. Tinyecc: Elliptic curve cryptography for sensor networks. Sept 15 2005.
8. D.J. Malan, M. Welsh, and M.D. Smith. A public-key infrastructure for key distribution in tinyos based on elliptic curve cryptography. In *SECON*, Santa Clara, CA, October 2004.
9. P. Montgomery. Modular multiplication without trial division. *Mathematics of Communication*, 44(170):519–521, April 1985.
10. F. Morain and J. Olivos. Speeding up the computations on an elliptic curve using addition-subtraction chains. *Theoretical Informatics and Applications*, 24:531–543, 1990.
11. S. Chang Shantz. From euclid's gcd to montgomery multiplication to the great divide. In *Technical report, Sun Lab TR-2001-95*, June 2001.
12. Haodong Wang and Qun Li. Distributed user access control in sensor networks. In *IEEE DCOSS*, pages 305–320, San Francisco, CA, June 2006.
13. Haodong Wang and Qun Li. Efficient Implementation of Public Key Cryptosystems on MicaZ and TelosB Motes. Technical Report WM-CS-2006, College of William and Mary, October 2006.
14. Haodong Wang, Bo Sheng, and Qun Li. Elliptic curve cryptography based access control in sensor networks. *Int. Journal of Security and Networks*, 1(2), 2006.

Threshold Implementations
Against Side-Channel Attacks and Glitches[*]

Svetla Nikova[1], Christian Rechberger[2], and Vincent Rijmen[2]

[1] Department Electrical Engineering, ESAT/COSIC,
Katholieke Universiteit Leuven, Belgium
Svetla.Nikova@esat.kuleuven.be
[2] Institute for Applied Information Processing and Communications (IAIK)
Graz University of Technology, Austria
{Christian.Rechberger, Vincent.Rijmen}@iaik.tugraz.at

Abstract. Implementations of cryptographic algorithms are vulnerable to side-channel attacks. Masking techniques are employed to counter side-channel attacks that are based on multiple measurements of the same operation on different data. Most currently known techniques require new random values after every nonlinear operation and they are not effective in the presence of glitches. We present a new method to protect implementations. Our method has a higher computational complexity, but requires random values only at the start, and stays effective in the presence of glitches.

Keywords: Masking, secret sharing, side-channel attacks.

1 Introduction

Several approaches to design circuits that counteract side-channel attacks, have been published recently. A popular approach is to make the intermediate results of the cryptographic algorithm being executed independent of the secret key. This can be done both at the algorithm level [2,5,10,18] and at the gate level [12,25]. These approaches have in common that they require the use of random values in order to *mask* the data that is being processed. A common feature of all these approaches is that in order to implement nonlinear circuits, they require the introduction of additional (*fresh*) random values. Among other reasons, these additional random values are needed in order to mask the intermediate results computed by the circuits. Without the fresh random values, these intermediate results would cause leakage of information. Additionally, it has been shown that the occurrence of glitches can lead to side-channel information in circuits that

---

[*] The work described in this paper has been supported in part by the European Commission under contract IST-2002-507932 (ECRYPT) and through the Austrian Science Fund (FWF) under grant number P16110-N04. The information in this paper is provided as is, and no warranty is given or implied that the information is fit for any particular purpose. The user thereof uses the information at its sole risk and liability.

P. Ning, S. Qing, and N. Li (Eds.): ICICS 2006, LNCS 4307, pp. 529–545, 2006.
© Springer-Verlag Berlin Heidelberg 2006

were previously believed to be secure [15,16]. Recently, also other ways to break gate level masking schemes have been devised [24].

In terms of software implementations, in [19], it is shown that many existing masking proposals are not secure against higher-order attack. A first proposal to secure AES software implementations against higher-order attacks is given in [22]. Gate-level solutions are proposed in [9,20]. Our method addresses this issue at the circuit level.

In this paper we describe a new approach to mask, based on secret sharing [3,23], threshold cryptography [8] and multi-party computation protocols [27]. The main contributions of this paper are the following. Firstly, we show circuits that resist side-channel attacks, even in the presence of glitches. Secondly, we achieve provable security against first-order side-channel attacks. Thirdly, our circuits also resist higher-order attacks that are based on a comparison of mean power consumption.

Compared to traditional masking approaches, our approach uses more random values during the setup. A related approach was presented in [6]. It requires new random values for remasking during the computation, which is costly in many environments. Furthermore, remasking can be effective only if the delays of all the circuits are fully controlled and if there are no glitches [15,16,18]. An alternative approach to avoid the generation of fresh random values is presented in [2]: they derive new masking values from the old ones by applying linear functions. Another related approach was presented in [11]. Also there, the effect of glitches is not considered.

We introduce notation and terminology in Section 2. In Sections 3–5 we present the main contribution of this paper: a new theory for designing implementations that are provably secure against first-order side-channel attacks, even in the presence of glitches. In Section 6 we illustrate our approach by discussing an important application: the implementation of the multiplicative inverse in the field $GF(2^m)$. We briefly discuss the resistance of our schemes against template attacks in Section 7 and conclude with suggestions for future work in Section 8.

2   Notation and Terminology

We use $\oplus, \bigoplus$ to denote addition in the field $GF(2^m)$ (XOR) and $+, \sum$ to denote addition of real numbers. A vector $(x_1, x_2, \ldots, x_n)$ is also denoted by $\overline{x}$, and the reduced vector $(x_1, x_2, \ldots, x_{i-1}, x_{i+1}, \ldots, x_n)$ by $\overline{x}_i$. We denote by $Pr(t(\overline{x}) = T)$ the probability that the variable t takes value T, i.e. the number of times that $t(\overline{x}) = T$ divided by the number of values the input of the circuit can take.

In our approach, the data is not masked by only one random value, but by two or more. Hence, during setup we need typically more random values than with traditional approaches. Our approach is inspired by methods used in secret sharing and threshold computing systems. We say that a variable x is split into n *shares* x_i if

$$x = \bigoplus_{i=1}^{n} x_i . \tag{1}$$

We will only use (n, n) secret sharing schemes, hence all n shares are needed in order to determine x uniquely. In a *perfect* (n, n) secret sharing scheme, knowledge of up to $n-1$ shares doesn't give any additional information on the value of x. Observe that a $(2, 2)$ secret sharing scheme corresponds to a traditional masking scheme. In a (k, t, n) *ramp scheme* [4], t honest parties are needed to recover the secret, but more than k malicious parties can already obtain information about the secret. In this paper, we use $(1, n, n)$ ramp schemes and secret sharing schemes where the conditional probability distribution $\Pr(\overline{X}|X)$ is uniform and hence:

$$\forall \overline{X} : \ \Pr(\overline{x} = \overline{X}) = c \Pr(x = \bigoplus_{i=1}^{n} X_i), \tag{2}$$

with c a normalization constant, which ensures that $\sum_{\overline{X}} \Pr(\overline{x} = \overline{X}) = 1$.

3   Basic Principle

We introduce our approach to implement linear and non-linear transformations in a secure way. We point out how this idea is related to threshold cryptography and we give an example that we will use in the remainder of this paper.

3.1   Linear Transformations

Consider a transformation $z = \mathrm{L}(x)$ over $\mathrm{GF}(2^m)$, which is linear over $\mathrm{GF}(2)$. The easiest way to implement a linear transformation securely is to process the n shares independently. Indeed, if

$$z_i = \mathrm{L}(x_i),\ 0 \le i < n, \tag{3}$$

then by definition of a linear transformation, we have

$$z = \bigoplus_{i=1}^{n} z_i = \bigoplus_{i=1}^{n} \mathrm{L}(x_i) = \mathrm{L}\left(\bigoplus_{i=1}^{n} x_i\right) = \mathrm{L}(x) . \tag{4}$$

Linear transformations taking more inputs can be treated in the same way. For a linear transformation $z = \mathrm{LL}(x, y, \dots)$, we take all $\mathrm{f}_i = \mathrm{LL}$.

Such an implementation of a linear transformation doesn't leak information that can be used in a side-channel attack, even if presence of glitches is taken into account [15,16]. A typical property of this implementation is that each output share z_i depends only on one input share of each variable (x_i, y_i, $\dots$).

3.2   Non-linear Transformations

Our idea is to construct circuits for non-linear transformations having a similar property as the secure circuits for linear transformations discussed in the previous section. Intuitively, it is clear that if a share z_i doesn't depend on the value of an input share $x_i, y_i, \ldots$, then z_i can't be correlated to $x, y, \ldots$ Neither will the computation of z_i leak information about the value of $x, y, \ldots$ By imposing additional constraints, we will also ensure that no correlation to the output z exists. In this section, we introduce two properties. In the next section, we will show that with functions satisfying these properties, we can construct secure circuits.

Let $z = N(x, y, \ldots)$ denote a transformation over $GF(2^m)$ which is not linear over $GF(2)$. Let $f_1, f_2, \ldots, f_n$ be a set of functions satisfying the following properties:

Property 1 (Non-completeness). Every function is independent of at least one share of each of the input variables $x, y, \ldots$

$$
\begin{aligned}
z_1 &= f_1(x_2, x_3, \ldots, x_n, y_2, y_3, \ldots, y_n, \ldots) &&= f_1(\overline{x}_1, \overline{y}_1, \ldots) \\
z_2 &= f_2(x_1, x_3, \ldots, x_n, y_1, y_3, \ldots, y_n, \ldots) &&= f_2(\overline{x}_2, \overline{y}_2, \ldots) \\
&\cdots \\
z_n &= f_n(x_1, x_2, \ldots, x_{n-1}, y_1, y_2, \ldots, y_{n-1}, \ldots) = f_n(\overline{x}_n, \overline{y}_n, \ldots)
\end{aligned}
\tag{5}
$$

Property 2 (Correctness). The sum of the output shares gives the desired output.

$$
z = \bigoplus_{i=1}^{n} z_i = \bigoplus_{i=1}^{n} f_i(\ldots) = N(x).
\tag{6}
$$

Property 1 and 2 impose a lower bound on the number of shares n.

Theorem 1. *The minimum number of shares required to implement a product of s variables with a realization satisfying Property 1 and 2 is given by*

$$
n \geq 1 + s \,.
$$

Proof. Multiplying s factors with n shares each can be done in the following way. Collect in the first output share all terms that don't contain the first share of any of the inputs. Collect in the second output share all terms that contain the first share of any of the inputs, but not the second share of any of the inputs. Continuing in this way, collect in output share i all the terms containing input shares $1, 2, \ldots$ and $i - 1$, but not input share i. Finally, collect in output share n the terms containing the terms with input shares $1, 2, \ldots$ and $n - 1$ but not input share n. Only if $n - 1 \geq s$, there are no terms left after step n.   □

It follows that we need at least 3 shares in order to implement a non-linear function. The construction used in the proof of Theorem 1 can also be used to implement more general monomials. For instance, the monomial $x^3 y$ can be implemented as a product of four variables. Because not all variables are independent, it might be that there exist other solutions with a lower number of shares. Hence, we have the following corollary.

Corollary 1. *The maximum number of shares required to implement a function* N *of* u *variables over* $GF(2^m)$, *equals* $1 + 2^{mu}$.

Proof. Since $\forall x \in GF(2^m) : x^{2^m} = x$, it is always possible to describe N as a multi-variate polynomial of degree at most 2^{mu}. For instance, we can use the Lagrange interpolation formula. We construct the functions f_i for each separate monomial of N by applying the same method as in the proof of Theorem 1. Summing up the functions for each monomial, we obtain the functions for N.   □

3.3   Effects on the Power Consumption

By definition, knowledge of up to $n-1$ shares of an input variable, doesn't reveal any information on this input variable. In a circuit satisfying Property 1, each share z_i of the output z is independent of at least one share of each input variable. Consequently, we have that the output shares are uncorrelated to the input variables. Such a circuit has the following advantages:

1. Each intermediate result of the computation is uncorrelated to the input variables. Hence, no additional random values are needed for masking the intermediate results of the computation.
2. Even the presence of glitches doesn't result in the leakage of information, provided that we can restrict an attacker to look at only one f_i at a time. We will discuss in Section 4.2 what we can do in case an attacker can measure the consumption of more than one f_i simultaneously.

We generalize now condition (2) in the following way:

$$\Pr(\overline{x} = \overline{X}, \overline{y} = \overline{Y}, \dots) = c \Pr(x = \bigoplus_i X_i, y = \bigoplus_i Y_i, \dots). \qquad (7)$$

In words, this means that any bias present in the joint distribution of $\overline{x}$ and $\overline{y}$ is due to biases in the joint distribution of x and y. Under this condition, we can prove the following.

Theorem 2. *In a circuit implementing a set of functions satisfying Property 1 and Property 2, when the input satisfies (7), all the intermediate results are independent of the inputs* x, y, ... *and the output* z. *Also the power consumption, or any other characteristic of each individual function* f_i *are independent of* x, y, ... *and* z.

The proof is given in Appendix A.

Example 1. Consider the multiplication of two operands in a finite field with characteristic 2: $z = N(x, y) = xy$. Let the number of shares $n = 3$ and define the 3 functions f_i as follows:

$$\begin{aligned}
z_1 &= f_1(x_2, x_3, y_2, y_3) = x_2 y_2 \oplus x_2 y_3 \oplus x_3 y_2 \\
z_2 &= f_2(x_1, x_3, y_1, y_3) = x_3 y_3 \oplus x_1 y_3 \oplus x_3 y_1 \\
z_3 &= f_3(x_1, x_2, y_1, y_2) = x_1 y_1 \oplus x_1 y_2 \oplus x_2 y_1
\end{aligned} \qquad (8)$$

The functions f_i satisfy Property 1. Furthermore, since

$$z_1 \oplus z_2 \oplus z_3 = (x_1 \oplus x_2 \oplus x_3)(y_1 \oplus y_2 \oplus y_3) = xy = z, \qquad (9)$$

also Property 2 is satisfied and the functions f_i form a secure realization of $N(x, y)$.

Example 2. The following example illustrates why we need condition (7). Consider the linear transformation $z = L(x, y) = x \oplus y$. The realization

$$z_i = f(x_{i+1}, y_{i+1}) = x_{i+1} \oplus y_{i+1} \qquad (10)$$

satisfies Properties 1 and 2. If $x = y$, then $z = \bigoplus_i z_i = 0$. Suppose now that $\Pr(\overline{x} = X, \overline{y} = Y) = \Pr(\overline{x} = X)$ if $\overline{X} = \overline{Y}$, and zero otherwise. With this dependency between $\overline{x}$ and $\overline{y}$, we get *always* $z_i = 0, \forall i$, and each z_i is perfectly correlated to z.

3.4 Relation to Multi-party Computation and Threshold Cryptography

Multi-Party Computation (MPC) protocols enable a set of players to securely evaluate an arbitrary function on their private inputs, but some of the players could be corrupted by an adversary. Consider n players, each player holding an input x_i. The players want to compute a function $F(x_1, \ldots, x_n) = z$ in a secure manner, which informally implies two things. The adversary cannot interrupt the computation, hence the computed value is correct. Additionally the adversary cannot learn any information about the inputs of the honest players, except of course what can be inferred from the function value. The results can be easily extended to more general types of functionality e.g. computing a function $F(x_1, \ldots, x_n) = (z_1, \ldots, z_n)$.

A (t, n) threshold system allows n parties to do secure computations when at least t parties are honest. We equate each function f_i with a party, thus we have an (n, n) threshold system. Our situation differs from the typical MPC case, because each input x_i is used by several parties (functions). Since each two functions together (possibly) use all inputs, we have an $(1, n, n)$ ramp scheme.

The functions are *corrupt* by means of side-channel attacks. A corrupt function still produces correct results, hence we have *passive corruption*. In a first-order attack, the attacker can corrupt at most one function at a time. Theorem 2 shows we achieve perfect security against first-order attacks.

If the attacker can corrupt several functions simultaneously, then the attack is called a *higher-order attack* [13,17]. We discuss issues that arise in this setting in Section 4.2.

4   Glitches

In this section, we first illustrate how glitches can cause leakage of information. Subsequently, we examine one traditional masking scheme and we show that our approach leads to improved security.

CMOS circuits consume very low amounts of power. Consequently, the power consumption caused by glitches is relatively large compared to the power consumption caused by the "normal" operation of CMOS circuits. Most masking schemes[1] presented in the cryptographic literature don't take the presence of glitches into account [5,18,25]. It has been shown that for many of these traditional masking schemes the presence of glitches or delays in logical circuits causes side-channel leakage in the power consumption [15,16].

Firstly, consider a simple AND gate, with inputs x, y and output z. Assume now that a glitch occurs in x, or that input x becomes stable significantly later than input y. If input y equals 1, then a variation or glitch in input x will cause the AND gate to temporarily change state, because $z = x$. However, if $y = 0$, then $z = 0$ and changes at input x will not affect the output. Consequently, the power consumption caused by glitches in input x depends on the value of input y. In the next subsection, we will study the effect of glitches in a masked AND gate.

4.1   Glitches in a Traditionally Masked AND-Gate

We consider a typical implementation of a masked AND gate [25], illustrated in Figure 1. To make the analysis easier, we assume here that XOR gates exist as basic primitives: we don't decompose them into smaller building blocks.

The circuit takes 5 inputs: the two random masks a, b, the two masked inputs $\widetilde{x} = a \oplus x, \widetilde{y} = b \oplus y$, and a new random value c to mask the output $z = x$ AND y. The circuit outputs the output mask and the masked output, which is computed as follows:

$$\widetilde{z} = \widetilde{x}\widetilde{y} \oplus (b\widetilde{x} \oplus (a\widetilde{y} \oplus (ab \oplus c))) \ . \tag{11}$$

Note that the order in which the XOR gates are evaluated, is not arbitrary. If the circuit would compute at any time the sum of any of the products, then there would be leakage. For instance, $\widetilde{x}\widetilde{y} \oplus b \cdot \widetilde{x} = y\widetilde{x}$, which leaks information about y. This is one of the reasons why the new random value c is introduced in the beginning and why all the products are added one by one to it.

Consider now what happens if a glitch occurs in input $\widetilde{x}$. The propagation of this glitch will depend on the values of b and $\widetilde{y}$. The power consumption caused by the glitch is related to the number of gates that "see" the glitch. It is clear from Table 1 that the energy consumption depends on the values of b and $\widetilde{y}$. Since the mean power consumption is different for $y = 0$ and $y = 1$, the power consumption leaks information on the value of y. Similar results can be obtained by analyzing the effect of a glitch in one of the other inputs, and the cases where some of the inputs arrive delayed with respect to the other inputs [15,16].

We conclude that switching characteristics of logical circuits may invalidate some of the assumptions commonly made in proofs of security against side-channel attacks. A slightly frustrating aspect of the findings in [15] is that it remains unclear how to construct security proofs that do take into account the

---

[1] In this section we use the terms "mask" and "masked gate" in order to stay close to the original description of the schemes.

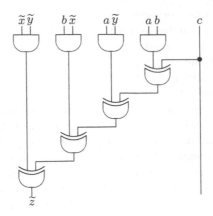

Fig. 1. Glitch propagation through a masked AND gate

Table 1. Number of affected gates in the circuit of Figure 1, when a glitch occurs in input $\tilde{x}$

$b\ \tilde{y}$	AND	XOR
0 0	0	0
0 1	1	1
1 0	1	2
1 1	2	2

presence of glitches. In order to avoid exhaustive analysis of all the possible combinations of signal arrival times, it seems beneficial to use a circuit that has Property 1.

4.2   Glitches in a Shared AND-Gate

The realization (8) can be used to implement multiplication in a finite field with characteristic two. Multiplication in GF(2) corresponds to the logical AND operation. Hence, the circuit can be used as a masked AND gate in order to implement arbitrary Boolean functions.

Theorem 3. *If the distributions of the input shares $\tilde{x}, \overline{y}$ satisfy (7), then the mean power consumption of a circuit implementing realization (8) is independent of x, y and z, even in the presence of glitches or the delayed arrival of some inputs.*

Proof. Theorem 2 states that all characteristics of the circuits implementing one of the functions f_i are independent of x, y, and z. Since no assumption is made on the behavior of the circuit and/or the presence of glitches, the theorem also holds in this case. Consequently, also the mean power consumption of each individual circuit is independent of x, y, z, even in the presence of glitches. Since the mean power consumption of the whole circuit equals the sum of the mean power consumptions of the individual functions, it is also independent of x, y, z.   □

Theorem 3 only applies to the mean power consumption of the circuit. We don't achieve indistinguishable distributions of the power consumption as demanded in [5]. Nevertheless, since the mean power consumption of the circuit is always the same, it resists the type of higher-order attacks that are based on the mean value of the addition or subtraction of the power consumption traces of the different circuits [17]. Although one can theoretically devise side-channel attacks that don't require a difference in the mean power consumption, such attacks have not been demonstrated in practice yet.

If the used logic style prevents the occurrence of glitches, then not only the mean power consumption, but also the variance are independent of the values of x, y, z. This can be shown by simply going through all possible state transitions.

5   Implementing Arbitrary Functions

Theorem 1 shows that implementing more complicated functions typically leads to an increase in the number of shares required, as well as an increase in the number of gates required. As a rough rule of thumb, going from 1 share to n shares will increase the number of gates with a factor n^2. This should't come as a big surprise, because introducing resistance gainst power attacks always comes at a price. For instance, in [20], the authors report an increase in area with a factor 5, for a decrease in performance with factor 0.6. The software solution proposed in [22] doubles the code size, multiplies the RAM requirements with a factor of 20 and decreases the performance with a factor 50. Other proposals add more complexity for the same security level. Nevertheless, for functions with large numbers of inputs, it is better to adopt pipelining.

Pipelining is often used to speed up hardware implementations. In order to allow large clock frequencies, combinatorial logic circuits shouldn't be many levels deep. Pipelining is an implementation technique where a logical circuit with l levels is divided into two circuits with $l/2$ levels, separated by a register, which stores the intermediate result of the first stage until the active phase of the next clock cycle. As an example, the AES implementation of [26] uses a pipeline with two stages to implement the S-boxes.

Dividing a combinatorial circuit into separate pipelining stages, can also reduce the number of shares and the number of gates required for a secure implementation. By definition, a register is insensible to glitches. The registers storing the intermediate results at the end of stage bound the propagation of glitches and delays. When considered individually, each of the pipeline stages represents a mathematical function that is less complex than the full circuit: the nonlinear degree will be lower and/or the number of monomials that needs to be summed. This will typically reduced the required number of shares and gates.

If the mean power consumption of each pipeline stage is constant, then also the mean of the total power consumption is constant, and the circuit is secure against first-order differential power attacks. Note that condition (7) needs now to be fulfilled at the input of each pipeline stage in order for Theorem 3 to hold. Since the input of the next pipeline stage is formed by the output of the previous pipeline stage, we can achieve this goal by demanding that the circuits satisfy an additional balance property.

Property 3 (Balance). A realization of $z = N(x, y, \dots)$ is balanced if for all distributions of the inputs x, y, $\dots$, and for all input share distributions satisfying (7) the conditional probability

$$\Pr(\overline{z} = \overline{Z} | z = \bigoplus_i Z_i)$$

is constant.

If the function N is invertible, then Property 3 is satisfied by invertible realizations. In an invertible realization of $z = N(x)$, every vector $\overline{z}$ is reached for exactly one input vector $\overline{x}$. This condition is stricter than the requirement that every value z is reached for exactly one input x.

Example 3. The realization (8) of the multiplication in Example 1 doesn't have Property 3. In fact, there is no realization for multiplication satisfying this property with 3 shares only. The following realization with 4 shares satisfies Property 1, 2 and 3:

$$
\begin{aligned}
z_1 &= (x_3 \oplus x_4)(y_2 \oplus y_3) \oplus y_2 \oplus y_3 \oplus y_4 \oplus x_2 \oplus x_3 \oplus x_4 \\
z_2 &= (x_1 \oplus x_3)(y_1 \oplus y_4) \oplus y_1 \oplus y_3 \oplus y_4 \oplus x_1 \oplus x_3 \oplus x_4 \\
z_3 &= (x_2 \oplus x_4)(y_1 \oplus y_4) \oplus y_2 \oplus x_2 \\
z_4 &= (x_1 \oplus x_2)(y_2 \oplus y_3) \oplus y_1 \oplus x_1.
\end{aligned}
\tag{12}
$$

Property 1 and 2 can be verified with pen and paper. Property 3 was verified by direct computation of all conditional probabilities.

6   Example: Inversion over Finite Fields

Finite field inversion is an important map, for instance because of its use in the AES. As illustration, we study here inversion in GF(16).

Firstly, let GF(4) be represented as $GF(2)[t]/(t^2 + t + 1)$. Operations in GF(4) then correspond to:

$$
\begin{aligned}
(at \oplus b) \oplus (ct \oplus d) &= (a \oplus c)t && \oplus (b \oplus d) \\
(at \oplus b) \times (ct \oplus d) &= (ad \oplus bc \oplus ac)t \oplus (bd \oplus ac) \\
(at \oplus b)^{-1} &= at && \oplus (a \oplus b) \\
(at \oplus b)^3 &= && ab \oplus a \oplus b.
\end{aligned}
\tag{13}
$$

Secondly, let GF(16) be represented by $GF(4)[s]/(s^2 \oplus s \oplus \alpha)$. Inversion in GF(16) then becomes:

$$(as \oplus b)^{-1} = a(a^2 \alpha \oplus ab \oplus b^2)^{-1} s \oplus (a \oplus b)(a^2 \alpha \oplus ab \oplus b^2)^{-1}.$$

Defining $c = a \oplus b$, we obtain:

$$(as \oplus (c \oplus a))^{-1} = a(a^2\alpha \oplus ac \oplus c^2)^{-1}s \oplus c(a^2\alpha \oplus ac \oplus c^2)^{-1}$$
$$= (a^2\alpha^2 \oplus a^3c^2 \oplus ac)s \oplus (ac\alpha^2 \oplus a^2c^3 \oplus c^2). \quad (14)$$

Combining (13) with (14) and choosing $\alpha = t$, we obtain

$$((xt \oplus y)s \oplus (zt \oplus v))^{-1} = (ft \oplus g)s \oplus (ht \oplus k),$$

where f, g, h, and k are Boolean functions defined as follows:

$$f = x \oplus y \oplus xv \oplus xyz$$
$$g = y \oplus xv \oplus yz \oplus xyz \oplus xyv$$
$$h = y \oplus xv \oplus yv \oplus xzv$$
$$k = z \oplus v \oplus xz \oplus yz \oplus yv \oplus xzv \oplus yzv.$$

Theorem 1 predicts we need at least 4 shares to implement these functions. Exhaustive search revealed that no realization with 4 shares can satisfy Property 3. We give a realization with 5 shares for f, g, h and k in Appendix B.

7 Considering Template Attacks

In the previous sections of this paper, we ignored the possibility of simple power attacks [14]. We assumed that an attacker can't use a single measurement to obtain a meaningful signal. Provided that a few basic rules are followed during the implementation, this is usually a realistic assumption, which is commonly made when discussing masking schemes. However, more sophisticated methods have been developed since then.

7.1 Template Attacks

Template attacks were introduced in [7], as an extension of simple power attacks. A template attack starts with a *profiling phase*, during which the attacker has at his disposal a freely programmable device which is identical to the targeted device. This device is used to build a model (templates) of its state while performing different operations on (parts of) the secret key. Afterwards, in the *hypothesis-testing phase*, these templates are used to classify the single trace of the targeted device which in turn reduces the entropy of the key. In order to improve classification results, multivariate instead of univariate statistics is employed to yield practical classification results.

Recent advances in template attacks highlight the importance of this topic in the context of masking schemes [1]. These results are summarized as follows. Using single-bit templates even masked implementations can be broken. The new, but in many practical circumstances reasonable setting is that an attacker can get hold of a device with a biased RNG which is generating the used masks. Using templates generated from such a card, it is shown that even devices with perfectly unbiased masks can be attacked.

7.2   Resistance Against Template Attacks

Our proposal to protect implementations does not prevent this type of attack if a biased RNG is in the hands of an attacker. However it makes it more difficult to implement the attack, because the parallel computation of the n shares lowers the signal-to-noise ratio. For example, consider a Hamming weight based leakage model. Let w denote the bit-width of a share. Ignoring noise, the relative leakage l is given by:

$$l = \frac{nw - \log_2(\sum_{i=0}^{nw} \frac{\binom{nw}{i}^2}{2^{n \cdot w}})}{nw}. \tag{15}$$

Since we assume that all shares are uncorrelated, the number of shares n effectively multiplies the bit-width. As a consequence the number of samples needed in the profiling step is greatly increased. If this number of samples can't be taken, then the classification results will get worse. In turn, the gain for the attacker, namely the reduction of the key entropy, is less.

8   Conclusions and Open Problems

We presented a new method to design implementations that counteract side-channel attacks. The big advantages are that we don't need fresh random values after every nonlinear transformation and that we achieve provable security against first order attacks, even in the presence of glitches. The scheme also resists certain types of higher-order attacks. To illustrate the design method, we applied it to the computation of the multiplicative inverse over $GF(2^4)$.

Disadvantages are the increased data storage requirements due to the higher number of shares, and the corresponding increase in computational complexity.

Investigating whether other attacks are feasible and how to protect against them is proposed as topic of further research. Future work also includes the design of more complicated circuits. Clearly, implementing more complex circuits in one go, will increase the complexity of our circuits dramatically. We propose to employ techniques from proactive secret sharing schemes [21] in order to reduce the circuit complexity. This has the added benefit to limit an attacker's possibilities even further, but has as disadvantage that now fresh random values are required.

References

1. Dakshi Agrawal, Josyula R. Rao, Pankaj Rohatgi, Kai Schramm, "Templates as Master Keys", J.R. Rao, B. Sunar, Eds., CHES 2005, LNCS 3659, Springer-Verlag, 2005, pp. 15–29.
2. Mehdi-Laurent Akkar, Christophe Giraud, "An implementation of DES and AES, secure against some attacks", Ç Koç, D. Naccache, Ch. Paar, Eds., CHES 2001, LNCS 2162, Springer-Verlag, 2001, pp. 309–318.
3. George Blakley, Safeguarding cryptographic keys, AFIPS 48, 1979, pp. 313-317.

4. George Blakley, Catherine Meadows, "Security of ramp schemes", CRYPTO '84, LNCS 196, Springer-Verlag, 1984, pp. 242–268.
5. Johannes Blömer, Jorge Guajardo Merchan, Volker Krummel, "Provably Secure Masking of AES", H. Handschuh, M. Anwar Hasan, Eds., Selected Areas in Cryptography (SAC 2004), LNCS 3357, Springer-Verlag, 2004, pp. 69-83.
6. Suresh Chari, Charanjit S. Jutla, Josyula R. Rao, Pankaj Rohatgi, "Towards Sound Approaches to Counteract Power- Analysis Attacks" CRYPTO '99, LNCS 1666, Springer-Verlag, 1999, pp. 398-412.
7. Suresh Chari, Josyula R. Rao, Pankaj Rohatgi, "Template Attacks", B. Kaliski, Ç Koç, Ch. Paar, Eds., CHES 2002, LNCS 2523, Springer-Verlag, 2003, pp. 13–28.
8. Yvo Desmedt, "Some recent research aspects of threshold cryptography", E. Okamoto, G. Davida, M. Mambo, Eds., Information Security, LNCS 1396, Springer-Verlag, 1997, pp. 158–173.
9. Wieland Fischer, Berndt M. Gammel, "Masking at Gate Level in the Presence of Glitches," J.R. Rao, B. Sunar, Eds., CHES 2005, LNCS 3659, Springer-Verlag, 2005, pp. 187–200.
10. Jovan D. Golić, Christophe Tymen, "Multiplicative masking and power analysis", B. Kaliski, Ç Koç, Ch. Paar, Eds., CHES 2002, LNCS 2523, Springer-Verlag, 2003, pp. 198–212.
11. Louis Goubin, Jacques Patarin, "DES and differential power analysis – the duplication method", Ç. Koç, Ch. Paar, Eds., CHES '99, LNCS 1717, Springer-Verlag, 1999, pp. 158–172.
12. Yuval Ishai, Amit Sahai, David Wagner, "Private circuits: securing hardware against probing attacks", D. Boneh, Ed., CRYPTO 2003, LNCS 2729, Springer-Verlag, 2003, pp. 463–481.
13. Marc Joye, Pascal Paillier, Berry Schoenmakers, "On second-order differential power analysis," J.R. Rao, B. Sunar, Eds., CHES 2005, LNCS 3659, Springer-Verlag, 2005, pp. 293–308.
14. Paul Kocher, Joshua Jaffe, Benjamin Jun, "Differential Power Analysis", M. Wiener, Ed., CRYPTO '99, LNCS 1666, Springer-Verlag, 1999, pp. 388–397.
15. Stefan Mangard, Thomas Popp, Berndt M. Gammel, "Side-channel leakage of masked CMOS gates", A.J. Menezes, Ed., CT-RSA 2005, LNCS 3376, Springer-Verlag, 2005, pp. 351–365.
16. Stefan Mangard, Norbert Pramstaller, Elisabeth Oswald, "Successfully attacking masked AES hardware implementations," J.R. Rao, B. Sunar, Eds., CHES 2005, LNCS 3659, Springer-Verlag, 2005, pp. 157–171.
17. Thomas S. Messerges, "Using second-order power analysis to attack DPA resistant software," Ç.K. Koç, Ch. Paar, Eds., CHES 2000, LNCS 1965, Springer-Verlag, 2000, pp. 238–251.
18. Elisabeth Oswald, Stefan Mangard, Norbert Pramstaller, Vincent Rijmen, "A Side-Channel Analysis Resistant Description of the AES S-box", FSE 2005, LNCS 3557, Springer-Verlag, pp. 413–423.
19. Elisabeth Oswald, Stefan Mangard, Christoph Herbst, Stefan Tillich, "Practical Second-Order DPA Attacks for Masked Smart Card Implementations of Block Ciphers", CT-RSA 2006, LNCS 3860, Springer-Verlag, pp. 192–207.
20. Thomas Popp, Stefan Mangard, "Masked dual-rail pre-charge logic: DPA-resistance without routing constraints," J.R. Rao, B. Sunar, Eds., CHES 2005, LNCS 3659, Springer-Verlag, 2005, pp. 172–186.
21. Rafail Ostrovsky, Moti Yung, "How to withstand mobile virus attacks", Proc. 10th ACM Symposium on Principles of Distributed Computing (PODC), 1991, pp. 51-59.

22. Kai Schramm, Christof Paar, "Higher Order Masking of the AES", CT-RSA 2006, LNCS 3860, Springer-Verlag, pp. 208–225.
23. Adi Shamir, "How to share a secret", *Commun. ACM* 22, 1979, pp. 612-613.
24. Kris Tiri, Patrick Schaumont, "Changing the Odds against Masked Logic", Selected Areas of Cryptagraphy 2006 (SAC), LNCS, Springer-Verlag, to appear.
25. Elena Trichina, Tymur Korkishko, "Small size, low power, side channel immune AES coprocessor design and synthesis results", Proc. fourth conference on the Advanced Encryption Standard (AES4), LNCS 3373, Springer-Verlag, 2005, pp. 113–127.
26. Johannes Wolkerstorfer, Elisabeth Oswald, Mario Lamberger, "An ASIC implementation of the AES S-boxes", B. Preneel, Ed., CT-RSA 2002, LNCS 2271, Springer-Verlag, 2002, pp. 67–78.
27. Andrew Yao, "Protocols for secure computation", *FOCS'82*, 1982, pp. 160-164.

A   Proof of Theorem 2

For sake of readability, we give the proof for the case of two input variables. The general case follows straightforwardly.

Let $t(\overline{x}_1, \overline{y}_1)$ be any intermediate result or any physical characteristic of the circuit implementing f_1. The only assumption we make about t is that it doesn't depend on the values of x_1 and y_1. Let $\delta(X, Y)$ be the function that is equal to 1 if $X = Y$ and 0 otherwise. Let A, A_1 denote the following sets:

$$A = \{(\overline{X}, \overline{Y}) \mid t(\overline{X}_1, \overline{Y}_1) = T\}$$
$$A_1 = \{(\overline{X}_1, \overline{Y}_1) \mid t(\overline{X}_1, \overline{Y}_1) = T\} \ .$$

and let B denote the set of possible values for (x_1, y_1). Since t doesn't depend on the values of x_1 and y_1, we have $A = B \times A_1$. By definition and using (2):

$$\Pr(t = T) = \sum_{\overline{X} \in A} \Pr(\overline{x} = \overline{X}) = \sum_{(\overline{X}, \overline{Y}) \in A} c \Pr(x = \bigoplus_i X_i, y = \bigoplus_i Y_i)$$

Splitting up the summation results in

$$\Pr(t = T) = \sum_{(\overline{X}_1, \overline{Y}_1) \in A_1} c \sum_{(X_1, Y_1) \in B} \Pr(x = \bigoplus_i X_i, y = \bigoplus_i Y_i) \ .$$

Since the shares $X_2, \ldots, X_n, Y_2, \ldots, Y_n$ give no information on X, Y, the latter summation equals 1 and hence:

$$\Pr(t = T) = \sum_{(\overline{X}_1, \overline{Y}_1) \in A_1} c \tag{16}$$

Similarly, we obtain:

$$\Pr(t = T, x = X, y = Y)$$
$$= \sum_{(\overline{X}_1, \overline{Y}_1) \in A_1} \Pr(\overline{x} = (X \oplus \bigoplus_{i=2}^n X_i, \overline{X}_1), \overline{y} = (Y \oplus \bigoplus_{i=2}^n Y_i, \overline{Y}_1))$$
$$= \sum_{(\overline{X}_1, \overline{Y}_1) \in A_1} c \Pr(x = X, y = Y)$$

Using (16), we obtain:

$$\Pr(t = T, x = X, y = Y) = \Pr(t = T)\Pr(x = X, y = Y).$$

Hence t is independent of x and y. Let $C(Z)$ denote the set

$$C(Z) = \{(X,Y) \mid N(X,Y) = Z\} = \{(X,Y) \mid \delta(N(X,Y),Z) = 1\} .$$

Then, we can write for z:

$$\Pr(z = Z) = \sum_{(X,Y) \in C(Z)} \Pr(x = X, y = Y) .$$

$$\Pr(t = T, z = Z)$$
$$= \sum_{(\overline{X},\overline{X}) \in A} \delta(N(\bigoplus_i X_i, \bigoplus_i Y_i), Z)\Pr(\overline{x} = \overline{X}, \overline{y} = \overline{Y})$$
$$= \sum_{(\overline{X}_1,\overline{X}_1) \in A_1} \sum_{(X_1,Y_1) \in B} \delta(N(\bigoplus_i X_i, \bigoplus_i Y_i), Z)c\Pr(x = \bigoplus_i X_i, y = \bigoplus_i Y_i) .$$

Since the shares $X_2, \ldots, X_n, Y_2, \ldots, Y_n$ give no information on X, Y, we can rewrite this as follows:

$$\Pr(t = T, z = Z) = \sum_{(\overline{X}_1,\overline{Y}_1) \in A_1} c \sum_{(X,Y) \in C(Z)} \Pr(x = X, y = Y)$$
$$= \Pr(t = T)\Pr(z = Z) .$$

B Realization of Inversion in GF(16) with 5 Shares for f, g, h, k

$$f_1 = x_2 \oplus y_2 \oplus (x_2 \oplus x_3 \oplus x_4 \oplus x_5)(v_2 \oplus v_3 \oplus v_4 \oplus v_5)$$
$$\oplus (x_2 \oplus x_3 \oplus x_4 \oplus x_5)(y_2 \oplus y_3 \oplus y_4 \oplus y_5)(z_2 \oplus z_3 \oplus z_4 \oplus z_5)$$
$$f_2 = x_3 \oplus y_3 \oplus x_1(v_3 \oplus v_4 \oplus v_5) \oplus v_1(x_3 \oplus x_4 \oplus x_5) \oplus x_1 v_1$$
$$\oplus x_1(y_3 \oplus y_4 \oplus y_5)(z_3 \oplus z_4 \oplus z_5) \oplus y_1(x_3 \oplus x_4 \oplus x_5)(z_3 \oplus z_4 \oplus z_5)$$
$$\oplus z_1(x_3 \oplus x_4 \oplus x_5)(y_3 \oplus y_4 \oplus y_5) \oplus x_1 y_1(z_3 \oplus z_4 \oplus z_5) \oplus x_1 z_1(y_3 \oplus y_4 \oplus y_5)$$
$$\oplus y_1 z_1(x_3 \oplus x_4 \oplus x_5) \oplus x_1 y_1 z_1$$
$$f_3 = x_4 \oplus y_4 \oplus x_2 v_1 \oplus x_1 v_2 \oplus x_1 y_1 z_2 \oplus x_1 y_2 z_1 \oplus x_2 y_1 z_1 \oplus x_1 y_2 z_2 \oplus x_2 y_1 z_2 \oplus x_2 y_2 z_1$$
$$\oplus x_1 y_2 z_4 \oplus x_2 y_1 z_4 \oplus x_1 y_4 z_2 \oplus x_2 y_4 z_1 \oplus x_4 y_1 z_2 \oplus x_4 y_2 z_1 \oplus x_1 y_2 z_5 \oplus x_2 y_1 z_5$$
$$\oplus x_1 y_5 z_2 \oplus x_2 y_5 z_1 \oplus x_5 y_1 z_2 \oplus x_5 y_2 z_1$$
$$f_4 = x_5 \oplus y_5 \oplus x_1 y_2 z_3 \oplus x_1 y_3 z_2 \oplus x_2 y_1 z_3 \oplus x_2 y_3 z_1 \oplus x_3 y_1 z_2 \oplus x_3 y_2 z_1$$
$$f_5 = x_1 \oplus y_1$$

$$g_1 = (x_2 \oplus x_3 \oplus x_4 \oplus x_5)(y_2 \oplus y_3 \oplus y_4 \oplus y_5)(z_2 \oplus z_3 \oplus z_4 \oplus z_5)$$
$$\oplus (x_2 \oplus x_3 \oplus x_4 \oplus x_5)(y_2 \oplus y_3 \oplus y_4 \oplus y_5)(v_2 \oplus v_3 \oplus v_4 \oplus v_5)$$
$$\oplus (x_2 \oplus x_3 \oplus x_4 \oplus x_5)(v_2 \oplus v_3 \oplus v_4 \oplus v_5)$$
$$\oplus (y_2 \oplus y_3 \oplus y_4 \oplus y_5)(z_2 \oplus z_3 \oplus z_4 \oplus z_5) \oplus y_2$$

$$g_2 = x_1(y_3 \oplus y_4 \oplus y_5)(z_3 \oplus z_4 \oplus z_5) \oplus y_1(x_3 \oplus x_4 \oplus x_5)(z_3 \oplus z_4 \oplus z_5)$$
$$\oplus z_1(x_3 \oplus x_4 \oplus x_5)(y_3 \oplus y_4 \oplus y_5) \oplus x_1 y_1(z_3 \oplus z_4 \oplus z_5) \oplus x_1 z_1(y_3 \oplus y_4 \oplus y_5)$$
$$\oplus y_1 z_1(x_3 \oplus x_4 \oplus x_5) \oplus x_1 y_1 z_1 \oplus x_1(y_3 \oplus y_4 \oplus y_5)(v_3 \oplus v_4 \oplus v_5)$$
$$\oplus y_1(x_3 \oplus x_4 \oplus x_5)(v_3 \oplus v_4 \oplus v_5) \oplus v_1(x_3 \oplus x_4 \oplus x_5)(y_3 \oplus y_4 \oplus y_5)$$
$$\oplus x_1 y_1(v_3 \oplus v_4 \oplus v_5) \oplus x_1 v_1(y_3 \oplus y_4 \oplus y_5) \oplus y_1 v_1(x_3 \oplus x_4 \oplus x_5) \oplus x_1 y_1 v_1$$
$$\oplus x_1(v_3 \oplus v_4 \oplus v_5) \oplus v_1(x_3 \oplus x_4 \oplus x_5) \oplus x_1 v_1 \oplus y_1(z_3 \oplus z_4 \oplus z_5)$$
$$\oplus z_1(y_3 \oplus y_4 \oplus y_5) \oplus y_1 z_1 \oplus y_3$$

$$g_3 = x_1 y_1 z_2 \oplus x_1 y_2 z_1 \oplus x_2 y_1 z_1 \oplus x_1 y_2 z_2 \oplus x_2 y_1 z_2 \oplus x_2 y_2 z_1 \oplus x_1 y_2 z_4 \oplus x_2 y_1 z_4$$
$$\oplus x_1 y_4 z_2 \oplus x_2 y_4 z_1 \oplus x_4 y_1 z_2 \oplus x_4 y_2 z_1 \oplus x_1 y_2 z_5 \oplus x_2 y_1 z_5 \oplus x_1 y_5 z_2 \oplus x_2 y_5 z_1$$
$$\oplus x_5 y_1 z_2 \oplus x_5 y_2 z_1 \oplus x_1 y_1 v_2 \oplus x_1 y_2 v_1 \oplus x_2 y_1 v_1 \oplus x_1 y_2 v_2 \oplus x_2 y_1 v_2 \oplus x_2 y_2 v_1$$
$$\oplus x_1 y_2 v_4 \oplus x_2 y_1 v_4 \oplus x_1 y_4 v_2 \oplus x_2 y_4 v_1 \oplus x_4 y_1 v_2 \oplus x_4 y_2 v_1 \oplus x_1 y_2 v_5 \oplus x_2 y_1 v_5$$
$$\oplus x_1 y_5 v_2 \oplus x_2 y_5 v_1 \oplus x_5 y_1 v_2 \oplus x_5 y_2 v_1 \oplus x_2 v_1 \oplus x_1 v_2 \oplus y_2 z_1 \oplus y_1 z_2 \oplus y_4$$

$$g_4 = x_1 y_2 z_3 \oplus x_1 y_3 z_2 \oplus x_2 y_1 z_3 \oplus x_2 y_3 z_1 \oplus x_3 y_1 z_2 \oplus x_3 y_2 z_1 \oplus x_1 y_2 v_3 \oplus x_1 y_3 v_2$$
$$\oplus x_2 y_1 v_3 \oplus x_2 y_3 v_1 \oplus x_3 y_1 v_2 \oplus x_3 y_2 v_1 \oplus y_5$$

$$g_5 = y_1$$

$$h_1 = (x_2 \oplus x_3 \oplus x_4 \oplus x_5)(v_2 \oplus v_3 \oplus v_4 \oplus v_5)(z_2 \oplus z_3 \oplus z_4 \oplus z_5) \oplus y_3 \oplus v_2$$
$$\oplus (x_2 \oplus x_3 \oplus x_4 \oplus x_5)(v_2 \oplus v_3 \oplus v_4 \oplus v_5)$$
$$\oplus (y_2 \oplus y_3 \oplus y_4 \oplus y_5)(v_2 \oplus v_3 \oplus v_4 \oplus v_5)$$

$$h_2 = x_1(v_3 \oplus v_4 \oplus v_5)(z_3 \oplus z_4 \oplus z_5) \oplus v_1(x_3 \oplus x_4 \oplus x_5)(z_3 \oplus z_4 \oplus z_5)$$
$$\oplus z_1(x_3 \oplus x_4 \oplus x_5)(v_3 \oplus v_4 \oplus v_5) \oplus x_1 v_1(z_3 \oplus z_4 \oplus z_5) \oplus x_1 z_1(v_3 \oplus v_4 \oplus v_5)$$
$$\oplus v_1 z_1(x_3 \oplus x_4 \oplus x_5) \oplus x_1 v_1 z_1 \oplus x_1(v_3 \oplus v_4 \oplus v_5) \oplus v_1(x_3 \oplus x_4 \oplus x_5) \oplus x_1 v_1$$
$$\oplus y_1(v_3 \oplus v_4 \oplus v_5) \oplus v_1(y_3 \oplus y_4 \oplus y_5) \oplus y_1 v_1 \oplus y_4 \oplus v_1 \oplus v_5$$

$$h_3 = x_1 v_1 z_2 \oplus x_1 v_2 z_1 \oplus x_2 v_1 z_1 \oplus x_1 v_2 z_2 \oplus x_2 v_1 z_2 \oplus x_2 v_2 z_1 \oplus x_1 v_2 z_4 \oplus x_2 v_1 z_4$$
$$\oplus x_1 v_4 z_2 \oplus x_2 v_4 z_1 \oplus x_4 v_1 z_2 \oplus x_4 v_2 z_1 \oplus x_1 v_2 z_5 \oplus x_2 v_1 z_5 \oplus x_1 v_5 z_2 \oplus x_2 v_5 z_1$$
$$\oplus x_5 v_1 z_2 \oplus x_5 v_2 z_1 \oplus x_2 v_1 \oplus x_1 v_2 \oplus y_2 v_1 \oplus y_1 v_2 \oplus y_5 \oplus v_1 \oplus v_2 \oplus v_5$$

$$h_4 = x_1 v_2 z_3 \oplus x_1 v_3 z_2 \oplus x_2 v_1 z_3 \oplus x_2 v_3 z_1 \oplus x_3 v_1 z_2 \oplus x_3 v_2 z_1 \oplus y_1 \oplus v_1$$

$$h_5 = y_2 \oplus v_1$$

$$k_1 = (x_2 \oplus x_3 \oplus x_4 \oplus x_5)(v_2 \oplus v_3 \oplus v_4 \oplus v_5)(z_2 \oplus z_3 \oplus z_4 \oplus z_5)$$
$$\oplus (v_2 \oplus v_3 \oplus v_4 \oplus v_5)(y_2 \oplus y_3 \oplus y_4 \oplus y_5)(z_2 \oplus z_3 \oplus z_4 \oplus z_5)$$
$$\oplus (x_2 \oplus x_3 \oplus x_4 \oplus x_5)(z_2 \oplus z_3 \oplus z_4 \oplus z_5)$$
$$\oplus (y_2 \oplus y_3 \oplus y_4 \oplus y_5)(z_2 \oplus z_3 \oplus z_4 \oplus z_5)$$
$$\oplus (y_2 \oplus y_3 \oplus y_4 \oplus y_5)(v_2 \oplus v_3 \oplus v_4 \oplus v_5) \oplus z_2 \oplus v_2$$

$$k_2 = x_1(v_3 \oplus v_4 \oplus v_5)(z_3 \oplus z_4 \oplus z_5) \oplus v_1(x_3 \oplus x_4 \oplus x_5)(z_3 \oplus z_4 \oplus z_5)$$
$$\oplus z_1(x_3 \oplus x_4 \oplus x_5)(v_3 \oplus v_4 \oplus v_5) \oplus x_1 v_1(z_3 \oplus z_4 \oplus z_5) \oplus x_1 z_1(v_3 \oplus v_4 \oplus v_5)$$
$$\oplus v_1 z_1(x_3 \oplus x_4 \oplus x_5) \oplus x_1 v_1 z_1 \oplus v_1(y_3 \oplus y_4 \oplus y_5)(z_3 \oplus z_4 \oplus z_5)$$
$$\oplus y_1(v_3 \oplus v_4 \oplus v_5)(z_3 \oplus z_4 \oplus z_5) \oplus z_1(v_3 \oplus v_4 \oplus v_5)(y_3 \oplus y_4 \oplus y_5)$$
$$\oplus v_1 y_1(z_3 \oplus z_4 \oplus z_5) \oplus v_1 z_1(y_3 \oplus y_4 \oplus y_5) \oplus y_1 z_1(v_3 \oplus v_4 \oplus v_5) \oplus v_1 y_1 z_1$$
$$\oplus x_1(z_3 \oplus z_4 \oplus z_5) \oplus z_1(x_3 \oplus x_4 \oplus x_5) \oplus x_1 z_1 \oplus y_1(z_3 \oplus z_4 \oplus z_5)$$
$$\oplus z_1(y_3 \oplus y_4 \oplus y_5) \oplus y_1 z_1 \oplus y_1(v_3 \oplus v_4 \oplus v_5) \oplus v_1(y_3 \oplus y_4 \oplus y_5) \oplus y_1 v_1$$
$$\oplus z_3 \oplus v_3$$

$$k_3 = x_1 v_1 z_2 \oplus x_1 v_2 z_1 \oplus x_2 v_1 z_1 \oplus x_1 v_2 z_2 \oplus x_2 v_1 z_2 \oplus x_2 v_2 z_1 \oplus x_1 v_2 z_4 \oplus x_2 v_1 z_4$$
$$\oplus x_1 v_4 z_2 \oplus x_2 v_4 z_1 \oplus x_4 v_1 z_2 \oplus x_4 v_2 z_1 \oplus x_1 v_2 z_5 \oplus x_2 v_1 z_5 \oplus x_1 v_5 z_2 \oplus x_2 v_5 z_1$$
$$\oplus x_5 v_1 z_2 \oplus x_5 v_2 z_1 \oplus v_1 y_1 z_2 \oplus v_1 y_2 z_1 \oplus v_2 y_1 z_1 \oplus v_1 y_2 z_2 \oplus v_2 y_1 z_2 \oplus v_2 y_2 z_1$$
$$\oplus v_1 y_2 z_4 \oplus v_2 y_1 z_4 \oplus v_1 y_4 z_2 \oplus v_2 y_4 z_1 \oplus v_4 y_1 z_2 \oplus v_4 y_2 z_1 \oplus v_1 y_2 z_5 \oplus v_2 y_1 z_5$$
$$\oplus v_1 y_5 z_2 \oplus v_2 y_5 z_1 \oplus v_5 y_1 z_2 \oplus v_5 y_2 z_1 \oplus x_2 z_1 \oplus x_1 z_2 \oplus y_2 z_1 \oplus y_1 z_2 \oplus y_2 v_1$$
$$\oplus y_1 v_2 \oplus z_4 \oplus v_4$$

$$k_4 = x_1 v_2 z_3 \oplus x_1 v_3 z_2 \oplus x_2 v_1 z_3 \oplus x_2 v_3 z_1 \oplus x_3 v_1 z_2 \oplus x_3 v_2 z_1 \oplus v_1 y_2 z_3 \oplus v_1 y_3 z_2$$
$$\oplus v_2 y_1 z_3 \oplus v_2 y_3 z_1 \oplus v_3 y_1 z_2 \oplus v_3 y_2 z_1 \oplus z_5 \oplus v_5$$

$$k_5 = z_1 \oplus v_1$$

Hardware-and-Software-Based Security Architecture for Broadband Router (Short Paper)*

Gu Xiaozhuo [1,2,3], Li Yufeng[1,3], Yang Jianzu [3], and Lan Julong[1,3]

[1] National Digital Switching System Engineering & Technological R&D Center, China
[2] Lanzhou City College, China
[3] Information Engineering University, China
No 783 Po Box 1001, 450002, Henan, China
{gxz, lyf}@mail.ndsc.com.cn, yjzxxgc@sohu.com,
ljl@mail.ndsc.com.cn

Abstract. Implementing IP security in broadband router without sacrificing the performance is main work we focused on. To meet the need of protecting wire speed forwarding data passing through fast path of the router, security module implemented with encryption chip was adopted; to protect non real time data passing through slow path of the router, the scheme of implementing IP security inside kernel of Master control module with software was introduced. Security architecture and several testing architectures were finely designed and depicted in the paper. Testing of security architecture was undergone in SR1880s router, which was developed by National Digital Switching System Engineering & Technological R&D Center of China (NDSC). Testing results show that the two schemes work well together.

Keywords: IP security (IPsec), Security architecture, Security module, IPsec module.

1 Introduction

With fast development of Next Generation Internet (NGI), routers are required to support IPsec as essential function. Owning to relatively mature technology of router manufacture, implementing IPsec in routers without changing the original framework is the recent work being focused on.

General security architecture shown in Fig. 1 has two main disadvantages. First, each Network processing unit with one Encryption chip will lead every packet passing through Network processing unit also passing Encryption chip, yet there is small part of traffic that needs to be protected by Encryption chip. Second, N Encryption chips together will aggravate the problems of power waste, heat dissipation, and electromagnetic compatibility in single-shelf

Comparing with the general security architecture, we put forward universal security architecture and adopted it in SR1880 series to make the testing. SR1880

* This work was supported by the National High Technology Research and Development Program of China (No. 2005AA121210).

P. Ning, S. Qing, and N. Li (Eds.): ICICS 2006, LNCS 4307, pp. 546–555, 2006.

series has breakthrough in system architecture of router, high-speed forwarding engine [4][6], switch fabric, and scheduling algorithm [5]. All of these innovations have been implemented successfully in SR1880 series routers. We designed universal security architecture and implemented it in SR1880 series, which are called SR1880s.

We will introduce system architecture of SR1880s router in section II, and discuss designing and implementing of IPsec in SR1880 series in section III. Section IV will present several test architectures for testing and section V will give the conclusion.

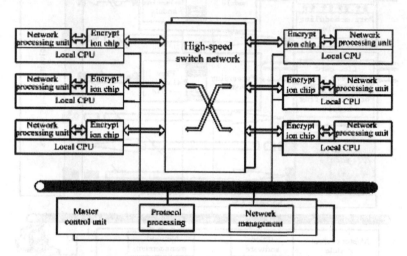

Fig. 1. General security architecture of broadband router

2 System Architecture of SR1880S

SR1880s router adopts decentralized module architecture shown in Fig. 2. Totally there are six main modules of the router, which are Line card interface module, Forwarding module, Photonic switching network, Security module, Inner communication module and Master control module.

Line card interface module includes 2.5G Packet over SONET/SDH (POS) interface, 155M Asynchronous Transfer Mode (ATM) interface and Gigabit Ethernet interface to process the packet in layer 1 and layer 2. Forwarding module is designed to forward the packet in layer 3, including wire speed forwarding, filtering and security checking, classification according to priority, identification of multicast and tagging, and inner packet forming. Photonic switching network provides service of exchanging packet according to different operation levels. Security module performs encryption and decryption of inbound and outbound packets. Master control module manages routing calculation, network management, device configuration and control, and IPsec module inside kernel. Inner communication module is the hinge to complete exchanges between every function board and Master control module.

Security module is consisted of Encryption adaptive board with dynamic Encryption chips to avoid the problems existed in general security architecture of the router. Security module is an independent part which has two outer interfaces, one is with Photonic switching network and the other is with Master control module. The number of Encryption chips in one Encryption adaptive board is changeable according to anticipated traffic passing through router. When one adaptive board full loaded can not meet the need, more Encryption adaptive boards can be added.

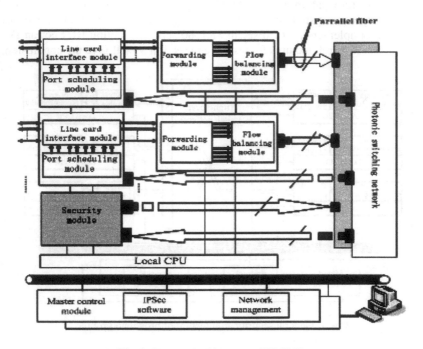

Fig. 2. System Architecture of SR1880s

3 Security Architecture of SR1880S

The architecture of SR1880S can be partitioned into two planes, data plane (fast path) and control plane (slow path), according to the design of separating the routing and forwarding data. Forwarding data are processed and forwarded in high speed through Line card interface module, Forwarding module, and Photonic switching network. In slow path, Master control module, Inner communication module, and local CPU cooperate together to fulfill the maintenance, control and management of the router through processing non-real time tasks. To provide protection for entire traffic passing through router, we put forward two schemes of implementing IPsec working together. One scheme uses hardware to process high-speed forwarding data in fast path, and the other scheme uses software inside Master control module to process non-real time data in slow path.

3.1 Security Architecture of Implementing IPsec with Security Module

This architecture is implemented using Encryption adaptive board with specific encryption chip, which is in the primary place in providing security protection. When system is powered on, Command line interface begins to add Security Policy (SP) to

IPsec engine. Then IPsec engine adds this SP to Forwarding module via Inner Ethernet and this SP is stored in the content-addressable memory (CAM) of Forwarding module. In the condition of manual key configuration, security association (SA) is also added to IPsec engine by Command line interface and then transferred to Security module. SA is a set of policy and keys used to protect traffic. It is stored in the CAM and static random access memory (SRAM) of Security module. Fig. 3 shows the security architecture and Fig. 4 shows the flow chart.

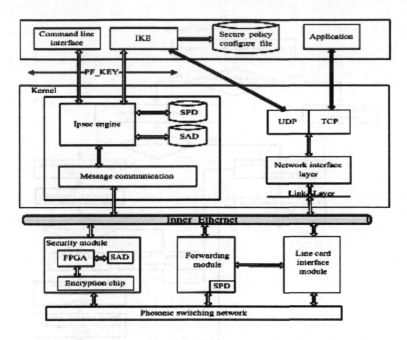

Fig. 3. Secure Architecture of Implementing IPsec with Security Module

For packet passing through the router, it is received by Line card interface module. Packet whose destination is not local router is transferred to Forwarding module. When receiving the packet, Forwarding module executes lookup in its security policy database (SPD) to see whether there has SP for this packet. If it has, the packet will be labeled encryption or decryption tag and forwarded to Security module. Receiving the packet, Security module looks up its security association database (SAD) for SA. If Command line interface didn't add SA manually or this is the first packet of an application, there wouldn't be any SA. In this case, Security module disposes the packet and asks IPsec engine to waken Internet Key Exchange (IKE) for negotiating SA. A major function of IKE is the establishment and maintenance of SAs. The process of IKE for negotiating SA is according to [2]. Otherwise Field Programmable Gate Array (FPGA) performs packet disassembly and controls encryption chip for encryption or decryption. For packet needs encryption, FPGA gets encryption type and encryption key from SAD according to source and destination addresses and protocol type to control Encryption chip for encryption. After encryption, the packet is assembled with packet header by FPGA to construct IPsec packet and the IPsec packet is sent out through Photonic switching network and Line card interface module. For packet needs decryption, FPGA gets decryption type and decryption key from SAD according to source and destination addresses, protocol type, and security parameter index (SPI), and then control Encryption chip for decryption. After decryption, the packet is assembled again with packet header to construct the original IP packet. Then the decrypted IP packet is also sent out through Photonic switching network and Line card interface module.

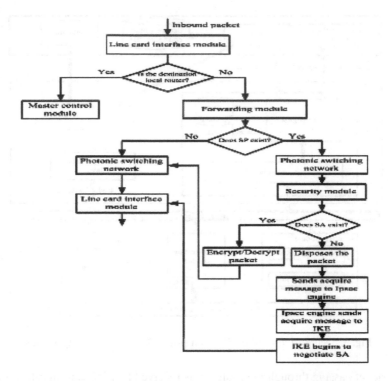

Fig. 4. Flow chart of processing packet with Security module

3.2 Security Architecture of Implementing IPsec Inside Master Control Module

Implementing IPsec inside kernel of Master control module is to deal with the case that data passing through slow path need encryption or decryption, such as the source or the destination address of data is local router. Because these data are almost control messages and are non-real time tasks, they can be encrypted or decrypted inside kernel of Master control module, which is relatively slower. Fig. 5 shows the security architecture.

Flow chart of processing inbound packet is shown in Fig. 6. For inbound packet whose destination is local, it is transferred to IPsec interface of Master control module by Line card interface module. When receiving packet, IPsec interface checks the next header of the packet. If the next header is Authentication Header (AH) or Encapsulating Security Payload (ESP), the packet will be delivered to IPsec inbound processing module. Then IPsec inbound processing module communicates with IPsec

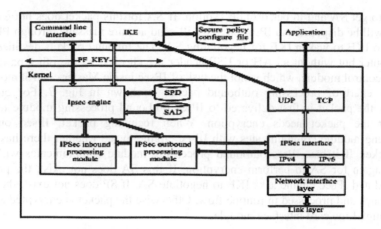

Fig. 5. Security Architecture of Implementing IPsec in Master Control Module

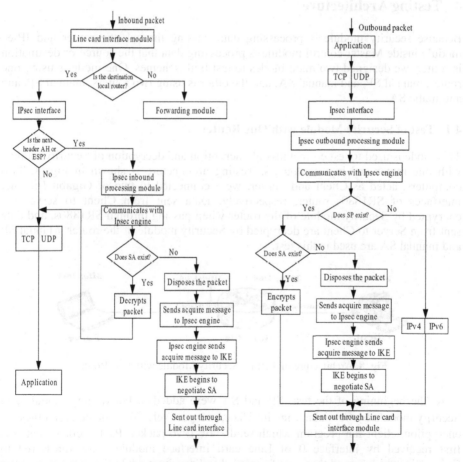

Fig. 6. Flow chart of processing inbound packet with Master Control Module

Fig. 7. Flow chart of processing outbound packet with Master control module

engine to get SA and to perform decryption. If SA for this packet does not exist, the packet will be disposed and IPsec engine will send acquire message through PF_KEY socket to IKE to waken IKE for negotiating SA. The Inbound packets destined to the local router but without an AH or ESP header are checked by the other parts of the Master control module, which is not the task of IPsec inside Master control module.

Flow chart of processing outbound packet is shown in Fig. 7. For outbound packets, the packet is first delivered to IPsec outbound processing module to check whether the packet needs encryption. When receiving packet, IPsec outbound processing module communicates with IPsec engine to see whether there has SP for this packet. If it has, IPsec outbound processing module communicates with IPsec engine again for SA to perform encryption. If this SA does not exist, the packet is disposed and IPsec engine asks IKE to negotiate SA. If SP does not exist, the packet is sent back and processed in routine flow. Otherwise the packet is encrypted and sent out through Line card interface module.

4   Testing Architecture

Because security module is processing data passing through the router and IPsec module inside Master control module is processing data that the source or destination is router, we designed two main modes to test both schemes. One mode is using one router, manual SP, and manual SA, and the other is using two routers, manual SP, and automatic SA.

4.1   Test of Security Module with One Router

This mode is used to test correctness of encryption and decryption of Security module with one router and two computers. Testing architecture is shown in Fig. 8. Two computers, acted as Client and Server, were connected to two of Gigabit Ethernet interfaces of SR1880s router, respectively. Data sent from Client to server are encrypted by Security module of the router when passing through SR1880s, and data sent from Server to Client are decrypted by Security module of the router. Manual SP and manual SA are used in this test.

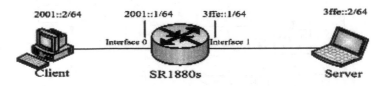

Fig. 8. Architecture of Testing Security Module with One Router

At the beginning of the test, SP and SA were added to Forwarding module and Security module by Command line interface, respectively. To validate correctness of encryption, client ran program which sends raw IPv6 packet. Packet client sent was first received by interface 0 of Line card interface module, was transferred to Forwarding module, and then was forwarded to Security module for encryption. After encryption, the packet was sent out through interface 1 and was finally received by server. File Client sent was stored in server in advance, so we encrypted the file in server and compared it with received cipher text.

The way to validate correctness of decryption had the similar flow as above. Server encrypted the file and sent it to Client with raw IPv6 packet. The encrypted packet was received by interface 1 of Line card interface module and was forwarded to Security module for decryption. Then the decrypted packet was sent out through interface 0. The packet received by client was in the form of plain text and was compared with the original file saved in advance.

We verified the correctness of encryption and decryption of Security module through testing architecture listed above.

4.2 Test of Security Module with Two Routers

This mode is designed to test the whole IPsec system, including IPsec engine, IKE, and Security module. Testing architecture, with two routers and two computers, is shown in Fig. 9. Two SR1880s were connected with Gigabit Ethernet interfaces and two computers were connected to one of Gigabit Ethernet interfaces of two SR1880s routers, respectively. SP was added to Forwarding module at the beginning of the test. The first packet passing the router would waken IKE to negotiate SA and this SA would be transferred to Security module. We have two methods to validate Security module. The first is using raw IPv6 socket program and the second is using ping.

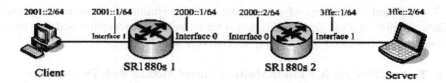

Fig. 9. Architecture of Testing Security Module with Two Routers

For the first method, Client sent the file using raw IPv6 socket program and server ran the reception program. The first packet wakened IKE to negotiate SA and was disposed by Security module of SR1880s 1. The rest packets were first encrypted by SR1880s 1, then were decrypted by SR1880s 2, and finally were received by server, where we stored the original file in advance to have comparison, in the form of plain text.

For the second method, Client pings server, Internet Control Message Protocol (ICMP) request packet sent by Client was encrypted by Security module of SR1880s 1, and then was decrypted by Security module of SR1880s 2. When server received the ICMP request packet, it sent the ICMP echo packet as reply. The reply packet was first encrypted by Security module of SR1880s 2, then was decrypted by Security module of SR1880s 1, and was finally accepted by client.

We tested the whole IPsec system using two methods listed above with the security architecture shown in Fig. 9. The whole system worked well together.

4.3 Test of IPsec Module Inside Master Control Module with One Router

Implementing IPsec inside Master control module is to process the data that the source or the destination address is local router. To test this module, architecture shown in Fig. 10 was adopted. Client was connected to one of Gigabit Ethernet interfaces of SR1880s, while server connected to SR1880s using telnet to manipulate the operation in the router. Manual SP and manual SA are also used in this mode. Packet sent from Client to SR1880s was decrypted in Master control module and packet sent from SR1880s to Client was encrypted in Master control module. Encrypted packet Client sent was first received by interface 0 of Line card interface module, and then was transferred to Master control module since the destination address is local. Then the packet was decrypted by IPsec inbound processing module in kernel and was received by reception program ran in application layer. Plain text Client sent was also stored in SR1880s in advance, so we compared the original file with received packet to check the correctness of decryption. Packet SR1880s 1 sent was first encrypted by IPsec outbound processing module in kernel, and then was sent out by Line card interface module through interface 0. Packet, in the form of cipher text, was finally received by Client to check the correctness of encryption.

Fig. 10. Architecture of testing IPsec inside Kernel with One Router

We verified correctness of encryption and decryption of IPsec module inside Master control module through this test. Due to perform encryption and decryption with software, the speed of processing is relatively slower.

4.4 Test of IPsec Module Inside Master Control Module with Two Routers

We also used two methods similar with Fig. 9 to test the whole IPsec module, including IKE, IPsec engine, IPsec inbound processing module, and IPsec outbound processing module. Test architecture is shown in Fig. 11. Client and server were connected to two routers respectively using telnet to manipulate the operation in the routers. Manual SP was added to SPD of IPsec engine in advance. The first packet SR1880s 1 sent would waken IKE to negotiate SA.

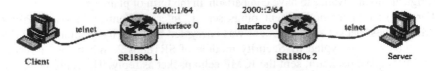

Fig. 11. Architecture of Testing IPsec inside Kernel with Two Routers

For the first method, we ran send program in SR1880s 1 and reception program in SR1880s 2. Packet sent by SR1880s 1 was encrypted by IPsec outbound processing module in kernel of Master control module, and then was sent out through interface 0 of Line card interface module. When interface 0 of SR1880s 2 received the encrypted packet, Line card interface module sent it to Master control module. Then Master control module called IPsec inbound processing module to execute decryption. After decryption, the packet was finally accepted by reception program ran in SR1880s 2, where stored the original file for checking.

The second method using ping method had the similar flow as in Fig. 9. Internet Control Message Protocol (ICMP) request packet sent by SR1880s 1 was encrypted by IPsec outbound processing module of SR1880s 1, and then was decrypted by IPsec inbound processing module of SR1880s 2. When SR1880s 2 received the ICMP request packet, it sent the ICMP echo packet as reply. The reply packet was first encrypted by IPsec outbound processing module of SR1880s 2, then was decrypted by IPsec inbound processing module of SR1880s 1, and was finally accepted by SR1880s 1.

We also tested the whole IPsec module using two methods above. Testing results show that the whole IPsec module works well together.

5 Conclusion

We presented security architecture which uses two schemes to implement IPsec and adopted it in SR1880s router. One scheme is implementing IPsec with hardware, which processing the data passing through fast path; the other is implementing IPsec inside kernel of Master control module of the router with software to process the data passing through slow path. Two schemes working together will process data in time with encryption chip and will also protect non-real time tasks in slow path. Testing results show that two schemes work well together and protect the traffic passing through the router.

Problem we still facing is the mismatch of processing speed between Security module, known as 2.5Gbps to 10Gbps, and Forwarding module, usually known as 10Gbps up to 40Gbps. How to improve the processing speed of Security module while not sacrificing the security is the next work we will research.

References

1. S. Kent and R. Atkinson "Security Architecture for the Internet Protocol", IETF RFC 2401, November 1998.
2. D. Harkins and D. Carrel, "The Internet Key Exchange (IKE)", IETF RFC 2409, November 1998.
3. Charlie Kaufman, "Internet Key Exchange (IKEv2) Protocol", IETF RFC 4306, Deembler 2005.
4. Ximing Hu, Jing Qu, Binqiang Wang, Xiaobei Li, "CISOQ: A Practical High-Performance Packet Switch Architecture for the Support of Multicast Traffic", in 2005 Proc. PDCAT Conf., Dalian, China, pp. 139-143
5. Chen Yue, Dong Yuguo, Lin Yusong, Lan Julong. "A Packet-Order-Keeping-Demultiplexer in Parallel-Structure Router Based on Flow Classification", in 2003 Proc. ICCNMC Conf. Shanghai, China, pp.
6. Li Yufeng, Yi Peng, Qiu Han, Lan Julong, "Sizing buffers for pipelined forwarding engine", in 2006 Proc. ICCCAS Conf.,Guilin, China, accepted.
7. Cássio Ditzel Kropiwiec, Edgard Jamhour, Carlos Maziero, "A Architecture for Protecting Web Sevices with IPsec", in 2004 Proc. EUROMICRO Conf., Rennes, France, pp. 290-297
8. Jonathon Trostle and Bill Gossman. "Techniques for improving the security and manageability of IPsec policy". International Journal of Information Security, vol. 4, no. 3, pp. 209–226, Jun. 2005.

Author Index